## Second Edition

# The
# Food
# Substitutions
# Bible

## More than **6,500** Substitutions for Ingredients, Equipment & Techniques

# David Joachim

*Robert*
**ROSE**

*Disclaimer*
The recipes in this book have been carefully tested by our kitchen and our tasters. To the best of our knowledge, they are safe and nutritious for ordinary use and users. For those people with food or other allergies, or who have special food requirements or health issues, please read the suggested contents of each recipe carefully and determine whether or not they may create a problem for you. All recipes are used at the risk of the consumer.

We cannot be responsible for any hazards, loss or damage that may occur as a result of any recipe use.

For those with special needs, allergies, requirements or health problems, in the event of any doubt, please contact your medical adviser prior to the use of any recipe.

Library and Archives Canada Cataloguing in Publication

Joachim, David
    The food substitutions bible : more than 6,500 substitutions for ingredients, equipment & techniques / David Joachim ; editor: Carol Sherman. — 2nd ed.

ISBN 978-0-7788-0245-7

1. Ingredient substitutions (Cookery).  I. Title.

TX652.J62 2010                  641.5                  C2010-903261-6

Editor: Carol Sherman
Copy Editor: Karen Campbell-Sheviak
Recipe Editor: Jennifer MacKenzie

Design and Production: PageWave Graphics Inc.
Cover Photography: Colin Ericson

We acknowledge the financial support of the Government of Canada through the Book Publishing Industry Development Program (BPIDP) for our publishing activities.

Published by Robert Rose Inc.
120 Eglinton Avenue East, Suite 800, Toronto, Ontario, Canada  M4P 1E2
Tel: (416) 322-6552  Fax: (416) 322-6936
www.robertrose.ca

Printed and bound in Canada

1  2  3  4  5  6  7  8  9  TCP  18  17  16  15  14  13  12  11  10

**Mixed Sources**
Product group from well-managed forests and other controlled sources
www.fsc.org  Cert no. SW-COC-000952
© 1996 Forest Stewardship Council

*For Bonnie, earth mother extraordinaire*

# Preface to the Second Edition

I STARTED WRITING THIS BOOK seven years ago. But it feels like 17 years. Since 2003, interest in food and cooking has mushroomed beyond belief. Exciting ingredients like agave nectar and XO sauce have circled the globe and soared in popularity. Cooks are even hungrier for information on how to substitute ingredients, equipment, and techniques in their kitchens.

Since then, I have also heard from many cooks, friends, and colleagues that this book holds a special place on their shelves, a spot reserved only for go-to books they thumb through regularly. That is the single most gratifying comment I could ever hear: this book has been truly useful to people.

With that feedback in mind, I set out to make this second edition even more useful. I added more than 1,500 new substitutions for ingredients like banyuls, pomegranate molasses, furikake, mustard essence, and vadouvan; and for equipment like a bench knife, cocktail strainer, ice cream maker, mandoline, popover pan, and a turkey baster. I added five new ingredient guides and measurement tables in the appendix to help decipher things like Picking Coffee (page 646), Can and Package Size Equivalents (page 680), and Alcohol Retention in Cooking (page 688). I also expanded the existing entries and reference material with additional information such as how many cups of caramelized onions you can expect to get from 1 pound (500 g) of raw onions (about $1\frac{1}{2}$ cups/375 mL when the onions are fully and beautifully browned). And I added more than 50 new recipes for things like Buttermilk Cheese (page 91), Red Chile Paste (page 124), Merken (page 343), a Chilean spice blend, and Steak Sauce (page 535).

With all this new material, the book is about 25% bigger than the 1$^{st}$ edition. Thankfully, the publisher agreed to enlarge the physical size (trim size) of the book. So all in all, you are holding in your hands a bigger, better, updated, revised, and expanded version of *The Food Substitutions Bible*. My greatest hope is that it puts even more useful cooking information right at your fingertips.

# Introduction

Ain't nothing like the real thing, Baby
Ain't nothing like the real thing

— Nickolas Ashford and Valerie Simpson,
*Ain't Nothing Like the Real Thing*

Substitute me for him
Substitute my coke for gin
Substitute you for my mum
At least I'll get my washing done

— The Who, *Substitute*

BOTH OF THE SONGS QUOTED above summarize my general philosophy of cooking. The lyrics of the first song make an impassioned plea to accept no substitutes, while the second song essentially says, "do whatever works."

When it comes to cooking, I truly believe that there "ain't nothing like the real thing." For instance, nothing tastes or acts quite like butter in cooking. But I am also a realist. I know from experience that sometimes you just have to get by with a substitute. Most cooks have, at one time or another, been in the middle of making a meal or special dish and found that they have run out of a key ingredient or don't have that special pan called for in the recipe. Other times, cooks simply want to create a different flavor or texture by experimenting with something new and exciting.

The answer to these dilemmas? Substitute.

Some of the greatest cooking discoveries have been and continue to be made by substituting one ingredient for another, one piece of equipment for another, or one cooking technique for another. Thousands of years ago, when our ancestors experimented with cooking food in clay pots rather than directly over an open flame, they opened the door to a slew of new moist-heat cooking methods, such as boiling, blanching, poaching, stewing, and steaming. Today, innovative cooks make all kinds of substitutions to suit their preferences. Those who like the taste of deep-fried food but don't care for the extra calories may turn to oven-frying, a lower-calorie technique that simulates deep-frying by lightly coating the food in oil then baking it in a very hot oven. Other cooks improvise in a pinch by using whatever they have on hand. They substitute vinegar for lemon juice, oil for butter, and hot sauce for ground red chile peppers. Don't have the mirin called for in the recipe? Use a mixture of sherry and sugar instead. Can't find your fondue pot? Use a heavy stoneware dish set on a warming tray or a heating pad. Cooks make these sorts of last-minute adjustments all the time. Whether you change your ingredients, equipment, or techniques, substituting is a matter of tailoring your cooking to meet your immediate needs.

This book compiles a wide range of substitutions into one comprehensive, easy-to-use guide organized from A to Z. Beginning with A1 and ending with Zwieback, it offers alternative ingredients, equipment, and techniques, including emergency substitutions, time-saving substitutions, healthy substitutions, alternatives for hard-to-find ingredients, alternatives for vegetarians, and ideas for varying the flavor of a dish in countless ways.

Many of the substitutions yield results that are remarkably similar to those you would achieve with the "real thing." For instance, 1 cup (250 mL) all-purpose flour mixed with $1\frac{1}{2}$ teaspoons (7 mL) baking powder and $\frac{1}{2}$ teaspoon (2 mL) salt makes a very close approximation of 1 cup (250 mL) store-bought self-rising flour. For those seeking a less-rich alternative to whipped cream, evaporated milk whips up surprisingly well and makes a creamy, lower-calorie substitute that you can dollop onto your favorite desserts.

Other substitutions in the book are not intended to imitate the original item. Instead, they are meant to inspire creativity or stimulate experimentation in the kitchen. For example, replacing apple butter with pumpkin butter will not approximate the original. But it may provide a flavor variation that takes your recipe where you want it to go.

Just keep this cardinal rule in mind: Substitutes will always produce slightly different results. Sometimes the results will be fabulous. Sometimes they may be even closer to what you are going for (if you are experimenting). No matter what you anticipate, expect the results to be at least slightly different when substituting one ingredient, piece of equipment, or technique for another. For instance, using all-purpose flour instead of cornstarch as a thickener produces a slightly coarser, fluffier texture and faintly wheat-like, somewhat earthy flavor. Cornstarch produces a finer, smoother texture and an ever-so-slightly sweet flavor.

Keep in mind, too, that food and cooking are subject to myriad minute variables of time and temperature; ingredient and equipment type, quality, age, and handling; and, of course, user skill level. Whenever you alter one of these variables by substituting, the results, however microscopic, are bound to be different. The fact is that in the ever-changing world of food production, there are few absolutes. And these are mostly mathematical equivalents. For example, 3 teaspoons (15 mL) will always equal 1 tablespoon (15 mL). But, believe it or not, many other mathematical measurements change, depending upon variables such as time, temperature, ingredients, cooking technique and even location. For instance, the boiling point of water is 212°F (100°C), right? Well, that's only at sea level. Go up 5,000 feet (1,525 meters) and water actually boils at about 203°F (95°C) because there is less atmospheric pressure on the surface of the water as it heats. Cooks who bake cookies and cakes at such elevation often increase their oven temperature by 25°F (14°C) and slightly reduce cooking times. The higher oven temperature helps batters and doughs set before the leavening gases overexpand as a result of the thin, dry air at that altitude.

As you can see, substituting is something that certain cooks do all the time without even thinking about it. If you live at high altitude, you are probably used to substituting amounts and temperatures for those given in recipes. If you are lowering your saturated fat intake, you probably substitute oil for butter when sautéing. If the herb cilantro tastes soapy to you, then you probably substitute another more agreeable herb such as parsley.

Substitutions can solve many problems in the kitchen. But they can't work magic. If you have run out of an ingredient and really want to replicate the original exactly, my advice is simple: don't substitute. If you absolutely must have the flavor of cardamom in a recipe, go buy some cardamom instead of substituting another spice such as cinnamon. Cinnamon will taste like cinnamon and not like cardamom. However, if you want to experiment with changing the flavor of your recipe, cinnamon may be an acceptable substitute.

Often, that's the reason I substitute one thing for another: just to try something new. With that in mind, I hope you find this book both practical and enjoyable, a reference that inspires you with fresh ideas and gives you all the information you need to improvise with confidence at home or in a commercial kitchen.

I have tried to make the book as comprehensive as possible, but reference books like this one are rarely "finished" in the final, complete, over-and-done-with sense of the word. Undoubtedly,

I have overlooked many fascinating items and substitutions. If you would like to suggest any additions (or point out any errors), please contact me through the publisher. The e-mail address is: foodsubstitutions@robertrose.ca.

I hope you have as much fun experimenting in your kitchen as I have in mine. Happy substituting!

— David Joachim

# How To Use This Book

**①**

## Annatto Oil

**③** *Also known as manteca de achiote. Food coloring made from the hard reddish pulp that surrounds the seeds of the annatto, a tropical American tree. In Jamaica, annatto oil is used to color codfish cakes.*

**④**
| 1 cup (250 mL) = 4 oz (125 g) |
| --- |

**②**

**⑤**

### If You Don't Have It

Substitute 1 tbsp (15 mL) annatto oil with:

- 1 tbsp (15 mL) Homemade Annatto Oil: Sauté 1½ tsp (7 mL) annatto seeds in 1 tbsp (15 mL) vegetable oil in a saucepan over medium heat, until oil turns a deep orange color, 8 to 10 minutes. Remove seeds with slotted spoon and discard. **⑥**
- 1 tbsp (15 mL) vegetable oil + 2 drops yellow food coloring + 1 drop red food coloring mixed into 1 tbsp (15 mL) water **⑦** or other non-oily liquid in recipe (food coloring will not mix with oil; add to watery liquids)

*See also* ANNATTO SEED. **⑧**

**①** The entries in this book are arranged alphabetically and cross-referenced like an index. The entries are alphabetized by the letter rather than by the word so that multiple word entries are treated like single words. For example, the entry Applejack appears after Apple, Dried and before Apple Juice.

**②** Each entry has been arranged into two columns. The left-hand column contains introductory and reference information. The right-hand column contains the substitutions.

**③** The introductory information in the left-hand column begins with a brief description, useful tip, or interesting fact about the item. If the item is known by any alternate names, these alternate names appear just before the description. For example, the entry for Annatto Oil begins, "Also known as manteca de achiote." These alternate names are followed by the item's description, in this case, "Food coloring made from the hard reddish pulp that surrounds the seeds of the annatto, a tropical American tree. In Jamaica, annatto oil is used to color codfish cakes."

**4** In many entries, the introduction is followed by a box of useful measurement equivalents, such as $\frac{1}{2}$ cup (125 mL) = 4 oz (125 mL). In some cases, the equivalents have been rounded for ease of measuring.

**5** The substitutions in the right-hand column appear in bulleted lists and have been categorized under one of five subheadings. Most substitutions fall under the subheading "If You Don't Have It," which appears in a shaded box at the top of the right-hand column. These substitutions are intended to replace items that you have run out of or cannot find in your market. However, in some cooking situations, you may want to intentionally vary the flavor of the finished dish, save time when preparing it, or improve its healthfulness. These types of substitutions appear under the subheadings "To Vary the Flavor," "To Save Time," and "For Better Health." If a particular item, such as Eggplant, has several varieties, those varieties and their characteristics appear beneath a fifth subheading, in this case, "Eggplant Varieties."

**6** In some entries, the suggested substitution is a basic recipe that may replace a common store-bought item. For instance, in the Annatto Oil entry, the first suggested substitution is a simple recipe for Homemade Annatto Oil. Every entry lists the preferred substitutions first, followed by those that less closely match the replaced item but still make a fair substitute. In most entries, canned, jarred, and frozen versions of fresh ingredients are not listed as substitutions. It is assumed that the reader will use discretion and preferences when choosing these common substitutes. In those few cases in which a canned, jarred, or frozen substitution is listed, the item being replaced is listed as fresh. For instance, in the Bell Pepper entry, the first substitution appears as follows: "Substitute 1 cup (250 mL) chopped fresh bell pepper with 1 cup (250 mL) chopped fresh, canned, or bottled pimiento."

**7** Every substitution includes proportions such as "Substitute 1 tbsp (15 mL) annatto oil with 1 tbsp (15 mL) vegetable oil + 2 drops yellow food coloring + 1 drop red food coloring mixed into 1 tbsp (15 mL) water or other non-oily liquid in recipe (food coloring will not mix with oil; add to watery liquids)." In some cases, additional adjustments are suggested in parentheses. Metric equivalents for each measurement, such as milliliters and Celsius, appear in parentheses after the Imperial measurement.

**8** Cross-references appear throughout the book in CAPITAL LETTERS. In most cases, cross-references direct the reader to the book entry that contains all of that item's information. For instance, readers looking up Active Dry Yeast will be referred to the entry for Yeast, Baker's. Cross-references may also direct readers to entries that provide related information. For example, under Annatto Oil, readers will find a cross-reference to see also the entry for Annatto Seed. These "see also" cross-references appear in the right-hand column after the bulleted list of substitutions.

Reference charts and tables appear at the back of the book. The first set of tables, called Ingredient Guides (page 635), profiles the different varieties of a particular food, such as apples. The profiles include alternate names for the food, texture and flavor characteristics, and the food's best uses or substitutes. The second set of tables, called Measurement Equivalents (page 677), offers Imperial and Metric equivalents for volume, weight, temperature, pan sizes and package sizes. It also includes charts of alcohol retention in cooking, stages of cooked sugar and adjustments for cooking and baking at high altitude. Many of the entries in A to Z section of the book refer you to these charts for more detailed information.

# A1 to Azuki Bean

## A1

*See* STEAK SAUCE.

## Ababai

*Also known as mountain papaya and mountain pawpaw. Thin-skinned fruit resembling a small papaya but with brown seeds filling the center. In its native Chile, the tropical fruit is preserved and candied, but it can also be eaten raw and is firm enough to be grilled, sautéed, or stewed.*

> 1 medium = 8 to 10 oz (250 to 300 g) = 1¼ to 1½ cups (300 to 375 mL) chopped or sliced

### If You Don't Have It

Substitute 1 lb (500 g) ababai with:
- 1 lb (500 g) papaya
- 1 lb (500 g) mango
- 1 lb (500 g) babaco
- 1 lb (500 g) pepino
- 1 lb (500 g) peaches
- 1 lb (500 g) nectarines

## Abalone

*Also known as awabi, loco, muttonfish, ormer, and paua. A mollusk sold in many Asian markets. Smaller ones taste better.*

### If You Don't Have It

Substitute 1 lb (500 g) abalone meat with:
- 1 lb (500 g) canned or frozen abalone (thaw and add juices to dish)
- 1 lb (500 g) clam or conch meat

## Abondance

*Also known as Tomme d'Abondance. French name-controlled cheese made from part-skim raw cow's milk. Made in 15-pound (7.5 kg) wheels, the cheese has a firm texture and wonderfully nutty, sweet, ripe, buttery taste. Great for melting.*

### If You Don't Have It
Substitute 1 oz (30 g) Abondance with:
- 1 oz (30 g) Raclette
- 1 oz (30 g) Comte
- 1 oz (30 g) Beaufort
- 1 oz (30 g) Fontina
- 1 oz (30 g) Appenzeller
- 1 oz (30 g) Emmental

## Absinthe

*See* ANISE LIQUEUR.

## Abura-age

*Pronounced "AH-boo-rah-AH-gay," this Japanese prepared food product is made of thin slices of deep-fried tofu with a crisp exterior and soft center. The deep-fried tofu can be sliced and added to soups or it can be slit open like a pita pocket and stuffed with sushi rice to make inari sushi.*

### If You Don't Have It
Substitute 8 oz (250 g) abura-age with:
- 8 oz (250 g) Homemade Abura-age: Cut a block of tofu through the side to make 3 slabs. Lay the slabs flat and put heavy weight on top for 30 minutes to press out excess liquid. Cut each slab in half then deep-fry or shallow-fry in oil until light golden brown on both sides, turning as necessary. Drain on paper towels and cool for 30 minutes. Fry a second time to a deeper golden brown, then drain and let cool. Rinse under hot water to remove excess oil. Refrigerate for up to 1 week.
- 8 oz (250 g) atsu-age

*See also* ATSU-AGE; TOFU.

## Açaí

*Small, round fruit of a palm tree native to Central and South America. Each deep-purple berry contains a single large seed and tastes reminiscent of blueberries, blackberries and cherries. Widely eaten fresh in Brazil, açaí berries are commonly juiced and consumed as beverages. Their antioxidant content is comparable to that of cranberries.*

### If You Don't Have It
Substitute 1 cup (250 mL) açaí berries or açaí juice with:
- 1 cup (250 mL) blueberries or blueberry juice
- 1 cup (250 mL) cranberries or cranberry juice
- 1 cup (250 mL) cherries or cherry juice

## Accent

*See* MONOSODIUM GLUTAMATE.

## Acerola

*Also known as West Indian cherry. A dark red fruit that's similar to cherries, higher in vitamin C than most other fruits, and slightly acidic.*

1 cup (250 mL) whole =
3½ oz (105 g)

1 pitted acerola =
¼ oz (7 g)

### If You Don't Have It
Substitute 1 cup (250 mL) pitted acerola with:
- 1 cup (250 mL) fresh rose hips
- 1 cup (250 mL) pitted cherries

## Achee

*See* ACKEE.

## Achiote Seed

*See* ANNATTO SEED.

## Acidophilus Milk

*See* MILK, WHOLE.

## Acidulated Water

*Water made slightly acidic by adding an acid ingredient, such as lemon juice or vinegar. Used to prevent the browning of cut foods such as apples and artichokes.*

### If You Don't Have It
Substitute 4 cups (1 L) acidulated water with:
- 4 cups (1 L) water + 1 tbsp (15 mL) salt (prevents browning without making the water acidic)
- 4 cups (1 L) Homemade Acidulated Water: Combine 4 cups (1 L) water, 1½ tbsp (22 mL) vinegar or 3 tbsp (45 mL) lemon juice or ½ cup (125 mL) white wine.
- 4 cups (1 L) water + 2 tablets (each 500 mg) vitamin C, crushed to a powder

## Acitrón

*See* NOPALE.

## Ackee

*Also known as achee and akee. A tropical fruit often served with salt cod in Jamaica. Only the ripe pale flesh of the fruit is edible.*

### If You Don't Have It
Substitute 1 cup (250 mL) fresh ackee with:
- 1 cup (250 mL) canned ackee

## Ackwai

*See* JIBNEH ARABIEH.

## Acorn

*Nuts produced by oak trees, some of which are edible by humans. Can be ground into meal, eaten raw, or roasted and eaten.*

### If You Don't Have It

Substitute 1 cup (250 mL) shelled white oak acorns with:
- 1 cup (250 mL) hazelnuts
- 1 cup (250 mL) chestnuts

## Acorn Squash

*Dark green winter squash, with orange spots, is deeply ridged and shaped like an acorn. For easy peeling, prick hard shell before cooking.*

> 1 lb (500 g) = 1 cup (250 mL) cooked and mashed

### If You Don't Have It

Substitute 1 cup (250 mL) acorn squash with:
- 1 cup (250 mL) butternut squash (more easily peeled; creamier)
- 1 cup (250 mL) buttercup squash (less moist)
- 1 cup (250 mL) pumpkin (creamier)

## Active Dry Yeast

*See* YEAST, BAKER'S.

## Adobo Sauce

*Traditional Mexican seasoning sauce or paste made from toasted and rehydrated chiles, garlic, cumin, oregano and other spices. Also used as the canning liquid for canned chipotle chiles.*

### If You Don't Have It

Substitute 1 cup (250 mL) adobo sauce with:
- 1 cup (250 mL) Homemade Adobo Sauce: Toast 8 to 10 unpeeled garlic cloves in a large dry skillet over medium heat, shaking occasionally, until skins are blackened, 10 to 15 minutes. Let cool and peel. Tear open and discard seeds from about 4 dried ancho chiles (2 oz/60 g), about 4 dried guajillo chiles (2 oz/60 g), and about 2 dried chipotle chiles (½ oz/15 g) (wear gloves to protect your hands). Toast chiles in the same skillet, pressing flat with spatula, until fragrant and lightly browned, about 2 minutes per side. Put chiles in a large bowl, cover with hot water, and let stand for 20 to 30 minutes. Transfer chiles to a blender or food processor. Add ½ cup (125 mL) beef, chicken, or vegetable broth, ¼ cup (60 mL) chile soaking liquid, toasted garlic, 1 to 2 tsp (5 to 10 mL) dried oregano, ½ tsp (2 mL) ground black pepper, ⅛ to ¼ tsp (0.5 to 1 mL) ground cumin, a pinch of ground coriander, and a pinch of ground cinnamon. Purée until smooth, scraping down sides. Strain mixture through a medium-mesh sieve into a bowl and discard solids. Stir in salt to taste. Makes about 1 cup (250 mL).

## Advocaat

*Dutch liqueur made from egg yolks and brandy. Similar to thick eggnog, advocaat is often dolloped into coffee or hot chocolate.*

### If You Don't Have It

Substitute 2 tbsp (30 mL) advocaat with:

- 2 tbsp (30 mL) nonalcoholic eggnog + ¼ to ½ tsp (1 to 2 mL) brandy
- 2 tbsp (30 mL) Irish cream liqueur

## Adzuki Bean

*See* THE WIDE WORLD OF DRIED BEANS (PAGE 637).

## African Bird's Eye Pepper

*See* CHOOSING DRIED CHILES (PAGE 642) AND CHOOSING FRESH CHILES (PAGE 640).

## African Blue Basil

*See* BASIL.

## African Horned Cucumber

*See* KIWANO.

## African Pepper

*See* SELIM KILI PEPPER.

## Agar

*Also known as kanten. An odorless sea vegetable used as a gelling agent. Use 1 tsp (5 mL) agar powder to gel 1 cup (250 mL) liquid.*

> 1½ tbsp (22 mL) agar flakes = 1 tsp (5 mL) agar powder = ½ kanten bar

### If You Don't Have It

Substitute 1 tsp (5 mL) agar powder with:

- 1½ tsp (7 mL) gelatin powder

## Agave Nectar

*Also known as agave syrup. A mild-tasting liquid sweetener extracted from agave cactus plants. Sweeter yet thinner than honey, agave nectar has a relatively low glycemic index (blood sugar load) due to its low proportion of glucose to fructose.*

> 1 lb (500 g) = 1⅓ cups (325 mL)

### If You Don't Have It

Substitute 1 cup (250 mL) agave nectar with:

- ¾ cup (175 mL) honey or maple syrup + 2 tbsp (30 mL) water or other liquid from the recipe (slightly thicker consistency; adds maple or honey flavor)
- ¾ cup (175 mL) barley malt syrup
- ½ cup (125 mL) molasses (stronger flavor; darker color; thicker consistency)
- 1¼ cups (300 mL) granulated sugar + ¼ cup (60 mL) liquid called for in recipe

*See also* HONEY; MAPLE SYRUP; SUGAR.

## Agrodolce

*Italian sweet-and-sour sauce made by reducing vinegar, sugar, and fruit or chocolate, sometimes with the addition of wine.*

### If You Don't Have It

Substitute 1 cup (250 mL) agrodolce with:

- 1 cup (250 mL) gastrique (French sweet-and-sour sauce)
- 1 cup (250 mL) Chinese sweet-and-sour sauce

## Aguardiente

*See* GRAPPA.

## Ahi

*See* TUNA, FRESH.

## Aïoli

*See* MAYONNAISE.

## Ají

*See* CHOOSING DRIED CHILES (PAGE 642) AND CHOOSING FRESH CHILES (PAGE 640).

## Aji-no-moto

*See* MONOSODIUM GLUTAMATE.

## Ajwain

*Also known as ajowan, Bishop's weed, and carom seed. A southern Indian spice that tastes somewhat like thyme. The seeds contain antioxidant and preservative qualities.*

### If You Don't Have It

Substitute 1 tsp (5 mL) ajwain with:

- 1 tsp (5 mL) lovage seeds
- 1¼ tsp (6 mL) dried thyme
- ½ tsp (2 mL) dried thyme or oregano + scant ½ tsp (2 mL) dried celery seeds + scant ¼ tsp (1 mL) ground black pepper
- ¾ tsp (3 mL) cumin seeds
- ¾ tsp (3 mL) caraway seeds

## Akala

*A large Hawaiian berry, varying in color from red to purple. Akala is eaten raw or cooked in pastries and jams.*

1 pint fresh = 2⅔ cups (650 mL)

### If You Don't Have It

Substitute 1 cup (250 mL) akala with:

- 1 cup (250 mL) raspberries

## Akee

*See* ACKEE.

## Akule

*A Hawaiian fish that is often salted and dried like cod.*

### If You Don't Have It

Substitute 1 lb (500 g) akule with:

- 1 lb (500 g) salted and dried mackerel
- 1 lb (500 g) salt cod

| | |
|---|---|
| **Akvavit** | *See* AQUAVIT. |
| **Alaska King Crab** | *See* CRAB; CHOOSING AMONG CRABS (PAGE 647). |
| **Alaska Smoked Cod** | *See* BLACK COD. |
| **Albacore** | *See* TUNA, CANNED; TUNA, FRESH. |
| **Alcohol** | *See* BEER; LIQUEUR; WINE; SPECIFIC TYPES. |
| **Ale** | *See* BEER. |
| **Aleppo** | *See* CHOOSING DRIED CHILES (PAGE 642). |
| **Alessandri** | *See* SALAMI. |

## Alfalfa Sprouts

*Germinated seeds of a green leafy forage crop, alfalfa sprouts are eaten as a salad vegetable or sandwich topping.*

### If You Don't Have It

Substitute ¼ cup (60 mL) alfalfa sprouts with:
- ¼ cup (60 mL) broccoli sprouts (more peppery)
- ¼ cup (60 mL) fenugreek sprouts (slightly bitter)
- ¼ cup (60 mL) buckwheat sprouts (more nutty)
- ¼ cup (60 mL) sunflower sprouts (more nutty)
- ¼ cup (60 mL) mung bean sprouts (thicker and more crisp)

| | |
|---|---|
| **Allemande Sauce** | *See* VELOUTÉ. |

## Alligator

*Alligator meat tastes similar to chicken or mild white fish. Tail meat is white and tender while body meat is somewhat tougher and darker. It is usually sold frozen as tail steak, stew meat, burger, wings (legs), or sausage.*

### If You Don't Have It

Substitute 1 lb (500 g) alligator tail meat with:
- 1 lb (500 g) crocodile tail meat
- 1 lb (500 g) turtle meat
- 1 lb (500 g) chicken breast
- 1 lb (500 g) swordfish

| | |
|---|---|
| **Alligator Pepper** | *See* GRAINS OF PARADISE. |
| **All-Purpose Flour** | *See* FLOUR, ALL-PURPOSE. |

## Allspice

*Also known as clove pepper, Jamaica pepper, myrtle pepper and pimento. A tiny dried, dark brown berry used often in desserts and Jamaican cooking.*

> 40 whole berries = 1 tsp (5 mL) ground

### If You Don't Have It

Substitute 1 tsp (5 mL) ground allspice with:

- ½ tsp (2 mL) ground cinnamon + ½ tsp (2 mL) ground cloves + pinch of ground nutmeg (optional)

## Almond

*See* ALMOND, BITTER; ALMOND, GREEN; ALMOND, SWEET; APRICOT KERNEL.

## Almond, Bitter

*A bitter almond contains about 6 milligrams of toxic cynanide. When heated, the toxin in is destroyed, making bitter almonds safe for use in almond extracts and liqueurs. The flavor of bitter almond is a key component in Italian amaretti cookies.*

> 1 lb (500 g) in shell =
> 1½ cups (375 mL) whole =
> ⅓ cup (75 mL)
> ground meal
>
> 1 lb (500 g) shelled =
> 3 cups (750 mL) whole =
> 4 cups (1 L) slivered =
> 4½ cups (1.125 L) sliced

### If You Don't Have It

Substitute 1 cup (250 mL) blanched bitter almonds with:

- 1 cup (250 mL) blanched or roasted apricot kernels (Chinese almonds)
- 1 cup (250 mL) almonds with skin (amber color, much less bitter flavor)
- 1 cup (250 mL) Homemade Blanched Bitter Almonds: Drop 1 cup (250 mL) bitter almonds in boiling water for 2 minutes. Drain and rub off skins in a kitchen towel.
- ¼ to ½ tsp (1 to 2 mL) bitter almond oil or extract (for baking and cooking; will add bitter almond flavor but not texture of whole nuts)
- 2 to 4 tbsp (30 to 60 mL) almond liqueur (for baking and cooking; adds some bitter almond flavor and alcohol but not texture of whole nuts; reduce liquid in recipe by 2 to 4 tbsp/30 to 60 mL)

*See also* APRICOT KERNEL.

## Almond Butter

*A spread of ground roasted almonds, oil, and salt, almond butter is slightly grainier than peanut butter.*

> 1 cup (250 mL) = 8 oz (250 g)

### If You Don't Have It

Substitute 1 cup (250 mL) almond butter with:

- 1 cup (250 mL) Homemade Almond Butter: Combine 2 cups (500 mL) roasted almonds and ¼ tsp (1 mL) salt in a blender or food processor fitted with metal blade. Process, gradually adding 6 tbsp (90 mL) almond or vegetable oil, until the mixture forms a paste, 1 to 2 minutes. Makes 1½ cups (375 mL).
- 1 cup (250 mL) peanut butter or cashew butter
- 1 cup (250 mL) tahini (pronounced sesame flavor)

## Almond, Chinese

See APRICOT KERNEL.

## Almond Extract

A concentrated flavoring, used mostly for desserts and pastries. It's made by combining bitter almond oil and ethyl alcohol.

### If You Don't Have It

Substitute ½ tsp (2 mL) almond extract with:
- 1 drop almond oil + ¼ tsp (1 mL) vodka
- 1 tbsp (15 mL) almond liqueur

### To Vary the Flavor

Substitute ½ tsp (2 mL) almond extract with:
- ¾ tsp (3 mL) vanilla extract

## Almond Flour

Fine flour ground from blanched almonds that have been pressed to extract excess oil.

10 oz (300 g) = 3 cups (750 mL)

### If You Don't Have It

Substitute 1 cup (250 mL) almond flour with:
- 1 cup (250 mL) almond meal (coarser texture, moister)

### To Vary the Flavor

Substitute 1 cup (250 mL) almond flour with:
- 1 cup (250 mL) chestnut flour (lower in protein, gluten-free)

See also NUT MEAL; CHOOSING AMONG WHOLE-GRAIN AND ALTERNATIVE FLOURS (PAGE 648).

## Almond, Green

Also known as fresh almonds. The immature sweet almond nut has a soft, fruit-like texture similar to grapes, and the outer hull is covered in downy green fuzz. Green almonds have a bright, grassy and slightly sour taste that can be tamed by salting or pickling them.

10 oz (300 g) = 3 cups (750 mL)

### If You Don't Have It

Substitute 1 cup (250 mL) green almonds with:
- 1 cup (250 mL) mature blanched or slivered almonds soaked for 10 to 12 hours in 2 cups (500 mL) warm water and 1 tsp (2 mL) baking soda (for use in cooked dishes)

See also ALMOND, SWEET.

## Almond Liqueur

A cordial widely used in Italy. Amaretto di Saronno is a popular brand.

### If You Don't Have It

Substitute 2 tbsp (30 mL) almond liqueur with:
- ½ to ¾ tsp (2 to 3 mL) almond extract (add 2 tbsp/30 mL water if necessary to replace lost liquid volume)

### To Vary the Flavor

Substitute 2 tbsp (30 mL) almond liqueur with:
- 2 tbsp (30 mL) hazelnut liqueur, coffee liqueur, or chocolate liqueur
- 2 tbsp (30 mL) crème d'amande or crème de noyaux (sweeter flavor, thicker texture, pink color)

## Almond Milk

*The liquid strained from ground blanched almonds, sugar, and water. It is gelled to make the classic French pudding blancmange.*

### If You Don't Have It

Substitute 1 cup (250 mL) almond milk with:
- 1 cup (250 mL) rice milk or sweetened soy milk

## Almond Oil

*See* OIL OF BITTER ALMONDS; SUBSTITUTING OILS (PAGE 658).

## Almond Paste

*A smooth blend of ground almonds and sugar used to make marzipan, macaroons, and fillings for Danish and other pastries.*

### If You Don't Have It

Substitute 1¼ cups (300 mL) almond paste with:
- 1¼ cups (300 mL) bitter almond paste (more intense almond flavor from oil of bitter almonds; often used for amaretti cookies)
- 1¼ cups (300 mL) marzipan (sweeter and more pliable)
- 1¾ cups (425 mL) ground blanched almonds + 1½ cups (375 mL) confectioner's sugar + 1 egg white + 1 tsp (5 mL) almond extract + ¼ tsp (1 mL) salt

## Almond, Sweet

*Commercially available almonds are known as sweet almonds. Most markets sell them with the natural brown skin intact or blanched (skin removed). Bitter almonds, on the other hand, contain a toxic acid and are generally unavailable to consumers.*

1 lb (500 g) in shell = 1½ cups (375 mL) whole = ⅓ cup (75 mL) ground meal

1 lb (500 g) shelled = 3 cups (750 mL) whole = 4 cups (1 L) slivered = 4½ cups (1.125 L) sliced

### If You Don't Have It

Substitute 1 cup (250 mL) blanched almonds with:
- 1 cup (250 mL) almonds with skin (if you don't mind the amber color and mildly bitter flavor)
- 1 cup (250 mL) Homemade Blanched Almonds: Drop 1 cup (250 mL) almonds in boiling water for 2 minutes. Drain and rub off skins in a kitchen towel.
- 2 to 4 tbsp (30 to 60 mL) almond oil (for baking and cooking; will add nut flavor but not texture of whole nuts; reduce fat in recipe by 2 to 4 tbsp/30 to 60 mL)
- 2 to 4 tbsp (30 to 60 mL) almond liqueur (for baking and cooking; adds nut flavor and alcohol but not texture of whole nuts; reduce liquid in recipe by 2 to 4 tbsp/30 to 60 mL)

### To Vary the Flavor

Substitute 1 cup (250 mL) shelled almonds with:
- 1 cup (250 mL) walnuts
- 1 cup (250 mL) pecans
- 1 cup (250 mL) hazelnuts
- 1 cup (250 mL) pistachios

*See also* ALMOND, BITTER; ALMOND, GREEN.

## Alouette

*See* CREAM CHEESE.

## Alpino

*See* SALAMI.

## Altitude

*See* BAKING AT HIGH-ALTITUDE (PAGE 686); COOKING AT HIGH-ALTITUDE (PAGE 686).

## Altramuz

*See* LUPINI BEAN.

## Aluminum Foil

*Also known as foil or tin foil. Around the turn of the 20th century, sheet foil manufactured from aluminum began to replace foil made from tin, which imparted a tinny aftertaste to foods wrapped in it.*

### If You Don't Have It

Substitute aluminum foil with:

- plastic wrap, especially sealable plastic wrap (for covering and refrigerating foods)
- parchment paper (for lining baking sheets, covering roasts, and wrapping foods)
- wax paper (for lining baking pans and wrapping foods)

### To Vary the Flavor

Substitute aluminum foil (as a food wrapper) with:

- corn husks (adds mild corn aroma)
- hoja santa leaves (adds aromas of root beer and fennel)
- banana leaves (adds herby-green flavor)

## Amaranth Flour

*See* CHOOSING AMONG WHOLE-GRAIN AND ALTERNATIVE FLOURS (PAGE 648).

## Amaranth Grain

*Also known as pigweed. Gluten-free, high-iron, high-lysine, high-quality-protein grain cultivated by the Aztecs.*

> 1 cup (250 mL) = about 9 oz (275 g)

### If You Don't Have It

Substitute 1 cup (250 mL) amaranth grain with:

- 1 cup (250 mL) quinoa
- 1 cup (250 mL) millet
- 1 cup (250 mL) couscous, especially whole wheat (cooks more quickly)
- 1 cup (250 mL) bulgur
- 1 cup (250 mL) rice
- 1 cup (250 mL) kasha (roasted buckwheat groats; takes longer to cook)

*See also* CHOOSING AMONG WHOLE-GRAIN AND ALTERNATIVE FLOURS (PAGE 648).

## Amaranth Leaf

*Also known as Chinese spinach and yin choy. The leaves are similar to spinach but sweeter and more delicate, and with beautiful pinkish purple veins. The seeds are used as cereal or ground to make amaranth flour.*

### If You Don't Have It

Substitute 1 lb (500 g) amaranth leaves with:

- 1 lb (500 g) red chard leaves (firmer leaves)
- 1 lb (500 g) baby spinach
- 1 lb (500 g) callaloo (taro leaves)
- 1 lb (500 g) Chinese kale
- 1 lb (500 g) chile leaves (more bitter)

## Amaretti

*Also known as Italian macaroons. The name means "little bitter," a reference to the bitter almond flavor. Often crushed for use in desserts and savory dishes.*

### If You Don't Have It
Substitute 1 lb (500 g) amaretti with:
- 1 lb (500 g) almond biscotti

### To Vary the Flavor
Substitute 1 lb (500 g) amaretti with
- 1 lb (500 g) graham crackers, ladyfingers, or other crisp cookies (especially for crushing)
- 1 lb (500 g) macaroons (softer; lighter)

## Amaretto

*See* ALMOND LIQUEUR.

## Amasake

*Japanese fermented rice milk. May be as thin as skim milk or as thick as a smoothie, depending upon the intended use.*

### If You Don't Have It
Substitute 1 cup (250 mL) amasake with:
- 1 cup (250 mL) sweetened rice milk, soy milk, or almond milk
- 1 cup (250 mL) milk

## Amberjack

*Atlantic fish in the Jack family ranging from 15 to 150 pounds (7 to 68 kg). Amberjacks have firm, white, very lean flesh.*

### If You Don't Have It
Substitute 1 lb (500 g) amberjack with:
- 1 lb (500 g) mahi-mahi
- 1 lb (500 g) grouper
- 1 lb (500 g) tilefish
- 1 lb (500 g) mullet
- 1 lb (500 g) shark

*See also* POMPANO.

## Ambrosia Melon

*Similar to cantaloupe but with pale orange flesh and an intense, floral perfume.*

1 medium = 2 lbs (1 kg)
= 3 cups (750 mL) diced

### If You Don't Have It
Substitute 1 cup (250 mL) chopped ambrosia melon with:
- 1 cup (250 mL) chopped cantaloupe
- 1 cup (250 mL) chopped Charentais melon
- 1 cup (250 mL) chpped Persian melon
- 1 cup (250 mL) chopped Crenshaw melon
- 1 cup (250 mL) chopped Santa Claus melon
- 1 cup (250 mL) chopped honeydew melon
- 1 cup (250 mL) chopped casaba melon

*See also* CHARENTAIS MELON.

## Amchur

*See* MANGO POWDER.

## American Bacon

*See* BACON.

## American Cheese

*Also known as processed cheese. Produced with up to 51% natural cheese that is combined with emulsifiers and other liquid.*

| 1 oz (30 g) = 1 slice |
|---|

### If You Don't Have It

Substitute 1 oz (30 g) with:

- 1 oz (30 g) processed cheese, such as Velveeta
- 1 oz (30 g) Cheddar cheese (sharper, deeper flavor)
- 1 oz (30 g) Swiss cheese (sharper, deeper flavor)

*See also* PROCESSED CHEESE.

## Amer Picon

*Also known as Picon. Very bitter reddish brown French apéritif produced with gentian, orange, and cinchona bark (also used to make quinine).*

### If You Don't Have It

Substitute 2 tbsp (30 mL) Amer Picon with:

- 2 tbsp (30 mL) Byrrh, Dubonnet blanc, or Lillet (each less bitter than Amer Picon)

## Ammonium Bicarbonate

*Leavener that preceded modern baking powder and baking soda.*

### If You Don't Have It

Substitute 1 tsp (5 mL) ammonium bicarbonate with:

- 1 tsp (5 mL) baking powder
- 1¼ tsp (6 mL) baking soda
- ¾ tsp (3 mL) baking powder + ¾ tsp (3 mL) baking soda

## Anago

*See* EEL.

## Anaheim Chile

*See* CHOOSING DRIED CHILES (PAGE 642); CHOOSING FRESH CHILES (PAGE 640).

## Anasazi Bean

*See* THE WIDE WORLD OF DRIED BEANS (PAGE 637).

## Ancho Chile

*See* CHOOSING DRIED CHILES (PAGE 642).

## Anchovy

*Small silver fish of many species found in warm oceans around the globe. Most popular in countries that rim the Mediterranean. Historically salted or canned in oil, fresh anchovies are gaining popularity.*

| 2 oz (60 g) = 10 to 12 anchovies = 3 to 4 tbsp (45 to 60 mL) anchovy paste |
|---|

### If You Don't Have It

Substitute 2 anchovy fillets with:

- 1 tsp (5 mL) anchovy paste
- ½ oz (15 g) smelt
- ½ oz (15 g) sardines

## Anchovy Paste

*A savory condiment of mashed anchovies, vinegar, spices and water available in tubes near the canned fish in most supermarkets.*

2 oz (60 g) =
4 tbsp (60 mL)

### If You Don't Have It
Substitute 1 tsp (5 mL) anchovy paste with:
- 1 mashed anchovy fillet (stronger anchovy flavor)

### To Vary the Flavor
Substitute 1 tsp (5 mL) anchovy paste with:
- 1 tsp (5 mL) shrimp paste (more pungent)

## Andouille

*French tripe-based large rustic sausages, smoked and eaten cold. In Louisiana, descendants of French Acadians created a spicy, smoked ground pork sausage of the same name.*

### If You Don't Have It
Substitute 1 lb (500 g) andouille with:
- 1 lb (500 g) spicy smoked kielbasa
- 1 lb (500 g) Spanish chorizo
- 1 lb (500 g) Portuguese chouriço or liguinça
- 1 lb (500 g) other spicy or smoked sausage

## Andouillette

*Small French fresh sausages most commonly made from tripe. Grilled andouillettes garnished with mustard and served with puréed potatoes are a classic bistro specialty.*

### If You Don't Have It
Substitute 1 lb (500 g) andouillette with:
- 1 lb (500 g) French andouille (larger)

### To Vary the Flavor
Substitute 1 lb (500 g) andouillette with:
- 1 lb (500 g) sweet Italian sausage

## Anesone

*See* ANISE LIQUEUR.

## Angel Food Cake

*Slice with a serrated knife or tines of a fork to prevent squashing the airy cake.*

### If You Don't Have It
Substitute 1 lb (500 g) angel food cake with:
- 1 lb (500 g) sponge cake
- 1 lb (500 g) pound cake (richer flavor; denser texture)

## Angelica

*Also known as French rhubarb. A tall, thick-stemmed, temperate plant sometimes eaten as a vegetable. Often used in European confectionery, the stalks are cut in short pieces and candied.*

### If You Don't Have It
Substitute 1 tbsp (15 mL) chopped fresh angelica with:
- 1 tbsp (15 mL) chopped fresh lovage (similar celery-like flavor)
- 1 tbsp (15 mL) chopped fresh tarragon (more licorice-like flavor)

## Angelica, Candied

*Tender green stems of the young angelica plant cooked in sugar syrup; often used to make decorative flour stems on cakes.*

### If You Don't Have It

Substitute 1 lb (500 g) candied angelica with:

- 1 lb (500 g) Homemade Candied Angelica: Cut 1 lb (500 g) young, tender angelica stems into even lengths and place in a 2-quart (2 L) shallow glass or ceramic dish. Boil 2 cups (500 mL) water with 2 tbsp (30 mL) salt then pour over the angelica. Completely submerge the angelica by weighting it down with a plate. Cover and let stand at room temperature for 2 hours. Drain, peel and discard the outer layer of the angelica, then rinse under cold water. Bring 1½ cups (375 mL) granulated sugar and 1½ cups (375 mL) water to a boil in a wide saucepan, add the angelica, and simmer until the angelica is tender, about 20 minutes. Using tongs, transfer the angelica to a wire rack and set aside until very dry, about 4 days (reserve the syrup). Return the syrup to a boil, add the dried angelica and simmer again for 10 minutes. Transfer to a wire rack and let dry for another 4 days. Coat with granulated sugar and store in an airtight container. Makes about 1 pound (500 g).
- 1 lb (500 g) candied fennel stalks
- 1 lb (500 g) green marzipan shaped into stalks and allowed to harden (for decorating cakes)

## Angled Luffa

*See* LUFFA, ANGLED.

## Anglerfish

*See* MONKFISH.

## Angostura Bitters

*See* BITTERS.

## Angula

*See* EEL.

## Anise Basil

*See* BASIL.

## Anise Extract

*A concentrated flavoring used for breads and pastries in European and Middle Eastern kitchens. Made by combining anise oil and ethyl alcohol.*

### If You Don't Have It

Substitute 1 tsp (5 mL) anise extract with:

- ⅛ to ¼ tsp (0.5 to 1 mL) anise oil
- 1 to 2 tbsp (15 to 30 mL) anise liqueur (reduce liquid in recipe by 1 to 2 tbsp/5 to 10 mL)
- 2 tsp (10 mL) ground anise seeds

### To Vary the Flavor

Substitute 1 tsp (5 mL) anise extract with:

- 1 tsp (5 mL) almond or vanilla extract

## Anise Liqueur

*Also known as arak, ouzo, and pastis. Cordial flavored with anise seeds. When mixed with water, clear anise-flavored liqueurs turn cloudy and white.*

### If You Don't Have It

Substitute 2 tbsp (30 mL) anise liqueur with:
- 1 to 1½ tsp (5 to 7 mL) anise extract (add 1½ tbsp/22 mL liquid to recipe if necessary)
- 2 tsp (10 mL) ground anise seeds (add 2 tbsp/30 mL liquid to recipe if necessary)
- 1 whole star anise (add 2 tbsp/30 mL liquid to recipe if necessary)

### Anise Liqueur Varieties

Choose 2 tbsp (30 mL) anise liqueur from these varieties:
- 2 tbsp (30 mL) anisette (French anise liqueur; sweet flavor; low alcohol)
- 2 tbsp (30 mL) anesone (Italian anise liqueur)
- 2 tbsp (30 mL) sambuca (Italian anise liqueur; more pronounced licorice flavor; higher alcohol)
- 2 tbsp (30 mL) ouzo (Greek anise liqueur; higher alcohol)
- 2 tbsp (30 mL) arak (anise-flavored liqueur of Middle Eastern origin; higher alcohol)
- 2 tbsp (30 mL) raki (anise-flavored liqueur of Middle Eastern origin; higher alcohol)
- 2 tbsp (30 mL) absinthe (anise-flavored liqueur popularized; once banned due to supposed hallucinogenic effects but now available in many countries; green colour; higher alcohol)
- 2 tbsp (30 mL) herbsaint (anise-flavored liqueur originating in New Orleans; similar to absinthe but without the narcotic; higher alcohol)
- 2 tbsp (30 mL) Ricard, Pernod, or other pastis (French anise liqueur; more pronounced licorice flavor; higher alcohol)

## Anise Oil

*Flavoring oil extracted from anise seeds.*

### If You Don't Have It

Substitute ¼ tsp (1 mL) anise oil with:
- 1 tsp (5 mL) anise extract
- 1 to 2 tbsp (15 to 30 mL) anise liqueur (reduce liquid in recipe by 1 to 2 tbsp/15 to 30 mL)
- 2 tsp (10 mL) ground anise seeds

## Anise Seed

*Seeds produced by a culinary herb in the parsley family. The anise plant has been cultivated since ancient Roman times. The sweet, distinctive flavor of anise comes from the essential oil anethole.*

### If You Don't Have It

Substitute ½ tsp (2 mL) anise seeds with:
- 1 small crushed star anise (bolder flavor)
- ½ tsp (2 mL) fennel seeds (milder, sweeter flavor)
- ½ tsp (2 mL) caraway seeds (milder, more nutty flavor)
- 1 tsp (5 mL) chopped fresh tarragon (adds green color)

*See also* STAR ANISE.

## Anisette

*See* ANISE LIQUEUR.

## Ankimo

*See* MONKFISH LIVER.

## Annatto Oil

*Also known as manteca de achiote. Food coloring made from the hard reddish pulp that surrounds the seeds of the annatto, a tropical American tree. In Jamaica, annatto oil is used to color codfish cakes.*

1 cup (250 mL) = 4 oz (125 g)

### If You Don't Have It

Substitute 1 tbsp (15 mL) annatto oil with:
- 1 tbsp (15 mL) Homemade Annatto Oil: Sauté 1½ tsp (7 mL) annatto seeds in 1 tbsp (15 mL) vegetable oil in a saucepan over medium heat, until oil turns a deep orange color, 8 to 10 minutes. Remove seeds with slotted spoon and discard.
- 1 tbsp (15 mL) vegetable oil + 2 drops yellow food coloring + 1 drop red food coloring mixed into 1 tbsp (15 mL) water or other non-oily liquid in recipe (food coloring will not mix with oil; add to watery liquids)

*See also* ANNATTO SEED.

## Annatto Seed

*Also known as achiote, atsuete seed, and roucou. To extract the rich yellow orange color, steep the seeds in boiling water for about 20 minutes, then discard the seeds. Or make annatto oil for cooking (see above).*

### If You Don't Have It

Substitute 1½ tsp (7 mL) annatto seeds with:
- ½ tsp (2 mL) turmeric + ½ tsp (2 mL) mild paprika (for yellow orange color; adds more pungent flavor)
- ½ to 1 tsp (2 to 5 mL) crushed dried safflower florets
- 2 drops yellow food coloring + 1 drop red food coloring mixed into water or other liquid in the recipe (for yellow orange color)

*See also* ANNATTO OIL.

## Antelope

*Ruminant mammals of Africa and Asia including gazelle, springbok, and wildebeest. The so-called North American antelope, the pronghorn, is also eaten as game meat. The lean meat can be larded for additional moistness and flavor.*

### If You Don't Have It

Substitute 1 lb (500 g) antelope with:
- 1 lb (500 g) gazelle
- 1 lb (500 g) caribou
- 1 lb (500 g) reindeer
- 1 lb (500 g) red, fallow, or white-tailed deer
- 1 lb (500 g) moose
- 1 lb (500 g) elk

*See also* VENISON.

## Appaloosa Bean

*See* THE WIDE WORLD OF DRIED BEANS (PAGE 637).

## Appenzeller

*Also known as Appenzell. Unpasteurized whole-milk cow's cheese from eastern Switzerland. The mildly fragrant flavor is partially due to washing the rind with spiced wine or cider.*

### If You Don't Have It
Substitute 1 oz (30 g) Appenzeller with:
- 1 oz (30 g) Emmental (nuttier flavor; large holes)
- 1 oz (30 g) Gruyère (sweeter, nuttier flavor; semifirm texture)
- 1 oz (30 g) raclette (sweeter, nuttier flavor; semifirm texture)

## Apple

*Apple varieties number between 7,000 and 8,000. Modern cultivated apples differ dramatically from their tiny, sour ancestors, which excelled botanically at producing seeds for propagation.*

1 lb (500 g) = 3 medium = 3 cups (750 mL) sliced = 1⅓ cups (325 mL) sauce

### If You Don't Have It
Substitute 1 lb (500 g) apples with:
- 1 lb (500 g) pears (generally softer flesh)
- 1 lb (500 g) Asian pears (generally crisper and juicier texture; tart flavor)
- 1 lb (500 g) quinces (best for cooking; more tart flavor)

*See also* PICKING APPLES (PAGE 636).

## Apple Brandy

*Also known as applejack, Calvados (French), cider brandy, cider spirits and cider whiskey. Distilled apple cider was a popular beverage in Colonial America and, as Calvados, it enjoys a distinguished history in the French apple-growing region of Normandy.*

### If You Don't Have It
Substitute 2 tbsp (30 mL) apple brandy with:
- 2 tbsp (30 mL) pear brandy
- 1 tbsp (15 mL) cognac or brandy + 1 tbsp (15 mL) apple juice concentrate

### Apple Brandy Varieties
Choose 2 tbsp (30 mL) apple brandy from these specific types:
- 2 tbsp (30 mL) Calvados (French apple brandy in varying degrees of good quality)
- 2 tbsp (30 mL) applejack (American apple brandy; generally of lesser quality than Calvados; look for straight instead of blended versions for higher quality)

### For Better Health
Substitute 2 tbsp (30 mL) apple brandy with:
- 2 tbsp (30 mL) apple juice or apple juice concentrate

## Apple Butter

*A preserve served as a bread topping or condiment. Prepared by slowly simmering apples with sugar, cider, cinnamon, cloves, and allspice.*

### If You Don't Have It

Substitute 1 tbsp (15 mL) apple butter with:

- 1 tbsp (15 mL) Homemade Apple Butter: Combine 1 cup (250 mL) sliced apples, 2 tbsp (30 mL) granulated sugar, and 2 tbsp (30 mL) apple juice or cider in a pot. Bring to a boil over high heat. Reduce heat to medium-low and simmer, stirring now and then, until apples are fall-apart tender, about 1 hour. Remove from heat. Stir in ¼ tsp (1 mL) cinnamon. Transfer to a blender or food processor and purée until smooth.

### To Vary the Flavor

Substitute 1 tbsp (15 mL) apple butter with:

- 1 tbsp (15 mL) pear butter
- 1 tbsp (15 mL) pumpkin butter

## Apple Cider

*Also known as sweet apple cider. Made by crushing several apple varieties into a pomace, then pressing out the juice. Tiny apple solids in the juice darken when exposed to air, giving cider its distinctive caramel color.*

### If You Don't Have It

Substitute 1 cup (250 mL) non-alcoholic apple cider with:

- 1 cup (250 mL) apple juice

### To Vary the Flavor

Substitute 1 cup (250 mL) nonalcoholic apple cider with:

- 1 cup (250 mL) pear cider

## Apple Corer

*A utensil, often stainless steel, designed to cut and easily remove the core, or center, from apples.*

### If You Don't Have It

Substitute an apple corer with:

- melon baller (to scoop the core from an apple halved lengthwise)
- paring knife (to cut the core from an apple halved lengthwise)
- countertop peeling-coring-slicing machine

## Apple, Dried

*Commercially produced, slices of peeled apples are treated with sulfur dioxide and dehydrated. Apple slices may also be dried in home food dehydrators.*

8 oz (250 g) =
2¼ cups (550 mL) =
4 cups (1 L) cooked

### If You Don't Have It

Substitute 1 oz (30 g) dried apples with:

- 1 oz (30 g) dried pears
- 1 oz (30 g) dried Asian pears

## Applejack

*See* APPLE BRANDY.

## Apple Juice

*Juice pressed from fresh apples that is filtered and heat-treated to be shelf stable. Also available in concentrate that is shelf-stable or frozen.*

### If You Don't Have It
Substitute 1 cup (250 mL) apple juice with:
- 1 cup (250 mL) apple cider
- 1 cup (250 mL) pear cider
- 1 cup (250 mL) white grape juice (sweeter)

## Apple Pear

*See* ASIAN PEAR.

## Apple Pie Spice

*A commercial or homemade combination of spices especially suited to enhance apple pie but also a wonderful seasoning for French toast, pancakes, waffles, sugar cookies, and other desserts. The mixture almost always contains cinnamon and nutmeg with a range of optional additions, including allspice, cardamom, cloves, mace, or ginger.*

### If You Don't Have It
Substitute 1 tbsp (15 mL) apple pie spice with:
- 1 tbsp (15 mL) Homemade Apple Pie Spice: Combine 2 tsp (10 mL) ground cinnamon, 1 tsp (5 mL) ground nutmeg and pinch ground allspice.

### To Vary the Flavor
Substitute 1 tbsp (15 mL) apple pie spice with:
- 1 tbsp (15 mL) pumpkin pie spice (adds ginger flavor)
- 2 tsp (10 mL) ground cinnamon + $\frac{1}{2}$ tsp (2 mL) ground nutmeg + $\frac{1}{2}$ tsp (2 mL) ground cardamom (adds pungent aroma)

## Applesauce

*Apples cooked to a smooth or chunky purée that may be sweetened or flavored with cinnamon or other spices.*

### If You Don't Have It
Substitute 1 cup (250 mL) applesauce with:
- 1 cup (250 mL) Homemade Applesauce: Peel, core and dice 4 medium-size sauce apples (See Picking Apples, page 636). Place in a saucepan over medium heat with $\frac{1}{4}$ cup (60 mL) water, $\frac{1}{4}$ cup (60 mL) granulated sugar (optional), and $\frac{1}{8}$ tsp (0.5 mL) salt. Simmer until soft, about 15 minutes. For chunky applesauce, smash with the back of a large spoon or a potato masher. For smooth applesauce, pass the mixture through a food mill. Add $\frac{1}{4}$ tsp (1 mL) cinnamon and more sugar, if desired. Makes $1\frac{1}{2}$ cups (375 mL).
- 1 cup (250 mL) pumpkin purée
- 1 cup (250 mL) plum purée
- 1 cup (250 mL) fat-free, fruit-based butter and oil replacement such as Smucker's "Baking Healthy' (for baking only).
- $\frac{1}{2}$ cup (125 mL) fat-free, fruit-based butter and oil replacement such as Sunsweet "Lighter Bake" (for baking only).

## Apple Schnapps

*Clear liqueur flavored with apples. Also available as sour apple schnapps.*

### If You Don't Have It
Substitute 2 tbsp (30 mL) apple schnapps with:
- 2 tbsp (30 mL) apple brandy (Calvados or applejack)

## Apricot

*Highly prized fruit with floral aroma and luscious orange flesh is a member of the rose family. First cultivated in China before 2000 BC. The versatile fruit is eaten out of hand, dried, simmered into preserves, and added to savory dishes.*

> 1 lb (500 g) fresh =
> 8 to 14 = 2½ cups
> (625 mL) sliced or halved

### If You Don't Have It
Substitute 1 lb (500 g) apricots with:
- 1 lb (500 g) apriums (a hybrid fruit that's a cross between apricot and plum; very apricot-like)
- 1 lb (500 g) pluots (a hybrid fruit that's a cross between apricot and plum; more plum-like)

### To Vary the Flavor
Substitute 1 lb (500 g) apricots with:
- 1 lb (500 g) small peaches
- 1 lb (500 g) small nectarines

*See also* APRICOT, DRIED.

## Apricot Brandy

*Dry distilled spirit made from apricot juice. Hungarian Barack Pálinka is renowned.*

### If You Don't Have It
Substitute 2 tbsp (30 mL) apricot brandy with:
- 2 tbsp (30 mL) apricot schnapps
- 2 tbsp (30 mL) apricot liqueur (sweeter)
- 1 tbsp (15 mL) brandy + 1 tbsp (15 mL) apricot nectar

### To Vary the Flavor
Substitute 2 tbsp (30 mL) apricot brandy with:
- 2 tbsp (30 mL) peach schnapps
- 2 tbsp (30 mL) cherry brandy

## Apricot, Dried

*A preservation method for fully ripe apricots; they are typically treated with sulphur dioxide and dried in the sun.*

> 1 lb (500 g) = 2½ to
> 3 cups (625 to 750 mL) =
> 5½ cups
> (1.375 L) cooked

### If You Don't Have It
Substitute 1 oz (30 g) dried apricots with:
- 1 oz (30 g) dried peaches
- 1 oz (30 g) dried nectarines
- 1 oz (30 g) dried apples

*See also* APRICOT.

## Apricot Kernel

*Also known as Chinese almond. Originating from the same genus (Prunus) as bitter almonds, apricot kernels taste remarkably similar. They're also mildly toxic (but less so than bitter almonds), containing about 0.5 milligrams of cyanide per kernel. To leach out the toxin, apricot kernels should always be roasted or blanched before eating.*

### If You Don't Have It
Substitute 1 cup (250 mL) apricot kernels with:
- 1 cup (250 mL) blanched or roasted bitter almonds
- 1 cup (250 mL) almonds with skin (much less bitter flavor)
- 1 cup (250 mL) Homemade Blanched Apricot Kernels: Drop 1 cup (250 mL) apricot kernels in boiling water for 2 minutes. Drain and rub off skins in a kitchen towel.
- ¼ to ½ tsp (1 to 2 mL) bitter almond oil or extract (for baking and cooking; will add bitter almond flavor but not texture of whole nuts)
- 2 to 4 tbsp (30 to 60 mL) almond liqueur (for baking and cooking; adds some bitter almond flavor and alcohol but not texture of whole nuts; reduce liquid in recipe by 2 to 4 tbsp/30 to 60 mL)

*See also* ALMOND, BITTER.

## Apricot Liqueur

*Alcoholic beverage made from mashed apricots and sweetened brandy.*

### If You Don't Have It
Substitute 2 tbsp (30 mL) apricot liqueur with:
- 2 tbsp (30 mL) apricot schnapps (less sweet; higher alcohol)
- 2 tbsp (30 mL) apricot brandy (less sweet; higher alcohol)
- 2 tbsp (30 mL) apricot nectar (heavier body; no alcohol)

### To Vary the Flavor
Substitute 2 tbsp (30 mL) apricot liqueur with:
- 2 tbsp (30 mL) peach or cherry liqueur

## Aprium

*A fruit cross between apricot and plum that more strongly resembles the apricot.*

1 lb (500 g) fresh = 8 to 14 = 2½ cups (625 mL) sliced or halved

### If You Don't Have It
Substitute 1 lb (500 g) apriums with:
- 1 lb (500 g) apricots
- 1 lb (500 g) pluots
- 1 lb (500 g) plums

## Aquavit

*Also known as akvavit. A caraway-flavored colorless liquor of Scandinavian origin distilled from grain or potatoes.*

### If You Don't Have It
Substitute 2 tbsp (30 mL) aquavit with:
- 2 tbsp (30 mL) vodka (lacks the aroma of caraway)
- 2 tbsp (30 mL) vodka + ⅛ tsp (0.5 mL) caraway seeds soaked at room temperature for at least 1 month

## Aqua Vitae

*See* BRANDY.

## Arak

*See* ANISE LIQUEUR.

## Arame

*A sweet and mild dried Japanese seaweed. The skinny dark brown strips can be rehydrated and added to salads or vegetable stir-fries.*

### If You Don't Have It

Substitute 1 oz (30 g) arame with:
- 1 oz (30 g) hijiki (stronger brine flavor; black color)
- 1 oz (30 g) wakame (green to dark brown color)
- 1 oz (30 g) dulse (stronger brine flavor; maroon color)
- 1 oz (30 g) kombu or kelp (stronger brine flavor; dark brown to black color)

## Arbol Chile

*See* CHOOSING DRIED CHILES (PAGE 642).

## Arborio Rice

*See* VARIETIES OF RICE (PAGE 664).

## Arctic Char

*See* CHAR.

## Ardennes Ham

*Also known as Jambon d'Ardennes. Belgian salt-cured, smoked ham with dark brown exterior. Best served in very thin slices.*

### If You Don't Have It

Substitute 1 lb (500 g) Ardennes ham with:
- 1 lb (500 g) Bayonne ham
- 1 lb (500 g) Westphalian ham (adds juniper and lighter smoked flavors)
- 1 lb (500 g) prosciutto (lacks smoke flavor)
- 1 lb (500 g) serrano or Iberico ham (lacks smoke flavor)
- 1 lb (500 g) other smoked or country ham

## Arepa

*Thick, Venezuelan flatbread reminiscent of a cross between polenta and a pancake. Often topped or filled with cheese and herbs.*

### If You Don't Have It

Substitute 1 arepa with:
- 1 sope
- 1 chalupa
- 1 gordita
- 1 corn tortilla (thinner and stiffer)

## Argan Oil

*Flavorful oil pressed from the nut found at the center of the fruit of the Argan tree, a gnarled desert evergreen native to Morocco and Algeria. Argan nuts are difficult to extract from the fruit and were once harvested from the droppings of the goats that ate the fruit.*

### If You Don't Have It

Substitute 1 tbsp (15 mL) argan oil with:
- 1 tbsp (15 mL) walnut oil
- 1 tbsp (15 mL) almond oil
- 1 tbsp (15 mL) extra virgin olive oil

*See also* SUBSTITUTING OILS (PAGE 658).

## Armagnac

*Brandy produced in southwestern France that is second only to cognac in stature.*

### If You Don't Have It

Substitute 2 tbsp (30 mL) Armagnac with:

- 2 tbsp (30 mL) cognac (lighter body)

## Armenian Cracker Bread

*See* LAVASH.

## Aroma Fish

*See* AYU.

## Arracacha

*Also known as Peruvian carrot and white carrot. A popular vegetable in South America and the Caribbean with a texture like that of potatoes and flavor similar to a combination of parsnip, celery, and carrot with a whiff of roasted chestnuts.*

### If You Don't Have It

Substitute 1 lb (500 g) arracacha with:

- 1 lb (500 g) potatoes (similar texture; lacks arracacha flavor)
- 4 oz (125 g) potatoes + 4 oz (125 g) parsnips + 4 oz (125 g) carrots + 4 oz (125 g) celeriac

## Arrowhead

*Also known as Chinese potato. A root vegetable that looks like an onion without the layers and tastes like a mix of sunchoke and potato with some bitterness.*

### If You Don't Have It

Substitute 1 cup (250 mL) chopped arrowhead with:

- ½ cup (125 mL) chopped potato + ½ cup (125 mL) chopped sunchoke

## Arrowroot Powder

*The roots of a dried, ground tropical tuber used as a thickening agent. Use 2 tsp (10 mL) arrowroot to thicken 1 cup (250 mL) liquid.*

### If You Don't Have It

Substitute 2 tsp (10 mL) arrowroot powder (for thickening) with:

- 1 tbsp (15 mL) quick-cooking tapioca
- 1 heaping tbsp (15 mL) all-purpose flour
- 1½ tsp (7 mL) cornstarch, potato starch, or rice starch
- 1 tsp (5 mL) instant mashed potato flakes

## Artichoke Heart

*Also known as artichoke bottom. The cup-shaped meaty base, with interior tender leaves attached, of a globe artichoke. The most tender and desirable*

### If You Don't Have It

Substitute 1 cup (250 mL) freshly cooked artichoke hearts with:

- 1 cup (250 mL) frozen artichoke hearts
- 1 cup (250 mL) canned artichoke hearts (saltier flavor from canning brine)
- 1 cup (250 mL) marinated artichoke hearts (more savory flavor from marinade)

*part of the otherwise fibrous-leafed vegetable.*

## To Vary the Flavor

Substitute 1 cup (250 mL) freshly cooked artichoke hearts with:

- 1 cup (250 mL) freshly cooked hearts of palm
- 1 cup (250 mL) canned hearts of palm

## Artificial Sweeteners

*See* SUCRALOSE.

## Arugula

*Also known as rocket. A pungent, peppery leafy green similar in shape to radish greens.*

> 1 oz (30 g) =
> 1 cup (250 mL)

### If You Don't Have It

Substitute 1 cup (250 mL) arugula with:

- 1 cup (250 mL) watercress
- 1 cup (250 mL) baby spinach leaves (milder flavor; add pepper for more bite)
- 1 cup (250 mL) Belgian endive, dandelion greens, escarole, or radicchio (for salads)

## Asadero

*Also known as Chihuahua cheese and Oaxaca cheese. A mild, semifirm Mexican white cow's milk cheese fashioned in rounds and braids.*

> 4 oz (125 g) = 1 cup
> (250 mL) shredded

### If You Don't Have It

Substitute 1 oz (30 g) asadero with:

- 1 oz (30 g) Sonoma or Monterey Jack cheese
- 1 oz (30 g) Teleme cheese
- 1 oz (30 g) mozzarella cheese

## Asafetida Powder

*Also known as devil's dung, ferula, hing, and stinking gum. Powdered gum resin with a pungent garlic and onion flavor. Often used in Indian dishes.*

### If You Don't Have It

Substitute ¼ tsp (1 mL) asafetida powder with:

- ¼ tsp (1 mL) garlic powder + ¼ tsp (1 mL) onion powder (less pungent)

## Asam Gelugor

*Also known as asam keping when dried. A Malaysian fruit often used dried as a souring agent in dishes such as the fish soup, asam laksa.*

> 1 oz (30 g) =
> ¼ cup (60 mL)

### If You Don't Have It

Substitute ½ oz (15 g) asam gelugor with:

- ½ oz (15 g) kokum
- 1 tbsp (15 mL) tamarind concentrate or paste (less floral aroma)
- 1½ tbsp (22 mL) mango powder or amchur (less floral aroma)
- 1 to 1½ tbsp (15 to 22 mL) lime or lemon juice (less floral aroma)

## Asam Jawa

*See* TAMARIND.

## Asem Candis

*See* KOKUM.

## Asiago

Sharp cow's milk cheese from the Veneto dating from the 1500s. Semisoft young Asiago can be sliced and used like provolone.

4 oz (125 g) = 1 cup (250 mL) grated

### If You Don't Have It
Substitute 1 oz (30 g) aged Asiago with:
- 1 oz (30 g) Parmesan (slightly sharper flavor)
- 1 oz (30 g) Grana Padano (slightly sharper flavor)
- 1 oz (30 g) Pecorino Romano (sharper flavor; less sweet)
- 1 oz (30 g) dry Jack cheese (more nutty flavor)

### For Better Health
Substitute 1 oz (30 g) aged Asiago with:
- 1 oz (30 g) Sapsago (more herbal flavor; lower in fat)

## Asian Barbecue Sauce

*See* CHINESE BARBECUE SAUCE.

## Asian Celery

*See* CHINESE CELERY.

## Asian Noodles

*See* A SNAPSHOT OF ASIAN NOODLES (PAGE 656).

## Asian Pear

Also known as apple pear. Ultra-juicy, crisp, sweet fruit that ranges from tiny to very large. The flesh is somewhat translucent.

### If You Don't Have It
Substitute 1 Asian pear with:
- 1 Bosc pear (less tart; softer flesh)
- 1 apple (similar texture; apple flavor)
- 1 quince (for cooking only; more tart flavor)

## Asparagus

A spear-shaped green vegetable that is a member of the lily family. The cultivated plants take several years to mature and require careful tending and harvesting. Many growers bury the stalks to prevent photosynthesis, resulting in the preferred white asparagus.

1 lb (500 g) fresh = 12 to 20 spears = 3½ cups (875 mL) chopped

### If You Don't Have It
Substitute 1 lb (500 g) asparagus with:
- 1 lb (500 g) broccoli
- 1 lb (500 g) canned hearts of palm
- 1 lb (500 g) green beans

### Asparagus Varieties
Choose 1 lb (500 g) asparagus from these varieties:
- 1 lb (500 g) green asparagus (grassy, slightly bitter taste)
- 1 lb (500 g) white asparagus (slightly more bitter flavor; more tender texture)
- 1 lb (500 g) purple asparagus (sweeter, juicier, and more tender)

## Asparagus Lettuce

*See* CELTUCE.

## Aspic Powder

*Commercial gelatin powder flavored with fish, poultry, meat, or vegetable stock.*

### If You Don't Have It

Substitute ¼ oz (7 g) aspic powder with:
- ¼ oz (7 g) flavored gelatin (meat, fish, or vegetable)

## Atemoya

*A fruit that's a cross between cherimoya and sweetsop. Native to South America and the West Indies, atemoya's sweet, creamy flesh is studded with black seeds and tastes like mango-scented vanilla custard. The grayish green skin is sturdy and covered with a petal-like pattern.*

### If You Don't Have It

Substitute 1 lb (500 g) atemoya with:
- 1 lb (500 g) cherimoya
- 1 lb (500 g) sweetsop
- 1 lb (500 g) mango + ¼ tsp (1 mL) vanilla extract

*See also* CHERIMOYA; SOURSOP; SWEETSOP.

## Atsu-age

*Also known as nama-age. A cake of tofu that is pressed then deep-fried for a crisp golden crust and soft white interior. It's often cut into cubes or triangles for soups and stir-fries.*

### If You Don't Have It

Substitute 8 oz (250 g) atsu-age with:
- 8 oz (250 g) Homemade Abura-age: Cut a block of tofu in half widthwise. Spread out the pieces slightly and put a heavy weight on top for 30 minutes to press out excess liquid. Cut each piece in half on a diagonal to make 4 triangles then deep-fry the triangles in oil until golden brown on both sides, turning as necessary. Drain on paper towels and let cool for 30 minutes. Before using, blanch or rinse under hot water to remove excess oil. Refrigerate for up to 1 week.
- 8 oz (250 g) abura-age
- 8 oz (250 g) extra-firm tofu (will not be as crisp or flavorful)

*See also* ABURA-AGE; TOFU.

## Atsuete Seed

*See* ANNATTO SEED.

## Aubergine

*See* EGGPLANT.

## Aurore Sauce

*See* BÉCHAMEL.

## Avocado

*A member of the laurel family native to Mexico but now grown in California and Florida, the avocado fruit boasts a 7,000-year history of cultivation. The delicately nutty, pale green buttery flesh is best enjoyed raw, particularly mashed into guacamole.*

> 1 lb (500 g) = 2 medium =
> 2½ cups (625 mL)
> chopped =
> 1½ cups (375 mL) puréed

### If You Don't Have It
Substitute 1 cup (250 mL) chopped avocado with:
- 1 cup (250 mL) cooked chayote squash (much lower in fat and less creamy; use cooked in soups and dips or prepare as you would yellow summer squash)

### Avocado Varieties
Choose 1 cup (250 mL) chopped avocado from these California varieties:
- 1 cup (250 mL) chopped Hass avocado (rich and creamy; best for guacamole, mashing, sauces, and soups)
- 1 cup (250 mL) chopped Fuerte avocado (slightly less rich and creamy)
- 1 cup (250 mL) chopped Pinkerton avocado (slightly less rich and creamy)
- 1 cup (250 mL) chopped Reed avocado (flesh stays firm when ripe; best for salads)
- 1 cup (250 mL) chopped or sliced avocadito (small Fuerte avocado or cocktail avocado best for salads and garnishing)

### For Better Health
Substitute 1 cup (250 mL) chopped California avocado with:
- 1 cup (250 mL) chopped Florida avocado (25 to 50% less fat than California avocados)
- ½ cup (125 mL) chopped California avocado + ½ cup (125 mL) chopped tomatillos (for lower-calorie guacamole)
- ½ cup (125 mL) chopped California avocado + ½ cup (125 mL) puréed raw peas (for lower-calorie guacamole)

## Avocado Leaf

*Often toasted and used like bay leaves.*

### If You Don't Have It
Substitute 1 toasted avocado leaf with:
- 1 hoja santa leaf (adds aromas of root beer and fennel)
- 2 bay leaves (adds more resinous pine-like aroma)

## Awabi

*See* ABALONE.

## Ayu

*Also known as aroma fish and sweet fish. A freshwater fish caught by Japanese Samurai using flies or decoy fish. Ayu has sweet, delicate flesh with hints of melon and cucumber.*

### If You Don't Have It
Substitute 1 lb (500 g) ayu with:
- 1 lb (500 g) trout
- 1 lb (500 g) smelts
- 1 lb (500 g) char

## Azuki Bean

*See* THE WIDE WORLD OF DRIED BEANS (PAGE 637).

# Babaco to Byrrh

## Babaco

Ecuadorian hybrid of papaya with a mild flavor hinting at banana, pineapple and strawberry.

### If You Don't Have It
Substitute 1 lb (500 g) babaco with:
- 1 lb (500 g) casaba melon
- 1 lb (500 g) papaya

## Babybel Cheese

Mild-flavored semi-soft processed cow's milk cheese sold in small wax-coated rounds. Available in Edam (original red wax), Cheddar (purple wax), Emmental/Swiss (yellow wax), Gouda (gold wax), and Goat (green wax).

1 lb (500 g) = 4 cups (1 L) grated or shredded

### If You Don't Have It
Substitute 1 oz (30 g) Babybel cheese with:
- 1 oz (30 g) Edam
- 1 oz (30 g) Gouda (richer)
- 1 oz (30 g) Fontina (richer)
- 1 oz (30 g) Brie (richer)
- 1 oz (30 g) Leyden (may be flavored with caraway or cumin)

## Baby Broccoli

See BROCCOLINI.

## Baby Kiwifruit

See KIWIFRUIT, BABY.

## Bacalao

See SALT COD.

## Back Bacon

*See* CANADIAN BACON.

## Bacon

*Also known as American bacon and streaky bacon. Pork belly that is brined and smoked, sometimes double smoked. Can be purchased in slabs or slices and must be cooked before eating.*

1 lb (500 g) raw =
18 to 22 regular slices =
10 to 14 thick slices

1 lb (500 g) cooked =
1½ cups (375 mL)
crumbled

1 slice cooked = 1 tbsp
(15 mL) crumbled

### If You Don't Have It
Substitute 1 slice (about ¾ oz /22 g) bacon with:
- 1 thin slice (about ¾ oz /22 g) pancetta (wonderful spice aromas; unsmoked)
- 1 thin slice (about ¾ oz/22 g) prosciutto (pork leg; unsmoked)
- 1 thin slice (about ¾ oz/22 g) speck (pork leg; smoked; adds juniper aromas)
- ¾ oz (22 g) salt pork (saltier; fattier; unsmoked; best as flavoring in soups, stews, and sauces)
- ¾ oz (22 g) smoked sausage
- ¾ oz (22 g) smoked ham
- ¾ oz (22 g) fatback (unsalted; fattier; unsmoked; best as flavoring in soups, stews, and sauces; or for barding)
- 2 to 3 tsp (10 to 15 mL) real bacon bits

### For Better Health
Substitute 1 slice (about ¾ oz /22 g) bacon with:
- 1 slice turkey bacon (less fat and fewer calories; retains shape better than sliced bacon)
- 1 slice vegetarian bacon (less fat and fewer calories; made from vegetable protein; flavored like smoked bacon)
- 1 slice Canadian or back bacon (less fat and calories)
- ¾ oz (22 g) smoked ham
- 2 to 3 tsp (10 to 15 mL) imitation bacon-flavored bits (vegetarian)

*See also* CANADIAN BACON; FATBACK; PANCETTA; SALT PORK.

## Bacon Bits

*Pieces of cooked bacon that have been preserved and dried. Imitation bacon-flavor bits are made from vegetable protein.*

### If You Don't Have It
Substitute 1 tbsp (15 mL) bacon bits or chips with:
- 1 to 2 slices bacon, crisply cooked, drained, and crumbled
- 1 tbsp (15 mL) imitation bacon-flavored bits (vegetarian)

## Bacon Press

*A flat, heavy piece of metal, often cast iron, with a handle for gripping that sits atop bacon to prevent curling as it fries.*

### If You Don't Have It
Substitute a bacon press with:
- heavy skillet (such as cast-iron)
- foil-wrapped brick or flat rock

## Bael Fruit

*Also known as Indian quince and holy fruit. Baseball-size rounded fruit with a woody yellow rind and orange, sweet-tart flesh similar to plums or grapes in texture. Often dried in slices or mashed fresh with sugar to make a curative beverage (smoothie). Bael trees are often cultivated near Hindu temples because they are considered sacred.*

### If You Don't Have It

Substitute 1 cup (250 mL) ripe bael fruit with:
- 1 cup (250 mL) ripe mangosteen segments
- 1 cup (250 mL) ripe peeled litchis

## Bagaceira

*See* GRAPPA.

## Bagel

*A yeast bun with a hole in the center. The dense, texture is achieved by boiling the risen dough before baking. Of Eastern European Jewish origin, the bagel first gained popularity in New York City.*

### If You Don't Have It

Substitute 1 bagel with:
- 1 bialy (flatter; filled with sautéed onions)
- 1 English muffin (slightly smaller; more light and airy crumb; less chewy)
- 1 soft pretzel (less dense)
- 2 slices dense, chewy bread (such as sourdough)

## Bagoong

*See* SHRIMP PASTE.

## Baguette

*See* FRENCH BREAD.

## Baharat

*Literally "spice" in Arabic, this finely ground seasoning blend flavors lamb and other meats throughout the Middle East. Turkish baharat often includes dried mint while the Tunisian version features dried rosebuds.*

### If You Don't Have It

Substitute 1 tbsp (15 mL) baharat with:
- 1 tbsp (15 mL) Homemade Baharat: Combine 1 tbsp (15 mL) freshly ground black pepper, 1 tbsp (15 mL) paprika, 1 tbsp (15 mL) ground cumin, 1½ tsp (7 mL) ground coriander, 1½ tsp (7 mL) ground cloves, 1½ tsp (7 mL) grated nutmeg, ½ tsp (2 mL) ground cinnamon, and ¼ tsp (1 mL) ground cardamom. Makes about ¼ cup (60 mL).
- 1 tbsp (15 mL) ras el hanout
- 1 tbsp (15 mL) garam masala

## Baijiu

*Strong Chinese distilled liquor averaging about 100 proof. The most famous unflavored baijiu, Maotai, is distilled from fermented sorghum and has a subtle umami flavor. The highest grade of baijiu, Wuliangye, can cost upwards of $3,000 a bottle.*

### If You Don't Have It

Substitute 3 tbsp (45 mL) baijiu with:

- 3 tbsp (45 mL) grappa
- 3 tbsp (45 mL) cognac
- 3 tbsp (45 mL) Armagnac

## Bainiku

*See* UMEBOSHI.

## Bajri Flour

*See* CHOOSING AMONG WHOLE-GRAIN AND ALTERNATIVE FLOURS (PAGE 648).

## Baker's Ammonia

*See* AMMONIUM BICARBONATE.

## Baker's Caramel

*A browning agent made from darkly caramelized sugar and used in baked goods such as pumpernickel bread.*

### If You Don't Have It

Substitute 1 tsp (5 mL) baker's caramel with:

- 1 tsp (5 mL) gravy browning such as Kitchen Bouquet or Gravy Master
- 1 tsp (5 mL): Homemade Baker's Caramel: Stir together ½ cup (125 mL) granulated sugar and ½ cup (125 mL) water in a small, heavy saucepan. Place over medium-low heat and cook, without stirring, until the sugar dissolves completely. Increase the heat to medium-high and bring to a boil. Reduce heat to medium and attach a candy thermometer to the inside of the pan. Boil gently until the mixture turns from clear to dark amber (about 360°F/182°C on the thermometer), 10 to 15 minutes. Do not stir. Every 5 minutes or so, dip a pastry brush in hot water and brush down the insides of the pan to dissolve any sugar crystals there (this helps prevent the caramel from crystallizing). Immediately remove from heat and let cool slightly but not to the point of hardening. Stand back and stir in 3 tbsp (45 mL) hot water to thin the mixture and prevent it from hardening (stand back because the mixture will sputter; wear oven mitts or heatproof silicone gloves to be perfectly safe). Let cool completely and refrigerate in an airtight glass bottle or other container for up to 6 months. Makes about ⅓ cup (75 mL).

## Baker's Wax

*See* PARAFFIN WAX.

## Baking Pans

*See* PAN SIZE EQUIVALENTS (PAGE 678); SPECIFIC TYPES.

## Baking Powder

*Most baking powder in North America is double-acting, which contains two acids that react as leavening agents at different times in the baking process. For delicate baked goods, use aluminum-free baking powder to avoid a tinny aftertaste.*

### If You Don't Have It

Substitute 1 tsp (5 mL) double-acting baking powder with:

- ¼ tsp (1 mL) baking soda + ¼ tsp (1 mL) cornstarch + ½ tsp (2 mL) cream of tartar
- 1¼ tsp (6 mL) single-acting baking powder
- 1½ tsp (7 mL) phosphate or tartrate baking powder
- 1 tsp (5 mL) ammonium bicarbonate (creates light, airy cookies; best for small baked goods so ammonia odor can evaporate during baking)

### To Vary the Flavor

Substitute 1 tsp (5 mL) double-acting baking powder with:

- ¼ tsp (1 mL) baking soda + ½ cup (125 mL) buttermilk or soured milk (reduce liquid in recipe by ½ cup/125 mL)
- ¼ tsp (1 mL) baking soda + ¼ cup (60 mL) molasses (reduce liquid in recipe by 3 tbsp/45 mL and adjust sweetener)

## Baking Sheet

*Insulated baking sheets, also known as air-bake cookie sheets, have a layer of air insulation between two sheets of metal to promote more even heating and browning.*

### If You Don't Have It

Substitute a thin, lightweight baking sheet with:

- insulated baking sheet (heats more slowly and evenly; helps prevent burning and premature browning)
- two lightweight baking sheets nested together (simulates an insulated baking sheet; especially good for cookies; helps prevent spreading, burning, and premature browning)
- heavy-gauge aluminum baking sheet (helps prevent burning and premature browning)

## Baking Soda

*Also known as bicarbonate of soda. When combined with acidic ingredients, baking soda creates carbon dioxide gas bubbles that cause batter or dough to rise.*

1 tsp (5 mL) = 5 g

### If You Don't Have It

Substitute 1 tsp (5 mL) baking soda with:

- 1 tsp (5 mL) potassium bicarbonate (potash)

## Baking Stone

*Also known as a pizza stone. Thick, heavy slab of stone that absorbs moisture and creates crisper, deeper brown crusts on bread and pizza.*

### If You Don't Have It

Substitute a baking stone with:

- unglazed quarry tiles (preferably, high-fired)
- brick oven
- outdoor ceramic cooker or smoker

## Baloney

See BOLOGNA.

## Balsamic Vinegar

See CHOOSING VINEGAR (PAGE 674).

## Balsam Pear

See BITTER MELON.

## Bamboo Leaf

*To use as a food wrapper, soak dried bamboo leaves in water until pliable.*

### If You Don't Have It
Substitute bamboo leaves (as a food wrapper) with:
- lotus leaves
- banana leaves
- aluminum foil
- parchment paper

## Bamboo Shoot

*The inner white section of certain edible young bamboo plants. A basic ingredient in Asian cooking, bamboo shoots have a mild flavor that is reminiscent of artichokes. Fresh ones must be cooked to eliminate their toxic hydrocyanic acid.*

> 8 oz (250 g) can =
> 1¼ cups
> (300 mL) sliced

### If You Don't Have It
Substitute 1 cup (250 mL) freshly cooked bamboo shoots with:
- 1 cup (250 mL) canned bamboo shoots

### To Vary the Flavor
Substitute 1 cup (250 mL) freshly cooked bamboo shoots with:
- 1 cup (250 mL) cooked jicama (sweeter)
- 1 cup (250 mL) peeled raw or canned water chestnuts (more crisp)
- 1 cup (250 mL) cooked taro (more starchy)
- 1 cup (250 mL) cooked artichoke hearts (more tender)

## Banana

*The sweet, starchy, seedless fruit of a tropical perennial herb that resembles a palm tree. North Americans favor yellow Cavendish bananas.*

> 1 lb (500 g) fresh =
> 3 to 4 medium =
> 2 cups (500 mL) sliced =
> 1¾ cups (425 mL) mashed =
> 1 cup dried slices
>
> 1 medium =
> ½ cup (125 mL) mashed

### If You Don't Have It
Substitute 1 lb (500 g) ripe Cavendish bananas with:
- 1 lb (500 g) very ripe black plantains (larger; less sweet; more starchy; best for baking, mashing, and frying)

### Banana Varieties
Choose 1 lb (500 g) ripe bananas from other varieties:
- 1 lb (500 g) burro bananas (shorter; adds slight lemon flavor)
- 1 lb (500 g) blue java or ice cream banana (adds sweet ice cream-like flavor)
- 1 lb (500 g) dwarf or finger bananas (sweeter)
- 1 lb (500 g) red bananas (sweeter; best for baking)
- 1 lb (500 g) manzano bananas (smaller; drier flesh; adds strawberry-apple flavor)
- 1 lb (500 g) Orinoco bananas (adds strawberry flavor)

*See also* PLANTAIN.

## Banana Bud

*Also known as banana blossom and banana heart. The interior of the male part of the banana flower is blanched several times to remove the bitterness.*

1 lb (500 g) = about 1 bud

### If You Don't Have It
Substitute 1 lb (500 g) banana buds with:
- 1 lb (500 g) artichokes

## Banana, Dried

*Also known as banana chips. One ounce (30 g) of banana chips fried in coconut oil (the most common method for making chips) contains about 150 calories and 10 grams of fat, while one ounce (30 g) of air-dried or freeze-dried banana slices contains about 100 calories and 2 grams of fat.*

1 lb (500 g) fresh =
1 cup (250 mL) dried slices
1 lb (500 g) dried =
4½ cups (1.125 L) slices

### If You Don't Have It
Substitute 1 oz (30 g) dried banana slices with:
- 1 oz (30 g) dried coconut chips
- 1 oz (30 g) dried apple slices

### For Better Health
Substitute 1 oz (30 g) banana chips fried in oil with:
- 1 oz (30 g) air-dried or freeze-dried banana slices

## Banana Leaf

*Often used for wrapping and flavoring steamed foods such as tamales. According to Mexican cooking authority Rick Bayless "banana leaves impart a very special herby-green flavor that you can't get from any other leaf."*

1 lb (500 g) = 10 to 12
12-inch (30 cm) squares

### If You Don't Have It
Substitute banana leaves (as a food wrapper) with:
- corn husks (much smaller; adds mild corn aroma)
- hoja santa leaves (much smaller; adds aromas of root beer and fennel)
- parchment paper (no flavor)
- aluminum foil (no flavor; reduce cooking time slightly)

## Banana Pepper

See SWEET PEPPER; CHOOSING FRESH CHILES (PAGE 640).

## Banana Squash

*This variety is so large that grocers usually cut it into smaller chunks before displaying it. It's tasty, but the biggest virtue of banana squash is its beautiful golden flesh.*

1 lb (500 g) = 1 cup (250 mL) cooked and mashed

### If You Don't Have It

Substitute 1 cup (250 mL) chopped banana squash with:

- 1 cup (250 mL) chopped butternut squash (less fruity flavor)
- 1 cup (250 mL) chopped buttercup squash (less fruity flavor; drier texture)
- 1 cup (250 mL) chopped delicata squash (less fruity flavor)

## B&B

*Also known as Bénédictine and Brandy. A liqueur that blends Bénédictine — a sweet French cognac-based liqueur flavored with herbs and fruit peels — with brandy.*

### If You Don't Have It

Substitute 2 tbsp (30 mL) B&B with:

- 1 tbsp (15 mL) Bénédictine + 1 tbsp (15 mL) brandy
- 2 tbsp (30 mL) Bénédictine

## Banon

See CHÈVRE.

## Banyuls

*A sweet fortified wine named for the French town of Banyuls-sur-Mer. Old vines of Grenache and Carignan grapes (and sometimes Muscat and Malvoisie) age for at least 10 months in oak barrels, resulting in a wine that is similar to port but lower in alcohol.*

### If You Don't Have It

Substitute 2 tbsp (30 mL) banyuls with:

- 2 tbsp (30 mL) port
- 2 tbsp (30 mL) Madeira
- 2 tbsp (30 mL) Lillet Rouge
- 2 tbsp (30 mL) dry vermouth
- 2 tbsp (30 mL) beef stock (for sauces)

See also PORT.

## Banyuls Vinegar

See CHOOSING VINEGAR (PAGE 674).

## Baobab Leaf

*Also known as kuka. The dried leaves of the thick-trunked baobab (Adansonia) tree, native to Madagascar, Africa, and Australia. The ground leaves provide a viscous, thickening "slime" in traditional West African stews.*

### If You Don't Have It

Substitute 1 tbsp (15 mL) ground baobab leaves with:
- 1 tbsp (15 mL) filé powder (for thickening)
- 2 cups (500 mL) okra (for stews, cook gradually to release okra's viscous, thickening "slime")

## Barbados Cherry

*See* ACEROLA.

## Barbados Sugar

*See* SUGAR, RAW.

## Barbari Bread

*Soft, oblong Afghani flatbread with rows of dimples made by fingertips pressed into the top of the dough.*

### If You Don't Have It

Substitute 1 lb (500 g) Barbari bread with:
- 1 lb (500 g) sangak bread (whole wheat sourdough)
- 1 lb (500 g) lavash (thinner)
- 1 lb (500 g) pita bread
- 1 lb (500 g) naan (thicker)
- 1 lb (500 g) flour tortilla (thinner)

## Barbary Fig

*See* PRICKLY PEAR.

## Barbecue Sauce

*A thick and sweet tomato-based sauce used to baste and/or accompany barbecued meat. Endless variations exist and can include ingredients such as onion, mustard, spices, garlic, beer, wine, and vinegar.*

### If You Don't Have It

Substitute 1 cup (250 mL) barbecue sauce with:
- 1 cup (250 mL) ketchup + $\frac{1}{2}$ to 1 tsp (2 to 5 mL) liquid smoke seasoning
- 1 cup (250 mL) canned barbecue Sloppy Joe sauce
- 1 cup (250 mL) Homemade Barbecue Sauce: Combine 2 cups (500 mL) ketchup, 3 tbsp (45 mL) dark brown sugar, 3 tbsp (45 mL) cider vinegar, 2 tbsp (30 mL) yellow prepared mustard, 2 tbsp (30 mL) Worcestershire sauce, 2 tsp (10 mL) paprika, $1\frac{1}{2}$ tsp (7 mL) salt, 1 tsp (5 mL) garlic powder, $\frac{1}{2}$ tsp (2 mL) onion powder, and $\frac{1}{2}$ tsp (2 mL) ground black pepper in a saucepan. Bring to a boil over high heat. Reduce heat to medium-low and simmer until thickened, about 20 minutes. Makes 3 cups (750 mL).

*See also* CHINESE BARBECUE SAUCE.

## Barbecuing

*A dry-heat cooking method that uses the indirect, low heat (200 to 230°F/90 to 110°C) of smoldering wood to slowly cook and smoke food.*

### If You Don't Have It

Substitute barbecuing with:

- gas or charcoal grilling (faster; higher heat; much less smoke flavor)
- gas or charcoal grilling + liquid smoke seasoning brushed onto food or added to marinade or sauce
- stovetop smoking (using a covered stovetop smoker with wood chips in the bottom and food in the top)

*See also* GRILL.

## Barberry

*Tiny, tart, red currant-like berry often used dried in Iranian dishes such as barberry rice.*

### If You Don't Have It

Substitute 1 cup (250 mL) dried barberries with:

- 1 cup (250 mL) dried cranberries
- 1 cup (250 mL) dried sour cherries
- 1 cup (250 mL) dried red currants

## Barley

*A robust grain dating from the Stone Age, barley is a versatile ingredient in cereals, breads, soups, and pilafs. When malted, it is used to make whiskey and beer. Pearl barley is the most common variety but hulled or whole-grain barley is more nutritious because the outer layer of bran is not polished away.*

> 1 cup (250 mL) medium pearl barley = 3½ to 4 cups (875 mL to 1 L) cooked
>
> 1 cup (250 mL) quick-cooking = 3 cups (750 mL) cooked

### If You Don't Have It

Substitute 1 cup (250 mL) pearl barley with:

- 1 cup (250 mL) Arborio or Carnaroli rice (less chewy; more starchy)
- 2 cups (500 mL) orzo pasta (less nutritious)
- 1 cup (250 mL) buckwheat groats (more earthy and chewy)
- 1 cup (250 mL) Scotch barley (more chewy and flavorful)
- 1 cup (250 mL) barley grits (more chewy and flavorful)

### To Save Time

Substitute 1 cup (250 mL) pearl barley with:

- 1¼ cups (300 mL) quick-cooking barley (takes 10 minutes to cook)

### For Better Health

Substitute 1 cup (250 mL) pearl barley with:

- 1 cup (250 mL) hulled or whole-grain barley (chewier; higher in fiber; increase liquid and cooking time)

## Barley Flakes

*Also known as rolled barley. Nearly identical to old-fashioned rolled oats but sweeter and chewier.*

> 1 cup (250 mL) = 1¾ cups (425 mL) cooked
>
> 1 lb (500 g) = 5 cups (1.25 L) uncooked

### If You Don't Have It

Substitute 1 cup (250 mL) barley flakes with:

- 1 cup (250 mL) old-fashioned rolled oats
- 1 cup (250 mL) barley grits (hulled, cracked barley)
- 1 cup (250 mL) steel-cut, Irish or Scotch oats (cut oat groats; smaller, firmer pieces)

## Barley Flour

*See* CHOOSING AMONG WHOLE-GRAIN AND ALTERNATIVE FLOURS (PAGE 648).

## Barley Grits

*Barley grains that have been hulled and cracked into pieces. Available in health food stores.*

### If You Don't Have It

Substitute 1 cup (250 mL) barley grits with:
- 1 cup (250 mL) buckwheat grits (more earthy, grassy flavor)
- 1 cup (250 mL) hominy grits (more creamy texture)

## Barley Malt Syrup

*Also known as malted cereal syrup and malt syrup. Similar to molasses, barley malt syrup is used mostly in beer and bread making.*

### If You Don't Have It

Substitute 1 cup (250 mL) barley malt syrup with:
- ⅔ cup (150 mL) molasses
- ¾ cup (175 mL) rice bran syrup
- ¾ cup (175 mL) maple syrup

*See also* SUGAR, GRANULATED.

## Barnacle

*Also known as goose barnacle and percebe. Inedible common barnacles (acorn barnacles) grow their thick shells onto rocks and the hulls of boats. But edible goose barnacles (percebes) attach themselves with an edible stalk. Barnacles are crustaceans and taste similar to crabs and lobsters.*

### If You Don't Have It

Substitute 1 lb (500 g) barnacle meat with:
- 1 lb (500 g) crab meat
- 1 lb (500 g) lobster meat
- 1 lb (500 g) shrimp
- 1 lb (500 g) scallops

### To Vary the Flavor

Substitute 1 lb (500 g) goose barnacle meat with:
- 1 lb (500 g) picoroco meat (*Austromegabalanus Psittacus*), a species of giant barnacle found off the coast of Chile and Peru

## Barquette

*Little "boat" puff pastry shells that can be filled with sweet or savory fillings.*

### If You Don't Have It

Substitute 1 barquette with:
- 1 round puff pastry shell
- 1 round phyllo pastry shell

*See also* PAN SIZE EQUIVALENTS (PAGE 678).

## Barracuda

*Also known as California or Pacific barracuda. Firm-fleshed, moderate-fat fish similar to mahi-mahi.*

### If You Don't Have It

Substitute 1 lb (500 g) barracuda with:
- 1 lb (500 g) mahi-mahi
- 1 lb (500 g) swordfish
- 1 lb (500 g) mako shark
- 1 lb (500 g) tuna
- 1 lb (500 g) pompano
- 1 lb (500 g) wahoo or other mackerel

## Bar Strainer

*See* COCKTAIL STRAINER.

## Basa

*See* CATFISH.

## Basa Genep

*A popular spice paste used in Balinese cuisine. Genep means "complete" or "perfect."*

### If You Don't Have It

Substitute ¼ cup (60 mL) basa genep with:

- ¼ cup (60 mL) Homemade Basa Genep: Grind 1 tsp (5 mL) black peppercorns, 3 small dried Thai or serrano chiles (stems and seeds removed), 1 tsp (5 mL) sesame seeds, and 1 tsp (5 mL) coriander seeds to a coarse powder in a mortar and pestle or spice grinder. If using a spice grinder, transfer to a food processor. Add 4 shallots, 3 garlic cloves, 3 candlenuts or macadamia nuts, 1 chopped lemongrass stalk, 1½ tbsp (22 mL) chopped fresh greater galangal or 2 tsp (10 mL) powdered, 1 tbsp (15 mL) chopped fresh turmeric or ½ tsp (2 mL) powdered, 1 tbsp (15 mL) grated fresh ginger, 2 tsp (10 mL) lesser galangal or 1 tsp (5 mL) powdered, ½ tsp (2 mL) fermented shrimp paste (terasi), ½ tsp (2 mL) salt, ½ tsp (2 mL) palm sugar or brown sugar, and ¼ tsp (1 mL) grated nutmeg. Grind to a coarse paste, adding just enough water to make a thick paste. Makes about ⅔ cup (150 mL).

## Basella

*Also known as Ceylon spinach, Malabar spinach, saan choi, and slippery vegetable. Tropical green leafy vegetable cooked like spinach but releasing a mucilaginous slime similar to okra.*

### If You Don't Have It

Substitute 1 lb (500 g) basella with:

- 1 lb (500 g) jute leaves
- 8 oz (250 g) cut okra + 8 oz (250 g) mature spinach leaves
- 1 lb (500 g) sorrel (no slime; more astringent taste)
- 1 lb (500 g) mature spinach or swiss chard (no slime; mild flavor)

## Basil

*An annual plant that originated in India, sweet basil — with tender green leaves and a flavor reminiscent of cloves — has become the signature fresh herb of the Italian kitchen. Most renowned as the base of pesto, a paste of pine nuts, garlic, extra virgin olive oil, and Parmesan and Pecorino cheeses.*

### If You Don't Have It

Substitute 1 tbsp (15 mL) chopped fresh basil with:

- 1 tsp (5 mL) dried basil
- 1 tsp (5 mL) dried Italian seasoning

### To Vary the Flavor

Substitute 1 tbsp (15 mL) chopped fresh basil with:

- 1 tbsp (15 mL) chopped fresh oregano
- 1 tbsp (15 mL) chopped fresh mint (works well in Thai dishes)
- 1 tbsp (15 mL) chopped fresh parsley or cilantro (especially for sauces such as pesto)
- 2 tsp (10 mL) chopped fresh thyme

| 1 cup (250 mL) packed =
¾ oz (22 g) |

## Basil Varieties

Choose 1 tbsp (15 mL) chopped fresh basil from these varieties:

- 1 tbsp (15 mL) chopped fresh Genovese basil (similar to sweet basil)
- 1 tbsp (15 mL) chopped fresh opal or purple basil (purple color; milder flavor than sweet basil; purple ruffle basil has serrated leaves)
- 1 tbsp (15 mL) chopped fresh Thai basil (more anise-like aroma than sweet basil)
- 1 tbsp (15 mL) chopped fresh anise or licorice basil (more anise-like aroma than sweet basil)
- 1 tbsp (15 mL) chopped fresh lemon basil (more lemony aroma than sweet basil)
- 1 tbsp (15 mL) chopped fresh African blue basil (more camphor aroma than sweet basil)

## Basmati Rice

*See* VARIETIES OF RICE (PAGE 664).

## Bass

*See* BLACK SEA BASS; GROUPER; STRIPED BASS.

## Baster

*Also known as a bulb baster or turkey baster. An oversized syringe used for drizzling liquid over food to keep it moist.*

### If You Don't Have It

Substitute a bulb baster with:

- Squeeze bottle
- Large syringe
- Ladle
- Large spoon
- Basting brush
- Clean paint brush
- Small, clean mop

## Batata

*See* BONIATO.

## Baton

*See* FRENCH BREAD.

## Bauchant

*See* ORANGE LIQUEUR.

## Bauerwurst

*Also known as bauernwurst. Fresh coarse-textured German pork sausage highly seasoned with mustard (and sometimes marjoram, pepper, paprika, and mace) and lightly smoked.*

### If You Don't Have It

Substitute 1 lb (500 g) bauerwurst with:

- 1 lb (500 g) knackwurst (made with beef)
- 1 lb (500 g) bockwurst (made with veal)
- 1 lb (500 g) bratwurst
- 1 lb (500 g) kielbasa (larger)
- 1 lb (500 g) frankfurters

## Bavarian Blue Cheese

*Mild, creamy German blue cheese.*

### If You Don't Have It

Substitute 1 oz (30 g) Bavarian blue cheese with:
- 1 oz (30 g) Blue Castello
- 1 oz (30 g) Danish blue (stronger flavor)
- 1 oz (30 g) Gorgonzola (more pungent flavor)

## Bay Leaf

*Also known as bay laurel and laurel leaf. Aromatic leaf of the Mediterranean evergreen bay laurel tree, used to season soups, stews, vegetables, and meats. Ancient Greeks and Romans revered the leaf as a symbol of triumph. Turkish bay leaves are about half the size yet have more complex flavor than the California variety. Use about two Turkish bay leaves to replace one California bay leaf.*

> 1 whole leaf = ¼ tsp (1 mL) crushed

### If You Don't Have It

Substitute 2 dried Turkish or Mediterranean bay leaves with:
- 1 dried California bay leaf
- ½ tsp (2 mL) crushed dried Turkish or Mediterranean bay leaf

### To Vary the Flavor

Substitute 1 dried Turkish or Mediterranean bay leaf with:
- 1 dried boldo leaf (more camphor aroma)
- ¼ tsp (1 mL) juniper berries (adds characteristic flavor of gin; especially good in a bouquet garni for stews or crushed in a spice rub for grilled meats)

### Bay Leaf Varieties

Choose bay leaves from these varieties:
- 2 dried Turkish or Mediterranean bay leaves (complex hints of clove, pine, and verbena)
- 1 dried California bay leaf, pepperwood, or Oregon myrtle (stronger but simpler woodsy and pine aromas)
- 2 dried Indian bay leaves (spicy hints of cinnamon and clove)
- 2 dried Indonesian bay leaves (mild hints of clove and lemon; nearly black when dried)

## Bayonne Ham

*Also known as jambon Bayonne. Mildly smoked boneless French ham that's cured in wine.*

### If You Don't Have It

Substitute 1 lb (500 g) Bayonne ham with:
- 1 lb (500 g) Ardennes ham
- 1 lb (500 g) York ham
- 1 lb (500 g) Westphalian ham (adds juniper flavor)
- 1 lb (500 g) prosciutto (lacks smoke flavor)
- 1 lb (500 g) serrano or Iberico ham (lacks smoke flavor)
- 1 lb (500 g) any mildly smoked ham

## Bean Curd

*See* TOFU.

## Bean, Dried

*To reduce the amount of hard-to-digest carbohydrates that cause gas and bloating in dried beans, soak dried beans for*

### If You Don't Have It

Substitute 1 cup (250 mL) dried beans with:
- 1 cup (250 mL) lentils or split peas (no soaking required; cooks faster)

8 to 10 hours and discard the water or rinse canned beans before using.

> 1 lb (500 g) dried = 2 to 2½ cups (500 to 625 mL) = 4½ to 5 cups (1.125 to 1.25 L) cooked
>
> 1 cup (250 mL) dried = 2 to 2½ cups (500 to 625 mL) cooked
>
> 15-oz (425 g) can = 1¾ to 2 cups (425 to 500 mL)

## To Vary the Flavor

Substitute 1 cup (250 mL) dried beans with:

- 1 cup (250 mL) fresh peas, edamame, or cranberry or other shelling beans (cooks faster)
- ½ cup (125 mL) cup nuts (for salads and dips)

*See also* FERMENTED BLACK BEAN; REFRIED BEANS; SWITCHING LENTILS (PAGE 653); THE WIDE WORLD OF DRIED BEANS (PAGE 637).

# Bean, Fresh Shelling

*Most shell beans contain all nine of the essential amino acids necessary to maintain human health, which has made them a popular source of protein throughout the world.*

> 1 lb (500 g) fresh in shell = 1 to 1¼ cups ( 250 to 300 mL) shelled

## If You Don't Have It

Substitute 1 cup (250 mL) fresh shell beans with:

- 1 cup (250 mL) sugar snap peas or snow peas (in the shell)

*See* BLACK-EYED PEA, FRESH; CRANBERRY BEAN, FRESH; EDAMAME; FAVA BEAN; LIMA BEAN; PEAS, EDIBLE POD; PEAS, SHELLING.

# Bean Herb

*See* EPAZOTE.

# Bean Sauce

*Also known as bean paste and sweet bean sauce. Seasonings prepared from fermented soybeans, popular in many Asian cuisines. Styles vary from thin to thick, smooth to chunky, salty to sweet.*

## If You Don't Have It

Substitute 1 tbsp (15 mL) Chinese brown bean sauce (sweet bean sauce) with:

- 1 tbsp (15 mL) hoisin sauce (milder)
- 1 tbsp (15 mL) Thai bean sauce (more salty)
- 1 tbsp (15 mL) black bean sauce (more salty; stronger flavor)
- 1 tbsp (15 mL) chile bean sauce (more salty and spicy)

*See also* BLACK BEAN SAUCE; CHILE PASTE; FERMENTED BEAN PASTE; RED BEAN PASTE.

# Bean, Snap

*See* GREEN BEAN; YARD-LONG BEAN.

# Bean Sprouts

*See* MUNG BEAN SPROUTS; SOYBEAN SPROUTS.

## Bean Threads

*See* A SNAPSHOT OF ASIAN NOODLES (PAGE 656).

## Bear

*Popular in Germany and Russia, bear meat is high in protein and low in fat and calories. Cook wild bear meat thoroughly to avoid trichinosis.*

### If You Don't Have It

Substitute 1 lb (500 g) bear meat with:
- 1 lb (500 g) venison such as elk, moose, or caribou
- 1 lb (500 g) buffalo
- 1 lb (500 g) beef (higher fat and calories)

## Béarnaise Sauce

*Daughter of the French mother sauce Hollandaise, Béarnaise is made with vinegar instead of lemon juice and flavored with shallots and tarragon.*

### If You Don't Have It

Substitute 1 cup (250 mL) Béarnaise sauce with:
- 1 cup (250 mL) Homemade Béarnaise Sauce: Put $\frac{1}{3}$ cup (75 mL) white wine vinegar, $\frac{1}{3}$ cup (75 mL) white wine, $1\frac{1}{2}$ tbsp (22 mL) chopped shallots, $1\frac{1}{2}$ tbsp (22 mL) fresh tarragon, 1 tbsp (15 mL) fresh chervil, and $\frac{1}{4}$ tsp (1 mL) cracked peppercorns in a saucepan. Boil over medium-high heat until the liquid is reduced to about 3 tbsp (45 mL). Remove from the heat, strain, return to the pan, and cool slightly. Mix 3 egg yolks with 2 tsp (10 mL) water, then whisk into the cooled liquid. Put the pan over simmering water or very low heat and gradually whisk in $\frac{2}{3}$ cup (150 mL) cold butter in 1 tbsp (15 mL) pieces until the sauce thickens. Season with salt and additional chopped tarragon, if you like. Makes about 1 cup (250 mL).

### To Vary the Flavor

Substitute 1 cup (250 mL) Béarnaise sauce with:
- 1 cup (250 mL) Hollandaise sauce (omits shallots and tarragon)
- 1 cup (250 mL) Choron sauce (béarnaise with tomato paste)
- 1 cup (250 mL) Foyot or Valois sauce (béarnaise with glace de viande)
- 1 cup (250 mL) Colbert sauce (béarnaise with glace de viande melted in white wine)
- 1 cup (250 mL) beurre blanc (no tarragon or egg yolks)

*See also* HOLLANDAISE SAUCE.

## Beaufort Cheese

*A fine French cheese similar to Swiss Gruyère with a rich nutty flavor and just a few small holes.*

### If You Don't Have It

Substitute 1 oz (30 g) Beaufort cheese with:
- 1 oz (30 g) Gruyère
- 1 oz (30 g) Comté

## Beau Monde® Seasoning

*A commercial spice blend including dried onion, celery seeds, and salt.*

### If You Don't Have It

Substitute 1 tsp (5 mL) Beau Monde® Seasoning with:
- ½ tsp (2 mL) celery salt + ½ tsp (2 mL) onion powder
- 1 tsp (5 mL) seasoned salt
- ½ tsp (2 mL) table salt
- ½ tsp (2 mL) Mei Yen seasoning

## Beaumont Cheese

*Also known as Tomme de Beaumont. French cow's milk cheese.*

### If You Don't Have It

Substitute 1 oz (30 g) Beaumont cheese with:
- 1 oz (30 g) Muenster
- 1 oz (30 g) Reblochon

## Béchamel

*Also known as balsamella, besciamella and white sauce. "Gastronomic literature is filled with tedious pages and trifling disputes," writes Raymond Sokolov in his classic 1976 book* The Saucier's Apprentice, *"Béchamel has inspired more than its fair share of this piffle."*

### If You Don't Have It

Substitute 1 cup (250 mL) béchamel with:
- 1 cup (250 mL) Homemade Basic Béchamel: Melt 2 tbsp (30 mL) butter in a heavy saucepan over low heat. Whisk in 3 tbsp (45 mL) flour and cook, stirring, for 2 to 3 minutes without darkening. Heat 2 cups (500 mL) milk just to a simmer in a small saucepan or microwave. Remove the flour mixture from the heat and whisk in the hot milk. Return to medium-high heat, bring to a boil, and boil, stirring, for 1 minute. Season with salt, pepper, and grated nutmeg. Makes about 2 cups (500 mL).

### To Vary the Flavor

Substitute 1 cup (250 mL) béchamel with:
- 1 cup (250 mL) Mornay sauce (béchamel with cheese such as Swiss and Parmesan)
- 1 cup (250 mL) Soubise sauce (béchamel with onions sweated in butter)
- 1 cup (250 mL) Aurore sauce (béchamel with tomato paste or purée)

*See also* VELOUTÉ.

## Beechnut

*Also known as beechmast. Nuts of the beech tree widely used as animal food and as food for people during times of famine.*

### If You Don't Have It

Substitute 1 cup (250 mL) shelled beechnuts with:
- 1 cup (250 mL) hazelnuts
- 1 cup (250 mL) chestnuts

## Beef

*The best cattle breeds for beef include Angus, Kobe (Wagyu), and Piedmontese.*

### If You Don't Have It
Substitute 1 lb (500 g) beef with:
- 1 lb (500 g) buffalo (leaner)
- 1 lb (500 g) venison (leaner; if wild-caught, marinate in wine or vinegar to tame the gamey taste)

*See also* BEEF, GROUND; JERKY.

## Beefalo

*See* BISON.

## Beef, Ground

*Tough yet flavorful cuts of meat are often ground to reduce their toughness while keeping the flavor. Among popular cuts of ground beef, ground chuck is the most flavorful, followed by ground round and ground sirloin.*

### If You Don't Have It
Substitute 1 lb (500 g) ground beef with:
- 1 lb (500 g) ground lamb, pork, or veal (a combination of ground beef, pork, and veal is traditional for meat loaf and meatballs)

### For Better Health
Substitute 1 lb (500 g) ground beef (30% fat) with:
- 1 lb (500 g) ground chuck (25 to 30% fat)
- 1 lb (500 g) lean ground round (20 to 25% fat)
- 1 lb (500 g) extra-lean ground sirloin (15% fat)
- 1 lb (500 g) ground turkey or ground turkey with dark meat
- 1 lb (500 g) ground pork loin
- 1 lb (500 g) ground chicken
- 1 lb (500 g) vegetarian ground beef or crumbles (less chewy)
- 1 lb (500 g) tofu, frozen, thawed, and crumbled with a few quick pulses in a food processor (less chewy; less flavorful)
- 1 cup (250 mL) textured vegetable protein granules, reconstituted in 1½ to 2 cups (375 to 500 mL) vegetable stock or other liquid (less chewy; much less flavorful)

## Beef Jerky

*See* BILTONG; JERKY; PEMMICAN.

## Beef Stock

*See* STOCK, BEEF.

## Beer

*Beverage with a low alcohol content (from 3 to 12%) brewed from water, malted barley or other cereal grains, hops, and yeast. Beers, including lager and Pilsner, are typically bottom-fermented (the yeast sinks in the fermentation tank). Ales, which are top-fermented (the yeast*

### If You Don't Have It
Substitute 1 cup (250 mL) beer (for soups and stews) with:
- 1 cup (250 mL) chicken or beef stock + 2 dashes Angostura bitters (optional)
- 1 cup (250 mL) red wine
- 1 cup (250 mL) sake (Japanese rice wine; less bitter, slightly sweet flavor; lighter body)

### Beer Styles
Choose 1 cup (250 mL) beer from these specific styles:
- 1 cup (250 mL) lager (light color; mild flavor; light body; bubbly)

*rises in the fermentation tank), are more full-flavored and frequently higher in alcohol.*

- 1 cup (250 mL) malt liquor (similar to lager; higher alcohol; fuller body)
- 1 cup (250 mL) pale ale (slightly bitter; fruity; medium body)
- 1 cup (250 mL) India pale ale (bitter; fruity; higher alcohol; medium to full body)
- 1 cup (250 mL) porter or stout (dark color; bitter flavor; full body)
- 1 cup (250 mL) wheat beer (light color; slightly sweet flavor; light body)
- 1 cup (250 mL) bock beer (dark color; slightly sweet flavor; full body)

### For Better Health
Substitute 1 cup (250 mL) beer with:
- 1 cup (250 mL) light beer (fewer calories)
- 1 cup (250 mL) nonalcoholic beer

## Beer Bean

*See* EDAMAME.

## Beer Cheese

*See* BIERKÄSE.

## Beet

*Also known as beetroot (British). Edible globular root, most commonly scarlet in color, but also yellow and sometimes white. For the best flavor and color, leave the beet's peel and stem on during cooking.*

> 1 lb (500 g) =
> 3 to 5 medium =
> 2 cups (500 mL) diced

### If You Don't Have It
Substitute 1 cup (250 mL) chopped red beets with:
- 1 cup (250 mL) chopped canned beets
- 1 cup (250 mL) chopped beefsteak tomatoes

### Beet Varieties
Choose 1 cup (250 mL) chopped beets from these varieties:
- 1 cup (250 mL) chopped golden beets (slightly sweeter; orange color)
- 1 cup (250 mL) chopped Chioggia beets (concentric red and white rings of color)
- 1 cup (250 mL) chopped baby beets (sweeter; quick-cooking)

## Beet Greens

*Edible green leafy tops of beets.*

> 1 lb (500 g) fresh =
> 1⅓ to 2 cups
> (325 to 500 mL) cooked

### If You Don't Have It
Substitute 1 lb (500 g) beet greens with:
- 1 lb (500 g) red or green chard
- 1 lb (500 g) turnip greens
- 1 lb (500 g) mature spinach

## Begonia

*See* PICKING EDIBLE FLOWERS (PAGE 650).

## Beignet

*See* DOUGHNUT.

## Belacan

*See* SHRIMP PASTE.

## Belgian Endive

*A variety of chicory with a long tight head that resembles a small ear of corn. Leaves are white with some yellow, green, or red tips. Pleasantly bitter flavor. Eaten raw in salads or braised as a vegetable.*

### If You Don't Have It
Substitute 1 cup (250 mL) Belgian endive with:
- 1 cup (250 mL) radicchio (red color; bitter flavor)
- 1 cup (250 mL) arugula (green color; more tender; less bitter; more peppery)
- 1 cup (250 mL) watercress (green color; more tender; less bitter; more peppery)

*See also* CHICORY; CURLY ENDIVE; ENDIGIA; FRISÉE.

## Bell Pepper

*Named for their shape, bell peppers all start out green but some varieties ripen to red, orange, or yellow and become sweeter.*

> 1 lb (500 g) = 2 large = 2½ cups (625 mL) chopped = 3 cups (750 mL) sliced
>
> 1 medium = 1 cup (250 mL) chopped

### If You Don't Have It
Substitute 1 cup (250 mL) chopped fresh bell pepper with:
- 1 cup (250 mL) chopped fresh, canned, or bottled pimiento
- 1 cup (250 mL) chopped fresh Cubanelle peppers
- 1 cup (250 mL) chopped fresh banana peppers
- 1 cup (250 mL) chopped fresh bull's horn peppers
- 1 cup (250 mL) chopped fresh Anaheim peppers (spicier)
- 1 cup (250 mL) chopped fresh poblano peppers (spicier)
- ½ cup (125 mL) dried bell peppers

*See also* SWEET PEPPER; CHOOSING FRESH CHILES (PAGE 640).

## Bell Pepper, Roasted Red

*Whole peppers charred quickly over an open flame, such as an oven broiler, barbecue, or open gas flame, then peeled. The partially cooked flesh develops a sweet, caramelized flavor.*

> 1 large = 1 cup (250 mL) chopped

### If You Don't Have It
Substitute 1 cup (250 mL) chopped roasted red peppers with:
- 1 cup (250 mL) chopped jarred pimientos (drained)

## Bellyfish

*See* MONKFISH.

## Belon Oyster

*See* OYSTER.

## Bel Paese

*A versatile, semisoft cheese of Italian origin with a mild flavor and buttery texture. It melts smoothly for pizza or casseroles and is also delicious with fruit.*

### If You Don't Have It

Substitute 1 oz (30 g) Bel Paese with:
- 1 oz (30 g) Monterey Jack
- 1 oz (30 g) mozzarella
- 1 oz (30 g) Muenster
- 1 oz (30 g) Gouda
- 1 oz (30 g) Fontina

## Beluga

*See* CHANGING ROE (PAGE 666).

## Bench Knife

*Also known as a bench scraper, dough knife, and pastry cutter. A flat, square-edged sturdy blade of metal (sometimes plastic) with a comfortable handle. Used by bakers to pick up, turn, and cut dough, and to scrape work surfaces clean or transfer ingredients.*

### If You Don't Have It

Substitute a bench knife with:
- sturdy square-edged spatula
- clean spackle knife

## Bénédictine

*A sweet cognac-based liqueur flavored with herbs and fruit peels, Bénédictine is named after the monks of the Abbey at Fecamp in Normandy, who developed it in the early 1500s.*

### If You Don't Have It

Substitute 2 tbsp (30 mL) Bénédictine with:
- 2 tbsp (30 mL) B&B (less sweet)
- 2 tbsp (30 mL) Chartreuse (green or yellow color)
- 2 tbsp (30 mL) Drambuie (mild licorice flavor)

*See also* B&B.

## Berbere

*Ethiopian blend of spices used to season soups and stews. May be a dry spice mix or a wet paste including cardamom, coriander, fenugreek, garlic, red pepper, and other spices.*

### If You Don't Have It

Substitute 1 tbsp (15 mL) berbere with:
- 1 tbsp (15 mL) Homemade Berbere Paste: Toast 1 tsp (5 mL) coriander seeds, 1 tsp (5 mL) black peppercorns, 1 tsp (5 mL) cardamom seeds, 1 tsp (5 mL) fenugreek seeds, ½ tsp (2 mL) cumin seeds, ¼ tsp (1 mL) allspice berries, and ¼ tsp (1 mL) whole cloves in a dry skillet over medium heat until fragrant, about 2 minutes. Remove spices from pan. Let cool, then coarsely grind in a spice grinder or with a mortar and pestle. Heat 1 tbsp (15 mL) vegetable oil in the same pan over medium-low heat and add ½ cup (125 mL) minced fresh onion. Cook until onion is soft, about 5 minutes. Add 2 minced garlic cloves and 2 tsp (10 mL) minced fresh

## Berbere (cont'd)

ginger. Cook for 1 minute. Remove from heat and stir in 2 tbsp (30 mL) mild paprika, ground spice blend, 2 tbsp (30 mL) vegetable oil, 1 tbsp (15 mL) kosher salt, $\frac{1}{2}$ to 1 tsp (2 to 5 mL) ground cayenne pepper and $\frac{1}{4}$ tsp (1 mL) grated nutmeg. Let cool. Refrigerate for up to 3 weeks in an airtight container. Makes about $\frac{3}{4}$ cup (175 mL).

- 1 tbsp (15 mL) mitmita (spicier)
- 1 tbsp (15 mL) harissa (spicier; less aromatic)

## Bergamot

*An herb in the mint family used in the cooking of Mexico and the Southwest United States.*

### If You Don't Have It

Substitute 1 tbsp (15 mL) chopped fresh bergamot with:

- 1 tbsp (15 mL) chopped fresh oregano, basil, or mint

*See also* ORANGE, SOUR.

## Bergamot Orange

*See* ORANGE, SOUR.

## Berliner

*See* DOUGHNUT.

## Berry

*See* SPECIFIC TYPES.

## Betel Leaf

*Also known as la-lot, pepper leaf and pupulu. Slightly bitter-tasting, heart-shaped leaf used as a wrapper for Thai snacks like miang kham, a mixture of dried shrimp, peanuts, and toasted coconut.*

### If You Don't Have It

Substitute 1 lb (500 g) betel leaves with:

- 1 lb (500 g) Chinese broccoli leaves (gai lan)
- 1 lb (500 g) shiso or perilla leaves (more minty)
- 1 lb (500 g) Boston lettuce leaves (milder)
- 1 lb (500 g) mature bok choy leaves (thicker; more cabbagey flavor)

## Beurre Blanc

*A reduction of shallots, white wine, and white wine vinegar whisked with butter until emulsified. According to* Larousse Gastronomique, *this simple butter sauce was created by chef Clémence Lefeuvre near Nantes, France as she "forgot to include the eggs when attempting to make a Béarnaise sauce."*

### To Vary the Flavor

Substitute 1 cup (250 mL) beurre blanc with:

- 1 cup (250 mL) beurre Nantais (adds heavy cream)
- 1 cup (250 mL) Béarnaise sauce (adds egg yolks and tarragon)
- 1 cup (250 mL) beurre noir (darker color, nuttier flavor)

## Beurre Manié

*Also known as kneaded butter. A paste of softened butter and flour that is used to thicken and enrich sauces.*

### If You Don't Have It
Substitute 2 tbsp (30 mL) beurre manié with:
- 2 tbsp (30 mL) roux
- 2 tbsp (30 mL) Homemade Beurre Manié: Combine 1 tbsp (15 mL) softened butter and 1 tbsp (15 mL) all-purpose flour. Knead together.
- 1½ tbsp (22 mL) tapioca starch whisked with 2 tbsp (30 mL) cold water
- 1½ tsp (7 mL) cornstarch whisked with 2 tsp (10 mL) cold water

## Beurre Noir

*Also known as black butter or brown butter. Melted butter cooked to a dark golden brown and mixed with vinegar or lemon juice and sometimes herbs such as parsley.*

### To Vary the Flavor
Substitute 1 cup (250 mL) beurre noir with:
- 1 cup (250 mL) beurre blanc (lighter color, milder flavor, adds shallots)
- 1 cup (250 mL) beurre Nantais (lighter color, adds heavy cream, shallots)
- 1 cup (250 mL) Béarnaise sauce (lighter color, adds egg yolks, tarragon, and shallots)

*See also* BEURRE NOISETTE.

## Beurre Noisette

*Melted butter cooked to a light golden brown for a nutty flavor.*

### To Vary the Flavor
Substitute 1 cup (250 mL) beurre noisette with:
- 1 cup (250 mL) ghee
- 1 cup (250 mL) clarified butter
- 1 cup (250 mL) beurre noir (darker brown, adds vinegar or lemon juice)

## Bialy

*Jewish-American yeast roll that's a first cousin to bagels. Instead of a center hole, bialys have a center depression that's often filled with onions. Named after the Polish city of Bialystok.*

### If You Don't Have It
Substitute 1 bialy with:
- 1 onion or plain bagel (thicker)
- 1 English muffin (smaller; more light and airy crumb; less chewy; no onion flavor)
- 2 slices dense, chewy bread (such as sourdough; no onion flavor)
- 1 soft pretzel

## Bibb Lettuce

*See* BUTTERHEAD LETTUCE.

## Bicarbonate of Soda

*See* BAKING SODA.

## Bierkäse

*Also known as beer cheese.
Soft ripened German
cheese with a sharp taste.*

### If You Don't Have It

Substitute 1 oz (30 g) Bierkäse with:
- 1 oz (30 g) Limburger

## Bierwurst

*Garlicky German dark
red cooked sausage most
frequently sliced and
served on sandwiches.*

### If You Don't Have It

Substitute 1 lb (500 g) Bierwurst with:
- 1 lb (500 g) jagdwurst
- 1 lb (500 g) krakauer
- 1 lb (500 g) cervelat
- 1 lb (500 g) Blockwurst
- 1 lb (500 g) bologna

## Bilberry

*Also known as blaeberry,
whinberry, and
whortleberry. A bluish
purple berry related to the
blueberry and cranberry.
Common in the British
Isles and far northern
climes of North America.*

1 pint fresh = 3 cups
(750 mL)

### If You Don't Have It

Substitute 1 cup (250 mL) bilberries with:
- 1 cup (250 mL) huckleberries (slightly sweeter)
- 1 cup (250 mL) cranberries (red color; more tart)
- 1 cup (250 mL) blueberries (larger and sweeter)
- 1 cup (250 mL) red currants (red color)

## Bilimbi

*Short cucumber-shaped
fruit related to star fruit
but much more acidic.*

### If You Don't Have It

Substitute 8 fresh bilimbi with:
- 1 tbsp (15 mL) lemon juice
- 1 tbsp (15 mL) lime juice
- 1 tbsp (15 mL) vinegar

## Biltong

*Dried and sometimes
smoked meat indigenous
to southern Africa. One
version is prepared by
coating a large cut of beef
with spice rub and vinegar,
then hanging it to air-dry
and later smoke. This type
is more tender than the type
made from drying seasoned
strips of zebra or other
game meat in the sun.*

### If You Don't Have It

Substitute 1 oz (30 g) biltong with:
- 1 oz (30 g) beef jerky (less spicy; more neutral flavor)
- 1 oz (30 g) pemmican (more complex flavor)

### For Better Health

- 1 oz (30 g) turkey jerky (leaner)
- 1 oz (30 g) vegetarian jerky (leaner)

*See also* JERKY; PEMMICAN.

## Bindenfleisch

*See* BÜNDNERFLEISCH.

## Bing Cherry

*See* CHERRY.

## Biscotti

*Crisp Italian cookies that are twice baked. Traditionally eaten by dunking in sweet dessert wine or coffee.*

### If You Don't Have It
Substitute 1 lb (500 g) biscotti with:
- 1 lb (500 g) mandlebrot (adds almond flavor)
- 1 lb (500 g) amaretti  (adds almond flavor)

## Biscuit

*See* CRACKER.

## Biscuit Cutter

*Circular implement that's typically smooth on the interior and scalloped on the outside. Used for cutting quick-bread biscuit dough.*

### If You Don't Have It
Substitute a biscuit cutter with:
- cookie cutter of any shape
- clean tuna can or other can with both ends removed
- inverted wine or drinking glass

*See also* COOKIE CUTTER.

## Biscuit Mix

*Boxed mixture of flour and leavening that requires only the addition of milk to make biscuit dough. With eggs added, the mix can also be used to prepare pancakes, waffles, and other quick breads.*

### If You Don't Have It
Substitute 1 cup (250 mL) biscuit mix with:
- 1 cup (250 mL) Homemade Biscuit Mix: Whisk together 3 cups (750 mL) cake or pastry flour, 1/3 cup (75 mL) powdered buttermilk or whole milk, 1 tbsp (15 mL) baking powder, and 1 tsp (5 mL) salt. When ready to bake, cut in 1/2 cup (125 mL) cold butter or vegetable shortening. Use immediately or refrigerate in an airtight container for up to 3 months (without butter). Makes about 3 1/3 cups (825 mL) (without butter).

## Bishop's Weed

*See* AJWAIN.

## Bison

*Also known as buffalo. Lean tender bison meat has more iron and less fat than beef and it doesn't taste gamey.*

### If You Don't Have It
Substitute 1 lb (500 g) bison with:
- 1 lb (500 g) beefalo (hybrid of 5/8 beef and 3/8 bison)
- 1 lb (500 g) beef (richer)
- 1 lb (500 g) venison (gamier)

## Bitter Almond

*See* ALMOND, BITTER.

## Bitter Chocolate

*See* CHOCOLATE, UNSWEETENED.

## Bitter Melon

*Also known as balsam pear. Sour fruit used in Chinese cooking. Bitter melon resembles a bumpy-skinned cucumber with green to yellow orange color.*

### If You Don't Have It
Substitute 1 cup (250 mL) chopped bitter melon with:
- 1 cup (250 mL) chopped winter melon (less bitter)

*See also* LUFFA, ANGLED.

## Bitter Orange

*See* ORANGE, SOUR.

## Bitters

*A distilled, high-alcohol blend of barks, flowers, herbs, seeds, roots, and other aromatics. Bitters are used to flavor many cocktails and foods. Also called upon to aid digestion, stimulate the appetite, and cure hangovers.*

### If You Don't Have It
- Substitute ¼ tsp (1 mL) bitters with:
- ½ tsp (2 mL) Worcestershire sauce (for cooking and savory drinks)

### Bitters Varieties
Choose ¼ tsp (1 mL) bitters from these specific types:
- ¼ tsp (1 mL) Angostura bitters
- ¼ tsp (1 mL) Peychaud's bitters
- ¼ tsp (1 mL) orange bitters (adds orange flavor)
- ¼ tsp (1 mL) Pommeranzen bitters (adds orange flavor)

*See also* AMER PICON; FERNET BRANCA.

## Bittersweet Chocolate

*See* CHOCOLATE, BITTERSWEET.

## Blacang

*See* SHRIMP PASTE.

## Blachan

*See* SHRIMP PASTE.

## Black Bean

*See* THE WIDE WORLD OF DRIED BEANS (PAGE 637).

## Black Bean Sauce

*A distinctively flavored condiment made by curing and fermenting soybeans in salt, which turns them black. Usually flavored with garlic and sometimes with star anise. Hot black bean sauce contains chile paste, as well as garlic, toasted sesame oil, and sugar.*

### If You Don't Have It
Substitute 1 tbsp (15 mL) black bean sauce with:
- 1 tbsp (15 mL) fermented black beans
- 1 tbsp (15 mL) Thai bean sauce (milder)
- 1 tbsp (15 mL) Chinese brown bean sauce (milder; less salty)

### To Vary the Flavor
Substitute 1 tbsp (15 mL) black bean sauce with:
- 1 tbsp (15 mL) hot black bean sauce (spicier)
- 1 tbsp (15 mL) black bean and garlic sauce (adds garlic flavor)

*See also* BEAN SAUCE; FERMENTED BLACK BEANS.

## Blackberry

*Also known as bramble. A large, deep purple berry that grows wild on thorny bushes. In England, blackberries are often combined with apples to make pie.*

> 1 pint fresh =
> 2 cups (500 mL)
> 10 oz (300 g) frozen =
> 2 cups (500 mL)

### If You Don't Have It

Substitute 1 cup (250 mL) blackberries with:
- 1 cup (250 mL) loganberries (red color)
- 1 cup (250 mL) boysenberries (slightly sweeter)
- 1 cup (250 mL) olallieberries (larger; sweeter)
- 1 cup (250 mL) raspberries (smaller; sweeter)

*See also* MARIONBERRY; OLALLIEBERRY.

## Blackberry Liqueur

*Sweetened blackberry-flavored spirit.*

### If You Don't Have It

Substitute 2 tbsp (30 mL) blackberry liqueur with:
- 2 tbsp (30 mL) crème de mûre (blackberry cream liqueur; sweeter; heavier body)
- 2 tbsp (30 mL) blackberry schnapps (less sweet; higher alcohol)
- 2 tbsp (30 mL) blackberry syrup (sweeter; no alcohol)
- 1 tsp (5 mL) blackberry extract (add 4 tsp/20 mL liquid to recipe if necessary)

### To Vary the Flavor

Substitute 2 tbsp (30 mL) blackberry liqueur with:
- 2 tbsp (30 mL) black raspberry liqueur (less astringent flavor)
- 2 tbsp (30 mL) cassis liqueur (blackcurrant liqueur; thicker; includes rum)
- 2 tbsp (30 mL) raspberry liqueur (sweeter)
- 2 tbsp (30 mL) crème de fraise (strawberry flavor; sweeter; heavier body)
- 2 tbsp (30 mL) cherry liqueur (sweeter)

## Black Bread

*Also known as Russian black bread. Like pumpernickel, this slightly sour dark bread has a high proportion of rye flour to wheat flour. The dark color can be enhanced by including molasses, cocoa, dark beer, and/or coffee.*

### If You Don't Have It

Substitute 1 lb (500 g) black bread with:
- 1 lb (500 g) pumpernickel bread
- 1 lb (500 g) dark rye bread (especially marbled or sourdough rye)
- 1 lb (500 g) limpa bread (more aromatic)

*See also* PUMPERNICKEL BREAD.

## Black Chicken

*See* CHICKEN, BLACK .

## Black Cod

*Mostly ranging from the southern coasts of New Zealand to sub-Antarctic waters. Like other cod icefish such as Patagonian toothfish (Chilean sea bass), black cod has adapted to its deep-sea environment by developing additional body fat and antifreeze glycoproteins in its blood and body fluids.*

### If You Don't Have It

Substitute 1 lb (500 g) black cod with:

- 1 lb (500 g) sablefish
- 1 lb (500 g) butterfish
- 1 lb (500 g) mackerel
- 1 lb (500 g) whitefish
- 1 lb (500 g) salmon
- 1 lb (500 g) blackfish
- 1 lb (500 g) grouper

### To Vary the Flavor

Substitute 1 lb (500 g) black cod with:

- 1 lb (500 g) smoked or kippered black cod or sablefish (cured fish; adds smoke flavor)

*See also* BUTTERFISH; SABLEFISH.

## Black Corinth

*See* CHAMPAGNE GRAPE.

## Black Currant

*See* CURRANT, FRESH.

## Black Currant Jelly

*See* CURRANT JELLY.

## Black-Eyed Pea, Fresh

*Also known as cowpeas and southernpeas. If you've only ever tried them dried, try to find some black-eyed beauties in the shell. They can be prepared like fresh lima beans but have a more complex, earthy, almost nutty taste.*

1 lb (500 g) fresh in shell = 1¼ cups (300 mL) shelled

### If You Don't Have It

Substitute 1 lb (500 g) fresh black-eyed peas (weighed in shell) with:

- 1 lb (500 g) fresh cranberry beans (cream and red-speckled color)
- 1 lb (500 g) fresh Dragon Tongue beans (deep reddish brown and cream color)
- 1 lb (500 g) fresh Tongue of Fire beans (green and red color)
- 1 lb (500 g) fresh Romano beans (green color)
- 1 lb (500 g) fresh Kentucky Wonder beans (green color)
- 1 lb (500 g) fresh lima beans (green color)
- 1 lb (500 g) fresh edamame (green color)

*See also* PEAS, SHELLING; THE WIDE WORLD OF DRIED BEANS (PAGE 637).

## Blackfin Tuna

*See* TUNA, FRESH.

## Blackfish

*Also known as black trout, Chinese steelhead, and tautog. Northwest Atlantic fish in the wrasse family with delicate flavor, tiny bones, and dark skin. Cunner is a closely related fish.*

### If You Don't Have It

Substitute 1 lb (500 g) blackfish with:
- 1 lb (500 g) grouper
- 1 lb (500 g) striped bass
- 1 lb (500 g) red snapper (flakier)

## Black Forest Ham

*A moist German ham that is prepared by salt-curing, air-drying, and smoking over fire or pine wood. The traditional practice of coating the ham in beef blood to produce a dark surface has given way to a spice rub and smoking that create a similar hue.*

### If You Don't Have It

Substitute 1 lb (500 g) Black Forest ham with:
- 1 lb (500 g) Bradenham ham (similar black exterior)
- 1 lb (500 g) Virginia ham (such as Smithfield ham; milder flavor)
- 1 lb (500 g) Westphalian ham (adds juniper aroma)
- 1 lb (500 g) prosciutto

## Black Garlic

*See* GARLIC, BLACK.

## Black Kingfish

*See* COBIA.

## Black Mullet

*See* MULLET.

## Black Mustard Seed

*See* MUSTARD SEED.

## Black Onion Seed

*See* NIGELLA.

## Black Pearl Caviar

*See* CHANGING ROE (PAGE 666).

## Black Pepper

*See* PEPPERCORN.

## Black Pudding

*See* BLOOD SAUSAGE.

## Black Raspberry Liqueur

*See* RASPBERRY LIQUEUR.

## Black Salmon

*See* COBIA.

## Black Sea Bass

*Caught off the Atlantic coast of the U.S., this popular fish responds well to any style of cooking. The succulent flesh is the result of a diet rich in shrimp, crabs, and mollusks.*

### If You Don't Have It

Substitute 1 lb (500 g) black sea bass with:

- 1 lb (500 g) rockfish
- 1 lb (500 g) red snapper
- 1 lb (500 g) grouper
- 1 lb (500 g) ocean perch
- 1 lb (500 g) striped bass
- 1 lb (500 g) tilefish
- 1 lb (500 g) catfish

## Black Sesame Seed

*See* SESAME SEED.

## Black Sturgeon Roe

*See* CHANGING ROE (PAGE 666).

## Black Sugar

*See* SUGAR, BLACK.

## Black Trout

*See* BLACKFISH.

## Black Trumpet Mushroom

*See* SHUFFLING MUSHROOMS (PAGE 654).

## Black Walnut

*See* WALNUT.

## Blaeberry

*See* BILBERRY.

## Blender

*A small electrical kitchen appliance with a tall cylinder shaped like a pitcher with short rotating blades at the base. Excellent for puréeing and for chopping small amounts of foods.*

### If You Don't Have It

Substitute a blender with:

- food processor fitted with a metal blade (best for puréeing soups and sauces; avoid overfilling; not recommended for crushing ice)
- immersion blender (for immersing into soups or sauces to purée)

## Bleu d'Auvergne

*A soft-rind cow's milk blue cheese from France that is designated with the* appellation d'origine contrôlée *(AOC).*

4 oz (125 g) = 1 cup (250 mL) crumbled

### If You Don't Have It

Substitute 1 oz (30 g) Bleu d'Auvergne with:

- 1 oz (30 g) Bleu des Causses
- 1 oz (30 g) Roquefort
- 1 oz (30 g) Fourme d'Ambert
- 1 oz (30 g) Maytag Blue

## Bleu de Bresse

*Soft-blue, full-fat cow's milk cheese from the Rhone-Alpes region of France.*

4 oz (125 g) = 1 cup (250 mL) crumbled

### If You Don't Have It

Substitute 1 oz (30 g) Bleu de Bresse with:

- 1 oz (30 g) Blue Castello
- 1 oz (30 g) Cambozola
- 1 oz (30 g) Gorgonzola
- 1 oz (30 g) Brie (less pungent)

## Bleu de Chèvre

*Aged goat's milk blue cheese from the Auvergne province of south central France.*

4 oz (125 g) = 1 cup (250 mL) crumbled

### If You Don't Have It

Substitute 1 oz (30 g) Bleu de Chèvre with:

- 1 oz (30 g) Roquefort
- 1 oz (30 g) Bleu d'Auvergne
- 1 oz (30 g) Bleu des Causses
- 1 oz (30 g) Gorgonzola

## Bleu de Gex

*French cow's milk appellation d'origine contrôlée (AOC) blue cheese from Franche-Comté. The word Gex is stamped into the rind.*

4 oz (125 g) = 1 cup (250 mL) crumbled

### If You Don't Have It

Substitute 1 oz (30 g) Bleu de Gex with:

- 1 oz (30 g) Fourme d'Ambert
- 1 oz (30 g) Stilton

## Bleu des Causses

*Likened to a cow's milk version of Roquefort, this appellation d'origine contrôlée (AOC) blue cheese is produced in the Midday-Pyrenees.*

4 oz (125 g) = 1 cup (250 mL) crumbled

### If You Don't Have It

Substitute 1 oz (30 g) Bleu des Causses with:

- 1 oz (30 g) Bleu d'Auvergne (milder)
- 1 oz (30 g) Roquefort
- 1 oz (30 g) Fourme d'Ambert
- 1 oz (30 g) Maytag Blue

## Blockwurst

*Spicy German pork sausage, sold ready-to-eat for sandwiches.*

### If You Don't Have It

Substitute 1 lb (500 g) Blockwurst with:

- 1 lb (500 g) cervelat
- 1 lb (500 g) Bierwurst
- 1 lb (500 g) bologna
- 1 lb (500 g) cooked salami

## Blood Orange

*See* ORANGE, BLOOD.

## Blood Sausage

*Also known as black pudding, blood pudding, and boudin noir. A style of sausage dating from ancient times and still produced in the British Isles and many European countries. Typically made with pork blood, cereal grain, and seasonings.*

### If You Don't Have It
Substitute 1 lb (500 g) blood sausage with these specific types:
- 1 lb (500 g) black pudding (British and Irish)
- 1 lb (500 g) Blutwurst (German)
- 1 lb (500 g) boudin rouge (French and Cajun)
- 1 lb (500 g) morcilla (Spanish)
- 1 lb (500 g) Zungenwurst (German; includes ox tongue)

## Blueberry

*Sweet-tart, smooth, blue berries with grayish blush. Cultivars of wild blueberries are a great success of commercial berry cultivation, having been introduced in New Jersey in 1920.*

| 1 pint fresh = 2 cups (500 mL) |
| 10 oz (300 g) frozen = 1½ cups (375 mL) |

### If You Don't Have It
Substitute 1 cup (250 mL) blueberries with:
- 1 cup (250 mL) huckleberries (more tart)
- 1 cup (250 mL) red currants (red color; more tart)
- 1 cup (250 mL) raspberries or strawberries (for serving fresh)

## Blueberry Liqueur

*See* CRÈME DE MYRTILLE.

## Blue Castello

*Rich triple-crème Danish blue cheese with a relatively mild flavor.*

### If You Don't Have It
Substitute 1 oz (30 g) Blue Castello with:
- 1 oz (30 g) Bleu de Bresse
- 1 oz (30 g) Cambozola
- 1 oz (30 g) Saga Blue
- 1 oz (30 g) Gorgonzola (more pungent)

## Blue Cheese

*A large class of cheeses that have been treated with molds that create blue or green veins and mildly to strongly pungent flavors.*

| 4 oz (125 g) = 1 cup (250 mL) crumbled |

### If You Don't Have It
Substitute 1 oz (30 g) blue cheese with:
- 1 oz (30 g) feta cheese (much milder)

### For Better Health
Substitute 1 oz (30 g) blue cheese with:
- ½ oz (15 g) blue cheese + ½ oz (15 g) reduced-fat cream cheese (for sauces and dressings)

*See also* SPECIFIC TYPES.

## Blue Cheshire
*See* CHESHIRE.

## Blue Crab
*See* CRAB.

## Blue Curaçao
*See* ORANGE LIQUEUR.

## Bluefin
*See* TUNA, FRESH.

## Bluefish

*Also known as elft, lûfer, and tailor. Nicknamed Bulldog of the Sea because of its voracious nature. The dark, oily strip that runs down the center of the fish should be removed to prevent the flesh from absorbing a fishy flavor.*

### If You Don't Have It
Substitute 1 lb (500 g) bluefish with:
- 1 lb (500 g) mackerel
- 1 lb (500 g) butterfish
- 1 lb (500 g) tilefish
- 1 lb (500 g) halibut
- 1 lb (500 g) cod

## Blue Ginger
*See* GALANGAL.

## Bluepoint Oyster
*See* OYSTER.

## Blutwurst
*See* BLOOD SAUSAGE.

## Boar

*Also known as wild boar. Renowned in classical myths and as the centerpiece of annual medieval European feasts.*

### If You Don't Have It
Substitute 1 lb (500 g) boar meat with:
- 1 lb (500 g) pork (preferably pastured; more pale; richer; milder-tasting)

*See also* PORK.

## Boboli
*See* PIZZA CRUST.

## Bockwurst

*German ground veal sausage seasoned with chives and parsley. A springtime tradition enjoyed with bock beer.*

### If You Don't Have It
Substitute 1 lb (500 g) Bockwurst with:
- 1 lb (500 g) fresh Bratwurst

## Boiling Water

*Often called for in recipes to cook rice or pasta or to soak dried mushrooms or sun-dried tomatoes.*

### To Vary the Flavor

Substitute 1 cup (250 mL) boiling water with:

- 1 cup (250 mL) boiling beef, chicken or vegetable stock
- 1 cup (250 mL) boiling vegetable juice

### To Save Time

Substitute 1 cup (250 mL) boiling water with:

- 1 cup (250 mL) hot tap water, brought to a boil if necessary (much faster, especially for pasta; for soaking dried mushrooms and sun-dried tomatoes, very hot tap water is sufficient; may slightly affect flavor if you haven't drawn hot water from the tap in a while)

## Bok Choy

*Also known as Chinese white cabbage, pak choi, pak choy, and Chinese mustard cabbage. Looks like a bulbous head of white or pale green celery with tender, pale green or dark green leaves. The tender inner "hearts" of bok choy are sometimes called white choy sum.*

1 lb (500 g) = 1 small = 6 baby = 3½ cups (875 mL) sliced

### If You Don't Have It

Substitute 1 lb (500 g) bok choy with:

- 1 lb (500 g) Chinese broccoli (darker green stems; slightly sweeter, less cabbagey flavor)
- 1 lb (500 g) napa cabbage (paler green yellow color; more tender; less juicy; great for stir-frying)
- 1 lb (500 g) green chard (less cabbagey flavor)
- 1 lb (500 g) collard greens (thinner, greener stems; larger leaves)
- 1 lb (500 g) celery (in place of bok choy stems in stir-fries)

### Bok Choy Varieties

Choose 1 lb (500 g) bok choy from these varieties:

- 1 lb (500 g) mature bok choy (the type common in American markets; sweet; juicy; mild cabbage flavor)
- 1 lb (500 g) choy sum or Chinese flowering cabbage (similar to mature bok choy but slightly smaller stems and leaves; often blossoms with clusters of small yellow flowers)
- 1 lb (500 g) Canton bok choy (slightly stronger cabbage flavor)
- 1 lb (500 g) Shanghai bok choy (short, squat, green stems; often sold as baby bok choy; mellow cabbage flavor)
- 1 lb (500 g) Taiwan bok choy (thinner stems; more delicate leaves; very mild cabbage flavor)

*See also* NAPA CABBAGE; TATSOI; YAU CHOY.

## Boldo Leaf

*From a tree native to central Chile, this small leaf exudes pleasant woodsy and camphor aromas but has a bitter taste. It is used like bay leaves to flavor Latin American dishes and shows up in herbal teas.*

1 whole leaf = ¼ tsp (1 mL) crushed

### If You Don't Have It

Substitute 2 dried boldo leaves with:

- 1 fresh bay leaf
- ½ tsp (2 mL) crushed dried bay leaf

## Bolillo

*Crusty, 6-inch (15 cm)
oval roll used for Mexican
sandwiches like tortas and
molletes.*

### If You Don't Have It
Substitute 1 lb (500 g) bolillo with:
- 1 lb (500 g) 6-inch (15 cm) sausage roll
- 1 lb (500 g) 6-inch (15 cm) submarine, grinder, or hoagie roll
- 1 lb (500 g) baguette, bâtarde, baton or other French bread cut into 6-inch (15 cm) lengths

## Bologna

*Also known as baloney.
Spiced sandwich meat that
is the mainstay of many a
bagged lunch. Named after
the Italian city of Bologna.*

### If You Don't Have It
Substitute 1 lb (500 g) bologna with:
- 1 lb (500 g) ring bologna (firmer and narrower; available fine or coarse)
- 1 lb (500 g) mortadella (similar but with cubes of pork fat and garlic flavor)
- 1 lb (500 g) galantina (more chunky)
- 1 lb (500 g) olive loaf (adds olive flavor)

### For Better Health
Substitute 1 lb (500 g) bologna with:
- 1 lb (500 g) Gelbwurst (lower in fat and calories)

*See also* RING BOLOGNA.

## Bombay Duck

*Also known as bummalo.
Not a duck but rather a
fish (Bommaloay Macchi)
that is native to Mumbai
(formerly Bombay), India.*

### If You Don't Have It
Substitute 1 lb (500 g) Bombay duck with:
- 1 lb (500 g) salt cod or another strongly flavored salted dried fish

## Bonbel Cheese

*See* BABYBEL CHEESE.

## Boneless Ham

*See* HAM, WET-CURED.

## Boniato

*Also known as batata
and camote. A sweet
potato cultivar with
brown or red skin and
white flesh. Popular
in Caribbean cooking.*

### If You Don't Have It
Substitute 1 cup (250 mL) chopped boniato with:
- 1 cup (250 mL) chopped white or cushcush yam
- 1 cup (250 mL) chopped russet potato
- 1 cup (250 mL) chopped sweet potato (orange flesh; much sweeter flavor; moister texture)

*See also* SWEET POTATO.

## Bonito

*A small variety of tuna (skipjack) often dried and used in Japanese dishes particularly to make dashi, a clear Japanese soup stock.*

### If You Don't Have It

Substitute 1 cup (250 mL) bonito flakes (katsuobushi, hanakatsuo, or kezuribushi) with:

- 1 cup (250 mL) dried dulse (a seaweed; adds briny but not fishy flavor)

*See also* TUNA, FRESH.

## Borage

*Herb with pretty blue flowers, large hairy leaves, and a cucumber-like flavor. Larger leaves may be cooked as a vegetable.*

### If You Don't Have It

Substitute 1 tbsp (15 mL) fresh borage with:

- 1 tbsp (15 mL) fresh salad burnet (to replace borage leaves as an herb)
- 2 tsp (10 mL) fresh thyme (to replace borage leaves as an herb)
- 1 tbsp (15 mL) fresh spinach (to replace borage leaves for cooking)
- 1 tbsp (15 mL) fresh nasturtiums (to replace flowers for salads)

*See also* PICKING EDIBLE FLOWERS (PAGE 650).

## Bordelaise Sauce

*A French brown sauce made with red wine, demi-glace, bone marrow, shallots, and herbs; often served with grilled meat. The very different Louisiana bordelaise is made with garlic, olive oil, butter, and herbs and is often served with seafood and pasta.*

### If You Don't Have It

Substitute 1 cup (250 mL) French Bordelaise sauce with:

- 1 cup (250 mL) French Bourguignonne sauce (adds mushrooms, onions, and bacon)
- 1 cup (250 mL) Chasseur or hunter's sauce (adds mushrooms and tomatoes)
- 1 cup (250 mL) Sauce Africaine (spicier)
- 1 cup (250 mL) red wine reduction sauce

*See also* ESPAGNOLE SAUCE.

## Borlotti Bean

*See* CRANBERRY BEAN, FRESH; THE WIDE WORLD OF DRIED BEANS (PAGE 637).

## Boston Brown Bread

*Dark, sweet steamed bread made with rye flour, wheat flour, cornmeal, and molasses or maple syrup. Sometimes raisins are added and the bread is usually cooked in a coffee can to produce a cylindrical loaf.*

### If You Don't Have It

Substitute 1 lb (500 g) Boston brown bread with:

- 1 lb (500 g) Russian black bread (denser; less sweet; may include cocoa, beer, and/or coffee)
- 1 lb (500 g) pumpernickel bread (denser; less sweet)
- 1 lb (500 g) dark rye bread (denser; less sweet)

## Boston Lettuce

*See* BUTTERHEAD LETTUCE.

## Bottarga

*See* CHANGING ROE (PAGE 666).

## Boxty

*Irish fried potato pancakes with many variations but usually including grated raw potatoes, mashed potatoes, wheat flour, and buttermilk.*

### If You Don't Have It

Substitute 1 lb (500 g) boxty with:
- 1 lb (500 g) Jewish latkes, Swedish raggmunk, or other potato pancakes

## Boudin Blanc

*A delicate French white sausage made with pork and chicken. In Louisiana, Cajun boudin blanc is made with pork and has a spicier, more complex flavor.*

### If You Don't Have It

Substitute 1 lb (500 g) boudin blanc with:
- 1 lb (500 g) German Weisswurst (mild flavor)
- 1 lb (500 g) white Bratwurst (mild flavor)

## Boudin Rouge

*See* BLOOD SAUSAGE.

## Bouillon

*See* STOCK.

## Bounceberry

*See* CRANBERRY.

## Bouquet Garni

*The classic flavoring trio of the French kitchen: bay leaf, parsley, and thyme.*

### If You Don't Have It

Substitute 1 bouquet garni with:
- 1 Homemade Classic Bouquet Garni: Combine 3 to 4 sprigs fresh parsley, 1 sprig fresh thyme, and 1 bay leaf. Tie together with string or a clean plastic twist-tie. Or tie shut in a cheesecloth or a clean coffee filter (use cheesecloth or a coffee filter if you want only the aroma of the herbs but not their texture in the dish).

## Bourbon

*See* WHISKEY.

## Boursault

*Triple-crème cheese with the consistency of thick sour cream. Look for paper-wrapped cylinders with no discoloration.*

### If You Don't Have It

Substitute 1 oz (30 g) Boursault with:
- 1 oz (30 g) Brillat-Savarin
- 1 oz (30 g) Explorateur
- 1 oz (30 g) Gratte-Paille
- 1 oz (30 g) Brie

## Boursin

*Triple-crème cheese with a whipped butter texture; seasoned with herbs, garlic, or cracked peppercorns.*

### If You Don't Have It

Substitute 1 oz (30 g) boursin with:
- 1 oz (30 g) Rondelé
- 1 oz (30 g) Alouette
- 1 oz (30 g) herbed cream cheese + 1½ tsp (7 mL) softened butter

## Bowls

*Essential kitchen equipment for mixing and serving. Stock a range of sizes, from small to large. For mixing, many cooks prefer sturdy and versatile stainless steel.*

### If You Don't Have It

Substitute bowls with:
- hollowed-out squash (for hot and cold soups)
- hollowed-out melons (for cold soups)
- hollowed-out citrus fruit (for cold soups)
- large coffee cups or mugs (for soup or creamy desserts)
- wineglasses (for soup or creamy desserts)
- large saucepan or pot (for mixing doughs and batters)

## Boysenberry

*In 1923, horticulturist Rudolph Boysen crossed a blackberry, loganberry, and raspberry to father his namesake fruit. The size of large raspberries, this sweet berry is purplish red.*

1 pint fresh =
2⅔ cups (650 mL)

### If You Don't Have It

Substitute 1 cup (250 mL) boysenberries with:
- 1 cup (250 mL) loganberries (redder color)
- 1 cup (250 mL) blackberries (more tart; larger seeds)
- 1 cup (250 mL) olallieberries (larger; sweeter)
- 1 cup (250 mL) raspberries (smaller; sweeter)

## Bramble

*See* BLACKBERRY.

## Bran

*See* OAT BRAN; WHEAT BRAN.

## Brandy

*Liquor distilled from wine or the juice of other fermented fruits. The word brandy is derived from the Dutch brandewijn (burned wine) because the wine is heated during distillation. The Latin term aqua vitae and the French term eau de vie ("water of life") both refer to colorless brandy such as Kirsch.*

### If You Don't Have It

Substitute ¼ cup (60 mL) brandy with:
- 2 to 3 tsp (10 to 15 mL) brandy extract + ¼ cup (60 mL) water or liquid in recipe

### To Vary the Flavor

Substitute ¼ cup (60 mL) brandy with:
- ¼ cup (60 mL) Scotch, bourbon or rum (especially with chocolate in baking)
- ¼ cup (60 mL) fruit juice or syrup (to replace fruit brandies)

*See also* ARMAGNAC; B&B; BRANDY DE JEREZ; COGNAC; METAXA; SPECIFIC FLAVORS.

## Brandy de Jerez

*Spanish brandy with a Protected Designation of Origin (PDO) from the Andalusian region of Jerez. Aged in American oak casks previously containing sherry, Brandy de Jerez Solera ages for at least 1 year, Solera Reserva for 3 years, and Gran Reserva for 10 years.*

### If You Don't Have It
Substitute 3 tbsp (45 mL) Brandy de Jerez with:
- 3 tbsp (45 mL) cognac (drier; lighter body)
- 3 tbsp (45 mL) Armagnac (drier; more complex flavor)
- 3 tbsp (45 mL) top-shelf brandy
- 3 tbsp (45 mL) top-shelf sherry

*See also* ARMAGNAC; COGNAC.

## Brandy Extract

*Concentrated brandy flavoring.*

### If You Don't Have It
Substitute ½ tsp (2 mL) brandy extract with:
- 1 to 1½ tbsp (15 to 22 mL) brandy (adds alcohol)
- ½ tsp (2 mL) rum extract (adds rum flavor)
- ½ tsp (2 mL) vanilla extract (adds vanilla flavor)

## Bratwurst

*German fresh pork and veal sausage seasoned with spices that may include caraway seeds, coriander, ginger, and nutmeg.*

### If You Don't Have It
Substitute 1 lb (500 g) Bratwurst with:
- 1 lb (500 g) smoked Bratwurst (adds smoke flavor)
- 1 lb (500 g) French boudin blanc (delicate flavor)
- 1 lb (500 g) Cajun boudin blanc (spicier, more complex flavor)
- 1 lb (500 g) German Weisswurst (mild flavor)
- 1 lb (500 g) Bockwurst (mild flavor)

## Braunschweiger

*Spreadable smoked liverwurst named after the German town of Braunschweig (Brunswick).*

### If You Don't Have It
Substitute 1 lb (500 g) Braunschweiger with:
- 1 lb (500 g) liverwurst (unsmoked)
- 1 lb (500 g) Mettwurst
- 1 lb (500 g) Teewurst (spicier)
- 1 lb (500 g) pâté

*See also* CERVELAT; LIVERWURST.

## Brazil Nut

*Also known as cream nut and para nut. Mostly a foraged crop in the Amazonian jungle. The nuts are actually segments similar to orange wedges found inside a round fruit the size of a coconut.*

### If You Don't Have It
Substitute 1 cup (250 mL) Brazil nuts with:
- 1 cup (250 mL) macadamia nuts
- 1 cup (250 mL) almonds
- 1 cup (250 mL) pecans

*See also* NUT; PARADISE NUT.

## Bread

*See* FRENCH BREAD; ITALIAN BREAD; SPECIFIC TYPES.

## Bread Crumbs, Dry

*A thrifty cook's binding agent. Dry crumbs are powdered like fine sand.*

1 slice dry bread or toast = ⅓ cup (75 mL) dry bread crumbs = 1 oz (30 g)

### If You Don't Have It
Substitute 1 cup (250 mL) plain dry bread crumbs with:
- 3 to 4 slices oven-dried bread, crushed to fine crumbs in a food processor
- 1¼ cups (300 mL) croutons or stuffing cubes, crushed
- 1 cup (250 mL) panko (Japanese bread crumbs; large crumbs; retains crispness better)
- ¾ cup (175 mL) cracker crumbs
- 1 tbsp (15 mL) quick-cooking oats (for thickening)

### To Vary the Flavor
Substitute 1 cup (250 mL) plain dry bread crumbs with:
- 1 cup (250 mL) seasoned dry bread crumbs
- 1 cup (250 mL) crushed melba toasts
- 1 cup (250 mL) matzo meal
- 1 cup (250 mL) crushed tortilla chips
- 1 cup (250 mL) crushed dry-bagged stuffing mix
- 1 cup (250 mL) crushed pretzels
- 1 cup (250 mL) crushed cornflakes
- 1 cup (250 mL) crushed potato chips

*See also* BREAD CRUMBS, FRESH; COOKIE CRUMBS; CORNFLAKE CRUMBS; CRACKER CRUMBS; PANKO.

## Bread Crumbs, Fresh

*Fresh bread crumbs are soft and the size of peas. Italian and French breads make the best crumbs.*

1 lb (500 g) bread, crust removed = 7 cups (1.75 L) fresh bread crumbs

1 slice fresh bread = ½ cup (125 mL) fresh bread crumbs

### If You Don't Have It
Substitute 1 cup (250 mL) fresh bread crumbs with:
- 2 slices slightly dry bread, crushed to coarse fresh crumbs in a food processor
- 1 cup (250 mL) fresh cornbread crumbs (from about a 3-inch/7.5 cm square and 1-inch/2.5 cm deep piece of cornbread)
- 1 cup (250 mL) fresh muffin crumbs

*See also* CORNBREAD CRUMBS; BREAD CRUMBS, DRY.

## Bread Flour

*See* FLOUR, BREAD.

## Breadfruit

*Rough green-skinned fruit, native to the Pacific. In 1789, Captain William Bligh of the HMS Bounty, was ordered to transport breadfruit plants from Polynesia to the British Caribbean colonies.*

### If You Don't Have It
Substitute 1 cup (250 mL) chopped breadfruit with:
- 1 cup (250 mL) chopped canned breadfruit
- 1 cup (250 mL) chopped jackfruit
- 1 cup (250 mL) chopped or sliced green or yellow plantains
- 1 cup (250 mL) chopped potatoes

*See also* JACKFRUIT.

## Breadstick

*Also known as grissini. Slender, twisted ropes of bread often seasoned with coarse salt, garlic, cheese, poppy or sesame seeds, and/or herbs.*

### If You Don't Have It
Substitute 1 lb (500 g) breadsticks with:
- 1 lb (500 g) baguettes, sliced into strips
- 1 lb (500 g) dinner rolls

### To Vary the Flavor
Substitute 1 lb (500 g) breadsticks with:
- 1 lb (500 g) cheese straws

## Bream

*See* CARP; PORGY.

## Bresaola

*The beef equivalent of prosciutto crudo originated in the Lombardy region of Italy.*

### If You Don't Have It
Substitute 1 lb (500 g) bresaola with:
- 1 lb (500 g) Bündnerfleisch
- 1 lb (500 g) Brési (French)
- 1 lb (500 g) biltong (Aftrican)
- 1 lb (500 g) prosciutto (richer; milder flavor)

## Brick Cheese

*Pale yellow brick-shaped cheese from Wisconsin ranges in flavor from mild to potent as it ages.*

> 4 oz (125 g) = 1 cup (250 mL) shredded

### If You Don't Have It
Substitute 1 oz (30 g) brick cheese with:
- 1 oz (30 g) German or Danish Tilsit
- 1 oz (30 g) Havarti
- 1 oz (30 g) Cheddar
- 1 oz (30 g) Limburger (combine with Cheddar for a milder flavor)

## Brie

*The granddaddy of this most fashionable of French cheeses, Brie de Meaux, dates from the 700s. While it is now a mold-ripened cheese, Brie de Meaux was originally eaten unripened.*

### If You Don't Have It
Substitute 1 oz (30 g) Brie with:
- 1 oz (30 g) Camembert
- 1 oz (30 g) Paglia-style cheese
- 1 oz (30 g) Explorateur
- 1 oz (30 g) Reblochon

## Brill

*European flatfish that tastes very much like turbot.*

### If You Don't Have It

Substitute 1 lb (500 g) brill with:

- 1 lb (500 g) turbot
- 1 lb (500 g) Dover sole

## Brillat-Savarin Cheese

*Lucious triple-crème cheese named in honor of French food philosopher Jean Anthelme Brillat-Savarin.*

### If You Don't Have It

Substitute 1 oz (30 g) Brillat-Savarin with:

- 1 oz (30 g) Excelsior
- 1 oz (30 g) Boursault
- 1 oz (30 g) Explorateur
- 1 oz (30 g) Gratte-Paille
- 1 oz (30 g) Saint-André
- 1 oz (30 g) Brie

## Brine

*A solution of salt, water and, sometimes, sugar. Used to moisten, flavor, or pickle various vegetables and meats.*

### If You Don't Have It

Substitute 4 quarts (4 L) brine with:

- 4 quarts (4 L) Homemade Basic Brine: Combine 4 cups (1 L) water, ¾ cup (175 mL) granulated sugar, and ¾ cup (175 mL) kosher salt in a saucepan. Boil over high heat until sugar and salt are dissolved, about 2 minutes. Remove from heat. Add 3 quarts (3 L) cold water, 1 tsp (5 mL) cracked peppercorns, 1 sliced celery rib, 1 sliced carrot, ½ sliced small onion, 6 sprigs fresh parsley and/or thyme, and 3 bay leaves. Place pork or poultry in the brine for 2 to 4 hours per pound (500 g) of meat, depending upon the meat's thickness. Discard the brine and cook the meat (browning it first improves the color).

## Brine-Cured Ham

*See* HAM, WET-CURED.

## Brinza Cheese

*See* BRYNDZA.

## Brioche

*A sweet French yeast bread enriched with plenty of butter and eggs. The classic baking mold produces a ridged loaf with a domed top.*

### If You Don't Have It

Substitute 1 lb (500 g) brioche with:

- 1 lb (500 g) challah (less rich)
- 1 lb (500 g) shokupan (rich Japanese white bread)
- 1 lb (500 g) croissants (less eggy, more airy texture)
- 1 lb (500 g) Kugelhopf (filled with dried and candied fruit and nuts)

## Brioche Pan

*See* PAN SIZE EQUIVALENTS (PAGE 678).

## Broad Bean

*See* FAVA BEAN.

## Broad-Leaved Endive

*See* ESCAROLE.

## Broccoflower™

*Also known as Cauli-Broc. Often labeled as a cross between cauliflower and broccoli, the brand named Broccoflower™ is actually a cultivar of Italian green cauliflower.*

1 lb (500 g) fresh = 2½ to 3 cups (625 to 750 mL) florets

### If You Don't Have It

Substitute 1 lb (500 g) Broccoflower™ with:
- 1 lb (500 g) cauliflower (white color; stronger cabbage flavor)
- 1 lb (500 g) broccoli (darker green color; softer texture; stronger flavor)
- 8 oz (250 g) cauliflower + 8 oz (250 g) broccoli (stronger flavor)

## Broccoletti

*See* BROCCOLI RAAB.

## Broccoli

*In an 18th century British gardening dictionary, an entry for broccoli described it as Italian asparagus.*

1 lb (500 g) fresh = 2 cups (500 mL) chopped

10 oz (300 g) frozen = 1½ cups (375 mL) chopped

### If You Don't Have It

Substitute 1 lb (500 g) broccoli with:
- 1 lb (500 g) Broccoflower™ (lighter green color; milder flavor; firmer texture)
- 1 lb (500 g) cauliflower (white color; stronger cabbage flavor; firmer texture)
- 1 lb (500 g) broccoli raab (more bitter flavor; includes leaves; cooks more quickly)

*See also* ROMANESCO.

## Broccolini

*Also known as asparation, baby broccoli, and mini-broccoli. The skinny stalks look like broccoli on a diet. This trademarked hybrid of broccoli and Chinese broccoli is crisp with a delicate broccoli flavor.*

1 lb (500 g) fresh = 2 cups (500 mL) chopped

### If You Don't Have It

Substitute 1 lb (500 g) Broccolini with:
- 1 lb (500 g) asparagus (straighter stalks; tighter heads)
- 1 lb (500 g) Chinese broccoli (darker green color; thicker stems)
- 1 lb (500 g) broccoli (shorter, thicker stems; more cabbagey flavor)
- 1 lb (500 g) broccoli raab (more bitter flavor; includes leaves)

*See also* CHINESE BROCCOLI.

## Broccoli Raab

*Also known as broccoletti, cime di rapa, and rapini. More closely related to the turnip family than the broccoli bunch, this sharp, pungent green resembles a bouquet of radish greens interspersed with small broccoli-like buds.*

1 lb (500 g) fresh = 2 cups (500 mL) chopped

### If You Don't Have It
Substitute 1 lb (500 g) broccoli raab with:
- 1 lb (500 g) Chinese broccoli (darker green color; milder flavor)
- 1 lb (500 g) bitter greens (such as dandelion, mustard, or turnip)
- 1 lb (500 g) green or red chard (sweeter flavor)
- 1 lb (500 g) broccoli (shorter, thicker stems; less bitter, more cabbagey flavor; takes longer to cook)

## Broccoli Romanesco

*See* ROMANESCO .

## Broccoli Sprouts

*The BroccoSprouts© brand was developed by scientists at the Johns Hopkins University School of Medicine to provide consistent levels of cancer-fighting sulforaphane.*

### If You Don't Have It
Substitute ¼ cup (60 mL) broccoli sprouts with:
- ¼ cup (60 mL) alfalfa sprouts (less peppery)
- ¼ cup (60 mL) radish sprouts (more peppery)
- ¼ cup (60 mL) fenugreek sprouts (slightly bitter)
- ¼ cup (60 mL) sunflower sprouts (more nutty)
- ¼ cup (60 mL) mung bean sprouts (thicker and crisper)

## Broiler

*A direct source of cooking heat, usually in the oven.*

### If You Don't Have It
Substitute a broiler with:
- grill (heat will come from below instead of above; otherwise, the cooking methods are very similar; grilling over coals will add smoke flavor)

## Broth

*See* STOCK.

## Brown Bean Sauce

*See* BEAN SAUCE.

## Brown Bread

*See* BOSTON BROWN BREAD.

## Brown Rice

*See* RICE.

## Brown Rice Syrup

*A sweetener made from fermented brown rice.*

### If You Don't Have It
Substitute 1 cup (250 mL) brown rice syrup with:
- ¾ cup (175 mL) maple syrup or honey + 2 tbsp (30 mL)

*Similar in consistency to honey but less sweet.*

water or other liquid from the recipe (slightly thinner consistency; adds maple or honey flavor)
- ¾ cup (175 mL) barley malt syrup
- ½ cup (125 mL) molasses

*See also* SUGAR, GRANULATED.

## Brown Sauce

*See* ESPAGNOLE SAUCE.

## Brown Sugar

*See* SUGAR, DARK BROWN; SUGAR, LIGHT BROWN.

## Brussels Sprouts

*Tiny sprouts are the tastiest of this cabbage family member.*

1 lb (500 g) = 24 to 28 medium sprouts = 3 cups (750 mL)

### If You Don't Have It
Substitute 1 lb (500 g) Brussels sprouts with:
- 1 lb (500 g) broccoli florets (darker green color; milder flavor; cooks more quickly)
- 1 lb (500 g) chopped green cabbage (cooks more quickly)

## Bryndza

*Also known as brinza cheese. Brine-cured sheep's milk cheese from Romania. Young Bryndza is soft enough to spread and gets increasingly crumbly when aged.*

### If You Don't Have It
Substitute 1 oz (30 g) Bryndza cheese with:
- 1 oz (30 g) feta
- 1 oz (30 g) aged chèvre
- 1 oz (30 g) ricotta salata
- 1 oz (30 g) cotija
- 1 oz (30 g) myzithra
- 1 oz (30 g) haloumi (adds mint flavor)

## Bûcheron

*See* CHÈVRE.

## Buckwheat Flour

*See* CHOOSING AMONG WHOLE-GRAIN AND ALTERNATIVE FLOURS (PAGE 648).

## Buckwheat Groats

*Although treated as a cereal grain, the buckwheat plant is actually an herb. Groats are the hulled, crushed kernels cooked like rice. When roasted they are known as Kasha.*

1 cup (250 mL) = 2½ to 3 cups (625 to 750 mL) cooked

### If You Don't Have It
Substitute 1 cup (250 mL) buckwheat groats with:
- 1 cup (250 mL) kasha (roasted buckwheat groats; adds sweeter, toasted flavor)
- 1 cup (250 mL) rice, millet or quinoa (cooks more quickly)
- 1 cup (250 mL) buckwheat grits, barley grits or hominy grits (each cooks more quickly)

## Buckwheat Sprouts

*A popular sprout among proponents of raw food because raw buckwheat germinates quickly and easily and has a pleasant nutty taste.*

### If You Don't Have It

Substitute ¼ cup (60 mL) buckwheat sprouts with:

- ¼ cup (60 mL) alfalfa sprouts (sweeter)
- ¼ cup (60 mL) broccoli sprouts (more peppery)
- ¼ cup (60 mL) fenugreek sprouts (slightly bitter)
- ¼ cup (60 mL) sunflower sprouts (more nutty)
- ¼ cup (60 mL) mung bean sprouts (thicker and crisper)

## Buddha's Hand

*See* CITRON.

## Buffalo

*See* BISON.

## Buffalo Fish

*Freshwater fish that's similar to carp. Popular as a smoked fish, it can also be prepared in a variety of other ways.*

### If You Don't Have It

Substitute 1 lb (500 g) buffalo fish with:

- 1 lb (500 g) carp

## Buffalo Milk Mozzarella

*See* MOZZARELLA.

## Bulb Baster

*See* BASTER.

## Bulbing Fennel

*See* FENNEL, FRESH.

## Bulgur

*Also known as bulgur wheat and burghul. Steamed, dried, crushed wheat kernels that reach their apex in the Middle Eastern salad tabbouleh.*

1 cup (250 mL) dry =
6½ oz (190 g) =
3 cups (750 mL) cooked

### If You Don't Have It

Substitute 1 cup (250 mL) bulgur with:

- 1 cup (250 mL) cracked wheat (takes longer to cook)
- 1 cup (250 mL) quinoa
- 1 cup (250 mL) rice
- 1 cup (250 mL) whole wheat couscous

*See also* CRACKED WHEAT.

## Bull's Horn

*See* SWEET PEPPER.

## Bummalo

*See* BOMBAY DUCK.

## Bunching Onion

*See* ONION, GREEN.

## Bündnerfleisch

*Also known as Bindenfleisch. Delicate Swiss beef jerky.*

### If You Don't Have It

Substitute 1 lb (500 g) Bündnerfleisch with:

- 1 lb (500 g) Bresaola (Italian)
- 1 lb (500 g) Brési (French)
- 1 lb (500 g) biltong (African)
- 1 lb (500 g) prosciutto (richer; milder flavor)

## Bundt Pan

*See* PAN SIZE EQUIVALENTS (PAGE 678).

## Buñuelos

*See* DOUGHNUT.

## Burbot

*Also known as eelpout. Every year since 1979, the town of Walker, Minnesota, has encouraged ice fisherman to catch this fresh fish at its International Eelpout Festival on Leech Lake.*

### If You Don't Have It

Substitute 1 lb (500 g) burbot with:

- 1 lb (500 g) walleye
- 1 lb (500 g) pike
- 1 lb (500 g) cusk (saltwater)
- 1 lb (500 g) cod (saltwater)

## Burdock

*Also known as gobo and great burdock. A skinny, long (up to a yard/90 cm long) root most valued in Japanese cooking.*

### If You Don't Have It

Substitute 1 lb (500 g) burdock with:

- 1 lb (500 g) salsify (white or black)
- 1 lb (500 g) asparagus (to replace wild green burdock)
- 1 lb (500 g) artichoke hearts
- 1 lb (500 g) carrots (orange color; sweeter flavor)

## Burghul

*See* BULGUR.

## Burnet

*See* SALAD BURNET.

## Burrata

*Literally "buttered" in Italian, burrata is a fresh buffalo or cow milk cheese from southeastern Italy's Puglia region. Made with curds of mozzarella and fresh cream, it features of soft, creamy center and is best eaten within 24 hours of making.*

### If You Don't Have It

Substitute 1 oz (30 g) burrata with:

- 1 oz (30 g) fresh buffalo mozzarella

*See also* MOZZARELLA.

## Butter

*Salt is added to butter as a preservative. Use unsalted butter for baking and for the freshest taste. When substituting butter with lower-fat alternatives in baking, replace no more than half of the total amount of butter for the best results.*

1 lb (500 g) = 2 cups (500 mL) = 4 sticks

1 lb (500 g) whipped = 3 cups (750 mL) regular

1 stick = 4 oz (125 g) = ½ cup (125 mL) = 8 tbsp (120 mL) = ¾ cup (175 mL) whipped = ⅓ cup (75 mL) clarified

## If You Don't Have It

Substitute ½ cup (125 mL) unsalted butter with:

- ½ cup (125 mL) salted butter (decrease salt in recipe by ¼ tsp/1 mL)
- ½ cup (125 mL) European-style butter such as Plugra (lower moisture content; creates flakier pastries, crisper cookies, and creamier sauces)
- ½ cup (125 mL) margarine (less flavorful; makes baked goods softer)
- ¾ cup (175 mL) whipped butter (for spreading only)
- ½ cup (125 mL) margarine spread (for spreading only)

## To Vary the Flavor

Substitute ½ cup (125 mL) butter with:

- ½ cup (125 mL) goat butter (more assertive aroma; silkier texture; whiter color; higher in calories, protein, unsaturated fats, calcium, potassium, and vitamin A; lower melting point)
- ½ cup (125 mL) sheep butter (much more assertive aroma; silkier texture; whiter color; higher in calories, protein, unsaturated fats, calcium, potassium, and vitamin A; lower melting point)
- ½ cup (125 mL) Homemade Flavored Butter: Stir ½ cup (125 mL) softened butter until smooth and mix in flavorings of choice. Reshape by rolling in plastic wrap if necessary. Garlic Butter: 1 minced garlic clove, ¼ tsp (1 mL) salt, and ¼ tsp (1 mL) pepper. Herb Butter: ¼ cup (60 mL) chopped fresh herbs, 1½ tsp (7 mL) orange or lemon juice, ¼ tsp (1 mL) salt, and ¼ tsp (1 mL) pepper. Citrus Butter: 1½ tsp (7 mL) grated lemon, lime or orange zest, 1½ tbsp (22 mL) lemon, lime or orange juice, ¼ tsp (1 mL) salt, and ¼ tsp (1 mL) pepper
- ½ cup (125 mL) Browned Butter: Melt ½ cup (125 mL) butter in a small saucepan over medium heat and cook until golden brown or dark golden brown, 10 to 15 minutes. Use like melted butter or chill until firm and use like butter.
- ½ cup (125 mL) coconut butter (not coconut oil; sweeter; adds coconut flavor)
- 7 tbsp (105 mL) bacon or pork fat or ⅓ cup (75 mL) chicken or poultry fat (for sautéing, frying, and sauces)
- 7 tbsp (105 mL) shortening or lard (for pastry and baking; creates flakier pastry and crisper cookies because shortening and lard lack the water content of butter; many cooks use half shortening or lard and half butter for flakiness and flavor)

## For Better Health

Substitute ½ cup (125 mL) butter with:

- ½ cup (125 mL) "light" butter (a product with half the calories and fat of butter due mostly to the addition of water; works best as a spread, in frostings and toppings, or melted for drizzling; in pie and pastry doughs, chill light butter and shred before quickly mixing with dry ingredients; in cookie dough, omit one egg white per $\frac{1}{2}$ cup (125 mL) light butter used; in pancake and quick bread batters, omit $\frac{1}{4}$ cup (60 mL) milk or other liquid from recipe per $\frac{1}{2}$ cup (125 mL) light butter used)

- $\frac{1}{4}$ cup (60 mL) butter or buttermilk + $\frac{1}{4}$ cup (60 mL) well-drained, unsweetened applesauce, prune purée or baby food prunes (for baking; applesauce works well with lighter-color or spice batters; puréed prunes work best with darker batters, such as chocolate; creates slightly chewier texture; use pastry or cake flour for lighter texture; increase sugar for more crispness)
- 3 tbsp (45 mL) butter + 3 tbsp (45 mL) vegetable oil (for baking, especially quick breads and some cookie doughs; reduce baking time slightly; baked goods will be slightly more chewy; use pastry or cake flour for lighter texture; increase sugar for more crispness)
- $\frac{1}{2}$ cup (125 mL) apple butter (for baking; reduce baking time slightly; baked goods will be slightly more chewy; use pastry or cake flour for lighter texture; adjust sugar if apple butter is sweetened)
- $\frac{1}{2}$ cup (125 mL) fat-free, fruit-based butter and oil replacement such as Smucker's "Baking Healthy" (for baking)
- $\frac{1}{4}$ cup (60 mL) fat-free, fruit-based butter and oil replacement such as Sunsweet "Lighter Bake" (for baking)
- $\frac{1}{2}$ cup (125 mL) marshmallow crème (for fillings and frostings)
- $\frac{1}{2}$ cup (125 mL) oil (for sautéing and frying). Or use a mixture of butter and oil. Or use a nonstick pan coated with cooking oil spray (or 1 to 2 tsp/5 to 10 mL oil or butter) and heat the pan thoroughly

*See also* BUTTER, CLARIFIED; GOAT BUTTER; MARGARINE; OIL; SHEEP BUTTER; VEGETABLE SHORTENING.

## Butter Bean

*See* FAVA BEAN; LIMA BEAN.

## Butter Cake

*Standard cake, usually frosted, which can be baked in round, rectangular, or novelty shaped pans.*

### If You Don't Have It
Substitute 1 lb (500 g) butter cake with:
- 1 lb (500 g) pound cake (denser texture; higher in fat)
- 1 lb (500 g) sponge cake (lighter texture; lower in fat)
- 1 lb (500 g) angel food cake (lighter, more airy texture; lower in fat)

## Butter, Clarified

*Also known as drawn butter. The clear golden butterfat that is skimmed from the milk solids after*

### If You Don't Have It
Substitute $\frac{1}{2}$ cup (125 mL) clarified butter with:
- $\frac{1}{2}$ cup (125 mL) Homemade Clarified Butter:
Melt $\frac{1}{2}$ cup (125 mL) + 2 tbsp (30 mL) butter in a skillet over low heat, skimming foam from surface. Heat until white

## Butter, Clarified (cont'd)

*unsalted butter is slowly melted. Useful for sautéing because it has a higher smoke point than solid butter. Ghee, a type of clarified butter, has an even higher smoke point (about 375°F/190°C) because it is simmered longer to evaporate excess moisture.*

milk solids sink to bottom of pan, 10 to 15 minutes. Let cool slightly, then strain and discard white milk solids, leaving golden clarified butter. Clarified butter keeps in an airtight container in the refrigerator for up to 6 months.

- ½ cup (125 mL) ghee (darker color; deeper, nuttier flavor; higher smoke point)
- ½ cup (125 mL) vegetable oil (less flavorful; use olive oil for richer flavor)
- ½ cup (125 mL) unsalted butter (adds rich flavor of milk solids; lower smoke point)

## Butter Cookie

*Also known as petit beurre. Thin crisp wafer-like cookies.*

### If You Don't Have It
Substitute 1 lb (500 g) butter cookies with:
- 1 lb (500 g) shortbread cookies (less crisp)

## Buttercup Squash

*Bulbous green winter squash topped with a small cap. Classic squash flavor with notes of honey, roasted chestnuts, and sweet potatoes.*

1 lb (500 g) = 1 cup (250 mL) cooked and mashed

### If You Don't Have It
Substitute 1 cup (250 mL) chopped buttercup squash with:
- 1 cup (250 mL) chopped butternut squash (more easily peeled; creamier)
- 1 cup (250 mL) chopped pumpkin (creamier)
- 1 cup (250 mL) chopped delicata squash (moister)
- 1 cup (250 mL) chopped sweet potato (sweeter; moister)

*See also* TURBAN SQUASH.

## Butterfish

*Also known as dollarfish, Pacific pompano, and pomfret. True to its name this family of small, buttery-textured fishes is rich in flavor. Their average size is about 8 ounces (250 g) and 6 to 9 inches (15 to 23 cm) long with bodies that are almost as broad as they are long, giving some species a nearly circular shape. Don't confuse butterfish with sablefish, which is a different fish altogether.*

### If You Don't Have It
Substitute 1 lb (500 g) butterfish with:
- 1 lb (500 g) pompano
- 1 lb (500 g) spot
- 1 lb (500 g) yellowfin or skipjack tuna
- 1 lb (500 g) mackerel
- 1 lb (500 g) bluefish
- 1 lb (500 g) striped bass

### Butterfish Varieties
Choose 1 lb (500 g) butterfish from these varieties:
- 1 lb (500 g) American butterfish (dollarfish; northern Atlantic)
- 1 lb (500 g) harvestfish (southern Atlantic)
- 1 lb (500 g) white or silver pomfret (Indo-Pacific)
- 1 lb (500 g) black pomfret (smaller than white pomfret; Indo-Pacific)
- 1 lb (500 g) Pacific pompano (Baja California to British Columbia)

*See also* POMPANO; SABLEFISH.

## Butterhead Lettuce

*Boston (large leaves) and Bibb (smaller leaves) are the two most popular types of this variety of head lettuce.*

> 1 lb (500 g) = 6 cups (1.5 L) pieces

### If You Don't Have It

Substitute 1 cup (250 mL) butterhead lettuce with:
- 1 cup (250 mL) mâche
- 1 cup (250 mL) leaf lettuce
- 1 cup (250 mL) crisphead lettuce such as iceberg

### Butterhead Varieties

Choose 1 cup (250 mL) butterhead lettuce from these varieties:
- 1 cup (250 mL) Bibb lettuce (smaller leaves; more complex flavor)
- 1 cup (250 mL) Boston lettuce (larger leaves; mild flavor)

## Buttermilk

*Originally the liquid that was left after churning whole milk into butter. Commercial buttermilk is a tart, thick dairy product created by adding special bacteria to nonfat or low-fat milk.*

### If You Don't Have It

Substitute 1 cup (250 mL) buttermilk with:
- 1 tbsp (15 mL) lemon juice or vinegar + enough milk to equal 1 cup (250 mL) (for baking; let stand for 5 to 10 minutes before using)
- 1 cup (250 mL) water + ¼ cup (60 mL) powdered buttermilk
- 1 cup (250 mL) kefir
- ½ cup (125 mL) plain yogurt + ½ cup (125 mL) milk
- 1 cup (250 mL) plain yogurt (thicker)
- 1 cup (250 mL) sour cream
- 1 cup (250 mL) milk + 1 to 1½ tsp (5 to 7 mL) cream of tartar (for baking)

## Buttermilk Cheese

*A tangy fresh cheese similar to yogurt cheese. Great for pasta fillings and cheesecakes.*

### If You Don't Have It

Substitute 1 oz (30 g) buttermilk cheese with:
- 1 oz (30 g) Homemade Buttermilk Cheese: Combine 2 quarts (2 L) whole milk, 3 cups (750 mL) low-fat buttermilk and 1 tbsp (15 mL) salt in a large saucepan. For flavored cheese, you can also add 1 tsp (5 mL) minced garlic, 1 tsp (5 mL) dried herbs, 1 tsp (5 mL) grated lemon zest, and/or 1 tsp (5 mL) black pepper. Heat over medium-high heat until the curds clump together and rise to the surface (about 180°F/90°C), 8 to 10 minutes, stirring occasionally to avoid scorching on the pan bottom. Line a colander with cheesecloth folded into four layers, leaving enough to hang over the sides of the colander. Place the lined colander in the sink and ladle or slowly pour the curds into the cheesecloth. Let drain a few minutes then gather up the edges of the cheesecloth and twist over the curds, pressing out any excess liquid. Unwrap and serve immediately; or, for firmer cheese, transfer the cloth-wrapped cheese to a plate and refrigerate until cold, about 20 minutes. Unwrap, transfer to plate, and discard cloth. Let stand for 5 minutes before serving. Refrigerate any remaining cheese loosely wrapped in plastic for up to 3 days. Makes about 2 cups (500 mL).

## Buttermilk Cheese (cont'd)

- 1 oz (30 g) yogurt cheese
- ½ oz (15 g) ricotta cheese + ½ oz (15 g) sour cream, blended
- ½ oz (15 g) cream cheese + ½ oz (15 g) cream, blended
- ½ oz (15 g) cottage cheese + ½ oz (15 g) yogurt, blended
- 1 oz (30 g) cream cheese
- 1 oz (30 g) mascarpone
- 1 oz (30 g) fromage blanc
- 1 oz (30 g) sour cream
- 1 oz (30 g) kefir cheese
- 1 oz (30 g) quark (richer texture)
- 1 cup (250 mL) crème fraîche
- 1 cup (250 mL) silken tofu, blended until smooth

## Butter Muslin

*See* CHEESECLOTH.

## Butternut

*Also known as white walnut. A New England nut with a high oil content.*

1 lb (500 g) shelled =
3½ cups (875 mL)
chopped

### If You Don't Have It
Substitute 1 cup (250 mL) chopped butternuts with:
- 1 cup (250 mL) chopped walnuts or black walnuts
- 1 cup (250 mL) chopped pecans

*See also* NUT; WALNUT.

## Butternut Squash

*A long winter squash that can grow up to a foot (30 cm) long and 5 inches (12.5 cm) wide. For easy peeling, prick hard shell several times with a fork; microwave on High for 2 to 3 minutes.*

1 lb (500 g) = 1 cup
(250 mL) cooked
and mashed

### If You Don't Have It
Substitute 1 cup (250 mL) chopped butternut squash with:
- 1 cup (250 mL) chopped buttercup squash (less moist)
- 1 cup (250 mL) chopped delicata squash (less fruity flavor)
- 1 cup (250 mL) chopped pumpkin (sweeter; moister)
- 1 cup (250 mL) chopped sweet potato (sweeter; moister)

## Byrrh

*A tangy, bittersweet French vermouth that's made with quinine and red wine. It's usually mixed with club soda.*

### If You Don't Have It
Substitute 2 tbsp (30 mL) byrrh with:
- 2 tbsp (30 mL) Dubonnet blanc or Lillet
- 2 tbsp (30 mL) Amer Picon (more bitter)

# Cabbage to Cynar

## Cabbage

The green cultivar of this crucifer is ubiquitous in coleslaw and sauerkraut, but cooks often prefer the red variety for its gorgeous garnet hue, a result of pigments known as anthocyanins.

> 1 lb (500 g) = 6 cups (1.5 L) shredded
>
> 1 lb (500 g) raw = 12 oz (375 g) cooked
>
> 1 medium head = 1¾ lbs (875 g)

### If You Don't Have It
Substitute 1 lb (500 g) green or red cabbage with:
- 1 lb (500 g) Brussels sprouts
- 1 lb (500 g) savoy cabbage (milder; more tender)
- 1 lb (500 g) napa cabbage (milder; more delicate)

See also BOK CHOY; NAPA CABBAGE; SAVOY CABBAGE.

## Cabbage Turnip

See KOHLRABI.

## Cabrales

Handmade in small amounts, this Spanish cheese is a blue for blue cheese lovers. Often crafted from a blend of cow's milk for acidity, goat's milk for piquancy, and sheep's milk for richness.

### If You Don't Have It
Substitute 1 oz (30 g) cabrales with:
- 1 oz (30 g) Picon
- 1 oz (30 g) Gamonedo
- 1 oz (30 g) Roquefort

## Cachaça

*Also known as pinga.
Brazilian sugarcane brandy
that forms the bedrock of
the country's fashionable
caipirinha cocktail.*

### If You Don't Have It

Substitute 3 tbsp (45 mL) cachaça with:
- 3 tbsp (45 mL) aguardiente de caña (may add anise flavor)
- 3 tbsp (45 mL) white rum
- 3 tbsp (45 mL) vodka

## Cachucha

*See* CHOOSING FRESH CHILES (PAGE 640).

## Caciocavallo

*This sharp Southern Italian
formaggio literally means
"cheese on horseback." The
name may be a reference to
the method of drying pairs
of cheeses tied to opposite
ends of a pole, in balance
like a saddlebag on a horse.*

4 oz (125 g) = 1 cup
(250 mL) shredded

### If You Don't Have It

Substitute 1 oz (30 g) Caciocavallo with:
- 1 oz (30 g) provolone
- 1 oz (30 g) scamorza

## Caciotta

*Semifirm central Italian
farmhouse cheese made with
sheep's and/or cow's milk.*

4 oz (125 g) = 1 cup
(250 mL) grated or
shredded

### If You Don't Have It

Substitute 1 oz (30 g) Caciotta with:
- 1 oz (30 g) Fontina
- ½ oz (15 g) Monterey Jack + ½ oz (15 g) feta
- 1 oz (30 g) young pecorino

## Cactus Leaf

*See* NOPALE.

## Cactus Pear

*See* PRICKLY PEAR.

## Caerphilly

*Tangy cow's milk cheese
named after a village
in Wales. In times past,
Caerphilly was the
traditional lunch of Welsh
coal miners. The cheese is
best eaten fresh.*

4 oz (125 g) = 1 cup
(250 mL) shredded

### If You Don't Have It

Substitute 1 oz (30 g) Caerphilly with:
- 1 oz (30 g) Cheddar, Cheshire, or Lancashire

## Caimito

*See* STAR APPLE.

## Cajeta

*Luscious Latin condiment of caramelized sugar and goat's or cow's milk.*

### If You Don't Have It

Substitute 1 cup (250 mL) cajeta with:
- 1 cup (250 mL) dulce de leche
- 1 cup (250 mL) caramel sauce (bottled commercial brands won't be nearly as flavorful as homemade goat's milk cajeta)

## Cajun Seasoning

*Also known as Cajun spice mix and Cajun spice seasoning. A blend of signature southern Louisiana herbs and spices that's likely to contain black pepper, cayenne pepper, garlic, mustard powder, and thyme. On the heels of widespread interest in Cajun cooking during the 1980s, Paul Prudhomme, Emeril Lagasse, and other celebrity chefs have marketed their own signature blends.*

### If You Don't Have It

Substitute 1 tbsp (15 mL) Cajun seasoning with:
- 1 tbsp (15 mL) Homemade Cajun seasoning: Combine $\frac{3}{4}$ tsp (3 mL) paprika, $\frac{3}{4}$ tsp (3 mL) ground black pepper, $\frac{1}{2}$ tsp (2 mL) garlic powder, $\frac{1}{8}$ to $\frac{1}{4}$ tsp (0.5 to 1 mL) cayenne pepper, $\frac{1}{4}$ tsp (1 mL) dried thyme, $\frac{1}{4}$ tsp (1 mL) dried oregano, $\frac{1}{4}$ tsp (1 mL) onion powder, and a pinch of mustard powder. Add salt to taste. Makes about 1 tablespoon (15 mL). Recipe can be doubled. Store seasoning in an airtight container for up to 6 months.
- 1 tbsp (15 mL) Creole seasoning (very similar)

*See also* CREOLE SEASONING.

## Cake Flour

*See* FLOUR, CAKE.

## Cake Pans

*See* PAN SIZE EQUIVALENTS (PAGE 678).

## Calabash

*See* CUCUZZA.

## Calabrese Sausage

*See* SALAMI.

## Calamari

*See* SQUID.

## Calamata Olive

*See* CHOOSING AMONG OLIVES (PAGE 659).

## Calamondin

*Also known as China orange, kalamansi, and musk lime. A hybrid of mandarin orange and kumquat that looks like a mandarin orange but has juicier, more acidic flesh.*

### If You Don't Have It

Substitute 1 calamondin with:
- 2 to 3 kumquats (for the flesh or zest)
- $\frac{1}{4}$ mandarin orange + $\frac{1}{2}$ lemon (for the flesh or zest)
- 1 tsp (5 mL) mandarin orange juice + 1 tbsp (15 mL) lemon juice (to replace 1 tbsp/15 mL calamondin juice)

## Calas

*See* DOUGHNUT.

## Calcot

*In 1898, a farmer in Valls, Spain (southwest of Barcelona) dug up his white onions, replanted them, protected the shoots with mounds of earth, and grew long, slender, white calcots. You can smell the sweet onions grilling over grapevines from November to March during calcot season.*

> 1 bunch = 5 oz (150 g) =
> 8 to 10 calcots =
> 3½ cups (875 mL)
> chopped

### If You Don't Have It

Substitute 10 calcots with:

- 10 large scallions
- 10 large green onions (less sweet)
- 12 to 14 ramps (stems only; milder flavor)
- 3 to 4 cups (750 mL to 1 L) chopped leeks (milder flavor)
- 3 cups (750 mL) chopped shallots (more complex flavor)
- 3 to 4 cups (750 mL to 1 L) chopped chives (milder flavor; best raw or lightly cooked)

*See also* ONION, GREEN; SCALLION.

## Calendula

*See* PICKING EDIBLE FLOWERS (PAGE 650).

## California Barracuda

*See* BARRACUDA.

## California Jack Cheese

*See* JACK CHEESE.

## California Sea Bass

*See* WHITE SEA BASS.

## Callaloo

*The large green leaves of the taro root are enjoyed in the Caribbean as a cooked vegetable. Also the namesake ingredient of callaloo soup, a melange of coconut milk, okra, yams, chiles, lime juice, and pork or seafood.*

### If You Don't Have It

Substitute 1 lb (500 g) callaloo with:

- 1 lb (500 g) Chinese kale
- 1 lb (500 g) mature spinach
- 1 lb (500 g) green chard
- 1 lb (500 g) mustard greens
- 1 lb (500 g) turnip greens
- 1 lb (500 g) collard greens

## Calvados

*See* APPLE BRANDY.

## Calypso Bean

*See* THE WIDE WORLD OF DRIED BEANS (PAGE 637).

## Cambozola

*A German cheese with
a downy rind and soft,
blue-veined paste.
Tastes like a cross
between Camembert and
Gorgonzola.*

### If You Don't Have It
Substitute 1 oz (30 g) Cambozola with:
- 1 oz (30 g) Blue Castello
- 1 oz (30 g) Bleu de Bresse
- 1 oz (30 g) Saga blue
- ½ oz (15 g) Gorgonzola + ½ oz (15 g) Camembert

## Camembert

*In the French village of
Camembert, a statue honors
Marie Harel as "the creator
of Camembert cheese."*

### If You Don't Have It
Substitute 1 oz (30 g) Camembert with:
- 1 oz (30 g) Brie
- 1 oz (30 g) Explorateur
- 1 oz (30 g) Reblochon

## Camouflage Melon

*See* SANTA CLAUS MELON.

## Campari

*Brand name of a vivid
red, bittersweet Italian
aperitivo. Milanese café
owner Gaspare Campari
created the drink in the
1860s and it's still very
fashionable.*

### If You Don't Have It
Substitute 3 tbsp (45 mL) Campari with:
- 3 tbsp (45 mL) Fernet Branca

## Canadian Bacon

*Also known as back bacon.
The Rolls-Royce of bacon
is prepared from lean
tenderloin of pork that has
been cured and smoked.
In addition to Canadian
bacon, back bacon includes
various cuts of British and
Irish back bacon, all of
which resemble ham more
closely than slab bacon.
In the United States,
Canadian bacon is sold
cooked.*

### If You Don't Have It
Substitute 1 slice (about 1 oz) Canadian bacon with:
- 1 oz (30 g) smoked ham
- 1 oz (30 g) Irish bacon (back bacon prepared from the eye of the loin)
- 1 oz (30 g) pancetta
- 1 oz (30 g) bacon

## Canary Melon

*Also known as Juan Canary melon. Named for their bright yellow skin, these sweet melons have pale white flesh that tastes similar to cantaloupe but sharper.*

1 medium = 3 lbs
(1.5 kg) = 4 to 5 cups
(1 to 1.25 L) cubed

### If You Don't Have It

Substitute 1 cup (250 mL) chopped canary melon with:
- 1 cup (250 mL) chopped Ogen melon
- 1 cup (250 mL) chopped galia melon
- 1 cup (250 mL) chopped Santa Claus melon
- 1 cup (250 mL) chopped Persian melon
- 1 cup (250 mL) chopped honeydew melon
- 1 cup (250 mL) chopped cantaloupe

## Candied Angelica

*See* ANGLICA, CANDIED.

## Candied Citrus Peel

*See* CITRUS PEEL, CANDIED.

## Candied Flowers

*See* FLOWERS, CANDIED.

## Candied Fruit

*See* FRUIT, CANDIED.

## Candlenut

*Also known as Indian walnut. The oily nuts were formerly used to make candles. Toxic unless cooked, the nuts are roasted and widely used in Javanese and other Southeast Asian kitchens.*

### If You Don't Have It

Substitute 1 cup (250 mL) candlenuts with:
- 1 cup (250 mL) macadamia nuts
- 1 cup (250 mL) Brazil nuts
- 1 cup (250 mL) cashews

## Canela

*See* CINNAMON.

## Cane Syrup

*See* GOLDEN SYRUP.

## Canistel

*Also known as egg fruit. Heart-shaped tropical fruit the size of a tennis ball with sweet, orange flesh the texture of a cooked egg yolk.*

### If You Don't Have It

Substitute 1 cup (250 mL) chopped fresh canistel with:
- 1 cup (250 mL) chopped mamey sapote
- 1 cup (250 mL) chopped white sapote
- 1 cup (250 mL) chopped sapodilla
- 1 cup (250 mL) chopped cherimoya
- 1 cup (250 mL) chopped persimmon

## Canned Heat

*See* STERNO©.

## Cannellini Bean

*See* THE WIDE WORLD OF DRIED BEANS (PAGE 637).

## Canning Wax

*See* PARAFFIN WAX.

## Canola Oil

*See* OIL; SUBSTITUTING OILS (PAGE 658).

## Cantal

*Also known as Cantal de Salers and Fourme du Cantal. Popular semifirm cow's milk cheese from the Auvergne region of France.*

### If You Don't Have It

Substitute 1 oz (30 g) Cantal with:
- 1 oz (30 g) Laguiole (sharper)
- 1 oz (30 g) Cheshire
- 1 oz (30 g) Lancashire
- 1 oz (30 g) Cheddar

## Cantaloupe

*Also known as musk melon. In the U.S., musk melons covered with raised netted webbing are marketed as cantaloupes. European cantaloupes, named for the town of Cantalupo near Rome, include the French Charentais.*

### If You Don't Have It

Substitute 1 cup (250 mL) chopped cantaloupe with:
- 1 cup (250 mL) chopped Persian melon
- 1 cup (250 mL) chopped Crenshaw melon
- 1 cup (250 mL) chopped Santa Claus melon
- 1 cup (250 mL) chopped honeydew melon
- 1 cup (250 mL) chopped casaba melon
- 1 cup (250 mL) chopped ambrosia melon

*See also* CHARENTAIS MELON.

## Cantaloupe, Dried

*As a melon's moisture evaporates, the flesh becomes denser, chewier, sweeter, and more concentrated in flavor.*

> 1 lb (500 g) = 2½ to
> 3 cups (625 to 750 mL) =
> 5½ cups (1.375 L)
> cooked

### If You Don't Have It

Substitute 1 oz (30 g) dried cantaloupe with:
- 1 oz (30 g) dried mango
- 1 oz (30 g) dried papaya
- 1 oz (30 g) dried peaches
- 1 oz (30 g) dried nectarines

## Canton Bok Choy

*See* BOK CHOY.

## Cap Classique

*See* WINE, SPARKLING.

## Cape Capensis

*Also known as cape hake and cape whiting. Among the best tasting in the hake family, this fish swims in South African waters.*

### If You Don't Have It
Substitute 1 lb (500 g) cape capensis with:
- 1 lb (500 g) sole
- 1 lb (500 g) flounder
- 1 lb (500 g) cod
- 1 lb (500 g) pollock

## Cape Gooseberry

*Also known as Chinese lantern, golden berry, ground cherry, husk tomato, physalis, and strawberry tomato. A tart golden berry covered with a parchment husk that looks like a Chinese lantern.*

### If You Don't Have It
Substitute 1 lb (500 g) cape gooseberries with:
- 1 lb (500 g) green or yellow tomatillos (adds lemon and apple aromas)
- 1 lb (500 g) gooseberries (more tart)
- 1 lb (500 g) yellow cherry tomatoes (sweeter)

*See also* GOOSEBERRY.

## Cape Hake

*See* CAPE CAPENSIS.

## Caper

*The unopened flower bud of a Mediterranean shrub that when pickled forms appetizingly bitter capric acid.*

1 cup (250 mL) drained =
4 oz (125 g)

### If You Don't Have It
Substitute 1 tsp (5 mL) capers with:
- 1 tsp (5 mL) green olives (leave whole to garnish a martini)
- 1 tsp (5 mL) caper berries (large Spanish capers with the stem on; used as a garnish)
- 1 tsp (5 mL) chopped pickles

## Capeshark

*See* DOGFISH.

## Cape Whiting

*See* CAPE CAPENSIS.

## Capicola

*Also known as capicollo and coppa. Italian pork shoulder that is salted and air-dried to cure. Produced in a "sweet" style coated with ground black pepper and a "hot" style coated with ground red pepper.*

### If You Don't Have It
Substitute 4 oz (125 g) capicola with:
- 4 oz (125 g) prosciutto
- 4 oz (125 g) bresaola (beef)
- 4 oz (125 g) Bündnerfleisch (beef; drier)
- 4 oz (125 g) Brési (beef; drier)
- 4 oz (125 g) biltong (beef; drier)

## Capon

*See* CHICKEN.

## Caprice des Dieux

*Literally "Caprice of the Gods." A brand of bloomy-rind, semi-soft French cow's milk cheese resembling Brie and Camembert except for its oval shape.*

### If You Don't Have It

Substitute 1 oz (30 g) Caprice des Dieux with:
- 1 oz (30 g) Camembert
- 1 oz (30 g) Brie
- 1 oz (30 g) Explorateur
- 1 oz (30 g) Brillat-Savarin
- 1 oz (30 g) Boursault

## Caprini

*Small Italian goat's milk cheeses molded into cylinders. From the Piedmont region. The whimsical name means "little goats."*

### If You Don't Have It

Substitute 1 oz (30 g) caprini with:
- 1 oz (30 g) Robiola Piemonte
- 1 oz (30 g) Petit Suisse

*See also* CHÈVRE; GOAT'S MILK.

## Capulin

*A subtropical cherry native to Mexico. Similar to the Jamaican cherry, it has dark red skin and firm flesh with a sweet, mild flavor.*

| 1 lb (500 g) fresh = 2½ tsp (12 mL) to 3 cups (750 mL) pitted |

### If You Don't Have It

Substitute 1 lb (500 g) capulin cherries with:
- 1 lb (500 g) Jamaican cherries
- 1 lb (500 g) sweet cherries such as Bing
- 1 lb (500 g) acerola

*See also* CHERRY.

## Carambola

*Also known as star fruit. Crosswise slices of this long yellow fruit look like stars. The tart variety, best as a citrus-like garnish, has ribs that are thinner than the sweet variety, which is wonderful for desserts and fruit salads.*

| 1 lb (500 g) = 2 to 3 carambolas |

### If You Don't Have It

Substitute 1 lb (500 g) carambola with:
- 1 lb (500 g) kiwifruit (greener color)
- 1¼ lbs (625 g) navel oranges, peeled (orange color; sweeter)
- 1¼ lbs (625 g) Spanish, Galia or Ogen melon (pale to bright green color)

## Caramel Coloring

*See* BAKER'S CARAMEL.

## Caraway Seed

*This herb and its delicate anise flavor are popular in German rye bread, the Arabic spice mix tabil, and the fiery North African harissa.*

### If You Don't Have It

Substitute 1 tsp (5 mL) caraway seeds with:
- 1 tsp (5 mL) dill seeds
- 1 tsp (5 mL) anise seeds

## Carbonated Water

*See* SODA WATER.

## Cardamom

*This relative of ginger is the third most expensive flavoring in the world after saffron and vanilla. The tiny, spicy-sweet seeds grow enclosed in green or more aromatic brown/black fibrous pods.*

### If You Don't Have It

Substitute 10 whole green or white cardamom pods (seeds removed and crushed) with:
- ½ tsp (2 mL) ground cardamom
- ½ tsp (2 mL) ground korerima

### To Vary the Flavor

Substitute ½ tsp (2 mL) ground cardamom with:
- ½ tsp (2 mL) ground cinnamon
- ¼ tsp (1 mL) ground cinnamon + ¼ tsp (1 mL) ground nutmeg or cloves

*See also* KORERIMA.

## Cardoon

*Resembling celery on steroids, mild-tasting cardoons are essential for dipping into the Piedmontese bagna caôda (a fondue of olive oil, anchovy, and garlic).*

### If You Don't Have It

Substitute 1 cup (250 mL) chopped cardoons with:
- 1 cup (250 mL) chopped artichoke hearts
- 1 cup (250 mL) chopped celery
- 1 cup (250 mL) chopped salsify
- ½ cup (125 mL) chopped artichoke hearts + ½ cup (125 mL) chopped celery

## Caribou

*A large member of the deer family closely related to reindeer. An important food source for Native Americans.*

### If You Don't Have It

Substitute 1 lb (500 g) caribou with:
- 1 lb (500 g) reindeer
- 1 lb (500 g) red, fallow, or white-tailed deer
- 1 lb (500 g) moose
- 1 lb (500 g) elk
- 1 lb (500 g) antelope
- 1 lb (500 g) gazelle

*See also* VENISON.

## Carissa

*Also known as Natal plum.
A native South African
plum-like fruit with red
flesh speckled with white.
The flavor is tart and the
texture slightly granular.*

### If You Don't Have It

Substitute 1 lb (500 g) carissa with:
- 1 lb (500 g) karanda
- 1 lb (500 g) gooseberries (especially for jellies and jams)
- 1 lb (500 g) cranberries (especially for jellies and jams)

## Carnation

*See* Picking Edible Flowers (page 650).

## Carne Seca

*See* Tasajo.

## Carob

*Also known as locust bean
and Saint John's bread. A
caffeine-free, chocolate-
like flavoring made from
the pods of the carob tree.*

### If You Don't Have It

Substitute 1 cup (250 mL) carob with:
- 1 cup (250 mL) minus 3 tbsp (45 mL) cocoa powder (to replace carob powder)
- 1 cup (250 mL) chocolate chips (to replace carob chips)

## Carom Seed

*See* Ajwain.

## Carp

*Originating in the
Danube and other central
European rivers, carp has
conquered the world as a
quick-growing aquaculture
fish. Perhaps best known
as the primary ingredient
of Jewish gefilte fish.*

### If You Don't Have It

Substitute 1 lb (500 g) carp with:
- 1 lb (500 g) carp bream (known as "bream" in the U.K.)
- 1 lb (500 g) buffalofish
- 1 lb (500 g) freshwater bass
- 1 lb (500 g) bluefish (higher in fat; softer flesh)

## Carrageen

*Also known as Irish moss.
An Atlantic seaweed that's
the base of carageenan, a
common food additive that
emulsifies, stabilizes, and
thickens countless food
products from soup to
ice cream.*

### If You Don't Have It

Substitute 1 oz (30 g) carrageen (for thickening) with:
- 1 tsp (5 mL) agar powder
- 1½ tsp (7 mL) gelatin powder

## Carré de l'Est

*Literally "square of the East," this French washed rind cow's milk cheese has a square shape, orange or white rind, and soft, oozing texture with a deliciously pungent flavor hinting at mushrooms and bacon.*

### If You Don't Have It

Substitute 1 oz (30 g) Carré de l'Est with:

- 1 oz (30 g) Epoisses de Bourgogne
- 1 oz (30 g) Ami du Chambertin
- 1 oz (30 g) Langres
- 1 oz (30 g) Maroilles
- 1 oz (30 g) Pont-l'Évêque

## Carrot

*Carrots are available in red, white, and purple colors in addition to the familiar orange variety. The orange "baby-cut" carrots sold in plastic bags are not truly baby carrots but mature carrots machine-cut for convenience.*

> 1 large carrot = 4 oz (125 g) = 1 cup (250 mL) grated = ¾ cup (175 mL) cooked and mashed

### If You Don't Have It

Substitute 1 cup (250 mL) chopped carrots with:

- 1 cup (250 mL) chopped parsnips
- 1 cup (250 mL) chopped daikon
- 1 cup (250 mL) chopped turnips
- 1 cup (250 mL) chopped celery

## Carrot Juice

*An easy-to-ingest source of beta-carotene. To flavor rice, couscous, or other grain pilafs, cook the grain in equal parts carrot juice and water.*

### If You Don't Have It

Substitute 1 cup (250 mL) fresh carrot juice with:

- 1 cup (250 mL) canned carrot juice
- 1 cup (250 mL) V8® Juice (red color; a commercial blend of tomato, spinach, celery, carrot, beet, lettuce, watercress, and parsley juices)

## Casaba Melon

*A type of winter melon similar to honeydew but with a rough skin.*

> 1 lb (500 g) = 1 to 1½ cups (250 to 375 mL) cubed

### If You Don't Have It

Substitute 1 cup (250 mL) chopped casaba melon with:

- 1 cup (250 mL) chopped Santa Claus melon
- 1 cup (250 mL) chopped Crenshaw melon
- 1 cup (250 mL) chopped Persian melon
- 1 cup (250 mL) chopped honeydew melon
- 1 cup (250 mL) chopped cantaloupe

## Cascabel Chile

*See* CHOOSING DRIED CHILES (PAGE 642).

## Casciotta Cheese

*See* CACIOTTA.

## Casero Cheese

*This semi-soft, mild, white Mexican cow's milk cheese has a slightly grainy texture and acidic bite. It is essentially housemade queso fresco (fresh cheese), named after the Spanish word for house, casa.*

4 oz (125 g) = 1 cup (250 mL) crumbled

### If You Don't Have It

Substitute 1 oz (30 g) casero with:
- 1 oz (30 g) queso fresco
- 1 oz (30 g) pressed, salted farmer's cheese
- 1 oz (30 g) young goat cheese
- 1 oz (30 g) feta cheese (rinsed to remove some salt)
- 1 oz (30 g) Monterey Jack cheese
- 1 oz (30 g) dry cottage cheese + $\frac{1}{8}$ tsp (0.5 mL) salt

## Cashel Bleu

*County Tipperary Irish blue cheese with a creamy texture and a thin pinkish red rind.*

### If You Don't Have It

Substitute 1 oz (30 g) Cashel Blue with:
- 1 oz (30 g) Gorgonzola
- 1 oz (30 g) Stilton
- 1 oz (30 g) Fourme d'Ambert
- 1 oz (30 g) Roquefort

## Cashew

*The shell of this buttery nut is highly toxic. Great care is taken in processing commercially sold shelled cashews, which are perfectly safe.*

1 lb (500 g) = 3⅓ cups (825 mL)

### If You Don't Have It

Substitute 1 cup (250 mL) cashew nuts with:
- 1 cup (250 mL) peanuts
- 1 cup (250 mL) pine nuts
- 1 cup (250 mL) pistachio nuts

*See also* NUT.

## Cashew Apple

*Also known as marañon. Not a true fruit, cashew apples are the yellow-orange swollen stems attached to cashew nuts on the cashew tree. Due to their delicate skin, cashew apples begin to ferment within 24 hours. The somewhat astringent juice is fermented into liquor in India and parts of Africa, and the raw juice is popular in Brazil and Thailand.*

### If You Don't Have It

Substitute 1 lb (500 g) cashew apples with:
- 1 lb (500 g) persimmons
- 1 lb (500 g) plums

## Cashew Butter

*A paste of ground roasted cashew nuts, oil, and salt.*

### If You Don't Have It

Substitute 1 cup (250 mL) cashew butter with:
- 1 cup (250 mL) Homemade Cashew Butter: Put 2 cups (500 mL) roasted cashews and ¼ tsp (1 mL) salt in a blender or food processor fitted with metal blade. Process, gradually adding 4 to 6 tbsp (60 to 90 mL) vegetable oil, until the mixture forms a paste. Add sugar to taste. Makes 1½ cups (375 mL).
- 1 cup (250 mL) peanut butter or almond butter
- 1 cup (250 mL) tahini (strong sesame flavor)

## Cassava

*Also known as mandioca, manioc, and yuca. A starchy root that is popular in Latin America and a staple in many parts of Africa. Tapioca is one by-product.*

### If You Don't Have It

Substitute 1 lb (500 g) cassava with:
- 1 lb (500 g) mandiba
- 1 lb (500 g) yautía or malanga
- 1 lb (500 g) taro
- 1 lb (500 g) potatoes

*See also* GARI; TAPIOCA.

## Casserole

*See* PAN SIZE EQUIVALENTS (PAGE 678).

## Cassia

*See* CINNAMON.

## Cassis Liqueur

*Also known as crème de cassis. A sweet liqueur made with black currants and rum.*

### If You Don't Have It

Substitute 3 tbsp (45 mL) cassis liqueur with:
- 3 tbsp (45 mL) black currant syrup (sweeter; no alcohol)
- 3 tbsp (45 mL) raspberry liqueur
- 3 tbsp (45 mL) crème de myrtille (tart blueberry flavor)

## Castelmagno

*Castelmagno fondue is a fixture in the restaurants of Piedmont, Italy. This pressed, raw cow's milk cheese has a remarkable granular texture that becomes smooth when melted yet remains granular when grated over salads. Sometimes tinged with blue mold.*

4 oz (125 g) = 1 cup (250 mL) crumbled

### If You Don't Have It

Substitute 1 oz (30 g) Castelmagno with:
- ¾ oz (22 g) Myzithra + ¼ oz (7 g) gorgonzola or other blue cheese
- ¾ oz (22 g) rinsed feta + ¼ oz (7 g) gorgonzola or other blue cheese
- ¾ oz (22 g) Haloumi + ¼ oz (7 g) gorgonzola or other blue cheese
- ¾ oz (22 g) Manouri + ¼ oz (7 g) gorgonzola or other blue cheese

## Cast Iron

*One of the least expensive and most durable cookware materials. Cast iron conducts and retains heat fairly well.*

### If You Don't Have It
Substitute cast-iron cookware with:
- enamelware
- heavy-gauge clad cookware (stainless steel with aluminum or copper core)
- hard anodized aluminum cookware

## Castries

*See* PEANUT LIQUEUR.

## Catarina Chile

*See* CHOOSING DRIED CHILES (PAGE 642).

## Catfish

*Growing to weights of up to 700 pounds (350 kg), the giant catfish of the Mekong River are reputed to be among the finest tasting fishes in the world.*

### If You Don't Have It
Substitute 1 lb (500 g) catfish with:
- 1 lb (500 g) tilapia
- 1 lb (500 g) sole
- 1 lb (500 g) grouper
- 1 lb (500 g) tilefish
- 1 lb (500 g) monkfish

### Catfish Varieties
Choose 1 lb (500 g) catfish from these common varieties:
- 1 lb (500 g) channel catfish (U.S. farm-raised and wild *Ictalurus punctatus*)
- 1 lb (500 g) basa fish (Thai and Vietnamese *Pangasius bocourti*, thick delicate flesh, mild flavor)
- 1 lb (500 g) tra, swai, striped catfish, or iridescent shark (Thai and Vietnamese *Pangasius hypophthalmus*, thinner, coarser flesh)

## Catsup

*See* KETCHUP.

## Caul

*The lacy, fatty lining of the abdominal cavity of pigs and sheep used to wrap pâtés and charcuterie.*

### If You Don't Have It
Substitute 4 oz (125 g) caul fat with:
- 4 oz (125 g) thinly sliced bacon (for barding)
- 4 oz (125 g) thinly sliced pancetta (for barding)

## Cauliflower

*The fleece (or curd) of cauliflower may be green, orange, pinkish, or yellow. Colored types often have a more pronounced flavor.*

1 head = 4 cups
(1 L) florets

### If You Don't Have It
Substitute 1 lb (500 g) cauliflower with:
- 1 lb (500 g) Broccoflower™ (light green color)
- 1 lb (500 g) broccoli Romanesco (light green color; conical florets)
- 1 lb (500 g) broccoli (dark green color; softer texture; cooks more quickly)

## Cava

*See* WINE, SPARKLING.

## Cavendish Banana

*See* BANANA.

## Caviar

*See* CHANGING ROE (PAGE 666).

## Cayenne Pepper

*A thin, pointed, and very hot chile pepper that's usually dried and crushed (crushed red pepper flakes) or ground (ground red pepper).*

### If You Don't Have It

Substitute ½ tsp (2 mL) ground cayenne pepper with:
- ½ tsp (2 mL) ground chipotle powder (much smokier)
- ½ tsp (2 mL) ground ancho powder (darker; milder)
- ½ tsp (2 mL) hot paprika (much milder)
- ¾ tsp (3 mL) crushed red pepper flakes
- ½ tsp (2 mL) chili powder (milder; adds flavors of cumin, oregano, and other spices)
- 1 very small whole dried red chile
- dash of hot pepper sauce
- 1 to 3 tsp (5 to 15 mL) chile paste

*See also* HOT PEPPER SAUCE; CHOOSING DRIED CHILES (PAGE 642); CHOOSING FRESH CHILES (PAGE 640).

## Cedar Plank

*See* WOOD PLANK.

## Cedro

*See* CITRON.

## Celeriac

*Also known as celery root, knob celery and turnip-rooted celery. Gnarly root celery — more full-flavored and herbaceous than celery stalks or leaves — is beloved in France. Céléri en remoulade (celery root in mustard mayonnaise) is a time-honored bistro appetizer.*

> 1½ lbs (750 g) = 4 cups
> (1 L) grated = 1¾ cups
> (425 mL) cooked
> and puréed

### If You Don't Have It

Substitute 1 cup (250 mL) chopped celeriac with:
- 1 cup (250 mL) chopped parsley root (stronger flavor)
- 1 cup (250 mL) chopped celery (milder flavor)
- 1 cup (250 mL) chopped turnips + pinch of celery seeds
- 1 cup (250 mL) chopped parsnips + pinch of celery seeds
- 1 cup (250 mL) chopped carrots + pinch of celery seeds

## Céleri Bâtard

*See* LOVAGE.

## Celery

*Garnishing a Bloody Mary cocktail with a stick of celery is said to have begun in the 1960s at the swanky Ambassador East Hotel in Chicago. A celebrity, who was served his Bloody Mary with no swizzle stick, grabbed a celery rib from the relish tray to stir his drink.*

1 rib = 1 oz (30 g) = ½ cup (125 mL) sliced

### If You Don't Have It

Substitute 1 cup (250 mL) chopped fresh celery with:
- ½ cup (125 mL) dehydrated celery flakes (for soups and stews; much less flavorful)
- ⅔ to 1 cup (150 to 250 mL) chopped Chinese celery (for cooking; stronger flavor)
- 1 cup (250 mL) chopped cardoons (adds mild artichoke flavor)
- 1 cup (250 mL) chopped fennel stalks (adds mild anise flavor)

## Celery Cabbage

*See* NAPA CABBAGE.

## Celery Root

*See* CELERIAC.

## Celery Salt

*A seasoning blend of ground celery seeds and salt.*

### If You Don't Have It

Substitute 1 tsp (5 mL) celery salt with:
- ¼ to ½ tsp (1 to 2 mL) ground celery seeds + ½ tsp (2 mL) salt
- 1 tsp (5 mL) Beau Monde® Seasoning (adds dried onion flavor)
- 1 tsp (5 mL) Old Bay Seasoning (adds paprika and other spices)

## Celery Seed

*The seeds of a wild celery called lovage have a stronger celery flavor than cultivated celery stalks.*

### If You Don't Have It

Substitute 1 tsp (5 mL) celery seeds with:
- 1 tsp (5 mL) celery salt (reduce salt in recipe by ½ tsp/2 mL)
- 1 tsp (5 mL) dill seeds
- 3 tbsp (45 mL) chopped celery leaves

## Cellophane Noodles

*See* A SNAPSHOT OF ASIAN NOODLES (PAGE 656).

## Celosia

*See* QUAIL GRASS.

## Celtuce

*Also known as celery lettuce, stem lettuce, and asparagus lettuce. The most popular form of lettuce in China, celtuce is grown for its crisp, tender stems rather than its leaves.*

### If You Don't Have It

Substitute 1 cup (250 mL) peeled, chopped celtuce with:
- 1 cup (250 mL) peeled, seeded, and chopped cucumber
- 1 cup (250 mL) peeled tender broccoli stems
- 1 cup (250 mL) celery
- 1 cup (250 mL) cardoons

## Çemen

*A Middle Eastern spice paste used to coat Turkish pastrami. A spicy Turkish tomato dip goes by the same name.*

### If You Don't Have It

Substitute 1 tbsp (15 mL) çemen with:
- 1 tbsp (15 mL) Homemade Çemen Paste: Mash in a mortar and pestle 1 large clove garlic, ¾ tsp (3 mL) ground black pepper, ¾ tsp (3 mL) ground cumin, ¾ tsp (3 mL) ground fenugreek, ¾ tsp (3 mL) salt, and ¾ tsp (3 mL) hot paprika (or cayenne pepper for more heat). Makes about 1½ tbsp (22 mL).
- 1 tbsp (15 mL) Homemade Çemen Dip: Grind ½ cup (125 mL) walnuts to a coarse meal (but not a powder) in a spice grinder or small food processor. Remove to a bowl and stir in 1 can (6 oz/175 g) tomato paste, 1½ tbsp (22 mL) Homemade Çemen Paste (recipe above), 1½ tsp (7 mL) dried mint (or ¼ cup/60 mL chopped fresh), 1½ tsp (7 mL) dried oregano, ¼ cup (60 mL) chopped fresh parsley, and ¼ cup (60 mL) canola oil. Makes about ¾ cup (175 mL).

## Cèpe

*See* SHUFFLING MUSHROOMS (PAGE 654).

## Ceriman

*See* MONSTERA.

## Cervelat

*A family of smoked German sausages made with pork and, sometimes, beef. Cervelat is typically a semidry sausage that's sliced and served raw like bologna, but spreadable versions are available. Popular varieties of cervelat include Thuringer and Landjäger. Not to be confused with France's cervelas, a related but smaller fresh sausage.*

### If You Don't Have It

Substitute 1 lb (500 g) cervelat with:
- 1 lb (500 g) bierwurst
- 1 lb (500 g) blockwurst
- 1 lb (500 g) mortadella
- 1 lb (500 g) bologna

*See also* BRAUNSCHWEIGER; LANDJÄGER; LEBANON BOLOGNA; MORTADELLA; SUMMER SAUSAGE; THURINGER.

## Ceylon Spinach

*See* BASELLA.

## Chaat Masala

*An Indian spice blend that tastes sour, salty, and sulfuric with the pungent flavor of Kala Namak or Indian black salt. It is typically served with Indian street snacks or chaat.*

### If You Don't Have It
Substitute 1 tbsp (15 mL) chaat masala with:
- 1 tbsp (15 mL) Homemade Chaat Masala: Toast 1 tbsp (15 mL) cumin seeds and 1 tbsp (15 mL) coriander seeds in a dry skillet until fragrant, 5 minutes. Transfer to a spice grinder and grind along with $\frac{1}{2}$ tsp (2 mL) black peppercorns. Pour into a bowl and mix in 1 tbsp (15 mL) amchur (mango powder), 2 tsp (10 mL) Kala Namak (black salt), 1 tsp (5 mL) coarse sea salt, $\frac{1}{2}$ tsp (2 mL) dried mint, $\frac{1}{4}$ tsp (1 mL) ground ginger, $\frac{1}{4}$ tsp (1 mL) asafetida powder (optional), and $\frac{1}{8}$ tsp (0.5 mL) cayenne pepper. Makes about $\frac{1}{4}$ cup (60 mL).
- $1\frac{1}{2}$ tsp (7 mL) garam masala + 1 tsp (5 mL) amchur (mango powder) + $\frac{1}{2}$ tsp (2 mL) Kala Namak (black salt)

*See also* GARAM MASALA; PANCH PHORAN; SAMBHAR MASALA.

## Chafing Dish

*Derived from the French* chauffeur, *which means "to heat," chafing dishes evolved to allow for simple, elegant tableside cooking away from the bustle and mess of the main cooking area.*

### If You Don't Have It
Substitute a chafing dish with:
- Large fondue pot
- Electric warming tray (for keeping food warm)
- Heating pad (for keeping food warm)

## Chai

*In India, "young boys (chai wallahs) brew tea on street corners using kettles and brass pots and mix it with buffalo milk and sugar,"* write Jane Pettigrew and Bruce Richardson in The New Tea Companion. *Chai is Indian for tea, but in the West refers to black tea spiced with cinnamon, cardamom, cloves, and pepper, a popular drink in India.*

### If You Don't Have It
Substitute 1 cup (250 mL) brewed spiced chai with:
- 1 cup (250 mL) Homemade Spiced Chai: In a medium saucepan, combine 1 cup (250 mL) water, 2 cinnamon sticks (3 inches/7.5 cm each), 1 slice crystallized ginger (2 inches/5 cm), 2 green cardamom pods, split open to expose seeds, $\frac{1}{2}$ tsp (2 mL) whole cloves, $\frac{1}{4}$ tsp (1 mL) whole allspice, $\frac{1}{4}$ tsp (1 mL) peppercorns (preferably white), and $\frac{1}{2}$ piece star anise. Bring to a boil over high heat then remove from heat and let stand 10 to 12 minutes. Add 5 cups (1.25 L) whole milk and bring to a boil over high heat. Remove from heat and let stand 5 to 7 minutes. Add sugar to taste and stir until dissolved. Strain into a warmed teapot and serve. Makes about 6 cups (1.5 L).
- 2 to 3 tsp (10 to 15 mL) dry spiced chai + $\frac{1}{2}$ cup (125 mL) boiling water, steeped for 4 to 6 minutes, strained and mixed with $\frac{1}{2}$ cup (125 mL) milk + sugar to taste

## Chai (cont'd)

- ½ cup (125 mL) liquid chai tea concentrate + ½ cup (125 mL) milk
- ⅞ cup (220 mL) hot brewed tea + pinch cinnamon + few drops vanilla + 3 tbsp (45 mL) whole milk

### To Vary the Flavor

Substitute 1 cup (250 mL) brewed spiced chai with:
- 1 cup (250 mL) brewed black tea (preferably with milk and sugar; no spice aroma)
- 1 cup (250 mL) brewed coffee (preferably with milk and sugar; no spice aroma)
- 1 cup (250 mL) brewed rooibos or other herbal tea
- 1 cup (250 mL) brewed roasted chicory

*See also* TEA; SWITCHING TEA (PAGE 670).

## Chaka

*See* YOGURT CHEESE.

## Challah

*Also known as challa and hallah. Jewish egg-rich bread that is often braided and served on the Sabbath and holidays. Traditionally, when challah is prepared, a pinch of dough is burned in the oven as the bread bakes. The word in Biblical Hebrew refers to this bit of dough and means "the priest's share."*

### If You Don't Have It

Substitute 1 lb (500 g) challah with:
- 1 lb (500 g) brioche (richer)
- 1 lb (500 g) Portuguese sweet bread
- 1 lb (500 g) raisin bread
- 1 lb (500 g) shokupan (rich Japanese white bread)
- 1 lb (500 g) croissants (less eggy, more airy texture)
- 1 lb (500 g) Kugelhopf (filled with dried and candied fruit and nuts)
- 1 lb (500 g) panettone
- 1 lb (500 g) soft white bread

## Chambord

*See* RASPBERY LIQUEUR.

## Champagne

*Sparkling wine made by the méthode champenoise, a meticulous production method that includes a second fermentation in the bottle and the removal of sediment.*

### If You Don't Have It

Substitute 1 cup (250 mL) champagne with:
- 1 cup (250 mL) sparkling wine, such as Asti Spumante, prosecco, or cava
- 1 cup (250 mL) white wine (no bubbles)

### Champagne Varieties

Choose 1 cup (250 mL) champagne from these varieties:
- 1 cup (250 mL) brut (the driest; contains less than 1.5% sugar)
- 1 cup (250 mL) extra dry or extra sec (slightly sweet; contains 1.2 to 2% sugar)

- 1 cup (250 mL) sec (medium sweet; contains 1.7 to 3.5% sugar)
- 1 cup (250 mL) demi-sec (sweet; contains 3.3 to 5% sugar)
- 1 cup (250 mL) doux (very sweet; contains more than 5% sugar)

## For Better Health
Substitute 1 cup (250 mL) champagne with:
- 1 cup (250 mL) sparkling cider (no alcohol)
- 1 cup (250 mL) sparkling grape juice (no alcohol)
- 1 cup (250 mL) ginger ale (no alcohol; ginger flavor)

*See also* WINE, SPARKLING.

## Champagne Grape

*Also known as Black Corinth and Zante grape. Tiny, sweet, juicy, purple eating grapes that, ironically, are not used to make champagne.*

### If You Don't Have It
Substitute 1 cup (250 mL) champagne grapes with:
- 1 cup (250 mL) Muscat grapes (adds musky flavor)
- 1 cup (250 mL) Flame seedless grapes (red color)
- 1 cup (250 mL) Thompson seedless grapes (larger; pale green color)

*See also* CURRANT, DRIED.

## Chana Flour

*See* CHOOSING AMONG WHOLE-GRAIN AND ALTERNATIVE FLOURS (PAGE 648).

## Chanterelle

*See* SHUFFLING MUSHROOMS (PAGE 654).

## Chaource

*Named after a town in the Champagne region of France, this soft-rind cow's milk cheese resembles Camembert.*

### If You Don't Have It
Substitute 1 oz (30 g) Chaource cheese with:
- 1 oz (30 g) Ervy-le-Châtel
- 1 oz (30 g) Camembert
- 1 oz (30 g) Brie

## Chapati

*Indian flatbread made with whole wheat flour and little or no fat.*

### If You Don't Have It
Substitute 1 chapati with:
- 1 roti (a generic term for Indian flatbread; similar to chapati; usually made with whole wheat flour)
- 1 paratha (griddle-cooked whole wheat flatbread with fat in the dough; richer; more flaky)
- 1 poori (deep-fried flatbread made with whole wheat flour; crisper)
- 1 naan (more puffy flatbread made from refined wheat flour and cooked on the walls of a tandoor or clay-lined oven; sometimes flavored with garlic, herbs, or other aromatics)
- 1 whole wheat pita bread (similar to naan)
- 1 whole wheat flour tortilla

## Chapati Flour

*Also known as atta. Finely milled whole wheat flour that is mixed with water to make Indian flatbread.*

### If You Don't Have It
Substitute 1 cup (250 mL) chapati flour with:
- ⅓ cup (75 mL) whole wheat flour + ⅓ cup (75 mL) all-purpose flour + ⅓ cup (75 mL) cake flour (makes tender breads)
- ⅓ cup (75 mL) whole wheat flour + ⅔ cup (150 mL) all-purpose flour (more firm breads)

## Char

*Also known as Arctic char. A fish with pink flesh and salmon-trout flavor aquacultured in Iceland.*

### If You Don't Have It
Substitute 1 lb (500 g) char with:
- 1 lb (500 g) salmon
- 1 lb (500 g) striped bass

## Chard

*Also known as leaf beet, spinach beet, and Swiss chard. Ranging in stem color from white to magenta, chard's green leafy stalks are related to the common beet. Both the stalks and leaves are beloved in Spain and Italy, where they are often sautéed in olive oil and garlic.*

### If You Don't Have It
Substitute 1 lb (500 g) chard with:
- 1 lb (500 g) turnip greens
- 1 lb (500 g) mature spinach
- 1 lb (500 g) bok choy
- 1 lb (500 g) mustard greens
- 1 lb (500 g) Tuscan kale

### Chard Varieties
Choose 1 lb (500 g) chard from these varieties:
- 1 lb (500 g) red chard (maroon stalks; slightly more tender than green chard)
- 1 lb (500 g) green chard (white stalks)

## Charentais Melon

*Small French melon with fragrant orange flesh and yellow rind.*

1 lb (500 g) =
1 to 1½ cups
(250 to 375 mL) cubed

### If You Don't Have It
Substitute 1 cup (250 mL) chopped Charentais melon with:
- 1 cup (250 mL) chopped cantaloupe
- 1 cup (250 mL) chopped Persian melon
- 1 cup (250 mL) chopped Crenshaw melon
- 1 cup (250 mL) chopped Santa Claus melon
- 1 cup (250 mL) chopped honeydew melon

## Charkassiye

*Soft, mild-tasting cow's milk cheese used in Syrian cuisine. Browns well but doesn't melt.*

1 lb (500 g) =
1 to 1½ cups
(250 to 375 mL) cubed

### If You Don't Have It
Substitute 1 oz (30 g) charkassiye with:
- 1 oz (30 g) haloumi
- 1 oz (30 g) feta cheese

## Charlotte Mold

*See* PAN SIZE EQUIVALENTS (PAGE 678).

## Charoli Nut

*Small, dark brown nuts with a flavor reminiscent of nutmeg. Often used in Indian desserts.*

### If You Don't Have It

Substitute 1 cup (250 mL) charoli nuts with:
- 1 cup (250 mL) unsalted pistachios + pinch of grated nutmeg

## Char Siu Sauce

*See* CHINESE BARBECUE SAUCE.

## Chartreuse

*An aromatic liqueur originally bottled by French Carthusian monks. The green variety is minty, spicy, and more intense than the yellow, which is lower in alcohol, sweetened with honey, and tinted with saffron. Chartreuse V.E.P. (in both colors) is aged for 12 years in oak to produce a more complex and mellow spirit.*

### If You Don't Have It

Substitute 3 tbsp (45 mL) Chartreuse with:
- 3 tbsp (45 mL) Izarra
- 3 tbsp (45 mL) Strega
- 3 tbsp (45 mL) Bénédictine
- 3 tbsp (45 mL) Drambuie (mild licorice flavor)

### Chartreuse Varieties

Choose 3 tbsp (45 mL) Chartreuse from these varieties:
- 3 tbsp (45 mL) green Chartreuse (green color; more bracing flavor and heavier body than yellow Chartreuse)
- 3 tbsp (45 mL) yellow Chartreuse (pale golden color; sweeter flavor and lighter body than green Chartreuse)

## Chaubier

*Known as a mi-chèvre (half goat), this French washed rind cheese is made with a 50/50 blend of goat's and cow's milk. It is cooked, pressed and aged for about 6 months. Great melter.*

### If You Don't Have It

Substitute 1 oz (30 g) Chaubier with:
- 1 oz (30 g) Saint-Nectaire
- 1 oz (30 g) Tomme de Savoie
- 1 oz (30 g) Beaumont

## Chaurice

*See* CHORIZO.

## Chaya

*Also known as tree spinach. The extremely nutritious leaves of a Central American shrub are covered with stinging hairs. When picked young, however, they are tender and may be cooked like spinach.*

### If You Don't Have It

Substitute 1 lb (500 g) chaya with:
- 1 lb (500 g) spinach
- 1 lb (500 g) green chard
- 1 lb (500 g) turnip greens

## Chayote

*Also known as mirliton and vegetable pear. A mild gourd-like fruit that's shaped like a pear.*

### If You Don't Have It

Substitute 1 lb (500 g) chayote with:
- 1 lb (500 g) bottle gourd or cucuzza
- 1 lb (500 g) zucchini
- 1 lb (500 g) yellow crookneck squash
- 8 oz (250 g) summer squash + 8 oz (250 g) kohlrabi

## Cheddar

*In 1840, English dairy farmers in Somerset created a tasty wedding present for Queen Victoria: a Cheddar cheese weighing 1,100 pounds (500 kg). In Wisconsin 120 years later, dairy farmers created a bigger 34,951-pound (16,000 kg) Cheddar.*

1 lb (500 g) = 4 cups
(1 L) shredded

### If You Don't Have It

Substitute 1 oz (30 g) Cheddar cheese with:
- 1 oz (30 g) Colby
- 1 oz (30 g) Cheshire
- 1 oz (30 g) Double Gloucester
- 1 oz (30 g) Leicester
- 1 oz (30 g) Lancashire
- 1 oz (30 g) Jack cheese
- 1 oz (30 g) American cheese

### For Better Health

Substitute 1 oz (30 g) Cheddar cheese with:
- 1 oz (30 g) reduced-fat Cheddar

*See also* CHESHIRE; GLOUCESTER; LANCASHIRE; LEICESTER; WENSLEYDALE.

## Chee Hou Sauce

*Also known as chu hou paste. Dark brown Chinese braising sauce made from soybeans, garlic, and ginger.*

### If You Don't Have It

Substitute ¼ cup (60 mL) chee hou sauce with:
- ¼ cup (60 mL) hoisin sauce (sweeter)

## Cheese

*Fresh cheeses, such as Italian ricotta, are meant to be enjoyed immediately. Other cheese curds are cooked, pressed, and aged to produce semifirm cheeses, such as Cheddar, and hard cheeses, such as Parmesan.*

### For Better Health

Substitute 1 oz (30 g) cheese with:
- 1 oz (30 g) reduced-fat cheese (made with partially skimmed milk; avoid fat-free cheeses, which do not melt well and have lost all semblance of cheese due to lack of fat)
- 1 oz (30 g) soy cheese (vegetarian; find a brand you like)

*See also* SPECIFIC TYPES.

## Cheesecloth

*Also known as butter muslin. Loosely woven cotton cloth used for straining, lining molds, and encasing a bouquet garni.*

### If You Don't Have It

Substitute cheesecloth with:
- nylon mesh, such as clean nylon stockings (for straining)
- clean kitchen towel (for straining)
- coffee filters (for straining and bouquet garni)

## Cheez Whiz

*See* PROCESSED CHEESE.

## Chemen

*See* ÇEMEN.

## Chenna

*Indian fresh cheese produced from cow's or water buffalo's milk. Similar to panir but softer and moister because it is not pressed.*

8 oz (250 g) = 1 cup (250 mL)

### If You Don't Have It
Substitute 1 cup (250 mL) chenna with:
- 1 cup (250 mL) ricotta cheese
- 1 cup (250 mL) dry-curd cottage cheese
- 1 cup (250 mL) panir, briefly puréed in a food processor (less moist)
- 1 cup (250 mL) soft tofu, cubed

*See also* PANIR.

## Cheremai

*See* OTAHEITE GOOSEBERRY.

## Cherimoya

*Also known as custard apple. This fruit has petal-patterned jade-green skin filled with granular creamy flesh that has a flavor suggesting mango, papaya, pineapple, and vanilla.*

1 = 12 oz (375 g) = 1½ cups (375 mL) chopped

### If You Don't Have It
Substitute 1 lb (500 g) cherimoya with:
- 1 lb (500 g) atemoya
- 1 lb (500 g) soursop
- 1 lb (500 g) sweetsop
- 1 lb (500 g) mango or papaya + ¼ tsp (1 mL) vanilla extract

*See also* ATEMOYA; SOURSOP; SWEETSOP.

## Chéri Suisse

*See* CHERRY LIQUEUR.

## Cherry

*The name cherry is derived from the ancient Greek word* kerasos, *which was also the name of a city in Asia Minor. Historians debate whether this small stone fruit was named for the city, or the city named for the fruit. Cherry varieties are generally classified as sweet or sour.*

### If You Don't Have It
Substitute 1 lb (500 g) cherries with:
- 1 lb (500 g) acerola
- 1 lb (500 g) chokecherries (to replace sour cherries for cooking)
- 1 lb (500 g) apricots
- 1 lb (500 g) plums
- 1 lb (500 g) peaches
- 1 lb (500 g) nectarines

### Cherry Varieties
Choose 1 lb (500 g) cherries from these varieties:
- 1 lb (500 g) sweet cherries such as Bing, Lambert, and Royal

## Cherry (cont'd)

1 lb (500 g) fresh =
2½ to 3 cups
(625 to 750 mL) pitted

10 oz (300 g) frozen =
1 cup (250 mL)

16-oz (454 mL) can =
1½ cups (375 mL) drained

Ann (best for snacking, but some varieties taste good cooked; yellow-and-red Royal Anns or Napoleons are often used to make maraschino cherries)

- 1 lb (500 g) sour cherries such as Early Richmond, Montmorency, and Morello (smaller, softer, and more tart than sweet cherries; best for cooking in pies, jams, and sauces)

*See also* CAPULIN; CHERRY, DRIED; CHOKECHERRY; JAMAICAN CHERRY.

## Cherry, Candied

*Also known as glacé cherries. These sugar-soaked cherries are sold in red and green versions.*

### If You Don't Have It

Substitute 1 cup (250 mL) candied cherries with:

- 1 cup (250 mL) dried cherries, dried cranberries, or other dried fruit

## Cherry, Dried

*Both sweet and sour varieties are available commercially dried like raisins.*

15 oz (426 g) =
2½ cups (625 mL)

### If You Don't Have It

Substitute 1 cup (250 mL) dried cherries with:

- 1 cup (250 mL) dried cranberries (more tart)
- 1 cup (250 mL) dried blueberries (dark blue color)
- 1 cup (250 mL) raisins
- 1 cup (250 mL) currants

## Cherry Extract

*The antioxidant powerhouse found in dietary supplements can also lend rich cherry flavor to cakes, cookies, muffins, pies, ice cream, and drinks.*

### If You Don't Have It

Substitute 1 tsp (5 mL) cherry extract with:

- 3 tbsp (45 mL) cherry juice (sweeter; reduce liquid in recipe by 3 tbsp/45 mL)
- 3 tbsp (45 mL) packing liquid from canned cherries or jarred maraschino cherries (sweeter; reduce liquid in recipe by 3 tbsp/45 mL)
- 3 tbsp (45 mL) Crème de cerise (sweeter; adds alcohol; reduce liquid in recipe by 3 tbsp/45 mL)
- 3 tbsp (45 mL) cherry cordial or cherry syrup (sweeter; adds alcohol; reduce liquid in recipe by 3 tbsp/45 mL)
- 3 tbsp (45 mL) Maraschino liqueur (sweeter; adds alcohol; reduce liquid in recipe by 3 tbsp/45 mL)
- 3 tbsp (45 mL) Chéri Suisse (adds alcohol and chocolate flavor; sweeter; reduce liquid in recipe by 3 tbsp/45 mL)
- 3 tbsp (45 mL) Kirsch (cherry brandy; sweeter; adds alcohol; reduce liquid in recipe by 3 tbsp/45 mL)
- 3 tbsp (45 mL) cherry schnapps (adds alcohol; reduce liquid in recipe by 3 tbsp/45 mL)
- 3 tbsp (45 mL) cherry vodka (adds alcohol; reduce liquid in recipe by 3 tbsp/45 mL)

## Cherry Liqueur

*Several types of cherry liqueur can be used interchangeably, including Cherry Heering, Cherry Marnier, Cherry Rocher, Kirschenliqueur.*

### If You Don't Have It

Substitute 3 tbsp (45 mL) cherry liqueur with:
- 3 tbsp (45 mL) crème de cerise (sweeter)
- 3 tbsp (45 mL) crème de griotte (sweet-tart; made with sour Morello cherries)
- 3 tbsp (45 mL) cherry cordial or cherry syrup (sweeter; nonalcoholic)
- 3 tbsp (45 mL) Maraschino liqueur (less sweet)
- 3 tbsp (45 mL) Chéri Suisse (adds chocolate flavor)
- 3 tbsp (45 mL) Kirsch (cherry brandy; less sweet)
- 3 tbsp (45 mL) cherry schnapps (less sweet)
- 3 tbsp (45 mL) cherry vodka (less sweet)
- 3 tbsp (45 mL) cherry whiskey (less sweet)
- 1 to 1½ tsp (5 to 7 mL) cherry extract + 3 tbsp (45 mL) water or liquid in recipe (less sweet)

## Cherry Pepper

*See* CHOOSING FRESH CHILES (PAGE 640).

## Cherrystone Clam

*See* CLAM.

## Cherry Tomato

*See* TOMATO.

## Chervil

*Also known as cicely, cicily, and sweet cicely. A relative of parsley, chervil's delicate anise note is finest in the fresh leaf form.*

### If You Don't Have It

Substitute 1 tbsp (15 mL) chopped fresh chervil with:
- 1 tbsp (15 mL) chopped fresh parsley
- 1 tbsp (15 mL) chopped fresh tarragon (stronger anise flavor)
- 1 tbsp (15 mL) chopped fresh fennel leaves
- 1 tbsp (15 mL) chopped fresh fines herbes (usually includes chervil, chives, parsley, and tarragon)
- 1 tbsp (15 mL) cicely (stronger anise flavor)
- 1 tsp (5 mL) dried chervil or parsley

*See also* CICELY.

## Cheshire

*Renowned English cow's milk cheese made only in its region of origin near the town of Chester. It's crumbly and tastes similar to Cheddar. The pale cheese is often colored orange with annatto. Blue Cheshire is as rich as Stilton but less robust.*

### If You Don't Have It

Substitute 1 oz (30 g) Cheshire cheese with:
- 1 oz (30 g) English Cheddar
- 1 oz (30 g) Wensleydale
- 1 oz (30 g) Leicester
- 1 oz (30 g) Colby (less flavorful)
- 1 oz (30 g) Jack, especially aged (pale color; less flavorful)

## Chestnut

*These sweet nuts generally contain more starch and less oil than other tree nuts and have played an important role as a food staple in rural areas of Europe, Asia, and North America.*

1 lb (500 g) in shell = 20 in shell = 12 oz (375 g) shelled = 35 to 40 chestnuts shelled and peeled = 2 cups (500 mL)

3 oz (90 g) dried = 1 cup (250 mL) fresh

8 oz (250 g) purée = about 1 cup (250 mL)

### If You Don't Have It

Substitute 1 cup (250 mL) fresh shelled chestnuts with:
- 1 cup (250 mL) canned or jarred chestnuts
- 1 cup (250 mL) hazelnuts
- 1 cup (250 mL) pecans
- 1 cup (250 mL) macadamia nuts
- 1 cup (250 mL) chufa nuts
- 1 cup (250 mL) jackfruit seeds

*See also* MAPE; NUT.

## Chestnut, Candied

*Also known as marrons glacés. Shelled and peeled chestnuts poached in syrup until candied.*

### If You Don't Have It

Substitute 1 cup (250 mL) candied chestnuts with:
- 1 cup (250 mL) chestnut cream
- 1 cup (250 mL) candied fruit such as cherries

## Chestnut Cream

*Also known as crème de marron. Puréed chestnuts sweetened with brown sugar and vanilla.*

### If You Don't Have It

Substitute 1 cup (250 mL) chestnut cream with:
- 1 cup (250 mL) candied chestnuts + dash of vanilla puréed in small food processor (add water or Homemade Simple Syrup, see recipe, page 552, if necessary to thin the purée)

## Chestnut Flour

*See* CHOOSING AMONG WHOLE-GRAIN AND ALTERNATIVE FLOURS (PAGE 648).

## Chestnut Purée

*Also known as purée de marron. Shelled and peeled chestnuts are cooked in milk and then puréed and passed through a sieve. Employed as a base for soups, stuffings, and desserts.*

### If You Don't Have It

Substitute 1 cup (250 mL) chestnut purée with:
- 1 cup (250 mL) chestnut cream (omit 1 to 3 tbsp/15 to 45 mL sugar from recipe)
- 1 cup (250 mL) Homemade Chestnut Purée: Put 1 cup (250 mL) shelled and peeled chestnuts (canned or jarred work in a pinch) in a small saucepan and cover with milk or water. Simmer over low heat until very tender, about 1 hour. Add more milk or water as necessary. Purée in a small food processor or blender and press through a sieve.

## Chèvre

*Also known as goat cheese. The generic French term for cheeses made from goat's milk. The term commonly refers to unaged or fresh goat cheeses that are snowy white, creamy in texture (with a slight chalkiness), and have a mild flavor with a pleasing tang. Aged chèvres have a firmer texture and sharper flavor.*

> 4 oz (125 g) = ½ cup
> (125 mL)

### If You Don't Have It
Substitute 1 oz (30 g) chèvre with:
- 1 oz (30 g) cream cheese or mascarpone (to replace fresh chèvre; smoother texture; simpler flavor)
- 1 oz (30 g) sheep's milk feta cheese (to replace aged chèvre; less pungent; saltier; rinse to reduce saltiness)

### Chèvre Varieties
Choose 1 oz (30 g) chèvre from these specific types:
- 1 oz (30 g) Montrachet (usually ash-covered)
- 1 oz (30 g) Banon (softer texture; wrapped in chestnut leaves)
- 1 oz (30 g) Bûcheron (softer texture; usually covered with black ash or a white rind)
- 1 oz (30 g) Selles-sur-Cher (semifirm texture; sweet, nutty flavor; covered with black ash)
- 1 oz (30 g) Crottin de Chavignol (soft to firm texture and mild to nutty flavor, depending on age)
- 1 oz (30 g) Sainte-Maure de Touraine (log-shaped with straw in the center to aerate the cheese)
- 1 oz (30 g) aged chèvre (firmer texture; stronger flavor)

### For Better Health
Substitute 1 oz (30 g) chèvre with:
- ½ oz (15 g) chèvre + ½ oz (15 g) reduced-fat cream cheese (less fat and fewer calories)

*See also* CAPRINI; GOAT'S MILK.

## Chicken

*Chickens are classified by age and size, which generally dictates their best uses. Tender two- to three-month old broiler-fryers generally weigh 3 to 4 pounds (1.5 to 2 kg) and are best for broiling, roasting, frying, and grilling. Four- to eight-month old roasters weigh 3 to 5 pounds (1.5 to 2.5 kg), have a slightly higher fat content, and taste best roasted. Ten- to eighteen-month old stewing chickens weigh 3 to 6 pounds (1.5 to 3 kg) and have tougher but more flavorful meat that takes best to*

### If You Don't Have It
Substitute 1 lb (500 g) chicken with:
- 1 lb (500 g) turkey
- 1 lb (500 g) rabbit

### To Vary the Flavor
Substitute 1 lb (500 g) Cornish hen with:
- 1 lb (500 g) quail (leaner)
- 1 lb (500 g) squab (more tender)
- 1 lb (500 g) grouse (leaner)
- 1 lb (500 g) young pheasant (leaner)

### For Better Health
Substitute 1 lb (500 g) chicken with:
- 1 lb (500 g) kosher chicken (raised more humanely with tighter bacterial controls; brined, which makes the meat slightly more salty)
- 1 lb (500 g) free-range chicken (raised more humanely; often fed a vegetarian diet; meat may be slightly less tender but more flavorful)

## Chicken (cont'd)

*longer, moist-heat cooking methods such as stewing and braising. Cornish game hens are small hybrid chickens sold at 4 to 6 weeks old and 1 to 2 pounds (500 g to 1 kg).*

> 1 lb (500 g) boneless chicken = 3 cups (750 mL) cubed

- 1 lb (500 g) pasture-raised chicken (raised outdoors on a diet with a high percentage of natural forage; meat may be slightly less tender but more flavorful)
- 1 lb (500 g) organic chicken (fed an organic diet)
- 1 lb (500 g) vegetarian chicken products (made with soy protein)
- 1 lb (500 g) extra-firm tofu (more tender; less flavorful)

## Chicken, Black

*Also known as black-skinned chicken, Silkie, and wu gu ji. With black skin, black bones, dark-bluish gray meat, and five-toed feet (instead of four), black chickens look nothing like traditional chickens. The common name "Silkie" comes from the feel of its fluffy soft feathers. They're leaner than conventional chickens, weighing in at 1 to 2 pounds (0.5 to 1 kg), but otherwise taste similar to lean, free-range chickens.*

> 1 lb (500 g) boneless chicken = 3 cups (750 mL) cubed

### If You Don't Have It

Substitute 1 lb (500) black chicken with:
- 1 lb (500 g) free-range chicken (paler meat, skin, and bones)
- 1 lb (500 g) conventional chicken (more tender; paler meat, skin, and bones)
- 1 lb (500 g) turkey (more tender; paler meat, skin, and bones)

## Chicken, Ground

*Skinless, boneless chicken parts run through a meat grinder. Sold packaged in supermarket meat sections. Chunks of raw chicken meat may also be finely chopped in a food processor fitted with a metal blade.*

### If You Don't Have It

Substitute 1 lb (500 g) ground chicken with:
- 1 lb (500 g) ground turkey (often includes dark meat)
- 1 lb (500 g) ground veal

### For Better Health

Substitute 1 lb (500 g) ground chicken with:
- 1 lb (500 g) ground turkey breast

## Chickpea

*See* THE WIDE WORLD OF DRIED BEANS (PAGE 637).

## Chickpea Flour

*See* CHOOSING AMONG WHOLE-GRAIN AND ALTERNATIVE FLOURS (PAGE 648).

## Chicory

*Leafy perennial plants often served as salads. Types of chicory include broad/narrow leaves, curly/noncurly leaves, heading/nonheading plants. Both red-leaf radicchio and green leafy Sugarloaf are types of chicory.*

### If You Don't Have It

Substitute 1 cup (250 mL) chicory with:
- 1 cup (250 mL) curly endive
- 1 cup (250 mL) escarole
- 1 cup (250 mL) radicchio (red color)

*See also* BELGIAN ENDIVE; CURLY ENDIVE; FRISÉE; RADICCHIO.

## Chicory Root, Roasted

*The large roots of some chicory are roasted and ground as a coffee substitute.*

### If You Don't Have It

Substitute 1 cup (250 mL) brewed roasted chicory root with:
- 1 cup (250 mL) brewed coffee

## Chihuahua Cheese

*See* ASADERO.

## Chikuwa

*See* SURIMI.

## Chilean Sea Bass

*See* PATAGONIAN TOOTHFISH.

## Chile

*See* BELL PEPPER; CAYENNE PEPPER; CHILE LEAF; CHILE OIL; CHILE POWDER; HOT PEPPER SAUCE; PAPRIKA; CHOOSING DRIED CHILES (PAGE 642); CHOOSING FRESH CHILES (PAGE 640).

## Chile Bean Paste

*See* CHILE PASTE.

## Chile Garlic Sauce

*See* CHILE PASTE.

## Chile Leaf

*More grassy and herbal than spicy, chile leaves come from various Capsicum plants and are used as cooking greens, featuring prominently in dishes like Filipino tinola soup.*

### If You Don't Have It

Substitute 1 lb (500 g) chile leaves with:
- 1 lb (500 g) bell pepper leaves
- 1 lb (500 g) mature spinach leaves (less pungent)
- 1 lb (500 g) amaranth leaves (sweeter)

## Chile Oil

*A mainstay of the Chinese kitchen, this condiment is prepared by steeping hot chiles in vegetable oil. Use sparingly. It's often very spicy.*

### If You Don't Have It

Substitute ½ tsp (2 mL) chile oil with:

- ½ tsp (2 mL) hot chili sesame oil (less spicy; adds sesame flavor)
- ½ tsp (2 mL) vegetable oil + pinch of cayenne pepper or dash of hot pepper sauce
- ½ tsp (2 mL) Homemade Chile Oil: Heat 1 cup (250 mL) vegetable oil (or toasted sesame oil for hot chile sesame oil) over medium-high heat until hot. Remove from heat and add 1 to 3 tbsp (15 to 45 mL) crushed red pepper flakes. Cover and set aside for 8 to 24 hours. Strain into a clean jar or bottle and discard pepper flakes. Add whole dried chiles (such as cayenne) to oil for decoration. Store oil in a cool place for up to 6 months. Makes 1 cup (250 mL).

## Chile Paste

*Also known as chili sauce, chile garlic sauce, chile bean paste (when made with fermented beans), and curry paste (when including several spices for curries). Usually refers to one of several Asian chile pastes, condiments made from crushed chiles that are widely used to flavor stir-fries, sauces, marinades, and dressings. May also refer to a Southwestern American chile paste that's used as the basis for chili and other regional Southwestern dishes.*

### If You Don't Have It

Substitute 1 tbsp (15 mL) chile paste with:

- 1 tbsp (15 mL) Homemade Red Chile Paste: Sauté ½ cup (125 mL) chopped shallots and 1 tbsp (15 mL) minced garlic in 1 tbsp (15 mL) oil until lightly browned. Transfer to a blender (with any residual oil) and purée with ¾ cup (175 mL) dried shrimp, ¼ cup (60 mL) dried red chiles (more if you like), 3 tbsp (45 mL) fish sauce, 1 tbsp (15 mL) sugar, 1 tbsp (15 mL) water, 1 tsp (5 mL) tamarind concentrate, and ¼ tsp (1 mL) salt until a paste forms, adding more water as necessary. Refrigerate for up to 3 months. Makes about ¾ cup (175 mL).
- 1 tbsp (15 mL) Homemade Red or Green Curry Paste: Sauté 3 tbsp (45 mL) chopped shallots, 3 tbsp (45 mL) minced garlic, and 1 tbsp (15 mL) chopped galangal and/or ginger in 1 tbsp (15 mL) oil until lightly browned. Transfer to a blender (with any residual oil) and purée with ½ cup (125 mL) dried shrimp, ¼ cup (60 mL) dried red chiles (more if you like), 1 tsp (5 mL) minced lemongrass, 1 tsp (5 mL) cilantro root (or 1 tbsp/15 mL cilantro leaves), 1 tsp (5 mL) ground coriander, 1 tsp (5 mL) ground cumin, ½ tsp (2 mL) chopped lime leaves, ½ tsp (2 mL) black peppercorns, and ½ tsp (2 mL) salt until a paste forms, adding water as necessary. Refrigerate for up to 3 months. Makes about ½ cup (125 mL).

### Chile Paste Varieties

Choose 1 tbsp (15 mL) chile paste from these specific types:

- 1 tbsp (15 mL) Szechuan chile paste (Chinese chile bean paste; medium-hot; made with chiles, garlic, vinegar, and fermented soybeans)

- 1 tbsp (15 mL) kochu chang (Korean chile bean paste; hot and sweet; made with chiles, sugar, fermented soybeans, and salt)
- 1 tbsp (15 mL) tuong ot toi (Vietnamese chile sauce; hot; one of the simplest; usually includes chiles, garlic, vinegar, and salt)
- 1 tbsp (15 mL) sambal oelek (Southeast Asian chile paste; hot; one of the simplest; usually includes chiles, sugar, and salt)
- 1 tbsp (15 mL) sambal bajak (Southeast Asian chile paste; hot; usually includes chiles, sugar, salt, garlic, onion, shrimp paste, nuts, and tamarind)
- 1 tbsp (15 mL) nam prik (Thai chile sauce; hot; usually includes chiles, garlic, lime, fish sauce, shrimp paste, tamarind, and sugar; known as nam prik pao when some of the ingredients are cooked)
- 1 tbsp (15 mL) nam prik kaeng khiao wan (thick, green Thai curry paste or sauce; very hot; usually includes chiles, garlic, lime, lemongrass, shrimp paste, coriander, galangal, sugar, and salt)
- 1 tbsp (15 mL) nam prik kaeng phet (thick red Thai curry paste or sauce; hot; usually includes chiles, garlic, lime, lemongrass, shrimp paste, coriander, galangal, and turmeric)
- 1 tbsp (15 mL) nam prik gaeng kari (thick yellow Thai curry paste or sauce; medium-hot; usually includes chiles, garlic, lime, lemongrass, shrimp paste, coriander, galangal, and turmeric)
- 1 to 3 tsp (5 to 15 mL) hot sauce
- 2 to 3 tsp (10 to 15 mL) harissa
- 1 tbsp (15 mL) berbere
- 1 tsp (5 mL) red pepper flakes
- ½ tsp (2 mL) ground cayenne pepper
- 1½ tsp (7 mL) bean sauce + 1½ tsp (7 mL) chile paste (adds fermented bean flavor)
- 2 small whole chiles + 1 small clove garlic

## Chile Pepper

*Sweet peppers and hot peppers share the same botanical family (Capsicum), but cooks often refer to spicy Capsicum as chile peppers to distinguish them from sweeter varieties.*

## If You Don't Have It

Substitute 1 tsp (5 mL) minced fresh chile pepper with:

- 1 tsp (5 mL) hot pepper sauce
- 1 to 3 tsp (5 to 15 mL) chile paste
- ¼ to ½ tsp (1 to 2 mL) ground cayenne
- ¾ tsp (3 mL) crushed red pepper flakes
- ½ tsp (2 mL) ground chipotle powder (much smokier)
- ½ tsp (2 mL) ground ancho powder (darker; milder)
- 1 tsp (5 mL) paprika (much milder)
- 1 tsp (5 mL) minced fresh bell pepper (much milder)
- 1 tsp (5 mL) chili powder (milder; adds flavors of cumin, oregano, and other spices)
- 1 very small whole dried red chile

*See also* BELL PEPPER; SWEET PEPPER; CHOOSING DRIED CHILES (PAGE 642); CHOOSING FRESH CHILES (PAGE 640).

## Chile Powder

*Also known as pure chile powder. Red chile powder is usually made from dried and ground red New Mexican chiles. Other pure chile powders often include the name of the dried chile, such as ancho powder and chipotle powder.*

### If You Don't Have It

Substitute 1 tsp (5 mL) pure chile powder with:
- ½ to 1 tsp (2 to 5 mL) cayenne pepper (most likely hotter)
- 1 to 2 tsp (5 to 10 mL) paprika (milder)
- 1 tsp (5 mL) chile oil
- 1 tsp (5 mL) chili powder (adds cumin, oregano, and salt)

*See also* CHILI POWDER.

## Chile Sauce

*A spicier version of ketchup that may be seasoned with chiles or chile powder, green bell peppers, and onions.*

### If You Don't Have It

Substitute 1 cup (250 mL) chile sauce with:
- 1 cup (250 mL) ketchup
- 1 cup (250 mL) Homemade Chile Sauce: Mix together 1 cup (250 mL) tomato sauce, ¼ cup (60 mL) brown sugar, 3 tbsp (45 mL) apple cider vinegar, 1 tbsp (15 mL) minced mild green chiles, and ¼ tsp (1 mL) ground allspice. Makes about 1¼ cups (300 mL).

## Chilcostle Chile

*See* CHOOSING DRIED CHILES (PAGE 642).

## Chilhuacle Chile

*See* CHOOSING DRIED CHILES (PAGE 642).

## Chili

*See* BELL PEPPER; CAYENNE PEPPER; CHILE OIL; CHILE POWDER; HOT PEPPER SAUCE; PAPRIKA; CHOOSING DRIED CHILES (PAGE 642); CHOOSING FRESH CHILES (PAGE 640).

## Chili Bean Paste

*See* CHILE PASTE.

## Chili Garlic Sauce

*See* CHILE PASTE.

## Chili Oil

*See* CHILE OIL.

## Chili Powder

*A spice blend used for making chili. Usually includes ground New Mexican chiles, dried oregano, other seasonings, and salt.*

### If You Don't Have It

Substitute 1 tsp (5 mL) chili powder with:
- 1 tsp (5 mL) Homemade Chili Powder: Mix together 1 tbsp (15 mL) paprika, 2 tsp (10 mL) cumin, 2 tsp (10 mL) dried oregano, 1 tsp (5 mL) garlic powder, 1 tsp (5 mL) onion powder, ½ tsp (2 mL) cayenne pepper, and ¼ tsp (1 mL) allspice. Makes about 3 tablespoons (45 mL).
- ½ to 1 tsp (2 to 5 mL) cayenne pepper (hotter)
- 1 to 2 tsp (5 to 10 mL) paprika (milder)
- 1 tsp (5 mL) chile oil (hotter)

## Chiltepín

*See* CHOOSING DRIED CHILES (PAGE 642); CHOOSING FRESH CHILES (PAGE 640).

## Chimichurri

*Argentina's answer to pesto. A thick and slightly spicy parsley-garlic sauce often served with grilled meat.*

### If You Don't Have It

Substitute 1 cup (250 mL) chimichurri with

- 1 cup (250 mL) Homemade Chimichurri: Put 1½ cups (375 mL) packed fresh parsley leaves and 4 garlic cloves in a small food processor and pulse until finely chopped (or finely chop by hand). Add ¼ cup (60 mL) white or red wine vinegar, 3 tbsp (45 mL) minced onion, 2 tsp (10 mL) chopped fresh oregano (or ¼ tsp/1 mL dried), ½ tsp (2 mL) salt, ⅛ to ¼ tsp (0.5 to 1 mL) cayenne pepper, and ⅛ to ¼ tsp (0.5 to 1 mL) ground black pepper. With machine running, gradually add ½ cup (125 mL) olive oil through the feed tube and process to a coarse purée. Makes about 1 cup (250 mL).
- 1 cup (250 mL) pebre (a similar Chilean sauce made with cilantro instead of parsley)
- 1 cup (250 mL) parsley pesto + ½ tsp (2 mL) hot pepper sauce

## China Orange

*See* CALAMONDIN.

## Chinese Almond

*See* APRICOT KERNEL.

## Chinese Apple

*See* POMEGRANATE.

## Chinese Artichoke

*Also known as chorogi, Japanese artichoke, and knot-root. A small Asian tuber with a flavor reminiscent of sunchokes (Jerusalem artichokes).*

### If You Don't Have It

Substitute 1 lb (500 g) Chinese artichokes with:

- 1 lb (500 g) sunchokes
- 1 lb (500 g) salsify

## Chinese Barbecue Sauce

*Also known as char siu sauce. Sweet like American barbecue sauce but based on fermented soybeans instead of tomatoes.*

### If You Don't Have It

Substitute 1 tbsp (15 mL) Chinese barbecue sauce with:

- 1 tbsp (15 mL) Homemade Chinese Barbecue Sauce: Scatter ¼ cup (60 mL) granulated sugar in a small heavy saucepan over medium heat. Let cook undisturbed until the sugar melts and turns amber caramel, 5 to 7 minutes. Meanwhile, stir together ⅓ cup (75 mL) hoisin sauce, 2 tbsp (30 mL) rice vinegar, 2 tbsp (30 mL) soy sauce, 1½ tbsp (22 mL) honey, ¼ cup (60 mL) chopped onion, 2 minced garlic cloves, 1 tbsp (15 mL) grated fresh ginger, and ⅛ tsp (0.5 mL) Chinese five-spice powder. Carefully stir into the

## Chinese Barbecue Sauce (cont'd)

caramel and cook over low heat, stirring now and then, until thickened, 5 to 7 minutes. Makes about 1 cup (250 mL).

- 1 tbsp (15 mL) Chee hou sauce (spicier)
- 1 tbsp (15 mL) Chinese brown bean sauce (spicier)
- 1 tbsp (15 mL) hoisin sauce (less complex)

*See also* HOISIN SAUCE.

## Chinese Black Bean

*See* FERMENTED BLACK BEAN.

## Chinese Broccoli

*Also known as Chinese kale, gai lan, kaii laan, and jie lan. This favored Chinese vegetable, probably a native of the Mediterranean, has narrow green stalks with kohlrabi-like sweetness, topped by fairly large collard-like leaves.*

### If You Don't Have It

Substitute 1 lb (500 g) Chinese broccoli with:

- 1 lb (500 g) broccoli raab (lighter green color; more bitter)
- 1 lb (500 g) broccoli (shorter, thicker stems; much fuller florets)
- 1 lb (500 g) Broccolini™ (lighter green color; skinnier stems)
- 1 lb (500 g) yau choy (paler green stems and leaves; more cabbagey flavor)
- 1 lb (500 g) choy sum or other bok choy (white stems and green leaves; more cabbagey flavor)
- 1 lb (500 g) red chard (sweeter flavor)

*See also* BROCCOLINI.

## Chinese Cabbage

*See* BOK CHOY; NAPA CABBAGE.

## Chinese Celery

*Also known as Asian celery, cutting celery, leaf celery, soup celery, kan tsai, and qin cai. Cooking celery valued for its aromatic green leaves, although the skinny stalks are also cooked as a vegetable and aromatic seasoning.*

### If You Don't Have It

Substitute 1 cup (250 mL) chopped Chinese celery with:

- 1 cup (250 mL) celery (milder flavor)
- 1 cup (250 mL) chopped cardoons (adds mild artichoke flavor)
- 1 cup (250 mL) chopped fennel stalks (adds mild anise flavor)
- 1 cup (250 mL) chopped celery leaves (to replace Chinese celery leaves)
- 1 cup (250 mL) chopped parsley (to replace Chinese celery leaves)
- ½ cup (125 mL) dehydrated celery flakes (for soups and stews; much less flavorful)

## Chinese Chives

*See* GARLIC CHIVES.

## Chinese Date, Dried

*Also known as senjed. When dried, apple-like Chinese dates taste similar to the more familiar medjool dates but less sweet.*

### If You Don't Have It
Substitute 1 cup (250 mL) dried Chinese dates with:
- 1 cup (250 mL) medjool dates (sweeter)
- 1 cup (250 mL) prunes
- 1 cup (250 mL) raisins

## Chinese Date, Fresh

*Also known as Chinese jujube and red date. Pale green fruit with crisp white flesh similar to apples. Chinese dates are more common dried.*

### If You Don't Have It
Substitute 1 cup (250 mL) chopped fresh Chinese dates with:
- 1 cup (250 mL) chopped fresh apples

## Chinese Duck Sauce

*See* PLUM SAUCE.

## Chinese Fermented Black Bean

*See* FERMENTED BLACK BEAN.

## Chinese Five-Spice Powder

*An exciting, aromatic seasoning blend of cinnamon, cloves, fennel seed, star anise, and Szechuan pepper.*

### If You Don't Have It
Substitute 1 tsp (5 mL) Chinese five-spice powder with:
- 1 tsp (5 mL) Homemade Chinese Five-Spice Powder: Mix together 1½ tbsp (22 mL) ground star anise, 2½ tsp (12 mL) ground fennel seed, 1½ tsp (7 mL) cinnamon, ½ tsp (2 mL) ground Szechuan pepper (or salt-free lemon pepper), and ¼ tsp (1 mL) ground cloves. Makes about 3 tablespoons (45 mL).

## Chinese Flowering Cabbage

*See* BOK CHOY.

## Chinese Garlic Stems

*Also known as garlic flower stems, green garlic, shen sum, and suan tai. Long, pencil-thin, green garlic stems with crunchy texture and garlic flavor.*

### If You Don't Have It
Substitute 1 cup (250 mL) chopped Chinese garlic stems with:
- 1 cup (250 mL) chopped garlic chives
- ¾ cup (175 mL) chopped green onions or scallions (green and white parts) + ¼ cup (60 mL) chopped garlic
- 1 cup (250 mL) chopped chives (not crunchy; more onion, less garlic flavor)

| | |
|---|---|
| **Chinese Ginger** | *See* FINGERROOT. |
| **Chinese Gooseberry** | *See* KIWIFRUIT. |
| **Chinese Grapefruit** | *See* PUMMELO. |
| **Chinese Ham** | *See* YUNNAN HAM. |
| **Chinese Jujube** | *See* CHINESE DATE, DRIED; CHINESE DATE, FRESH. |
| **Chinese Kale** | *See* CHINESE BROCCOLI. |
| **Chinese Key** | *See* FINGERROOT. |
| **Chinese Lantern** | *See* CAPE GOOSEBERRY. |
| **Chinese Mustard Cabbage** | *See* BOK CHOY. |
| **Chinese Okra** | *See* LUFFA, ANGLED. |
| **Chinese Parsley** | *See* CILANTRO. |
| **Chinese Pea Pod** | *See* PEAS, EDIBLE POD. |
| **Chinese Pear** | *See* ASIAN PEAR. |
| **Chinese Pickle** | *See* TEA MELON. |
| **Chinese Potato** | *See* ARROWHEAD. |
| **Chinese Red Date** | *See* CHINESE DATE, FRESH. |
| **Chinese Sausage** | *See* LAP CHEONG. |
| **Chinese Spider Strainer** | *See* STRAINER. |

## Chinese Spinach

*See* AMARANTH LEAF.

## Chinese Steelhead

*See* BLACKFISH.

## Chinese Vermicelli

*See* A SNAPSHOT OF ASIAN NOODLES (PAGE 656).

## Chinese White Cabbage

*See* BOK CHOY.

## Chinois

*A cone-shaped metal mesh sieve for straining and puréeing cooked foods. The finest mesh chinois is called a bouillon strainer.*

### If You Don't Have It
Substitute a chinois with:
- fine or medium mesh-strainer

## Chinook Salmon

*See* SALMON.

## Chipolata

*Also known as little fingers. Tiny, well-seasoned pork sausages. In French cuisine, à la chipolata is a garnish of chipolata, chestnuts, and glazed vegetables that accompanies roasts.*

### If You Don't Have It
Substitute 1 lb (500 g) chipolata with:
- 1 lb (500 g) hot links (larger)
- 1 lb (500 g) spicy kielbasa (much larger)
- 1 lb (500 g) highly seasoned sausage
- 1 lb (500 g) Vienna sausage (less flavorful)

## Chipotle

*Also known as chile ahumado, chile meco, morita, and tipico. Smoke-dried red jalapeño peppers commonly sold dried, powdered, or preserved in cans in adobo sauce.*

### If You Don't Have It
Substitute 1 oz (30 g) whole dried chipotle chiles with:
- 1 oz (30 g) pasilla de Oaxaca (smoked, larger, darker color)
- 1 oz (30 g) Cobán (smoked, smaller, hotter)
- 1 oz (30 g) capons (smoked seedless red jalapeño, more expensive)
- 1 oz (30 g) smoked green jalapeños
- 1 oz (30 g) chipotle powder
- 1 oz (30 g) ancho powder (not smoked, milder)

### To Vary the Flavor
Substitute 1 chipotle in adobo sauce with:
- 1 fresh jalapeño pepper (preferably red) + 2 tsp (10 mL) ketchup + ¼ tsp (1 mL) liquid smoke

*See also* CHOOSING DRIED CHILES (PAGE 642).

## Chipped Beef

*Also known as dried beef. Razor-thin slices of salted, smoked dried beef. Basis of the infamous American military staple creamed chipped beef on toast.*

### If You Don't Have It
Substitute 4 oz (125 g) chipped beef with:
- 4 oz (125 g) beef jerky (tougher)
- 4 oz (125 g) biltong (tougher; more complex, spicy flavor)
- 4 oz (125 g) pemmican (tougher; more complex flavor)

### For Better Health
Substitute 4 oz (125 g) chipped beef with:
- 4 oz (125 g) turkey jerky (tougher; leaner)
- 4 oz (125 g) vegetarian jerky (leaner)

## Chive Blossom

*See* PICKING EDIBLE FLOWERS (PAGE 650).

## Chives

*Both the skinny green leaves and violet flowers offer mild onion flavor. To simplify chopping chives, snip them with kitchen scissors.*

### If You Don't Have It
Substitute 1 tbsp (15 mL) chopped fresh chives with:
- 1 tbsp (15 mL) chopped green onions or scallions (green tops only)
- 1 tbsp (15 mL) chopped garlic chives (adds garlic flavor)
- 1 tbsp (15 mL) Chinese garlic stems (adds crunch and garlic flavor)
- 3 tbsp (45 mL) chopped dried chives (much less flavorful)

*See also* GARLIC CHIVES; ONION, GREEN.

## Chocolate, Bittersweet

*Intensely flavored chocolate made with slightly less sugar than semisweet chocolate and at least 35% chocolate liquor, which is the brown paste remaining after cocoa butter is extracted from cocoa beans.*

### If You Don't Have It
Substitute 1 oz (30 g) bittersweet chocolate with:
- 1 oz (30 g) semisweet chocolate (add $\frac{1}{4}$ tsp to $\frac{1}{2}$ tsp/1 to 2 mL unsweetened cocoa powder for richer chocolate flavor)
- $\frac{2}{3}$ oz (20 g) unsweetened chocolate + 2 tsp (10 mL) granulated sugar
- 2 heaping tbsp (30 mL) unsweetened cocoa powder + 1 to $1\frac{1}{3}$ tbsp (15 to 20 mL) granulated sugar + $1\frac{1}{2}$ tsp (7 mL) butter, shortening, or vegetable oil

*See also* COCOA NIBS; COCOA POWDER, UNSWEETENED; CUPUAÇU.

## Chocolate, Couverture

*Dark "covering" chocolate with at least 32% cocoa butter that is used by pastry chefs to coat candies and glaze cakes.*

### If You Don't Have It
Substitute 1 oz (30 g) couverture chocolate with:
- 1 oz (30 g) bittersweet or semisweet chocolate + $\frac{1}{4}$ to $\frac{1}{2}$ tsp (1 to 2 mL) butter, shortening, or vegetable oil
- 1 oz (30 g) chocolate confectionery coating (contains no cocoa butter; less rich taste and mouth-feel; melts at a higher temperature)

*See also* CONFECTIONERY COATING.

## Chocolate Curls

*Also known as chocolate shavings. Made by warming a thick chocolate bar or square then shaving curls from it with a vegetable peeler.*

### If You Don't Have It

Substitute ½ cup (125 mL) chocolate curls (for garnishing desserts) with:

- ⅓ cup (75 mL) grated chocolate
- 1 to 3 tbsp (15 to 45 mL) sifted cocoa powder (for dusting)

## Chocolate-Hazelnut Spread

*See* GIANDUJA.

## Chocolate Liqueur

*Includes brands such as Godiva, Mozart, and Haagen Daz.*

### If You Don't Have It

Substitute 3 tbsp (45 mL) chocolate liqueur with:

- 3 tbsp (45 mL) water + ¾ tsp (3 mL) chocolate extract
- 3 tbsp (45 mL) chocolate syrup (thicker; sweeter; nonalcoholic)

### To Vary the Flavor

Substitute 3 tbsp (45 mL) chocolate liqueur with:

- 3 tbsp (45 mL) crème de cacao (sweeter)
- 3 tbsp (45 mL) Chéri Suisse (combines chocolate and cherry flavors)
- 3 tbsp (45 mL) Vandermint (combines chocolate and mint flavors)
- 3 tbsp (45 mL) Tiramisù liqueur (combines chocolate, coffee, and almond flavors)
- 3 tbsp (45 mL) coffee liqueur
- 3 tbsp (45 mL) almond liqueur
- 3 tbsp (45 mL) hazelnut liqueur

## Chocolate, Mexican

*Also known as Ibarra chocolate, a popular brand. A grainy sweetened chocolate flavored with cinnamon, almonds, and vanilla.*

1 tablet = 3.1 oz (93 g)

### If You Don't Have It

Substitute 1 oz (30 g) Mexican chocolate with:

- 1 oz (30 g) semisweet chocolate, + ½ tsp (2 mL) ground cinnamon + 1 drop almond extract + 1 drop vanilla extract
- 1 tbsp (15 mL) cocoa powder (for mole sauces)

## Chocolate, Milk

*Similar to semisweet chocolate but with more sugar, a minimum of 10% chocolate liquor, and at least 12% added milk solids.*

### If You Don't Have It

Substitute 6 oz (175 g) milk chocolate with:

- 6 oz (175 g) semisweet or white chocolate
- 6 oz (175 g) sweet chocolate

## Chocolate Pudding Fruit

*See* SAPOTE, WHITE.

## Chocolate, Semisweet

*Sweetened chocolate made with slightly more sugar than bittersweet chocolate and at least 35% chocolate liquor (the brown paste remaining after cocoa butter is extracted from cocoa beans). If the chocolate is to be melted, chips, squares, and bars are generally interchangeable. However, chips contain stabilizers that help them retain their shape during baking. These stabilizers may create a less velvety texture in delicate chocolate sauces and custards.*

> 6 oz (175 g) = 1 cup (250 mL) chips

### If You Don't Have It
Substitute 1 oz (30 g) semisweet chocolate with:
- 1 oz (30 g) bittersweet chocolate (richer chocolate flavor)
- ½ oz (15 g) unsweetened chocolate + 1 tbsp (15 mL) granulated sugar
- 3 tbsp (45 mL) unsweetened cocoa powder + 1 to 1½ tbsp (15 to 22 mL) granulated sugar + 1½ tsp (7 mL) butter, shortening, or vegetable oil

### To Vary the Flavor
Substitute 6 oz (175 g) or 1 cup (250 mL) semisweet chocolate chips with:
- 6 oz (175 g) chocolate bar or squares, chopped into chunks (chunks from untempered chocolate bars may lose their shape more than chocolate chips)
- 6 oz (175 g) mint-flavored semisweet chocolate chips
- 6 oz (175 g) milk chocolate chips
- 6 oz (175 g) M&Ms
- 6 oz (175 g) peanut butter chips
- 6 oz (175 g) butterscotch chips
- 6 oz (175 g) cinnamon chips
- 6 oz (175 g) white chocolate chips
- 1 cup (250 mL) chopped nuts

### For Better Health
Substitute 6 oz (175 g) or 1 cup (250 mL) semisweet chocolate chips with:
- 3 oz (90 g) or ½ cup (125 mL) semisweet mini chocolate chips (for better distribution throughout baked goods)
- 6 oz (175 g) or 1 cup (250 mL) carob chips
- 1 cup (250 mL) raisins
- 1 cup (250 mL) chocolate-covered raisins
- 9 tbsp (135 mL) unsweetened cocoa powder + 7 tbsp (105 mL) sugar + 1 tbsp (15 mL) butter, shortening, or vegetable oil (when needed to replace melted semisweet chocolate chips; for same fat content as semisweet chips, use 3 tbsp/45 mL butter, shortening, or oil)

*See also* CUPUAÇU.

## Chocolate Shavings

*See* CHOCOLATE CURLS.

## Chocolate, Sweet

*Also known by some brands as sweet German chocolate. Similar to semisweet chocolate but containing more sugar and a minimum of 15% chocolate liquor.*

### If You Don't Have It
Substitute 1 oz (30 g) sweet chocolate with:
- 1 oz (30 g) semisweet or bittersweet chocolate (richer chocolate and less sweet flavor)
- ½ oz (15 g) unsweetened chocolate + 4 tsp (20 mL) granulated sugar
- 3 tbsp (45 mL) unsweetened cocoa powder + 4 tsp (20 mL) granulated sugar + 1 tbsp (15 mL) butter, shortening, or vegetable oil

## Chocolate Syrup

*A sweet syrup made from cocoa powder, corn syrup, and other flavorings and thickeners. Available in cans and jars in thin or thick versions. Often used on desserts or to make chocolate milk.*

### If You Don't Have It
Substitute 1 cup (250 mL) chocolate syrup with:
- 1 cup (250 mL) Homemade Chocolate Syrup: Whisk together ½ cup (125 mL) light corn syrup and ½ cup (125 mL) unsweetened cocoa powder (preferably Dutch-process) in a medium saucepan. (Mixture will be very thick.) Whisk in 1 cup (250 mL) milk, 1⅓ cups (325 mL) granulated sugar, and ⅛ to ¼ tsp (0.5 to 1 mL) salt. Bring to a gentle boil over medium-high heat. Reduce heat to medium-low and simmer until thickened to thin syrup, 5 to 10 minutes. Mixture will thicken further as it cools. Remove from heat and stir in 3 tbsp (45 mL) butter and ½ tsp (2 mL) vanilla extract. Let cool and refrigerate in a glass jar for up to 1 week. Makes about 1½ cups (375 mL).
- ½ to 1 cup (125 to 250 mL) crème de cacao (adds alcohol)

## Chocolate, Unsweetened

*Also known as baking chocolate or bitter chocolate. Pure solidified chocolate liquor containing 50 to 58% cocoa butter (the natural fat in cocoa beans).*

### If You Don't Have It
Substitute 1 oz (30 g) or 1 square unsweetened chocolate with:
- 3 tbsp (45 mL) unsweetened cocoa powder + 1 tbsp (15 mL) butter, shortening, or vegetable oil (dissolve cocoa in liquid that is in recipe)
- 1½ to 2 oz (45 to 60 g) bittersweet or semisweet chocolate (decrease sugar in recipe by 3 tbsp/45 mL and butter by ½ tsp/2 mL)

### For Better Health
- 3 tbsp (45 mL) unsweetened cocoa powder + 3 tbsp (45 mL) water
- 3 tbsp (45 mL) carob powder + 3 tbsp (45 mL) water

*See also* CHOCOLATE, BITTERSWEET; COCOA POWDER, UNSWEETENED; CUPUAÇU.

## Chocolate, White

*Look for white chocolate that contains cocoa butter as the only type of fat. Cheap imitations are made with palm kernel oil or other vegetable fats and little or no cocoa butter.*

### If You Don't Have It
Substitute 1 oz (30 g) white chocolate with:
- 1 oz (30 g) milk chocolate (adds chocolate color and flavor)

## Chokecherry

*These North American wild cherries are far too sour (hence the name) to eat out-of-hand but are terrific simmered into jams and jellies.*

### If You Don't Have It
Substitute 1 lb (500 g) chokecherries (for jams and jellies) with:
- 1 lb (500 g) sour cherries
- 1 lb (500 g) cranberries

## Chop Suey Vegetable

*See* CHRYSANTHEMUM GREENS.

## Chop Suey Yam

*See* JICAMA.

## Chopsui Potato

*See* JICAMA.

## Chorizo

*Very flavorful, usually red, and often spicy-hot coarse-ground pork sausage. There are dozens of variations on the theme, two most common of which are Mexican chorizo, a fresh pork sausage, and Spanish chorizo, a dry-cured pork sausage that can be sliced and eaten cold like salami and pepperoni.*

8 oz (250 g) = 10 inches (25 cm) = 20 slices (½ inch/1 cm)

### If You Don't Have It
Substitute 1 lb (500 g) chorizo with:
- 1 lb (500 g) andouille
- 1 lb (500 g) merguez
- 1 lb (500 g) spicy kielbasa
- 1 lb (500 g) hot Italian sausage
- 1 lb (500 g) hot links

### Chorizo Varieties
Choose 1 lb (500 g) chorizo from these varieties:
- 1 lb (500 g) fresh Mexican chorizo (spicy; must be cooked)
- 1 lb (500 g) fresh Creole/Cajun chaurice (spicy; must be cooked)
- 1 lb (500 g) cured Spanish chorizo (less spicy; smoked; can be eaten cold)
- 1 lb (500 g) cured Portuguese chouriço or linguiça (less spicy; less paprika than Spanish chorizo; smoked; can be eaten cold)

## Chorogi

*See* CHINESE ARTICHOKE.

**Choron Sauce**

*See* BEARNAISE SAUCE.

**Chowder Clam**

*See* SWAPPING CLAMS (PAGE 645).

**Choy Sum**

*See* BOK CHOY; YAU CHOY.

**Christian IX**

*See* DANBO.

**Christmas Melon**

*See* SANTA CLAUS MELON.

**Chrysanthemum Greens**

*Also known as chop suey vegetable and cooking chrysanthemum. The edible, yet bitter, species of the common decorative flower is a popular leafy green in Asian cooking.*

### If You Don't Have It
Substitute 1 lb (500 g) chrysanthemum greens with:
- 1 lb (500 g) arugula
- 1 lb (500 g) watercress
- 1 lb (500 g) spinach (mature spinach will approximate bitterness better; add pepper for more bite)
- 1 lb (500 g) Belgian endive, dandelion greens, escarole, or radicchio (for salads)

**Chufa**

*Also known as chufa nuts, earth almonds, earthnuts, and tiger nuts. Small tuberous roots of an African sedge plant, chufa "nuts" are popular in Spain and Mexico.*

### If You Don't Have It
Substitute 1 cup (250 mL) chufa with:
- 1 cup (250 mL) chestnuts
- 1 cup (250 mL) almonds (for horchata)

**Chu Hou Paste**

*See* CHEE HOU SAUCE.

**Churros**

*See* DOUGHNUT.

**Chutney**

*In Indian cooking, a spicy relish made from a myriad of fruits or vegetables, spices, and aromatics. Types vary greatly by region. British colonials embraced chutney with enthusiasm and popularized a jam-like sweet-and-sour version, the most well-known of which is made with mango.*

### If You Don't Have It
Substitute 1 cup (250 mL) chutney with:
- 1 cup (250 mL) fruit salsa (may be chunkier; mash or chop to coarse purée if you like; add sugar or lime juice to sweeten or sour the salsa to taste)
- 1 cup (250 mL) dried fruit compote (may be chunkier; mash or chop to coarse purée if you like; may be sweeter; add vinegar, lemon or lime juice to sour it)
- 1 cup (250 mL) marmalade (add lime juice, salt, and red pepper flakes to taste)
- 1 cup (250 mL) Asian sweet chili sauce (add coarsely puréed mango or other fruit if you like)

## Chymosin

*See* RENNET.

## Ciabatta

The name of this Italian bread means "slipper." The loaf is about 8 inches (20 cm) long with a light, crispy crust.

### If You Don't Have It

Substitute 1 lb (500 g) ciabatta with:
- 1 lb (500 g) other Italian bread
- 1 lb (500 g) French bread

*See also* ITALIAN BREAD.

## Ciambellone

Rich, ring-shaped Italian Easter cake traditionally flavored with lemon zest.

### If You Don't Have It

Substitute 1 lb (500 g) ciambellone with:
- 1 lb (500 g) lemon pound cake
- 1 lb (500 g) lemon poppy seed cake
- 1 lb (500 g) panettone

## Cicely

Also known as Spanish chervil, sweet chervil, and sweet cicely. A ferny-leaf herb with an anise flavor more assertive than chervil. Flavors desserts in Scandinavia.

### If You Don't Have It

Substitute 1 tbsp (15 mL) chopped fresh cicely with:
- 1 tbsp (15 mL) chopped fresh chervil (milder anise flavor)
- 1 tbsp (15 mL) chopped fresh tarragon (stronger anise flavor)
- 1 tbsp (15 mL) chopped fresh fennel leaves
- 1 tbsp (15 mL) chopped fresh fines herbes (usually includes chervil, chives, parsley, and tarragon)
- 1 tbsp (15 mL) chopped fresh parsley

*See also* CHERVIL.

## Cider

*See* APPLE CIDER.

## Cider Brandy

*See* APPLE BRANDY.

## Cider Spirits

*See* APPLE BRANDY.

## Cider Vinegar

*See* CHOOSING VINEGAR (PAGE 674).

## Cider Whiskey

*See* APPLE BRANDY.

## Cilantro

Also known as fresh coriander and Chinese parsley. The distinctively flavored leaves of the coriander plant are said by supporters to taste of citrus

### If You Don't Have It

Substitute 1 tbsp (15 mL) chopped fresh cilantro with:
- 1 tbsp (15 mL) chopped fresh culantro (sawleaf herb)
- 1 tbsp (15 mL) chopped fresh rice paddy herb
- 1 tbsp (15 mL) chopped fresh parsley
- 1 tbsp (15 mL) chopped fresh mint + dash of lemon juice
- 1 tbsp (15 mL) chopped fresh basil or lemon basil

*and spice. Detractors compare the flavor to bug-infested linens and soap. The herb is essential in many Asian and South American cuisines, and alone among European kitchens, in Portugal.*

*See also* CORIANDER SEED.

## Cime di Rapa

*See* BROCCOLI RAAB.

## Cinnamon

*What is labeled as "cinnamon" in many North American markets is actually cassia, a very similar spice. True cinnamon (also known as Ceylon cinnamon, Seychelles Islands cinnamon and Mexican canela) has a lighter brown color compared with the darker, more reddish cassia. True cinnamon also has a more delicate yet more complex aroma. Curiously, in a sensory study conducted by Alan R. Hirsch, MD of the Smell & Taste Treatment and Research Foundation, the aroma of cinnamon buns ranked number one as a sexual turn-on for male subjects.*

1 3-inch (7.5 cm) stick =
½ tsp (2 mL) ground

### If You Don't Have It
Substitute 1 cinnamon stick (3 inches/7.5 cm) with:
- ½ tsp (2 mL) ground cinnamon (for mulling, wrap ground cinnamon in cheesecloth or coffee filter and tie with kitchen string or clean twist-tie)
- ⅛ tsp (0.5 mL) cinnamon extract

### To Vary the Flavor
Substitute ½ tsp (2 mL) ground cinnamon with:
- ¼ to ½ tsp (1 to 2 mL) ground cardamom (more musky aroma)
- ¼ to ½ tsp (1 to 2 mL) ground allspice
- ¼ to ½ tsp (1 to 2 mL) ground nutmeg
- ½ tsp (2 mL) apple pie spice (adds nutmeg and allspice)
- ½ tsp (2 mL) pumpkin pie spice (adds nutmeg and ginger)

### Cinnamon Varieties
Substitute ½ tsp (2 mL) ground cinnamon with:
- ½ tsp (2 mL) Ceylon cinnamon, Mexican canela, or Seychelles Islands cinnamon (lighter color than the more common cassia; more delicate yet more complex aroma)
- ½ tsp (2 mL) cassia (darker, redder color than Ceylon cinnamon or Mexican canela; slightly more aggressive, almost bitter flavor)

## Cinnamon Extract

*A concentrated cinnamon flavoring.*

### If You Don't Have It
Substitute ½ tsp (2 mL) cinnamon extract with:
- ¹⁄₁₆ to ⅛ tsp (0.25 to 0.5 mL) cinnamon oil
- 1½ to 2 tsp (7 to 10 mL) ground cinnamon (adds color of ground spice to recipe)

## Cinnamon Oil

*A flavoring derived from the pods of the cinnamon tree.*

### If You Don't Have It
Substitute ⅛ tsp (0.5 mL) cinnamon oil with:
- ½ tsp (2 mL) cinnamon extract

## Cinnamon Sugar

See SUGAR, GRANULATED.

## Cipollini

See ONION, LITTLE.

## Citron

*A large citrus fruit that looks like a green-tinged bumpy lemon. The Buddha's hand, or fingered, citron is ribbed and more elongated.*

### If You Don't Have It
Substitute 1 tbsp (15 mL) citron peel with:
- 2½ tsp (12 mL) lemon peel + a pinch of cinnamon + a pinch of black pepper

See also CITRUS PEEL, CANDIED.

## Citrónge

See ORANGE LIQUEUR.

## Citrus Peel, Candied

*Varying amounts of the white pith are left on candied citrus peels to add bitterness.*

### If You Don't Have It
Substitute ½ cup (125 mL) candied citrus peel with:
- ½ cup (125 mL) Homemade Candied Citrus Peel: Using a vegetable peeler, remove the outer zest (and some of the white pith if you like for bitterness) from 3 grapefruits, 4 oranges or citrons, 5 lemons, or 6 limes (reserve fruit for another use). Put the zest in a medium saucepan and cover with cold water. Bring to a boil over medium heat and simmer for 20 minutes (40 minutes for grapefruit). Drain then soak in cold water until cooled. Slice the peels lengthwise into strips. Bring 3 cups (750 mL) granulated sugar and 1½ cups (375 mL) water to a boil in a medium saucepan, stirring to dissolve the sugar. Add peels and simmer over medium-low heat, stirring occasionally, until strips are translucent and the syrup thickens, about 30 minutes. Remove from heat and let cool overnight in the syrup. Store refrigerated in the syrup. Or remove with a slotted spoon and drip away excess syrup, then coat with sugar and let dry. Makes about ¾ cup (175 mL).
- 1 tsp (5 mL) grated fresh citrus peel + ½ cup (125 mL) golden raisins (for panettone and fruit cakes)

### To Vary the Flavor
- ½ cup (125 mL) soft crystallized ginger

## Citrus Peel, Dried

*Fresh citrus peels retain much more aromatic oil*

### If You Don't Have It
Substitute 1 tsp (5 mL) dried citrus peel with:
- Homemade Dried Citrus Peel: Use a citrus zester or

*than dried. But dried peels can be useful in dry spice mixes.*

vegetable peeler to remove the outer zest (but not the bitter white pith) from 1 organic or unsprayed orange, lemon, lime, tangerine, grapefruit, or other citrus. Let zest dry until hard, 3 to 4 days. Store in an airtight container.
- ½ to 1 tsp (2 to 5 mL) fresh citrus peel (moister; brighter aroma)
- ½ tsp (2 mL) citrus extract (adds liquid)

## Citrus Zester

*See* ZESTER.

## Clam

*Edible bivalves that are most appreciated in North America, a legacy that Native Americans passed on to European settlers.*

| |
|---|
| 1 lb (500 g) pismo, surf, or geoduck clams = 2 to 3 |
| 1 lb (500 g) butter, chowder, or manila clams = 3 to 4 |
| 1 lb (500 g) cherrystone, mahogany, or razor clams = 4 to 5 |
| 1 lb (500 g) littlenecks or steamers = 10 to 12 |
| 3 dozen medium in shell = 4 cups (1 L) shucked |

### If You Don't Have It
Substitute 1 lb (500 g) clams with:
- 1 lb (500 g) mussels (more delicate)
- 1 lb (500 g) cockles
- 1 lb (500 g) oysters
- 1 lb (500 g) scallops
- 1 lb (500 g) abalone (tougher)

*See also* SWAPPING CLAMS (PAGE 645).

## Clam Juice

*To reduce the saltiness of bottled clam juice, replace the amount called for with half clam juice and half water.*

### If You Don't Have It
Substitute 1 cup (250 mL) clam juice with:
- 1 cup (250 mL) fish stock
- 1 cup (250 mL) dashi
- ½ cup (125 mL) chicken broth + ½ cup (125 mL) water
- 1 cup (250 mL) oyster liquor

## Clam Knife

*A specially designed cutting implement for prying open clam shells.*

### If You Don't Have It
Substitute a clam knife with:
- another thick, dull knife such as small spreading knife or spackling knife
- microwaving the clams until they open (about 20 seconds)
- steaming the clams until they open (about 4 minutes)

## Claret

*See* WINE, RED.

---

## Clary

*See* PICKING EDIBLE FLOWERS (PAGE 650).

---

## Clay Pot

*A cooking container fashioned from unglazed earthenware. Because it is porous, it must be soaked in water before each use.*

### If You Don't Have It

Substitute a clay pot with:
- a deep casserole dish (reduce oven temperature by about 100°F/50°C and cooking time by about 30 minutes)
- a Dutch oven (reduce oven temperature by about 100°F/50°C and cooking time by about 30 minutes)

*See also* CLOCHE.

---

## Clear Jel

*This modified cornstarch is the secret to perfect pie fillings. Unlike regular cornstarch, it helps prevent thickened mixtures from weeping and it tolerates high temperatures (in canning for instance). The instant version thickens without heating and is freezer-stable; you can see it at work in many commercial instant pudding mixes.*

### If You Don't Have It

Substitute 3 tbsp (45 mL) Clear Jel with:
- 3 tbsp (45 mL) cornstarch
- ¼ cup (60 mL) tapioca flour
- ⅓ cup (75 mL) all-purpose flour

---

## Cleaver

*The blade of this ax-like knife can be used to chop everything from vegetables to bone-in poultry. The flat side can be a tenderizer or a crushing tool for garlic.*

### If You Don't Have It

Substitute a cleaver with:
- a sturdy chef's knife
- a small, clean, hand-held ax

---

## Clementine

*See* MANDARIN ORANGE.

---

## Cloche

*A dome-shaped clay oven used for baking a single loaf of bread. The moisture-trapping clay simulates baking bread in a stone or brick oven.*

### If You Don't Have It

Substitute a 10- by 5-inch (25 by 12.5 cm) cloche clay oven with:
- 5-quart (5 L) 10- by 4-inch (25 by 10 cm) cast-iron Dutch oven with a lid (for bread baking)

*See also* PAN SIZE EQUIVALENTS (PAGE 678).

## Cloudberry

*Also known as bake-apple berry, mountain berry, and yellow berry. A deliciously tart golden berry related to the raspberry. It grows wild in upper North America and Europe.*

### If You Don't Have It

Substitute 1 cup (250 mL) cloudberries with:
- 1 cup (250 mL) yellow raspberries (sweeter)
- 1 cup (250 mL) red raspberries (red color; sweeter)
- 1 cup (250 mL) loganberries (red color; slightly sweeter)
- 1 cup (250 mL) blackberries (purple color; large seeds)

## Cloud Ear

*See* SHUFFLING MUSHROOMS (PAGE 654).

## Clove

*Named after the Latin word for nail, clavus, which it resembles, this brown spice is the dried, flower bud of a tropical evergreen.*

> 1 tsp whole = 25 cloves
>
> 35 to 40 whole cloves = 1 tsp (5 mL) ground

### If You Don't Have It

Substitute ½ tsp (2 mL) ground cloves with:
- ½ tsp (2 mL) ground allspice

## Clove Pepper

*See* ALLSPICE.

## Club Soda

*See* SODA WATER.

## Coalfish

*See* COBIA.

## Cobia

*Also known as black kingfish, black salmon, coalfish, and lemonfish. Cobia typically run 3 to 4 feet (91 to 122 cm) in length, and weigh 30 to 50 lbs (14 to 23 kg). Torpedo-shaped fish resembling a mackerel in looks and rich taste but with mild, firm white flesh. Adult cobias in the wild average about 40 lbs (18 kg) but the fish is increasingly farmed and harvested at around 4 to 5 lbs (2 to 2.5 kg).*

### If You Don't Have It

Substitute 1 lb (500 g) cobia with:
- 1 lb (500 g) swordfish
- 1 lb (500 g) shark
- 1 lb (500 g) monkfish
- 1 lb (500 g) tuna
- 1 lb (500 g) mahi-mahi
- 1 lb (500 g) Spanish mackerel

## Cockle

*These gritty bivalves must be well washed to rid them of sand.*

### If You Don't Have It

Substitute 1 lb (500 g) cockles with:

- 1 lb (500 g) clams
- 1 lb (500 g) mussels
- 1 lb (500 g) oysters
- 1 lb (500 g) scallops
- 1 lb (500 g) abalone (tougher)

## Cocktail Sauce

*The classic condiment to accompany chilled shrimp is a mixture of ketchup or chili sauce, prepared horseradish, lemon juice, and Tabasco sauce.*

### If You Don't Have It

Substitute 1 cup (250 mL) cocktail sauce with:

- 1 cup (250 mL) Homemade Cocktail Sauce: Mix together 1 cup (250 mL) ketchup (or, for better flavor, $\frac{1}{2}$ cup/125 mL ketchup and $\frac{1}{2}$ cup/125 mL chili sauce), $\frac{1}{4}$ cup (60 mL) prepared horseradish, 1 tbsp (15 mL) lemon juice and dash of hot pepper sauce. Makes about $1\frac{1}{4}$ cups (300 mL).

## Cocktail Strainer

*Also known as a bar strainer. The two main types are the Hawthorn, a flat metal disc with stabilizing prongs and a metal spring around the rim, and the Julep, which resembles a large rounded spoon perforated with holes. Both do a fine job of straining the ice from shaken or stirred cocktails.*

### If You Don't Have It

Substitute a cocktail strainer with:

- A small, clean mesh strainer nestled into the top of the shaker or glass
- A second smaller shaker or glass positioned bottom-down over the ice in the main shaker or glass
- Slotted spoon

## Cocoa Mix

*Also known as instant cocoa. A mixture of unsweetened cocoa powder, confectioner's (icing) sugar, and powdered milk for making hot cocoa.*

### If You Don't Have It

Substitute $\frac{1}{4}$ cup (60 mL) cocoa mix with:

- 3 tbsp (45 mL) powdered milk + $1\frac{1}{2}$ tbsp (22 mL) confectioner's (icing) sugar + $1\frac{1}{2}$ tsp (7 mL) unsweetened cocoa powder + $1\frac{1}{2}$ tsp (7 mL) powdered nondairy creamer
- 4 oz (125 g) Mexican chocolate

## Cocoa Nibs

*Most chocolate products are made by fermenting, drying, roasting, and then grinding the beans of the cacao tree. Before grinding, the beans can also be lightly crushed to make pure cacao (cocoa) nibs, which have a deliciously bitter chocolate crunch.*

> 1 lb (500 g) =
> 4 cups (1 L)

### If You Don't Have It

Substitute 1 cup (250 mL) cocoa nibs with:
- 1 cup (250 mL) roasted cocoa beans, lightly crushed
- 1 cup (250 mL) finely chopped bittersweet chocolate
- 1 cup (250 mL) small bittersweet chocolate chips

### To Vary the Flavor

Substitute $\frac{1}{2}$ tsp (2 mL) ground cinnamon with:
- 1 cup (250 mL) roasted coffee beans, lightly crushed
- 1 cup (250 mL) toasted nuts
- 1 cup (250 mL) raisins

*See also* CHOCOLATE, BITTERSWEET.

## Cocoa Powder, Unsweetened

*Dried, powdered chocolate liquor with 10 to 22% cocoa butter. Natural (nonalkalized) cocoa includes the natural acidity of cocoa beans. Dutch-process cocoa has an alkali added to neutralize the acidity, mellowing the flavor.*

> 1 oz (30 g) =
> $\frac{1}{4}$ cup (60 mL)

### If You Don't Have It

Substitute 3 tbsp (45 mL) unsweetened natural cocoa powder with:
- 1 oz (30 g) unsweetened chocolate (decrease fat in recipe by 1 tbsp/15 mL)
- 2 oz (60 g) semisweet chocolate (decrease fat in recipe by 1 tbsp/15 mL and sugar in recipe by 3 tbsp/45 mL)
- 3 heaping tbsp (45 mL) carob powder (reduce sugar by 1 tbsp/15 mL and increase fat by 1 tbsp/15 mL)
- 3 tbsp (45 mL) Dutch-process cocoa powder + $\frac{1}{8}$ tsp (0.5 mL) cream of tartar (or in lieu of adding cream of tartar, omit baking soda from recipe)

*See also* CHOCOLATE, UNSWEETENED; CUPUAÇU.

## Coconut Butter

*The difference between coconut oil and coconut butter is similar to the difference between peanut oil and peanut butter. Coconut oil is extracted from coconut meat, while coconut butter is dried and puréed coconut meat.*

### If You Don't Have It

Substitute $\frac{1}{2}$ cup (125 mL) coconut butter with:
- $\frac{1}{2}$ cup (125 mL) Homemade Coconut Butter: Purée 2 cups (500 mL) unsweetened dessicated coconut (flakes or shreds) in a food processor to a fine paste. Makes about $1\frac{3}{4}$ cups (425 mL).
- $\frac{1}{2}$ cup (125 mL) vegetable shortening + $\frac{1}{4}$ tsp (1 mL) coconut extract
- $\frac{1}{2}$ cup (125 mL) unsalted butter + $\frac{1}{4}$ tsp (1 mL) coconut extract (adds butter flavor)

*See also* SUBSTITUTING OILS (PAGE 658).

## Coconut Cream

*Flavoring liquid made by simmering and straining 4 parts coconut meat and 1 part water or milk.*

### If You Don't Have It
Substitute 1 cup (250 mL) coconut cream with:
- 1 cup (250 mL) coconut milk (especially the thicker cream that rises to the top of coconut milk)
- 1 cup (250 mL) light whipping cream or heavy whipping cream (35% butterfat) + ½ tsp (2 mL) coconut extract

### For Better Health
Substitute 1 cup (250 mL) coconut cream with:
- 1 cup (250 mL) reduced-fat coconut milk (less rich; thinner consistency)

*See also* CREAM OF COCONUT; SUBSTITUTING OILS (PAGE 658).

## Coconut Egg Jam

*Also known as kaya. The Southeast Asian answer to Nutella, coconut egg jam is rich coconut curd often available in jars and cans. It is irresistible on toast.*

### If You Don't Have It
Substitute ½ cup (125 mL) coconut egg jam with:
- ½ cup (125 mL) Homemade Coconut Egg Jam: First, sterilize 4 half-pint (250 mL) mason jars or other glass jars and their lids: put them in a large saucepan, cover with water, bring to a boil, and boil gently for 10 minutes. Turn off the heat and let the jars and lids sit in the hot water. Combine 1½ cups (375 mL) granulated sugar, 3 tbsp (45 mL) light (white) corn syrup, 3 tbsp (45 mL) water, and ¼ tsp (1 mL) fresh lemon juice in a small heavy saucepan. Put over medium-low heat and cook without stirring until the sugar dissolves. Increase heat to medium-high and bring to a boil. Reduce heat to medium and attach a candy thermometer to inside of pan. Boil gently until mixture turns from clear to medium amber (about 350°F/180°C on the thermometer), 8 to 10 minutes. Do not stir. Every 5 minutes or so, dip a pastry brush in hot water and brush down the inside of the pan to dissolve any sugar crystals and prevent the caramel from crystallizing. Immediately remove from heat and let cool slightly. Put on oven mitts, stand back and stir in 3 tbsp (45 mL) hot water to thin the mixture and prevent hardening (hot mixture will sputter). Set aside until cool to the touch. In the bowl of an electric mixer, beat together 10 eggs and 1⅔ cups (400 mL) fresh or thick canned coconut milk. Pour into the top of a double boiler and place over but not touching simmering water. Gradually scrape in the cooled caramel, stirring gently until incorporated. Cook and stir gently until the mixture thickens to the consistency of pudding, 20 to 30 minutes. Remove from the heat and strain through a medium-mesh sieve into a heatproof bowl. Divide the hot curd among the hot sterilized jars, cover with the lids, and let cool to room temperature. Store unopened in the refrigerator up to 6 months. After opening, keep refrigerated for up to 3 weeks. Makes about 3½ cups (875 mL).
- ½ cup (125 mL) coconut butter (not coconut oil)

## To Vary the Flavor

Substitute ½ cup (125 mL) coconut egg jam with:

- ½ cup (125 mL) lemon curd
- ½ cup (125 mL) nutella

## Coconut, Fresh

*The shaggy brown coconut sold in markets is actually only the hard stone center of the fruit of the coconut palm. The outer husk is removed to be used for other purposes.*

1 medium coconut =
4 to 5 cups (1 to 1.25 L)
shredded

6 cups (1.5 L) shredded =
1 lb (500 g)

### If You Don't Have It

Substitute 1 cup (250 mL) fresh shredded coconut with:

- 1⅓ cups (325 mL) packaged unsweetened shredded coconut

## Coconut Juice

*See* COCONUT WATER.

## Coconut Milk

*Flavoring liquid made by simmering, and then straining, equal parts coconut meat and water.*

### If You Don't Have It

Substitute 1 cup (250 mL) fresh coconut milk with:

- 1 cup (250 mL) canned coconut milk
- 1 cup (250 mL) coconut cream (richer)
- ¼ cup (60 mL) powdered coconut cream + ¾ to 1 cup (175 to 250 mL) boiling water or milk
- 1 cup (250 mL) Homemade Coconut Milk: Pour 1 cup (250 mL) boiling water or milk over 1 packed cup (250 mL) fresh grated coconut. Let stand for 30 minutes. Then pour the mixture into cheesecloth or a clean damp cloth and squeeze the liquid into a bowl. Discard the grated coconut. Makes about 1 cup (250 mL).

### For Better Health

Substitute 1 cup (250 mL) coconut milk with:

- 1 cup (250 mL) reduced-fat canned coconut milk
- ½ cup (125 mL) coconut milk + ½ cup (125 mL) coconut water
- 1 cup (250 mL) milk or half-and-half cream + ½ tsp (2 mL) coconut extract

*See also* COCONUT WATER.

## Coconut Oil

*See* COCONUT BUTTER; SUBSTITUTING OILS (PAGE 658).

## Coconut Rum

*White rum flavored with coconut. Malibu and CocoRibe are popular brands.*

### If You Don't Have It

Substitute 1 cup (250 mL) coconut rum with:
- 1 cup (250 mL) white rum + ½ tsp (2 mL) coconut extract
- ⅞ cup (220 mL) white rum + 2 tbsp (30 mL) coconut milk or coconut cream (adds fat)

## Coconut Shoots

*New leaves at the top of the coconut palm are tender, white, and pleasantly sweet.*

### If You Don't Have It

Substitute 1 cup (250 mL) coconut shoots with:
- 1 cup (250 mL) bamboo shoots (less sweet)

## Coconut, Shredded

*Also known as flaked coconut.*

| 7 oz (210 g) shredded or flaked = 3 cups (750 mL) |
| 2 oz (60 g) shredded or flaked = ½ cup (125 mL) |
| 3.5 oz (99 g) = 1⅓ cups (325 mL) |

### If You Don't Have It

Substitute 1 cup (250 mL) packaged shredded coconut with:
- ⅔ cup (150 mL) fresh shredded coconut

### To Vary the Flavor

Substitute 1 cup (250 mL) packaged shredded coconut with:
- 1 cup (250 mL) finely chopped macadamia nuts

### For Better Health

Substitute 1 cup (250 mL) packaged shredded coconut with:
- 1 tsp (5 mL) coconut extract (fewer calories)

## Coconut Sugar

*See* SUGAR, PALM.

## Coconut Syrup

*Sweetened coconut cream poured on pancakes and used to make mixed drinks in Hawaii.*

### If You Don't Have It

Substitute 1 cup (250 mL) coconut syrup with:
- 1 cup (250 mL) Homemade Coconut Syrup: Simmer ⅓ cup (75 mL) water and ⅓ cup (75 mL) granulated sugar over medium heat until reduced in volume by about half. Stir in 1¼ cups (300 mL) coconut cream or strained separated coconut milk and cook until the syrup is thick enough to drip slowly from a spoon. Remove from the heat and stir in ½ tsp (2 mL) lemon juice, ½ tsp (2 mL) vanilla extract and ⅛ tsp (0.5 mL) salt. (If you don't have coconut cream, drain off the thin liquid from the thick fat layer from canned coconut milk and measure 1¼ cups/300 mL of the thick milk). Makes about 1½ cups (375 mL).
- 1 cup (250 mL) cream of coconut (for mixed drinks)

## Coconut Water

*Also known as agua de pipa, agua de coco, and coconut juice. The potassium-rich juice of young, green coconuts is the second best-selling juice in Brazil.*

1 green coconut =
1½ cups (375 mL)
coconut water

## Cocoyam

## Cod

*The title of a book by food historian Mark Kurlansky,* Cod: A Biography of the Fish That Changed the World, *sums up the global impact of this sea creature that has been fished heavily since medieval times. Before modern refrigeration, cod was preserved by drying it into stockfish, or salting and drying into salt cod.*

## Coffee

*Coffee is the world's second largest traded commodity. Oil is the first. Of the two widely cultivated species, high-altitude coffea arabica beans are more complex in flavor than the harsher low altitude coffea robusta.*

1 lb (500 g) = 5 cups
(1.25 L) grounds =
40 brewed cups
(6 oz/175 g each)

### If You Don't Have It

Substitute 1 cup (250 mL) coconut water with:
- ¾ cup (175 mL) water + ¼ cup (60 mL) coconut milk
- 1 cup (250 mL) water + ⅛ tsp (0.5 mL) coconut extract

### Coconut Water Varieties

Choose 1 cup (250 mL) coconut water from among these varieties:
- 1 cup (250 mL) Indian coconut water (sweet)
- 1 cup (250 mL) Brazilian coconut water (mild)
- 1 cup (250 mL) Bangladeshi coconut water (very sweet; slightly briny)

*See* TARO; YAUTÍA.

### If You Don't Have It

Substitute 1 lb (500 g) cod with:
- 1 lb (500 g) pollock
- 1 lb (500 g) haddock
- 1 lb (500 g) hake
- 1 lb (500 g) scrod (young cod)
- 1 lb (500 g) Cape capensis
- 1 lb (500 g) orange roughy
- 1 lb (500 g) tilapia
- 1 lb (500 g) sole
- 1 lb (500 g) flounder
- 1 lb (500 g) tilefish
- 1 lb (500 g) grouper
- 1 lb (500 g) halibut
- 1 lb (500 g) red snapper
- 1 lb (500 g) striped bass

*See also* SALT COD.

### If You Don't Have It

Substitute 1 cup (250 mL) strong brewed coffee with:
- 1 cup (250 mL) hot water + 2 tsp (10 mL) instant coffee powder or espresso powder

### To Vary the Flavor

Substitute 1 cup (250 mL) strong brewed coffee with:
- 1 cup (250 mL) strong brewed black tea

### For Better Health

Substitute 1 cup (250 mL) strong brewed coffee with:
- 1 cup (250 mL) brewed decaffeinated coffee
- 1 cup (250 mL) brewed roasted chicory (caffeine-free)
- 1 cup (250 mL) strong brewed rooibos

*See also* ESPRESSO; PICKING COFFEE (PAGE 646).

## Coffee Filter

*Paper liners used to hold ground coffee, and prevent grounds from entering the brewed coffee, in automatic drip coffee machines.*

### If You Don't Have It

Substitute coffee filters with:

- thick paper towels
- triple layer of cheesecloth or folded three times
- nylon mesh, such as clean nylon stockings
- clean kitchen towel

## Coffee Liqueur

*Neutral spirit or sweetened rum beverage flavored with natural or artificial coffee flavoring.*

### If You Don't Have It

Substitute 3 tbsp (45 mL) coffee liqueur with:

- 3 tbsp (45 mL) water + ¾ tsp (3 mL) instant coffee granules
- 3 tbsp (45 mL) chocolate liqueur, hazelnut liqueur, or almond liqueur
- 3 tbsp (45 mL) cognac
- 3 tbsp (45 mL) rum

### Coffee Liqueur Varieties

Choose 3 tbsp (45 mL) coffee liqueur from these varieties:

- 3 tbsp (45 mL) Kahlúa
- 3 tbsp (45 mL) Crème de café (sweeter; heavier body)
- 3 tbsp (45 mL) Tia Maria (lighter body; adds rum flavor)
- 3 tbsp (45 mL) Tiramisù liqueur (combines chocolate, coffee, and almond flavors)

## Cognac

*This king of brandies is double distilled and aged a minimum of three years in Limousin oak. The label term X.O. (extra and reserve) means that the cognac is the oldest a producer distributes. Older cognacs are ranked on the label with the following terms: V.S. = very superior; V.S.O.P = very superior old pale; V.V.S.O.P. = very, very, superior old pale.*

### If You Don't Have It

Substitute 3 tbsp (45 mL) cognac with:

- 3 tbsp (45 mL) Brandy de Jerez (sweeter; heavier body)
- 3 tbsp (45 mL) Armagnac (drier; more complex flavor)
- 3 tbsp (45 mL) top-shelf brandy
- 3 tbsp (45 mL) top-shelf Scotch, bourbon, or other whiskey

*See also* ARMAGNAC; BRANDY DE JEREZ.

## Coho Salmon

*See* SALMON.

## Cointreau

*See* ORANGE LIQUEUR.

## Colander

*A bowl-shaped strainer used to wash produce or drain noodles or vegetables after boiling. Large metal ones are best.*

### If You Don't Have It
Substitute a colander with:
- a medium-mesh strainer
- tongs, pasta spoon, or slotted spoon (for plucking or scooping foods out of hot liquid)

*See also* STRAINER.

## Colby

*A soft, springy cheese with mild sweet taste. Because of its high moisture content, Colby cheese should be eaten soon after purchase.*

### If You Don't Have It
Substitute 1 oz (30 g) Colby cheese with:
- 1 oz (30 g) Cheddar (sharper)
- 1 oz (30 g) Cheshire (sharper)
- 1 oz (30 g) Jack (pale color; milder flavor)
- 1 oz (30 g) American cheese (milder flavor)

### For Better Health
Substitute 1 oz (30 g) Colby cheese with:
- 1 oz (30 g) reduced-fat Colby, Cheddar, or Jack

## Cold Cuts

*See* SPECIFIC TYPES.

## Collards

*Also known as collard greens. A type of dark green cabbage with tall, dense stalks. Frozen collards can be substituted for fresh with a tolerable loss of flavor.*

> 1 lb (500 g) fresh =
> 1⅓ to 2 cups (325 to
> 500 mL) cooked

### If You Don't Have It
Substitute 1 lb (500 g) collards with:
- 1 lb (500 g) kale
- 1 lb (500 g) mature spinach
- 1 lb (500 g) green chard leaves
- 1 lb (500 g) mustard greens
- 1 lb (500 g) turnip greens
- 1 lb (500 g) callaloo
- 1 lb (500 g) Chinese kale
- 1 lb (500 g) bok choy

## Comal

*Flat, round griddle for cooking tortillas.*

### If You Don't Have It
Substitute a comal with:
- a small, thin metal skillet such as a crêpe pan

## Comice Pear

*See* PICKING PEARS (PAGE 661).

## Comté

*Also known as Gruyère de Comté. Nutty, buttery cheese produced for many centuries in the French Jura Mountains adjacent to Switzerland.*

> 4 oz (125 g) =
> 1 cup (250 mL) grated

### If You Don't Have It
Substitute 1 oz (30 g) Comté with:
- 1 oz (30 g) Gruyère
- 1 oz (30 g) Beaufort
- 1 oz (30 g) Emmental

## Conch

*Pronounced "konk," this beautiful mollusk is a snail-like creature housed in a shell. The tough flesh must be tenderized before eating.*

### If You Don't Have It
Substitute 4 oz (125 g) conch meat with:
- 4 oz (125 g) abalone
- 4 oz (125 g) clams
- 4 oz (125 g) whelk

## Condensed Milk

*See* SWEETENED CONDENSED MILK.

## Confectioner's Sugar

*See* SUGAR, CONFECTIONER'S.

## Confectionery Coating

*Also known as compound chocolate (when flavored with chocolate). A variously flavored and colored dip for candies and confections that contains sugar, powdered milk, and solid fat but no cocoa butter.*

### If You Don't Have It
Substitute 1 oz (30 g) confectionery coating with:
- 1 oz (30 g) couverture chocolate (contains cocoa butter; richer taste and mouth-feel; melts at a lower temperature)

*See also* CHOCOLATE, COUVERTURE.

## Conger

*See* EEL.

## Convection Oven

*Gas or electric oven equipped with a fan to circulate the hot air evenly around the food.*

### If You Don't Have It
Substitute a convection oven with:
- a gas or electric oven (does not provide circulation of hot air to speed cooking; increase oven temperature by about 25°F/14°C; increase cooking time by about 25%)

## Cookie Crumbs

*To make crumbs from stale cookies, grind them in a food processor fitted with a metal blade or place in a plastic bag and crush with a rolling pin. Use the crumbs to top fresh-cut fruits, pudding, yogurt, or ice cream. Or, use to "flour" greased cake pans.*

> 22 vanilla wafers =
> 1½ cups (375 mL)
> crumbs
>
> 18 to 20 chocolate
> waters = 1 cup (250 mL)
> crumbs

### To Vary the Flavor

Substitute 1½ cups (375 mL) cookie crumbs with:

- 1½ cups (375 mL) crushed graham crackers (about 21 squares)
- 1½ cups (375 mL) crushed gingersnaps (about 22)
- 1½ cups (375 mL) crushed vanilla wafer cookies (about 33)
- 1½ cups (375 mL) crushed chocolate wafer cookies (about 32)
- 1½ cups (375 mL) crushed Oreo cookies (about 21, including cookie filling); omit sugar from crust
- 1½ cups (375 mL) crushed wheat, bran or corn flakes (about 4½ cups/1.125 L)
- 1½ cups (375 mL) crushed saltine crackers (about 42); omit sugar from crust and adjust salt in filling (for savory fillings)
- 1½ cups (375 mL) cake crumbs (to replace soft cookie crumbs)
- 1½ cups (375 mL) muffin crumbs (to replace soft cookie crumbs)

### For Better Health

Substitute 1 crumb crust with:

- half of cookie crumbs in recipe plus equal amount of crushed saltine or other table crackers (omit salt from recipe)

*See also* BREAD CRUMBS, DRY; BREAD CRUMBS, FRESH; PIE CRUST, CRUMB.

## Cookie Cutter

*A metal implement to cut rolled cookie dough into circles. Cutters also are manufactured in hundreds of novelty shapes. To prevent sticking to soft doughs, dip the cutter in flour or granulated sugar.*

### If You Don't Have It

Substitute a cookie cutter with:

- biscuit cutter
- clean tuna can or other can with both ends removed
- inverted wine or drinking glass

*See also* BISCUIT CUTTER; CRUMPET RING.

## Cookie Sheet

*See* BAKING SHEET.

## Cooking Spray

*See* VEGETABLE OIL SPRAY.

## Cookware and Bakeware

*See* SPECIFIC TYPES.

## Cooling Rack

*Raised racks of sturdy parallel or woven wires that allow air to circulate. Used for cooling cookies, cakes, breads, and pastries so the bottoms won't get soggy.*

### If You Don't Have It

Substitute a cooling rack with:

- oven rack or toaster oven rack (remove from cool oven)
- flat roasting or broiling rack

## Coon

*A hybrid Cheddar cheese rarely produced outside of the Midwest United States.*

### If You Don't Have It

Substitute 1 oz (30 g) coon cheese with:

- 1 oz (30 g) Cheddar
- 1 oz (30 g) Colby
- 1 oz (30 g) Cheshire
- 1 oz (30 g) Jack

## Copha

*Australians are wild about this highly saturated solid coconut oil, using it in the preparation of candies and pastries.*

### If You Don't Have It

Substitute 1 cup (250 mL) copha with:

- 1 cup (250 mL) vegetable shortening or lard + ⅛ to ¼ tsp (0.5 to 1 mL) coconut extract

## Copoasu

*See* CUPUAÇU.

## Coppa

*See* CAPICOLA.

## Copper Bowl

*Properly executed, beating egg whites by hand with a balloon whisk in an unlined copper bowl produces one-third more volume of foam.*

### If You Don't Have It

Substitute a copper bowl for stabilizing whipped egg whites with:

- glass bowl + pinch of powdered copper supplement (available in health food stores)
- silver-plated bowl

## Corer

*See* APPLE CORER.

## Coriander Root

*Mild-tasting, juicy root of the coriander plant sometimes used in Southeast Asian cooking.*

### If You Don't Have It

Substitute 1 tbsp (15 mL) coriander root with:

- 2 tbsp (30 mL) thick cilantro stems

### To Vary the Flavor

Substitute 1 tbsp (15 mL) coriander root with:

- 1 tbsp (15 mL) mint root
- 1 tbsp (15 mL) basil
- 1 tbsp (15 mL) parsley root

## Coriander Seed

*Also known as ketumbar. The dried seeds of the herb coriander are pleasantly spicy. They are a standard item in garam masala and are also called upon to season savory dishes, breads, and cakes.*

### If You Don't Have It
Substitute 1 tsp (5 mL) coriander seeds with:
- 1 tsp (5 mL) caraway seeds
- 1 tsp (5 mL) fennel seeds
- ¾ tsp (3 mL) cumin seeds
- ½ to ¾ tsp (2 to 3 mL) cardamom seeds

*See also* CILANTRO; GARAM MASALA.

## Corkscrew

*The oenophile's best friend, this implement uncorks one of humanity's finest gastronomic achievements.*

### If You Don't Have It
Substitute a corkscrew with:
- using the blunt end of a table knife or another blunt narrow object, push the cork into the bottle. If the cork breaks into pieces, strain the wine into a decanter, glass pitcher or other spouted container

## Corn

*Also known as sweet corn. To easily remove the silk from corn-on-the-cob, husk the corn then rub the ears with a damp paper towel. The silk will stick to the towel and the whole lot can be tossed into the trash.*

2 medium ears = 1 to 1¼ cups (250 to 300 mL) kernels

10 oz (300 g) frozen kernels = 1¾ cups (425 mL)

### If You Don't Have It
Substitute 1 cup (250 mL) fresh corn with:
- 1 cup (250 mL) frozen and thawed corn
- 1 cup (250 mL) canned corn (not as good as frozen and thawed)
- 1 cup (250 mL) other cooked grain such as barley
- 1 cup (250 mL) peas

*See also* POPCORN.

## Cornbread Crumbs

*Cornbread dries out quickly but, fortunately, the crumbs make tasty stuffings, when moistened and seasoned, for vegetables or poultry.*

1 3-inch (7.5 cm) square (1-inch/2.5 cm deep) piece of cornbread = 1 cup (250 mL) crumbs

### If You Don't Have It
Substitute 1 cup (250 mL) fresh cornbread crumbs with:
- 1 cup (250 mL) crumbled corn muffin
- 1 cup (250 mL) fresh bread crumbs

*See also* BREAD CRUMBS, FRESH.

## Corn Chips

*January 29 is designated as National Corn Chip Day in the United States.*

### If You Don't Have It

Substitute 1 cup (250 mL) corn chips with:

- 1 cup (250 mL) tortilla chips
- 1 cup (250 mL) potato chips

## Corned Beef

*Beef brisket that is cured in a seasoned brine. The term "corned" refers in old English to the "corns," or small particles of salt, in the brine.*

### If You Don't Have It

Substitute 1 lb (500 g) corned beef with:

- 1 lb (500 g) pastrami (more tender)

## Cornflake Crumbs

*Since 1884, when surgeon and health food zealot John Harvey Kellogg applied for a patent for his toasted flaked corn cereal, the crumbs — useful in many recipes — have been the bonus at the bottom of the box.*

> 3 cups (750 mL)
> cornflakes = 1 cup
> (250 mL) crushed

### If You Don't Have It

Substitute 1 cup (250 mL) cornflake crumbs with:

- 1 cup (250 mL) cornmeal
- 1 cup (250 mL) dry bread crumbs
- 1 cup (250 mL) crushed wheat flakes or other cereal flakes
- 1 cup (250 mL) panko (Japanese bread crumbs; large crumbs; retains crispness better)
- 1 cup (250 mL) cracker crumbs
- 1 cup (250 mL) crushed tortilla chips or corn chips
- 1 cup (250 mL) crushed melba toast
- 1 cup (250 mL) matzo meal
- 1 cup (250 mL) crushed dry-bagged stuffing cubes
- 1 cup (250 mL) crushed potato chips
- 1 cup (250 mL) crushed pretzels

*See also* BREAD CRUMBS; CRACKER CRUMBS; PANKO.

## Corn Flour

*Finely ground yellow or white cornmeal. In Great Britain, corn flour is the term for cornstarch.*

### If You Don't Have It

Substitute 1 cup (250 mL) corn flour with:

- 1 cup (250 mL) cornmeal ground in a blender or small food processor until finely textured

*See also* MASA HARINA; CHOOSING AMONG WHOLE-GRAIN AND ALTERNATIVE FLOURS (PAGE 648).

## Corn Grits

*Dried, ground corn available in fine, medium, and coarse grinds. Not to be confused with hominy grits made from ground hominy.*

> 1 cup (250 mL) = 4½ cups
> (1.125 L) cooked

### If You Don't Have It

Substitute 1 cup (250 mL) corn grits with:

- 1 cup (250 mL) hominy grits
- 1 cup (250 mL) coarse polenta meal (preferably stone-ground)
- 1 cup (250 mL) barley grits
- 1 cup (250 mL) buckwheat grits

*See also* BARLEY GRITS; HOMINY GRITS.

## Corn Husk

*When used as a food wrapper, as in tamales, corn husks add a mild corn flavor to the food.*

### If You Don't Have It
Substitute corn husks (for wrapping foods) with:
- hoja santa leaves (adds aromas of root beer and fennel)
- banana leaves (adds herby-green flavor)
- parchment paper (adds no flavor)
- aluminum foil (adds no flavor)

## Cornichon

*The French word for "gherkins," cornichons are tiny, crisp, tart pickles.*

### If You Don't Have It
Substitute 1 cup (250 mL) cornichons with:
- 1 cup (250 mL) sweet gherkins (sweeter)
- 1 cup (250 mL) small whole or sliced dill pickles

*See also* CUCUMBER.

## Cornish Game Hen

*See* CHICKEN.

## Cornmeal

*For the most nutrients and a whiff of nuttiness, choose old-fashioned water-ground (also called stone-ground) cornmeal. It retains some of the hull and germ. Store in the refrigerator for up to 4 months.*

1 lb (500 g) = 3¼ cups (800 mL)

### If You Don't Have It
Substitute 1 cup (250 mL) yellow cornmeal with:
- 1 cup (250 mL) blue cornmeal
- 1 cup (250 mL) corn grits (heavier texture)
- 1 cup (250 mL) polenta meal (heavier texture)
- 1 cup (250 mL) mielie-meal (similar to grits and polenta meal)
- 1 cup (250 mL) corn flour (lighter texture)
- 1 cup (250 mL) crushed tortilla chips or corn chips (for breading; crush chips in a food processor or blender until fine)
- 1 cup (250 mL) self-rising cornmeal (for quick breads; omit 1½ tbsp/22 mL baking powder and ½ tsp/2 mL salt from recipe)

*See also* CORN GRITS; POLENTA MEAL.

## Cornmeal, Self-Rising

*For making cornmeal bread, muffins, and other baked goods, this variety of cornmeal is conveniently packaged with baking powder.*

### If You Don't Have It
Substitute 1 cup (250 mL) self-rising cornmeal with:
- 1 cup (250 mL) minus 3 tbsp (45 mL) cornmeal + 1½ tbsp (22 mL) baking powder + ½ tsp (2 mL) salt
- ¾ cup (175 mL) cornmeal + ¼ cup (60 mL) all-purpose flour + ½ tsp (2 mL) salt + ½ tsp (2 mL) baking powder + ¼ tsp (1 mL) baking soda (to replace cornmeal "mix" made with cornmeal and wheat flour)

## Corn Oil

*See* SUBSTITUTING OILS (PAGE 658).

## Corn Salad

*See* MÂCHE.

## Corn Smut

*See* HUITLACOCHE.

## Cornstarch

*To avoid lumps, dissolve cornstarch (and all other starches or flours used for thickening) in twice the amount of cold liquid before stirring into the hot liquid.*

1 lb (500 g) = 3 cups (750 mL))

1 oz (30 g) = 3 tbsp (45 mL)

To thicken 1 cup (250 mL) liquid: 1 tsp (5 mL) for thin; 2 tsp (10 mL) for medium; 1 tbsp (15 mL) for medium-thick; 1½ tbsp (22 mL) for thick

### If You Don't Have It
Substitute 1 tbsp (15 mL) cornstarch (for thickening) with:
- 1½ tbsp (22 mL) Instant Clear Jel
- 3 tbsp (45 mL) all-purpose flour (cook a few minutes after thickening to cook out raw flour taste)
- 1 to 1½ tbsp (15 to 22 mL) arrowroot (a better choice if thickened food will be cooked for a long time; also makes sauces more glossy)
- 1½ to 2 tbsp (22 to 25 mL) quick-cooking tapioca
- 2 tsp (10 mL) potato starch, rice starch, or instant mashed potato flakes

*See also* CLEAR JEL.

## Corn Stick Pan

*See* PAN SIZE EQUIVALENTS (PAGE 678).

## Corn Syrup, Dark

*Similar to light corn syrup but with added caramel coloring and flavoring.*

16 oz (500 mL) = 2 cups (500 mL)

### If You Don't Have It
Substitute 1 cup (250 mL) dark corn syrup with:
- ¾ cup (175 mL) light corn syrup + ¼ cup (60 mL) light molasses
- 1 cup (250 mL) light corn syrup (no caramel flavoring; lighter color)
- 1 cup (250 mL) golden syrup (thicker; sweeter)
- 1 cup (250 mL) honey (sweeter; lighter color)
- 1¼ cups (300 mL) packed brown sugar dissolved in ¼ cup (60 mL) hot water or liquid used in recipe

## Corn Syrup, Light

*Thick, sweet, clear syrup derived from cornstarch.*

16 oz (500 mL) = 2 cups (500 mL)

### If You Don't Have It
Substitute 1 cup (250 mL) light corn syrup with:
- 1¼ cups (300 mL) granulated sugar dissolved in ¼ cup (60 mL) hot water or liquid used in recipe
- 1 cup (250 mL) golden syrup (thicker; sweeter)
- 1 cup (250 mL) liquid glucose

## To Vary the Flavor

Substitute 1 cup (250 mL) light corn syrup with:

- 1 cup (250 mL) dark corn syrup (adds caramel flavor and color)
- 1 cup (250 mL) honey (sweeter; adds amber color)
- 1 cup (250 mL) molasses (deepens flavor and adds darker brown color)

## Corsu Vecchio

*Corsican semifirm sheep's milk cheese with a rough grayish white rind, ivory paste, and earthy, nutty flavor with hints of thyme.*

### If You Don't Have It

Substitute 1 oz (30 g) corsu vecchio with:

- 1 oz (30 g) Tomme de Savoie
- 1 oz (30 g) Saint Nectaire
- 1 oz (30 g) Beaumont

## Costeño Chile

*See* CHOOSING DRIED CHILES (PAGE 642).

## Cotechino

*A fresh pork sausage from the Italian city of Modena.*

### If You Don't Have It

Substitute 4 oz (125 g) cotechino with:

- 4 oz (125 g) mild Italian sausage

## Cotija

*See* QUESO AÑEJO.

## Cottage Cheese

*Strict lacto-ovo vegetarians can enjoy cottage cheese because it contains no rennet. It's an acid curd cheese, meaning the curds are formed by the natural tendency of warmed milk to curdle on its own.*

8 oz (250 g) =
1 cup (250 mL)

### If You Don't Have It

Substitute 1 cup (250 mL) cottage cheese with:

- 1 cup (250 mL) ricotta
- 1 cup (250 mL) pot cheese
- 1 cup (250 mL) chenna
- 1 cup (250 mL) panir, briefly puréed in a food processor

## Coulommiers

*A French cheese that's a stand-in for Brie except that the round is thicker and smaller.*

### If You Don't Have It

Substitute 1 oz (30 g) Coulommiers with:

- 1 oz (30 g) Brie
- 1 oz (30 g) Camembert
- 1 oz (30 g) Chaource

## Country Ham

*See* HAM, DRY-CURED.

## Courgette

*See* ZUCCHINI.

## Couscous

*North African granular semolina steamed and served as a grain side dish. Also the name of a spicy stew that it accompanies.*

> 1 cup (250 mL) = 2½ cups (625 mL) cooked

### If You Don't Have It
Substitute 1 cup (250 mL) instant couscous with:
- 1 cup (250 mL) couscous (takes longer to cook)
- 1 cup (250 mL) white rice (takes longer to cook)

### For Better Health
Substitute 1 cup (250 mL) instant couscous with:
- 1 cup (250 mL) whole wheat couscous
- 1 cup (250 mL) quinoa
- 1 cup (250 mL) bulgur (takes longer to cook)
- 1 cup (250 mL) brown rice (takes longer to cook)

*See also* COUSCOUSSIÈRE.

## Couscoussière

*A North African cooking pot in two parts. The bottom pot is used to simmer a spicy stew and the perforated top part is used to steam the accompanying couscous.*

### If You Don't Have It
Substitute a couscoussièrre with:
- colander lined with cheesecloth or thick paper towels and set over a pot
- steamer pot with an insert basket lined with cheesecloth or thick paper towels

*See also* COUSCOUS.

## Couverture

*See* CHOCOLATE, COUVERTURE.

## Cowberry

*See* LINGONBERRY.

## Cowpea

*See* BLACK-EYED PEA, FRESH.

## Crab

*Refrigerated pasteurized premium crabmeat in a tub or can makes a suitable substitute for fresh lump crabmeat.*

> 1 lb (500 g) = 2 cups (500 mL) meat

### If You Don't Have It
Substitute 1 lb (500 g) crabmeat with:
- 1 lb (500 g) shrimp (firmer texture)
- 1 lb (500 g) lobster (more expensive; firmer)
- 1 lb (500 g) scallops
- 1 lb (500 g) surimi (imitation crabmeat; less flavorful)
- 1 lb (500 g) monkfish
- 1 lb (500 g) cod

*See also* SURIMI; CHOOSING AMONG CRABS (PAGE 647).

## Crab Boil Seasoning

*Also known as fish boil and shrimp boil. A zesty mixture of herbs and spices added to water in which seafood is simmered. May include allspice, bay leaves, red chiles, cloves, dried ginger, mustard seeds, and peppercorns.*

### If You Don't Have It

Substitute 1 tbsp (15 mL) crab boil seasoning with:

- 1 tbsp (15 mL) Homemade Crab Boil Seasoning: Combine 2 bay leaves, ½ tsp (2 mL) black peppercorns or ground pepper, ½ tsp (2 mL) mustard seeds, ½ tsp (2 mL) dill seeds, ½ tsp (2 mL) coriander seeds, ¼ tsp (1 mL) whole cloves, ¼ tsp (1 mL) allspice berries, and ⅛ tsp (0.5 mL) ground ginger in a piece of cheesecloth or coffee filter. Tie with kitchen string or a clean twist-tie. Makes about 1 tablespoon (15 mL).
- 1 tbsp (15 mL) Old Bay seasoning (adds salt, paprika, celery seed, and other flavors)
- 1 tbsp (15 mL) pickling spice

*See also* OLD BAY SEASONING.

## Crab Sticks

*See* SURIMI.

## Cracked Wheat

*Wheat berries that are broken into fine, medium, and coarse bits. Can be prepared as cereal, in pilafs, or mixed into whole-grain bread doughs.*

### If You Don't Have It

Substitute 1 cup (250 mL) cracked wheat with:

- 1 cup (250 mL) wheat berries (takes longer to cook)
- 1 cup (250 mL) bulgur (takes less time to cook)
- 1 cup (250 mL) whole wheat couscous (takes less time to cook)
- 1 cup (250 mL) quinoa (takes less time to cook)
- 1 cup (250 mL) brown rice

*See also* BULGUR.

## Cracker

*Also known as biscuits (in England). In North America, crackers refer to thin, unsweetened, unleavened wafers. Centuries ago, the term "cracker" referred to a liar or boaster.*

### If You Don't Have It

Substitute 1 lb (500 g) crackers with:

- 1 lb (500 g) melba toast
- 1 lb (500 g) crisp lavash
- 1 lb (500 g) tortilla chips

### Cracker Varieties

Choose 1 lb (500 g) crackers from these common varieties:

- 1 lb (500 g) water crackers (very crisp, dry, and relatively low in salt)
- 1 lb (500 g) soda crackers (crisp, dry, and relatively low in salt)
- 1 lb (500 g) oyster crackers (usually small, round or hexagonal, somewhat crisp, and relatively low in salt)
- 1 lb (500 g) saltines (crisp, dry, and salty)
- 1 lb (500 g) Triscuits (crisp, dry and relatively low in salt; made with whole-grain flour)
- 1 lb (500 g) Ritz crackers (buttery-soft and salty)

*See also* CRACKER CRUMBS; GRAHAM CRACKER.

## Cracker Bread

*See* LAVASH.

## Cracker Crumbs

*To re-crisp soggy crackers to make crumbs, spread on a baking sheet and place in a 350°F (180°C) oven for 5 to 10 minutes. Let cool before crumbling.*

> 20 soda/saltine crackers = 1 cup (250 mL) crumbs

### If You Don't Have It
Substitute 1 cup (250 mL) cracker crumbs with:
- 1¼ cups (300 mL) dry bread crumbs
- 1½ cups (375 mL) croutons or stuffing cubes, crushed
- 1 cup (250 mL) panko (Japanese bread crumbs; large crumbs; retains crispness better)
- 1 tbsp (15 mL) quick-cooking oats (for thickening)

### Cracker Crumb Varieties
Choose 1 cup (250 mL) cracker crumbs from these varieties:
- 1 cup (250 mL) water cracker crumbs (very crisp, dry, and relatively low in salt)
- 1 cup (250 mL) soda cracker crumbs (crisp, dry, and relatively low in salt)
- 1 cup (250 mL) saltine cracker crumbs (crisp, dry, and salty)
- 1 cup (250 mL) Ritz cracker crumbs (buttery-soft and salty)
- 1 cup (250 mL) seasoned dry bread crumbs
- 1 cup (250 mL) finely crushed melba toasts
- 1 cup (250 mL) matzo meal
- 1 cup (250 mL) finely crushed tortilla chips
- 1 cup (250 mL) crushed dry-bagged stuffing mix
- 1 cup (250 mL) finely crushed pretzels
- 1 cup (250 mL) finely crushed cornflakes
- 1 cup (250 mL) finely crushed potato chips

## Craisins®

*See* CRANBERRY, DRIED.

## Cranberry

*Also known as bearberries, bounceberries and craneberries. Frozen and thawed cranberries make a fair substitute for fresh cranberries, especially in sauces, compotes or dishes including liquid.*

> 12 oz (375 g) fresh or frozen = 3 cups (750 mL) = 4 cups (1 L) sauce

### If You Don't Have It
Substitute 1 cup (250 mL) cranberries with:
- 1 cup (250 mL) lingonberries (smaller; more complex flavor)
- 1 cup (250 mL) carissa
- 1 cup (250 mL) blueberries (sweeter)
- 1 cup (250 mL) red currants

## Cranberry Bean, Fresh

*Also known as borlotti bean and horticultural bean. A cream and red-speckled shell bean that's often harvested when the beans are mature then shelled and enjoyed fresh. Also available dried.*

1 lb (500 g) fresh in shell = 1¼ cups (300 mL) shelled

### If You Don't Have It
Substitute 1 lb (500 g) fresh cranberry beans (weighed in shell) with:
- 1 lb (500 g) fresh Dragon Tongue beans (deep reddish brown and cream color)
- 1 lb (500 g) fresh Tongue of Fire beans (green and red color)
- 1 lb (500 g) fresh Romano beans (green color)
- 1 lb (500 g) fresh Kentucky Wonder beans (green color)
- 1 lb (500 g) fresh black-eyed peas or other cowpeas (southernpeas; pale green and cream or pink color with black "eye" at center)
- 1 lb (500 g) fresh lima beans (green color)
- 1 lb (500 g) fresh edamame (green color)
- 1 lb (500 g) fresh garden peas (green color)

*See also* PEAS, SHELLING; THE WIDE WORLD OF DRIED BEANS (PAGE 637).

## Cranberry, Dried

*Also known as Craisins®. Drying fresh cranberries allows producers to maximize sales of the harvest.*

### If You Don't Have It
Substitute 1 cup (250 mL) dried cranberries with:
- 1 cup (250 mL) raisins
- 1 cup (250 mL) dried cherries
- 1 cup (250 mL) dried blueberries
- 1 cup (250 mL) currants (smaller, drier)

## Cranberry Juice

*High in vitamin C, cranberry juice is reputed to promote urinary tract health. It also lends a lovely pink hue to Cosmopolitan cocktails and pink lemonade.*

### If You Don't Have It
Substitute 1 cup (250 mL) cranberry juice with:
- 1 cup (250 mL) cranberry juice cocktail (up to 27% cranberry juice; may include added water, sweeteners, flavors, and colors)
- 1 cup (250 mL) pomegranate juice (sweeter)
- 1 cup (250 mL) red grape juice + 1 tsp (5 mL) lemon juice
- 1 cup (250 mL) açai juice

## Cranberry Liqueur

*Sweetened cranberry-flavored spirit.*

### If You Don't Have It
Substitute 2 tbsp (30 mL) cranberry liqueur with:
- 2 tbsp (30 mL) cranberry schnapps (less sweet; higher alcohol)
- 2 tbsp (30 mL) cranberry syrup (sweeter; no alcohol)
- 1 tsp (5 mL) cranberry extract (add 4 tsp/20 mL liquid to recipe if necessary)

### To Vary the Flavor
Substitute 2 tbsp (30 mL) cranberry liqueur with:
- 2 tbsp (30 mL) raspberry liqueur (slightly more astringent flavor)
- 2 tbsp (30 mL) black raspberry liqueur (more astringent flavor)
- 2 tbsp (30 mL) blackberry liqueur

## Crane Melon

*Sonoma County farmer Oliver Crane developed the Crane Melon in the early 1900s by crossing Japanese melon, white melon, Persian melon, and ambrosia melon, among others. The sweet, juicy, aromatic orange flesh is highly prized but rarely found outside of Northern California.*

1 medium = 2 lbs
(1 kg) = 3 cups
(750 mL) diced

### If You Don't Have It

Substitute 1 cup (250 mL) chopped Crane melon with:
- 1 cup (250 mL) chopped Persian melon
- 1 cup (250 mL) chopped Crenshaw melon
- 1 cup (250 mL) chopped Santa Claus melon
- 1 cup (250 mL) chopped casaba melon
- 1 cup (250 mL) chopped ambrosia melon
- 1 cup (250 mL) chopped cantaloupe

## Cranshaw Melon

*See* CRENSHAW MELON.

## Crawdad

*See* CRAYFISH.

## Crayfish

*Also known as crawdads, crawfish, écrevisses, mudbugs, and yabbies. Freshwater crustaceans that look exactly like miniature lobsters, from 3 to 6 inches (7.5 to 15 cm) long and weighing from 2 to 8 ounces (60 to 250 g). Breaux Bridge, Louisiana is known as "The Crawfish Capital of the World."*

1 lb (500 g) = 15 large
crayfish = 3 oz (90 g)
peeled tails

### If You Don't Have It

Substitute 1 lb (500 g) crayfish with:
- 1 lb (500 g) shrimp (especially rock shrimp)
- 1 lb (500 g) lobster (especially spiny or rock lobster for the tails)
- 1 lb (500 g) crab

## Cream

*The luscious milk fat that rises to the top of standing milk that hasn't been homogenized.*

### If You Don't Have It

Substitute 1 cup (250 mL) cream with:
- 1 cup (250 mL) strained yogurt or yogurt cheese (for uncooked or gently heated sauces, cold soups, and other mixtures; thicker; adds slight tanginess)

*Ultra-pasteurized creams don't whip as easily and have a detectable cooked milk flavor.*

---

1 cup (250 mL) =
8 oz (250 g)

---

- 1 cup (250 mL) yogurt (for uncooked or gently heated sauces, cold soups, and other mixtures; adds slight tanginess)

## For Better Health

Substitute 1 cup (250 mL) cream with:

- 1 cup (250 mL) evaporated milk (fewer calories; thinner consistency; whips less easily; adds slight cooked milk flavor)

*See also* CREAM, CLABBER; CREAM, CLOTTED; CREAM, DOUBLE; CREAM, HALF-AND-HALF; CREAM, LIGHT; CREAM, LIGHT WHIPPING; CREAM, WHIPPING; CRÈME FRAÎCHE; KAYMAK; SMETANA; SOUR CREAM; WHIPPED CREAM.

---

## Cream Cheese

*In 1872, New York State dairyman William A. Lawrence developed a method for making cream cheese while attempting to duplicate French Neufchâtel. In 1880, New York cheese distributor A. L. Reynolds packaged the cheese in tin-foil wrappers and called it Philadelphia Brand Cream Cheese because the public equated the City of Brotherly Love with high-quality food products.*

---

1 lb (500 g) = 2 cups
(500 mL)

---

## If You Don't Have It

Substitute 1 lb (500 g) cream cheese with:
- 1 lb (500 g) mascarpone cheese (richer)
- 1 lb (500 g) boursin cheese (adds garlic and herb flavors)
- 1 lb (500 g) Alouette cheese (adds various flavors)
- 1 lb (500 g) Rondele cheese (adds various flavors)

## For Better Health

Substitute 1 lb (500 g) cream cheese with:
- 1 lb (500 g) reduced-fat (Neufchâtel) or fat-free cream cheese (block or tub-style; lower in fat and moisture)
- 8 oz (250 g) reduced-fat cream cheese + 8 oz (250 g) fat-free cream cheese
- 1 lb (500 g) reduced-fat ricotta cheese (for cooking)
- 1 lb (500 g) dry-curd cottage cheese (for cooking)
- 1 lb (500 g) puréed silken or soft tofu
- 1 lb (500 g) tofu cream cheese

---

## Cream, Clabber

*Cream that has soured and thickened naturally.*

## If You Don't Have It

Substitute 1 cup (250 mL) clabber cream with:
- 1 cup (250 mL) crème fraîche (thinner consistency)

---

## Cream, Clotted

*Also known as Devon cream or Devonshire cream. The heavy cream that is skimmed from gently heated unpasteurized milk.*

## If You Don't Have It

Substitute 1 cup (250 mL) clotted cream with:
- 1 cup (250 mL) crème fraîche
- ½ cup (125 mL) whipped cream

*See also* CREAM; CRÈME FRAÎCHE; KAYMAK; SMETANA.

## Cream, Double

*Cream that contains 42% to 48% butterfat. Not widely available to consumers in the United States.*

### If You Don't Have It
Substitute 1 cup (250 mL) double cream with:
- 1 cup (250 mL) heavy or whipping cream (35% butterfat)
- 1 cup (250 mL) crème fraîche

### For Better Health
Substitute 1 cup (250 mL) double cream with:
- 1 cup (250 mL) strained yogurt or yogurt cheese (less fat and calories; for uncooked or gently heated dishes)

## Cream, Half-and-Half

*A mixture of equal parts milk and cream that contains 10 to 12% butterfat.*

### If You Don't Have It
Substitute 1 cup (250 mL) half-and-half with:
- ½ cup (125 mL) light or table cream + ½ cup (125 mL) whole milk
- 1 tbsp (15 mL) melted unsalted butter + enough whole milk to equal 1 cup (250 mL)
- ¾ cup (175 mL) whole milk + ¼ cup (60 mL) heavy or whipping cream (35% butterfat)
- 1 cup (250 mL) evaporated milk (for baking)

### For Better Health
Substitute 1 cup (250 mL) half-and-half with:
- 1 cup (250 mL) fat-free half-and-half
- 1 cup (250 mL) fat-free evaporated milk (for baking)
- 1 cup (250 mL) strained yogurt or yogurt cheese (less fat and calories; thicker; for uncooked or gently heated dishes)

## Cream, Light

*Also known as coffee cream and table cream. Can contain anywhere from 18 to 30% fat; most common content is 20%. In Canada, this cream is known as table cream, while light cream refers to a lighter cream with 5% fat.*

### If You Don't Have It
Substitute 1 cup (250 mL) light or table cream with:
- 3 tbsp (45 mL) melted unsalted butter + whole milk to equal 1 cup (250 mL)
- ½ cup (125 mL) heavy or whipping cream (35% butterfat) + ½ cup (125 mL) whole milk
- ½ cup (125 mL) evaporated milk + ½ cup (125 mL) whole milk

### For Better Health
Substitute 1 cup (250 mL) light or table cream with:
- 1 cup (250 mL) half-and-half
- 1 cup (250 mL) fat-free half-and-half
- ½ cup (125 mL) fat-free evaporated milk + ½ cup (125 mL) whole or 2% milk

## Cream, Light Whipping

*The most common type of cream sold commercially in the U.S., it contains 30 to 36% fat and frequently stabilizers and emulsifiers.*

### If You Don't Have It

Substitute 1 cup (250 mL) light whipping cream when not for whipping with:
- ¾ cup (175 mL) whole milk + ¼ cup (60 mL) melted unsalted butter
- 1 cup (250 mL) heavy or whipping cream (35% butterfat; heavier body)

### For Better Health

Substitute 1 cup (250 mL) light whipping cream when not for whipping with:
- 1 cup (250 mL) half-and-half

## Cream Nut

*See* BRAZIL NUT.

## Cream of Coconut

*Ultra-sweet, thick blend of coconut paste, water, and sugar that forms the basis of the tropical piña colada cocktail. Not to be confused with coconut cream, a thick type of coconut milk.*

### If You Don't Have It

Substitute 1 cup (250 mL) cream of coconut with:
- 1 cup (250 mL) sweetened condensed milk + ¼ to ½ tsp (1 to 2 mL) coconut extract
- 1 cup (250 mL) coconut cream + ¼ to ½ cup (60 to 125 mL) confectioner's (icing) sugar blended together
- 1 cup (250 mL) coconut milk + ¼ to ½ cup (60 to 125 mL) confectioner's (icing) sugar blended together

### For Better Health

Substitute 1 cup (250 mL) cream of coconut with:
- 1 cup (250 mL) reduced-fat coconut milk + ¼ to ½ cup (60 to 125 mL) confectioner's (icing) sugar blended together (less rich; thinner consistency)

*See also* COCONUT CREAM.

## Cream of Tartar

*An acidic white powder scraped from the inside of wine barrels, it's added to candy and frosting for creaminess and to egg whites before beating to achieve higher volume and stability. Also added to some baking powders.*

### If You Don't Have It

Substitute 1 tsp (5 mL) cream of tartar with:
- 1 tbsp (15 mL) distilled white vinegar or lemon juice (to add acidity to liquids)

## Cream, Whipping

*Also known as heavy cream. Cream that contains 35 to 40% butterfat. There is also a light whipping cream with 30 to 35% butterfat available in the U.S. When substituting lower-fat creams for whipping cream in sauces, prevent curdling by heating the sauce over low heat only.*

> 1 cup (250 mL) = 2 cups (500 mL) whipped

### If You Don't Have It
Substitute 1 cup (250 mL) heavy or whipping cream (35% butterfat) when not for whipping with:
- 1 cup (250 mL) double cream
- 1 cup (250 mL) crème fraîche
- ⅔ cup (150 mL) whole milk + ⅓ cup (75 mL) melted unsalted butter
- ⅔ cup (150 mL) evaporated milk

### For Better Health
Substitute 1 cup (250 mL) heavy or whipping cream (35% butterfat) when not for whipping with:
- 1 cup (250 mL) light or table cream
- 1 cup (250 mL) half-and-half
- 1 cup (250 mL) fat-free half-and-half
- 1 cup (250 mL) 2% or 1% milk + 1 tbsp (15 mL) cornstarch
- ⅔ cup (150 mL) fat-free evaporated milk
- 1 cup (250 mL) strained yogurt or yogurt cheese (less fat and calories; thicker; for uncooked or gently heated dishes)

*See also* CREAM, LIGHT WHIPPING; WHIPPED CREAM.

## Crema Danica

*Also known as Crema Dania. From Denmark, small rectangular 72% butterfat cheese cloaked in a downy white rind.*

### If You Don't Have It
Substitute 1 oz (30 g) Crema Danica with:
- 1 oz (30 g) Brie
- 1 oz (30 g) Camembert

## Crema Mexicana

*See* CRÈME FRAÎCHE.

## Crema Salvadoreña

*See* SOUR CREAM.

## Crème d'Abricots

*Sweet, syrupy apricot liqueur.*

### If You Don't Have It
Substitute 3 tbsp (45 mL) crème d'abricots with:
- 3 tbsp (45 mL) apricot liqueur (less sweet)

## Crème d'Amande

*See* ALMOND LIQUEUR.

## Crème d'Ananas

*Syrupy, pineapple liqueur.*

### If You Don't Have It
Substitute 3 tbsp (45 mL) crème d'ananas with:
- 3 tbsp (45 mL) crème de banane (banana flavor)

## Crème de Banane

*Sweet, syrupy liqueur with the flavor of ripe bananas but no dairy products.*

### If You Don't Have It

Substitute 3 tbsp (45 mL) crème de banane with:
- 3 tbsp (45 mL) crème d'ananas (pineapple flavor)

## Crème de Cacao

*See* CHOCOLATE LIQUEUR.

## Crème de Café

*See* COFFEE LIQUEUR.

## Crème de Cassis

*See* CASSIS LIQUEUR.

## Crème de Cerise

*See* CHERRY LIQUEUR.

## Crème de Cumin

*Syrupy liqueur flavored with caraway seeds.*

### If You Don't Have It

Substitute 3 tbsp (45 mL) crème de cumin with:
- 3 tbsp (45 mL) kümmel (less sweet; cumin flavor)

## Crème de Fraise

*Sweet, thick strawberry liqueur made without dairy products.*

### If You Don't Have It

Substitute 3 tbsp (45 mL) crème de fraise with:
- 3 tbsp (45 mL) crème de framboise (raspberry flavor)
- 3 tbsp (45 mL) strawberry liqueur (less sweet; lighter body)
- 3 tbsp (45 mL) strawberry schnapps (less sweet; lighter body)
- 3 tbsp (45 mL) crème de cassis (black currant flavor)

## Crème de Framboise

*Syrupy raspberry made without dairy products.*

### If You Don't Have It

Substitute 3 tbsp (45 mL) crème de framboise with:
- 3 tbsp (45 mL) crème de fraise (strawberry flavor)
- 3 tbsp (45 mL) raspberry liqueur (less sweet; lighter body)
- 3 tbsp (45 mL) raspberry schnapps (less sweet; lighter body)
- 3 tbsp (45 mL) crème de cassis (black currant flavor)

## Crème de Griotte

*See* CHERRY LIQUEUR.

## Crème de Mandarin

*See* MANDARIN LIQUEUR.

## Crème de Marron

*See* CHESTNUT CREAM.

## Crème de Menthe

*Mint liqueur comes in clear (also called "white") and green.*

### If You Don't Have It

Substitute 3 tbsp (45 mL) crème de menthe with:
- 3 tbsp (45 mL) peppermint schnapps (less sweet; lighter body)
- 3 tbsp (45 mL) Jägermeister (much more bitter and complex)
- ¼ to ½ tsp (1 to 2 mL) peppermint extract + 3 tbsp (45 mL) water or other liquid
- 2 drops peppermint oil + 3 tbsp (45 mL) water or other liquid

## Crème de mûre

*See* BLACKBERRY LIQUEUR.

## Crème de Myrtille

*Syrupy blueberry liqueur often made with bilberries, the smaller tart cousins of blueberries.*

### If You Don't Have It

Substitute 3 tbsp (45 mL) crème de myrtille with:
- 3 tbsp (45 mL) cassis liqueur (black currant flavor; made with rum)
- 3 tbsp (45 mL) raspberry liqueur
- 3 tbsp (45 mL) blueberry syrup (sweeter; no alcohol)
- 3 tbsp (45 mL) black currant syrup (sweeter; no alcohol)

## Crème de Noix

*See* WALNUT LIQUEUR.

## Crème de Noyaux

*See* ALMOND LIQUEUR.

## Crème de Pêche

*Syrupy peach liqueur made without dairy products.*

### If You Don't Have It

Substitute 3 tbsp (45 mL) crème de pêche with:
- 3 tbsp (45 mL) crème d'abricots (apricot flavor)
- 3 tbsp (45 mL) apricot liqueur (apricot flavor; less sweet)

## Crème de Prunelle

*Thick, sweet liqueur made with sloe plums.*

### If You Don't Have It

Substitute 3 tbsp (45 mL) crème de prunelle with:
- 3 tbsp (45 mL) sloe gin (less sweet)
- 3 tbsp (45 mL) plum brandy (less sweet)

*See also* PLUM BRANDY.

## Crème de Rose

*This liqueur by any other name would still taste of rose petals scented with vanilla and spices.*

### If You Don't Have It

Substitute 3 tbsp (45 mL) crème de rose with:
- 3 tbsp (45 mL) crème de vanille + 2 to 3 drops rose water

## Crème de Vanille

*Vanilla scented liqueur containing no dairy products.*

### If You Don't Have It

Substitute 3 tbsp (45 mL) crème de vanille with:
- ½ tsp (2 mL) vanilla extract + 3 tbsp (45 mL) water or other liquid

## Crème de Violette

*Liqueur flavored with violets.*

### If You Don't Have It

Substitute 3 tbsp (45 mL) crème de violette with:
- 3 tbsp (45 mL) Parfait d'Amour (adds citrus flavor)
- 3 tbsp (45 mL) crème de rose (lighter color; adds vanilla flavor)

## Crème Fraîche

*Also known as crema Mexicana (in Mexico and Central America). Matured thickened cream, a specialty of France. Unlike sour cream, crème fraîche won't curdle if boiled.*

> 1 cup (250 mL) = 8 oz (250 g)

### If You Don't Have It

Substitute 1 cup (250 mL) crème fraîche with:
- 1 cup (250 mL) sour cream or yogurt (for cold or gently heated sauces and cold soups)
- ½ cup (125 mL) sour cream + ½ cup (125 mL) heavy or whipping cream (35% butterfat)
- 1 cup (250 mL) clabber cream (thicker)
- 1 cup (250 mL) Homemade Crème Fraîche: Mix together 1 cup (250 mL) heavy or whipping cream (35% butterfat) and 3 tbsp (45 mL) buttermilk (for a tangy flavor) or ½ cup (125 mL) sour cream (for less tangy flavor). Cover and let stand at room temperature (68° to 72°F/20° to 22°C) overnight or for up to 24 hours. Stir, recover and chill for at least 8 hours before using. Keeps refrigerated for about 10 days.

### To Vary the Flavor

Substitute 1 cup (250 mL) crème fraîche with:
- 1 cup (250 mL) Homemade Crème Fraîche (see recipe above) mixed with 1 tbsp (15 mL) chopped fresh herbs, crystallized ginger, or honey before chilling.

*See also* CREAM, CLOTTED; KAYMAK; SMETANA; SOUR CREAM.

## Crenshaw Melon

*Also known as cranshaw melon. Sweet oval melon with golden-green, lightly ribbed rind and salmon-color flesh. The aroma is spicy. Can weigh up to 9 pounds (4.5 kg).*

> 1 lb (500 g) = 1 to 1½ cups (250 to 375 mL) cubed

### If You Don't Have It

Substitute 1 cup (250 mL) chopped Crenshaw melon with:
- 1 cup (250 mL) chopped Persian melon
- 1 cup (250 mL) chopped casaba melon
- 1 cup (250 mL) chopped Santa Claus melon
- 1 cup (250 mL) chopped cantaloupe
- 1 cup (250 mL) chopped honeydew melon

## Creole Seasoning

*The New Orleans city cousin of country Cajun Seasoning.*

### If You Don't Have It

Substitute 1 tbsp (15 mL) Creole seasoning with:

- 1 tbsp (15 mL) Homemade Creole seasoning: Combine ¾ tsp (3 mL) paprika, ½ tsp (2 mL) ground black pepper, ½ tsp (2 mL) cayenne pepper, ½ tsp (2 mL) garlic powder, ½ tsp (2 mL) onion powder, ½ tsp (2 mL) dried oregano, ½ tsp (2 mL) dried thyme, and ¼ tsp (1 mL) celery seeds (optional). Add salt to taste. Makes about 1 tablespoon (15 mL). To make more, multiply recipe and store in an airtight container for up to 6 months.
- 1 tbsp (15 mL) Cajun seasoning (very similar)

*See also* CAJUN SEASONING.

## Crescenza

*See* STRACCHINO.

## Cress

*Derived from the Greek word "to creep." Low-growing plants with small leaves, commonly used on salads but can also be cooked. Includes watercress, upland cress, curly cress, and land cress. Cress is highly perishable, so try to use it as soon as possible after you buy it.*

> 1 oz (30 g) =
> 1 cup (250 mL)

### If You Don't Have It

Substitute 1 cup (250 mL) cress with:

- 1 cup (250 mL) arugula
- 1 cup (250 mL) nasturtium leaves
- 1 cup (250 mL) baby spinach leaves + pinch of pepper
- 1 cup (250 mL) radish sprouts
- 1 cup (250 mL) tender dandelion greens

### Cress Varieties

Choose 1 cup (250 mL) cress from these varieties:

- 1 cup (250 mL) watercress (peppery; small tender leaves; crunchy stems; use fresh or gently cooked)
- 1 cup (250 mL) upland cress or land cress (elegantly peppery with a bite that comes on slow; often sold as small, micro-cress; tender, round or oval pale green leaves and stems; use fresh)
- 1 cup (250 mL) garden cress or pepper cress (sweetly peppery; often sold as sprouts; tiny, tender leaves and stems; use fresh)
- 1 cup (250 mL) winter cress (bitterly peppery; green leaves similar to arugula in size and shape; use gently cooked to tame the bitterness or mix young winter cress with milder greens to use fresh)

*See also* NASTURTIUM.

## Crisco

*See* VEGETABLE SHORTENING.

## Crisphead Lettuce

*One of the "cabbage" lettuces, with crisp leaves that form compacted heads or long-leaved without heads.*

### If You Don't Have It

Substitute 1 lb (500 g) crisphead lettuce with:

- 1 lb (500 g) romaine lettuce (crunchy; more flavorful)
- 8 oz (250 g) leaf lettuce (less crunchy; less watery)

### Crisphead Lettuce Varieties

Choose 1 lb (500 g) crisphead lettuce from these varieties:

- 1 lb (500 g) Iceberg, Great Lakes, Imperial, Vanguard, or Western lettuce (similar varieties of crisphead lettuce)

*See also* BUTTERHEAD LETTUCE.

## Croaker

*Also known as drum. A category of fish that make a deep croaking or drumming noise, especially during breeding season.*

### If You Don't Have It

Substitute 1 lb (500 g) croaker with:

- 1 lb (500 g) porgy
- 1 lb (500 g) hake

### Croaker Varieties

Choose 1 lb (500 g) croaker from these varieties:

- 1 lb (500 g) Atlantic croaker
- 1 lb (500 g) black drum
- 1 lb (500 g) red drum or redfish
- 1 lb (500 g) spot
- 1 lb (500 g) kingfish
- 1 lb (500 g) weakfish

*See also* WHITE SEA BASS.

## Crocodile

*Farm-raised crocodile are an established commodity in Australia, where it is illegal to sell the wild meat.*

### If You Don't Have It

Substitute 1 lb (500 g) crocodile tail meat with:

- 1 lb (500 g) alligator tail meat
- 1 lb (500 g) turtle meat
- 1 lb (500 g) chicken breast
- 1 lb (500 g) swordfish

## Croissant

*From the French word meaning "crescent." A breakfast roll that is traditionally made with butter.*

### If You Don't Have It

Substitute 1 lb (500 g) croissants with:

- 1 lb (500 g) crescent rolls from refrigerated dough (less flavorful)
- 1 lb (500 g) brioche (more eggy; denser texture)
- 1 lb (500 g) challah (more eggy; denser texture)

## Crostini

*A toasted Italian bread similar to bruschetta but often smaller, thinner, and sometimes with the crust removed. Usually topped and served as an appetizer or canapé.*

### If You Don't Have It

Substitute 16 crostini with:

- 16 Homemade Crostini: Cut a baguette into ¼-inch (1 cm) thick slices (remove crust if you like). Bake slices at 400°F (200°C), turning once, until just crisp, about 5 minutes. Rub with a cut garlic clove and brush, drizzle, or spray with olive oil. Makes about 16 crostini.
- 16 slices bruschetta (usually larger, thicker, with crust, and typically charcoal-grilled)
- 16 melba toasts
- 16 bagel chips
- 16 crackers

## Crottin de Chavignol

*See* CHÈVRE.

## Croustade

*An edible container used for stew, creamed meats, or vegetable mixtures. It can be made from pastry, a hollowed bread loaf, or puréed potatoes. Before filling, it is deep-fried or toasted until golden and crisp.*

### If You Don't Have It

Substitute 16 croustades with:

- 16 frozen prepared phyllo mini-shells (before filling, bake phyllo shells at 350°F/180°C on a baking sheet for 3 to 5 minutes)
- 8 small dinner rolls, each cut in half and hollowed out to leave the crust; brush with melted butter or olive oil and bake at 375°F (190°C) on a baking sheet until crisp, 8 to 12 minutes
- 16 small barquettes (boat-shaped pastry shells)
- 16 crostini (for hors d'oeuvres)
- 16 water crackers (for hors d'oeuvres)
- 16 rounds from slices of white bread (cut rounds with a cookie cutter) pressed into greased regular or mini-muffin cups and baked at 350°F (180°C) until crisp, 8 to 12 minutes
- 6 frozen prepared puff pastry shells (larger and more tender; bake pastry shells at 400°F/200°C on a baking sheet until puffed and golden, about 20 minutes. Remove tops and bake shells for 5 minutes more)

## Croutons

*Small browned pieces of bread. Usually served with salad. Smaller, commercially prepared croutons or "stuffing cubes" are turned into dressings and stuffings.*

### If You Don't Have It

Substitute 1 cup (250 mL) croutons with:

- 1 cup (250 mL) Homemade Croutons: Cut your favorite bread (dense, flavorful bread works best) into 1 cup (250 mL) of cubes (up to ½-inch/1 cm thick cubes for stuffing; up to 1½-inch/4 cm cubes for salad croutons) or other shapes. Toss with 2 to 3 tsp (10 to 15 mL) melted butter or oil and, if you like, salt, pepper, herbs, garlic, and/or Parmesan cheese, or other seasonings. Bake on a baking sheet at 350°F (180°C), tossing or turning once or twice to brown evenly, until crisp, about 15 minutes. Makes 1 cup (250 mL).

- 1 cup (250 mL) coarse bread crumbs (to top casseroles)
- 1 cup (250 mL) broken bagel chips (to top salads and casseroles)
- 1 cup (250 mL) broken crostini (to top salads and casseroles)

## Crumbs

*See* BREAD CRUMBS; COOKIE CRUMBS; CORNFLAKE CRUMBS; CRACKER CRUMBS; MATZO MEAL; PANKO; PIE CRUST, CRUMB.

## Crumpet

*In Britain, a thick, perforated yeast-risen pancake cooked until the underside is pale gold.*

### If You Don't Have It

Substitute 1 crumpet with:
- 1 English muffin (American)
- 1 American biscuit (less airy)
- 1 scone (sweeter; less airy)

## Crumpet Ring

*Also known as English muffin rings. Stainless-steel rings that are 4 inches (10 cm) in diameter and 1 inch (2.5 cm) deep.*

### If You Don't Have It

Substitute a crumpet ring with:
- biscuit cutter or cookie cutter
- clean 6-oz (170 g) tuna can with both ends removed

## Crust

*See* PIE CRUST, CRUMB; PIE CRUST, PASTRY.

## Crystallized Ginger

*See* GINGER, CRYSTALLIZED.

## Cubanelle Chile

*See* CHOOSING FRESH CHILES (PAGE 640).

## Cubeb

*Also known as Java pepper. Native to Indonesia, these dried grey-black berries (piper cubeba) are slightly longer than true black peppercorns and retain a "tail," which is the stem of the berries. Crushed cubeb emits aromas of camphor, mint, and allspice and tastes pleasantly hot.*

### If You Don't Have It

Substitute 1 tsp (5 mL) cubeb with:
- 1 tsp (5 mL) long pepper (adds citrus aromas)
- 1 tsp (5 mL) Tasmanian peppercorns (softer, more fruity aroma)
- 1 tsp (5 mL) grains of paradise (adds cardamom aromas)
- 1 tsp (5 mL) crushed selim kili pepper (adds eucalyptus and nutmeg aromas; slightly bitter)
- 1 tsp (5 mL) black peppercorns (less complex)

## Cucumber

*At about 4,000 years old, the cucumber is one of the oldest cultivated vegetables. It is 96% water. Used commonly for salads, garnishes, soups and sandwiches, and dressed with yogurt or vinegar.*

1 lb (500 g) = 2 medium = 2 cups (500 mL) sliced

### If You Don't Have It
Substitute 1 lb (500 g) cucumber with:
- 1 lb (500 g) small zucchini (for cooking; less sweet)

### Cucumber Varieties
Choose 1 lb (500 g) cucumber from these varieties:
- 1 lb (500 g) American slicing or garden cucumber (often sold waxed to extend shelf-life; thick, heavy body; bumpy dark green, thick and sometimes bitter-tasting skin; flesh is very mild in flavor; crunchy texture; best peeled and seeded for soups or when mixed with other ingredients)
- 1 lb (500 g) English or European or hothouse cucumber (often sold shrink-wrapped; longer and more slender than American slicing cucumbers; smooth or slightly ridged dark green thin skin; nearly seedless; mildly sweet flavor; less bitter than American slicing cucumbers; needs no peeling or seeding)
- 1 lb (500 g) Asian or Korean or Japanese cucumber (longer and more narrow than American slicing cucumbers; bumpy pale green to dark green thin skin; nearly seedless; complex, earthy flavor ranging from mild to bitter; juicy, crunchy texture; needs no peeling or seeding; best for sushi)
- 1 lb (500 g) Armenian cucumber or snake melon (long, slender, curved body; ridged, light yellow to pale green razor-thin skin; sweet, mild citrus flavor; extra-crisp texture; needs no peeling or seeding)
- 1 lb (500 g) American pickling or so-called "Kirby" cucumber (short, thick, blunt or slightly curved and pointed body; bumpy, pale-striped yellow to dark green somewhat-thin skin; crunchy, juicy texture; mildly sweet flavor; small seeds; good for slicing, cooking, and pickling)
- 1 lb (500 g) gherkins (often pickled and sold by the French name *cornichon*; small, short, relatively narrow body; bumpy, somewhat thin dark green skin; crunchy texture; sweet flavor; small seeds; good for slicing, cooking, and pickling)
- 1 lb (500 g) lemon cucumber (round and baseball-sized; bright yellow; tender and sweet, large core of seeds; good for slicing and pickling)

*See also* CORNICHON; SWEET GHERKIN.

## Cucuzza

*Also known as calabash, opo squash, long melon, snake gourd. Sicilian term for squash that looks like an elongated bottle gourd with a taste similar to zucchini when young.*

### If You Don't Have It
Substitute 1 lb (500 g) cucuzza with:
- 1 lb (500 g) bottle gourd
- 1 lb (500 g) winter melon
- 1 lb (500 g) chayote
- 1 lb (500 g) zucchini
- 1 lb (500 g) yellow squash

## Cuitlacoche

*See* HUITLACOCHE.

## Culantro

*See* SAWLEAF HERB.

## Culatello

*"Little backside." An Italian product made from pork hindquarters pressed like ham. The lean meat is salted, soaked in wine, and, traditionally, packed in the pig's bladder. It is moist, delicate, pink, and eaten raw. Originated in Parma.*

### If You Don't Have It
Substitute 4 oz (125 g) culatello with:
- 4 oz (125 g) prosciutto (fattier; not soaked in wine during aging)

### To Vary the Flavor
Substitute 4 oz (125 g) culatello with:
- 4 oz (125 g) Serrano or Iberico ham
- 4 oz (125 g) Ardennes ham (adds smoke flavor)
- 4 oz (125 g) Bayonne ham (adds mild smoke flavor)
- 4 oz (125 g) Westphalian ham (adds juniper and mild smoke flavors)

## Cumberland Sausage

*Traditional British spicy sausage made of coarse-cut pork. Sometimes sold by length from a long coil.*

### If You Don't Have It
Substitute 4 oz (125 g) Cumberland sausage with:
- 4 oz (125 g) Cambridge, Oxford, or other British sausage
- 4 oz (125 g) relatively mild pork sausage

## Cumin

*Also known as jeera and cumin seeds. Spice made from dried tiny seedlike fruits of an herb in the parsley family. Cumin is mentioned in the Bible and was probably used by the Romans. It is used in the Netherlands to flavor certain cheeses, in India in garam masala, and in Mexican and Tex-Mex dishes of North America.*

1 oz (30 g) = 4½ tbsp
(67 mL) whole seed =
4 tbsp (60 mL) ground

### If You Don't Have It
Substitute 1 tsp (5 mL) amber cumin seeds (ground) with:
- 1 tsp (5 mL) chili powder (most commercial chili powder blends contain a high percentage of amber cumin; adds oregano, mild chile pepper, salt, and pepper flavors)
- 1 tsp (5 mL) ground coriander (adds musky, lemony aroma)
- ½ tsp (2 mL) caraway (adds mild licorice aroma)

### Cumin Varieties
Choose 1 tsp (5 mL) amber cumin seeds (whole or ground) from these varieties:
- 1 tsp (5 mL) white cumin (similar to the common amber cumin; available in Asian markets)
- 1 tsp (5 mL) black cumin or royal cumin (shahi jeera or kala jeera; sweeter; more peppery; often used in curries; available in Asian markets)

## Cunner

*See* BLACKFISH.

## Cupuaçu

*Also known as copoasu. A tree and its fruit from the tropical rainforest of northern Brazil. Potato-shaped cupuaçu fruits weigh about 3 lbs (1.5 kg) with a tough coconut-like shell covered in brown fuzz. The fragrant white fruit inside hints at banana and melon and is puréed for juice, jams, ice creams, and tarts. The seeds are processed into chocolate-like products known to Brazilians as cupulate, which looks redder, has little caffeine, and taste milder and less bitter. Like its sister, cocoa* (Theobroma cacao), *cupuaçu* (Theobroma grandiflorum) *is high in disease-fighting antioxidants and polyphenols. It also contains theacrine, an alkaloid associated with sedative and hypnotic properties.*

### If You Don't Have It

Substitute 1 oz (30 g) cupulate with:
- 1 oz (30 g) semisweet chocolate (more complex chocolate flavor)
- 3 tbsp (45 mL) unsweetened cocoa powder + 1 to $1\frac{1}{2}$ tbsp (15 to 22 mL) granulated sugar + $1\frac{1}{2}$ tsp (7 mL) butter, shortening, or vegetable oil
- 3 heaping tbsp (45 mL) carob powder + 1 to $1\frac{1}{2}$ tbsp (15 to 22 mL) granulated sugar + $1\frac{1}{2}$ tsp (7 mL) butter, shortening, or vegetable oil

### To Vary the Flavor

Substitute 1 cup (250 mL) cupuaçu juice with:
- 1 cup (250 mL) açai juice
- 1 cup (250 mL) pomegranate juice
- 1 cup (250 mL) cranberry juice (more tart)
- 1 cup (250 mL) red grape juice + 1 tsp (5 mL) lemon juice

*See also* CHOCOLATE, BITTERSWEET; CHOCOLATE, SEMISWEET; CHOCOLATE, UNSWEETENED.

## Curaçao

*See* ORANGE LIQUEUR.

## Curly Endive

*A green that grows in loose heads of lacy leaves with prickly texture and slightly bitter taste. Frisée is blanched curly endive. It has paler yellow or light green leaves and is slightly sweet and less bitter. It can be used interchangeably with curly endive.*

### If You Don't Have It

Substitute 1 cup (250 mL) curly endive with:
- 1 cup (250 mL) chicory
- 1 cup (250 mL) escarole (less bitter; softer leaves)
- 1 cup (250 mL) radicchio (red color)

*See also* BELGIAN ENDIVE; CHICORY; ESCAROLE; FRISÉE.

## Currant, Dried

*The dried fruit of the seedless Zante grape. Not to be confused with fresh currants.*

¼ cup (60 mL) =
1½ oz (45 g)

### If You Don't Have It

Substitute 1 cup (250 mL) dried currants with:
- 1 cup (250 mL) raisins (dark or golden; larger than currants)
- 1 cup (250 mL) finely chopped soft prunes
- 1 cup (250 mL) finely chopped soft dates
- 1 cup (250 mL) dried blueberries, cherries, or cranberries

*See also* CHAMPAGNE GRAPE; CURRANT, FRESH; RAISIN.

## Currant, Fresh

*Small round red, white, or black berries that grow in northern temperate regions. Red currants were domesticated in Europe in the 16^{th} century. White currants are an uncommon variant of red currants. Black currants were cultivated a century later than red currants and thought inferior; they were used in Britain to treat sore throats and have an abundance of vitamin C. Frozen currants can be substituted for fresh, especially in jams.*

### If You Don't Have It

Substitute 1 cup (250 mL) fresh currants with:
- 1 cup (250 mL) elderberries (purple black color; bitter flavor)
- 1 cup (250 mL) gooseberries (light yellow to pale green color; tart flavor)
- 1 cup (250 mL) bilberries (purple color; sharp, sweet flavor)
- 1 cup (250 mL) blueberries (purple color; sweet flavor)

### Currant Varieties

Choose 1 cup (250 mL) fresh currants from these varieties:
- 1 cup (250 mL) black currants or cassis (dark color; tart)
- 1 cup (250 mL) red currants (red color; slightly sweet; slightly tart)
- 1 cup (250 mL) white currants (white color; slightly sweet; less tart)

## Currant Jelly

*The two main types are red currant jelly and less common black currant jelly. Red currant jelly is often used to accompany lamb and other meats.*

### If You Don't Have It

Substitute 1 cup (250 mL) currant jelly with:
- 1 cup (250 mL) grape jelly + 1 tsp (5 mL) lemon juice
- 1 cup (250 mL) scuppernong or muscadine jelly

## Curry Leaf

*Also known as kari leaf. Green shiny leaf of a small tree that grows wild in South Asia. The leaves are aromatic and used for flavor in cooking. The curry leaf's function corresponds to the Western use of bay leaf, often fried, and removed before the dish is served.*

### If You Don't Have It

Substitute 10 fresh curry leaves with:
- 10 good-quality dried curry leaves

### To Vary the Flavor

Substitute 10 fresh curry leaves with:
- 5 to 10 makrut (kaffir) lime leaves (adds lime, mandarin orange, and lemon aromas)
- 5 fresh bay leaves (adds piney, resinous, woodsy aromas)
- 1 tbsp (15 mL) chopped fresh cilantro (adds grassy, lemony aromas)

## Curry Paste

*See* CHILE PASTE.

## Curry Powder

*Originally, this powder was an attempt to produce a ready-made spice mix similar to homemade spice blends in India. Likely to include coriander, cumin, mustard seeds, pepper, fenugreek, and turmeric. Commercial "Madras" curry powder is usually spicier than curry powder without the Madras label.*

### If You Don't Have It

Substitute 1 tsp (5 mL) curry powder with:
- 1 tsp (5 mL) Homemade Curry Powder: Combine $3\frac{1}{2}$ tsp (17 mL) ground coriander, $2\frac{1}{2}$ tsp (12 mL) ground turmeric, 1 tsp (5 mL) ground cumin, 1 tsp (5 mL) crushed fenugreek seeds, $\frac{1}{2}$ tsp (2 mL) ground black pepper, $\frac{1}{2}$ tsp (2 mL) mustard powder, $\frac{1}{2}$ tsp (2 mL) ground allspice, $\frac{1}{4}$ tsp (1 mL) ground ginger, and $\frac{1}{8}$ to $\frac{1}{4}$ tsp (0.5 to 1 mL) cayenne pepper. Add salt to taste. Makes about 3 tablespoons (45 mL).
- $\frac{1}{2}$ tsp (2 mL) turmeric (just for yellow color; adds much less flavor)

## Cusk

*Also known as torsk or tusk. A saltwater fish similar to cod that's found in Arctic waters. The flesh is firm and moderately oily. Best for grilling or baking.*

### If You Don't Have It

Substitute 1 lb (500 g) cusk with:
- 1 lb (500 g) cod
- 1 lb (500 g) pollock
- 1 lb (500 g) haddock
- 1 lb (500 g) hake
- 1 lb (500 g) scrod (young cod)
- 1 lb (500 g) Cape capensis
- 1 lb (500 g) tilapia
- 1 lb (500 g) sole
- 1 lb (500 g) flounder
- 1 lb (500 g) tilefish
- 1 lb (500 g) turbot
- 1 lb (500 g) grouper
- 1 lb (500 g) halibut
- 1 lb (500 g) red snapper
- 1 lb (500 g) striped bass

## Custard Apple

*See* CHERIMOYA.

## Custard Powder

Not powdered custard,
but an eggless mixture
of cornstarch (or other
starch), dry milk, annatto
coloring, and other
ingredients that make a
custard-like sauce. It is
usually mixed with milk
and sugar then stirred into
hot milk. Instant custard
powder requires only hot
water. It was invented
in 1837 by British food
chemist Alfred Bird because
his wife was allergic to
eggs.

### If You Don't Have It
Substitute ½ cup (125 mL) instant custard powder with:
- ½ cup (125 mL) instant vanilla pudding mix

## Custard Squash

*See* PATTYPAN SQUASH.

## Cuttlefish

Also known as inkfish.
An edible cephalopod
with ink sacs and ten
appendages, it resembles
a large squid. Japan is the
largest market. Available
both fresh and dried.

### If You Don't Have It
Substitute 1 lb (500 g) cuttlefish with:
- 1 lb (500 g) squid (smaller; firmer; tenderize by simmering salted water or by pounding)
- 1 lb (500 g) octopus, preferably young (firmer; tenderize by simmering in salted water or by pounding)

## Cynar

An Italian aperitivo or
digestivo made from
artichokes and various
herbs. Served plain or
with a splash of soda
water over ice.

### If You Don't Have It
Substitute 3 tbsp (45 mL) Cynar with:
- 3 tbsp (45 mL) Byrrh

# Daikon to Dwenjang

| | |
|---|---|
| **Daikon** | *See* RADISH. |
| **Daikon Sprouts** | *See* RADISH SPROUTS. |
| **Daisy** | *See* PICKING EDIBLE FLOWERS (PAGE 650). |
| **Dal** | *See* PEAS, SPLIT; SWITCHING LENTILS (PAGE 653); THE WIDE WORLD OF DRIED BEANS (PAGE 637). |

**Danbo**

*Also known as Christian IX. Mildly sweet, pale yellow cheese from Denmark with red or yellow wax cover.*

**If You Don't Have It**

Substitute 1 oz (30 g) Danbo with:
- 1 oz (30 g) Tybo or Samsoe + small pinch of caraway seeds
- 1 oz (30 g) mild Cheddar or American cheese + small pinch of caraway seeds

**Dandelion**

*Young, tender dandelion greens work well in salads or gently cooked. Older, more bitter dandelion greens taste best when mellowed by cooking.*

**If You Don't Have It**

Substitute 1 cup (250 mL) dandelion greens with:
- 1 cup (250 mL) arugula
- 1 cup (250 mL) watercress or upland cress
- 1 cup (250 mL) nasturtium leaves
- 1 cup (250 mL) curly endive
- 1 cup (250 mL) baby spinach leaves + pinch of pepper

*See also* PICKING EDIBLE FLOWERS (PAGE 650).

## Danish Blue

*Also known as Danablu. A widely distributed cow's milk blue cheese from Denmark that's delicious paired with fruit, dark breads, and red wines.*

### If You Don't Have It
Substitute 1 oz (30 g) Danish blue with:
- 1 oz (30 g) aged Gorgonzola
- 1 oz (30 g) Roquefort
- 1 oz (30 g) Stilton
- 1 oz (30 g) Saga blue
- 1 oz (30 g) Blue Castello

## Danish Port Salut

*See* ESROM.

## Dasheen

*See* TARO.

## Dashi

*Japanese broth made with dried bonito tuna flakes. Dashi-no-moto is the instant form, sold as concentrate, granulated, or powdered.*

### If You Don't Have It
Substitute 1 cup (250 mL) dashi with:
- 1 cup (250 mL) Homemade Dashi: Put one 2-inch (5 cm) square piece of kombu (kelp) and 2¼ cups (550 mL) fresh water in a small pot. Bring to a boil over high heat. Remove from heat and stir in 3 tbsp (45 mL) bonito flakes. Let stand for a few minutes until bonito flakes sink. Remove and discard kombu. Strain stock into an airtight container. Cool, seal, and refrigerate for up to 5 days. Makes about 2 cups (500 mL).
- 1 cup (250 mL) reconstituted instant dashi (dashi-no-moto)
- 1 cup (250 mL) chicken stock + 3 tbsp (45 mL) dulse (seaweed) flakes or a 1-inch (2.5 cm) square of kombu, brought to a boil, removed from heat and cooled for 5 minutes, then strained (not as flavorful)

## Date

*Multiple varieties of fresh and dried dates are enjoyed in the Middle East and North Africa. Westerners are generally more familiar with dried medjool or deglet noor varieties. When dried, dates become softer and sweeter.*

> 8 oz (250 g) = 24 medium = 1¼ cups (300 mL) chopped

### If You Don't Have It
Substitute 1 cup (250 mL) dried dates with:
- 1 cup (250 mL) dried figs
- 1 cup (250 mL) raisins

## Date Sugar

*Dehydrated and ground date pieces.*

### If You Don't Have It

Substitute 1 cup (250 mL) date sugar with:

- 1 cup (250 mL) light brown or granulated sugar (fewer nutrients)

## Daylily

*See* PICKING EDIBLE FLOWERS (PAGE 650).

## Decanter

*A glass or crystal container with a bulbous bottom and a stopper that fits in the narrow neck. Used to serve or display wines and other spirits.*

### If You Don't Have It

Substitute a decanter with:

- tall decorative glass jar with a cork, as used for flavored oils and vinegars
- decorative glass pitcher

## Decorating Sugar

*See* SUGAR, DECORATING.

## Deep-Frying

*See* FRYING.

## Deer

*The main species eaten by humans are fallow deer, red deer, roe deer, and white-tailed deer. Since prehistoric times, deer meat has provided protein to people around the world.*

### If You Don't Have It

Substitute 1 lb (500 g) deer with:

- 1 lb (500 g) reindeer (technically a species of deer; eaten mostly in northern Europe and Asia, particularly in Sweden, Finland, and Russia)
- 1 lb (500 g) caribou
- 1 lb (500 g) elk
- 1 lb (500 g) antelope
- 1 lb (500 g) gazelle

### Deer Subspecies

Choose 1 lb (500 g) deer from these subspecies:

- 1 lb (500 g) white-tailed deer (the most common deer in North America)
- 1 lb (500 g) red deer (among the largest deer; found mostly in the Scottish Highlands)
- 1 lb (500 g) fallow deer (found near the Mediterranean and other parts of Europe)
- 1 lb (500 g) roe deer (among the smallest; considered the best-tasting by many cooks)

*See also* VENISON.

## Degreasing Pitcher

*See* FAT SEPARATOR.

## Delicata Squash

*Also known as sweet potato squash. The yellow flesh tastes like a combination of butternut squash and sweet potatoes.*

### If You Don't Have It
Substitute 1 cup (250 mL) chopped delicata squash with:
- 1 cup (250 mL) chopped sweet dumpling squash
- 1 cup (250 mL) chopped butternut squash
- 1 cup (250 mL) chopped buttercup squash
- 1 cup (250 mL) chopped pumpkin
- 1 cup (250 mL) chopped sweet potato

## Demerara Sugar

*See* SUGAR, RAW.

## Demi-Glace

*The classic French mother sauce, prepared by reducing equal measures of sauce espagnole (brown sauce) and brown veal stock.*

### For Better Health
Substitute 1 cup (250 mL) veal demi-glace with:
- 1 cup (250 mL) veggie glace (commercially available roasted vegetable demi-glace)

*See also* GLACE DE VIANDE.

## Derby

*Sage Derby (strongly flavored with sage) is a popular variety of this mild, semifirm cow's milk cheese.*

### If You Don't Have It
Substitute 1 oz (30 g) Derby cheese with:
- 1 oz (30 g) mild Cheddar
- 1 oz (30 g) Colby
- 1 oz (30 g) Cheshire
- 1 oz (30 g) Vermont Sage (to replace Sage Derby)

## Dessert Wine

*See* WINE, DESSERT.

## Deviled Ham

*The devil logo from Underwood canned deviled ham is the oldest food trademark still in use in the United States. Like deviled eggs, deviled ham incorporates devilishly hot seasonings like mustard and chiles.*

### If You Don't Have It
Substitute 12 oz (375 g) deviled ham with:
- 12 oz (375 g) Homemade Deviled Ham: Combine 12 oz (375 g) chopped wet-cured or canned ham (preferably smoked), $\frac{1}{4}$ cup (60 mL) chopped onion, $\frac{1}{3}$ cup (75 mL) mayonnaise or sour cream, 2 tbsp (30 mL) Dijon mustard, 1 tsp (5 mL) hot sauce, and 1 tsp (5 mL) Worcestershire sauce in a food processor. Pulse until finely minced but not uniformly puréed. Makes about $1\frac{1}{2}$ cups (375 mL).
- 12 oz (375 g) minced spam

### To Vary the Flavor
Substitute 12 oz (375 g) deviled ham with:
- 12 oz (375 g) liverwurst
- 12 oz (375 g) paté

*See also* SPAM.

## Devil's Dung

*See* ASAFETIDA POWDER.

## Devon Cream

*See* CREAM, CLOTTED.

## Dewberry

*A close relative of the blackberry that produces smaller berries.*

### If You Don't Have It

Substitute 1 cup (250 mL) dewberries with:
- 1 cup (250 mL) blackberries (larger)
- 1 cup (250 mL) tayberries (larger; red color)
- 1 cup (250 mL) youngberries (larger; red color)
- 1 cup (250 mL) loganberries (dark red color)
- 1 cup (250 mL) raspberries (sweeter; red color)

## Dextrose

*See* GLLUCOSE, LIQUID.

## Dianthus

*See* PICKING EDIBLE FLOWERS (PAGE 650).

## Digestive Biscuit

*Also known as sweetmeal biscuit and wheatmeal biscuit. The commercial name of a British favorite: slightly sweet whole wheat biscuits that are eaten with cheese.*

### If You Don't Have It

Substitute 1 lb (500 g) digestive biscuits with:
- 1 lb (500 g) graham crackers (sweeter)
- 1 lb (500 g) teething biscuits

## Dijon Mustard

*See* MUSTARD, PREPARED.

## Dika

*See* OGBONO NUT.

## Dill

*A member of the parsley family, dill is related to fennel but exudes aromas of caraway and lemon rather than anise.*

### If You Don't Have It

Substitute 1 tbsp (15 mL) fresh dill with:
- 1 tbsp (15 mL) fresh tarragon (particularly with eggs, fish, and chicken)
- 1 tbsp (15 mL) fresh fennel leaves (for garnishing)

## Dill Seed

*Along with the leaves of this annual herb, dill seeds have a special affinity with Scandinavian and eastern European cooking.*

### If You Don't Have It

Substitute 1 tsp (5 mL) dill seeds with:
- 1 tsp (5 mL) caraway seeds (stronger aroma)
- 1 tsp (5 mL) celery seeds (adds celery aroma)

## Doenjang

*See* FERMENTED BEAN PASTE.

---

## Dogfish

*Also known as capeshark and sand shark. The name of these various small sharks is reference to the small size and shape.*

### If You Don't Have It

Substitute 1 lb (500 g) dogfish with:
- 1 lb (500 g) shark
- 1 lb (500 g) swordfish
- 1 lb (500 g) mahi-mahi (sweeter)

---

## Dollarfish

*See* BUTTERFISH.

---

## Dolphinfish

*See* MAHI-MAHI.

---

## Donut

*See* DOUGHNUT.

---

## Donut Peach

*See* PEACH.

---

## Dorado

*See* MAHI-MAHI.

---

## Dorrigo Pepper

*See* TASMANIAN PEPPER.

---

## Dory

*See* JOHN DORY.

---

## Doubanjiang

*See* FERMENTED BEAN PASTE.

---

## Double Boiler

*Two nesting pots in which the bottom holds simmering water to gently heat or melt the ingredient — perhaps, custard, chocolate, or sauce — in the top pot.*

### If You Don't Have It

Substitute a double boiler with:
- stainless-steel or heatproof bowl set over a saucepan of simmering water (make sure that the bowl does not touch the water)
- microwave oven (for melting chocolate; put small, similar-size pieces of chocolate into a bone-dry microwave-safe bowl and microwave on Medium power in 30-second increments, stopping to stir after every increment; microwave only until chocolate can be stirred smooth)
- 250°F (120°C) oven (for melting chocolate; place small, similar-size pieces of chocolate into a bone-dry heatproof bowl; place in a preheated 250°F (120°C) oven for 8 to 10 minutes, or just until chocolate can be stirred smooth)
- heating pad set to high (for melting chocolate; place small, similar-size pieces of chocolate into a bone-dry glass bowl; set the bowl on the heating pad for 10 minutes, or just until chocolate can be stirred smooth; keep the chocolate melted

## Double Boiler (cont'd)

for several hours by setting the heating pad to low and putting the bowl on the pad)

- warming tray set to low (for melting chocolate; place small, similar-size pieces of chocolate into a bone-dry heatproof bowl; set the bowl on the warming tray for 5 to 10 minutes, or just until chocolate is almost melted; stir smooth off the heat)

## Double Gloucester

*See* GLOUCESTER.

## Douchi

*See* FERMENTED BLACK BEAN.

## Doughnut

*Also known as donut. Although leavened fried balls of dough have a long and festive history around the world, the ring-shaped pastry seems particularly American.*

### If You Don't Have It

Substitute 1 lb (500 g) doughnuts with:

- 1 lb (500 g) zeppoli (Italian deep-fried dough; chewier, fluffier, greasier)
- 1 lb (500 g) beignets (French and New Orleans deep-fried dough)
- 1 lb (500 g) Oliebollen (Dutch deep-fried dough)
- 1 lb (500 g) Berliner (German deep-fried dough filled with jam)
- 1 lb (500 g) buñuelos (Bolivian deep-fried dough)
- 1 lb (500 g) sonho (Brazilian deep-fried dough)
- 1 lb (500 g) loukoumathes (Greek deep-fried dough)
- 1 lb (500 g) sufganiyah (Israeli deep-fried dough filled with jam or custard)
- 1 lb (500 g) churros (Spanish or Mexican slender, ridged sticks of deep-fried dough piped through a star-shaped nozzle)
- 1 lb (500 g) paczki (Polish deep-fried dough filled with jam)
- 1 lb (500 g) calas (New Orleans deep-fried dough made from cooked rice)
- 1 lb (500 g) funnel cakes (German-American deep-fried batter drizzled through a funnel in a circular pattern; fluffier; greasier)
- 1 lb (500 g) génoise, sponge cake, or pound cake

## Dough Scraper

*See* BENCH KNIFE.

## Dove

*See* SQUAB.

## Dover Sole

*See* SOLE.

## Dragées

*Tiny hard round candies, in silver and other colors, used to decorate confections.*

### If You Don't Have It

Substitute 1 tbsp (15 mL) dragées with:
- 1 tbsp (15 mL) jimmies
- 1 tbsp (15 mL) nonpareils
- 1 tbsp (15 mL) M&Ms
- 1 tbsp (15 mL) colored sugar sprinkles

## Dragon Fruit

*See* PITAYA.

## Dragon's Eye

*See* LONGAN.

## Drambuie

*A liqueur of Scotch blended with heather honey and herbs.*

### If You Don't Have It

Substitute 3 tbsp (45 mL) Drambuie with:
- 3 tbsp (45 mL) Grandtully
- 3 tbsp (45 mL) Lochan Ora
- 3 tbsp (45 mL) Glayva

## Drawn Butter

*See* BUTTER, CLARIFIED.

## Dried Bonito

*See* BONITO.

## Dried Citrus Peel

*See* CITRUS PEEL, DRIED.

## Dried Crayfish

*In Louisiana, crayfish season runs from late October to early July. The rest of the year, dried crayfish remains an option.*

### If You Don't Have It

Substitute 1 oz (30 g) dried crayfish with:
- 1 oz (30 g) dried shrimp

## Dried Fruit

*See* SPECIFIC TYPES.

## Dried Lily Bud

*See* LILY BUD.

## Dried Shrimp

*A pungent flavoring in Asian and Latin American cooking. To reconstitute dried shrimp, soak them in warm water. The soaking water is used in some preparations as additional flavoring.*

### If You Don't Have It

Substitute 1 oz (30 g) dried shrimp with:
- 1 oz (30 g) dried crayfish

## Drum

*See* CROAKER.

## Drumstick

*Long, green pod vegetable from the Moringa tree. The pods are cooked, split, and scraped for their mild-flavored, aromatic pulp. Popular in Indian and the Phillipines, Moringa leaves can also be cooked like spinach.*

### If You Don't Have It
Substitute 1 lb (500 g) drumsticks with:
- 1 lb (500 g) asparagus

## Dry-Cured ham

*See* HAM, DRY-CURED.

## Dry Milk

*Also known as powdered milk. Long a staple of thrifty homemakers, dehydrated milk is available in full-fat and fat-free versions. Although the flavor of the reconstituted powder doesn't duplicate fresh fluid milk, the powder is a convenient ingredient in baked goods, pancakes, and waffles.*

1 lb (500 g) = 3⅔ cups (900 mL) = 14 cups (3.5 L) reconstituted

1⅓ cups (325 mL) = 4 cups (1 L) reconstituted

⅓ cup (75 mL) = 1 cup (250 mL) reconstituted

### If You Don't Have It
Substitute 1 cup (250 mL) dry milk (reconstituted) with:
- 1 cup (250 mL) whole milk (3.5% fat)

### For Better Health
Substitute 1 cup (250 mL) nonfat dry milk (reconstituted) with:
- 1 cup (250 mL) fat-free milk (less than 0.5% fat)

*See also* BUTTERMILK.

## Dry Mustard

*See* MUSTARD, POWDERED.

## Dublin Bay Prawn

*Also known as langoustine, lobsterette, and scampi. Small salt-water crustaceans resembling 6- to 8-inch (15 to 20 cm) lobsters.*

### If You Don't Have It
Substitute 1 lb (500 g) Dublin Bay prawns with:
- 1 lb (500 g) crayfish
- 1 lb (500 g) spiny or rock lobster (larger)
- 1 lb (500 g) Maine lobster (larger)
- 1 lb (500 g) jumbo shrimp or prawns

## Dubonnet

*A bittersweet, herbal apéritif. Dubonnet rouge (red) is based on red wine, flavored with quinine. Dubonnet blanc (blond) resembles dry vermouth.*

### If You Don't Have It

Substitute 3 tbsp (45 mL) Dubonnet with:
- 3 tbsp (45 mL) Lillet
- 3 tbsp (45 mL) Byrrh
- 3 tbsp (45 mL) Raphael
- 3 tbsp (45 mL) Punt e Mes

## Duck

*Also known as duckling. Most duck is sold frozen although fresh duck is available in some markets. Broilers and fryers are less than 8 weeks of age; roosters no more than 16 weeks. Ducks generally weigh between 3 and 5 pounds (1.5 to 2.5 kg). The USDA classifications for duck quality are A, B, and C. The highest grade, A, is usually what is found in markets. Look for the grade stamp on the wrapping or on a tag attached to the wing.*

### If You Don't Have It

Substitute 1 lb (500 g) duck with:
- 1 lb (500 g) squab
- 1 lb (500 g) goose (less fatty)
- 1 lb (500 g) turkey
- 1 lb (500 g) rabbit
- 1 lb (500 g) chicken

## Duck Egg

*Prepared with almost ritualistic precision, the preparation of 17-day-old fertilized duck egg, called balut, is a Filipino delicacy.*

### If You Don't Have It

Substitute 1 duck egg with:
- 1 extra-large chicken egg, especially from a pasture-raised hen (less rich; less flavorful)
- 5 quail eggs (smaller; less rich; less flavorful)

## Duck Fat

*Most renowned in the cooking of Gascony in southwestern France, where it is utilized as a cooking medium and a preservative. Confit de canard is duck that is cooked and stored in its own fat.*

### If You Don't Have It

Substitute 1 tbsp (15 mL) duck fat with:
- 1 tbsp (15 mL) goose fat
- 1 tbsp (15 mL) lard or pork fat
- 1 tbsp (15 mL) chicken fat

## Duckling

*See* DUCK.

## Duck Press

*One of the brassy classics of French table service, in which pieces of roasted duck—bones and all—are placed and pressed to extract every last drop of duck juices, blood and marrow, which are then made into a flavorful reduction sauce with red wine.*

### If You Don't Have It

Substitute a duck press with:
- Cider press
- Wine press
- Heavy-duty commercial juice press or citrus press

## Duck Sauce

*See* PLUM SAUCE.

## Dukka

*Also known as dukkah. Coarsely ground Egyptian seasoning mix often based on almonds, chickpeas, or hazelnuts with spicy additions such as coriander, cumin, pepper, and sesame seeds.*

### If You Don't Have It

Substitute 1 tbsp (15 mL) dukka with:
- 1 tbsp (15 mL) Homemade Dukka: Toast 1 cup (250 mL) hazelnuts or almonds in a dry frying pan over medium heat until fragrant, about 3 minutes. Remove and let cool slightly. Then rub off skins in a kitchen towel if you like (skins may be slightly bitter). Toast $\frac{1}{2}$ cup (125 mL) sesame seeds and $\frac{1}{4}$ cup (60 mL) coriander seeds in same pan. Transfer to a plate to cool. Combine cooled nuts and seeds in a food processor, in a mortar with a pestle or in a large electric spice grinder. Add 1 tbsp (15 mL) cumin seeds, $\frac{1}{2}$ tsp (2 mL) salt, and $\frac{1}{2}$ tsp (2 mL) ground black pepper. Process or pound to a coarse powder. Makes about $1\frac{1}{4}$ cups (300 mL).

## Duku

*See* LANGSAT.

## Dulce de Membrillo

*Also known as carne de membrillo, cotognata, marmelada, and quince paste. Firm marmalade of quince often cubed and served with cheese or used to fill pastries*

### If You Don't Have It

Substitute $\frac{1}{4}$ cup (60 mL) dulce de membrillo with:
- $\frac{1}{4}$ cup (60 mL) guava paste
- $\frac{1}{4}$ cup (60 mL) apple butter
- $\frac{1}{4}$ cup (60 mL) strawberry preserves
- $\frac{1}{4}$ cup (60 mL) other tropical fruit preserves

*See also* QUINCE.

## Dulse

*Maroon-color sea vegetable. Rich in iron. Often powdered and used as a salt substitute.*

### If You Don't Have It
Substitute 1 oz (30 g) dulse with:
- 1 oz (30 g) arame (milder brine flavor; dark brown color)
- 1 oz (30 g) wakame (similar brine flavor; dark green to brown color)
- 1 oz (30 g) hijiki (stronger brine flavor; black color)
- 1 oz (30 g) kombu (stronger brine flavor; dark brown to black color)

## Dumpling Wrappers

*See* WON TON SKINS.

## Dungeness Crab

*See* CHOOSING AMONG CRABS (PAGE 647).

## Durum Flour

*See* FLOUR, DURUM.

## Dutch Oven

*A large cast-iron pot with a tight-fitting lid traditionally used for Pennsylvania Dutch stews and braises.*

### If You Don't Have It
Substitute a Dutch oven with:
- any large, heavy, ovenproof pot with a tight-fitting lid

## Dutch-Process Cocoa

*See* COCOA POWDER, UNSWEETENED.

## Dwenjang

*See* FERMENTED BEAN PASTE.

# Early Richmond Cherry
## to Extracts

### Early Richmond Cherry

*See* CHERRY.

### Earthenware

*High-fired earthenware cooking pots are sturdier than those fired at low temperatures.*

**If You Don't Have It**

Substitute earthenware with:
- stoneware
- porcelain
- heatproof glass

### Eau de Vie

*See* BRANDY.

### Edam

*Next to Gouda, this mild yellow cheese is the second most popular cheese export from the Netherlands.*

1 lb (500 g) = 4 cups (1 L) grated or shredded

**If You Don't Have It**

Substitute 1 oz (30 g) Edam with:
- 1 oz (30 g) Gouda (richer; less tangy)
- 1 oz (30 g) Leyden (spicier; may be flavored with caraway or cumin)
- 1 oz (30 g) Fontina (richer; less tangy)

## Edamame

*Also known as green soybean. In Japan, young soybean pods are picked at the start of summer then boiled and salted for snacking like peanuts.*

> 1 lb (500 g) in shell =
> 1 cup (250 mL) shelled

### If You Don't Have It
Substitute 1 lb (500 g) shelled and cooked edamame with:
- 1 lb (500 g) cooked green peas
- 1 lb (500 g) cooked fresh lima beans
- 1 lb (500 g) cooked fresh fava beans
- 1 lb (500 g) cooked beans such as cannellini, kidney, or black-eyed peas

## Eel

*A notorious burglar in 18th century Japan claimed that he could see in the dark because he ate so much eel, which are rich in vision-enhancing vitamin A.*

### If You Don't Have It
Substitute 1 lb (500 g) eel with:
- 1 lb (500 g) lamprey (milder flavor)
- 1 lb (500 g) monkfish (more tender)
- 1 lb (500 g) mullet (more flaky)

### Eel Types
Choose 1 lb (500 g) eel from these types:
- 1 lb (500 g) freshwater eel (mostly farmed or seasonal; slightly fishier taste than saltwater eels)
- 1 lb (500 g) angula, elver or baby eel (tender; sweet)
- 1 lb (500 g) conger eel (tougher)
- 1 lb (500 g) smoked eel (less rich; adds smoke flavor)

## Egg

*See* EGG WHITE; EGG, WHOLE; EGG YOLK.

## Egg Barley

*Also known as egg drops and tarhonya. Hungarian dried egg pasta that is cut or shredded so small it resembles barley grains.*

### If You Don't Have It
Substitute 1 lb (500 g) egg barley with:
- 1 lb (500 g) Homemade Egg Barley: Stir together 4 cups (1 L) all-purpose flour and 1 tsp (5 mL) salt on a work surface and make a well in the center. Add 3 eggs and beat lightly, gradually working in the flour until combined. Knead until smooth then let stand for 30 minutes. Roll the dough several times until no more than $\frac{1}{8}$-inch (3 mm) thick then slice into $\frac{1}{8}$-inch (3 mm) cubes. Makes about 1 pound (500 g).
- 1 lb (500 g) spaetzle, cut into $\frac{1}{8}$-inch (3 mm) cubes
- 1 lb (500 g) egg noodles, broken into very small pieces
- 1 lb (500 g) won ton skins or fresh pasta cut into $\frac{1}{8}$-inch (3 mm) cubes
- 1 lb (500 g) dried soup pasta such as acini de pepe, pastina or orzo

## Egg Beater

*See* ROTARY BEATER.

## Egg Fruit

*See* CANISTEL.

## Eggnog

*In early American cookbooks, this luscious combination of eggs, cream, and spices was recommended for invalids.*

### If You Don't Have It
Substitute 1 cup (250 mL) eggnog with:
- 1 cup (250 mL) heavy or whipping cream (35% butterfat), light or table cream, or whole milk (less rich; thinner consistency)
- ½ cup (125 mL) to 1 cup (250 mL) advocaat (Dutch liqueur made with egg yolks and brandy)

### For Better Health
Substitute 1 cup (250 mL) eggnog with:
- 1 cup (250 mL) reduced-fat eggnog (less fat; fewer calories)

## Egg Noodle

*Although some Asian noodles contain egg, the term egg noodles generally refers to Eastern European flat pasta strips.*

| |
|---|
| 1 lb (500 g) dried = 5 cups (1.25 L) cooked |

### If You Don't Have It
Substitute 1 lb (500 g) dried egg noodles with:
- 8 oz (250 g) dried strand pasta such as linguine, fettuccine, or pappardelle

*See also* EGG BARLEY; PASTA, DRIED RIBBONS; PASTA, DRIED SHAPES; PASTA, DRIED STRANDS; PASTA, FRESH.

## Eggplant

*Also known as aubergine. To remove bitterness (especially in older, larger or very bitter varieties of eggplant), sprinkle the cut eggplant with salt and let drain briefly in a colander. Rinse off the salt if necessary.*

| |
|---|
| 1 lb (500 g) globe eggplant = 1 medium = 4½ cups (1.125 L) peeled and cubed = 1¾ cups (425 mL) roasted |
| 1 medium globe eggplant = about 3 Asian eggplants |

### If You Don't Have It
Substitute 1 lb (500 g) eggplant with:
- 1 lb (500 g) portobello mushrooms (particularly the caps to replace eggplant slices)
- 1 lb (500 g) zucchini or yellow squash

### Eggplant Varieties
Choose 1 lb (500 g) eggplant from these varieties:
- 1 lb (500 g) American, Italian-American, or globe eggplant (bell shape; dark purple skin; relatively tough flesh with mild to bitter flavor)
- 1 lb (500 g) baby or Italian purple eggplant (round or bell shape; thin to thick purple skin; relatively tender to tough flesh with mild to bitter flavor)
- 1 lb (500 g) Japanese or Asian eggplant (usually long, slender shape; tender, light violet to medium purple skin with sweet flavor; creamy flesh; cooks faster than globe eggplant)
- 1 lb (500 g) Chinese eggplant (usually long, slender shape; tender, white to lavender or violet skin; sweet, delicate, creamy flesh with few seeds; cooks faster than globe eggplant)

- 1 lb (500 g) elongated green-skinned eggplant (long, slender shape; tender, pale green skin; sweet, meaty flesh; cooks faster than globe eggplant)
- 1 lb (500 g) round green-skinned or Thai eggplant (size and shape of limes; thick green skin, flecked with yellow or white; mild, sweet, meaty, and seedy flesh)
- 1 lb (500 g) pea eggplant or baby Thai eggplant (the size, shape and color of small green grapes, growing in clusters; bitter flesh)
- 1 lb (500 g) white-skinned eggplant (round or elongated shape; thick white skin; mild flesh)
- 1 lb (500 g) striped Spanish or European eggplant (large round or bell shape; relatively tough skin with white to purple color and purple or pink stripes; mild, creamy flesh with few seeds)

## Egg Replacer, Powdered

*Eggs were first commercially dried and processed into powder in St. Louis, Missouri, around 1880. A vegetarian version of powdered eggs known as "egg replacer" combines various starches, such as potato starch, and leavening agents. Egg replacer is popular among vegans and available in most health food stores.*

### If You Don't Have It
Substitute 1½ tsp (7 mL) egg replacer powder mixed with 3 tbsp (45 mL) cold water with:
- 3 tbsp (45 mL) liquid egg substitute
- 2 egg whites (zero fat and cholesterol)
- 1 large egg (adds fat and cholesterol; makes richer baked goods)

*See also* EGG WHITE.

## Egg Ring

*A round metal form, with or without a handle, to hold and shape an egg as it's fried.*

### If You Don't Have It
Substitute an egg ring with:
- biscuit cutter
- cookie cutter
- clean tuna can or other short can with both ends removed

## Egg Roll Wrappers

*Also known as egg roll skins. A simple dough made from flour and water. When stuffing egg roll skins, keep the stack moist by covering with a damp towel.*

### If You Don't Have It
Substitute 1 lb (500 g) egg roll wrappers with:
- 1 lb (500 g) empanada wrappers (round)
- 1 lb (500 g) rolled pasta (cut to desired shape)
- 1 lb (500 g) won ton skins (thinner; square or rectangular)
- 1 lb (500 g) dumpling wrappers (thinner; round)
- 1 lb (500 g) rice paper (thinner, large; cut to desired shape; makes extra-crispy rolls)

*See also* WON TON SKINS.

## Egg Scissors

*A gadget with a scissors-like handle used to snip the top of the shell from soft-cooked eggs.*

### If You Don't Have It

Substitute egg scissors with:
- sharp knife and a steady hand
- kitchen scissors

## Egg Separator

*A small cup centered in a round frame made of plastic, metal, or ceramic. The cup catches the yolk while slots around the frame let the white slip through to a container beneath.*

### If You Don't Have It

Substitute an egg separator with:
- small, clean funnel (pour cracked egg into funnel; gently shake white through funnel spout; yolk remains in funnel)
- clean hands (pour cracked egg into palm; part fingers slightly to let whites slip through)

## Egg Slicer

*A device that cuts a hard-cooked egg into neat slices with one swift stroke. Its cutting mechanism of parallel wires is drawn down over the egg, which rests in an indented tray.*

### If You Don't Have It

Substitute an egg slicer with:
- sharp knife for slicing

## Egg Substitute

*Liquid egg products formulated as substitutes for whole eggs. Such products contain mostly egg white. The yolk is replaced with other ingredients such as nonfat milk, tofu, vegetable oils, emulsifiers, stabilizers, antioxidants, gum, artificial color, minerals, and vitamins.*

### If You Don't Have It

Substitute 3 tbsp (45 mL) egg substitute with:
- 2 egg whites (zero fat and cholesterol)
- 3 tbsp (45 mL) liquid pasteurized eggs (reduces risk of bacterial contamination; especially for uncooked or gently cooked preparations)
- 1 large egg (adds fat and cholesterol; makes richer baked goods)
- 1½ tsp (7 mL) powdered egg replacer + 3 tbsp (45 mL) cold water (for baking and thickening)

*See also* EGG REPLACER, POWDERED.

## Egg Wash

*Egg yolk or white, beaten with some water or milk, that is brushed on breads and other baked goods to promote a golden, shiny crust.*

### If You Don't Have It

Substitute ¼ cup (60 mL) egg wash with:
- 1 tbsp (15 mL) milk or cream + 1 to 2 tsp (5 to 10 mL) granulated sugar: brush milk over pastry, sprinkle with sugar (produces a more homestyle country glaze)

## Egg White

*The albumen content of an egg, which accounts for nearly 70% of the liquid weight. It contains more than half the egg's protein and many other nutrients.*

1 dozen large eggs =
1½ cups (375 mL)
egg whites

1 egg = 3 tbsp (45 mL)
egg whites

1 cup (250 mL) =
7 egg whites

1 egg white = 1 oz (30 g)

### If You Don't Have It

Substitute 1 large egg white with:
- 3 tbsp (45 mL) frozen and thawed egg white
- 1 tbsp (15 mL) powdered egg white + 3 tbsp (45 mL) water (reduces risk of bacterial contamination)
- 2 tsp (10 mL) meringue powder + 3 tbsp (45 mL) water (reduces risk of bacterial contamination; adds small amount of sugar)
- 1 tbsp (15 mL) ground flaxseed simmered in 3 tbsp (45 mL) water (adds body but no leavening)

*See also* EGG, WHOLE; MERINGUE POWDER.

## Egg, Whole

*Egg shell and yolk color may vary, but color has nothing to do with egg quality or flavor. The color comes from pigments in the outer layer of the shell and ranges in breeds from white to deep brown. The breed of hen determines the color of the shell. Breeds with white feathers and ear lobes lay white eggs; breeds with red feathers and ear lobes lay brown eggs. To measure half an egg, beat 1 whole egg, then measure out 1½ tbsp (22 mL).*

1 large egg = 3 tbsp
(45 mL) yolks and
whites = 1¾ oz (52 g)

4 jumbo eggs = 5 large
eggs = 6 medium
eggs = 7 small eggs =
1 cup (250 mL) yolks
and whites

1 dozen large eggs =
2⅓ cups (575 mL) yolks
and whites

### If You Don't Have It

Substitute 1 large whole egg (2 oz/60 g) with:
- 2 large egg yolks + 1 tbsp (15 mL) cold water, optional (for cooking and baking; makes richer baked goods)
- 2 large egg yolks (for thickening sauces and custards)
- 3 tbsp (45 mL) vegetable oil + 1 tbsp (15 mL) water (for baking)
- 2 to 3 tbsp (30 to 45 mL) mayonnaise (for cakes)
- 3½ tbsp (52 mL) frozen and thawed egg
- 2½ tbsp (37 mL) powdered whole egg + 2½ tbsp (37 mL) water
- 1 tsp (5 mL) cornstarch + 3 tbsp (45 mL) additional liquid in recipe (for thickening)
- 3 tbsp (45 mL) water, milk, or other liquid + 3 tbsp (45 mL) flour + 1½ tsp (7 mL) shortening, + ½ tsp (2 mL) baking powder (for baking)
- 1 tsp (5 mL) baking powder + 1 tsp (5 mL) vinegar (if using to replace 1 additional egg when at least 1 egg is already in recipe)

### To Vary the Flavor

Substitute 1 large egg with:
- 1 duck egg (larger; richer; more flavorful)
- 3 to 4 quail eggs (smaller)

### For Better Health

Substitute 1 large whole egg (2 oz/60 g) with:
- 2 egg whites (zero fat and cholesterol; makes baked goods less tender; add 1 tbsp/15 mL oil to improve texture)
- 3 tbsp (45 mL) egg white (for precise measurement in baking

## Egg, Whole (cont'd)

recipes; to make measuring easier, whisk egg white with a pinch of salt to loosen texture)
- 3 tbsp to ¼ cup (45 to 60 mL) liquid egg substitute (zero cholesterol; results in more gummy baked goods; add 1 tbsp/15 mL oil to improve texture)
- 3 tbsp (45 mL) liquid pasteurized eggs (to reduce risk of bacterial contamination; especially for uncooked or gently cooked preparations)
- 3 tbsp (45 mL) ground flaxseed + ⅛ tsp (0.5 mL) baking powder + 3 tbsp (45 mL) water (for baking, especially quick breads)
- half a ripe banana, mashed + ¼ tsp (1 mL) baking powder (for baking, especially quick breads)
- ¼ cup (60 mL) firm tofu, crumbled and sautéed with aromatics (vegan substitute for scrambled eggs; add turmeric or saffron for yellow color)

*See also* DUCK EGG; EGG SUBSTITUTE; EGG WHITE; EGG YOLK; QUAIL EGG.

## Egg Yolk

*With the exception of riboflavin and niacin, the yolk contains a higher proportion of the egg's vitamins than the white. Egg yolks are one of the few foods naturally containing vitamin D.*

> 1 dozen large eggs = ⅞ cup (220 mL) egg yolks
>
> 1 egg = 1 tbsp (15 mL) egg yolk = ¾ oz (20 g)
>
> 1 cup (250 mL) = 14 egg yolks

### If You Don't Have It
Substitute 2 egg yolks with:
- 1 large whole egg (for thickening sauces)
- 3 tbsp (45 mL) frozen and thawed egg yolk
- ¼ cup (60 mL) powdered egg yolk + 4 tsp (20 mL) water (for baking)

### For Better Health
Substitute 2 egg yolks with:
- 1 egg white (for baking and cooking; zero fat and cholesterol; may result in less tender baked goods)

*See also* EGG, WHOLE.

## Egusi Seed

*In West Africa, the term egusi refers to the fat- and protein-rich seeds of certain gourds, which are ground to thicken a soup of the same name.*

### If You Don't Have It
Substitute ½ cup (125 mL) egusi seeds with:
- ½ cup (125 mL) pumpkin seeds
- ½ cup (125 mL) sunflower seeds
- ½ cup (125 mL) pine nuts

## Einkorn

*See* FARRO.

## Elbow Macaroni

*See* PASTA, DRIED SHAPES.

## Elderberry

*Both elderberries and elderflowers must be cooked before eating to destroy the tiny amount of poisonous alkaloid they contain. The tart-tasting, purple-black berries make excellent jelly. The elderflowers are wonderful in teas (employed by Native Americans as an antidote to colds) or cooked into fritters, muffins, or pancakes.*

### If You Don't Have It
Substitute 1 cup (250 mL) elderberries with:
- 1 cup (250 mL) fresh black currants or cassis (dark color; tart)
- 1 cup (250 mL) fresh red currants (red color; slightly sweet; slightly tart)
- 1 cup (250 mL) fresh white currants (white color; slightly sweet; less tart)
- 1 cup (250 mL) gooseberries (light yellow to pale green color; tart)
- 1 cup (250 mL) cranberries (red color; tart)
- 1 cup (250 mL) lingonberries (red color; tart)

## Elk

*The North American game animal, which can stand 5 feet (1.5 m) at the shoulder, is larger than the European elk. American president and renowned sportsman Theodore Roosevelt was partial to elk tongue, pronouncing it, "excellent to take out as a lunch on a long hunting trip."*

### If You Don't Have It
Substitute 1 lb (500 g) elk with:
- 1 lb (500 g) reindeer
- 1 lb (500 g) caribou
- 1 lb (500 g) red, fallow, or white-tailed deer
- 1 lb (500 g) moose
- 1 lb (500 g) antelope
- 1 lb (500 g) gazelle

*See also* VENISON.

## Elver

*See* EEL.

## Emmental

*Also known as Emmentaler and Emmenthaler. Named for Switzerland's Emmental Valley, versions of this buttery, nutty cheese are produced in Austria, France, Germany, and the United States.*

4 oz (125 g) = 1 cup (250 mL) grated

### If You Don't Have It
Substitute 1 oz (30 g) Emmental with:
- 1 oz (30 g) Jarlsberg
- 1 oz (30 g) Gruyère
- 1 oz (30 g) Swiss
- 1 oz (30 g) French Comté
- 1 oz (30 g) Beaufort

## Emmer

*See* FARRO.

## Empanada Wrappers

*Dough rounds that are stuffed with savory or sweet fillings before they are baked or fried. Sold frozen in some supermarkets.*

### If You Don't Have It
Substitute 1 lb (500 g) empanada wrappers with:
- 1 lb (500 g) egg roll wrappers (square)
- 1 lb (500 g) won ton skins (thinner; round)
- 1 lb (500 g) dumpling wrappers (thinner; round)
- 1 lb (500 g) rolled pasta (cut to desired shape)
- 1 lb (500 g) rice paper (thinner, large; cut to desired shape; makes crispy empanadas)

## Emu

*A nonflying game bird. Emu is now farm-raised in its native Australia and in North America. It tastes like beef but is softer in texture.*

### If You Don't Have It
Substitute 1 lb (500 g) emu with:
- 1 lb (500 g) ostrich
- 1 lb (500 g) beef (firmer texture; richer)
- 1 lb (500 g) turkey
- 1 lb (500 g) chicken

## Enamelware

*For best heat conduction, choose enamelware cooking pans with a cast-iron core.*

### If You Don't Have It
Substitute enamelware with:
- cast-iron cookware (may react with acidic foods, altering their flavor and color)

## Endigia

*Also known as red endive. A gorgeous cross between radicchio and Belgian endive in a compact football shape with ruffled, claret-colored leaf tips that fade to snow white stems. Sweet, bitter, juicy, and crunchy.*

### If You Don't Have It
Substitute 1 lb (500 g) endigia with:
- 1 lb (500 g) Belgian endive
- 1 lb (500 g) radicchio

*See also* BELGIAN ENDIVE; RADICCHIO.

## Endive

*See* BELGIAN ENDIVE; CURLY ENDIVE; ESCAROLE.

## English Bean

*See* FAVA BEAN.

## English Cucumber

*See* CUCUMBER.

## English Muffin

*Round yeast buns that are "baked" on a griddle. The preferred method for cutting the muffin in half before toasting is to split it gently with a fork. This creates a textured surface that catches plenty of butter and jam.*

### If You Don't Have It

Substitute 1 English muffin with:

- 1 crumpet
- 1 biscuit (less airy)
- 1 bagel (denser; chewier)
- 1 scone (sweeter; less airy)
- 1 croissant (richer; flakier)
- 2 slices sturdy bread (especially toasted)

## English Muffin Ring

*See* CRUMPET RING.

## Enoki

*See* SHUFFLING MUSHROOMS (PAGE 654).

## Epazote

*Also known as bean herb, Mexican tea, pigweed, wormseed, and worm weed. A strongly flavored wild herb called for in many Mexican bean dishes because it counters flatulence.*

### If You Don't Have It

Substitute 1 tbsp (15 mL) chopped fresh epazote with:

- 1 tsp (5 mL) dried epazote
- 1 tbsp (15 mL) chopped fresh savory
- 1 tbsp (15 mL) chopped fresh parsley

## Épices Fines

*See* SPICE PARISIENNE.

## Epoisses de Bourgogne

*A pungent soft paste cheese from the French region of Burgundy. The rind is washed with marc, a clear eau de vie.*

### If You Don't Have It

Substitute 1 oz (30 g) Epoisses de Bourgogne with:

- 1 oz (30 g) Ami du Chambertin
- 1 oz (30 g) Langres
- 1 oz (30 g) Pont-l'Évêque
- 1 oz (30 g) French-Alsatian Muenster

## Escargots

*See* SNAILS.

## Escarole

*Also known as Batavian endive. A type of endive that forms flat-leaf, relatively compact heads with dark green outer leaves and pale hearts.*

### If You Don't Have It

Substitute 1 cup (250 mL) escarole with:

- 1 cup (250 mL) curly endive
- 1 cup (250 mL) chicory
- 1 cup (250 mL) radicchio (red color)
- 1 cup (250 mL) arugula (more tender)

## Escolar

*Also known as snake mackerel and walu. Sometimes marketed as "white tuna" or "butterfish," this exceptionally rich Hawaiian fish has a bad reputation as "Ex-lax fish." While escolar is high in oil, it is often unscrupulously replaced with a very similar fish called oilfish or castor oil fish (Ruvettus pretiosus), which is so high in oil that has a laxative effect. True escolar fillets look similar to those of bluefish, while oilfish appears somewhat red.*

### If You Don't Have It

Substitute 1 lb (500 g) escolar with:
- 1 lb (500 g) butterfish
- 1 lb (500 g) black cod
- 1 lb (500 g) halibut

## Espagnole Sauce

*Also known as basic brown sauce. "The name has nothing to do with Spain,"* writes Alan Davidson in the Oxford Companion to Food, *"any more than the counterpart term allemande (see Velouté) has anything to do with Germany. It is generally believed that the terms were chosen because in French eyes Germans are blond and Spaniards are brown."*

### If You Don't Have It

Substitute 1 cup (250 mL) espagnole sauce with:
- 1 cup (250 mL) Homemade Espagnole Sauce: Melt ¼ cup (60 mL) butter in a saucepan over medium-low heat. Add ½ cup (125 mL) chopped onion, ½ cup (125 mL) chopped carrot, and ⅓ cup (75 mL) chopped celery. Cover and sweat for 10 minutes. Stir in 3 tbsp (45 mL) all-purpose flour and cook, stirring, until flour turns nutty brown, 8 to 10 minutes. Whisk in 4½ cups (1.125 L) hot beef stock and 2½ tbsp (37 mL) tomato paste until blended smooth. Tie a few fresh parsley sprigs, ½ tsp (2 mL) peppercorns, and 1 bay leaf in cheesecloth or a clean coffee filter and add to the sauce. Simmer gently over low heat, stirring occasionally, until slightly thickened and reduced to about 3½ cups (875 mL), about 2 hours. Strain, pressing on the vegetables, then taste and season with salt and pepper as necessary. Makes about 3 cups (750 mL).
- 1 cup (250 mL) French Bourguignonne sauce (adds a reduction of red wine, shallots, and herbs)
- 1 cup (250 mL) sauce aux champignons (adds mushrooms and cream)
- 1 cup (250 mL) Chasseur or hunter's sauce (adds mushrooms, shallots, red wine, herbs, and tomatoes)
- 1 cup (250 mL) sauce à l'Orange (adds orange zest)
- 1 cup (250 mL) Sauce Africaine (spicier)
- 1 cup (250 mL) port wine sauce (adds reduced port or Madeira)
- 1 cup (250 mL) bordelaise sauce (made with red wine, demi-glace, bone marrow, shallots, and herbs)

## Espresso

*The standard cuppa coffee in Italy is prepared by forcing steam through finely ground, packed coffee to make a robust brew. A properly executed espresso is crowned with foam called* crema *or* schiuma.

### If You Don't Have It
Substitute ¼ cup (60 mL) brewed espresso with:
- ¼ cup (60 mL) strong brewed coffee
- ¼ cup (60 mL) hot water + 1 to 2 tsp (5 to 10 mL) instant espresso powder

### For Better Health
Substitute ¼ cup (60 mL) brewed espresso with:
- ¼ cup (60 mL) brewed decaffeinated espresso
- ¼ cup (60 mL) brewed roasted chicory (caffeine-free)
- ¼ cup (60 mL) brewed concentrated rooibos or "red espresso"

*See also* COFFEE.

## Espumante

*See* WINE, SPARKLING.

## Esrom

*Also known as Danish Port Salut. Pleasantly pungent when young, this pale yellow Danish cheese, named for Esrom, Denmark, intensifies in flavor as it ages.*

### If You Don't Have It
Substitute 1 oz (30 g) Esrom with:
- 1 oz (30 g) Tilsit
- 1 oz (30 g) Havarti
- 1 oz (30 g) Fontina
- 1 oz (30 g) French Port Salut or Saint Paulin

## Essences

*See* FLAVORING OILS.

## Ethiopian Flat Bread

*See* INJERA.

## Ethiopian Pepper

*See* SELIM KILI PEPPER.

## Ethyl Alcohol

*See* NEUTRAL SPIRITS.

## Etima

*See* OGBONO NUT.

## Evaporated Milk

*Homogenized milk that is cooked (to reduce the water content by 60%) and then canned. It has a slightly caramelized flavor.*

> 12-oz (375 g) can =
> 1½ cups (375 mL)

### If You Don't Have It
Substitute 1 cup (250 mL) evaporated whole milk (8% to 10% fat) with:
- 1 cup (250 mL) Milnot, a brand of evaporated milk that whips better than others
- 2¼ cups (550 mL) whole milk, gently simmered in a saucepan until reduced to 1 cup (250 mL)
- 1 cup (250 mL) whole milk (3.5% to 4% fat; not for whipping)
- 1 cup (250 mL) half-and-half (10 to 12% fat; not for whipping)

## Evaporated Milk
### (cont'd)

- 1 cup (250 mL) light or table cream (20% fat; not for whipping)
- 1 cup (250 mL) light whipping cream (30% fat) or heavy whipping cream (35% fat)

### For Better Health
Substitute 1 cup (250 mL) evaporated whole milk with:
- 1 cup (250 mL) fat-free evaporated milk (0.5% fat)

*See also* SWEETENED CONDENSED MILK.

## Everclear

*See* NEUTRAL SPIRITS.

## Excelsior Cheese

*Double- or triple-cream cow's milk cheese made in Normandy but named by Parisian cheese authority Henri Androuët. It has a cylindrical shape and mild, almond-like flavor.*

### If You Don't Have It
Substitute 1 oz (30 g) excelsior with:
- 1 oz (30 g) Brillat-Savarin
- 1 oz (30 g) Boursault
- 1 oz (30 g) Explorateur

## Explorateur

*Luscious white rind cylinders of triple-crème cheese.*

### If You Don't Have It
Substitute 1 oz (30 g) Explorateur with:
- 1 oz (30 g) Boursault
- 1 oz (30 g) Brillat-Savarin
- 1 oz (30 g) Gratte-Paille
- 1 oz (30 g) Brie
- 1 oz (30 g) Camembert

## Extracts

*Various concentrated flavorings derived from foods through evaporation or distillation. Because of their intensity, a tiny amount of extract can greatly impact the flavor of a dish without changing its consistency.*

### If You Don't Have It
Substitute 1 tsp (5 mL) flavoring extract with:
- $\frac{1}{8}$ tsp (0.5 mL) flavoring oil

*See also* SPECIFIC TYPES.

# Falernum to Fuzzy Gourd

## Falernum

*A West Indian flavoring syrup that tastes of almonds, ginger, and lime.*

**If You Don't Have It**

Substitute 3 tbsp (45 mL) falernum with:
- 5 tsp (25 mL) orgeat syrup (preferably, add 1 tsp/5 mL lime juice and ½ tsp/2 mL ginger juice)
- 5 tsp (25 mL) Homemade Simple Syrup (see recipe, page 552; preferably, add 1 tsp/5 mL lime juice, ½ tsp/2 mL ginger juice, and ⅛ tsp/0.5 mL almond extract)
- 3 tbsp (45 mL) grenadine (adds red color and pomegranate flavor; preferably, add 1 tsp/5 mL lime juice, ½ tsp/2 mL ginger juice, and ⅛ tsp/0.5 mL almond extract)

## Farfel

*Matzo or dried noodles broken into small pieces. Often used in Jewish cookery.*

**If You Don't Have It**

Substitute 1 cup (250 mL) farfel with:
- 1 cup (250 mL) broken crackers
- 1 cup (250 mL) broken fried (crisp) chow mein noodles
- 1 cup (250 mL) broken tortilla chips
- 1 cup (250 mL) broken cornflakes
- 1 cup (250 mL) broken potato chips

## Farina

*Derived from the Latin, the word means "flour" in English and Italian.*

**If You Don't Have It**

Substitute 1 cup (250 mL) farina with:
- 1 cup (250 mL) semolina
- 1 cup (250 mL) durum wheat flour
- 1 cup (250 mL) cornmeal (preferably coarsely ground)
- 1 cup (250 mL) corn grits

## Farmer Cheese

*Also known as farmer's cheese. A drier version of cottage cheese usually pressed into a loaf.*

### If You Don't Have It

Substitute 1 oz (30 g) farmer cheese with:

- 1 oz (30 g) Homemade Farmer Cheese: Wrap 1 cup (250 mL) cottage cheese in a piece of cheesecloth or a coffee filter and put in a strainer or colander. Set the colander over a bowl and refrigerate until the liquid drains into the bowl and the cheese firms up. Makes about ¾ cup (175 mL).
- 1 oz (30 g) ricotta cheese, drained in cheesecloth (may add more liquid)
- 1 oz (30 g) dry-curd cottage cheese
- 1 oz (30 g) cream cheese (especially for dips; may add more liquid)
- 1 oz (30 g) sour cream (especially for dips; may add more liquid)
- 1 oz (30 g) Monterey Jack cheese

## Farro

*Also known as emmer. A form of wheat cultivated since at least 9500 BC in Neolithic Western Asia. It eventually migrated to Europe and became a staple of the Roman poor. Three related grains are sometimes labeled as farro, including farro piccolo (einkorn or* Triticum monococcum*), farro medio (emmer or* Triticum dicoccum*), and farro grande (spelt or* Triticum spelta*). Farro medio (emmer) grown in the Garfagnana mountains of northwest Tuscany has its geographic identity protected by law.*

> 1 cup (250 mL) farro (emmer) =
> 2½ cups (625 mL) cooked

### If You Don't Have It

Substitute 1 cup (250 mL) farro (emmer) with:

- 1 cup (250 mL) spelt berries or groats (larger grains)
- 1 cup (250 mL) hulled or whole-grain barley
- 1 cup (250 mL) wheat berries
- 1 cup (250 mL) cracked wheat (takes less time to cook)
- 1 cup (250 mL) bulgur (takes less time to cook)
- 1 cup (250 mL) rye berries
- 1 cup (250 mL) kasha
- 1 cup (250 mL) triticale berries or groats
- 1 cup (250 mL) Kamut® berries or groats

*See also* WHEAT BERRIES.

## Fat

*See* BUTTER; LARD; VEGETABLE SHORTENING; SPECIFIC TYPES.

## Fatback

The layer of fresh fat that runs down a pig's back. It is typically unsalted and used to make cracklings or rendered into lard. In Italy, a delicate type of fatback called lardo is salt-cured, seasoned, and eaten like prosciutto.

### If You Don't Have It
Substitute 4 oz (125 g) fatback with:
- 4 oz (125 g) salt pork (drop into boiling water for 30 seconds to extract excess salt)
- 4 oz (125 g) caul fat
- 4 oz (125 g) bacon (adds smoke flavor; drop into boiling water for 30 seconds to extract excess salt)

## Fat Choy

Also known as black moss, hair moss, and hair vegetable. A blue-green algae that looks like black hair when dried. When rehydrated, it has a noodle-like texture but remains black. It is often served in the Cantonese dish Buddha's Delight for Chinese New Year in part because the term "fat choy" sounds like the term "prosperity" when pronounced in Chinese.

### If You Don't Have It
Substitute 1 oz (30 g) fat choy with:
- 1 oz (30 g) cellophane noodles or bean threads (transparent color)

## Fat Mop

*See* GREASE MOP.

## Fat Separator

Also known as a degreasing pitcher. Ingenious heatproof pitcher with a spout that reaches to the bottom of the cup. You pour in fatty liquid, such as sauce, stock or pan drippings, let the fat rise to the top, then pour out the defatted liquid.

### If You Don't Have It
Substitute a fat separator with:
- grease mop or fat mop
- chilling pan of soup, stock or other liquid until fat congeals on top, then spooning off fat
- skimming fat from surface with a ladle, large spoon, or bulb baster
- dragging folded paper towels across surface of liquid until fat is removed (for small amounts of fat)
- placing ice cubes in a slotted spoon and dragging across surface of liquid, then discarding ice as it becomes covered with fat (for small amounts of fat)

## Fat Substitutes

*See* BUTTER; LARD; VEGETABLE SHORTENING.

## Fava Bean

*Also known as broad bean, butter bean, English bean, and Windsor bean. Beloved in Mediterranean France and in Italy, fresh young favas need only be shelled before eating. More mature beans may also need to be peeled. Favas are also available dried.*

1 lb (500 g) in shell =
4 to 6 oz (125 to 175 g)
shelled = 1 to 1½ cups
(250 to 375 mL) shelled

1 lb (500 g) dried =
2 cups (500 mL) =
4½ cups (1.125 L) cooked

### If You Don't Have It

Substitute 1 cup (250 mL) shelled and peeled fresh fava beans with:

- 1 cup (250 mL) fresh edamame (shelled green soybeans)
- 1 cup (250 mL) fresh baby lima beans (sweeter)
- 1 cup (250 mL) sugar snap peas (in the shell)
- 1 cup (250 mL) chickpeas, red kidney beans, or cannellini beans (to replace dried favas in soups and stews)

*See also* THE WIDE WORLD OF DRIED BEANS (PAGE 637).

## Feijoa

*Also known as pineapple guava. A green-skinned tropical fruit that's the size and shape of an egg with cream-color granular flesh that tastes of Concord grapes, lemon pineapple, and quince.*

### If You Don't Have It

Substitute 1 lb (500 g) feijoa with:

- 1 lb (500 g) guava
- 1 lb (500 g) kiwifruit
- 1 lb (500 g) pineapple
- 1 lb (500 g) blueberries or strawberries

## Fennel, Fresh

*Also known as bulbing fennel and finocchio. Often mislabeled as anise, both the bulb and copious aromatic greens of this crisp, sweet vegetable are extremely versatile. To replace fresh fennel leaves, use hoja santa leaves, dill, or parsley.*

1 lb (500 g) = 3 cups
(750 mL) sliced

### If You Don't Have It

Substitute 1 lb (500 g) fresh fennel bulb with:

- 1 lb (500 g) celery (cooks faster; preferably, add 1 tsp/5 mL crushed fennel seeds or 1 tbsp/15 mL anise liqueur, such as Pernod or Ricard, to add anise flavor)
- 1 lb (500 g) bok choy stems (preferably, add 1 tsp/5 mL crushed fennel seeds or 1 tbsp/15 mL anise liqueur, such as Pernod or Ricard, to add anise flavor)
- 1 lb (500 g) udo

## Fennel Seeds

*The seeds of the common fennel plant add delicate licorice flavor to a variety of preparations from liqueurs to sausages.*

### If You Don't Have It

Substitute 1 tsp (5 mL) fennel seeds with:

- 1 tsp (5 mL) anise seeds
- 1 tsp (5 mL) caraway seeds (less sweet)
- 1 tsp (5 mL) dill seeds (milder)
- 1 tsp (5 mL) cumin seeds (more earthy aroma)
- 1 tsp (5 mL) yellow mustard seeds (less complex aroma)

## Fenugreek Leaf

*Also known as fenugreek greens and methi leaves. These bitter greens are common in Indian and Pakistani cooking. They are typically added to breads or chickpea fritters.*

### If You Don't Have It

Substitute 1 tbsp (15 mL) chopped fresh fenugreek leaves with:

- 1 tsp (5 mL) dried fenugreek leaves
- 1 tbsp (15 mL) chopped fresh Chinese celery leaves
- 1 tbsp (15 mL) chopped fresh celery leaves
- 1 tbsp (15 mL) packed watercress

## Fenugreek Seed

*Yellowish brown seeds used to flavor Indian curries. The aroma is similar to celery. Slow toasting brings out the full flavor, but too much heat can turn the seeds bitter.*

### If You Don't Have It

Substitute 1 tsp (5 mL) fenugreek seeds with:

- 1 tsp (5 mL) yellow mustard seeds

## Fenugreek Sprouts

*For centuries, folk medicine has recommended the seeds, leaves, and sprouts of fenugreek for women's health, most recently for breast health among pregnant and nursing women.*

### If You Don't Have It

Substitute $\frac{1}{4}$ cup (60 mL) fenugreek sprouts with:

- $\frac{1}{4}$ cup (60 mL) alfalfa sprouts (sweeter)
- $\frac{1}{4}$ cup (60 mL) broccoli sprouts (more peppery)
- $\frac{1}{4}$ cup (60 mL) buckwheat sprouts (more nutty)
- $\frac{1}{4}$ cup (60 mL) sunflower sprouts (more nutty)
- $\frac{1}{4}$ cup (60 mL) mung bean sprouts (thicker and crisper)

## Fermented Bean Paste

*A broad category of Asian pastes based on fermented soybeans and a primary source of umami flavor in Asian cuisines.*

### If You Don't Have It

Substitute $\frac{1}{2}$ cup (125 mL) fermented bean paste with:

- $\frac{1}{2}$ cup (250 mL) fermented black beans
- $\frac{1}{2}$ cup (250 mL) hoisin sauce
- $\frac{1}{2}$ cup (250 mL) sweet bean sauce
- $\frac{1}{2}$ cup (250 mL) red or dark miso
- $\frac{1}{2}$ cup (250 mL) natto

## Fermented Bean Paste (cont'd)

### Fermented Bean Paste Varieties

Choose ½ cup (125 mL) fermented bean paste from these varieties:

- ½ cup (125 mL) doubanjiang (Szechuan paste often including fermented broad beans)
- ½ cup (125 mL) yellow soybean paste (Beijing specialty often substituted with sweet bean sauce or hoisin sauce)
- ½ cup (125 mL) doenjang (thick paste found throughout Korean cuisine)
- ½ cup (125 mL) gochujang (thick and spicy Korean paste made with glutinous rice)
- ½ cup (125 mL) tuong (Vietnamese thick or thin paste made with glutinous rice)

*See also* BEAN SAUCE; FERMENTED BLACK BEAN; MISO.

## Fermented Black Bean

*Also known as douchi, Chinese or salty black bean. Small black soybeans preserved in salt. The flavor is pungent and complex.*

### If You Don't Have It

Substitute ½ cup (125 mL) fermented black beans with:

- ½ cup (125 mL) black bean sauce (may add garlic and anise flavors)
- ½ cup (125 mL) cooked soybeans + 1 tbsp (15 mL) soy sauce

*See also* FERMENTED BLACK BEAN PASTE.

## Fernet Branca

*An astringent Italian bitters concocted from 40-some ingredients that include chamomile and rhubarb. Reputed to soothe upset tummies and tame a hangover.*

### If You Don't Have It

Substitute 3 tbsp (45 mL) Fernet Branca with:

- 3 tbsp (45 mL) Branca Menta (adds mint flavor)
- 3 tbsp (45 mL) Amer Picon
- 3 tbsp (45 mL) Campari
- 3 tbsp (45 mL) Unicum
- 3 tbsp (45 mL) Punt e Mes

## Ferula

*See* ASAFETIDA.

## Feta Cheese

*The salty cheese most closely associated with Greek cooking, feta is traditionally made from sheep's or goat's milk. It's often referred to as a pickled cheese because it is cured and stored in its own salty whey.*

### If You Don't Have It

Substitute 1 oz (30 g) feta cheese with:

- 1 oz (30 g) aged chèvre
- 1 oz (30 g) Brinza
- 1 oz (30 g) ricotta salata
- 1 oz (30 g) cotija
- 1 oz (30 g) myzithra
- 1 oz (30 g) haloumi (may add mint flavor)
- 1 oz (30 g) crumbly blue cheese (less salty; more pungent)

| 4 oz (125 g) =
1 cup (250 mL) crumbled |

## For Better Health
Substitute 1 oz (30 g) feta cheese with:
- ½ oz (15 g) feta cheese + ½ oz (15 g) reduced-fat or fat-free cream cheese (for blending with other ingredients

---

### Fetticus
*See* MÂCHE.

---

### Fiddlehead Fern

*Also known as ostrich fern and pohole. The coiled head of an unopened wild fern. Savored as a gourmet vegetable, fiddleheads must be cooked.*

## If You Don't Have It
Substitute 1 cup (250 mL) fiddlehead ferns with:
- 1 cup (250 mL) pencil-thin asparagus
- 1 cup (250 mL) haricot verts (slender French green beans)

---

### Field Lettuce
*See* MÂCHE.

---

### Field Peas
*See* PEAS, SPLIT.

---

### Fig, Dried

*Stored in a low-humidity location at about 55°F (13°C), figs keep well for up to 6 months.*

| 1 lb (500 g) =
40 medium = 3 cups
(750 mL) chopped |

## If You Don't Have It
Substitute 1 lb (500 g) dried figs with:
- 1 lb (500 g) pitted dried dates
- 1 lb (500 g) pitted prunes
- 1 lb (500 g) raisins
- 1 lb (500 g) dried apricots

---

### Fig, Fresh

*Eaten as a luscious fruit, a fig is actually the flower of the fig tree inverted into itself. These sweet treats are composed of 55% sugar and come in hundreds of different varieties. According to the United Nations' Food and Agriculture Organization, Turkey produces more figs than any other country in the world.*

| 1 lb (500 g) = 9 medium
= 2½ cups (625 mL)
chopped |

## If You Don't Have It
Substitute 1 lb (500 g) fresh figs with:
- 1 lb (500 g) pears, nectarines, apricots or other ripe, soft-fleshed fruit

## Fig Varieties
Choose 1 lb (500 g) fresh figs from these varieties:
- 1 lb (500 g) Smyrna figs (dark green skin; white-pink flesh; large and squat; includes Calimyrna, Marabout, and Zidi cultivars)
- 1 lb (500 g) common figs (light green to dark purple skin; amber to red flesh; various sizes; includes Adriatic, Black Mission, Brown Turkey, Celeste, Kadota, and Magnolia cultivars)
- 1 lb (500 g) San Pedro figs (includes Lampeira and King cultivars)

## Fig Leaf

*Adam and Eve aren't the only ones who made use of fig leaves to cover flesh. Countless cooks use fig leaves like grape leaves and banana leaves to wrap foods before grilling them.*

### If You Don't Have It

Substitute 10 fig leaves with:
- 10 brined grape leaves, simmer in salted water until tender (as food wrappers)
- 10 green cabbage leaves, simmered in salted water until tender (as food wrappers)
- 4 to 6 banana leaves
- 15 to 20 corn husks
- sheets of aluminum foil

## Fiji Chestnut

*See* MAPE.

## Filbert

*See* HAZELNUT.

## Filé Powder

*The ground dried leaves of the sassafras tree. Often used to flavor and thicken Creole gumbo.*

### If You Don't Have It

Substitute 1 tbsp (15 mL) filé powder (for thickening) with:
- 1 tbsp (15 mL) ground baobab leaves
- 2 cups (500 mL) okra (especially in gumbo and African stews; cook gradually to release okra's viscous, thickening "slime")
- 2 tsp (10 mL) cornstarch mixed with 1 tbsp (15 mL) cold water

## Filo

*See* PHYLLO.

## Fines Herbes

*A seasoning blend of delicate minced fresh chervil, chives, parsley, and tarragon.*

### If You Don't Have It

Substitute 1 tbsp (15 mL) fines herbes with:
- 1 tbsp (15 mL) Homemade Classic Fines Herbes: Combine ³⁄₄ tsp (3 mL) chopped fresh chervil, ³⁄₄ tsp (3 mL) chopped fresh chives, ³⁄₄ tsp (3 mL) chopped fresh tarragon, and ³⁄₄ tsp (3 mL) chopped fresh parsley.

## Fingered Citron

*See* CITRON.

## Fingerroot

*Also known as Chinese ginger or Key. This long, finger-shaped relative of gingerroot is popular in Thai cooking.*

### If You Don't Have It

Substitute 1 tbsp (15 mL) chopped fresh fingerroot with:
- 1 tbsp (15 mL) chopped fresh galangal
- 1 tbsp (15 mL) chopped fresh ginger

## Finnan Haddie

*Also known as finnan haddock. Salted, smoked Scottish haddock was originally smoked over peat fires.*

### If You Don't Have It
Substitute 1 lb (500 g) finnan haddie with:
- 1 lb (500 g) smoked mackerel
- 1 lb (500 g) smoked sturgeon
- 1 lb (500 g) smoked bluefish
- 1 lb (500 g) smoked salmon

## Finocchio

*See* FENNEL, FRESH.

## Fiore Sardo

*See* PECORINO.

## Fish

*See* SPECIFIC TYPES.

## Fish Boil

*See* CRAB BOIL.

## Fish Sauce

*Also known as nam pla, nuoc nam, patis, and shottsuru. A common seasoning in Southeast Asian cooking made from the liquid of salted fermented anchovies.*

### If You Don't Have It
Substitute 1 tbsp (15 mL) fish sauce with:
- 1 tbsp (15 mL) Homemade Fish Sauce Substitute: Combine ¼ cup (60 mL) soy sauce, 3 tbsp (45 mL) anchovy paste or 18 whole anchovy fillets, 3 tbsp (45 mL) water, 1 smashed garlic clove, and a pinch of brown sugar in a saucepan. Simmer over medium heat for 10 minutes. Then strain, pressing gently through a small sieve. Makes about ½ cup (125 mL).
- 1 tbsp (15 mL) soy sauce (preferably, add ½ tsp/2 mL powdered dulse seaweed for briny flavor)
- 1 tbsp (15 mL) fermented tofu
- 1 tbsp (15 mL) Homemade Vegetarian Fish Sauce Substitute: Combine ¼ cup (60 mL) soy sauce and 1 tsp (5 mL) rice vinegar in a small bowl. Press 3 tbsp (45 mL) fermented black beans through small sieve or garlic press into bowl. Mix in 1 tbsp (15 mL) yellow miso. Let stand for 15 to 20 minutes. Stir and strain through small sieve. Makes about ⅓ cup (75 mL).
- 1 tsp (5 mL) shrimp sauce (more pungent)

### Fish Sauce Varieties
Choose 1 tbsp (15 mL) fish sauce from these varieties:
- 1 tbsp (15 mL) Thai fish sauce (nam pla)
- 1 tbsp (15 mL) Vietnamese fish sauce (nuoc nam)
- 1 tbsp (15 mL) Vietnamese vegetarian fish sauce (nuoc mam an chay)
- 1 tbsp (15 mL) Japanese fish sauce (shottsuru)
- 1 tbsp (15 mL) Filipino fish sauce (patis)

## Five-Spice Powder

*See* CHINESE FIVE-SPICE POWDER.

## Flageolet

*See* THE WIDE WORLD OF DRIED BEANS (PAGE 637).

## Flatfish

*See* BRILL; FLOUNDER; HALIBUT; PLAICE; SOLE; TURBOT.

## Flavored Syrup

*Manufactured in dozens of varieties that include fruits, nuts, and other aromatics. Often added to complement Italian coffee or specialty drinks.*

### If You Don't Have It
Substitute 3 tbsp (45 mL) flavored syrup with:
- 3 tbsp (45 mL) Homemade Flavored Syrup: Combine ½ cup (125 mL) granulated sugar and ½ cup (125 mL) water in a medium saucepan. Bring to a boil over high heat. Reduce heat to medium-low and simmer for 5 minutes. Let cool, then stir in ¼ to ¾ tsp (1 to 3 mL) flavored extract, such as vanilla, almond, or hazelnut. Makes about ½ cup (125 mL).
- 3 tbsp (45 mL) nut, fruit, or other flavored liqueur (adds alcohol)
- 3 tbsp (45 mL) syrup from canned fruit packed in syrup (to replace fruit-flavored syrup)

## Flavoring Extracts

*See* EXTRACTS.

## Flavoring Oils

*Also known as essences. Concentrated oil extracted from plants and other foods. Used in small amounts to flavor recipes.*

### If You Don't Have It
Substitute ⅛ tsp (0.5 mL) flavoring oil with:
- ½ to 1 tsp (2 to 5 mL) flavoring extract

## Flaxseed

*Tiny, brown, oval seeds packed with omega-3 fatty acids, which our bodies metabolize more easily when the seed is ground.*

### If You Don't Have It
Substitute 3 tbsp (45 mL) ground flaxseed with:
- 3 tbsp (45 mL) wheat germ (lower in omega-3s)
- 3 tbsp (45 mL) wheat bran (lower in omega-3s)
- 3 tbsp (45 mL) oat bran (lower in omega-3s)
- 3 tbsp (45 mL) rice bran (lower in omega-3s)
- 1 tbsp (15 mL) butter, margarine, or oil (to replace ground flaxseed as fat in recipe)
- 3 whole eggs (to replace ground flaxseed as egg substitute in recipe; reduce added water by 6 tbsp/90 mL)

## Fleischwurst

*See* RING BOLOGNA.

## Florida Key Lime

*See* LIME.

## Flounder

*A tasty, fine-textured flatfish that is at home in kitchens from Australia to Spain. Types include winter flounder, summer flounder, yellowtailed flounder, and greenback flounder.*

### If You Don't Have It

Substitute 1 lb (500 g) flounder with:
- 1 lb (500 g) plaice or dab
- 1 lb (500 g) sole
- 1 lb (500 g) brill
- 1 lb (500 g) turbot

*See also* SOLE.

## Flour, All-Purpose

*Bleached all-purpose flour is whiter and lower in vitamin E than unbleached flour. Otherwise, the two can be used interchangeably. Most flour is sold pre-sifted, so sifting is generally unnecessary unless a recipe specifically calls for sifted flour. In Italy, milled flour is numbered 1 (coarse), 0 (fine), or 00 (very fine). Many Italian pasta recipes call for tipo 00 flour, and in The Essentials of Classic Italian Cooking, Marcella Hazan recommends all-purpose flour as "the most consistently satisfying" substitute.*

> 1 lb (500 g) = 3⅓ cups (825 mL)

### If You Don't Have It

Substitute 1 tbsp (15 mL) unsifted all-purpose flour (for thickening) with:
- 1 tbsp (15 mL) instant flour (such as Wondra; reduces lumps)
- 1½ tsp (7 mL) cornstarch, potato starch, or rice starch mixed with 1 tbsp (15 mL) cold water
- 1 tsp (5 mL) instant mashed potato flakes
- 2 tsp (10 mL) arrowroot
- 1 tbsp (15 mL) quick-cooking tapioca
- 1 tbsp (15 mL) cornmeal
- 2 egg yolks

Substitute 1 cup (250 mL) unsifted all-purpose flour (for baking) with:
- 1 cup (250 mL) + 3 tbsp (45 mL) sifted all-purpose flour
- 1 cup (250 mL) + 3 tbsp (45 mL) cake flour (creates much lighter texture; not recommended for cookies and quick breads)
- 1 cup (250 mL) unsifted self-rising flour (omit baking powder and salt from recipe)
- 1 cup (250 mL) pastry flour (creates lighter texture; not recommended for cookies)
- 1½ cups (375 mL) dry bread crumbs
- 1 cup (250 mL) rolled oats

### For Better Health

Substitute 1 cup (250 mL) unsifted all-purpose flour with:
- ½ cup (125 mL) whole wheat flour + ½ cup (125 mL) all-purpose flour (adds fiber; add 1 tbsp/15 mL liquid to recipe)
- 1 cup (250 mL) unsifted whole wheat pastry flour (omit 3 tbsp/45 mL liquid from recipe; for quick breads and desserts; has lower gluten content than whole wheat flour)
- ½ cup (125 mL) unsifted whole wheat pastry flour + ½ cup (125 mL) unsifted oat flour (omit 3 tbsp/45 mL) liquid from

## Flour, All-Purpose (cont'd)

recipe; for delicate baked goods such as cakes; oat flour creates a lighter texture; sift the flours to lighten the texture further)

- ½ cup (125 mL) unsifted cake flour + ½ cup (125 mL) unsifted whole wheat flour (mix gently; wheat flour contains additional gluten which can make baked goods tough if batter is overmixed)
- ¼ cup (60 mL) wheat germ + ¾ cup (175 mL) unsifted all-purpose flour (adds fiber)
- 1 cup (250 mL) minus 3 tbsp (45 mL) sifted oat flour
- 1 cup (250 mL) minus 3 tbsp (45 mL) rice flour (use to replace up to half of all-purpose flour in recipe)

*See also* BISCUIT MIX; FLOUR, SEMOLINA; CHOOSING AMONG WHEAT FLOURS (PAGE 648); CHOOSING AMONG WHOLE-GRAIN AND ALTERNATIVE FLOURS (PAGE 648).

## Flour, Almond

*See* ALMOND FLOUR.

## Flour, Bread

*Unbleached, high-gluten hard-wheat flour blended with a small amount of malted barley (to boost yeast activity) and vitamin C or potassium bromate (to make gluten more elastic and retain air bubbles in the dough).*

> 1 lb (500 g) = 3 cups (750 mL) sifted

### If You Don't Have It
Substitute 1 cup (250 mL) unsifted bread flour with:
- 1 cup (250 mL) all-purpose flour (preferably, add 2 tsp/10 mL gluten flour to improve structure)

### For Better Health
Substitute 1 cup (250 mL) unsifted bread flour with:
- 1 cup (250 mL) whole wheat flour (adds fiber; preferably, add 2 tsp/10 mL gluten flour to improve structure)

*See also* CHOOSING AMONG WHEAT FLOURS (PAGE 648).

## Flour, Cake

*A soft-wheat flour with a high starch content that produces tender cakes and baked goods.*

> 1 lb (500 g) = 4½ cups (1.125 L)

### If You Don't Have It
Substitute 1 cup (250 mL) sifted cake flour with:
- 1 cup (250 mL) pastry flour (to improve texture, mix batter gently and separate the eggs, beating the whites to soft peaks then folding them into batter; cakes will be less delicate than with cake flour)
- 1 cup (250 mL) minus 3 tbsp (45 mL) sifted all-purpose flour + 3 tbsp (45 mL) cornstarch (to improve texture, mix batter gently and separate the eggs, beating the whites to soft peaks then folding them into batter; cakes will be less delicate than with cake flour)

*See also* CHOOSING AMONG WHEAT FLOURS (PAGE 648).

## Flour, Durum

*Finely ground durum (high-gluten) wheat.*

### If You Don't Have It
Substitute 1 cup (250 mL) durum wheat flour with:
- 1 cup (250 mL) semolina (more coarse)

*See also* CHOOSING AMONG WHEAT FLOURS (PAGE 648).

## Flour, Gluten

*See* SEITAN.

## Flour, Graham

*Coarsely ground whole wheat flour developed by the Reverend Sylvester Graham, an early health food advocate.*

1 lb (500 g) = 3¾ cups (925 mL)

### If You Don't Have It
Substitute 1 cup (250 mL) unsifted graham flour with:
- 1 cup (250 mL) whole wheat flour
- ½ cup (125 mL) unsifted whole wheat flour + ½ cup (125 mL) unsifted all-purpose flour
- 1 cup (250 mL) minus 3 tbsp (45 mL) unsifted all-purpose flour + 3 tbsp (45 mL) wheat germ

*See also* FLOUR, WHOLE WHEAT; GRAHAM CRACKER; CHOOSING AMONG WHEAT FLOURS (PAGE 648).

## Flour, Instant

*A granular flour that dissolves quickly to thicken gravies, sauces, and other dishes.*

### If You Don't Have It
Substitute 1 tbsp (15 mL) instant flour (for thickening) with:
- 1 tbsp (15 mL) all-purpose flour mixed with 3 tbsp (45 mL) cold water
- 1½ tsp (7 mL) cornstarch, potato starch, or rice starch mixed with 1 tbsp (15 mL) cold water
- 1 tsp (5 mL) instant mashed potato flakes
- 2 tsp (10 mL) arrowroot mixed with 1 tbsp (15 mL) cold water
- 1 tbsp (15 mL) quick-cooking tapioca
- 1 tbsp (15 mL) cornmeal

## Flour, Pastry

*Contains slightly more protein than cake flour. Particularly good for biscuits, cookies, and pie crusts.*

1 lb (500 g) = 4¼ cups (1.05 L)

### If You Don't Have It
Substitute 1 cup (250 mL) unsifted pastry flour with:
- ⅔ cup (150 mL) unsifted all-purpose flour + ⅓ cup (75 mL) cake flour (to improve texture, handle dough gently, use very cold fat, and only as little liquid as necessary)

### For Better Health
Substitute 1 cup (250 mL) unsifted pastry flour with:
- 1 cup (250 mL) unsifted whole wheat pastry flour (adds fiber)

*See also* CHOOSING AMONG WHEAT FLOURS (PAGE 648).

## Flour, Self-Rising

*All-purpose flour with baking powder and salt added.*

> 1 lb (500 g) = 3 cups (750 mL) sifted

### If You Don't Have It
Substitute 1 cup (250 mL) unsifted self-rising flour with:
- 1 cup (250 mL) unsifted all-purpose flour + 1½ tsp (7 mL) baking powder + ½ tsp (2 mL) salt

*See also* BISCUIT MIX; CHOOSING AMONG WHEAT FLOURS (PAGE 648).

## Flour, Semolina

*Durum (high-gluten) wheat flour that is more coarsely ground than most flours. Often added to all-purpose flour to give fresh pasta a little more chew.*

> 1 lb (500 g) = 2⅛ cups (530 mL)

### If You Don't Have It
Substitute 1 cup (250 mL) semolina flour with:
- 1 cup (250 mL) durum wheat flour (finer grind)

### For Better Health
Substitute 1 cup (250 mL) semolina flour with:
- 1 cup (250 mL) spelt flour (low-gluten content; for those with wheat allergies)
- 1 cup (250 mL) Kamut© flour (medium-low gluten content; for those with wheat allergies)

*See also* CHOOSING AMONG WHEAT FLOURS (PAGE 648).

## Flour Sifter

*See* SIFTER.

## Flour, Whole Wheat

*Because it contains the wheat germ, this hearty flour has more fiber, nutrients, and oil than white flour. Best stored in the refrigerator or freezer to prevent rancidity.*

> 1 lb (500 g) = 3⅓ cups (825 mL)

### If You Don't Have It
Substitute 1 cup (250 mL) unsifted whole wheat flour with:
- 1 cup (250 mL) minus 3 tbsp (45 mL) unsifted all-purpose flour + 3 tbsp (45 mL) wheat germ
- ½ cup (125 mL) unsifted whole wheat flour + ½ cup (125 mL) unsifted all-purpose flour
- 1 cup (250 mL) graham flour

*See also* FLOUR, GRAHAM; CHOOSING AMONG WHEAT FLOURS (PAGE 648).

## Flowering Chinese Cabbage

*See* BOK CHOY; YAU CHOY.

## Flowering Chives

*See* GARLIC CHIVES.

## Flowering Kale

*See* KALE.

## Flower Pepper

*See* SZECHUAN PEPPER.

## Flowers, Candied

*Edible rose petals, violas, calendulas, pansies, and lavender make sparkling cake decorations when candied. Be sure to use fresh flowers that are not treated with pesticides.*

### If You Don't Have It

Substitute 1 cup (250 mL) candied flowers with:

- 1 cup (250 mL) Homemade Candied Flowers: Mix together 1 tsp (5 mL) meringue powder and 1 tbsp (15 mL) water in a cup. Brush all over 20 to 25 edible flowers to coat completely. Sprinkle with ¾ cup (175 mL) superfine sugar (or granulated sugar ground fine in a spice grinder). Let dry on wax paper for 2 days.
- An equal number of icing or frosting flowers piped with a star or rose tip

*See also* PICKING EDIBLE FLOWERS (PAGE 650).

## Flowers, Edible

*See* PICKING EDIBLE FLOWERS (PAGE 650).

## Focaccia

*A dimpled, flat Italian bread often garnished with savory toppings or ingredients worked into the dough. From the Latin* focus *for hearth.*

### If You Don't Have It

Substitute 1 lb (500 g) focaccia with:

- 1 lb (500 g) fougasse (French focaccia)
- 1 lb (500 g) prebaked pizza crust (such as Boboli)
- 1 lb (500 g) bread dough (roll flat before baking)
- 1 lb (500 g) sliced sourdough or other chewy bread (to replace sliced focaccia used to make sandwiches)

*See also* FOUGASSE.

## Foie de Lotte

*See* MONKFISH LIVER.

## Foie Gras

*See* PÂTÉ.

## Fondue Pot

*A communal pot set over a low flame to hold molten cheese, oil, or chocolate into which diners dip breads, vegetables, meats, or other foods. The classic cheese fondue was originally a Swiss family-style meal.*

### If You Don't Have It

Substitute a fondue pot with:

- heavy earthenware or stoneware pot set over a low flame, on a warming tray, or a on a heating pad set to high
- heavy-bottomed saucepan (enameled cast iron works particularly well) set over a low flame, on a warming tray, or on a heating pad set to high
- chafing dish set over a low flame

## Fontina

*This beautiful melting cheese is the base for* fonduta, *the Valle d'Aosta fondue.*

1 lb (500 g) =
4 cups (1 L) shredded

### If You Don't Have It

Substitute 1 oz (30 g) fontina with:
- 1 oz (30 g) raclette
- 1 oz (30 g) Gruyère or Emmental
- 1 oz (30 g) Appenzeller
- 1 oz (30 g) Morbier
- 1 oz (30 g) Beaufort
- 1 oz (30 g) Bel Paese
- 1 oz (30 g) provolone

## Food Mill

*A kitchen utensil used to strain skins, seeds, and other solids from foods. Resembles a perforated saucepan with a hand-cranked strainer plate at the bottom.*

### If You Don't Have It

Substitute a food mill with:
- pressing food through a medium-mesh sieve
- blender or food processor (for puréeing foods; will not separate out skins or seeds)

## Food Processor

*The ubiquitous home food processor was introduced in 1973 by Carl G. Sontheimer under the brand name Cuisinart®.*

### If You Don't Have It

Substitute a food processor with:
- blender (not recommended for blending doughs and batters)

### To Save Time

Substitute a food processor with:
- hand-blender (especially for soups and sauces)

## Fortified Wine

*See* BANYULS; MADEIRA; MARSALA; PORT; SHERRY; VERMOUTH.

## Fougasse

*French yeast bread traditionally baked first to test the temperature of the wood-fired oven. Often includes cheese, bacon, olives, or dried fruit.*

### If You Don't Have It

Substitute 1 lb (500 g) fougasse with:
- 1 lb (500 g) focaccia (Italian fougasse)
- 1 lb (500 g) prebaked pizza crust (such as Boboli)
- 1 lb (500 g) bread dough (shaped as desired before baking)
- 1 lb (500 g) sliced sourdough or other chewy bread (to replace sliced fougasse)

*See also* FOCACCIA.

## Fourme d'Ambert

*French blue-veined cheese that dates from Roman times. Easily recognized by its tall cylindrical shape.*

### If You Don't Have It

Substitute 1 oz (30 g) Fourme d'Ambert with:
- 1 oz (30 g) Bleu de Gex
- 1 oz (30 g) Bleu d'Auvergne
- 1 oz (30 g) Cambozola
- 1 oz (30 g) Stilton

## Foxberry

*See* LINGONBERRY.

## Foyot Sauce

*See* BÉARNAISE SAUCE.

## Fraise des Bois

*Also known as wild or alpine strawberries. Tiny, wild strawberries from France with a sweet, musky flavor.*

### If You Don't Have It
Substitute 1 cup (250 mL) cup fraise des bois with:
- 1 cup (250 mL) strawberries (larger)

*See also* STRAWBERRY.

## Framboise

*Also known as raspberry brandy. A clear, powerful eau de vie made from raspberries.*

### If You Don't Have It
Substitute 3 tbsp (45 mL) framboise with:
- 3 tbsp (45 mL) raspberry liqueur (sweeter)
- 3 tbsp (45 mL) raspberry syrup (sweeter; no alcohol)
- 1 tsp (5 mL) raspberry extract (add 5 tsp/25 mL liquid to recipe if necessary)

### To Vary the Flavor
Substitute 3 tbsp (45 mL) framboise with:
- 3 tbsp (45 mL) kirsch (cherry flavor)

*See also* RASPBERRY LIQUEUR.

## Franciacorta

*See* WINE, SPARKLING.

## Frangelico

*See* HAZELNUT LIQUEUR.

## Frangipane

*See* NUT MEAL.

## Frankfurter

*Also known as frank, wiener, and hot dog (when served in a bun). A mildly seasoned smoked sausage, probably of German origin, that became a star in the United States. Kosher and all-beef frankfurters enjoy the best reputation.*

### If You Don't Have It
Substitute 1 lb (500 g) frankfurters with:
- 1 lb (500 g) Knackwurst
- 1 lb (500 g) kielbasa (larger)
- 1 lb (500 g) Bockwurst (made with veal)
- 1 lb (500 g) Bratwurst
- 1 lb (500 g) cocktail wieners (smaller)
- 1 lb (500 g) Vienna sausages (smaller)
- 1 lb (500 g) chipolata (spicier)

### For Better Health
Substitute 1 lb (500 g) frankfurters with:
- 1 lb (500 g) reduced-fat frankfurters
- 1 lb (500 g) vegetarian hot dogs

## French Bread

*"True French bread contains neither sugar nor milk," writes French chef Madeleine Kamman. "It is a white bread with a long-baked crispy and crackling crust, which makes the best sandwiches with butter, salami, boiled ham, or country pâté."*

### If You Don't Have It
Substitute 1 lb (500 g) French bread with these types:
- 1 lb (500 g) baguette (narrow loaf about 2 feet/61 cm long)
- 1 lb (500 g) baton (similar to a baguette but smaller)
- 1 lb (500 g) pain Parisienne (wider than baguette)
- 1 lb (500 g) ficelle (narrower than baguette)
- 1 lb (500 g) bâtarde (wider than baguette)
- 1 lb (500 g) boule (round loaf)

### To Vary the Flavor
Substitute 1 lb (500 g) French bread with:
- 1 lb (500 g) Italian bread (usually shorter and rounder than French bread)

## Freshwater Eel

*See* EEL.

## Frisée

*Blanched curly endive with pale yellow or light green leaves and a slightly sweet, less bitter flavor than curly endive.*

### If You Don't Have It
Substitute 1 cup (250 mL) frisée with:
- 1 cup (250 mL) curly endive or curly chicory (more bitter)
- 1 cup (250 mL) escarole (softer leaves)
- 1 cup (250 mL) radicchio (red color)

*See also* BELGIAN ENDIVE; CHICORY; ESCAROLE.

## Friselle

*These peppery, ring-shaped Italian crackers resemble mini-bagels. Like biscotti, they are twice-baked and can be dunked in savory flavored liquid or soup. Italians often rehydrate them briefly in water then top them with olive oil, tomatoes, herbs, and/or cheese for a snack.*

### If You Don't Have It
Substitute 1 lb (500 g) friselle with:
- 1 lb (500 g) mini-bagels (preferably pepper-flavored), toasted
- 1 lb (500 g) focaccia (preferably pepper-flavored), toasted
- 1 lb (500 g) croutons (preferably pepper-flavored)

## Frog

*The hind legs are the edible part with a flavor akin to tender young chicken.*

1 lb (500 g) = 8 legs

### If You Don't Have It
Substitute 1 lb (500 g) frog's legs with:
- 1 lb (500 g) chicken breast or tenders
- 1 lb (500 g) scallops

## Frogfish

*See* MONKFISH.

## Frog Skin Melon

*See* SANTA CLAUS MELON.

## Fromage Blanc

*This soft fresh cream cheese is delightful when sweetened and served with fresh fruit. For the French dessert coeur à la crème, it's folded with meringue and chilled in a heart-shaped mold.*

### If You Don't Have It
Substitute 1 oz (30 g) fromage blanc with:
- 1 oz (30 g) yogurt cheese
- 1 oz (30 g) quark
- ½ oz (15 g) cream cheese + ½ oz (15 g) cream, blended
- ½ oz (15 g) cottage cheese + ½ oz (15 g) yogurt, blended

## Frozen Whipped Topping

*See* WHIPPED TOPPING.

## Fructose

*Also known as fruit sugar and levulose. This by-product of fruits and honey is sweeter than sucrose but contains only half the calories.*

### If You Don't Have It
Substitute 1 cup (250 mL) fructose with:
- 1⅓ cups (325 mL) granulated sugar (baked goods will be drier)
- 1⅓ cups (325 mL) Sucanat (powdered organic sugarcane juice, which retains all its vitamins and minerals; baked goods will be drier)
- 1 cup (250 mL) + 2 tbsp (30 mL) honey (for baking, reduce liquid in recipe by ⅓ cup/75 mL; add heaping ¼ tsp/1 mL baking soda to neutralize acidity of honey)
- ⅔ cup (150 mL) granulated sugar + ⅔ cup (150 mL) sugar-free sugar substitute such as Splenda or DiabetiSweet

## Fruit Brandy

*See* SPECIFIC TYPES.

## Fruit, Candied

*Also known as glacé fruit. Simmering and soaking fruit repeatedly in sugar syrup for several weeks evaporates its moisture and saturates it with so much sugar that it becomes preserved, translucent, and even more delicious.*

### If You Don't Have It
Substitute 1 cup (250 mL) candied fruit with:
- 1 cup (250 mL) Italian fruit mostarda (more pungent)
- 1 cup (250 mL) chopped dried apricots
- 1 cup (250 mL) dried cherries
- 1 cup (250 mL) dried cranberries

*See also* CITRUS PEEL, CANDIED; SPECIFIC CANDIED FRUITS.

## Fruit, Fresh

*For the finest fruit, you don't have to look far. Locally grown fruit harvested at the peak of its season will taste better and be more nutritious than fruits that are picked before they ripen to be shipped thousands of miles to market. Choose plump, healthy looking fruits that are fragrant, a prime indicator of flavor.*

### If You Don't Have It
Substitute 1½ cups (375 mL) fresh chopped fruit with:
- 1 (16 oz/454 g) can, drained

*See also* SPECIFIC TYPES.

## Fruit Liqueur

*Alcoholic beverage flavored with fruit and composed of spirits, sweeteners, and water. Usually enjoyed in small glasses as an after-dinner drink.*

### If You Don't Have It
Substitute 3 tbsp (45 mL) fruit liqueur with:
- 3 tbsp (45 mL) fruit syrup (sweeter)
- 3 tbsp (45 mL) fruit wine (thinner consistency)
- 1 tsp (5 mL) fruit extract

*See also* SPECIFIC TYPES.

## Fruit Sugar

*See* FRUCTOSE.

## Fruta Bomba

*See* PAPAYA.

## Frying

*Cooking food in a shallow layer or deep layer of hot fat (deep-fat frying).*

### For Better Health
Substitute frying with:
- oven-frying. Mimic the technique of deep-fat frying by using a very hot oven and a thin coating of fat on the surface of the food. Preheat oven to 475°F (240°C). Preheat a rimmed baking sheet in oven for 10 minutes. Dip food in batter, if using, then spray or brush generously with cooking oil spray or another fat. Put food on hot baking sheet and bake, turning once, until brown and crisp. Works well for oven-fried French fries, tortilla chips, vegetable chips (such as plantain chips or potato chips), turnovers, and breaded meats, poultry, seafood, and vegetables.

## Frying Pan

*Also known as a skillet. A long-handled and usually round heavy pan with sides that slope so steam (the enemy of crisping) doesn't accumulate inside.*

### If You Don't Have It
Substitute a frying pan with:
- wok (for frying, stir-frying, and sautéing)
- sauté pan (for frying and sautéing)
- griddle (for light sautéing; has lower rims or none at all)

## Funnel

*Pennsylvania cooks used their funnels to create a deep-fried pastry that has become a popular concession treat. Made by pouring batter through a funnel held over a pot of hot fat, the resulting freeform pastry, dusted with confectioner's sugar or honey, looks like the abstract painting of the doughnut world.*

### If You Don't Have It

Substitute a funnel with:

- paper, wax paper, or aluminum foil rolled into a cone shape

## Funnel cake

*See* DOUGHNUT.

## Furikake

*Dry or wet Japanese condiment for rice that usually includes seaweed, sesame seeds, bonito flakes, dried shrimp, and salt or soy sauce.*

### If You Don't Have It

Substitute 1 tbsp (15 mL) furikake with:

- 1 tbsp (15 mL) Homemade Furikake: Put 5 sheets nori seaweed and 2 shiso leaves (perilla or Japanese basil) in a food processor and pulse until crumbled. Transfer to a bowl. Toast 2 tbsp (30 mL) white sesame seeds and 1 tbsp (15 mL) black sesame seeds in a dry skillet until fragrant, 3 to 4 minutes. Add to the bowl along with 1 tbsp (15 mL) bonito flakes (katsuobushi), 2 tsp (10 mL) dried shrimp, 2 tsp (10 mL) hot red pepper flakes (optional), and 2 tsp (10 mL) coarse salt or soy salt (or add soy sauce along with the furikake). Can also add 1 tsp (5 mL) mushroom powder to enhance the savory flavor. Makes about ½ cup (125 mL).
- 1 tbsp (15 mL) gomashio (less complex)
- 1 tbsp (15 mL) tamari or soy sauce (wet and much less complex)

*See also* GOMASHIO.

## Fuzzy Gourd

*Also known as fuzzy melon, hairy melon (or squash or gourd), and little winter melon. A green cylindrical Chinese squash that sports a five o'clock shadow. Peel before using. The flesh tastes like a combination of zucchini and cucumber with a tinge of lemon.*

### If You Don't Have It

Substitute 1 lb (500 g) fuzzy gourd with:

- 1 lb (500 g) zucchini
- 8 oz (250 g) zucchini + 8 oz (250 g) cucumber
- 1 lb (500 g) cucuzza
- 1 lb (500 g) yellow squash
- 1 lb (500 g) pattypan squash
- 1 lb (500 g) Armenian cucumber or snake melon (long, slender, curved body; ridged, light yellow to pale green razor-thin skin; sweet, mild citrus flavor; extra-crisp texture; needs no peeling or seeding)

*See also* WINTER MELON.

# Gai Choy to Gyoza Wrappers

## Gai Choy

*See* MUSTARD GREENS.

## Gai Lan

*See* CHINESE BROCCOLI.

## Galangal

*Also known as blue ginger, galanga root and galingale. A rhizome that exists in two forms: white-flesh greater galangal (Thai ginger), and the stronger orange-flesh lesser galangal.*

> 1 tbsp (15 mL)
> chopped fresh =
> 1½ tsp (7 mL) powdered

### If You Don't Have It
Substitute 1 tbsp (15 mL) chopped fresh galangal (greater galangal) with:
- 1 tbsp (15 mL) chopped fresh ginger + ⅛ to ¼ tsp (0.5 to 1 mL) lemon juice (less pungent)
- 1 tbsp (15 mL) chopped fresh lesser galangal (more pungent; orange flesh)
- 1 tbsp (15 mL) chopped fresh fingerroot

## Galantina

*An Italian cooked salami that contains pancetta, pistachios, spices, and veal.*

### If You Don't Have It
Substitute 1 lb (500 g) galantina with:
- 1 lb (500 g) mortadella (less chunky; has cubes of pork fat and garlic flavor)
- 1 lb (500 g) bologna (less complex flavor)
- 1 lb (500 g) olive loaf (adds olive flavor)

### For Better Health
Substitute 1 lb (500 g) galantina with:
- 1 lb (500 g) Gelbwurst (lower in fat and calories)

## Galia Melon

*A hybrid melon developed in Israel to thrive in desert growing conditions. Tastes like a sweeter version of cantaloupe.*

> 1 lb (500 g) =
> 1 to 1½ cups
> (250 to 375 mL) cubed

### If You Don't Have It

Substitute 1 cup (250 mL) chopped Galia melon with:
- 1 cup (250 mL) chopped honeydew
- 1 cup (250 mL) chopped Santa Claus melon
- 1 cup (250 mL) chopped cantaloupe
- 1 cup (250 mL) chopped Persian melon

## Galingale

*See* GALANGAL.

## Galip Nut

*See* PILI NUT.

## Galliano

*Also known as Liquore Galliano. Spicy, herbal proprietary Italian liqueur. A mixer in the Harvey Wallbanger, Golden Cadillac, and other cocktails.*

### If You Don't Have It

Substitute 3 tbsp (45 mL) Galliano with:
- 3 tbsp (45 mL) Roiano (sweeter)
- 3 tbsp (45 mL) Neopolitan liqueur or other less expensive imitation Galliano
- 3 tbsp (45 mL) sambuca (stronger licorice flavor; fewer herbal flavors)
- 3 tbsp (45 mL) anesone, anisette, or other anise-flavored liqueur (more anise flavor; fewer herbal flavors)

## Game

*See* SPECIFIC TYPES.

## Game Hen

*See* CHICKEN.

## Gammel Dansk®

*Danish bitters made from dozens of spices, roots, and wild rowanberries from the island of Zealand, steeped in neutral spirits for 3 months.*

### If You Don't Have It

Substitute 3 tbsp (45 mL) Gammel Dansk® with:
- 3 tbsp (45 mL) Fernet Branca

## Gamonedo

*Lightly smoked cave-aged cheese from northeast Spain made with set proportions of cow's, sheep's, and goat's milk.*

### If You Don't Have It

Substitute 1 oz (30 g) Gamonedo with:
- 1 oz (30 g) Cabrales
- 1 oz (30 g) Picón
- 1 oz (30 g) Roquefort
- 1 oz (30 g) Gorgonzola

## Garam Masala

*Scintillating blend of toasted ground spices that originated in northern India. Many variations exist. Garam masala is added to a dish toward the end of the cooking or sprinkled on top just before serving.*

### If You Don't Have It
Substitute 1 tbsp (15 mL) garam masala with:
- 1 tbsp (15 mL) Homemade Basic Garam Masala: Combine 1 tsp (5 mL) cumin seeds, 1 tsp (5 mL) coriander seeds, 1 tsp (5 mL) black peppercorns, 1 tsp (5 mL) cardamom seeds (scraped from pods), ½ tsp (2 mL) whole cloves, and two 3-inch (7.5 cm) cinnamon sticks (broken into pieces) in a skillet. Toast over medium heat, shaking often, until fragrant, about 3 minutes. Let cool then grind in a spice grinder. Makes about ¼ cup (60 mL).

### To Save Time
Substitute 1 tbsp (15 mL) garam masala with:
- 1 tbsp (15 mL) Homemade Quick Garam Masala: Combine ½ tsp (2 mL) ground cumin, ½ tsp (2 mL) ground coriander, ½ tsp (2 mL) ground black pepper, ½ tsp (2 mL) ground cardamom, ½ tsp (2 mL) ground cinnamon, and ¼ tsp (1 mL) ground cloves. Toast spices just before using. Makes about 1 tablespoon (15 mL).

*See also* CHAAT MASALA; PANCH PHORAN; SAMBHAR MASALA.

## Garbanzo Bean

*See* THE WIDE WORLD OF DRIED BEANS (PAGE 637).

## Garbanzo Bean Flour

*See* CHOOSING AMONG WHOLE-GRAIN AND ALTERNATIVE FLOURS (PAGE 648).

## Garden Peas

*See* PEAS, SHELLING.

## Gari

*Nigerian flour made from fermented, roasted, and ground cassava.*

### If You Don't Have It
Substitute 1 cup (250 mL) gari with:
- 1 cup (250 mL) tapioca or cassava flour (lacks fermented flavor)
- 1 cup (250 mL) cream of wheat (lacks fermented flavor)

*See also* CASSAVA; GINGER, PICKLED.

## Garlic

*Hundreds of varieties of "the stinking rose" are grown worldwide, including hardneck types, such as rocambole, porcelain, and purple stripe, as well as softneck varieties, such as*

### If You Don't Have It
Substitute 1 clove fresh garlic (minced or pressed) with:
- ½ tsp (2 mL) jarred minced garlic or liquid garlic seasoning
- ½ to 1 tsp (2 to 5 mL) roasted garlic (mellower, sweeter flavor)
- ½ tsp (2 mL) garlic chives (less pungent; adds green color)
- ½ to 1 tsp (2 to 5 mL) minced shallots (less pungent)
- ⅛ tsp (0.5 mL) garlic powder

*artichoke and silverskin. To remove garlicky aromas from your fingers, rub them on stainless steel (such as the bowl of a stainless-steel spoon) under cool running water.*

1 head = 8 to 12 cloves

1 clove = ½ tsp (2 mL) minced

- ¼ tsp (1 mL) granulated garlic
- ½ tsp (2 mL) garlic flakes or instant garlic
- ½ tsp (2 mL) garlic salt (omit ½ tsp/2 mL salt from recipe)
- ½ tsp (2 mL) garlic juice (less pungent)
- ⅛ tsp (0.5 mL) asafetida powder (more pungent; combines onion and garlic flavors)

## Garlic Varieties

Choose 1 clove fresh garlic from these varieties:
- 1 clove white-skinned American or California garlic (very pungent)
- 1 clove purple-skinned Italian or Mexican garlic (less pungent)
- ½ tsp (2 mL) clove elephant garlic (actually a type of leek; mild)
- ½ tsp (2 mL) minced fresh green or immature garlic (very mild)

## Garlic, Black

*Popular in Korea for its antioxidant content, black garlic is fermented at high temperatures until the cloves turn mission-fig black and develop a custard-like texture and sweet caramel flavor permeated with savoriness.*

1 head = 8 to 12 cloves = ¼ cup (60 mL) roasted garlic paste

1 clove = ½ tsp (2 mL) minced

### If You Don't Have It

Substitute 1 clove black garlic with:
- ½ tsp (2 mL) mashed well-roasted garlic
- ½ tsp (2 mL) minced garlic + ¼ tsp (1 mL) molasses

## Garlic Blossom

*See* PICKING EDIBLE FLOWERS (PAGE 650).

## Garlic Butter

*See* BUTTER.

## Garlic Chives

*Also known as Chinese chives and ku chai. An herb that looks like chives but tastes of garlic instead of onion. Snip garlic chives with kitchen scissors for quick cutting.*

### If You Don't Have It

Substitute 1 cup (250 mL) chopped garlic chives with:
- 1 cup (250 mL) chopped chives (less garlicky, more oniony flavor)
- 1 cup (250 mL) chopped green onions or scallions (green tops only; less garlicky, more oniony flavor; add 2 to 3 tsp/ 10 to 15 mL chopped fresh garlic for more garlic flavor)
- 1 cup (250 mL) chopped Chinese garlic stems (more pungent garlic flavor; adds crunch)

## Garlic Chives (cont'd)

### Garlic Chive Varieties

Choose 1 cup (250 mL) chopped garlic chives from these varieties:

- 1 cup (250 mL) chopped green garlic chives (flat green leaves; mellow garlic flavor when cooked)
- 1 cup (250 mL) chopped yellow garlic chives (green garlic chives grown under wraps to prevent photosynthesis; flat yellow, tender leaves; mellow garlic flavor when cooked)
- 1 cup (250 mL) chopped flowering garlic chives (round green leaves; mellow garlic flavor when cooked; works best in soups, stews, or with moist-heat cooking methods)

## Garlic, Green

*Also known as baby garlic, garlic sprouts, and spring garlic. Immature green garlic is often sold at farmers markets and resembles a scallion or baby leek. The leafy green stalks fade to a white stem tinged with purple near the bulb end, which is straight. The undeveloped garlic flavor tastes agreeably mild and even slightly sweet when cooked.*

> 1 bunch = 5 oz (150 g) =
> 5 pieces green garlic =
> 1 cup (250 mL) chopped
> (white/purple part only) =
> 3½ cups (875 mL) chopped
> (white and green parts)

### If You Don't Have It

Substitute 1 bunch green garlic (white and green parts) with:

- 3 to 4 cups (750 mL to 1 L) chopped garlic chives
- 3 to 4 cups (750 mL to 1 L) garlic scapes (mild garlic flavor and crunch)
- 3 to 4 cups (750 mL to 1 L) chopped Chinese garlic stems (pungent garlic flavor and crunch)

### To Vary the Flavor

Substitute 1 bunch green garlic with:

- 1 bunch scallions or green onions + 1 tbsp (15 mL) minced garlic (adds onion flavor; slightly stronger garlic flavor)
- 1 bunch ramps or leeks (white part only) + 1 tbsp (15 mL) minced garlic (adds leek flavor; slightly stronger garlic flavor)
- 3 to 4 cups (750 mL to 1 L) chopped chives + 1 tbsp (15 mL) minced garlic (adds mild onion flavor; best raw or lightly cooked)

## Garlic Mayonnaise

*See* MAYONNAISE.

## Garlic Mustard

*See* MUSTARD GREENS.

## Garlic Oil

*Commercially available gourmet oil — often extra virgin olive oil — in which garlic has been macerated. A convenient ingredient for dipping, salad dressings, or sautéing vegetables.*

### If You Don't Have It

Substitute ¼ cup (60 mL) garlic oil with:

- ¼ cup (60 mL) roasted garlic oil (mellower, sweeter flavor)
- ¼ cup (60 mL) Homemade Garlic Oil: Combine 1 small garlic clove and ¼ cup (60 mL) olive oil in small saucepan over low heat. Heat until garlic is mildly fragrant, about 10 minutes. Discard garlic and use oil immediately. Or let cool, refrigerate in an airtight glass jar, and use within 1 day.

## Garlic Press

*When buying a garlic press, look for the easy-cleaning type, which has prongs to push bits of garlic back out through the holes.*

### If You Don't Have It

Substitute a garlic press with:

- finely mincing the food with a chef's knife, then pressing the mound of minced food with the flat side of the knife

## Garlic Salt

*A seasoning of ground dried garlic and salt sold on the supermarket spice shelf.*

### If You Don't Have It

Substitute 1 tsp (5 mL) garlic salt with:

- ¼ tsp (1 mL) garlic powder + ¾ tsp (3 mL) salt

## Garlic Scapes

*Resembling crazy straws, curvy green garlic scapes are stalks that grow out of hardneck garlic bulbs. Savor their crunch and mild garlic flavor by using them raw in spring pestos and quickly cooked stir-fries.*

1 bunch = 5 oz (150 g) = 18 to 20 pieces green garlic = 3 cups (750 mL) chopped (green and white parts)

### If You Don't Have It

Substitute 1 bunch garlic scapes (green and white parts) with:

- 1 bunch green garlic (green and white/purple parts)
- 3 to 4 cups (750 mL to 1 L) chopped Chinese garlic stems (pungent garlic flavor and crunch)
- 3 to 4 cups (750 mL to 1 L) chopped garlic chives

### To Vary the Flavor

Substitute 1 bunch garlic scapes with:

- 1 bunch scallions or green onions + 1 tbsp (15 mL) minced garlic (adds onion flavor; slightly stronger garlic flavor)
- 1 bunch ramps or leeks (white part only) + 1 tbsp (15 mL) minced garlic (adds leek flavor; slightly stronger garlic flavor)
- 3 to 4 cups (750 mL to 1 L) chopped chives + 1 tbsp (15 mL) minced garlic (adds mild onion flavor; best raw or lightly cooked)

## Gastrique

*French sweet-and-sour sauce made by caramelizing sugar then adding and reducing vinegar and fruit or fruit juice (and sometimes wine).*

### If You Don't Have It

Substitute 1 cup (250 mL) gastrique with:

- 1 cup (250 mL) agrodolce (Italian sweet-and-sour sauce)
- 1 cup (250 mL) Chinese sweet-and-sour sauce

## Gelatin

*Before the introduction of commercial gelatin in the late 1800s, cooks who wanted jelled dishes had to boil calves' feet or knuckles to extract the gelatin. Use*

### If You Don't Have It

Substitute ¼ oz (8 g) pkg (1 tbsp/15 mL) unflavored gelatin with:

- 4 sheets (9- by 4-inches/23 by 10 cm) leaf gelatin
- 1 tbsp (15 mL) kosher or vegetarian powdered gelatin (for those eating kosher and vegetarians who prefer gelling agents from non-animal sources)

## Gelatin (cont'd)

*1 tbsp (15 mL) unflavored powdered gelatin to gel 2 cups (500 mL) of liquid.*

- 2 tsp (10 mL) agar powder (a sea vegetable; suitable for vegetarians)
- 1 oz (30 g) carrageen (a sea vegetable; suitable for vegetarians; reconstitute the dried carrageen in cool water; cook the reconstituted carrageen with the liquid to be gelled; then strain out the carrageen)

## Gelatin, Flavored

*Also known as gelatin dessert mix and Jell-O®. The Jell-O Gallery in LeRoy, New York, houses exhibits dedicated to "America's Favorite Dessert."*

### If You Don't Have It
Substitute 3 oz (90 g) pkg powdered flavored gelatin, prepared, with:
- 1 tbsp (15 mL) unflavored gelatin + 2 cups (500 mL) fruit juice

## Gelato

*See* ICE CREAM.

## Gelbwurst

*Mild pork and veal sausage dubbed "diet bologna" in Germany because of its relatively low-fat content.*

### If You Don't Have It
Substitute 1 lb (500 g) Gelbwurst with:
- 1 lb (500 g) bologna (higher in fat and calories)
- 1 lb (500 g) mortadella (has cubes of pork fat and garlic flavor)
- 1 lb (500 g) galantina (chunkier; more complex flavor)
- 1 lb (500 g) olive loaf (adds olive flavor)

## Génoise

*This versatile sponge cake is named génoise by the French, reputedly after its origin in Genoa, Italy. However, the Italian word for the same sponge cake is pan di Spagna, which means "Spanish bread."*

### If You Don't Have It
Substitute 1 lb (500 g) génoise with:
- 1 lb (500 g) sponge cake (less moist)
- 1 lb (500 g) ladyfingers (especially for tiramisù)
- 1 lb (500 g) pound cake (moister, denser texture)

## Genovese Basil

*See* BASIL.

## Geoduck

*See* SWAPPING CLAMS (PAGE 645).

## Gervais

*See* PETIT SUISSE.

## Ghee

*See* BUTTER, CLARIFIED.

## Gherkin

*See* CUCUMBER; SWEET GHERKIN.

## Ghora Angur

*See* SUMAC.

## Gianduja

*Also known as chocolate-hazelnut spread or paste. The most widely distributed brand is Nutella©.*

### If You Don't Have It
Substitute 1 cup (250 mL) gianduja with:
- 1 cup (250 mL) creamy peanut butter (omits chocolate and hazelnut flavors)
- 3 oz (90 g) or ½ cup (125 mL) milk chocolate + ½ cup (125 mL) creamy peanut butter, cashew butter, or almond butter; melt in a double boiler and stir until smooth

## Gin

*Juniper berries give gin its distinctive bouquet. Essential in the dry martini and countless classic cocktails. Not to be confused with sloe gin, which is a sweetened liqueur.*

### If You Don't Have It
Substitute 3 tbsp (45 mL) gin with:
- 3 tbsp (45 mL) vodka
- 3 tbsp (45 mL) white rum
- 3 tbsp (45 mL) brandy

### Gin Varieties
Choose 3 tbsp (45 mL) gin from these varieties:
- 3 tbsp (45 mL) London gin (dry; complex flavor)
- 3 tbsp (45 mL) American gin (less dry; slightly less complex flavor)
- 3 tbsp (45 mL) Dutch or Hollands gin (sweeter; more complex flavor than dry gin)
- 3 tbsp (45 mL) golden gin (golden color; aged in wood)

*See also* SLOE GIN.

## Ginger Ale

*James Vernor created ginger ale in 1866 and sold it in his Detroit, Michigan drug store for 30 years before opening a factory to produce and bottle it.*

### If You Don't Have It
Substitute 1 cup (250 mL) ginger ale with:
- 1 cup (250 mL) ginger beer (stronger ginger flavor)
- 1 cup (250 mL) lemon and lime flavored soda such as 7-Up© (no ginger flavor)
- 1 cup (250 mL) soda water (adds no flavor)

## Ginger Beer

*Ginger ale with attitude. Ginger beer comes in alcoholic and nonalcoholic versions.*

### If You Don't Have It
Substitute 1 cup (250 mL) ginger beer with:
- 1 cup (250 mL) ginger ale (milder ginger flavor)
- 1 cup (250 mL) lemon and lime flavored soda, such as 7-Up© (no ginger flavor)
- 1 cup (250 mL) soda water (adds no flavor)

## Ginger Biscuit

*See* GINGERSNAP, CRUMBS.

## Ginger, Crystallized

*Also known as candied ginger. Fresh ginger pieces simmered in syrup until tender and then drained and coated with granulated sugar.*

### If You Don't Have It

Substitute 3 tbsp (45 mL) minced crystallized ginger with:

- 3 tbsp (45 mL) Homemade Crystallized Ginger: Mix together ⅔ cup (150 mL) granulated sugar and ½ cup (125 mL) water in a small saucepan. Bring to a boil over high heat. Then add ½ cup (125 mL) peeled, sliced ginger. Reduce heat and simmer for 20 to 30 minutes. Strain ginger pieces, then dry on a rack and sprinkle with sugar. When completely cool, store in an airtight container for up to 1 month. Mince as needed. Makes about ½ cup (125 mL).
- 2 tsp (10 mL) minced fresh ginger + ⅛ to ½ tsp (0.5 to 2 mL) granulated sugar (stronger ginger flavor)
- ⅛ tsp (0.5 mL) ground ginger

## Ginger Flower

*See* GINGER, WILD BUD.

## Ginger, Fresh

*Also known as gingerroot. Young ginger, also known as green ginger or spring ginger, is relatively mild with tender pink tips and doesn't need to be peeled. The more common mature ginger should be peeled to reveal the spicy golden flesh. Unpeeled ginger may be refrigerated for up to 3 weeks or frozen for up to 6 months.*

> 1 oz (30 g) =
> ¼ cup (60 mL) sliced
>
> 1 tbsp (15 mL)
> minced fresh =
> ⅛ tsp (0.5 mL) ground

### If You Don't Have It

Substitute 1 tbsp (15 mL) fresh ginger (minced or grated) with:

- 1 tbsp (15 mL) fresh galangal (minced or grated)
- 3 tbsp (45 mL) rinsed crystallized ginger, minced (for baking or where a little sugar is acceptable in recipe)
- ⅛ tsp (0.5 mL) ground ginger (for baking)

## Ginger, Ground

*The dried, ground form of fresh ginger is a distinctive spice in its own right lending its name and zing to gingerbread, gingersnaps, and other gingery treats.*

### If You Don't Have It

Substitute 1 tsp (5 mL) ground ginger (for baking) with:

- ⅓ cup (75 mL) minced crystallized ginger, rinsed to remove sugar
- 1 tbsp (15 mL) grated or minced fresh ginger (preferably add

½ tsp/2 mL ground ginger to help better distribute the flavor)
- 1 to 2 tsp (5 to 10 mL) ginger juice (add to wet ingredients)

## To Vary the Flavor
Substitute 1 tsp (5 mL) ground ginger with:
- 1 tsp (5 mL) pumpkin pie spice (adds cinnamon, clove, and nutmeg aromas)
- 1 tsp (5 mL) allspice (adds cinnamon, clove, and nutmeg aromas)
- 1 tsp (5 mL) ground cardamom (adds musky citrus aroma)

## Ginger Jam

*Also known as ginger jelly, marmalade, or preserves. A sweet-hot favorite equally at home on toast and grilled meats.*

### If You Don't Have It
Substitute 1 cup (250 mL) ginger jam with:
- ¾ cup (175 mL) apple jelly + ¼ cup (60 mL) soft chopped candied ginger + 1 tsp (5 mL) ground ginger

### To Vary the Flavor
Substitute 1 cup (250 mL) ginger jam with:
- ¾ cup (175 mL) orange marmalade + ¼ cup (60 mL) soft chopped candied ginger + 1 tsp (5 mL) ground ginger
- ¾ cup (175 mL) apricot preserves + ¼ cup (60 mL) soft chopped candied ginger + 1 tsp (5 mL) ground ginger

## Ginger Juice

*Look for the juice squeezed from fresh ginger in specialty markets or natural food stores.*

> 1 oz (30 g)
> (about ¼ cup/60 mL)
> fresh ginger =
> 2 tsp (10 mL) juice

### If You Don't Have It
Substitute 1 tbsp (15 mL) ginger juice with:
- 1 tbsp (15 mL) Homemade Ginger Juice: Press 1½ oz (45 g), about ⅓ cup (75 mL) minced fresh ginger, in a garlic press and squeeze out juice. Makes about 1 tablespoon (15 mL).

## Ginger, Pickled

*Also known as gari and sushi ginger. The palate-cleansing partner to nose-clearing wasabi on sushi plates. Young ginger naturally shades toward pink when pickled but commercial versions often add red coloring or beet juice.*

### If You Don't Have It
Substitute 1 tbsp (15 mL) pickled ginger with:
- 1 tbsp (15 mL) Homemade Pickled Ginger: Peel 8 to 10 oz (250 to 300 g) young fresh ginger then slice paper-thin, preferably on a mandoline, transferring the slices to 2 warm, sterilized pint-size (500 mL) jars (you should have about 2 cups/500 mL paper-thin slices). Put 2 cups (500 mL) rice vinegar, ½ cup (125 mL) sugar, 1 tbsp (15 mL) salt, and 2 slices peeled red beet (each about ⅛ inch/3 mm thick) in a medium saucepan. Bring to a boil and boil for 1 minute. Pluck out and discard the beet slices. Divide the hot vinegar

## Ginger, Pickled (cont'd)

mixture equally among the jars, completely covering the ginger. Screw on the lids and let cool. Refrigerate for up to 1 month. Makes about 2 cups (500 mL).

- 1 tbsp (15 mL) fresh young ginger sliced paper-thin + ½ tsp (2 mL) rice vinegar + pinch of sugar + pinch of salt

## Gingerroot

*See* GINGER, FRESH.

## Gingersnap Crumbs

*Also known as ginger biscuit or ginger nut (British). Crisp and spicy cookie often sweetened with molasses. Closely related to German* pfeffernüesse *and Scandinavian* peppernott.

### If You Don't Have It

Substitute 1½ cups (375 mL) crushed gingersnaps with:

- 1½ cups (375 mL) crushed graham crackers (about 21 squares)
- 1½ cups (375 mL) crushed vanilla wafer cookies (about 33)
- 1½ cups (375 mL) crushed chocolate wafer cookies (about 32)
- 1½ cups (375 mL) crushed Oreo cookies (about 21, including cookie filling); omit sugar from crust
- 1½ cups (375 mL) crushed wheat, bran or corn flakes (about 4½ cups/1.125 L)
- 1½ cups (375 mL) crushed saltine crackers (about 42); omit sugar from crust and adjust salt in filling (for savory fillings)

## Ginger, Wild Bud

*Also known as bunga siantan, ginger flower, red ginger lily, and torch ginger. A gorgeous flower with brilliant pinkish red leaves and neon yellow tips often used in Malaysian dishes such as laksa for its floral yet spicy ginger aromas.*

### If You Don't Have It

Substitute 1 cup (250 mL) wild ginger buds with:

- 1 cup (250 mL) miyoga (buds that grow from the roots of a related rhizome)
- ½ cup (125 mL) minced green or young ginger (no crunchy texture; less complex aroma)

*See also* MIYOGA.

## Ginkgo Nut

*An American petrified ginkgo forest in Washington state is estimated to be 15 million years old.*

### If You Don't Have It

Substitute 1 oz (30 g) ginkgo nuts with:

- 1 oz (30 g) cashew nuts
- 1 oz (30 g) blanched almonds
- 1 oz (30 g) blanched hazelnuts
- 1 oz (30 g) pine nuts

## Girolle

*A specialized cheese or chocolate shaver that consists of a round base with a center spindle and thin, rotating blade with a handle. You place a wheel of cheese or chocolate over the spindle then scrape the blade in a circular motion to create paper-thin rosettes (girolles). While the Swiss tête de moine cheese it shaves has been made for more than 800 years, the girolle was only invented in 1982.*

### If You Don't Have It
Substitute a girolle with:
- Sharp chef's knife dragged across the surface
- Sharp bench knife
- Cheese slicer
- Vegetable peeler

*See also* TÊTE DE MOINE.

## Gjetost

*A Norwegian cheese made from goat's and cow's milk whey that is cooked until caramelized. The texture may be spreadable or semifirm.*

### If You Don't Have It
Substitute 1 oz (30 g) gjetost with:
- 1 oz (30 g) mysost

*See also* MYSOST.

## Glacé Cherry

*See* CHERRY, CANDIED.

## Glace de Viande

*Brown stock (usually beef, veal, or poultry) reduced to a syrup that gels when chilled. Often used to glaze meats or gloss up and flavor sauces at the last minute. Commercial versions are available.*

### If You Don't Have It
Substitute 1 tbsp (15 mL) glace de viande with:
- 1 tbsp (15 mL) Homemade Glace de Viande: Strain and degrease 4 cups (1 L) brown beef, veal, or chicken stock. Then bring to a boil in a medium saucepan over medium-high heat. Reduce heat and boil gently until reduced by about half (about 2 cups/500 mL), skimming foam from surface. Strain into a smaller saucepan and simmer vigorously until reduced by half again, reducing the heat as necessary to avoid burning (this will take 2 to 4 hours). When reduced to 1 cup (250 mL) and lightly coating the back of a spoon, strain into a jar or other airtight container and refrigerate up to 2 months or freeze for up to 6 months (glaze will gel when chilled). Makes about 1 cup (250 mL).

## Glacé Fruit

*See* FRUIT, CANDIED.

## Glass Noodles

*See* A SNAPSHOT OF ASIAN NOODLES (PAGE 656).

## Glasswort

*See* SALICORNIA.

## Glayva™

*Scottish whiskey liqueur flavored with almonds, Seville oranges, herbs, and spices.*

### If You Don't Have It
Substitute 3 tbsp (45 mL) Glayva™ with:
- 3 tbsp (45 mL) Drambuie
- 3 tbsp (45 mL) Grandtully
- 3 tbsp (45 mL) Lochan Ora

## Globe Artichoke

*See* ARTICHOKE.

## Globe Squash

*See* ZUCCHINI.

## Gloucester

*Also known as double Gloucester. A fine mellow English cheese originally made only with the milk from Gloucester cows, which are now nearly extinct. The harder-to-find single Gloucester is made with skimmed milk instead of the whole milk and cream used to make double Gloucester.*

1 lb (500 g) = 4 cups (1 L) shredded

### If You Don't Have It
Substitute 1 oz (30 g) Gloucester with:
- 1 oz (30 g) Cheshire (more complex flavor)
- 1 oz (30 g) Cheddar

### Gloucester Varieties
Choose 1 oz (30 g) Gloucester from these varieties:
- 1 oz (30 g) double Gloucester (creamier, milder, more complex flavor)
- 1 oz (30 g) Huntsman cheese (a layer of Stilton sandwiched between two layers of double Gloucester)

### For Better Health
Substitute 1 oz (30 g) Gloucester with:
- 1 oz (30 g) single Gloucester (lower in fat; drier and crumblier than double Gloucester)

## Glucose, Liquid

*Also known as dextroglucose and dextrose. Common sweetener used in the production of soft drinks. It doesn't crystallize easily, so it is also used in candies, frostings, and baked goods.*

### If You Don't Have It
Substitute ½ cup (125 mL) liquid glucose with:
- ½ cup (125 mL) light corn syrup

## Gluten Flour

*See* SEITAN.

## Glutinous Rice

*See* VARIETIES OF RICE (PAGE 664).

## Goat

*Because they thrive in mountainous habitats on thorny scrub, the meat of goats has been an important protein source for many cultures around the world.*

### If You Don't Have It

Substitute 1 lb (500 g) baby goat with:
- 1 lb (500 g) lamb

## Goat Butter

*Also known as staka. White, silky goat's milk butter tastes fabulous on toast. Compared to cow's milk butter, it is slightly higher in calories, protein, unsaturated fats, calcium, potassium, and vitamin A. Goat butter also has a lower melting point and pleasant barnyardy aroma.*

### If You Don't Have It

Substitute ½ cup (125 mL) goat butter with:
- ½ cup (125 mL) sheep butter (slightly more assertive)
- ½ cup (125 mL) cow butter (milder aroma; waxier texture; yellow color; lower in calories, protein, unsaturated fats, calcium, potassium, and vitamin A; higher melting point)

*See also* BUTTER; SHEEP BUTTER.

## Goat Cheese

*See* CHÈVRE.

## Goatfish

*See* RED MULLET.

## Goat's Milk

*Liquid goat's milk is a good source of calcium for people who are allergic to cow's milk. Goat's milk is also typically transformed into a wide variety of fresh local cheeses. Goat's milk cheese is chalk white because it contains no carotene pigments like cow's or sheep's milk.*

### If You Don't Have It

Substitute 1 cup (250 mL) goat's milk with:
- 1 cup (250 mL) sheep's milk (for cheese making)
- 1 cup (250 mL) cow's milk (for drinking and baking; milder)
- 1 cup (250 mL) soy milk (for drinking and baking; milder, slightly beany tasting; may be sweetened or unsweetened)
- 1 cup (250 mL) almond milk (for drinking and baking; sweeter)
- 1 cup (250 mL) rice milk (for drinking and baking; sweeter)

*See also* CHÈVRE.

## Gobo

*See* BURDOCK.

## Gochujang

*See* FERMENTED BEAN PASTE.

## Godiva Liqueur

*See* CHOCOLATE LIQUEUR.

## Goetta

*The pride of Cincinnati, Ohio, goetta is a rustic pâté of simmered pork, oats, and spices. The city hosts two annual festivals dedicated to the local specialty.*

### If You Don't Have It
Substitute 1 lb (500 g) goetta with:
- 1 lb (500 g) scrapple (sausage and cornmeal)
- 1 lb (500 g) loose breakfast sausage

## Golden Berry

*See* CAPE GOOSEBERRY.

## Golden Delicious Squash

*Eye-shaped winter squash with fine-textured yellow-orange flesh and thick red-orange skin.*

### If You Don't Have It
Substitute 1 lb (500 g) golden delicious squash with:
- 1 lb (500 g) golden hubbard
- 1 lb (500 g) buttercup squash
- 1 lb (500 g) Jarrahdale
- 1 lb (500 g) Queensland Blue
- 1 lb (500 g) pumpkin
- 1 lb (500 g) butternut squash

*See also* HUBBARD SQUASH.

## Golden Needle

*See* LILY BUD.

## Golden Nugget Squash

*It may sound like a Las Vegas casino but this sweet winter squash is named for its bright orange skin and flesh.*

### If You Don't Have It
Substitute 1 cup (250 mL) chopped golden nugget squash with:
- 1 cup (250 mL) chopped buttercup squash
- 1 cup (250 mL) chopped butternut squash
- 1 cup (250 mL) chopped Baby blue hubbard squash
- 1 cup (250 mL) chopped acorn squash
- 1 cup (250 mL) chopped kabocha squash

## Golden Raspberry

*See* RASPBERRY.

## Golden Syrup

*Also known as light treacle (British). Made by cooking the water from sugarcane juice, golden syrup has a rich, toasty flavor. It can be used as a topping or ingredient in cooking or baking.*

### If You Don't Have It
Substitute 1 cup (250 mL) golden syrup with:
- 1 cup (250 mL) Swedish light syrup (ljus sirap)
- ¾ cup (175 mL) light corn syrup + ¼ cup (60 mL) light molasses (slightly thinner; less sweet)
- ½ cup (125 mL) dark corn syrup + ½ cup (125 mL) honey (slightly thinner; less sweet)
- 1 cup (250 mL) pure maple syrup (thinner; less sweet; adds maple flavor)

*See also* TREACLE.

## Goldschläger®

*A Swiss brand of cinnamon schnapps with 24-karat gold leaf flakes.*

**If You Don't Have It**
Substitute 3 tbsp (45 mL) Goldschläger with:
- 3 tbsp (45 mL) cinnamon schnapps

## Goldwasser

*Generic name for an herbal Swiss or German liqueur in which particles of gold leaf flakes are suspended. Danziger® is a well-known producer.*

**If You Don't Have It**
Substitute 3 tbsp (45 mL) Goldwasser with:
- 3 tbsp (45 mL) Silverwasser (has silver flakes)
- 3 tbsp (45 mL) Liqueur d'Or
- 3 tbsp (45 mL) Strega
- 3 tbsp (45 mL) Kümmel
- 3 tbsp (45 mL) aquavit

## Goliath Grouper

*In 2001, the common name of this fish, jewfish, was replaced by the more politically correct goliath grouper.*

**If You Don't Have It**
Substitute 1 lb (500 g) goliath grouper with:
- 1 lb (500 g) striped bass
- 1 lb (500 g) cod
- 1 lb (500 g) catfish
- 1 lb (500 g) red snapper

## Goma

*See* GOMASHIO; SESAME SEED.

## Gomashio

*Japanese seasoning mixture of toasted sesame seeds and sea salt.*

**If You Don't Have It**
Substitute 1 tsp (5 mL) gomashio with:
- 1 tsp (5 mL) Homemade Gomashio: Toast 1½ tbsp (22 mL) sea salt in a heavy skillet over medium heat until fragrant and gray in color, 5 to 7 minutes. Remove and let cool. Toast 1 cup (250 mL) unhulled brown sesame seeds in same skillet until fragrant, 4 to 6 minutes. Remove and let cool. Coarsely grind toasted salt and sesame seeds in a mortar and pestle or spice grinder until sandy in texture. Store in an airtight container in a cool dry place for up to 4 months. Makes about 1 cup (250 mL).
- 1 tsp (5 mL) sesame seeds + pinch of salt

*See also* FURIKAKE.

## Goose

*Foie gras (rich goose liver) and confit (goose cooked and preserved in its own rendered fat) are specialties of southwestern France.*

**If You Don't Have It**
Substitute 1 lb (500 g) goose with:
- 1 lb (500 g) duck (smaller; fattier)
- 1 lb (500 g) squab (smaller; less fatty)
- 1 lb (500 g) turkey dark meat (less fatty; more tender)
- 1 lb (500 g) rabbit (less fatty)
- 1 lb (500 g) chicken dark meat (less fatty; more tender)

## Goose Barnacle

*See* BARNACLE.

## Gooseberry

*Wild and domesticated bush berries that thrive in northern European climes. Canned gooseberries make a good substitute when the berries will be cooked.*

### If You Don't Have It
Substitute 1 cup (250 mL) gooseberries with:
- 1 cup (250 mL) fresh red or white currants (smaller)
- 1 cup (250 mL) kiwifruit (larger; sweeter)
- 1 cup (250 mL) chopped rhubarb (to replace sour gooseberries to be cooked with sugar)

*See also* CAPE GOOSEBERRY.

## Goose Fat

*The fat rendered from these large plump birds is prized as a flavorful cooking medium in many European kitchens.*

### If You Don't Have It
Substitute 1 tbsp (15 mL) goose fat with:
- 1 tbsp (15 mL) duck fat
- 1 tbsp (15 mL) lard or pork fat
- 1 tbsp (15 mL) chicken fat

## Goosefish

*See* MONKFISH.

## Gordita

*A plump corn tortilla that's first cooked on a griddle and then fried in oil before being filled with ground pork, chorizo, or other savory stuffings.*

### If You Don't Have It
Substitute 1 gordita with:
- 1 arepa (split, for stuffing)
- 1 chalupa (split, for stuffing; elongated shape)
- 1 corn tortilla (thinner and stiffer)
- 1 flour tortilla (thinner)
- 1 small pita bread (split, for stuffing)

## Gorgonzola

*One of the world's greatest blue-veined cheeses made from cow's milk in the region of Lombardy. Mild, creamy Gorgonzola dolce is aged for 3 months. More pungent, aged types are variously labeled* di monte, naturale, piccante, *and* stagionata.

### If You Don't Have It
Substitute 1 oz (30 g) Gorgonzola with:
- 1 oz (30 g) Roquefort (less creamy)
- 1 oz (30 g) Stilton (less creamy)
- 1 oz (30 g) Gorgonzola dolce or Dolcelatte (young gorgonzola; milder)
- 1 oz (30 g) Cambozola (less complex flavor)
- 1 oz (30 g) Saga (less complex flavor)

## Gouda

*Young Gouda melts well in cooking. Aged Gouda (a.k.a. Saenkanter) is harder and tastes infinitely more complex with delicious butterscotch aromas.*

### If You Don't Have It

Substitute 1 oz (30 g) Gouda with:
- 1 oz (30 g) farmer's Gouda or Boerenkaas
- 1 oz (30 g) Edam (less rich)
- 1 oz (30 g) Leyden (adds caraway or cumin flavors)
- 1 oz (30 g) Samsoe

## Gourmandise

*Spreadable processed cow's milk cheese made with Gruyère, Cheddar, and cream. Available flavored with walnuts or kirsch.*

### If You Don't Have It

Substitute 1 oz (30 g) Gourmandise with:
- 1 oz (30 g) spreadable Cheddar cheese with nuts
- 1 oz (30 g) Rondelé served with nuts or kirsch (adds garlic and/or herb flavors)
- 1 oz (30 g) Alouette served with nuts or kirsch (adds garlic and/or herb flavors)
- 1 oz (30 g) flavored cream cheese served with nuts or kirsch

## Graham Cracker

*The Reverend Sylvester Graham concocted the sweet, crisp whole wheat cracker in the 1830s and proclaimed it a health food.*

### If You Don't Have It

Substitute 1 lb (500 g) graham crackers with:
- 1 lb (500 g) digestive biscuits (sweeter)
- 1 lb (500 g) teething biscuits
- 1 lb (500 g) wheatmeal biscuits (Australian graham crackers)

### To Vary the Flavor

Substitute 1½ cups (375 mL) crushed graham crackers for pie crust (about 21 squares) with:
- 1½ cups (375 mL) crushed gingersnaps (about 22)
- 1½ cups (375 mL) crushed vanilla wafer cookies (about 33)
- 1½ cups (375 mL) crushed chocolate wafer cookies (about 32)
- 1½ cups (375 mL) crushed Oreo cookies (about 21, including cookie filling); omit sugar from crust
- 1½ cups (375 mL) crushed wheat, bran or corn flakes (about 4½ cups/1.125 L)
- 1½ cups (375 mL) crushed saltine crackers (about 42); omit sugar from crust and adjust salt in filling (for savory fillings)

## Graham Flour

*See* FLOUR, GRAHAM.

## Grain Alcohol

*See* NEUTRAL SPIRITS.

## Grains of Paradise

*Also known as alligator pepper, Guinea pepper, and melegueta pepper. Pungent aromatic seeds of a West African reed-like herb.*

### If You Don't Have It

Substitute 1 tsp (5 mL) ground grains of paradise with:
- ½ tsp (2 mL) ground cardamom + ½ tsp (2 mL) ground black peppercorns

*See also* SELIM KILI PEPPER.

## Grains of Selim

*See* SELIM KILI PEPPER.

## Gram Flour

*See* CHOOSING AMONG WHOLE-GRAIN AND ALTERNATIVE FLOURS (PAGE 648).

## Granadilla

*See* PASSION FRUIT.

## Grana Padano

*A Parmesan-style, hard grating cheese produced in the Italian regions of Lombardy and Piedmont.*

### If You Don't Have It

Substitute 1 oz (30 g) Grana Padano with:
- 1 oz (30 g) Parmesan
- 1 oz (30 g) Pecorino Romano (sharper flavor; less sweet)
- 1 oz (30 g) aged Asiago (slightly milder)
- 1 oz (30 g) dry Jack cheese (more nutty flavor)

### For Better Health

Substitute 1 oz (30 g) Grana Padano (for grating) with:
- 1 oz (30 g) Sapsago (more herbal flavor; lower in fat)

## Grand Marnier

*See* ORANGE LIQUEUR.

## Granita

*Italian water-based dessert frozen without incorporating air so that it has a grainy texture. Some granitas include milk or cream but are frozen so that the texture remains slushy.*

### If You Don't Have It

Substitute 1 cup (250 mL) granita with:
- 1 cup (250 mL) sorbet or sherbet (smooth water-based frozen dessert, sometimes incorporating milk or cream)
- 1 cup (250 mL) gelato (ice cream made without eggs)
- 1 cup (250 mL) frozen yogurt
- 1 cup (250 mL) ice cream

*See also* SORBET.

## Granola

*Embraced by back-to-nature types in the 1960s and '70s, this breakfast/snack food typically combines oats and other grains, nuts, and dried fruits.*

### If You Don't Have It

Substitute 1 cup (250 mL) granola with:
- 1 cup (250 mL) muesli (the original Swiss granola)

## Gran Torres

*See* ORANGE LIQUEUR.

## Grapefruit

*The only citrus fruit to originate in the New World, grapefruit is likely a natural mutation between a pummelo and another citrus fruit. It takes its name from its habit of growing in clusters like grapes.*

### If You Don't Have It

Substitute 1 cup (250 mL) grapefruit segments with:

- ½ cup (125 mL) pummelo segments + ½ cup (125 mL) orange segments
- 1 cup (250 mL) Ugli fruit™ segments
- 1 cup (250 mL) tangelo segments

## Grapefruit Juice

*Grapefruit juice decreases the production of a certain enzyme in the intestines that helps metabolize many prescription and nonprescription drugs. Some research shows that eating mushrooms can counter this effect. Always consult your physician or pharmacist before taking medication with grapefruit juice.*

### If You Don't Have It

Substitute 1 cup (250 mL) grapefruit juice with:

- ½ cup (125 mL) pummelo juice + ½ cup (125 mL) orange juice

### To Vary the Flavor

Substitute 1 cup (250 mL) grapefruit juice with:

- 1 cup (250 mL) pummelo juice
- 1 cup (250 mL) orange juice
- 1 cup (250 mL) pineapple juice

## Grapefruit Knife

*A flexible knife, serrated on both sides of the blade, that makes quick work of sectioning grapefruit.*

### If You Don't Have It

Substitute a grapefruit knife with:

- small serrated knife
- grapefruit spoon

## Grapefruit Peel

*See* CITRUS PEEL, CANDIED.

## Grape Jelly

*Comedian Adam Sandler speaks for the six-year-old in all of us with the line "I Love Grape Jelly" from his silly song Grape Jelly.*

### If You Don't Have It

Substitute 1 cup (250 mL) grape jelly with:

- 1 cup (250 mL) scuppernong or muscadine jelly
- 1 cup (250 mL) red currant jelly

## Grape Juice

*More than 85% of the content of grapes is juice.*

### If You Don't Have It

Substitute 1 cup (250 mL) grape juice with:

- 1 cup (250 mL) de-alcoholized wine (less sweet)
- 1 cup (250 mL) apple juice (less sweet; apple flavor)

## Grape Juice (cont'd)

### Grape Juice Varieties
Choose 1 cup (250 mL) grape juice from these varieties:
- 1 cup (250 mL) white grape juice
- 1 cup (250 mL) red grape juice
- 1 cup (250 mL) sparkling grape juice (carbonated)
- 1 cup (250 mL) juice blend (many juice blends are based on grape juice; flavors will vary)

## Grape Leaf

*Also known as vine leaves. Edible food wrappers associated with Greek and Middle Eastern cookery. Packed commercially in brine. Rinse under cool running water to remove excess salt before using.*

### If You Don't Have It
Substitute 10 brined grape leaves with:
- 10 Homemade Prepared Grape Leaves: Bring 4 cups (1 L) water to a boil in a deep, wide sauté pan over high heat. Add 1½ tsp (7 mL) salt and 10 fresh, unsprayed grape leaves. Reduce heat to medium and simmer until soft, 5 to 10 minutes. Drain. Makes 10.
- 10 fig leaves, simmer in salted water until tender (as food wrappers)
- 10 green cabbage leaves, simmered in salted water until tender (as food wrappers)
- 10 small green chard leaves, thick ribs removed, simmered in salted water until tender (as food wrappers)
- 4 to 6 banana leaves
- 15 to 20 corn husks
- sheets of aluminum foil

## Grapeseed Oil

*See* SUBSTITUTING OILS (PAGE 658).

## Grape, Table

*The bestselling grape in the U.S. is the Thompson Seedless. The average American eats about 8 pounds (4 kg) of grapes each year.*

> 1 lb (500 g) = 75
> medium = 2½ to 3 cups
> (625 to 750 mL)

### If You Don't Have It
Substitute 1 cup (250 mL) green table grapes with:
- 1 cup (250 mL) blueberries (purple color; blueberry flavor)

### Table Grape Varieties
Choose 1 cup (250 mL) green table grapes from:
- 1 cup (250 mL) red table grapes (red color)
- 1 cup (250 mL) Flame Tokay grapes (red color; thick skin; mild flavor)
- 1 cup (250 mL) Muscat grapes (more complex, musky flavor)
- 1 cup (250 mL) Muscadine or scuppernong grapes (strong, musky flavor; often made into jelly or wine)
- 1 cup (250 mL) champagne grapes (smaller)

## Grappa

*A distilled spirit produced in northern Italy from fermented grape pomace. The last several decades*

### If You Don't Have It
Substitute 3 tbsp (45 mL) grappa with:
- 3 tbsp (45 mL) cognac
- 3 tbsp (45 mL) Armagnac

*have seen producers using finer grapes to make more elegant grappas.*

## Grappa Varieties

Choose 3 tbsp (45 mL) grappa from these varieties:

- 3 tbsp (45 mL) marc (French)
- 3 tbsp (45 mL) aguardiente (Spanish)
- 3 tbsp (45 mL) testerbranntwein (German)
- 3 tbsp (45 mL) bagaceira (Portuguese)

## Grater

*Plastic or metal kitchen tool perforated with sharp holes or slits. When cheeses, vegetables, or other foods are drawn over the perforations, they are cut into fine bits or strips.*

### If You Don't Have It

Substitute a grater with these different types:

- box grater (for shredding, grating, and slicing)
- food processor fitted with a shredding or slicing disc (for shredding or slicing)
- food processor fitted with a metal blade (for grinding foods such as nuts into small pieces)
- flat grater (for shredding or grating)
- Microplane® or rasp (for finely grating cheese, chocolate, nuts, or nutmeg)
- mouli or rotary grater (for grating small amounts of cheese, chocolate, nuts, or nutmeg)
- nutmeg grater (for finely grating small amounts of nutmeg)

## Gratin Dish

*Shallow ovenproof dish for baking gratins, casserole-type dishes topped with cheese or buttered crumbs.*

### If You Don't Have It

Substitute a gratin dish with:

- any shallow, wide, heatproof dish such as a quiche dish or pie plate

## Graviera

*Popular Greek hard cheese similar to Gruyère. Graviera from Crete is made with sheep's milk and has a caramel aroma. In Naxos, it's often combined with up to 30% goat milk.*

### If You Don't Have It

Substitute 1 oz (30 g) graviera with:

- 1 oz (30 g) aged Kefalotyri
- 1 oz (30 g) Kasseri
- 1 oz (30 g) Gruyère
- 1 oz (30 g) Jarlsberg

## Gravlax

*A Swedish delicacy. Salmon cured in a mixture of salt, sugar, and fresh dill. Should be sliced and served in transparently thin slices.*

### If You Don't Have It

Substitute 1 lb (500 g) gravlax with:

- 1 lb (500 g) lox or other smoked salmon, especially brined and hot-smoked salmon such as "kippered salmon" or "squaw candy" (preferably, add fresh or dried dill; adds mild smoke flavor)
- 1 lb (500 g) cured or smoked arctic char (preferably, add fresh or dried dill)

*See also* SMOKED SALMON.

## Gravy Browning

*Commercial condiment designed to boost the dark color and rich flavor of homemade gravy and sauces. Includes Kitchen Bouquet© and Gravy Master©.*

### If You Don't Have It

Substitute 1 tsp (5 mL) gravy browning (for brown color) with:
- ½ to 1 tsp (2 to 5 mL) baker's caramel (less salty)
- 2 drops red food coloring + 1 drop green food coloring (adds only brown color, no flavor; will darken 1 cup/250 mL liquid a light brown)
- 1 tsp (5 mL) Worcestershire sauce (adds other flavors)
- 1 tsp (5 mL) steak sauce (adds other flavors)

## Grease Mop

*Also known as fat mop. A mini-mop with absorbent strips for sopping up oil floating on the surface of soups or stews.*

### If You Don't Have It

Substitute a grease mop with:
- fat separator
- dragging folded paper towels across surface of liquid until fat is removed (for small amounts of fat)
- skimming fat from surface with a ladle, large spoon, or bulb baster
- placing ice cubes in a slotted spoon and dragging across surface of liquid, then discarding ice as it becomes covered with fat (for small amounts of fat)
- chilling pan of soup, stock or other liquid until fat congeals on top, then spooning off fat

## Greek Seasoning

*A bottled herb blend of characteristic Greek flavorings.*

### If You Don't Have It

Substitute 1 tsp (5 mL) Greek seasoning with
- 1 tsp (5 mL) Homemade Greek Seasoning: Combine 1 tsp (5 mL) dried oregano, ¾ tsp (3 mL) onion powder, ¾ tsp (3 mL) garlic powder, ½ tsp (2 mL) ground black pepper, ¼ tsp (1 mL) dried mint, small pinch of cinnamon, and small pinch of nutmeg. Add salt to taste. Makes about 1 tablespoon (15 mL).

## Greek Yogurt

*See* YOGURT CHEESE.

## Green Almond

*See* ALMOND, GREEN.

## Green Bean

*Also known as snap beans or string beans. Long ago, there really was a fibrous string that ran down the seam of the string bean pod but it has been bred out*

### If You Don't Have It

Substitute 1 lb (500 g) green beans with:
- 1 lb (500 g) yard-long beans (longer; starchier and less sweet)
- 1 lb (500 g) thin asparagus
- 1 lb (500 g) nopales, sliced
- 1 lb (500 g) okra
- 1 lb (500 g) broccoli

*of the species. Cooks
no longer have to
de-string their beans.*

```
1 lb (500 g) =
3 cups (750 mL)
```

## Green Bean Varieties

Choose 1 lb (500 g) green beans from these varieties:
- 1 lb (500 g) green snap beans (crisp; mildly sweet)
- 1 lb (500 g) purple snap beans (similar to green snap beans; green when cooked)
- 1 lb (500 g) yellow wax beans (pale yellow color; mild flavor)
- 1 lb (500 g) haricot verts, filet beans, or French beans (green, yellow, or purple color; slender; tender; more complex flavor)
- 1 lb (500 g) Romano or Italian flat beans (green or yellow color; flatter than green snap beans; juicy and meaty; mild flavor)
- 1 lb (500 g) Tongue of Fire beans (green with flecks of pink or purple; flatter than green snap beans; green when cooked)
- 1 lb (500 g) Dragon Tongue beans (pale yellow or cream with maroon or dark purple splotches; similar to yellow wax beans; yellow when cooked)

### Green Cabbage

*See* BOK CHOY; CABBAGE; NAPA CABBAGE; RED CABBAGE; SAVOY CABBAGE.

### Green Coconut

*See* COCONUT WATER.

### Green Garlic

*See* GARLIC, GREEN.

### Green Ginger

*See* GINGER, FRESH.

### Green Leaf Lettuce

*See* LEAF LETTUCE.

### Green Mussel

*See* MUSSEL.

### Green Onion

*See* ONION, GREEN.

### Green Pepper

*See* BELL PEPPER.

### Green Peppercorn

*See* PEPPERCORN.

### Greens

*See* SPECIFIC TYPES.

### Gremolata

*A savory Italian blend
of minced fresh garlic,
lemon zest, and parsley
that garnishes osso buco.*

### If You Don't Have It

Substitute 1 tbsp (15 mL) gremolata with:
- 1 tbsp (15 mL) Homemade Gremolata: Combine 3 tbsp (45 mL) finely chopped flat-leaf parsley, 1 minced garlic clove, and 1 tsp (5 mL) grated lemon zest. Season to taste with salt and ground black pepper to taste. Makes about 3 tablespoons (45 mL).

## Grenadine

*Garnet-color, pomegranate-flavored syrup used to flavor beverages and sweets. At one time, made only with pomegranates grown on the island of Grenada.*

### If You Don't Have It
Substitute 1 tsp (5 mL) grenadine with:
- ¼ to ½ tsp (1 to 2 mL) pomegranate molasses or concentrate
- 2 to 3 tsp (10 to 15 mL) pomegranate juice (reduce liquid in recipe by 1 to 2 tsp/5 to 10 mL and add sugar if necessary)
- 1 tsp (5 mL) red currant syrup
- 1 tsp (5 mL) raspberry syrup

## Greve

*Semifirm Swedish cow's milk cheese similar to Swiss Emmental.*

### If You Don't Have It
Substitute 1 oz (30 g) Greve with:
- 1 oz (30 g) Emmental
- 1 oz (30 g) Jarlsberg
- 1 oz (30 g) Gruyère
- 1 oz (30 g) Swiss
- 1 oz (30 g) French Comté

## Griddle

*Cast-iron or cast-aluminum rimless cooking pan or surface that can be a portable unit to sit atop heating elements or a unit built into a stovetop cooking surface. Commonly used to cook pancakes, bacon, French toast, and hot sandwiches.*

### If You Don't Have It
Substitute a griddle with:
- large frying pan or skillet
- large sauté pan

## Grill

*A sturdy metal grate that holds foods set over hot charcoal or other heat source. Both indoor and outdoor units are available.*

### If You Don't Have It
Substitute a grill with:
- broiler (heat comes from above instead of below; to add smoke flavor that would have been achieved by grilling over coals, add 1 to 2 drops liquid smoke to marinade or sauce; or include a smoked food such as chipotle chiles)
- ridged grill pan (gives good grill marks; can steam foods; to add smoke flavor that would have been achieved by grilling over coals, add 1 to 2 drops liquid smoke to marinade or sauce; or include a smoked food such as chipotle chiles)
- electric tabletop grill (gives good grill marks; can steam foods; best for sandwiches; to add smoke flavor that would have been achieved by grilling over coals, add 1 to 2 drops liquid smoke to marinade or sauce; or include a smoked food such as chipotle chiles)

## Grissini

*See* BREADSTICK.

## Grits

*See* BARLEY GRITS; CORN GRITS; HOMINY GRITS.

## Groats

*See* BUCKWHEAT GROATS; OAT GROATS.

## Grosella

*See* OTAHEITE GOOSEBERRY.

## Ground Cherry

*See* CAPE GOOSEBERRY.

## Ground Ginger

*See* GINGER, GROUND.

## Ground Red Pepper

*See* CAYENNE PEPPER.

## Grouper

*A lean, firm-fleshed fish of the bass family. The strongly flavored skin is often removed before cooking.*

### If You Don't Have It
Substitute 1 lb (500 g) grouper with:
- 1 lb (500 g) striped bass
- 1 lb (500 g) cod
- 1 lb (500 g) catfish
- 1 lb (500 g) red snapper

*See also* GOLIATH GROUPER.

## Grouse

*A distinctively flavored dark-meat game bird widely enjoyed in Great Britain. Young grouse are excellent roasted or braised.*

### If You Don't Have It
Substitute 1 lb (500 g) grouse with:
- 1 lb (500 g) quail
- 1 lb (500 g) squab
- 1 lb (500 g) young pheasant
- 1 lb (500 g) Cornish game hen (fattier)

## Gruyère

*One of the finest cheeses in the world, Gruyère has been produced in Switzerland since the 12th century.*

4 oz (125 g) =
1 cup (250 mL) grated

### If You Don't Have It
Substitute 1 oz (30 g) Gruyère with:
- 1 oz (30 g) Comté
- 1 oz (30 g) Beaufort
- 1 oz (30 g) Emmental

## Guacamole

*See* AVOCADO.

## Guajes

*Seeds that grow in flat green or reddish-brown pods on the leguminous Leucaena tree. In Mexico, guaje seeds are eaten both fresh and dried. They are often ground add added to Mexican sauces for a flavor reminiscent of shallots.*

### If You Don't Have It
Substitute 1 cup (250 mL) guaje seeds with:
- 1 cup (250 mL) pumpkin seeds + 1 tbsp (15 mL) chopped shallots

## Guajillo Chile

*See* CHOOSING DRIED CHILES (PAGE 642).

## Guanabana

*See* SOURSOP.

## Guanciale

*Salt-cured, air-dried pig's jowl and cheek. In Italian cooking, guanciale is used much like pancetta.*

### If You Don't Have It
Substitute 4 oz (125 g) guanciale with:
- 4 oz (125 g) pancetta
- 4 oz (125 g) hog jowl (adds smoke flavor)
- 4 oz (125 g) bacon (adds smoke flavor)
- 2 to 4 oz (60 to 125 g) salt pork (drop in boiling water for a few minutes to reduce saltiness or reduce salt in recipe if necessary)
- 4 oz (125 g) bacon

*See also* HOG JOWL.

## Guar Gum

*Made from the ground endosperm of beans that grow on the guar or custer plant, guar gum has eight times the water-thickening power of cornstarch. It thickens, emulsifies, and stabilizes hundreds of commercial products from ice creams and puddings to sauces and salad dressings. Those intolerant of gluten use guar gum to replace gluten in breads and baking, using about ½ tsp (2 mL) per cup (250 mL) of gluten-free flour. To thicken 1 cup (250 mL) liquid, use about ¼ tsp (1 mL) guar gum.*

### If You Don't Have It
Substitute 1 tsp (5 mL) guar gum with:
- 1½ tsp (7 mL) xanthan gum
- 1½ tsp (7 mL) pre-gel starch
- 1½ tsp (7 mL) ground flaxseed
- 2½ tbsp (37 mL) cornstarch

## Guava

*Also known as goyave
and guayaba. Guava
may be one of 140-odd
species with sweet or sour
aromatic flesh tasting of
strawberries, pineapple,
banana, or all three.*

> 1 medium =
> ½ cup (125 mL) pulp

### If You Don't Have It

Substitute ½ cup (125 mL) guava pulp with:
- ½ cup (125 mL) chopped pineapple
- ½ cup (125 mL) strawberries

*See also* GUAVA PASTE.

## Guavaberry Liqueur

*The national rum drink
of St. Martin, where
guavaberries (rumberries)
thrive. The liqueur is
popular at Christmastime
and often accompanied by
the song "Good mornin',
good mornin', I come for me
guavaberry; good mornin',
good mornin' to you and
all your family," written by
Bill La Motta. Guavaberries
themselves are unrelated to
guava and grow on a plant
related to eucalyptus and
clove. The yellow-orange
or red-purple berries are
about the size of cranberries
and contain a single seed
surrounded by juicy, sweet,
aromatic flesh. They're also
used to make juice, jams,
cakes, and tarts around
the holidays.*

### If You Don't Have It

Substitute 1 cup (250 mL) guavaberry liqueur with:
- 1 cup (250 mL) Homemade Guavaberry Liqueur: Squeeze the seeds from 1 lb (500 g) red and/or yellow guavaberries. Put ½ cup (125 mL) of the berries in a bowl and mash with a potato masher. Add 1 bottle (750 mL) dark rum (such as Myers's) and let stand. Meanwhile, put the remaining berries in a large saucepan along with 1 cup (250 mL) dark brown sugar and bring to a boil over medium high heat. Boil until the berries are soft and the liquid becomes medium-thick. Remove from the heat and let cool to room temperature. Put 4 cups (1 L) dried hibiscus flower (Jamaican sorrel), 1¼ cups (300 mL) prunes, 1¼ cups (300 mL) raisins, ½ cup (125 mL) sliced gingerroot, 2 cinnamon sticks, and 1 whole vanilla bean in a half-gallon (2 quart/2 L) jar with a lid. Pour in the mashed berry mixture and the cooled mixture. Screw on the lid to seal and store in a dark place for 4 to 8 months. Strain into two 750-mL bottles. Makes 1½ quarts (two 750-mL bottles).
- 1 cup (250 mL) dark rum puréed with ½ cup (125 mL) guavaberry or lingonberry preserves, ⅛ tsp (0.5 mL) vanilla extract, a pinch of ground ginger, and a pinch of ground cinnamon.
- 1 cup (250 mL) mulled wine + 1 tbsp (15 mL) dark rum
- 1 cup (250 mL) cranberry liqueur
- 1 cup (250 mL) cherry liqueur

## Guava Paste

*Like a bar of firm jelly,
guava paste is prepared
by slowly simmering
guava, sugar, pectin,
and citric acid. Sold in
Latin American and some
specialty markets.*

### If You Don't Have It

Substitute ¼ cup (60 mL) guava paste with:
- ¼ cup (60 mL) quince paste (dulce de membrillo)
- ¼ cup (60 mL) strawberry preserves
- ¼ cup (60 mL) other tropical fruit preserves

*See also* GUAVA.

## Guayaba

*See* GUAVA.

## Güero Chile

*See* CHOOSING FRESH CHILES (PAGE 640).

## Guinea Fowl

*Small bird related to chicken and partridge, said to have originated in Guinea, Africa. The meat is dark and pleasingly gamey.*

### If You Don't Have It

Substitute 1 lb (500 g) guinea fowl with:

- 1 lb (500 g) pheasant
- 1 lb (500 g) Cornish game hen (moister)
- 1 lb (500 g) chicken (preferably pasture-raised; moister)

## Guinea Pepper

*See* GRAINS OF PARADISE; SELIM KILI PEPPER.

## Gur

*See* JAGGERY.

## Gyoza Wrappers

*See* WON TON SKINS.

# Habanero Chile
## to Hyssop

---

### Habanero Chile

*See* CHOOSING DRIED CHILES (PAGE 642); CHOOSING FRESH CHILES (PAGE 640).

---

### Haddock

*This saltwater fish is a smaller relative of cod. It is low in fat, mild in flavor, and has a firm texture.*

**If You Don't Have It**

Substitute 1 lb (500 g) haddock with:
- 1 lb (500 g) cod
- 1 lb (500 g) pollock
- 1 lb (500 g) blackfish
- 1 lb (500 g) grouper
- 1 lb (500 g) red snapper
- 1 lb (500 g) sea bass
- 1 lb (500 g) tilefish
- 1 lb (500 g) turbot

**To Vary the Flavor**

Substitute 1 lb (500 g) haddock with:
- 1 lb (500 g) finnan haddie (smoked haddock)

---

### Hairy Melon

*See* FUZZY GOURD.

## Hake

*A relative of cod that swims in both the Atlantic and Pacific Oceans. The delicate white flesh is low in fat.*

### If You Don't Have It

Substitute 1 lb (500 g) hake with:

- 1 lb (500 g) cod
- 1 lb (500 g) pollock
- 1 lb (500 g) red snapper
- 1 lb (500 g) whiting
- 1 lb (500 g) dogfish
- 1 lb (500 g) rockfish
- 1 lb (500 g) sea bass
- 1 lb (500 g) tilefish
- 1 lb (500 g) weakfish

## Half-and-Half

*See* CREAM, HALF-AND-HALF.

## Halibut

*This very large flatfish can weigh up to 1,000 pounds (500 kg) but typically ranges from 50 to 100 pounds (25 to 50 kg).*

### If You Don't Have It

Substitute 1 lb (500 g) halibut with:

- 1 lb (500 g) lingcod
- 1 lb (500 g) cod
- 1 lb (500 g) turbot
- 1 lb (500 g) dogfish
- 1 lb (500 g) haddock
- 1 lb (500 g) striped bass

## Haloumi

*A firm, salty sheep's milk cheese eaten widely in Cyprus, Egypt, and other Middle Eastern countries.*

### If You Don't Have It

Substitute 1 oz (30 g) haloumi with:

- 1 oz (30 g) feta
- ½ oz (15 g) feta + ½ oz (15 g) mozzarella

## Ham

*Ham may be a first-rate cured pork product, but it is also synonymous with a second-rate actor.*

1 lb (500 g) boneless =
1½ to 3 cups
(375 to 750 mL) chopped =
1 to 2 cups
(250 to 500 mL) ground

### If You Don't Have It

Substitute 1 lb (500 g) ham with:

- 1 lb (500 g) Canadian bacon (usually leaner than ham)
- 1 lb (500 g) canned ham (moister; saltier than wet-cured or dry-cured ham; may be a whole boneless portion or pieces formed into a single shape)
- 1 lb (500 g) picnic ham or picnic shoulder (cured like ham; tougher and fattier)

*See also* HAM, DRY-CURED; HAM, WET-CURED.

## Hamburger

*See* BEEF, GROUND.

## Hamburg Parsley

*See* PARSLEY ROOT.

## Ham, Canned

*See* DEVILED HAM; HAM, WET-CURED; SPAM.

## Ham, Dry-Cured

*Also known as country ham. Firmer texture and more complex flavor than wet-cured ham and may be smoked or unsmoked.*

### If You Don't Have It

Substitute 1 lb (500 g) dry-cured ham with:

- 1 lb (500 g) well-aged wet-cured ham (moister; generally milder, less complex flavor)

*See also* ARDENNES HAM; BAYONNE HAM; BLACK FOREST HAM; CULATELLO; HAM, WET-CURED; IBERICO HAM; KENTUCKY HAM; PROSCIUTTO; SERRANO HAM; SPECK; VIRGINIA HAM; WESTPHALIAN HAM; YORK HAM; YUNNAN HAM.

## Ham Hock

*The lower hind leg of a hog, usually cured, smoked, or both. Contributes hearty campfire flavor to beans, soups, and stews.*

### If You Don't Have It

Substitute 1 smoked ham hock with:

- 4 oz (125 g) chopped smoked ham
- 4 oz (125 g) cured, smoked hog jowl or guanciale
- 4 to 6 oz (125 to 175 g) smoked turkey drumsticks
- 4 oz (125 g) smoked sausage
- 4 oz (125 g) chopped smoked bacon
- 4 oz (125 g) pancetta (no smoke flavor)
- 2 to 4 oz (60 to 125 g) chopped salt pork (no smoke flavor; reduce salt in recipe if necessary)
- 1 ham bone (no smoke flavor)

## Ham, Wet-Cured

*Also known as brine-cured ham and city ham. Fully cooked hams sold bone-in, boneless, spiral-sliced, and as ham steak.*

### If You Don't Have It

Substitute 1 lb (500 g) wet-cured ham with:

- 1 lb (500 g) dry-cured ham (saltier; firmer; more complex flavor)
- 1 lb (500 g) picnic ham or picnic shoulder (cured like ham; tougher and fattier)

*See also* HAM, DRY-CURED.

## Hanakatsuo

*See* BONITO.

## Handkäse

*Also known as Mainz. Handkäse is German for "hand cheese" because it's manually molded into irregular shapes. Made from sour milk, the*

### If You Don't Have It

Substitute 1 oz (30 g) Handkäse with:

- 1 oz (30 g) Harzer
- 1 oz (30 g) Kochkäse
- 1 oz (30 g) Liederkranz
- 1 oz (30 g) Limburger

## Handkäse (cont'd)

*pungent taste and aroma pleases some more than others. The first historical mention of Hessischer Handkäse was in 1813 when people from the town of Groß-Gerau in Hesse, Germany sold their hand-formed cheese on the market in Mainz.*

*See also* HARZER; KOCHKÄSE.

## Hanpen

*See* SURIMI.

## Hard-Shell Clam

*See* SWAPPING CLAMS (PAGE 645).

## Hardtack

*Also known as sea bread and ship biscuit. Flat, hard biscuit that helped to keep sailors alive on long sea voyages.*

### If You Don't Have It

Substitute 1 lb (500 g) hardtack with:

- 1 lb (500 g) zweiback

## Hard Wheat Flour

*See* FLOUR, BREAD.

## Hare

*A well-liked game animal in Europe, this larger relative of the rabbit has never been domesticated. Several closely related species are known as jackrabbits. The dark, full-flavored meat is delicious in English civet, French* daube, *German* hansenpfeffer, *and Italian* lepre in agrodolce.

### If You Don't Have It

Substitute 1 lb (500 g) hare or jackrabbit with:

- 1 lb (500 g) rabbit
- 1 lb (500 g) chicken

*See also* RABBIT.

## Haricot Vert

*See* GREEN BEAN.

## Harinilla

*See* MASA HARINA.

## Harissa

*A blistering red chile paste that ignites North African palates. One common brand features a picture of an erupting volcano on the can.*

### If You Don't Have It

Substitute 1 tbsp (15 mL) harissa with:

- 1 tbsp (15 mL) Homemade Harissa: Toast 1 tsp (5 mL) caraway seeds, 1 tsp (5 mL) coriander seeds and ½ tsp (2 mL) cumin seeds in a dry skillet over medium heat until fragrant, about 2 minutes. Grind to a powder in a spice grinder, blender, or with a mortar and pestle. If using a spice grinder, transfer to a blender or small food processor and add 2 chopped garlic cloves, 3 tbsp (45 mL) paprika, 1 tbsp (15 mL) vegetable oil and 1 to 1½ tsp (5 to 7 mL) cayenne pepper. Grind to a paste and add salt to taste. Makes about ⅓ cup (75 mL).
- 1 tbsp (15 mL) tabil (a similar spice paste from Tunisia)
- 1 tbsp (15 mL) chile paste
- 1 tbsp (15 mL) berbere
- 1 to 3 tsp (5 to 15 mL) hot sauce (less aromatic)

## Harusame

*See* A SNAPSHOT OF ASIAN NOODLES (PAGE 656).

## Harvestfish

*See* BUTTERFISH.

## Harzer

*A sour-milk curd cheese made from skimmed cow's milk. Like handkäse, harzer is low in fat but high in pungency and often enjoyed with bread, mustard, and gherkins. A similar cheese known as harz is made from fresh whole milk in Harz, the highest mountain range in northern Germany.*

### If You Don't Have It

Substitute 1 oz (30 g) harzer with:

- 1 oz (30 g) Handkäse
- 1 oz (30 g) Liederkranz
- 1 oz (30 g) Limburger

*See also* HANDKÄSE; KOCHKÄSE.

## Havarti

*Often referred to as the Danish version of Tilsit, this tangy cheese is named after the experimental farm on which it was developed.*

### If You Don't Have It

Substitute 1 oz (30 g) Havarti with:

- 1 oz (30 g) Tilsit
- 1 oz (30 g) Esrom
- 1 oz (30 g) Monterey Jack

## Hawaiian Salmon

*See* RAINBOW RUNNER.

## Hawaij

*Yemenite spice mix used for grilling and in soups, stews, rice, and simmered dishes. A different mix of spices used to flavor Yemeni coffee goes by the same name.*

### If You Don't Have It

Substitute 1 tbsp (15 mL) hawaij with:

- 1 tbsp (15 mL) Homemade Hawaij: Toast $\frac{1}{4}$ cup (60 mL) cumin seeds, 1 tbsp (15 mL) black peppercorns, 2 tsp (10 mL) coriander seeds, $1\frac{1}{2}$ tsp (7 mL) green cardamom pods and $\frac{1}{2}$ tsp (2 mL) whole cloves in a dry skillet over medium heat until fragrant, 3 to 5 minutes. Cool slightly, transfer to a spice grinder, and grind to a powder. Stir in $\frac{1}{4}$ cup (60 mL) ground turmeric. Makes about $\frac{1}{2}$ cup (125 mL).
- $1\frac{1}{2}$ tsp (7 mL) ground cumin + $1\frac{1}{2}$ tsp (7 mL) ground turmeric + $\frac{1}{4}$ tsp (1 mL) ground black pepper + $\frac{1}{8}$ tsp (0.5 mL) ground cardamom
- 1 tbsp (15 mL) berbere (hotter)
- 1 tbsp (15 mL) harissa (much hotter)
- 1 tbsp (15 mL) garam masala

## Hazelnut

*Also known as cobnut, filbert, nocciola, and noisette. To easily peel the dark, bitter skin from hazelnuts, scatter them on a baking sheet and bake in a 350°F (180°C) oven for 12 to 15 minutes, or until the skins begin to part from the nuts. Remove and rub the nuts, a few at a time, between the folds of a dish towel to completely loosen the skins.*

> 1 lb (500 g) shelled =
> $3\frac{1}{2}$ cups (875 mL) nuts =
> 4 cups (1 L) ground

### If You Don't Have It

Substitute 1 cup (250 mL) shelled hazelnuts with:

- 2 to 4 tbsp (30 to 60 mL) hazelnut oil (for baking and cooking; will add nut flavor but not texture of whole nuts; reduce fat in recipe by 2 to 4 tbsp/30 to 60 mL)
- 1 cup (250 mL) beechnuts
- 1 cup (250 mL) cashews
- 1 cup (250 mL) macadamia nuts
- 1 cup (250 mL) almonds
- 1 cup (250 mL) walnuts

*See also* NUT.

## Hazelnut Butter

*Sweetened paste of ground roasted hazelnuts, oil, and salt.*

### If You Don't Have It

Substitute 1 cup (250 mL) hazelnut butter with:

- 1 cup (250 mL) Homemade Hazelnut Butter: Put 2 cups (500 mL) roasted hazelnuts (skins removed) and $\frac{1}{4}$ tsp (1 mL) salt in a blender or food processor fitted with metal blade. Process, gradually adding 4 to 6 tbsp (60 to 90 mL) vegetable oil (and/or hazelnut oil), until the mixture forms a paste. Add sugar to taste. Makes $1\frac{1}{2}$ cups (375 mL).
- 1 cup (250 mL) cashew butter, almond butter, or peanut butter
- 1 cup (250 mL) gianduja (chocolate-hazelnut paste)

*See also* HAZELNUT PASTE.

## Hazelnut Liqueur

*Also known as noisette. Frangelico is a widely known brand.*

### If You Don't Have It

Substitute 3 tbsp (45 mL) hazelnut liqueur with:

- ½ to ¾ tsp (2 to 3 mL) hazelnut extract (add 3 tbsp/45 mL water or other liquid if necessary to replace lost volume in recipe)
- ½ to ¾ tsp (2 to 3 mL) hazelnut extract and reduce liquid in recipe by a scant 3 tbsp (45 mL)

### To Vary the Flavor

Substitute 3 tbsp (45 mL) hazelnut liqueur with:

- 3 tbsp (45 mL) almond liqueur, walnut liqueur, coffee liqueur, or chocolate liqueur

## Hazelnut Oil

*See* SUBSTITUTING OILS (PAGE 658).

## Hazelnut Paste

*Also known as pasta nocciola. A sensuous filling for pastries and confections prepared with ground roasted hazelnuts, egg whites, confectioner's sugar, and hazelnut liqueur.*

### If You Don't Have It

Substitute 1 cup (250 mL) hazelnut paste with:

- 1 cup (250 mL) Homemade Hazelnut Paste: Grind 2 cups (500 mL) roasted hazelnuts in a food processor or blender until the texture of cornmeal. Add 2 large egg whites, 1 cup (250 mL) confectioner's (icing) sugar, and 1 tsp (5 mL) hazelnut liqueur and blend until smooth. Makes about 1½ cups (375 mL).
- 1 cup (250 mL) gianduja (chocolate-hazelnut paste)

## Headcheese

*Also known as pork brawn. The head of a pig contains nearly enough gelatin to make aspic (meat jelly). To make headcheese, the head is boiled and mixed with small pieces of cured meat from the hog's head (and sometimes pieces of the trotters, tongue, and heart) and molded into a sliceable cold cut. International versions include Austrian presswurst and German sülze. In the southern United States, a sweet-and-sour version made with vinegar goes by the name of pork souse.*

### If You Don't Have It

Substitute 4 oz (125 g) headcheese with:

- 4 oz (125 g) jellied pork tongue
- 4 oz (125 g) mortadella
- 4 oz (125 g) zungenwurst
- 4 oz (125 g) wet-cured ham
- 4 oz (125 g) jellied corned beef

## Head Lettuce

*See* BUTTERHEAD LETTUCE; CRISPHEAD LETTUCE.

## Hearts of Palm

*This delicacy is most often the center portion of the stems of Florida's state tree, the cabbage palm. More coveted stems come from other varieties of palm such as the açai palm. The hearts look like white asparagus and taste faintly of artichoke. Canned versions make a fair substitute for fresh.*

### If You Don't Have It

Substitute 1 cup (250 mL) hearts of palm with:
- 1 cup (250 mL) canned or marinated artichoke hearts
- 1 cup (250 mL) cooked asparagus (for salads)

## Heavy Cream

*See* CREAM, WHIPPING.

## Herba Buena

*See* MINT.

## Herbal Salt Substitute

*Commercial seasoning condiment, such as Mrs. Dash® Original Blend, for those who wish to reduce sodium intake. Proprietary mixtures can contain various spices, herbs, seeds, and dehydrated aromatic vegetables.*

### If You Don't Have It

Substitute 1 tsp (5 mL) herbal salt substitute with:
- 1 tsp (5 mL) Italian seasoning (salt-free)
- 1 tsp (5 mL) Spike® (a blend of 39 seasonings; salt-free)
- 1 tsp (5 mL) Beau Monde® Seasoning (adds salt)
- ½ tsp (2 mL) table salt

## Herbal Tea

*See* TEA.

## Herbes de Provence

*Not quite like a trip to the Riviera, this seasoning blend does, however, evoke the warm, vibrant flavors of the South of France.*

### If You Don't Have It

Substitute 1 tsp (5 mL) herbes de Provence with:
- 1 tsp (5 mL) Homemade Herbes de Provence: Combine 2 tsp (10 mL) dried thyme, 2 tsp (10 mL) dried savory, 1 tsp (5 mL) dried marjoram, 1 tsp (5 mL) dried lavender, ½ tsp (2 mL) dried rosemary, ½ tsp (2 mL) fennel seeds, and 1 crushed bay leaf. Makes about 3 tablespoons (45 mL).

## Herbs

From alexanders (a wild European herb that tastes like bitter celery) to za'atar (Arabic wild thyme) there flourishes a wide world of culinary seasonings derived from the aromatic leaves and stems of tender green plants.

### If You Don't Have It
Substitute 1 tbsp (15 mL) chopped fresh herbs with:
- 1 tsp (5 mL) dried herbs
- ¼ to ½ tsp (1 to 2 mL) ground or powdered

See also SPECIFIC TYPES.

## Herbsaint

See ANISE LIQUEUR.

## Herring

This large family of mostly small fish has more than 100 varieties. American shad is a type of herring, as is the alewife. Herring is particularly beloved in northern and eastern Europe, where it is transformed by pickling, salting, and smoking into Bismarck herring, rollmops, kippered herring, schmaltz herring, and many other cured tidbits.

### If You Don't Have It
Substitute 1 lb (500 g) herring with:
- 1 lb (500 g) sardines (smaller)
- 1 lb (500 g) shad (larger)
- 1 lb (500 g) smelt
- 1 lb (500 g) mackerel

### Herring Varieties
Choose 1 lb (500 g) cured herring from these varieties:
- 1 lb (500 g) red herring (brined and heavily smoked)
- 1 lb (500 g) kippers (split, salted, and cold smoked)
- 1 lb (500 g) bloaters (split, salted, and lightly smoked; larger than kippers)
- 1 lb (500 g) Bismarck herring (unskinned double fillets marinated in spiced vinegar with onions)
- 1 lb (500 g) rollmops (unskinned double fillets wrapped around pickled cucumber or onion and marinated in spiced vinegar)
- 1 lb (500 g) pickled herring (cured and marinated in sauce of sour cream, mustard, or wine)

See also SHAD; SPRAT.

## Herve

Cheese, similar to Limburger that is soft and pungent with a reddish-brown natural coating sometimes flavored with herbs.

### If You Don't Have It
Substitute 1 oz (30 g) Herve with:
- 1 oz (30 g) Limburger
- 1 oz (30 g) Liederkranz

## Hibachi

*"Fire bowl" in Japanese, these compact portable grills are easy to use and versatile.*

### If You Don't Have It

Substitute a hibachi with:

- grill, especially a portable grill (usually larger and with a lid)
- broiler (heat comes from above instead of below; to add smoke flavor that would have been achieved by grilling over coals in a hibachi, add 1 to 2 drops liquid smoke to marinade or sauce; or include a smoked food such as chipotle chiles)
- ridged grill pan (gives good grill marks; can steam foods; to add smoke flavor that would have been achieved by grilling over coals in a hibachi, add 1 to 2 drops liquid smoke to marinade or sauce; or include a smoked food such as chipotle chiles)
- electric tabletop grill (gives good grill marks; can steam foods; best for sandwiches; to add smoke flavor that would have been achieved by grilling over coals in a hibachi, add 1 to 2 drops liquid smoke to marinade or sauce; or include a smoked food such as chipotle chiles)

## Hibiscus

*Also known as Jamaica sorrel, red sorrel, and roselle. Often made into red herbal teas and Christmas beverages, the dried flowers of hibiscus go by the name of sorrel in the Caribbean Islands and roselle in Africa and Australia. In her book* Tropical Cooking, *Panamanian food writer Gladys R. Graham notes that "Sorrel is such an important beverage and jam-jelly ingredient that highway crews widening Central American roads will cut down every other shrub and tree in their way, leaving the sorrel to blossom on the road shoulders."*

1 cup (250 mL) =
1½ oz (45 grams)

### If You Don't Have It

Substitute 1 cup (250 mL) dried hibiscus flowers with:

- 1 cup (250 mL) rose hips
- 1 cup (250 mL) Red Zinger herbal tea bags (adds rosehips, peppermint, and other herbs)

## Hickory Nut

*This family of nuts includes the superb pecan. The common hickory nut is hard to find and tough to crack.*

### If You Don't Have It

Substitute 1 cup (250 mL) shelled hickory nuts with:
- 1 cup (250 mL) pecans
- 1 cup (250 mL) walnuts

*See also* PECAN.

## Hierba Santa

*See* HOJA SANTA.

## High-Altitude Baking and Cooking

*See* BAKING AT HIGH ALTITUDE (PAGE 686); COOKING AT HIGH ALTITUDE (PAGE 686).

## Hijiki

*Also known as hiziki. A Japanese seaweed that is sun-dried before and after boiling. Rich in minerals, it offers a salty, light anise taste. Food safety agencies in Canada, Britain, New Zealand and other countries have cautioned against excessive consumption of hijiki due to high levels of inorganic arsenic, a carcinogen. Other types of seaweed such as kelp (kombu), dulse, and nori do not contain inorganic arsenic and are safe to eat.*

### If You Don't Have It

Substitute 1 oz (30 g) hijiki with:
- 1 oz (30 g) arame (milder flavor; dark brown color)
- 1 oz (30 g) dulse (stronger flavor; maroon color)
- 1 oz (30 g) wakame (stronger flavor; dark green to brown color)
- 1 oz (30 g) kombu (stronger flavor; dark brown to black color)

## Hog Jowl

*Cured and smoked hog cheek is a country cooking legacy in the Southern U.S. Fattier than bacon, it's called upon to flavor beans, stews, greens, and other long-simmered dishes.*

### If You Don't Have It

Substitute 4 oz (125 g) cured, smoked hog jowl with:
- 4 oz (125 g) chopped smoked bacon
- 4 oz (125 g) chopped smoked ham
- 4 oz (125 g) guanciale (no smoke flavor)
- 4 oz (125 g) pancetta (no smoke flavor)
- 4 oz (125 g) prosciutto (no smoke flavor)
- 2 to 4 oz (60 to 125 g) salt pork (no smoke flavor; reduce salt in recipe if necessary)

*See also* GUANCIALE.

## Hoisin Sauce

*A dark and complex variety of sweet bean sauce made from fermented beans, salt, sugar, and garlic. This thick, rich paste often seasons sauces and marinades for roasted and barbecued meats.*

### If You Don't Have It

Substitute 1 tbsp (15 mL) hoisin sauce with:
- 1 tbsp (15 mL) Homemade Hoisin Sauce Substitute: Combine 1 cup (250 mL) minus 3 tbsp (45 mL) thick barbecue sauce (preferably without smoke flavor), 3 tbsp (45 mL) molasses, 4 tsp (20 mL) soy sauce, 4 tsp (20 mL) yeast extract and 2½ tsp (12 mL) Chinese five-spice powder. Makes about 1 cup (250 mL).
- 1 tbsp (15 mL) Chee hou sauce (spicier)
- 1 tbsp (15 mL) Chinese brown bean sauce (spicier)

## Hoja Santa

*Also known as hierba santa and yerba santa. The large leaves, which taste of anise or sassafrass, flavor soups or wrap whole fish in Latin American preparations.*

### If You Don't Have It

Substitute ½ cup (125 mL) chopped hoja santa leaves (for sauces and stews) with:
- ½ cup (125 mL) chopped Mexican avocado leaves
- ½ cup (125 mL) chopped Mexican or French tarragon
- ½ cup (125 mL) chopped green fennel tops + ⅛ to ¼ tsp (0.5 to 1 mL) ground black pepper

### If You Don't Have It

Substitute hoja santa leaves (as a food wrapper) with:
- corn husks (adds mild corn aroma)
- banana leaves (adds herby-green flavor)
- parchment paper (adds no flavor)
- aluminum foil (adds no flavor)

## Holland Chile

*See* CHOOSING FRESH CHILES (PAGE 640).

## Hollandaise Sauce

*In classic French service, hollandaise is set on the plate beside the food it accompanies,* never *ladled over it.*

### To Vary the Flavor

Substitute 1 cup (250 mL) hollandaise sauce with:
- 1 cup (250 mL) Béarnaise sauce (adds tarragon)
- 1 cup (250 mL) Choron sauce (adds tarragon and tomato)
- 1 cup (250 mL) Foyot or Valois sauce (adds tarragon and glace de viande)
- 1 cup (250 mL) Colbert sauce (adds tarragon and glace de viande melted in white wine)
- 1 cup (250 mL) beurre blanc (no egg yolks)

### To Save Time

- 1 cup (250 mL) Homemade Quick Hollandaise Sauce: Put 3 egg yolks, juice of small lemon, ½ tsp (2 mL) salt, and a pinch of mustard powder into a blender or small food processor. Blend ingredients and drizzle in ½ cup (125 mL) melted butter until thickened. Makes about 1 cup (250 mL).

## For Better Health
Substitute 1 cup (250 mL) hollandaise sauce with:
- 1 cup (250 mL) Homemade Avgolemono Sauce (fewer calories): Whisk together 3 egg yolks, juice of ½ small lemon, ½ tsp (2 mL) salt, and 1 tsp (5 mL) arrowroot powder or ¾ tsp (3 mL) cornstarch in a small saucepan. Put pan over medium heat. Gradually whisk in 1 cup (250 mL) chicken stock, stirring until thickened. Stir in 1 tbsp (15 mL) chopped fresh herbs if you like. Makes about 1 cup (250 mL).

*See also* BÉARNAISE SAUCE.

## Hollyhock
*See* PICKING EDIBLE FLOWERS (PAGE 650).

## Holy Basil
*See* BASIL.

## Hom Ha
*See* SHRIMP SAUCE.

## Hominy

*A beloved staple of the American South, hominy is dried white or yellow corn kernels that are treated with an alkali, such as lye, to remove the hull. Hominy also features prominently in the hearty Mexican soup known as posole. It is available canned (ready to eat) or dried.*

1 lb (500 g) whole = 2½ cups (625 mL)

1 cup (250 mL) whole = 6⅔ cups (1.65 L) cooked

### If You Don't Have It
Substitute 1 cup (250 mL) dried or canned hominy with:
- 1 cup (250 mL) samp (broken hominy)
- 1 cup (250 mL) dried or canned beans (for soups and stews)

*See also* HOMINY GRITS.

## Hominy Grits

*Hominy that is ground fine, medium, or coarse. Cooked in milk or water until thick, the resulting mush is served hot, or chilled, then sliced and fried.*

1 cup (250 mL) = 4½ cups (1.125 L) cooked

### If You Don't Have It
Substitute 1 cup (250 mL) hominy grits with:
- 1 cup (250 mL) polenta meal (preferably stone-ground)

### To Vary the Flavor
Substitute 1 cup (250 mL) hominy grits with:
- 1 cup (250 mL) barley grits
- 1 cup (250 mL) buckwheat grits

*See also* BARLEY GRITS; CORN GRITS; HOMINY.

## Honey

*To produce one pound (500 g) of honey, the bees must visit flowers about 2 million times to extract the nectar.*

1 lb (500 g) =
1⅓ cups (325 mL)

1 cup (250 mL) =
11.7 oz (333 g)

### If You Don't Have It
Substitute 1 cup (250 mL) honey with:
- 1¼ cups (300 mL) granulated sugar + ¼ cup (60 mL) liquid called for in recipe
- ½ cup (125 mL) granulated sugar + ¾ cup (175 mL) maple syrup, light or dark corn syrup, or light molasses

*See also* AGAVE NECTAR; MAPLE SYRUP; SUGAR; SPOONING UP HONEY (PAGE 651).

## Honeyball Melon

*Similar to honeydew melon but small and netted.*

### If You Don't Have It
Substitute 1 cup (250 mL) chopped honeyball melon with:
- 1 cup (250 mL) chopped honeydew melon
- 1 cup (250 mL) chopped Ogen melon
- 1 cup (250 mL) chopped galia melon
- 1 cup (250 mL) chopped Santa Claus melon
- 1 cup (250 mL) chopped cantaloupe
- 1 cup (250 mL) chopped Persian melon

## Honeydew Melon

*Choose honeydew that feel heavy in relation to size. Perfectly ripe specimens will subtly wrinkle on the surface of the rind.*

1 medium = 3 lbs
(1.5 kg) = 4 to 5 cups
(1 to 1.25 L) cubed

### If You Don't Have It
Substitute 1 cup (250 mL) chopped honeydew melon with:
- 1 cup (250 mL) chopped honeyball melon
- 1 cup (250 mL) chopped Ogen melon
- 1 cup (250 mL) chopped Galia melon
- 1 cup (250 mL) chopped Santa Claus melon
- 1 cup (250 mL) chopped cantaloupe
- 1 cup (250 mL) chopped Persian melon

## Hon-Shimeji

*See* SHUFFLING MUSHROOMS (PAGE 654).

## Hontaka Chile

*See* CHOOSING FRESH CHILES (PAGE 640).

## Hoop Cheese

*An almost archaic cheese that is very similar to farmer cheese. In the 1800s, special cutting devices were manufactured to cut precise portions of hoop cheese.*

### If You Don't Have It
Substitute 1 oz (30 g) hoop cheese with:
- 1 oz (30 g) farmer cheese or pot cheese
- 1 oz (30 g) dry-curd cottage cheese
- 1 oz (30 g) ricotta cheese, drained in cheesecloth (may add more liquid)

## Horchata

*A family of sweet, refreshing drinks made from soaked, puréed and strained grains, seeds, and spices. One of the most popular versions from Mexico is made with rice.*

### If You Don't Have It

Substitute 1 cup (250 mL) horchata with:

- 1 cup (250 mL) Homemade Mexican Horchata: Soak ½ cup (125 mL) raw white rice, 2 strips orange peel, 2 strips lime peel, 2 cinnamon sticks, 3 whole cloves, 3 allspice berries, and ¼ cup (60 mL) agave nectar or sugar in 4½ cups (1.125 L) hot water. Let cool to room temperature then cover and refrigerate until the rice is very soft, about 4 hours. Transfer to a blender or food processor and purée until smooth. Strain through a medium-mesh sieve into a bowl or pitcher and stir in ½ tsp (2 mL) vanilla extract and ½ tsp (2 mL) almond extract. Refrigerate for up to 1 week. Makes about 4 cups (1 L).
- 1 cup (250 mL) vanilla-flavored rice milk + pinch of ground cinnamon
- 1 cup (250 mL) vanilla-flavored soy milk + pinch of ground cinnamon
- 1 cup (250 mL) vanilla-flavored cow's milk + pinch of ground cinnamon

## Horned Melon

*See* KIWANO.

## Horseradish

*An ancient herb that is cultivated mostly for its white pungent roots. The roots can be purchased fresh or grated, processed, and jarred as a condiment.*

| 1 tbsp (15 mL) bottled = 2 tsp (10 mL) freshly grated |
| :---: |
| 1 oz (30 g) = ¼ cup (60 mL) sliced |

### If You Don't Have It

Substitute 1 tbsp (15 mL) grated fresh horseradish with:

- 1 tbsp (15 mL) prepared white horseradish (less pungent; adds vinegar flavor, reduce vinegar in recipe 1½ tsp/7 mL if necessary)
- 1 tbsp (15 mL) prepared red horseradish (red color from beet juice; adds vinegar flavor, reduce vinegar in recipe 1½ tsp/7 mL if necessary)
- 1 to 3 tbsp (15 to 45 mL) creamed horseradish (adds sour cream or mayonnaise flavors)
- 1 to 3 tbsp (15 to 45 mL) grated fresh wasabi
- 1 to 3 tbsp (15 to 45 mL) peeled and grated fresh black radish

## Hot Chili Sauce

*See* CHILE SAUCE.

## Hot Chocolate Mix

*See* COCOA MIX.

## Hot Dog

*See* FRANKFURTER.

## Hot Garlic Sauce

*See* CHILE SAUCE.

## Hot Pepper Sauce

*The basic recipe for hot sauce is to chop or crush hot chiles, mix with salt and allow to ferment, sometimes for years. Then you blend the mash with vinegar, age it longer, strain it, and bottle it. But the type of chile, aging barrel, and whether solids are retained can create vastly different hot sauces. Like snowflakes, no two hot pepper sauces are ever the same.*

### If You Don't Have It

Substitute 1 tsp (5 mL) hot pepper sauce with:

- 1 to 3 tsp (5 to 15 mL) chile paste
- ¼ to ½ tsp (1 to 2 mL) ground cayenne pepper
- ¾ tsp (3 mL) crushed red pepper flakes
- ½ tsp (2 mL) ground chipotle powder (much smokier)
- ½ tsp (2 mL) ground ancho powder (darker; milder)
- 1 tsp (5 mL) paprika (much milder)
- 1 tsp (5 mL) chili powder (milder; adds flavors of cumin, oregano, and other spices)
- 1 tsp (5 mL) minced fresh chile
- 1 very small whole dried red chile

*See also* CHOOSING DRIED CHILES (PAGE 642); CHOOSING FRESH CHILES (PAGE 640).

## Huauzontle

*Pronounced "wah-ZONT-lay," this Mexican vegetable is related to the common lambs quarter and goosefoot weeds. The leaves are typically trimmed away and only the long tufted green flower buds are eaten. Mexican cooks often make them into Tortas de Huauzontles by wrapping a bundle of huauzontles around a wedge of cheese then dipping it into egg batter and deep-frying it.*

### If You Don't Have It

Substitute 1 lb (500 g) huauzontle with:

- 1 lb (500 g) budding quinoa greens
- 1 lb (500 g) budding epazote
- 1 lb (500 g) broccolini
- 1 lb (500 g) Chinese broccoli

## Hubbard Squash

*A large winter squash with a lumpy dark green or orange shell and slightly grainy, orange flesh. It can be stored whole, unwrapped, at 50°F (10°C) or cooler, for as long as six months.*

### If You Don't Have It

Substitute 1 lb (500 g) hubbard squash with:

- 1 lb (500 g) Jarrahdale
- 1 lb (500 g) Queensland Blue
- 1 lb (500 g) golden delicious
- 1 lb (500 g) buttercup squash
- 1 lb (500 g) pumpkin
- 1 lb (500 g) butternut squash
- 1 lb (500 g) buttercup squash

*See also* GOLDEN DELICIOUS SQUASH.

## Huckleberry

*A wild berry that's often mistaken for the blueberry. But upon closer inspection, the huckleberry has thicker skin, is more tart, and has 10 small, hard seeds in the center.*

### If You Don't Have It

Substitute 1 cup (250 mL) huckleberries with:
- 1 cup (250 mL) blueberries (sweeter)
- 1 cup (250 mL) bilberries (more tart)
- 1 cup (250 mL) juneberries (apple-like flavor)
- 1 cup (250 mL) red currants (red color; more tart)

## Huitlacoche

*Once considered a blight, huitlacoche is now cultivated as a delicacy. The fungus attacks corn during the rainy season, causing kernels to swell into spongy misshapen galls with a slightly smoky, slightly funky aroma.*

### If You Don't Have It

Substitute 4 oz (125 g) huitlacoche with:
- 4 oz (125 g) black trumpet mushrooms
- 4 oz (125 g) morel mushrooms
- 4 oz (125 g) porcini mushrooms

## Huli-Huli Sauce

*Hawaiian for "turn-turn," huli-huli refers to barbecued chicken that is constantly turned as well as the popular teriyaki-like sauce that flavors the meat. Huli-huli chicken is among the most beloved fundraiser foods in Hawaii.*

### If You Don't Have It

Substitute 1 cup (250 mL) huli-huli sauce with:
- 1 cup (250 mL) Homemade Huli-Huli Sauce: Combine ¼ cup (60 mL) ketchup, ¼ cup (60 mL) tamari, shoyu, or soy sauce, ¼ cup (60 mL) rice wine or sherry, 1 tbsp (15 mL) lime juice, ½ tsp (2 mL) ground ginger, ¼ tsp (1 mL) garlic powder, ¼ tsp (1 mL) onion powder, ¼ tsp (1 mL) Worcestershire sauce, ⅛ tsp (0.5 mL) ground black pepper in a small saucepan. Bring to a boil over high heat, then reduce the heat to low and simmer for 5 minutes. Thin the sauce with 1 to 3 tbsp (15 to 45 mL) water as desired. Makes about ¾ cup (175 mL).
- 1 cup (250 mL) teriyaki sauce (thinner)
- 1 cup (250 mL) hoisin sauce (thicker)
- 1 cup (250 mL) soy sauce (thinner; less flavorful)

## Humboldt Fog

*An artisanal surface-ripened goat cheese from California's Cypress Grove. The creamy, tangy cheese has an exterior rind and central layer of edible vegetable ash.*

### If You Don't Have It

Substitute 1 oz (30 g) Humboldt Fog with:
- 1 oz (30 g) Purple Haze (adds lavender and fennel pollen)
- 1 oz (30 g) Robiola Piemonte (made with a high percentage of goat's or sheep's milk)
- 1 oz (30 g) aged goat cheese
- 1 oz (30 g) Morbier (made with cow's milk; similar central layer of ash)

## Hummus

*In her landmark* Book of Middle Eastern Food, *Claudia Roden writes that "this salad purée...is the constant companion of shish kebab and ta'amia in Oriental restaurants."*

### If You Don't Have It
Substitute 1 cup (250 mL) hummus with:

- 1 cup (250 mL) Homemade Hummus: Combine 2 cups (500 mL) cooked or canned chickpeas, $\frac{1}{3}$ cup (75 mL) fresh lemon juice, 3 tbsp (45 mL) tahini (sesame paste), 1 tbsp (15 mL) olive oil, 2 cloves garlic, $\frac{1}{4}$ tsp (1 mL) salt, and $\frac{1}{8}$ tsp (0.5 mL) ground black pepper in a small food processor or blender. Purée until smooth, adding 1 to 2 tbsp (15 to 30 mL) water as necessary to make the dip easily spoonable. Garnish with olive oil, chopped parsley, and paprika if you like. Makes about $2\frac{1}{2}$ cups (625 mL).

### To Vary the Flavor
Substitute 1 cup (250 mL) hummus with:

- 1 cup (250 mL) puréed white bean dip
- 1 cup (250 mL) puréed black bean dip
- 1 cup (250 mL) puréed pinto bean dip
- 1 cup (250 mL) tapenade (olive-caper spread)

## Humpback Salmon

*See* SALMON.

## Hungarian Pepper

*See* PAPRIKA.

## Husk Tomato

*See* CAPE GOOSEBERRY; TOMATILLO.

## Hyssop

*Originating in the eastern Mediterranean, the leaves of this aromatic plant have been used since pre-Christian times. Reminiscent of mint, the leaves are reputed to aid in digesting fat. Used to season a wide variety of dishes including fruits, salads, sausages, and meats.*

### If You Don't Have It
Substitute 1 tbsp (15 mL) chopped fresh hyssop with:

- $1\frac{1}{2}$ tsp (7 mL) chopped fresh sage + $1\frac{1}{2}$ tsp (7 mL) chopped fresh mint

# Ibarra to Izarra

## Ibarra

*See* CHOCOLATE, MEXICAN.

## Iberico Ham

*Also known as jamón iberico. An artisanal ham that is salted and naturally dried and aged. Produced from the Iberian pig that is native to southwestern Spain.*

### If You Don't Have It
Substitute 1 oz (30 g) Iberico ham with:
- 1 oz (30 g) serrano ham
- 1 oz (30 g) prosciutto (di Parma or di San Daniele)
- 1 oz (30 g) Ardennes ham (adds smoked flavor)
- 1 oz (30 g) Bayonne ham (adds smoked flavor)

## Iceberg Lettuce

*See* CRISPHEAD LETTUCE.

## Ice Cream

*This frozen dairy treat has universal appeal — from the intensely flavored gelato of Italy to the lighter kulfi of India to the helado of the Philippines flavored with corn or purple yams.*

### If You Don't Have It
Substitute 1 cup (250 mL) ice cream with:
- 1 cup (250 mL) soy ice cream
- 1 cup (250 mL) frozen yogurt

### For Better Health
Substitute 1 cup (250 mL) ice cream with:
- 1 cup (250 mL) reduced-fat ice cream or frozen yogurt (less fat and fewer calories)
- 1 cup (250 mL) gelato (ice cream made without eggs; less fat and fewer calories)
- 1 cup (250 mL) sorbet (water-based frozen dessert sometimes incorporating milk or cream; less fat and fewer calories)
- 1 cup (250 mL) granita (grainy Italian water-based frozen dessert; less fat and fewer calories)

## Ice Cream Machine

In the 1840s, Nancy Johnson and William Young both patented hand-cranked ice cream freezers that established the basic method of making ice cream still used today. Adding salt to ice to lower the freezing point of water and stirring frequently both help to achieve the smooth, creamy results we have come to enjoy in frozen sweetened cream. Modern ice cream machines merely automate the stirring and freezing.

### If You Don't Have It
Substitute an ice cream machine with:
- frequent stirring + a clean metal container surrounded by ice and salt set in a larger container
- frequent stirring + liquid nitrogen gradually added directly to ice cream mixture (inexpensive liquid nitrogen is available through welding supply stores and specialty gas companies)

## Icing Sugar

See SUGAR, CONFECTIONER'S.

## Idiazabal Cheese

Spanish raw sheep's milk cheese with a firm texture, nutty flavor, and hundreds of tiny holes throughout. Usually smoked.

### If You Don't Have It
Substitute 1 oz (30 g) Idiazabal with:
- 1 oz (30 g) Roncal + few drops liquid smoke
- 1 oz (30 g) Manchego + few drops liquid smoke
- 1 oz (30 g) Zamorano + few drops liquid smoke
- 1 oz (30 g) smoked provolone

## Ilama

Mexican and Central American fruit similar to cherimoya but covered with downy white fuzz. Green-skinned ilamas have sweet, white flesh, while pink-skinned varieties have more tart, rose-colored flesh. Soncoya (cabeza de negro), a similar fruit with bumpy gray-brown skin sometimes goes by the same name.

### If You Don't Have It
Substitute 1 lb (500 g) ilama with:
- 1 lb (500 g) cherimoya
- 1 lb (500 g) sweetsop
- 1 lb (500 g) atemoya (hybrid of sweetsop and cherimoya)
- 1 lb (500 g) soncoya + $\frac{1}{4}$ tsp (1 mL) vanilla extract
- 1 lb (500 g) mango or papaya + $\frac{1}{4}$ tsp (1 mL) vanilla extract

## Imitation Bacon Bits

See BACON BITS.

| | |
|---|---|
| **Imitation Crab Meat** | *See* SURIMI. |
| **Immersion Blender** | *See* BLENDER. |
| **Indian Bay Leaf** | *See* BAY LEAF. |
| **Indian Date** | *See* TAMARIND CONCENTRATE. |
| **Indian Fig** | *See* PRICKLY PEAR. |
| **Indian Flatbread** | *See* CHAPATI. |
| **Indian Long Pepper** | *See* LONG PEPPER. |
| **Indian Saffron** | *See* TURMERIC. |
| **Indonesian Bay Leaf** | *See* BAY LEAF. |
| **Indonesian Long Pepper** | *See* LONG PEPPER. |
| **Indonesian Sweet Soy Sauce** | *See* KECAP. |

**Injera**

*Large Ethiopian sourdough crêpes are made with teff flour and serve as both plate and spoon for stews. Some cooks ferment the injera batter for days to develop a deep sour flavor.*

**If You Don't Have It**

Substitute 2 injera with:

- 2 large blini or thin buckwheat pancakes made with lemon juice
- 2 large wheat flour crêpes, preferably made with lemon juice

| | |
|---|---|
| **Instant Flour** | *See* FLOUR, INSTANT. |
| **Instant Gluten Flour** | *See* SEITAN. |
| **Iridescent Shark** | *See* CATFISH. |

## Irish Bacon

See CANADIAN BACON.

## Irish Cream Liqueur

*A category of commercial liqueurs that blend Irish whiskey, cream, spices, and sweeteners.*

### If You Don't Have It

Substitute 3 tbsp (45 mL) Irish cream liqueur with:

- 3 tbsp (45 mL) advocaat
- 3 tbsp (45 mL) nonalcoholic eggnog + $\frac{1}{8}$ to $\frac{1}{4}$ tsp (0.5 to 1 mL) brandy

## Irish Mist

*A liqueur that kisses Irish whiskey with a touch of heather honey.*

### If You Don't Have It

Substitute 3 tbsp (45 mL) Irish Mist with:

- 3 tbsp (45 mL) Drambuie
- 3 tbsp (45 mL) Grandtully
- 3 tbsp (45 mL) Glayva
- 3 tbsp (45 mL) Lochan Ora

## Irish Whiskey

See WHISKEY.

## Iron Cookware

See CAST IRON.

## Irvingia

See OGBONO NUT.

## Isinglass

*Collagen from the dried swim bladders of sturgeon, cod, and other fish often used to clarify beer and some Kosher wines. The word* isinglass *comes from the Middle Dutch word* huysenblas, *a combination of* huysen *(sturgeon) and* blas *(bladder). In the 1500s, when the word was introduced to English, "the spelling was changed to isinglass," writes Mark Morton in* Cupboard Love: A Dictionary of Culinary Curiosities, *"partly because the see-through nature of the gelatin reminded people of glass."*

### If You Don't Have It

Substitute 1 oz (30 g) isinglass with:

- 1 oz (30 g) carrageen
- 1 tsp (5 mL) agar powder
- $1\frac{1}{2}$ tsp (7 mL) gelatin powder

## Italian Bread

*"In a country where the family is the primary source of physical and emotional sustenance, bread celebrates the richest and simplest pleasure of daily living," writes Carol Field in* The Italian Baker. *"No Italian would contemplate a meal without bread."*

### If You Don't Have It
Substitute 1 lb (500 g) Italian bread with:
- 1 lb (500 g) French bread (usually longer and narrower than Italian bread)

### Italian Bread Types
Choose 1 lb (500 g) Italian bread from these types:
- 1 lb (500 g) ciabatta (chewy crust; crumb has large holes)
- 1 lb (500 g) Pugliese (thin chewy-crunchy crust; pillowy crumb)

## Italian Herb Seasoning

*A packaged herbal blend with a pan-Italian flavor profile.*

### If You Don't Have It
Substitute 2 tsp (10 mL) Italian herb seasoning with:
- 1 tsp (5 mL) dried oregano + ½ tsp (2 mL) dried basil + ½ tsp (2 mL) dried thyme

## Italian Parsley

*See* PARSLEY.

## Italian Sausage

*Spiced ground pork mixture piped into casings, generally composed of 60% lean meat and 40% fat. Seasoned with salt, garlic, and fennel seeds. Peperoncini (hot chiles) are added to produce a hot version.*

### If You Don't Have It
Substitute 1 lb (500 g) Italian sausage with:
- 1 lb (500 g) pork sausage (sweet or hot)

## Izarra

*An Armagnac-based herbal liqueur that comes in mild yellow and stronger green colors.*

### If You Don't Have It
Substitute 3 tbsp (45 mL) Izarra with:
- 3 tbsp (45 mL) Chartreuse
- 3 tbsp (45 mL) Strega
- 3 tbsp (45 mL) Bénédictine

### Izarra Varieties
Choose 3 tbsp (45 mL) Izarra from these varieties:
- 3 tbsp (45 mL) green Izarra (green color; more bracing flavor and heavier body than yellow Chartreuse)
- 3 tbsp (45 mL) yellow Izarra (pale golden color; sweeter flavor and lighter body than green Chartreuse)

# Jaboticaba to Jute Leaf

## Jaboticaba

*Also known as Brazilian grape. Dark purple, round fruit of a native Brazilian tree in the myrtle family. With thick, astringent skin, soft pink flesh, and a size approximating a ping-pong ball, jaboticabas look and taste like a cross between Damson plums and muscadine grapes.*

### If You Don't Have It

Substitute 1 lb (500 g) jaboticabas with:
- 1 lb (500 g) purple grapes
- 1 lb (500 g) plums
- 8 oz (250 g) muscadine grapes + 8 oz (250 g) Damson plums

## Jack

*See* AMBERJACK; POMPANO.

## Jack Cheese

*Also known as California Jack and Monterey Jack. Buttery semisoft cheese named for David Jacks, a 19th century California cheesemaker. Both unaged and aged (dry) are produced.*

1 lb (500 g) = 4 cups (1 L) grated or shredded

### If You Don't Have It

Substitute 1 oz (30 g) Jack cheese with:
- 1 oz (30 g) Muenster
- 1 oz (30 g) Gouda
- 1 oz (30 g) Havarti
- 1 oz (30 g) Samsoe
- 1 oz (30 g) Tybo
- 1 oz (30 g) Teleme (softer)

## Jack Cheese Varieties

Choose 1 oz (30 g) Jack cheese from these varieties:

- 1 oz (30 g) Monterey or Sonoma Jack (soft, white and mild with an acidic tanginess; tiny flattened holes throughout)
- 1 oz (30 g) Wisconsin Jack (slightly firmer and with fewer or no holes as in Monterey Jack)
- 1 oz (30 g) Pepper Jack or Jalapeño Jack (Monterey Jack with chopped jalapeño peppers)
- 1 oz (30 g) aged or dry Jack (Monterey Jack aged for 7 to 10 months; hard, sharp, and excellent for grating)

## Jackfruit

*Also known as jak and nangka. Related to the breadfruit, southeast Asian specimens can grow up to 90 pounds (45 kg), making it the largest tree-borne fruit. The unripe flesh is cooked as a starchy vegetable, dried, or pickled. The ripe fruit smells terrible but tastes wonderful — like pineapple and banana.*

### If You Don't Have It

Substitute 1 cup (250 mL) chopped jackfruit with:

- 1 cup (250 mL) chopped breadfruit (smaller)
- 1 cup (250 mL) green or yellow plantains (to replace green jackfruit)
- 1 cup (250 mL) potatoes (to replace green jackfruit)
- 1 cup (250 mL) winter melon (to replace green jackfruit)
- 1 cup (250 mL) fuzzy gourd (to replace green jackfruit)
- 1 cup (250 mL) summer squash (to replace green jackfruit)
- 1 cup (250 mL) canned jackfruit (to replace fresh ripe jackfruit)
- 1 cup (250 mL) papaya (to replace ripe jackfruit)

*See also* BREADFRUIT.

## Jackfruit Seed

*These prolific seeds (up to 500 in a single jackfruit) resemble chestnuts and can be candied or dried and ground for flour. Fresh ones are often boiled and roasted. They taste somewhat mealy like chestnuts, but drier, less sweet and slightly more acidic with a hint of tropical jackfruit flavor. When extracting fresh jackfruit seeds, use vegetable oil to remove the sticky latex covering the seeds.*

### If You Don't Have It

Substitute 1 cup (250 mL) roasted jackfruit seeds with:

- 1 cup (250 mL) roasted chestnuts
- 1 cup (250 mL) roasted breadnut seeds
- 1 cup (250 mL) pecans
- 1 cup (250 mL) macadamia nuts
- 1 cup (250 mL) chufa nuts

## Jackrabbit

*See* HARE.

## Jagdwurst

*Literally "hunting sausage." This German cooked beef and pork sausage is flavored with garlic, mustard seed, and sometimes other spices like mace. It's mostly smooth like bologna but also incorporates little bits of cured meat and fat.*

### If You Don't Have It

Substitute 1 lb (500 g) jagdwurst with:
- 1 lb (500 g) krakauer (larger chunks of fat)
- 1 lb (500 g) mortadella (large chunks of fat)
- 1 lb (500 g) bierwurst (usually smoked)
- 1 lb (500 g) galantina (more chunky)
- 1 lb (500 g) bologna (milder)

### For Better Health

Substitute 1 lb (500 g) jagdwurst with:
- 1 lb (500 g) gelbwurst (lower in fat and calories)

## Jägermeister

*Forceful, bitter German liqueur — concocted from a combination of 56 herbs, spices, barks, resins, and seeds — lives up to its name of "hunt master."*

### If You Don't Have It

Substitute 3 tbsp (45 mL) Jägermeister with:
- 3 tbsp (45 mL) Bénédictine
- 3 tbsp (45 mL) green Chartreuse
- 3 tbsp (45 mL) Fernet Branca

## Jaggery

*Also known as gur (when made from palm tree sap) and palm sugar. Dark coarse sugar extract from palm trees or sugarcane juice that is favored in India. The soft type is spreadable, while the solid cake is crushed to use as a topping or a confectionery ingredient.*

### If You Don't Have It

Substitute 1 cup (250 mL) jaggery with:
- 1 cup (250 mL) piloncillo
- 1 cup (250 mL) black sugar (solid block, stronger molasses flavor)
- 1 cup (250 mL) dark brown sugar + 2 tsp (10 mL) molasses
- 1 cup (250 mL) light brown sugar + 5 tsp (25 mL) molasses
- 1 cup (250 mL) granulated sugar + 4 to 5 tbsp (60 to 75 mL) molasses
- 1 cup (250 mL) palm sugar

*See also* PILONCILLO; SUGAR, BLACK; SUGAR, DARK BROWN; SUGAR, GRANULATED; SUGAR, LIGHT BROWN; SUGAR, PALM.

## Jak

*See* JACKFRUIT.

## Jalapeño Pepper

*See* CHOOSING DRIED CHILES (PAGE 642); CHOOSING FRESH CHILES (PAGE 640).

## Jam

*U.S. Department of Agriculture regulations stipulate that these chunky conserves must contain at least 45% fruit.*

### If You Don't Have It

Substitute 1 cup (250 mL) jam with:
- 1 cup (250 mL) preserves (larger chunks)
- 1 cup (250 mL) jelly (thinner consistency)

## Jamaican Cherry

*Bullet-shaped sweet cherry with aromas reminiscent of cotton candy.*

1 lb (500 g) fresh =
2½ to 3 cups
(625 to 750 mL) pitted

### If You Don't Have It

Substitute 1 lb (500 g) Jamaican cherries with:

- 1 lb (500 g) sweet cherries such as Royal Ann or Bing
- 1 lb (500 g) capulin cherries
- 1 lb (500 g) acerola

*See also* CHERRY.

## Jamaican Jerk

*Also known as Jamaican jerk seasoning. Traditionally a seasoning paste slathered on grilled chicken, pork, and other meats. Now also sold as a dry seasoning typically combining hot chiles with allspice, cinnamon, cloves, garlic, ginger, onion, and thyme.*

### If You Don't have It

Substitute 1 tbsp (15 mL) dry Jamaican jerk seasoning with:

- 1 tbsp (15 mL) Homemade Jamaican Jerk Dry Rub: Combine 1 tbsp (15 mL) dried thyme, 1 tbsp (15 mL) dark brown sugar, 2 tsp (10 mL) ground allspice, 1 tsp (5 mL) ground cinnamon, 1 tsp (5 mL) ground nutmeg, 1 tsp (5 mL) ground coriander, 1 tsp (5 mL) ground black pepper, 1 tsp (5 mL) salt, ½ tsp (2 mL) onion powder, ½ tsp (2 mL) garlic powder, ½ to 1 tsp (2 to 5 mL) cayenne pepper, and ¼ tsp (1 mL) ground ginger. To make a marinade, add ¼ cup (60 mL) vegetable oil, 3 tbsp (45 mL) soy sauce, 3 tbsp (45 mL) lime juice, and 1 tbsp (15 mL) dark rum. Makes about ⅓ cup (75 mL) dry rub.

## Jamaica Sorrel

*See* HIBISCUS.

## Japanese Cucumber

*See* CUCUMBER.

## Japanese Eggplant

*See* EGGPLANT.

## Japanese Horseradish

*See* WASABI.

## Japanese Pepper

*See* SZECHUAN PEPPER.

## Japanese Plum

*See* LOQUAT.

## Japanese Sweet Rice Wine

*See* MIRIN.

## Japanese Vermicelli

*See* A SNAPSHOT OF ASIAN NOODLES (PAGE 656).

## Jarlsberg

*The Norwegian version of Swiss-style cheese is a fine all-purpose cheese for melting and snacking.*

### If You Don't Have It

Substitute 1 oz (30 g) Jarlsberg with:
- 1 oz (30 g) Emmental
- 1 oz (30 g) Gruyère
- 1 oz (30 g) Swiss
- 1 oz (30 g) French Comté

## Jarrahdale Squash

*Australian heirloom winter squash with stone-gray skin and Halloween pumpkin shape. The full taste of its deep-orange flesh make it great for pies and baking.*

### If You Don't Have It

Substitute 1 lb (500 g) Jarrahdale squash with:
- 1 lb (500 g) Queensland blue squash
- 1 lb (500 g) golden delicious
- 1 lb (500 g) buttercup squash
- 1 lb (500 g) sugar pumpkin
- 1 lb (500 g) butternut squash

## Jasmine Rice

*See* VARIETIES OF RICE (PAGE 664).

## Java Almond

*See* PILI NUT.

## Java Cubeb Pepper

*See* CUBEB.

## Java Long Pepper

*See* LONG PEPPER.

## Java Sugar

*See* SUGAR, PALM.

## Jeera

*See* CUMIN.

## Jelly

*A conserve made from fruit juice, sugar, and often pectin for gelling. Delicious spread on morning toast and to top cakes, cookies, or doughnuts.*

### If You Don't Have It

Substitute 1 cup (250 mL) jelly with:
- 1 cup (250 mL) jam (thicker)
- 1 cup (250 mL) preserves (larger chunks)

## Jelly Melon

*See* KIWANO.

## Jelly Roll Pan

*See* PAN SIZE EQUIVALENTS (PAGE 678).

## Jerky

*Native Americans educated the European colonists on how to preserve meat by drying strips in the sun or at a fire. The name is derived from a Spanish adaptation of the native Peruvian word charqui for dried meat. The most common variety is beef.*

### If You Don't Have It
Substitute 1 oz (30 g) beef jerky with:
- 1 oz (30 g) biltong (spicier; more complex flavor)
- 1 oz (30 g) pemmican (more complex flavor)

### For Better Health
Substitute 1 oz (30 g) beef jerky with:
- 1 oz (30 g) turkey jerky (leaner)
- 1 oz (30 g) vegetarian jerky (leaner)

*See also* BILTONG; PEMMICAN; TASAJO.

## Jeruk Purut

*See* MAKRUT LIME.

## Jerusalem Artichoke

*See* SUNCHOKE.

## Jewfish

*See* GOLIATH GROUPER.

## Jibneh Arabieh

*Popular Middle Eastern cheese originally made from goat's or sheep's milk but now commonly made from cow's milk. It has a mild flavor and porous texture. A very smooth but salty (brined) cow's milk version known as ackawi is now the best-selling Middle Eastern cheese among Arab-Americans.*

### If You Don't Have It
Substitute 1 oz (30 g) jibneh arabieh or ackawi with:
- 1 oz (30 g) sheep's milk feta cheese
- 1 oz (30 g) aged goat cheese
- 1 oz (30 g) haloumi

## Jicama

*A crisp, sweet and juicy tuber with white flesh akin to water chestnut. It can be eaten raw or cooked.*

1 lb (500 g) = 4 cups
(1 L) shredded

### If You Don't Have It
Substitute 1 cup (250 mL) chopped jicama with:
- 1 cup (250 mL) chopped water chestnuts
- 1 cup (250 mL) chopped sunchokes
- 1 cup (250 mL) chopped Asian radishes such as daikon (add a pinch of sugar to balance the peppery flavor if you like)
- 1 cup (250 mL) chopped turnips

## Jinhua Ham

*Fine, dry-cured ham from the Zhejiang province of eastern China. It is made from a breed of pig known as "two ends black" in a manner similar to Spanish Iberico ham.*

### If You Don't Have It

Substitute 4 oz (125 g) Jinhua ham with:

- 4 oz (125 g) Yunnan ham
- 4 oz (125 g) Iberico or serrano ham
- 4 oz (125 g) Smithfield ham or other Virginia ham

## Jocoque

*Also known as labin. Thick Mexican buttermilk introduced to Mexico by Lebanese immigrants.*

### If You Don't Have It

Substitute 1 cup (250 mL) jocoque with:

- ½ cup (125 mL) buttermilk + ½ cup (125 mL) Mexican crema or sour cream + pinch of salt
- ½ cup (125 mL) buttermilk + ½ cup (125 mL) crème fraîche + pinch of salt
- ½ cup (125 mL) buttermilk + ½ cup (125 mL) yogurt + pinch of salt

## John Dory

*Also known as Saint-Pierre. A long, slender body enables this fish to sneak up on prey and snatch them with a huge retractable jaw.*

### If You Don't Have It

Substitute 1 lb (500 g) John Dory with:

- 1 lb (500 g) porgy
- 1 lb (500 g) grouper
- 1 lb (500 g) monkfish
- 1 lb (500 g) halibut

## Johnny Jump-Up

*See* PICKING EDIBLE FLOWERS (PAGE 650).

## Jonah Crab

*See* CHOOSING AMONG CRABS (PAGE 647).

## Jujube

*See* CHINESE DATE, FRESH.

## Juneberry

*Also known as Saskatoon, shadberry, and western serviceberry. Dark purple mild-flavored berry with a bloom on the skin; similar to blueberry. Foraged for centuries by Native Americans in northern U.S. states and Canada. Now mostly cultivated in home gardens.*

### If You Don't Have It

Substitute 1 cup (250 mL) juneberries with:

- 1 cup (250 mL) blueberries
- 1 cup (250 mL) huckleberries

## Juniper Berry

*The aromatic berry of a coniferous shrub is usually dried before use as an herb to flavor meats, game, pâtés, sauerkraut, and, most famously, gin.*

### If You Don't Have It

Substitute 6 juniper berries with:
- 1 tsp (5 mL) caraway seeds + 1 tsp (5 mL) crushed bay leaf
- 1 tbsp (15 mL) gin (for marinades and sauces; adds alcohol)

## Jute Leaf

*Also known as ewedu, fakahoy, meloukhia or mulukhiyya, and saluyot. Jute fiber is a common rope material and the world's second most produced natural fiber after cotton. The plant's nutritious leaves are also simmered into soups, sauces, and side dishes in West Africa, Egypt, the Philippines, and Southeast Asia. Jute leaves have a slightly sour taste and, like okra, a mucilaginous thickening quality when heated. Quick, high-heat cooking minimizes the slime.*

### If You Don't Have It

Substitute 1 lb (500 g) jute leaves with:
- 1 lb (500 g) basella (Malabar spinach)
- 8 oz (250 g) cut okra + 8 oz (250 g) mature spinach leaves

# Kabocha Squash
# to **Kumquat Liqueur**

## Kabocha Squash

*The generic term for winter squash in Japan, kabocha is the North American marketing term for a variety of cultivars that range from rough-skinned/drum shaped to smoother/globe shaped. These different squash have in common a honey-sweet flesh that's almost as smooth as custard.*

> 1 lb (500 g) =
> 1 cup (250 mL)
> cooked and mashed

### If You Don't Have It
Substitute 1 cup (250 mL) chopped kabocha squash with:
- 1 cup (250 mL) chopped buttercup squash
- 1 cup (250 mL) chopped butternut squash
- 1 cup (250 mL) chopped Baby Blue Hubbard squash
- 1 cup (250 mL) chopped calabaza
- 1 cup (250 mL) chopped acorn squash
- 1 cup (250 mL) chopped sweet dumpling squash

## Kabosu

*Japanese citrus fruit with small seeds and a flavor similar to Key lime with hints of melon and mint. Kabosu can be harvested when the rind is green (and the juice is sour) or when it ripens to yellow (sweeter juice).*

### If You Don't Have It
Substitute 1 kabosu with:
- 1 to 2 Key limes
- 1 Persian lime
- 1 small yuzu (less juicy; more sour and floral)
- 2 tbsp (30 mL) rice vinegar (to replace juice of 1 kabosu)

| | |
|---|---|
| **Kadota Fig** | *See* FIG, FRESH. |
| **Kaffir Lime** | *See* MAKRUT LIME. |
| **Kahlúa** | *See* COFFEE LIQUEUR. |
| **Kaimaki** | *See* KAYMAK. |
| **Kaiware** | *See* RADISH SPROUTS. |
| **Kajiki** | *See* MARLIN. |
| **Kala Jeera** | *See* CUMIN. |
| **Kalamansi** | *See* CALAMONDIN. |
| **Kalamata Olive** | *See* CHOOSING AMONG OLIVES (PAGE 659). |

## Kale

*Members of the cabbage family that grow in loose bunches of leaves rather than heads. Types include curly kale, Russian red kale, and Tuscan black kale. Sweetest if harvested after the frost, these deep green leaves are nutritional superstars bursting with nutrients and phytochemicals. Kale is an excellent source of calcium, folic acid, vitamin C, and potassium.*

1 lb (500 g) =
1½ to 2 cups
(375 to 500 mL) cooked

### If You Don't Have It
Substitute 1 lb (500 g) kale with:
- 1 lb (500 g) collard greens
- 1 lb (500 g) callaloo
- 1 lb (500 g) Chinese kale
- 1 lb (500 g) green chard
- 1 lb (500 g) turnip greens
- 1 lb (500 g) mustard greens
- 1 lb (500 g) spinach

### Kale Varieties
Choose 1 lb (500 g) kale from these varieties:
- 1 lb (500 g) curly kale (green to light blue green leaves; mildly sweet flavor; resilient texture)
- 1 lb (500 g) Tuscan, cavolo nero, or lacinato (dark green to dark purple black leaves that are curled under and have a nubbly surface; deep, complex, mildly sweet flavor; softer texture than curly kale)
- 1 lb (500 g) flowering or ornamental kale (pretty, frilly, light green leaves with cream-color or pinkish purple stems; firm texture; used mostly as a garnish; leaves can be steamed or simmered in salted water.
- 1 lb (500 g) Russian Red kale (light green, oak-leaf-shaped leaves with cream-color to magenta stems; firm texture; deep, mildly sweet flavor)

## Kalonji

*See* NIGELLA.

## Kamaboko

*See* SURIMI.

## Kamagong

*See* MABOLO.

## Kamanu

*See* RAINBOW RUNNER.

## Kamut© Flour

*See* CHOOSING AMONG WHOLE-GRAIN AND ALTERNATIVE FLOURS (PAGE 648).

## Kangaroo

*A staple food of Aboriginal Australians, European colonists took to the kangaroo as game. After a downturn in interest for much of the 20$^{th}$ century, the meat is enjoying a resurgence on tables down under.*

### If You Don't Have It

Substitute 1 lb (500 g) kangaroo with:
- 1 lb (500 g) antelope
- 1 lb (500 g) gazelle
- 1 lb (500 g) deer
- 1 lb (500 g) elk
- 1 lb (500 g) caribou
- 1 lb (500 g) moose
- 1 lb (500 g) reindeer

## Kanten

*See* AGAR.

## Kapi

*See* SHRIMP PASTE.

## Kasar

*See* KASSERI.

## Kasha

*See* BUCKWHEAT GROATS.

## Kashk

*Fermented, concentrated, salted whey product available as a liquid or powder. Adds a sour flavor and creamy texture to traditional Persian dishes like the eggplant spread kashk-e bademjan.*

### If You Don't Have It

Substitute ½ cup (125 mL) kashk with:
- ½ cup (125 mL) sour cream + pinch of salt
- ½ cup (125 mL) crème fraîche + pinch of salt
- ½ cup (125 mL) yogurt cheese + pinch of salt
- ½ cup (125 mL) reconstituted qurut

*See also* QURUT.

## Kashkaval

*Sheep's milk cheese of Bulgarian origin is a pasta filata type, meaning the curds are stretched*

### If You Don't Have It

Substitute 1 oz (30 g) young Kashkaval with:
- 1 oz (30 g) Caciocavallo
- 1 oz (30 g) Scamorza
- 1 oz (30 g) provolone

*into strands before they are molded.*

1 lb (500 g) = 4 cups
(1 L) shredded

### If You Don't Have It
Substitute 1 oz (30 g) aged Kashkaval with:
- 1 oz (30 g) Kefalotyri
- 1 oz (30 g) Pecorino Romano
- 1 oz (30 g) Parmesan
- 1 oz (30 g) Asiago

## Kasseri

*Greek semihard cheese made from sheep's milk sometimes combined with goat's milk. Salty and pungent with an underlying sweetness. Known as kasar in Turkey.*

1 lb (500 g) = 4 cups
(1 L) grated or shredded

### If You Don't Have It
Substitute 1 oz (30 g) Kasseri with:
- 1 oz (30 g) Kefalotyri
- 1 oz (30 g) kashkaval
- 1 oz (30 g) graviera
- 1 oz (30 g) Pecorino Romano
- 1 oz (30 g) Parmesan
- 1 oz (30 g) Asiago

*See also* KEFALOTYRI.

## Katsuobushi

*See* BONITO.

## Kaya

*See* COCONUT EGG JAM.

## Kaymak

*Also known as kaimaki and qaimaaq. Middle Eastern clotted cream traditionally prepared from goat's milk or water buffalo milk.*

8 oz (250 g) =
1 cup (250 mL)

### If You Don't Have It
Substitute 1 cup (250 mL) kaymak with:
- 1 cup (250 mL) clotted cream
- 1 cup (250 mL) crème fraîche

*See also* CREAM, CLOTTED; CRÈME FRAÎCHE; SMETANA; SOUR CREAM.

## Kecap

*Also known as ketjap manis. A dark, syrupy Indonesian condiment made from soybeans. It is sweeter, thicker, and more complexly flavored than soy sauce. Pronounced "ketchap," the word passed into English usage as ketchup, the name for an entirely different sauce.*

### If You Don't Have It
Substitute 1 cup (250 mL) kecap with:
- 1 cup (250 mL) Homemade Kecap: Combine ¾ cup (175 mL) tamari or soy sauce, ⅓ cup (75 mL) brown sugar, 3 tbsp (45 mL) molasses, ¼ tsp (1 mL) crushed garlic, and ⅛ tsp (0.5 mL) ground star anise or 1 whole star anise in a saucepan over medium-low heat. Stir until smooth and heated through; if using whole star anise, remove before using. Makes 1⅓ cups (325 mL).
- 1 cup (250 mL) minus 3 tbsp (45 mL) Maggi seasoning + 3 tbsp (45 mL) molasses

## Kefalotyri

*Made from sheep's milk, sometimes mixed with goat's milk, younger kefalotyri is served as table cheese and in the fried appetizer saganaki. Aged longer, it is an excellent grating cheese.*

1 lb (500 g) = 4 cups
(1 L) grated or shredded

### If You Don't Have It
Substitute 1 oz (30 g) Kefalotyri with:
- 1 oz (30 g) Kasseri
- 1 oz (30 g) Graviera
- 1 oz (30 g) Pecorino Romano
- 1 oz (30 g) Parmesan
- 1 oz (30 g) Grana Padano
- 1 oz (30 g) Asiago

*See also* KASSERI.

## Kefir

*A cultured milk beverage that originated in the Caucasus Mountains.*

8 oz (250 g) =
1 cup (250 mL)

### If You Don't Have It
Substitute 1 cup (250 mL) kefir with:
- ¾ cup (175 mL) yogurt + 4 to 5 tbsp (60 to 75 mL) milk
- 1 cup (250 mL) kumiss

*See also* KEFIR CHEESE; KUMISS.

## Kefir Cheese

*Soft white cheese made by draining the kefir curds from the whey.*

### If You Don't Have It
Substitute 1 cup (250 mL) kefir cheese with:
- 1 cup (250 mL) yogurt cheese
- 1 cup (250 mL) cream cheese

*See also* KEFIR.

## Kekuna Nut

*See* PILI NUT.

## Kelp

*See* KOMBU.

## Kenari Nut

*See* PILI NUT.

## Kentucky Ham

*A dry-cured country ham smoked with hickory and apple wood.*

1 lb (500 g) boneless =
1½ to 3 cups
(375 to 750 mL)
chopped = 2 cups
(500 mL) ground

### If You Don't Have It
Substitute 1 lb (500 g) Kentucky Ham with:
- 1 lb (500 g) Virginia ham, especially Smithfield ham
- 1 lb (500 g) York ham
- 1 lb (500 g) Yunnan ham

## Kentucky Whiskey

*See* WHISKEY.

## Ketchup

*Also known as catsup and catchup. Sweet tomato ketchup is the sole survivor of a broad category of thin salty sauces with a long shelf life. Ketchups of yore included those made from mushrooms, oysters, mussels, and walnuts.*

### If You Don't Have It

Substitute 1 cup (250 mL) ketchup with:
- 1 cup (250 mL) tomato sauce + ¼ cup (60 mL) granulated sugar + 3 tbsp (45 mL) apple cider vinegar + ½ tsp (2 mL) salt + pinch of ground cloves
- 1 cup (250 mL) chili sauce (adds chopped pickles)
- 1 cup (250 mL) barbecue sauce (darker; more complex flavor)

## Ketumbar

*See* CORIANDER SEED.

## Ketza

*See* NIGELLA.

## Kewra

*See* SCREWPINE LEAF.

## Key Lime

*See* LIME.

## Kezuribushi

*See* BONITO.

## Kharbouza Melon

*Football-shaped melon with a hard yellow skin and patches of dark green. The flesh is pale green, firm, crunchy, and fairly sweet with hints of chardonnay wine.*

### If You Don't Have It

Substitute 1 cup (250 mL) chopped kharbouza melon with:
- 1 cup (250 mL) chopped Ogen melon
- 1 cup (250 mL) chopped galia melon
- 1 cup (250 mL) chopped Santa Claus melon
- 1 cup (250 mL) chopped Persian melon
- 1 cup (250 mL) chopped honeydew melon

## Kidney Bean

*See* THE WIDE WORLD OF DRIED BEANS (PAGE 637).

## Kielbasa

*Also known as kielbasy and Polish sausage. Fresh or smoked robust garlicky sausage commonly made of pork.*

### If You Don't Have It

Substitute 1 lb (500 g) kielbasa with:
- 1 lb (500 g) Kolbasz
- 1 lb (500 g) Cajun andouille (spicier)
- 1 lb (500 g) Spanish chorizo
- 1 lb (500 g) linguiça

## Kili Pepper

*See* SELIM KILI PEPPER.

## Kimba Pepper

*See* SELIM KILI PEPPER.

## King Crab

*See* CHOOSING AMONG CRABS (PAGE 647).

## Kingfish

*See* CROAKER.

## King Mackerel

*See* MACKEREL.

## King Salmon

*See* SALMON.

## Kinome Leaf

*The serrated leaves of the Japanese prickly ash tree, the same tree that produces Szechuan peppercorns. The leaves are less tingly-hot than the peppercorns with a fresh, minty aroma.*

2 oz (60 g) = 1½ cups (375 mL) chopped

### If You Don't Have It
Substitute 1 tbsp (15 mL) chopped fresh kinome leaf with:
- 1 tbsp (15 mL) chopped fresh lemon mint + pinch of sansho or ground Szechuan peppercorns
- 1 tbsp (15 mL) chopped fresh mint + pinch of fresh grated lemon zest + pinch of ground black pepper
- 1 tsp (5 mL) dried kinome

*See also* SZECHUAN PEPPER.

## Kippered Black Cod

*See* BLACK COD.

## Kippered Herring

*See* HERRING.

## Kippered Sablefish

*See* SABLEFISH.

## Kippered Salmon

*See* SMOKED SALMON.

## Kirby Cucumber

*See* CUCUMBER.

## Kirsch

*Also known as Kirschwasser. Clear German brandy named "cherry water" is at home in recipes for fondue, cherries jubilee, and cherry tart.*

### If You Don't Have It
Substitute 3 tbsp (45 mL) Kirsch with:
- 1 to 1½ tsp (5 to 7 mL) cherry extract + 3 tbsp (45 mL) brandy
- 3 tbsp (45 mL) cherry liqueur (sweeter)
- 3 tbsp (45 mL) cherry syrup (sweeter; nonalcoholic)
- 3 tbsp (45 mL) Maraschino liqueur
- 3 tbsp (45 mL) cherry vodka

### To Vary the Flavor
Substitute 3 tbsp (45 mL) Kirsch with:
- 3 tbsp (45 mL) framboise (raspberry flavor)
- 3 tbsp (45 mL) plum brandy (plum flavor)

## Kitchen Bouquet

*See* GRAVY BROWNING.

## Kitchen Shears

*See* POULTRY SHEARS.

## Kiwano

*Also known as African horned cucumber, horned melon, and jelly melon. More of a curiosity than a cause for gustatory celebration, the flesh of this spiked fruit tastes like the odd offspring of cucumber and banana.*

### If You Don't Have It

Substitute 1 cup (250 mL) kiwano flesh with:
- 1 cup (250 mL) cucumber flesh, gel, and seeds, especially Armenian cucumber or snake melon + dash of lime juice (paler green color)

## Kiwifruit

*Also known as Chinese gooseberry and monkey peach. Kiwifruit has ten times the vitamin C of lemons.*

> 2 whole fruit =
> ¾ cup (175 mL)
> chopped or sliced

### If You Don't Have It

Substitute 1 cup (250 mL) peeled kiwifruit with:
- 1 cup (250 mL) peeled gold kiwifruit (fuzzless skin, golden flesh with a hint of mango)
- ½ cup (125 mL) strawberries + ½ cup (125 mL) gooseberries (especially when kiwifruit will be puréed)
- 1 cup (250 mL) pitaya

## Kiwifruit, Baby

*Also known as cocktail kiwi, hardy kiwi, dessert kiwi, and kiwi berry. These mini kiwifruits resemble greenish red grapes in color, size, and consistency. They can also be eaten whole like grapes due to their fuzzless, thin skin. The flavor is sweeter than mature kiwis with hints of strawberry, lime, and pineapple.*

> 2 whole fruit =
> ¾ cup (175 mL)
> chopped or sliced

### If You Don't Have It

Substitute 1 cup (250 mL) unpeeled baby kiwifruit with:
- 1 cup (250 mL) grapes
- 1 cup (250 mL) peeled green or gold kiwifruit
- ½ cup (125 mL) strawberries + ½ cup (125 mL) gooseberries (especially when baby kiwifruit will be puréed)

## Kkaennip

*See* PERILLA.

## Knackwurst

*Also known as knoblauch and knockwurst. Garlicky smoked beef sausages that look much like hot dogs. Often grilled or served with sauerkraut.*

### If You Don't Have It

Substitute 1 lb (500 g) Knackwurst with:

- 1 lb (500 g) frankfurters
- 1 lb (500 g) Bockwurst (made with veal)
- 1 lb (500 g) kielbasa (larger)
- 1 lb (500 g) Bratwurst
- 1 lb (500 g) bauerwurst (seasoned with mustard)

## Knafa

*See* PHYLLO.

## Knob Celery

*See* CELERIAC.

## Kobe Beef

*See* BEEF.

## Kochkäse

*German spreadable cow's milk cheese made from sour milk and baking soda and seasoned with caraway seeds.*

### If You Don't Have It

Substitute 1 oz (30 g) Kochkäse with:

- 1 oz (30 g) Harzer
- 1 oz (30 g) Handkäse
- 1 oz (30 g) Liederkranz
- 1 oz (30 g) Limburger

## Kochu Chang

*See* CHILE PASTE.

## Kohlrabi

*Also known as cabbage turnip. A type of common cabbage in which the base of the stem grows above ground into a globe from which other skinny, leaf-topped stems emerge. Delicious and crisp served raw. Sweet and satisfying when cooked.*

4 medium bulbs = 2 lbs (1 kg) = 3½ cups (875 mL) cubed and cooked

### If You Don't Have It

Substitute 1 lb (500 g) kohlrabi bulb with:

- 1 lb (500 g) turnip (more bitter)
- 1 lb (500 g) broccoli stems
- 1 lb (500 g) celeriac

*See also* KOHLRABI GREENS.

## Kohlrabi Greens

*The leaves of the kohlrabi bulb taste like collards and can be cooked like them.*

### If You Don't Have It

Substitute 1 lb (500 g) kohlrabi greens with:

- 1 lb (500 g) turnip greens
- 1 lb (500 g) collards

1 lb (500 g) =
1½ to 2 cups
(375 to 500 mL) cooked

- 1 lb (500 g) green chard
- 1 lb (500 g) mature spinach
- 1 lb (500 g) bok choy
- 1 lb (500 g) mustard greens
- 1 lb (500 g) kale

*See also* KOHLRABI.

## Kokum

*Also known as black kokum and asem candis. The dried skin of a fruit related to mangosteen used as a souring agent in southern Indian cooking. Kokum leaves behind a light purple color and sometimes a few seeds.*

1 oz (30 g) =
¼ cup (60 mL)

### If You Don't Have It
Substitute ½ oz (15 g) kokum with:

- ½ oz (15 g) asam gelugor
- 1 tbsp (15 mL) tamarind concentrate or paste (less floral aroma)
- 1½ tbsp (22 mL) mango powder or amchur (less floral aroma)
- 1 to 1½ tbsp (15 to 22 mL) lime or lemon juice (less floral aroma)

## Kolbasz

*See* KIELBASA.

## Kombu

*Also known as kelp and konbu. A large, diverse, and significant group of Japanese brown seaweeds harvested primarily off the shores of Hokkaido. It is preserved by sun drying. Essential in many dishes, including dashi (soup stock).*

### If You Don't Have It
Substitute 1 oz (30 g) kombu with:

- 1 oz (30 g) hijiki (stronger brine flavor; black color)
- 1 oz (30 g) wakame (milder brine flavor; dark green to brown color)
- 1 oz (30 g) dulse (milder brine flavor; maroon color)
- ½ tsp (2 mL) salt

## Kontomire

*See* TARO.

## Korerima

*Native to the southern rain forests of Ethiopia, korerima is a close relative of cardamom and often ground as a seasoning for Ethiopian stews.*

### If You Don't Have It
Substitute ½ tsp (2 mL) ground korerima with:

- ½ tsp (2 mL) ground cardamom

## Koseret

*The leaves of a wild African shrub (Lippia javanica) known as lemon bush. The dried, citrusy leaves are used along with korerima or Ethiopian cardamom to season the Ethiopian clarified butter known as niter kebbeh that forms the basis of many Ethiopian dishes.*

### If You Don't Have It
Substitute 1 tbsp (15 mL) chopped fresh koseret with:
- 1 tsp (5 mL) dried koseret

### To Vary the Flavor
Substitute 1 tbsp (15 mL) chopped fresh koseret with:
- 1 tbsp (15 mL) chopped fresh lemon verbena or 1 tsp (5 mL) dried
- 1 tbsp (15 mL) chopped fresh lemon basil or 1 tsp (5 mL) dried

## Kosher Salt

*See* SALT.

## Koumiss

*See* KUMISS.

## Krakauer

*Originally from Krakow, Poland, a finely ground cooked pork and beef sausage with chunks of cured meat and fat. The sausage is seasoned with garlic, pepper and other spices and sliced cold as lunchmeat. In Germany, street vendors fry krakauer and serve it on a roll with mustard.*

### If You Don't Have It
Substitute 1 lb (500 g) krakauer with:
- 1 lb (500 g) jagdwurst (smaller chunks of fat)
- 1 lb (500 g) mortadella (large chunks of fat)
- 1 lb (500 g) bierwurst (usually smoked)
- 1 lb (500 g) galantina (more chunky)
- 1 lb (500 g) bologna (milder)

### For Better Health
Substitute 1 lb (500 g) krakauer with:
- 1 lb (500 g) gelbwurst (lower in fat and calories)

## Kreplach Wrappers

*Dough used to make Jewish dumplings similar to small Italian ravioli or Chinese wontons. Kreplach are often filled with ground meat or potatoes and served in brothy chicken soup.*

### If You Don't Have It
Substitute 1 lb (500 g) kreplach wrappers with:
- 1 lb (500 g) egg roll wrappers (relatively thick; often used for egg rolls)
- 1 lb (500 g) empanada wrappers (round)
- 1 lb (500 g) rolled sheet pasta (cut to desired shape)
- 1 lb (500 g) gyoza wrappers (thick; round; often used for pot stickers)
- 1 lb (500 g) suey gow wrappers or won ton wrappers (may be thick or thin; used for dumplings)
- 1 lb (500 g) water dumpling wrappers (relatively thin; round; often used for soups or cooked in liquid)
- 1 lb (500 g) shao mai skins (relatively thin; round; often used for steamed dumplings)
- 1 lb (500 g) rice paper (thinner; larger; cut to desired shape; makes crispy dumplings)

## Kudzu Powder

*Also known as gok fun (China) and ko fen (Japan). A starch extracted from the kudzu root and used for thickening. Use 1½ tbsp (22 mL) to thicken 1 cup (250 mL) liquid.*

### If You Don't Have It

Substitute 1½ tbsp (22 mL) kudzu powder (for thickening) with:
- 2 tsp (10 mL) arrowroot powder
- 1½ tsp (7 mL) cornstarch, potato starch, or rice starch
- 1 tbsp (15 mL) quick-cooking tapioca
- 1 heaping tbsp (15 mL) all-purpose flour
- 1 tsp (5 mL) instant mashed potato flakes

## Kugelhopf

*Also known as gugelhupf. A decoratively swirled, ring-shaped yeast cake renowned in Central Europe from Eastern France to Austria.*

### If You Don't Have It

Substitute 1 lb (500 g) kugelhopf with:
- 1 lb (500 g) panettone (Italian sweet yeast bread; tall, cylindrical shape)
- 1 lb (500 g) kulich (Russian sweet yeast bread; usually has icing; tall, cylindrical shape)
- 1 lb (500 g) brioche (French yeast bread; richer; less sweet or not sweet; )

*See also* PAN SIZE EQUIVALENTS (PAGE 678).

## Kuka

*See* BAOBAB LEAF.

## Kulich

*A light yeast bread that's prepared to celebrate Russian Easter. The dough is flavored with candied fruit, raisins, and saffron, then baked in a tall cylindrical loaf. It is iced and garnished with almonds and more candied fruit.*

### If You Don't Have It

Substitute 1 lb (500 g) kulich with:
- 1 lb (500 g) panettone (Italian sweet yeast bread)
- 1 lb (500 g) Kugelhopf (central European sweet yeast bread; tall, ring shape)
- 1 lb (500 g) brioche (French yeast bread; richer; less sweet or not sweet)

## Kuminost

*See* NÖKKELOST.

## Kumiss

*Also known as koumiss. Of Mongol origin, a slightly alcoholic beverage traditionally fermented from camel's or mare's milk. Cow's milk is now used to make kumiss.*

8 oz (250 g) =
1 cup (250 mL)

### If You Don't Have It

Substitute 1 cup (250 mL) kumiss with:
- 1 cup (250 mL) kefir
- ¾ cup (175 mL) yogurt + 4 to 5 tbsp (60 to 75 mL) milk

*See also* KEFIR.

## Kümmel

*The name refers to the cumin seeds — among a list of other herbs — that flavor this clear liqueur of Dutch lineage.*

### If You Don't Have It

Substitute 3 tbsp (45 mL) Kümmel with:

- 3 tbsp (45 mL) aquavit
- 3 tbsp (45 mL) vodka + pinch of caraway seeds + small pinch of cumin seeds + small pinch of fennel seeds, soaked at room temperature for at least 1 month
- 3 tbsp (45 mL) Goldwasser (includes gold flakes)
- 3 tbsp (45 mL) Silverwasser (includes silver flakes)
- 3 tbsp (45 mL) Liqueur d'Or
- 3 tbsp (45 mL) Strega

## Kumquat

*Although they look like Lilliputian oranges, kumquats are categorized in the* Fortunella *genus, not* Citrus. *Both the sweet skin and tart flesh are completely edible.*

> 1 lb (500 g) = 1 to
> 1½ cups (250 to 375 mL)
> chopped

### If You Don't Have It

Substitute 2 to 3 kumquats with:

- 1 calamondin (hybrid of mandarin orange and kumquat; for flesh or zest)
- ¼ mandarin orange + ½ tsp (2 mL) lemon (for flesh or zest)
- 2 to 3 limequats (hybrid of lime and kumquat; for flesh or zest)
- 2 to 3 lemonquats (hybrid of lemon and kumquat; for flesh or zest)

## Kumquat Liqueur

*A popular bottled cordial in Corfu, Greece. It can also be made at home by infusing kumquats into sweetened vodka in the manner of Italian limoncello.*

### If You Don't Have It

Substitute 3 tbsp (45 mL) kumquat liqueur with:

- 3 tbsp (45 mL) Homemade Kumquat Liqueur: Quarter 2 lbs (1 kg) kumquats and place in a 2-quart (2 L) glass bottle or jar with a cap or lid. Add enough pure grain alcohol or good-quality 100-proof vodka to cover the kumquats (about three-fourths of a 750-mL bottle should do it). Cover and keep in a dark spot for 3 to 5 weeks. Combine 2 cups (500 mL) water and 1 cup (250 mL) granulated sugar. Bring to a boil and simmer over medium-high heat until slightly thickened, about 5 minutes. Let cool then add to the steeping vodka along with the rest of the 750-mL bottle of pure grain alcohol or 100-proof vodka (about another ¾ cup/175 mL). Cover and return to the dark spot for 3 to 5 more weeks. Strain the liqueur into bottles, gently pressing on the kumquats (the vodka-soaked kumquats make a delicious snack). Seal and store in the freezer or at room temperature for up to 6 to 8 months. Serve icy cold or toss with fruit or use in a frozen dessert. Makes about 5 cups (1.25 L).
- 1 tbsp (15 mL) orange vodka + 1 tbsp (15 mL) sugar syrup

# Labin to Lyle's Golden Syrup

| | |
|---|---|
| **Labin** | *See* JOCOQUE. |
| **Labneh** | *See* YOGURT CHEESE. |
| **Ladyfinger pan** | *See* PAN SIZE EQUIVALENTS (PAGE 678). |

## Ladyfingers

*Also known as biscotti di Savoia, savoiardi (both Italian) and sponge fingers. Strips of sponge cake used in the preparation of charlottes, tiramisù, and many other desserts. American ladyfingers are moister than Italian ones.*

> 1 lb (500 g) =
> 60 to 65 ladyfingers

**If You Don't Have It**

Substitute 1 lb (500 g) ladyfingers with:

- 1 lb (500 g) sponge cake, cut into small pieces and baked for 10 minutes if necessary to crisp (best for desserts such as tiramisù in which the cake will be soaked in espresso, syrups, or other flavored liquids)
- 1 lb (500 g) génoise, baked for 10 minutes if necessary to crisp
- 1 lb (500 g) pound cake, baked for 10 minutes if necessary to crisp

| | |
|---|---|
| **Lager** | *See* BEER. |

## Lagerkaese

*Semisoft German cow's milk cheese with a somewhat pungent aroma.*

**If You Don't Have It**

Substitute 1 oz (30 g) Lagerkaese with:

- 1 oz (30 g) Brick
- 1 oz (30 g) Havarti
- 1 oz (30 g) Limburger (more pungent)

## Laguiole

*French semifirm raw cow's milk cheese with a crumbly yet creamy texture and a biting, verdant taste. Wheels of laguiole age for 6 to 12 months and weigh 80 to 100 pounds (40 to 50 kg).*

### If You Don't Have It
Substitute 1 oz (30 g) laguiole with:
- 1 oz (30 g) Salers
- 1 oz (30 g) Cantal
- 1 oz (30 g) Cheshire
- 1 oz (30 g) Lancashire
- 1 oz (30 g) aged Cheddar

## Lahvosh

*See* LAVASH.

## Laksa Leaf

*See* VIETNAMESE MINT.

## Laksa Paste

*A tantalizing seasoning prepared by grinding candlenuts, lemongrass, hot chiles, galangal, shrimp paste, fresh ginger, garlic, cilantro, turmeric, tamarind, and other spices. Used to spike the broth in the famous Malaysian noodle soup.*

### If You Don't Have It
Substitute 1 tbsp (15 mL) laksa paste with:
- 1 tbsp (15 mL) Homemade Laksa Paste: Combine ½ cup (125 mL) red curry paste, 2 to 3 tbsp (25 to 45 mL) macadamia nuts or candlenuts, 3 tbsp (45 mL) chopped Vietnamese mint (or 1 tbsp/15 mL chopped mint and 1 tbsp/15 mL chopped cilantro), 3 tbsp (45 mL) vegetable oil, and 1 tbsp (15 mL) shrimp paste in a small food processor or blender. Purée until smooth. Makes about ¾ cup (175 mL).
- 1 tbsp (15 mL) vegetarian laksa paste (has no shrimp paste)

## La-Lot Leaf

*See* BETEL LEAF.

## Lamb

*The meat of sheep younger than 1 year includes suckling lamb fed only its mother's milk.*

### If You Don't Have It
Substitute 1 lb (500 g) lamb with:
- 1 lb (500 g) beef
- 1 lb (500 g) pork
- 1 lb (500 g) veal
- 1 lb (500 g) mutton (sheep over 2 years old; tougher, fattier texture; stronger flavor)

## Lambert Cherry

*See* CHERRY.

## Lamb's Lettuce

*See* MÂCHE.

## Lamprey

*Often erroneously referred to as eel, this primitive, rather grotesque fish survives as an ocean parasite, sucking blood from larger fish.*

### If You Don't Have It
Substitute 1 lb (500 g) lamprey with:
- 1 lb (500 g) eel (stronger flavor)
- 1 lb (500 g) monkfish (more tender)
- 1 lb (500 g) mullet (more flaky)

## Lancashire

*Because of its melting quality, this British cheese is often selected for Welsh Rabbit.*

> 1 lb (500 g) = 4 cups (1 L) shredded

### If You Don't Have It
Substitute 1 oz (30 g) Lancashire cheese with:
- 1 oz (30 g) Cheshire
- 1 oz (30 g) Cheddar
- 1 oz (30 g) Caerphilly
- 1 oz (30 g) Leicester

## Landjäger

*Semidry, smoked beef and pork sausage sold in slightly flattened links. Landjäger originated in Switzerland but the name, "country hunters" also refers to mounted police in some regions of Germany.*

### If You Don't Have It
Substitute 1 lb (500 g) landjäger with:
- 1 lb (500 g) Thuringer
- 1 lb (500 g) Lebanon bologna
- 1 lb (500 g) Spanish chorizo
- 1 lb (500 g) other semidry or summer sausage
- 1 lb (500 g) salami or other dry sausage
- 1 lb (500 g) pepperoni

*See also* CERVELAT; SUMMER SAUSAGE.

## Langouste

*See* SPINY LOBSTER.

## Langoustine

*See* DUBLIN BAY PRAWN.

## Langsat

*Also known as duku. Sweet-tart fruit growing in clusters on the Lansium tree, which is native to Malaysia. The firm yellowed skin houses five soft, translucent segments of pale, juicy flesh and sometimes an intolerably bitter seed. The peels make a reasonable mosquito repellant.*

### If You Don't Have It
Substitute 1 cup (250 mL) peeled and seeded fresh langsat with:
- 1 cup (250 mL) peeled and seeded rambutans
- 1 cup (250 mL) peeled and seeded longans
- 1 cup (250 mL) peeled and seeded litchis
- 1 cup (250 mL) peeled and seeded pulasans

### Langsat Varieties
Choose 1 cup (250 mL) langsat from these varieties:
- 1 cup (250 mL) duku (more widely cultivated; round, 2-inch (5 cm) diameter; thin skin; more tart than langsat; about 10 fruits per cluster)
- 1 cup (250 mL) langsat or wild langsat (less widely cultivated; oval, 1-inch (2.5 cm) diameter; thicker skin; sweeter than duku; about 20 fruits per cluster)

## Lap Cheong

*Also known as lap cheung and lop chong. Dry-cured, smoked, sweet Chinese sausages made with pork, pork fat, soy sauce, paprika, grains, and alcohol.*

### If You Don't Have It

Substitute 1 lb (500 g) lap cheong with:

- 1 lb (500 g) Spanish chorizo
- 1 lb (500 g) pepperoni
- 1 lb (500 g) salami

## Lappi

*Finnish cheese from Lapland is semisoft, semisweet, slices beautifully and melts delightfully.*

> 1 lb (500 g) = 4 cups
> (1 L) shredded

### If You Don't Have It

Substitute 1 oz (30 g) Lappi with:

- 1 oz (30 g) Emmental
- 1 oz (30 g) Jarlsberg
- 1 oz (30 g) Gruyère
- 1 oz (30 g) Swiss

## Lard

*Also known as manteca (Spanish) and strutto (Italian). Rendered, filtered pork fat used for frying and in baked goods. The finest quality lard is called leaf lard, which comes from fat encasing hog's kidneys. Not to be confused with lardo, an Italian delicacy of pig's rump fat cured with salt, pepper, herbs, and spices (a similar delicacy goes by the name of speck in Germany).*

> 1 lb (500 g) =
> 2 cups (500 mL)

### If You Don't Have It

Substitute 1 cup (250 mL) lard with:

- 1 cup (250 mL) vegetable shortening

### To Vary the Flavor

Substitute 1 cup (250 mL) lard with:

- ½ cup (125 mL) lard + ½ cup (125 mL) unsalted butter (for both flakiness and flavor in biscuits, pie crust and pastries)
- 1 cup (250 mL) + 3 tbsp (45 mL) unsalted butter
- 1 cup (250 mL) bacon fat (especially for sautéing)

### For Better Health

Substitute 1 cup (250 mL) lard with:

- ½ cup (125 mL) lard + ½ cup (125 mL) vegetable oil (especially in Mexican cooking to retain lard's flavor while lowering saturated fat)

## Lardo

*See* FATBACK; LARD.

## Lardons

*Also known as lardoons. Narrow strips of fat that are larded, or inserted, into large cuts of meat to season and baste them internally as they roast.*

### If You Don't Have It

Substitute 1 lb (500 g) lardons with:

- 1 lb (500 g) sliced fatback (for larding or barding)
- 1 lb (500 g) fatty bacon (for barding)

## Lasagna

*See* PASTA, DRIED RIBBONS; PASTA, FRESH.

## Laughing Cow

*See* LA VACHE QUI RIT.

## Laurel Leaf

*See* BAY LEAF.

## La Vache Qui Rit

*Also known as The Laughing Cow. French pasteurized processed spreadable cow's milk cheese sold in single-serving foil-wrapped wedges and other shapes.*

### If You Don't Have It

Substitute 1 oz (30 g) la vache qui rit with:

- 1 oz (30 g) Vacherin Fribourgeois
- 1 oz (30 g) Vacherin Mont d'Or
- 1 oz (30 g) processed Swiss cheese spread

## Lavash

*Also known as Armenian cracker bread. Middle Eastern flatbread that can be as wide as 14 inches (35 cm).*

### If You Don't Have It

Substitute 1 lb (500 g) lavash with:

- 1 lb (500 g) sangak bread (thicker whole wheat sour dough)
- 1 lb (500 g) Barbari bread (thicker)
- 1 lb (500 g) large pita bread or naan (thicker)
- 1 lb (500 g) flour tortillas (especially for making wrap sandwiches)
- 1 lb (500 g) matzo (to replace crisp lavash)

## Lavender

*Fragrant flowers often candied or used to flavor beverages, salads, and ice creams.*

1 oz (30 g) fresh = 1/3 cup (75 mL)

1 oz (30 g) dried = 9 tbsp (135 mL)

### If You Don't Have It

Substitute 1 tbsp (15 mL) fresh lavender with:

- 1 tsp (5 mL) dried lavender
- 1 drop lavender essential oil

*See also* PICKING EDIBLE FLOWERS (PAGE 650).

## Laver

*Also known as jee choy and purple laver. Nutritious dried seaweed that must be soaked in cold water before using in a recipe.*

### If You Don't Have It

Substitute 1 oz (30 g) laver with:

- 1 oz (30 g) dulse (mild brine flavor; maroon color)
- 1 oz (30 g) nori (mild brine flavor; deep green color)
- 1 oz (30 g) arame (mild brine flavor; dark brown color)
- 1/2 tsp (2 mL) salt

*See also* NORI.

## Leaf Lard

*See* LARD.

## Leaf Lettuce

*Also known as looseleaf lettuce and Simpson lettuce. Popular types are green leaf, oak leaf, red leaf, and salad bowl. When shopping, choose leaves that look vibrant and evenly colored with no signs of wilting or yellowing.*

> 1 lb (500 g) =
> 6 cups (1.5 L) pieces

### If You Don't Have It

Substitute 1 lb (500 g) leaf lettuce with:

- 1 lb (500 g) butterhead lettuce such as Bibb or Boston (generally larger, slightly thicker leaves)
- 1 lb (500 g) crisphead lettuce such as Great Lakes, Iceberg, Imperial, Vanguard, or Western lettuce (crunchy; less flavorful)
- 1 lb (500 g) romaine lettuce (crunchy; more flavorful than crisphead lettuce)
- 1 lb (500 g) mâche (tender leaves; bittersweet, slightly nutty flavor)

### Leaf Lettuce Varieties

Choose 1 lb (500 g) leaf lettuce from these varieties:

- 1 lb (500 g) oak leaf lettuce (tender, oak-leaf shaped leaves with green or red color; mild flavor)
- 1 lb (500 g) lollo rosso (pale green stems; beautiful purplish red, frilly leaves; very mild flavor)
- 1 lb (500 g) lollo biondo (similar to lollo rosso but pale green in color)
- 1 lb (500 g) tango lettuce (crisp, green leaves with ruffled edges; mild flavor)

## Leaveners

*See* SPECIFIC TYPES.

## Lebanon Bologna

*Smoked, semidry or summer sausage made of coarsely chopped beef. It was created by German immigrants in Lebanon, Pennsylvania.*

### If You Don't Have It

Substitute 1 lb (500 g) Lebanon bologna with:

- 1 lb (500 g) Thuringer
- 1 lb (500 g) Landjäger
- 1 lb (500 g) other semidry or summer sausage
- 1 lb (500 g) salami or other dry sausage
- 1 lb (500 g) pepperoni

*See also* CERVELAT; RING BOLOGNA; SUMMER SAUSAGE.

## Leberkäse

*German for "liver cheese," this pâté is made with pork, eggs, garlic, and onion.*

### If You Don't Have It

Substitute 1 lb (500 g) Leberkäse with:

- 1 lb (500 g) mortadella (has cubes of pork fat and garlic flavor)
- 1 lb (500 g) bologna (less complex flavor)
- 1 lb (500 g) olive loaf (adds olive flavor)
- 1 lb (500 g) galantina (more chunky; more complex flavor)

### For Better Health

Substitute 1 lb (500 g) Leberkäse with:

- 1 lb (500 g) Gelbwurst (lower in fat and calories)

## Lebni

*See* YOGURT CHEESE.

## Lecithin

*An emulsifier that is found naturally in eggs and many other foods. Also, commercially extracted from soybeans.*

### If You Don't Have It

Substitute 1 cup (250 mL) lecithin with:
- 1 cup (250 mL) vegetable oil (for baking; adds fat)

## Lechosa

*See* PAPAYA.

## Leechee

*See* LITCHI.

## Leech Lime

*See* MAKRUT LIME.

## Leek

*On March 1, St. David's Day, many Welshmen wear leeks in their hats to celebrate a famous battle victory in which the Welsh soldiers wore leeks in their hats.*

1 lb (500 g) = 2 large leeks = 2 cups (500 mL) trimmed and chopped = 1 cup (250 mL) cooked

### If You Don't Have It

Substitute 1 cup (250 mL) chopped leeks with:
- 1 cup (250 mL) chopped green onions or scallions (white and light green parts only)
- 1 cup (250 mL) chopped shallots (sweeter, more complex flavor)
- 1 cup (250 mL) chopped sweet or storage onions (stronger, less complex flavor)
- 1 cup (250 mL) chopped ramps or wild leeks (lights parts only; but consider leaving ramps whole or cutting into just two pieces to show off their beautiful bulbs and leaves; best as a substitute for leeks that will be served as a side dish; stronger, more complex flavor than cultivated leeks)

*See also* RAMP.

## Leerdammer

*See* MAASDAM.

## Lefse

*Norwegian flatbread made from mashed potatoes. To rehydrate dried lefse, moisten it and heat briefly in a microwave oven.*

### If You Don't Have It

Substitute 1 lefse with:
- 1 chapati
- 1 soft lavash
- 1 flour tortilla

## Legume

*See* CRANBERRY BEAN, FRESH; EDAMAME; FAVA BEAN; GREEN BEAN; LIMA BEAN; PEANUT; PEAS, SHELLING; YARD-LONG BEAN; SWITCHING LENTILS (PAGE 653); THE WIDE WORLD OF DRIED BEANS (PAGE 637).

## Leicester

*Orange cheese that tastes like Cheddar but is moister. Great for snacking or dishes that call for melted cheese.*

1 lb (500 g) = 4 cups
(1 L) shredded

### If You Don't Have It

Substitute 1 oz (30 g) Leicester cheese with:

- 1 oz (30 g) Cheshire
- 1 oz (30 g) Lancashire
- 1 oz (30 g) Caerphilly
- 1 oz (30 g) Cheddar

## Lekvar

*See* PRUNE PURÉE.

## Lemon

*Eureka and Lisbon lemons are the familiar variety found in most markets. Meyer lemons are about twice the size and have an almost floral aroma and sweeter juice.*

1 medium Eureka or
Lisbon lemon =
2 to 3 tbsp (30 to 45 mL)
juice = 1 to 2 tsp
(5 to 10 mL) zest

1 medium Meyer lemon =
$\frac{1}{4}$ to $\frac{1}{3}$ cup
(60 to 75 mL) juice =
1 to 3 tbsp
(15 to 45 mL) zest

### If You Don't Have It

Substitute 1 fresh lemon with:

- $\frac{1}{2}$ Meyer lemon (larger; sweeter)
- 1 lime (slightly smaller; sweeter)
- 1 calamondin (hybrid of kumquat and mandarin orange)
- $\frac{1}{2}$ tsp (2 mL) orange (larger; sweeter)
- $\frac{1}{4}$ grapefruit (larger; sweeter)
- $\frac{1}{4}$ pummelo (larger; sweeter)

### To Vary the Flavor

Substitute 1 fresh lemon with:

- 1 tbsp (15 mL) chopped fresh lemon basil, lemon balm, or lemon thyme (for hint of lemon flavor)
- 2 to 3 leaves chopped fresh lemon verbena (stronger lemon flavor)

*See also* LEMON EXTRACT; LEMON JUICE; LEMON ZEST; MEYER LEMON; PRESERVED LEMON.

## Lemon Balm

*Also known as balm. In Europe, this minty lemon herb seasons salads, poultry, and meats. Also brewed into soothing tea.*

1 oz (30 g) = 2 cups
(500 mL) chopped

1 cup (250 mL) fresh =
$\frac{1}{4}$ cup (60 mL) dried

### If You Don't Have It

Substitute 1 tbsp (15 mL) chopped fresh lemon balm with:

- $2\frac{1}{2}$ tsp (12 mL) chopped fresh mint + $\frac{1}{2}$ tsp (2 mL) chopped fresh lemon verbena
- 2 tsp (10 mL) chopped fresh mint + 1 tsp (5 mL) chopped fresh lemon basil or holy basil
- 1 to 2 tsp (5 to 10 mL) lemon zest

### To Vary the Flavor

Substitute 1 tbsp (15 mL) chopped fresh lemon balm with:

- 1 tbsp (15 mL) chopped fresh basil
- 1 tbsp (15 mL) chopped fresh mint
- 1 tbsp (15 mL) chopped fresh bergamot (aromas of orange, thyme, sage, and rosemary)

## Lemon Basil

*See* BASIL.

## Lemon Extract

*For finest flavor, select "pure" lemon extract, which is derived from the fresh fruit.*

### If You Don't Have It
Substitute ½ tsp (2 mL) lemon extract with:
- 1 to 2 drops lemon oil + ¼ tsp (1 mL) vodka (optional)
- 1 tbsp (15 mL) limoncello (reduce liquid in recipe by 2½ tsp/12 mL and sugar by ¾ tsp/3 mL)
- 1 tsp (5 mL) lemon zest

### To Vary the Flavor
Substitute ½ tsp (2 mL) lemon extract with:
- ½ tsp (2 mL) orange extract
- ¾ tsp (3 mL) vanilla extract

## Lemon Cucumber

*See* CUCUMBER.

## Lemonfish

*See* COBIA.

## Lemongrass

*Also known as citronella and sereh (especially when powdered). A perennial tropical grass with delightful lemon scent and flavor. Widely utilized in Thai and other Southeast Asian cuisines.*

> 1 trimmed stalk =
> 1 tbsp (15 mL) dried =
> 1 tsp (5 mL) powder
> (sereh powder)

### If You Don't Have It
Substitute 1 lemongrass stalk with:
- 1½ tsp (7 mL) lemon zest + ⅛ tsp (0.5 mL) minced fresh ginger
- 1 tsp (5 mL) lemon balm
- 2 lemon leaves
- 2 lemon verbena leaves

## Lemon Juice

*If you don't own a citrus reamer, cut the lemon in half, stick a fork into the cut side and twist and squeeze to release the juice.*

> 1 medium Eureka or
> Lisbon lemon = 2 to
> 3 tbsp (30 to 45 mL) juice
>
> 1 medium Meyer lemon =
> ¼ to ⅓ cup
> (60 to 75 mL) juice

### If You Don't Have It
Substitute 1 tbsp (15 mL) fresh lemon juice with:
- 1 tbsp (15 mL) bottled or frozen lemon juice (much weaker flavor)
- 3 tbsp (45 mL) brewed lemon herbal tea (adds other flavors)

### To Vary the Flavor
Substitute 1 tbsp (15 mL) fresh lemon juice with:
- 2¼ tsp (11 mL) fresh lime juice
- 1½ tsp (7 mL) white wine vinegar, sherry vinegar, or champagne vinegar

## Lemon Liqueur

*A sweetened spirit flavored with lemon.*

### If You Don't Have It

Substitute 3 tbsp (45 mL) lemon liqueur with:
- 3 tbsp (45 mL) limoncello
- 1 tbsp (15 mL) lemon vodka + 1 tbsp (15 mL) sugar syrup
- 3 tbsp (45 mL) lemon vodka (less sweet)
- 5 tsp (25 mL) vodka + 1 tsp (5 mL) lemon juice (less sweet)
- 3 tbsp (45 mL) lemon schnapps

*See also* LIMONCELLO.

## Lemon Oil

*Concentrated oil of lemon peels often used in candies.*

### If You Don't Have It

Substitute 1 drop lemon oil with:
- ½ tsp (2 mL) lemon extract (less concentrated; evaporates at high temperatures; reduce liquid in recipe by ½ tsp/2 mL if necessary)
- 1 tbsp (15 mL) limoncello (reduce liquid in recipe by 1 tbsp/15 mL and sugar by ¾ tsp/3 mL if necessary)
- 1 tsp (5 mL) lemon zest

### To Vary the Flavor

Substitute 1 drop lemon oil with:
- 1 drop orange oil
- ¾ tsp (3 mL) vanilla extract (evaporates at high temperatures; reduce liquid in recipe by ¾ tsp/3 mL if necessary)

## Lemon Peel

*See* CITRUS PEEL, CANDIED; LEMON ZEST.

## Lemon Pepper Seasoning

*Commercial seasoning blend of ground black peppercorns and lemon zest. Tasty on chicken and vegetables.*

| 1 oz (30 g) = 3 tbsp (45 mL) |
| --- |

### If You Don't Have It

Substitute 1 tsp (5 mL) lemon pepper seasoning with:
- ½ tsp (2 mL) grated fresh lemon zest + ¼ tsp (1 mL) salt + ⅛ tsp (0.5 mL) ground black pepper
- ½ tsp (2 mL) ground sumac berries + ½ tsp (2 mL) ground black pepper

### For Better Health

Substitute 1 tsp (5 mL) lemon pepper seasoning with:
- 1 tsp (5 mL) salt-free lemon pepper seasoning
- 1 tsp (5 mL) herbal salt substitute

## Lemon Thyme

*See* THYME.

## Lemon Verbena

*Introduced to Great Britain from Chile in the 1700s. The leaves of this small deciduous shrub are popular in Europe for flavoring lemon tea, salads, sauces, and desserts.*

1 oz (30 g) = 2 cups (500 mL) chopped

1 cup (250 mL) fresh = ¼ cup (60 mL) dried

### If You Don't Have It
Substitute 2 leaves lemon verbena with:
- 1 stalk lemongrass
- 2 tsp (10 mL) lemon balm (adds minty flavor)
- 1½ tsp (7 mL) lemon zest

## Lemon Zest

*The yellow outer layer of lemon peel contains the essential flavoring oils. When grating or slicing the zest, take care to only remove the yellow skin, not the underlying bitter white membrane.*

1 medium Eureka or Lisbon lemon = 1 to 2 tsp (5 to 10 mL) zest

1 medium Meyer lemon = 1 to 3 tbsp (15 to 45 mL) zest

### If You Don't Have It
Substitute 1 tsp (5 mL) grated lemon zest with:
- ½ to 1 tsp (2 to 5 mL) dried lemon peel
- ½ tsp (2 mL) lemon extract
- 1 drop lemon oil

### To Vary the Flavor
Substitute 1 tsp (5 mL) grated lemon zest with:
- 1 tsp (5 mL) grated lime zest
- 1 tsp (5 mL) grated citron zest
- 1 tsp (5 mL) grated orange zest
- 1 tsp (5 mL) grated kumquat zest
- 1 small stalk lemongrass
- 1 tbsp (15 mL) chopped fresh lemon basil, lemon balm, or lemon thyme (for hint of lemon flavor)
- 2 lemon verbena leaves (stronger lemon flavor)

## Lentil

*See* SWITCHING LENTILS (PAGE 653).

## Lesser Galangal

*See* GALANGAL.

## Lettuce

*See* BUTTERHEAD LETTUCE; CRISPHEAD LETTUCE; LEAF LETTUCE; ROMAINE LETTUCE.

## Leyden

*Distinctive Dutch cheese fashioned from part-skim cow's milk and buttermilk that's seasoned with caraway or cumin seeds.*

1 lb (500 g) = 4 cups (1 L) shredded

### If You Don't Have It
Substitute 1 oz (30 g) young Leyden with:
- 1 oz (30 g) Gouda (no caraway or cumin flavors)
- 1 oz (30 g) Edam (less rich; no caraway or cumin flavors)
- 1 oz (30 g) Fontina (less tangy)

## Lichi

*See* LITCHI.

## Licor 43®

*Sweet, yellow Spanish liqueur formulated from "cuarenta y tres"; ingredients include citrus, fruits, herbs, and vanilla.*

### If You Don't Have It
Substitute 3 tbsp (45 mL) Licor 43® with:
- 3 tbsp (45 mL) Tuaca
- 3 tbsp (45 mL) crème de vanille or other vanilla liqueur
- 3 tbsp (45 mL) vanilla vodka (less sweet)

## Licorice Basil

*See* BASIL.

## Licorice Liqueur

*See* ANISE LIQUEUR.

## Liederkranz

*An American cheese that's mildly pungent when young and full-bodied when aged. Created in the late 19th century by New York cheesemaker Emil Frey. Named after a singing society whose members loved the cheese.*

1 lb (500 g) = 4 cups (1 L) shredded

### If You Don't Have It
Substitute 1 oz (30 g) Liederkranz with:
- 1 oz (30 g) Limburger
- 1 oz (30 g) Handkäse

## Light Cream

*See* CREAM, LIGHT.

## Light Rum

*See* RUM.

## Lilac

*See* PICKING EDIBLE FLOWERS (PAGE 650).

## Lillet

*An apéritif that originated in the French village of Podensac. Blended from white or red wine, brandy, herbs, and fruits.*

### If You Don't Have It
Substitute 3 tbsp (45 mL) Lillet with:
- 3 tbsp (45 mL) Dubonnet
- 3 tbsp (45 mL) sweet vermouth or sherry (to replace Lillet blanc)
- 3 tbsp (45 mL) Byrrh (to replace sweet Lillet rouge)
- 3 tbsp (45 mL) port (to replace sweet Lillet rouge)

## Lily Bud

*Buds of the yellow day lily picked before the short-lived flowers open. When dried, lily buds remain pliable and appear brownish yellow, lending a floral, slightly fruity aroma to dishes like traditional Chinese hot and sour soup.*

½ oz (15 g) dried lily buds = ½ cup (125 mL) = 30 dried lily buds

### If You Don't Have It
Substitute ½ cup (125 mL) dried lily buds with:
- ½ cup (125 mL) dried yellow rose buds

### To Vary the Flavor
Substitute ½ cup (125 mL) dried lily buds with:
- 1 cup (250 mL) thinly shredded green cabbage (for soups; no floral or fruity aroma)

## Lima Bean

*Also known as butter beans (dried) and Madagascar beans. Plump, kidney-shaped beans come in two distinct types: smaller baby lima beans and the larger, more flavorful Fordhooks. Lima beans can be purchased in season in their pods, also dried or frozen.*

1 lb (500 g) in shell = 1 cup (250 mL) shelled

1 lb (500 g) dried = 2⅓ cups (575 mL) = 5½ cups (1.375 L) cooked

### If You Don't Have It
Substitute 1 cup (250 mL) lima beans with:
- 1 cup (250 mL) fresh green peas
- 1 cup (250 mL) fresh edamame (shelled green soybeans)
- 1 cup (250 mL) shelled and peeled fresh fava beans
- 1 cup (250 mL) fresh sugar snap peas (in shell)
- 1 cup (250 mL) chickpeas, red kidney beans, black-eyed peas, or cannellini beans (to replace dried limas in soups and stews)

*See also* THE WIDE WORLD OF DRIED BEANS (PAGE 637).

## Limburger

*Considered by some people to be the embodiment of stinky cheese, this aromatic dairy product originated in Belgium, took hold in Germany, and is also produced by one American dairy cooperative in Wisconsin.*

1 lb (500 g) = 4 cups (1 L) shredded

### If You Don't Have It
Substitute 1 oz (30 g) Limburger with:
- 1 oz (30 g) Liederkranz
- 1 oz (30 g) Handkäse
- 1 oz (30 g) Bierkäse

# Lime

*Persian or Tahiti limes are the familiar variety found in most markets. Mexican or Key limes are smaller and have a more concentrated lime flavor than Persians.*

> 1 lb (500 g) = 6 to 8 medium Persian limes = ½ to ⅔ cup (125 to 150 mL) juice
>
> 1 medium Persian lime = 1 to 3 tbsp (15 to 45 mL) juice = 1 to 2 tsp (5 to 10 mL) zest
>
> 1 lb (500 g) = 12 to 16 medium Key limes = ½ to ⅔ cup (125 to 150 mL) juice
>
> 1 medium Key lime = 2 to 3 tsp (10 to 15 mL) juice = ¾ to 1 tsp (3 to 5 mL) zest

## If You Don't Have It

Substitute 1 Persian lime with:

- 1 to 2 Key limes (smaller; more intense lime flavor)
- 1 lemon (slightly larger; lemon flavor)
- ½ tsp (2 mL) Meyer lemon (larger; sweeter than familiar Eureka or Lisbon lemon)
- 1 calamondin (hybrid of kumquat and mandarin orange)
- ½ tsp (2 mL) orange (larger; sweeter)
- ¼ grapefruit (larger; sweeter)
- ¼ pummelo (larger; sweeter)

*See also* KABOSU; LIME JUICE; LIME ZEST; MAKRUT LIME.

# Lime Juice

*Freshly squeezed lime juice perks up everything from margaritas to seviche. The commercial Rose's lime juice is Key lime juice.*

> 1 medium Persian lime = 1 to 3 tbsp (15 to 45 mL) juice
>
> 1 lb (500 g) = 12 to 16 medium Key limes = ½ to ⅔ cup (125 to 150 mL) juice
>
> 1 medium Key lime = 2 to 3 tsp (10 to 15 mL) juice

## If You Don't Have It

Substitute 1 tbsp (15 mL) fresh Persian lime juice with:

- 1 tbsp (15 mL) bottled or frozen lime juice (less intense lime flavor)
- 1 tbsp (15 mL) Rose's lime juice (bottled sweetened Key lime juice; less intense lime flavor)

Substitute 1 tbsp (15 mL) fresh Key lime juice with:

- 1½ tsp (7 mL) Persian lime juice + 1½ tsp (7 mL) lemon juice
- 1½ tbsp (22 mL) Persian lime juice (less intense lime flavor)
- 1 tbsp (15 mL) Rose's lime juice (bottled sweetened Key lime juice; less intense lime flavor)

## To Vary the Flavor

Substitute 1 tbsp (15 mL) fresh Persian lime juice with:

- 3 to 4 tsp (15 to 20 mL) fresh lemon juice
- 1 tbsp (15 mL) calamondin juice
- 1 to 3 tbsp (15 to 45 mL) orange juice (sweeter)

*See* CITRUS PEEL, CANDIED; LIME ZEST.

# Lime Peel

## Limequat

*This hybrid belongs to the genus known as Fortunella, named in 1915 after Scottish botanist Robert Fortune. Like kumquats, limequats have sweet skin and bitter-sweet pulp and the small green oval-shaped fruit can be eaten whole.*

> 1 lb (500 g) =
> 1 to 1½ cups
> (250 to 375 mL) chopped

### If You Don't Have It

Substitute 2 to 3 limequats with:

- ¼ mandarin orange + ½ tsp (2 mL) lime zest (for the flesh or zest)
- 2 to 3 lemonquats (hybrid of lemon and kumquat; for flesh or zest)
- 2 to 3 kumquats (orange flavor; for flesh or zest)
- 1 calamondin (hybrid of mandarin orange and kumquat; for flesh or zest)

## Lime Zest

*The colored outer layer of the lime rind is rich in flavonoids, bioflavonoids, and limonoids.*

> 1 medium Persian lime =
> 1 to 2 tsp
> (5 to 10 mL) zest
>
> 1 medium Key lime =
> ¾ to 1 tsp (3 to 5 mL)
> zest

### If You Don't Have It

Substitute 1 tsp (5 mL) grated Persian lime zest with:

- ½ to 1 tsp (2 to 5 mL) dried lime peel
- ½ tsp (2 mL) lime extract

### To Vary the Flavor

Substitute 1 tsp (5 mL) grated Persian lime zest with:

- 1 tsp (5 mL) grated Key lime zest (more intense lime flavor)
- 1 tsp (5 mL) grated lemon zest
- 1 tsp (5 mL) grated citron zest
- 1 tsp (5 mL) grated orange zest
- 1 tsp (5 mL) grated kumquat zest
- 1 tsp (5 mL) grated calamondin zest

## Limoncello

*A stylish liqueur produced on Italy's Amalfi coast and in Sicily. It's made by steeping lemon zest in alcohol and then adding sugar syrup. Better brands use real lemon while cheaper versions rely on lemon extract.*

### If You Don't Have It

Substitute 3 tbsp (45 mL) Limoncello with:

- 3 tbsp (45 mL) Homemade Limoncello: Place the zest (no bitter white membrane) of 6 to 8 clean lemons and 1½ cups (375 mL) of pure grain alcohol or good-quality 100-proof vodka (half of a 750 mL bottle) into a 2-quart (2 L) glass bottle or jar with a cap or lid. Cover and keep in a dark spot for 3 to 5 weeks. Combine 2 cups (500 mL) water and 1 cup (250 mL) granulated sugar. Bring to a boil and simmer over medium-high heat until slightly thickened, about 5 minutes. Let cool then add to the steeping vodka along with another 1½ cups (375 mL) pure grain alcohol or 100-proof vodka. Cover and return to the dark spot for 3 to 5 more weeks. Strain the limoncello into bottles, discarding lemon zest. Seal and store limoncello in the freezer or at room temperature for up to 6 to 8 months.

## Limoncello (cont'd)

Serve icy cold or toss with fruit or use in a frozen dessert. Makes about 5 cups (1.25 L).

- 1 tbsp (15 mL) lemon vodka + 1 tbsp (15 mL) sugar syrup

### To Vary the Flavor
Substitute 3 tbsp (45 mL) limoncello with:
- 1 tbsp (15 mL) kumquat liqueur
- 1 tbsp (15 mL) mandarin liqueur

## Limpa Bread

*Also known as Swedish limpa. A moist and fragrant rye bread seasoned with cumin, fennel or anise, and orange zest.*

### If You Don't Have It
Substitute 1 lb (500 g) limpa bread with:
- 1 lb (500 g) rye bread with caraway seeds much less aromatic)
- 1 lb (500 g) pumpernickel bread (much less aromatic)

## Limpet

*A delicacy in Hawaii and Portugal, this saltwater snail is shaped like a slightly melted Hershey's Kiss. Slipper limpets are particularly tender and pile upon one another on shallow sea rocks.*

### If You Don't Have It
Substitute 1 lb (500 g) limpets with:
- 1 lb (500 g) periwinkles (smaller)
- 1 lb (500 g) whelks
- 1 lb (500 g) snails
- 1 lb (500 g) scallops
- 1 lb (500 g) cockles
- 1 lb (500 g) clams
- 1 lb (500 g) oysters

## Lingcod

*Not a cod, but a type of greenling with sweet and firm white flesh. Sold whole, also cut into fillets or steaks.*

### If You Don't Have It
Substitute 1 lb (500 g) lingcod with:
- 1 lb (500 g) cod (flakier texture)
- 1 lb (500 g) sablefish or black cod (fuller flavor)

## Lingonberry

*Also known as cowberry, foxberry, and mountain cranberry. A wild relative of the cranberry that flourishes in Canada, Maine, and Scandinavia. Processed into preserves and sauces.*

1 pint fresh =
2 cups (500 mL)

### If You Don't Have It
Substitute 1 cup (250 mL) lingonberries with:
- 1 cup (250 mL) cranberries (larger, more tart; less complex flavor)
- 1 cup (250 mL) red currants
- 1 cup (250 mL) black currants or cassis
- 1 cup (250 mL) elderberries
- 1 cup (250 mL) carissa
- 1 cup (250 mL) bilberries
- 1 cup (250 mL) blueberries (sweeter)

## Linguiça

*See* CHORIZO.

## Liqueur

*If you only need a small amount of a liqueur for a recipe, buy a miniature bottle at the liquor store checkout.*

### If You Don't Have It

Substitute 3 tbsp (45 mL) liqueur with:
- 2 tsp (10 mL) liqueur extract
- 1 tbsp (15 mL) fruit syrup (to replace fruit liqueurs)

### To Vary the Flavor
- 2 tsp (10 mL) vanilla extract

*See also* BITTERS; SPECIFIC TYPES.

## Liquid Smoke

*A natural product made by dissolving real wood smoke (usually hickory) in water. Liquid smoke is often used in barbecue sauces and other food products that have "grilled" or "barbecued" flavor. Look for it in the spice aisle or near the barbecue sauce in well-stocked grocery stores.*

### If You Don't Have It

Substitute 2 drops liquid smoke (for smoke flavor) with:
- 1 smoked ham hock (adds fat and ham flavor)
- 2 slices bacon (adds fat and bacon flavor)
- 1 tsp (5 mL) canning liquid from canned chipotle peppers (adds spices and considerable heat)
- ½ tsp (2 mL) ground chipotle peppers (adds considerable heat)
- ½ tsp (2 mL) smoked salt
- ½ tsp (2 mL) smoked pepper, paprika, or other smoked spices
- grilling or smoking the food using hickory or other wood

*See also* WOOD SMOKE.

## Liquor

*See* LIQUEUR; SPECIFIC TYPES.

## Litchi

*Also known as lychee. The fruit of a grand ornamental tree beloved in China. The fruit grows in clusters of burr-like pods that are about the size of ping pong balls.*

> 1 lb (500 g) fresh =
> 2½ cups (625 mL) sliced

### If You Don't Have It

Substitute 1 cup (250 mL) peeled and seeded fresh litchis with:
- 1 cup (250 mL) canned litchis (less aromatic)
- 1 cup (250 mL) peeled and seeded pulasans
- 1 cup (250 mL) peeled and seeded rambutans (less sweet)
- 1 cup (250 mL) peeled and seeded longans (sweeter; less aromatic)

*See also* LONGAN; PULASAN; RAMBUTAN.

## Livarot

*From the Calvados region of Normandy, this cheese is related to Camembert but is more pungent and larger in size.*

### If You Don't Have It

Substitute 1 oz (30 g) Livarot with:
- 1 oz (30 g) Limburger
- 1 oz (30 g) Maroilles
- 1 oz (30 g) Liederkranz
- 1 oz (30 g) Handkäse

## Liverwurst

*A broad category of liver-based sausages, sometimes smoked, that can range in texture from spreadable to sliceable.*

### If You Don't Have It

Substitute 1 lb (500 g) liverwurst with:

- 1 lb (500 g) Braunschweiger (smoked liverwurst)
- 1 lb (500 g) pâté
- 1 lb (500 g) Mettwurst
- 1 lb (500 g) Teewurst (spicier)

## Ljus Sirap

*See* SWEDISH SYRUP.

## Loaf Pan

*A deep rectangular baking pan most commonly sized 9-by 5-inches (2 L) and 3 inches (7.5 cm) deep.*

### If You Don't Have It

Substitute a loaf pan with:

- large, clean coffee can with one end removed

*See also* PAN SIZE EQUIVALENTS (PAGE 678).

## Lobster

*Also known as American lobster and Maine lobster. Maine lobsters have large claws, while spiny lobsters have no claws.*

1 to 1½ lbs
(500 to 750 g) =
2½ to 3 cups
(625 to 750 mL) meat

### If You Don't Have It

Substitute 1 lb (500 g) Maine lobster with:

- 1 lb (500 g) Dublin Bay prawns
- 1 lb (500 g) crayfish
- 1 lb (500 g) jumbo shrimp
- 1 lb (500 g) crab
- 1 lb (500 g) scallops

### Lobster Varieties

Choose 1 lb (500 g) lobster from these varieties:

- 1 lb (500 g) Maine lobster (large claws)
- 1 lb (500 g) spiny or rock lobster (no claws, large tails)

*See also* SPINY LOBSTER; CHANGING ROE (PAGE 666).

## Lobster Coral

*See* CHANGING ROE (PAGE 666).

## Locatelli

*See* PECORINO.

## Lochan Ora®

*The only liqueur from Chivas Brothers, this blend includes Scotch whiskey tamed by heather honey, herbs, and spices.*

### If You Don't Have It

Substitute 3 tbsp (45 mL) Lochan Ora with:

- 3 tbsp (45 mL) Drambuie
- 3 tbsp (45 mL) Grandtully
- 3 tbsp (45 mL) Glayva

## Locust Bean

*See* CAROB.

## Loganberry

*Large reddish purple fruit is reputed to be a hybrid of blackberry and red raspberry produced in the backyard of California Judge J.H. Logan in the summer of 1880.*

1 pint fresh =
2 cups (500 mL)

### If You Don't Have It
Substitute 1 cup (250 mL) loganberries with:
- 1 cup (250 mL) boysenberries (hybrid of blackberries, raspberries, and loganberries; reddish purple color)
- 1 cup (250 mL) blackberries (dark purple; more tart; larger seeds)
- 1 cup (250 mL) raspberries (red; sweeter)
- 1 cup (250 mL) tayberries (hybrid of blackberries and raspberries)
- 1 cup (250 mL) olallieberries (larger; sweeter)

## Lollo Biondo

*See* LEAF LETTUCE.

## Lollo Rosso

*See* LEAF LETTUCE.

## Longan

*These fruits can be as tiny as an olive or as large as a plum with an easy-to-peel skin. The gray flesh is sweet with overtones of perfumed flowers and pine.*

1 lb (500 g) fresh =
2½ cups (625 mL) sliced

### If You Don't Have It
Substitute 1 cup (250 mL) peeled and seeded fresh longans with:
- 1 cup (250 mL) peeled and seeded rambutans (less sweet)
- 1 cup (250 mL) peeled and seeded fresh or canned litchis
- 1 cup (250 mL) peeled and seeded pulasans

*See also* LITCHI.

## Long Melon

*See* CUCUZZA.

## Long Pepper

*Also known as Indian, Indonesian and Java Long Pepper and Pippali. Resembling tiny, elongated grey-black pine cones, long pepper (piper longum) is closely related to black pepper (piper nigrum) but with more citrus aromas and simple searing heat.*

### If You Don't Have It
Substitute 1 tsp (5 mL) long pepper with:
- 1 tsp (5 mL) cubeb (adds mint and allspice aromas)
- 1 tsp (5 mL) Tasmanian peppercorns (softer, more fruity aroma)
- 1 tsp (5 mL) grains of paradise (adds cardamom aromas)
- 1 tsp (5 mL) crushed selim kili pepper (adds eucalyptus and nutmeg aromas; slightly bitter)
- 1 tsp (5 mL) black peppercorns (less complex)

*See also* CUBEB.

## Looseleaf Lettuce

*See* LEAF LETTUCE.

## Lop Chong

*See* LAP CHEONG.

## Loquat

*Also known as Japanese plum and Japanese medlar. The earliest of spring fruits to ripen, the loquat is popular in almost all corners of the world except the U.S. It looks like a pear-shaped apricot but contains several very large seeds. The flesh is crisp-tender and juicy, tasting like a blend of cherry, grape, litchi, and plum.*

> 1 lb (500 g) fresh =
> 2½ cups (625 mL)
> sliced or halved

### If You Don't Have It
Substitute 1 lb (500 g) loquats with:
- 1 lb (500 g) sour cherries
- 1 lb (500 g) acerola
- 1 lb (500 g) apricots
- 1 lb (500 g) plums

## Lotte

*See* MONKFISH.

## Lotus Leaf

*When young and tender, the leaves of the Asian flower are used as herbs. More mature leaves are large enough to use as wrappers for foods to be steamed.*

### If You Don't Have It
Substitute lotus leaves (as a food wrapper) with:
- softened bamboo leaves
- banana leaves
- parchment paper

## Lotus Root

*Also known as renkon (Japan). The underwater rhizome of an Asian flower that is torpedo-shape and aerated with a series of round tunnels.*

> 1 lb (500 g) = 3 cups
> (750 mL) sliced

### If You Don't Have It
Substitute 1 cup (250 mL) chopped lotus root with:
- 1 cup (250 mL) chopped water chestnuts
- 1 cup (250 mL) chopped jicama
- 1 cup (250 mL) chopped sunchokes
- 1 cup (250 mL) chopped Asian radishes such as daikon (add a pinch of sugar to balance the peppery flavor)

## Lotus Seed

*Dried seeds of the lotus plant often stewed and mashed to make lotus seed paste for Chinese desserts (sweet bean paste makes a workable substitute for lotus bean paste). White peel lotus seeds are harvested while they are still green and have their shells and membranes removed. Brown peel seeds are harvested when ripe, retain their membrane, and are usually sold cracked.*

### If You Don't Have It
Substitute 1 cup (250 mL) lotus seeds with:
- 1 cup (250 mL) blanched almonds
- 1 cup (250 mL) blanched hazelnuts

## Loukanika

*This fresh Greek link sausage, made with lamb or pork, is flavored with orange zest.*

### If You Don't Have It
Substitute 1 lb (500 g) loukanika with:
- 1 lb (500 g) pork sausage + 1 to 2 tsp (5 to 10 mL) grated fresh orange zest

## Loukoumathes

*See* DOUGHNUT.

## Lovage

*Also known as céleri bâtard, smallage, and smellage. An extremely tall, leafy stalk that tastes like very strong celery. The stalks can be cooked as a vegetable; the leaves can season savory dishes.*

> 1 lb (500 g) stalk untrimmed = 2 cups (500 mL) sliced or diced

### If You Don't Have It
Substitute 1 tbsp (15 mL) chopped fresh lovage leaves with:
- 1 to 3 tbsp (15 to 45 mL) chopped fresh celery leaves
- ½ tbsp (7 mL) chopped fresh celery leaves + ½ tbsp (7 mL) chopped fresh parsley or chervil

### To Vary the Flavor
Substitute 1 cup (250 mL) chopped fresh lovage stalks with:
- 1 cup (250 mL) chopped fresh Chinese celery
- 1 cup (250 mL) chopped fresh celery stalks (milder flavor)

## Lovage Seed

*A rare spice closely related in appearance and aroma to celery seed.*

### If You Don't Have It
Substitute 1 tsp (5 mL) lovage seed with:
- 1 tsp (5 mL) celery seed
- 1 tsp (5 mL) ajwain
- 1 tsp (5 mL) caraway seed

## Lox

*See* SMOKED SALMON.

## Luffa, Angled

*Also known as angled loofa. A type of Asian bitter melon with ridged skin.*

1 lb (500 g) = 3 cups (750 mL) sliced

### If You Don't Have It
Substitute ½ cup (125 mL) chopped angled loofah with:
- ¼ cup (60 mL) chopped zucchini + ¼ cup (60 mL) chopped English cucumber
- ½ cup (125 mL) chopped zucchini

*See also* BITTER MELON.

## Luganega

*Also known as lucanica. Thin Italian pork sausage reputed to be most delicious when made in Lombardy. Often added to risotto.*

### If You Don't Have It
Substitute 1 lb (500 g) luganega with:
- 1 lb (500 g) mild Italian sausage

## Lumpfish Roe

*See* CHANGING ROE (PAGE 666).

## Lumpia Wrapper

*Thin pastry skin made of flour or cornstarch, eggs, and water. Encases savory fillings for the Filipino and Indonesian versions of egg rolls.*

### If You Don't Have It
Substitute 1 lb (500 g) lumpia wrappers with:
- 1 lb (500 g) lettuce leaves
- 1 lb (500 g) rice paper
- 1 lb (500 g) dumpling wrappers
- 1 lb (500 g) won ton skins (thicker)
- 1 lb (500 g) empanada wrappers (thicker)
- 1 lb (500 g) egg roll wrappers (thicker)
- 1 lb (500 g) rolled pasta

## Lupini Bean

*Also known as altramuz, tirmis, and tremmocos. Like soybeans, lupini beans are considered a "complete protein," containing a full range of essential amino acids.*

### If You Don't Have It
Substitute 1 cup (250 mL) shelled and peeled fresh lupini beans with:
- 1 cup (250 mL) fresh edamame (shelled green soybeans)
- 1 cup (250 mL) shelled and peeled fresh fava beans
- 1 cup (250 mL) fresh baby lima beans (sweeter)
- 1 cup (250 mL) chickpeas, red kidney beans, or cannellini beans (to replace dried lupini in soups and stews)

## Lychee

*See* LITCHI.

## Lyle's Golden Syrup

*See* GOLDEN SYRUP.

# Maasdam to Myzithra

## Maasdam

Also known as Leerdammer, the trademarked name for Maasdam, a young Dutch semifirm cow's milk cheese with a mild nutty taste and large holes.

> 4 oz (125 g) =
> 1 cup (250 mL) grated

### If You Don't Have It
Substitute 1 oz (30 g) Maasdam with:
- 1 oz (30 g) Emmental (slightly drier)
- 1 oz (30 g) Jarlsberg (slightly drier)
- 1 oz (30 g) Gruyère (drier)
- 1 oz (30 g) Swiss (drier)

## Mabolo

Also known as kamagong and velvet apple. Covered in rust-colored downy fuzz, the skins of these native Filipino fruits have a pungent aroma but the pink flesh inside tastes sweet, soft, and creamy.

### If You Don't Have It
Substitute 1 lb (500 g) mabolo with:
- 1 lb (500 g) ripe peaches
- 1 lb (500 g) ripe persimmons (more astringent)

## Macadamia Nut

A smooth, buttery nut that is indigenous to Australia but rose to prominence in Hawaii, where 90% of

### If You Don't Have It
Substitute 1 cup (250 mL) macadamia nuts with:
- 2 to 4 tbsp (30 to 60 mL) macadamia nut oil (for baking and cooking; will add nut flavor but not texture of whole nuts; reduce fat in recipe by 2 to 4 tbsp/30 to 60 mL)

## Macadamia Nut (cont'd)

*the world's crop is now harvested.*

5 oz (150 g) can =
1 cup (250 mL) whole

7 oz (210 g) jar =
1½ cups (375 mL) whole

- 1 cup (250 mL) candlenuts
- 1 cup (250 mL) Brazil nuts
- 1 cup (250 mL) chestnuts
- 1 cup (250 mL) cashews
- 1 cup (250 mL) almonds
- 1 cup (250 mL) pecans
- 1 cup (250 mL) walnuts

## Macaroni

*See* PASTA, DRIED SHAPES.

## Macaroon

*Thought to have originated in Venice around 1400, these cookies were traditionally prepared with ground almonds, sugar, and egg whites.*

### If You Don't Have It

Substitute 1 lb (500 g) macaroons with:
- 1 lb (500 g) amaretti (crisper; heavier)
- 1 lb (500 g) mandelbrot (crisper; heavier)
- 1 lb (500 g) almond or coconut biscotti (crisper; heavier)

## Mace

*A spunkier version of nutmeg, this spice is the dried, ground reddish skin that covers the nutmeg seed. Generally sold ground but sometimes the whole "blade" is available.*

1 oz (30 g) =
4½ tbsp (67 mL)

### If You Don't Have It

Substitute 1 tsp (5 mL) ground mace with:
- 1 tsp (5 mL) ground nutmeg (milder aroma)
- 1 tsp (5 mL) ground allspice
- 1 tsp (5 mL) apple pie spice (combination of cinnamon, nutmeg, and allspice)
- 1 tsp (5 mL) ground cinnamon

## Mâche

*Also known as corn salad, fetticus, field lettuce, field salad, and lamb's lettuce. This tender, sweet salad green, which forms multi-leafed sprigs, has nothing to do with corn or lambs. Highly regarded in Europe, mâche has become a chic lettuce in the United States.*

1 lb (500 g) =
6 cups (1.5 L) leaves

### If You Don't Have It

Substitute 1 lb (500 g) mâche with:
- 1 lb (500 g) leaf lettuce such as oak leaf or lollo rosso
- 1 lb (500 g) butterhead lettuce such as Bibb or Boston (generally larger, slightly thicker leaves)
- 1 lb (500 g) baby spinach leaves (adds slight bitterness)
- 1 lb (500 g) mild arugula (adds pepperiness)
- 1 lb (500 g) crisphead lettuce such as Great Lakes, Iceberg, Imperial, Vanguard, or Western (much larger leaves; crunchy; less flavorful)
- 1 lb (500 g) romaine lettuce (crunchy; more flavorful than crisphead lettuce)

## Mackerel

*A high-fat fish with firm texture and pronounced flavor. Includes Atlantic mackerel, chub (Pacific) mackerel, king mackerel (kingfish), Spanish mackerel, cero (painted mackerel), and wahoo (ono).*

### If You Don't Have It

Substitute 1 lb (500 g) fresh mackerel with:

- 1 lb (500 g) bluefish
- 1 lb (500 g) butterfish
- 1 lb (500 g) shad
- 1 lb (500 g) mahi-mahi
- 1 lb (500 g) pompano
- 1 lb (500 g) striped bass
- 1 lb (500 g) tuna

### To Vary the Flavor

Substitute 1 lb (500 g) fresh mackerel with:

- 1 lb (500 g) smoked mackerel (cured fish; adds smoke flavor)

## Madagascar Bean

*See* LIMA BEAN.

## Madeira

*Fortified wine produced on the Portuguese island of the same name. Distinctive and versatile, Madeira styles range in color from pale to tawny, in taste from dry to sweet, and in application from sipping to cooking.*

### If You Don't Have It

Substitute 3 tbsp (45 mL) Madeira with:

- 3 tbsp (45 mL) dry port
- 3 tbsp (45 mL) Marsala
- 3 tbsp (45 mL) dry vermouth
- 3 tbsp (45 mL) dry sherry

### Madeira Varieties

Choose 3 tbsp (45 mL) Madeira from these varieties:

- 3 tbsp (45 mL) Sercial (light and dry)
- 3 tbsp (45 mL) Verdelho (medium-dry to medium-sweet)
- 3 tbsp (45 mL) Boal or Bual (medium-sweet)
- 3 tbsp (45 mL) Malmsey or Malvasia (dark, sweet, rich)

## Madeleine Pan

*See* PAN SIZE EQUIVALENTS (PAGE 678).

## Maggi Seasoning

*A bottled condiment made from vegetable extract. It is used to enhance sauces, soups, and stews.*

### If You Don't Have It

Substitute 1 tbsp (15 mL) Maggi Seasoning with:

- 1 tbsp (15 mL) tamari (dark soy sauce)
- 1 tbsp (15 mL) soy sauce

## Maguey Leaf

*Also known as mixiote and penca. The tough, parchment-like outer skin of the leaves of the maguey or century plant (*Agave americana*) and the essential ingredient in Mexican mixiotes, little bundles of seasoned meat (often goat, lamb or chicken) wrapped in maguey leaves and pit-barbecued, roasted, or steamed.*

### If You Don't Have It
Substitute maguey leaves with:
- banana leaves
- avocado leaves
- parchment paper
- papel para mixiotes or plastic baggies + a wrapping of aluminum foil

## Mahi-Mahi

*Also known as dolphinfish and dorado. The Hawaiian name for a type of dolphin (not the familiar mammal!), this medium-fat, firm-fleshed fish is delicious grilled or broiled.*

### If You Don't Have It
Substitute 1 lb (500 g) mahi-mahi with:
- 1 lb (500 g) swordfish
- 1 lb (500 g) mako shark
- 1 lb (500 g) tuna
- 1 lb (500 g) pompano

## Mahlab

*Also spelled mahleb and mahlepi. The dried kernels of sour cherry pits popular in Middle Eastern breads and desserts for their floral, almond-like aroma. They release the most aroma when freshly ground.*

### If You Don't Have It
Substitute 1 tbsp (15 mL) freshly ground mahlab with:
- 1 tbsp (15 mL) blanched or roasted apricot kernels, freshly ground
- 1 tbsp (15 mL) blanched or roasted bitter almonds, freshly ground
- 1½ tsp (7 mL) tonka beans + 1½ tsp (7 mL) bitter almonds, freshly ground
- ⅛ tsp (0.5 mL) bitter almond oil or extract + ⅛ tsp (0.5 mL) cherry extract
- 1 tsp (5 mL) almond liqueur + 1 tsp (5 mL) kirsch or cherry liqueur

### To Vary the Flavor
- 1 tbsp (15 mL) freshly ground cardamom

## Mahón

*Unpasteurized cow's milk cheese from the Spanish island of Minorca. It has a hard orange rind with a cheesecloth mesh imprint and traditional cushion shape. Young mahón is sweet and fruity.*

1 lb (500 g) = 4 cups (1 L) shredded

### If You Don't Have It
Substitute 1 oz (30 g) Mahón cheese with:
- 1 oz (30 g) Gouda
- 1 oz (30 g) Edam
- 1 oz (30 g) Boerenkaas

## Mainz

*See* HANDKÄSE.

## Makrut Lime

*Also known as jeruk purut, kaffir lime and leech lime. The term "makrut lime" is preferred over "kaffir lime" because kaffir has a pejorative connotation. The leaves of this bitter citrus are irreplaceable in Southeast Asian cookery, but some passable alternatives are offered here. The distinctive figure-eight shape looks like two leaves joined at the stem end. The grated zest is also used in cooking.*

1 oz (30 g) fresh or frozen = about 75 leaves

### If You Don't Have It
Substitute 1 tbsp (15 mL) makrut (kaffir) lime zest with:
- 1 tbsp (15 mL) citron zest
- 1 tbsp (15 mL) lime zest
- 5 to 6 makrut (kaffir) lime leaves + 1 tbsp (15 mL) lime zest

### If You Don't Have It
Substitute 6 fresh or frozen makrut (kaffir) lime leaves with:
- 12 dried makrut (kaffir) lime leaves
- 1 tbsp (15 mL) makrut (kaffir) lime zest
- 1 tbsp (15 mL) citron zest
- 1 tbsp (15 mL) lime zest
- 1 tbsp (15 mL) lemon zest
- 1 to 3 tbsp (15 to 45 mL) fresh lemon verbena or lemon thyme

## Malabar Plum

*See* ROSE APPLE.

## Malabar Spinach

*See* BASELLA.

## Malagueta Chile

*See* CHOOSING FRESH CHILES (PAGE 640).

## Malanga

*See* YAUTÍA.

## Malay Gooseberry

*See* OTAHEITE GOOSEBERRY.

## Malibu Rum

*See* COCONUT RUM.

## Mallet

*A sturdy handle attached to a heavy metal plate that is sometimes ridged. Used to crush, grind, flatten, or tenderize foods.*

### If You Don't Have It
Substitute a mallet with:
- clean hammer
- rolling pin
- heavy skillet

## Malt Liquor

*See* BEER.

## Malt Syrup

*See* BARLEY MALT SYRUP.

## Malt Vinegar

*See* CHOOSING VINEGAR (PAGE 674).

## Malt Whiskey

*See* WHISKEY.

## Mamey Sapote

*Also known as mamee, mamey apple, and marmalade plum. A soft Caribbean fruit with a rough brown rind. The smooth reddish gold flesh tastes like a cross between apricots and almonds.*

> 1 medium = 12 oz (375 g)
> = ⅔ cup (150 mL) pulp

### If You Don't Have It
Substitute 1 cup (250 mL) chopped fresh mamey sapote with:
- 1 cup (250 mL) chopped white sapote

*See also* SAPOTE, WHITE.

## Manchego

*Cheese originally made only from the milk of the Manchego breed of sheep that grazed on the Spanish plains of La Mancha. Smooth, rich, and mellow, it is enjoyed as a table cheese when young* (curado) *and for grating when aged* (viejo).

> 1 lb (500 g) curado =
> 4 cups (1 L) shredded
>
> 4 oz (125 g) viejo =
> 1 cup (250 mL) grated

### If You Don't Have It
Substitute 1 oz (30 g) Manchego with:
- 1 oz (30 g) Roncal
- 1 oz (30 g) Zamorano
- 1 oz (30 g) Castellano
- 1 oz (30 g) Monterey Jack
- 1 oz (30 g) Cheddar
- 1 oz (30 g) Pecorino Romano (for grating)
- 1 oz (30 g) Parmigiano-Reggiano (for grating)
- 1 oz (30 g) Asiago (for grating)

## Mandarin Lime

*See* RANGPUR.

## Mandarin Liqueur

*Also known as crème de mandarin. Mandarin orange-flavored, sweetened spirits, or sometimes brandy, such as Belgian Mandarin Napolèon and South African Van der Hum.*

### If You Don't Have It
Substitute 3 tbsp (45 mL) with:
- 3 tbsp (45 mL) orange liqueur such as Grand Marnier, Cointreau, curaçao, or Triple Sec

## Mandarin Orange

*Also known as tangerine. Canned mandarin oranges are typically made with sweet, tropical-tasting satsuma mandarins.*

### If You Don't Have It
Substitute 1 mandarin orange with:
- ½ to 1 navel orange (orange flesh)
- ½ to 1 Moro or blood orange (red flesh; more tart; complex flavor)
- ½ to 1 Minneola tangelo (orange flesh; sweet-tart flavor with honey aromas)
- 1 Rangpur or mandarin lime (sweet-tart; complex mandarin and lime aromas)
- 1 calamondin (orange flesh; acidic)

### Mandarin Orange Varieties
Choose 1 mandarin orange from these varieties:
- 1 clementine (sweet; apricot aromas)
- 1 Dancy tangerine (sweet-tart; plum aromas)
- 1 honey tangerine (sweet and juicy; floral aromas)
- 1 satsuma (sweet; tropical aromas)
- 1 temple orange (most likely a hybrid of orange and mandarin; somewhat tart, orange-like aromas)

*See also* CALAMONDIN; TANGELO; UGLI FRUIT.

## Mandarin Pancake

*Chinese style wheat-flour crêpe used as a wrapper for Peking duck and other dishes.*

### If You Don't Have It
Substitute 1 lb (500 g) mandarin pancakes with:
- 1 lb (500 g) crêpes
- 1 lb (500 g) thin dumpling wrappers
- 1 lb (500 g) flour tortillas (thicker)

## Mandelbrot

*Sometimes dubbed "Jewish biscotti," these dry, crisp pastries are named for the German words* mandel *(almond) and* brot *(bread).*

### If You Don't Have It
Substitute 1 lb (500 g) mandelbrot with:
- 1 lb (500 g) amaretti (crisper)
- 1 lb (500 g) almond biscotti (crisper)
- 1 lb (500 g) almond macaroons (softer; lighter)

## Mandlen

*Also known as Passover crackers and soup nuts. Yiddish for "almond," mandlen are almond-shaped or round crackers often served with soups at Passover celebrations.*

### If You Don't Have It
Substitute 1 lb (500 g) mandlen with:
- 1 lb (500 g) farfel (small soup noodles or crushed matzo)
- 1 lb (500 g) matzo
- 1 lb (500 g) croutons

## Mandoline

*An indispensible kitchen tool for making quick, uniform, paper-thin slices. Professional models come with attachments for making waffle cuts, crinkle cuts, and juliennes of varying widths and thicknesses.*

### If You Don't Have It
Substitute a mandoline with:
- food processor fitted with the slicing disk (use light to no pressure when feeding food into the feed tube; difficult to do paper-thin slices)
- cheese slicer and light pressure (for smaller foods)
- vegetable peeler and light pressure (for smaller foods)
- thin-bladed, razor-sharp knife (and a steady hand)

## Mangetout

*See* PEAS, EDIBLE POD.

## Mango

*The American cooking teacher James Beard wrote, "… to most enjoy a mango one should probably eat it in a bathtub, or at the very least in private."*

> 1 mango = ¾ to 1 cup (175 to 250 mL) purée

### If You Don't Have It
Substitute 1 cup (250 mL) chopped fresh mango with:
- 1 cup (250 mL) chopped frozen mango

### To Vary the Flavor
Substitute 1 cup (250 mL) chopped fresh mango with:
- 1 cup (250 mL) chopped papaya
- 1 cup (250 mL) chopped peaches
- 1 cup (250 mL) chopped nectarines

## Mango Chutney

*See* CHUTNEY.

## Mango, Dried

*Freeze-dried mango pieces sometimes coated with sugar.*

### If You Don't Have It
Substitute 1 cup (250 mL) dried mango with:
- 1 cup (250 mL) dried papaya
- 1 cup (250 mL) dried peaches
- 1 cup (250 mL) dried nectarines
- 1 cup (250 mL) dried apricots
- 1 cup (250 mL) dried cantaloupe

*See also* MANGO POWDER.

## Mango Powder

*Also called amchur. Ground flesh of unripe sun-dried mango from northern India. Used as a souring agent.*

### If You Don't Have It

Substitute 1 tsp (5 mL) mango powder with:
- 1 tsp (5 mL) lemon juice or lime juice (for acidity)
- ½ to ¾ tsp (2 to 3 mL) tamarind concentrate or paste (for acidity)

*See also* MANGO, DRIED.

## Mangosteen

*This small fruit has a tough reddish purple rind that encloses white-skinned segments with the texture of ripened plums.*

### If You Don't Have It

Substitute 1 cup (250 mL) mangosteen segments with:
- 1 cup (250 mL) bacurí or bacuripari segments

## Mangosteen, Dried

*Ancient Chinese doctors sometimes prescribed dried and powdered mangosteen rind to alleviate dysentery. Today, dried mangosteen usually consists of the dried white pulp eaten as a snack for its citrusy, peachy taste.*

### If You Don't Have It

Substitute 1 cup (250 mL) dried mangosteen with:
- 1 cup (250 mL) dried peaches
- 1 cup (250 mL) dried nectarines
- 1 cup (250 mL) dried apricots

*See also* KOKUM.

## Manioc

*See* CASSAVA.

## Manouri

*Also known as manoypi. A rindless Greek cheese made either from sheep's or goat's milk. The cheese is white and creamy and has a fresh, dairy flavor with a hint of citrus.*

8 oz (250 g) =
1 cup (250 mL)

### If You Don't Have It

Substitute 1 oz (30 g) Manouri cheese with:
- 1 oz (30 g) feta (less creamy; rinse to reduce saltiness if you like)
- 1 oz (30 g) haloumi (may add mint flavor)
- 1 oz (30 g) ricotta salata (less creamy)

## Manteca

*See* LARD.

## Manzanilla

*See* SHERRY.

## Manzano Banana

*See* BANANA.

## Maotai

*See* BAIJIU.

## Mape

*Also known as Fiji, Polynesian or Tahitian chestnut. Popular in the Fiji islands, mape are typically eaten roasted and taste similar to Italian chestnuts.*

### If You Don't Have It

Substitute 1 cup (250 mL) shelled mape with:
- 1 cup (250 mL) shelled, canned, or jarred Italian chestnuts
- 1 cup (250 mL) chufa nuts
- 1 cup (250 mL) jackfruit seeds
- 1 cup (250 mL) macadamia nuts
- 1 cup (250 mL) hazelnuts

*See also* CHESTNUT.

## Maple Sugar

*Nearly twice as sweet as granulated sugar.*

### If You Don't Have It

Substitute 1 cup (250 mL) finely grated maple sugar with:
- 1 cup (250 mL) minus 3 tbsp (45 mL) granulated or light brown sugar + ⅓ cup (75 mL) maple syrup (reduce liquid in recipe by 3 to 4 tbsp/45 to 60 mL)
- 1 cup (250 mL) minus 3 tbsp (45 mL) granulated or light brown sugar + ¼ cup (60 mL) corn syrup + ¼ to ½ tsp (1 to 2 mL) pure maple extract (reduce liquid in recipe by 3 to 4 tbsp/45 to 60 mL)

*See also* MAPLE SYRUP.

## Maple Syrup

*The reduced sap of dormant sugar maple or black maple trees is North America's sweet gift to the world. It requires a remarkable 40 gallons (182 L) of sap to produce a single gallon (4.54 L) of the amber syrup. Quebec, Vermont, New York, and Ontario are the leading processors.*

> 16 fluid oz (454 mL) = 2 cups (500 mL)

### If You Don't Have It

Substitute 1 cup (250 mL) pure maple syrup with:
- 1¼ cups (300 mL) granulated sugar (for baking, increase liquid in recipe by ¼ cup/60 mL; add ¼ to ½ tsp/1 to 2 mL pure maple extract to add maple flavor if you like; reduce baking soda in recipe by heaping ¼ tsp/1 mL to balance acidity)
- 1 cup (250 mL) pancake syrup (corn syrup flavored with artificial maple flavor)
- 1 cup (250 mL) Swedish light syrup (ljus sirap)
- ¾ cup (175 mL) corn syrup + ¼ to ½ tsp (1 to 2 mL) maple extract (for pancakes, also add 3 tbsp/45 mL melted butter)
- 1 cup (250 mL) minus 3 tbsp (45 mL) light molasses
- 1 cup (250 mL) honey
- 1 cup (250 mL) brown rice syrup
- 1¼ cups (300 mL) barley malt syrup

### Maple Syrup Varieties

Choose 1 cup (250 mL) maple syrup from these grades:
- 1 cup (250 mL) Grade AA (light amber color; mild flavor)

- 1 cup (250 mL) Grade A (medium to dark amber color; gentle flavor)
- 1 cup (250 mL) Grade B (dark amber color; rich flavor)
- 1 cup (250 mL) Grade C (darkest amber color; strong flavor)

| | |
|---|---|
| **Mapuey** | *See* YAM. |
| **Maracuja** | *See* PASSION FRUIT. |
| **Marañon** | *See* CASHEW APPLE. |
| **Maraschino Cherry** | *See* CHERRY. |
| **Maraschino Liqueur** | *See* CHERRY LIQUEUR. |
| **Marc** | *See* GRAPPA. |

## Margarine

*Also known as oleo and oleomargarine. It is a culinary irony that a cheap fake butter was invented in France, the country whose classic cuisine is unimaginable without real butter. The developer named his solidified white mixture of beef fat, skimmed milk, and water after* margarites, *the Greek word for pearl. Most margarines are now made with vegetable oil, such as "soy margarine" made from soybean oil.*

1 lb (500 g) = 2 cups
(500 mL) = 4 sticks

1 stick = ¼ lb (125 g) =
½ cup (125 mL) =
8 tbsp (120 mL) =
¾ cup (175 mL) whipped

### If You Don't Have It

Substitute ½ cup (125 mL) unsalted margarine with:

- ½ cup (125 mL) salted margarine (decrease salt in recipe by ¼ tsp/1 mL)
- ½ cup (125 mL) butter (more flavorful; makes baked goods crisper)
- ½ cup (125 mL) European-style butter (lower moisture content; creates flakier pastries, crisper cookies, and creamier sauces)
- ¾ cup (175 mL) whipped butter (for spreading)

### To Vary the Flavor

Substitute ½ cup (125 mL) margarine with:

- ½ cup (125 mL) Homemade Flavored Butter: Stir ½ cup (125 mL) softened butter or margarine until smooth and mix in flavorings of choice. Reshape by rolling in plastic wrap if necessary. Garlic Butter: Mix together 1 minced garlic clove, ¼ tsp (1 mL) salt, and ¼ tsp (1 mL) ground black pepper. Herb Butter: Mix together ¼ cup (60 mL) chopped fresh herbs, 1½ tsp (7 mL) orange or lemon juice, ¼ tsp (1 mL) salt, and ¼ tsp (1 mL) ground black pepper. Citrus Butter: Mix together 1½ tsp (7 mL) grated lemon, lime or orange zest, 1½ tbsp (22 mL) lemon, lime or orange juice, ¼ tsp (1 mL) salt, and ¼ tsp (1 mL) ground black pepper.
- ½ cup (125 mL) Browned Butter: Melt ½ cup (125 mL) butter in small saucepan over medium heat and cook until

**Margarine (cont'd)**

golden brown or dark golden brown. Use like melted margarine or chill until firm and use like margarine

- 7 tbsp (105 mL) bacon or pork fat or ⅓ cup (75 mL) chicken or poultry fat (for sautéing, frying, and sauces)
- 7 tbsp (105 mL) shortening or lard (for pastry and baking; creates flakier pastry and crisper cookies because shortening and lard lack water; consider using half shortening or lard and half margarine or butter for flakiness and flavor)

### For Better Health
Substitute ½ cup (125 mL) margarine with:

- ½ cup (125 mL) reduced-fat margarine (fewer calories; more water; for spreading only; not for baking)
- ½ cup (125 mL) whipped margarine or margarine spread (fewer calories; more air; for spreading only; not for baking)
- ¼ cup (60 mL) margarine or buttermilk + ¼ cup (60 mL) well-drained, unsweetened applesauce or baby food prunes (for baking; applesauce works well with lighter-color or spice batters; puréed prunes work best with darker batters, such as chocolate; creates slightly chewier texture; use pastry or cake flour for lighter texture; increase sugar for more crispness)
- 3 tbsp (45 mL) margarine + 3 tbsp (45 mL) oil (for baking, especially cookie doughs; reduce baking time slightly; product will be slightly more chewy; use pastry or cake flour for lighter texture; increase sugar for more crispness)
- ½ cup (125 mL) apple butter (for baking; reduce baking time slightly; product will be slightly more chewy; use pastry or cake flour for lighter texture; adjust sugar if apple butter is sweetened)
- ½ cup (125 mL) fat-free, fruit-based butter and oil replacement such as Smucker's "Baking Healthy" (for baking only)
- ¼ cup (60 mL) fat-free, fruit-based butter and oil replacement such as Sunsweet "Lighter Bake" (for baking only)
- ½ cup (125 mL) marshmallow crème (for fillings and frostings)
- ½ cup (125 mL) oil (for sautéing and frying). Or use a mixture of margarine and oil. Or use a nonstick pan coated with cooking oil spray (or 1 to 2 tsp/5 to 10 mL oil or margarine) and heat the pan thoroughly

*See also* BUTTER; OIL; VEGETABLE SHORTENING.

**Marigold**

*See* PICKING EDIBLE FLOWERS (PAGE 650).

## Marinade

*A seasoned liquid in which various foods are soaked to absorb flavor or to tenderize them prior to cooking. Typical ingredients are oil, wine, citrus juice, vinegar, aromatics, herbs, and spices.*

### If You Don't Have It

Substitute 1 cup (250 mL) marinade with:
- 1 cup (250 mL) salad dressing or vinaigrette with similar flavors
- ½ cup (125 mL) spice rub with similar flavors (for flavoring meats; pat over entire surface)

## Marionberry

*Also known as Marion blackberry. Named after Marion County, Oregon, where it was developed, this blackberry variety is a cross between the Chehalem blackberry and olallieberry.*

> 1 pint fresh =
> 2 cups (500 mL)

### If You Don't Have It

Substitute 1 cup (250 mL) marionberries with:
- 1 cup (250 mL) blackberries (smaller)
- 1 cup (250 mL) loganberries (red color)
- 1 cup (250 mL) boysenberries (slightly sweeter)
- 1 cup (250 mL) olallieberries (sweeter)
- 1 cup (250 mL) raspberries (smaller; sweeter)

*See also OLALLIEBERRY.*

## Marjoram

*A distinctive, widely used culinary herb from the genus Origanum, of which four main species exist. One species, Origanum majorana, tastes similar to thyme, while the others have varying degrees of oregano flavor.*

> 1 oz (30 g) = 6 tbsp
> (90 mL) chopped

### If You Don't Have It

Substitute 1 tbsp (15 mL) chopped fresh marjoram with:
- 1 tsp (5 mL) dried marjoram

### To Vary the Flavor

Substitute 1 tbsp (15 mL) chopped fresh marjoram with:
- 2 to 3 tsp (10 to 15 mL) chopped fresh oregano
- 1 tbsp (15 mL) chopped fresh sweet basil
- 2 to 3 tsp (10 to 15 mL) chopped fresh thyme
- 1 tbsp (15 mL) chopped fresh summer savory
- 1 to 2 tsp (5 to 10 mL) chopped fresh sage
- 1 tsp (5 mL) dried Italian seasoning (adds oregano, thyme, and basil flavors)
- 1 tsp (5 mL) Herbes de Provence (adds other flavors such as thyme, savory, lavender, fennel, and bay leaf)

## Marlin

*Also known as kajiki and spearfish. The name for several large firm-flesh billfish pursued around the globe as a prized game catch.*

### If You Don't Have It

Substitute 1 lb (500 g) marlin with:
- 1 lb (500 g) swordfish
- 1 lb (500 g) mako shark
- 1 lb (500 g) tuna
- 1 lb (500 g) mahi-mahi

## Marmalade

*Citrus fruit preserve that includes strips of zest along with the fruit. Seville, or bitter, orange is the most common.*

### If You Don't Have It
Substitute 1 tbsp (15 mL) marmalade with:
- 1 tbsp (15 mL) chutney (more complex flavor; add sugar or honey to taste)
- 1 tbsp (15 mL) preserves or jam

## Marmalade Plum

*See* MAMEY SAPOTE.

## Maroilles

*Named after an abbey in northern France, this square, semisoft cheese has a piercing surface aroma that belies the rich, yellow cheese inside.*

### If You Don't Have It
Substitute 1 oz (30 g) Maroilles with:
- 1 oz (30 g) Gris de Lille
- 1 oz (30 g) Livarot
- 1 oz (30 g) Limburger
- 1 oz (30 g) Pont-l'Évêque
- 1 oz (30 g) Herve
- 1 oz (30 g) Liederkranz

## Marron

*See* CHESTNUT.

## Marrow Bean

*See* THE WIDE WORLD OF DRIED BEANS (PAGE 637).

## Marrow Squash

*See* ZUCCHINI.

## Marsala

*A Denominazione di Origine Controllata (DOC) fortified wine from Sicily enjoyed both for sipping and cooking. Marsala Fine and Superiore are made with sifone (sweet wine and alcohol) and/or vino cotto (reduced grape must) in varying percentages and a blend of red and white wines. Marsala Vergine or Solera is formulated like Spanish sherry, with a blend of aged wines from different barrels. Stravecchio is a Marsala Vergine aged for a decade in wooden barrels.*

### If You Don't Have It
Substitute 3 tbsp (45 mL) Marsala with:
- 3 tbsp (45 mL) Madeira
- 1 tbsp (15 mL) dry sherry + 1 tbsp (15 mL) sweet vermouth
- 3 tbsp (45 mL) dry sherry

## Marshmallow

*Originally a confection made by boiling the pulpy roots of the marsh mallow plant with sugar. Today's marshmallows are a combination of sugar, corn syrup, and gelatin.*

> 1 lb (500 g) =
> 4 cups (1 L) =
> 100 miniature marshmallows
>
> 1 large = 10 miniature

### If You Don't Have It

Substitute 8 to 10 regular marshmallows with:
- 1 cup (250 mL) mini-marshmallows
- ¾ cup (175 mL) marshmallow creme (sweeter; spreadable)

## Marshmallow Crème

*Also known as marshmallow cream. A convenient topping of whipped melted marshmallows, such as Marshmallow Fluff®.*

> 7.5 oz (225 g) jar =
> 2½ cups (625 mL)

### If You Don't Have It

Substitute 1 cup (250 mL) marshmallow crème with:
- 16 large or 160 miniature marshmallows + 2 tsp (10 mL) corn syrup, stirred until smooth in a double boiler or stainless-steel bowl over simmering water

## Marsh Rabbit

*See* MUSKRAT.

## Mary Ann Pan

*See* PAN SIZE EQUIVALENTS (PAGE 678).

## Marzipan

*A paste of ground almonds and sugar that has myriad confectionery uses in Europe, North Africa, the Middle East, India, and Mexico. It is a filling for yeast breads, cakes, petits fours, macaroons, and sweet meats. It is also an edible sculpting medium for pastry artists.*

> 7 oz (210 g) =
> ⅞ cup (220 mL)

### If You Don't Have It

Substitute 2½ cups (625 mL) marzipan with:
- 2 cups (500 mL) almond paste + 1 cup (250 mL) confectioner's (icing) sugar + 3 tbsp (45 mL) light corn syrup, combined with a pastry blender or kneaded together by hand until pliable

## Masa

Traditional Mexican dough for corn tortillas. It is prepared from dried corn kernels that are cooked and soaked overnight in limewater. The corn is then drained and ground.

1 lb (500 g) = 2 cups (500 mL)

### If You Don't Have It
Substitute 1 cup (250 mL) fresh masa with:
- 1 cup (250 mL) masa harina + 1 cup (250 mL) plus 3 tbsp (45 mL) hot water

See also MASA HARINA.

## Masa Harina

"Dough flour" made from dried masa is a convenient ingredient for preparing corn tortillas and other dishes.

1 lb (500 g) = 3 cups (750 mL)

### If You Don't Have It
Substitute 1 cup (250 mL) masa harina with:
- 1 cup (250 mL) prepared fresh masa
- 1 cup (250 mL) harinilla (masa harina made from blue corn)
- 1 cup (250 mL) corn flour (texture will be less appealing)

See also MASA.

## Masala

See CHAAT MASALA; GARAM MASALA; PANCH PHORAN; SAMBHAR MASALA.

## Mascarpone

Luscious Italian fresh, soft cow's milk cheese with only slightly less fat than butter. The finest is said to come from Lombardy and Emilia-Romagna.

8 oz (250 g) = 1 cup (250 mL)

### If You Don't Have It
Substitute 1 cup (250 mL) mascarpone cheese with:
- 1 cup (250 mL) crème fraîche
- ½ cup (125 mL) cream cheese + ½ cup (125 mL) sour cream, blended by hand or in a small food processor until smooth
- ¾ cup (175 mL) cream cheese + ¼ cup (60 mL) heavy or whipping cream (35% butterfat), blended by hand or in a small food processor until smooth
- ½ cup (125 mL) ricotta cheese + ½ cup (125 mL) heavy or whipping cream (35% butterfat), blended by hand or in a food processor until smooth

### For Better Health
Substitute 1 cup (250 mL) mascarpone cheese with:
- ½ cup (125 mL) mascarpone cheese + ½ cup (125 mL) Neufchâtel cheese

## Masticha

Greek brandy-based liqueur flavored with gum mastic, an amber-color plant resin that tastes of licorice. The island of Chios is the main producer.

### If You Don't Have It
Substitute 3 tbsp (45 mL) Masticha with:
- 3 tbsp (45 mL) ouzo
- 3 tbsp (45 mL) Metaxa
- 3 tbsp (45 mL) arak, sambuca, or other anise liqueur

## Matar Dal

*See* PEAS, SPLIT; SWITCHING LENTILS (PAGE 653).

## Matsutake Mushroom

*See* SHUFFLING MUSHROOMS (PAGE 654).

## Matzo

*Also known as matzoh. Cracker-like unleavened Jewish bread is traditionally eaten for Passover.*

### If You Don't Have It
Substitute 1 lb (500 g) matzo with:
- 1 lb (500 g) crisp lavash

*See also* MATZO MEAL.

## Matzo Meal

*Fine or medium-consistency crumbs made from crushing matzo. Matzo meal is a thickener, a breading agent, and an ingredient in many Jewish dishes, such as gefilte fish and matzo balls.*

> 1 cup (250 mL) =
> 3 crushed matzos

### If You Don't Have It
Substitute 1 cup (250 mL) matzo meal with:
- 3 matzos, crushed (in a food processor or using a bag and a rolling pin) to the texture of fine or medium-fine crumbs
- 1 cup (250 mL) cracker crumbs

### To Vary the Flavor
Substitute 1 cup (250 mL) matzo meal with:
- 1 cup (250 mL) plain dry bread crumbs
- 1 cup (250 mL) crushed melba toasts
- 1 cup (250 mL) crushed tortilla chips
- 1 cup (250 mL) crushed dry-bagged stuffing mix
- 1 cup (250 mL) crushed pretzels
- 1 cup (250 mL) crushed cornflakes
- 1 cup (250 mL) crushed potato chips

*See also* MATZO.

## Maui Onion

*See* ONION, SWEET.

## Mayonnaise

*New York delicatessen owner Richard Hellmann began mass-producing mayonnaise in 1912 from his wife, Nina's, recipe. The condiment was an immediate hit and was said to boost the popularity of coleslaw.*

> 32 oz (1 kg) jar =
> 4 cups (1 L)

### If You Don't Have It
Substitute 1 cup (250 mL) mayonnaise with:
- 1 cup (250 mL) Homemade Mayonnaise: Whisk together 1 egg yolk, 1 tbsp (15 mL) lemon juice, and ½ tsp (2 mL) salt using a whisk or in a food processor. While whisking or with the machine running, blend in ½ cup (125 mL) olive oil or vegetable oil in a thin steady stream until mixture is blended and thick. Makes about 1 cup (250 mL).
- 1 cup (250 mL) sour cream
- 1 cup (250 mL) yogurt
- 1 cup (250 mL) cottage cheese, puréed in a blender or small food processor
- ½ cup (125 mL) mayonnaise + ½ cup (125 mL) yogurt or sour cream

## Mayonnaise (cont'd)

## To Vary the Flavor

Substitute 1 cup (250 mL) mayonnaise with:

- 1 cup (250 mL) Homemade Aïoli: Make 1 cup (250 mL) Homemade Mayonnaise (above) or use store-bought, adding 2 minced garlic cloves or 2 to 4 tsp (10 to 20 mL) mashed roasted garlic along with the egg yolk and reducing lemon juice to 1 tsp (5 mL). Add salt to taste. Makes about 1 cup (250 mL).
- 1 cup (250 mL) Homemade Tartar Sauce: Make 1 cup (250 mL) Homemade Mayonnaise (above) or use store-bought, stirring in 3 tbsp (45 mL) minced cornichons, gherkins, or pickle relish, 1 tbsp (15 mL) minced scallions or shallots, and 1 tsp (5 mL) drained capers. Add salt to taste. Makes about 1 cup (250 mL).
- 1 cup (250 mL) Homemade Rouille: Make 1 cup (250 mL) Homemade Mayonnaise (above) or use store-bought, adding $\frac{1}{3}$ to $\frac{1}{2}$ cup (75 to 125 mL) roasted red bell peppers, 1 large garlic clove, and a pinch of cayenne pepper. Add salt to taste. Makes about 1 cup (250 mL).
- 1 cup (250 mL) Homemade Rémoulade: Make 1 cup (250 mL) Homemade Mayonnaise (above) or use store-bought, stirring in 1 tbsp (15 mL) minced cornichons, 1 tbsp (15 mL) drained capers, 1 tbsp (15 mL) chopped fresh parsley, $1\frac{1}{2}$ tsp (7 mL) chopped fresh tarragon, 1 tsp (5 mL) Dijon mustard, 1 minced garlic clove, and 1 finely chopped hard-boiled egg. Add salt to taste. Makes about 1 cup (250 mL).
- 1 cup (250 mL) Homemade Chipotle Mayonnaise: Make 1 cup (250 mL) Homemade Mayonnaise (left) or use store-bought, stirring in 2 to 3 tsp (10 to 15 mL) finely chopped canned chipotle peppers in adobo sauce. If you like, also stir in 1 tbsp (15 mL) lime juice, 1 tbsp (15 mL) chopped fresh cilantro, 1 to 2 tsp (5 to 10 mL) tomato purée, and $\frac{1}{2}$ tsp (2 mL) minced garlic. Add salt to taste. Makes about 1 cup (250 mL).

## For Better Health

Substitute 1 cup (250 mL) mayonnaise with:

- 1 cup (250 mL) Homemade Mayonnaise Substitute: Whisk together 1 tbsp (15 mL) cornstarch, $1\frac{1}{4}$ tsp (6 mL) mustard powder, 1 tsp (5 mL) honey, and $\frac{1}{2}$ tsp (2 mL) salt in a small saucepan. Gradually whisk in $\frac{3}{4}$ cup (175 mL) buttermilk and 1 egg. Cook over medium heat, whisking constantly, until thickened and bubbly, 3 to 5 minutes. Remove from heat and whisk in 3 tbsp (45 mL) lemon juice and 1 tbsp (15 mL) olive oil. Makes about 1 cup (250 mL).
- 1 cup (250 mL) reduced-fat mayonnaise
- $\frac{1}{2}$ cup (125 mL) reduced-fat mayonnaise + $\frac{1}{2}$ cup (125 mL) low-fat yogurt

## Maytag Blue

*An esteemed American cheese produced by heirs to the appliance company in Newton, Iowa.*

> 4 oz (125 g) = 1 cup (250 mL) crumbled

### If You Don't Have It

Substitute 1 oz (30 g) Maytag Blue cheese with:

- 1 oz (30 g) Roquefort
- 1 oz (30 g) Fourme d'Ambert
- 1 oz (30 g) Bleu d'Auvergne
- 1 oz (30 g) Bleu des Causses

## Measuring Cups

*See* VOLUME EQUIVALENTS (PAGE 682).

## Meat

*Originally, the edible portion of something. In the 1300s, meat began to refer only to the edible portion of animals.*

### For Better Health

Substitute 1 lb (500 g) meat with:

- 1 lb (500 g) tofu or vegetarian beef, pork, or poultry products (these generally have fewer calories)

*See also* BEEF; LAMB; PORK; VEAL.

## Meat Tenderizer, Powdered

*Sold in supermarkets, this white powder contains papain — an enzyme found in papaya that breaks down the fibers of meat — as well as salt, sweetener, and anti-caking agents.*

### If You Don't Have It

Substitute 1 cup (250 mL) powdered meat tenderizer with:

- 2 cups (500 mL) papaya or kiwi purée or juice (add to marinade or spread over surface of meat; marinate in refrigerator 30 minutes to 1 hour)

## Meat Thermometer

*See* THERMOMETER.

## Mei Yen Seasoning

*See* MONOSODIUM GLUTAMATE.

## Mekong Catfish

*See* CATFISH.

## Melano

*See* KIWANO.

## Melba Toast

*The great French chef Auguste Escoffier created this thin, dry toast to honor opera star Dame Nellie Melba.*

### If You Don't Have It

Substitute 16 Melba toasts with:

- 16 thinly cut crostini or bruschetta
- 16 bagel chips
- 16 crackers
- 16 zwieback

## Melegueta Pepper

*See* GRAINS OF PARADISE.

## Mellowfruit

*See* PEPINO.

## Melon

*See* SPECIFIC TYPES.

## Melon Pear

*See* PEPINO.

## Meloukhia

*See* JUTE LEAF.

## Membrillo

*See* DULCE DE MEMBRILLO; QUINCE.

## Menudo Mix

*Also known as menudo spices. The typical seasoning blend that flavors Mexican tripe stew.*

### If You Don't Have It

Substitute 1 tbsp (15 mL) menudo mix with:

- 1 tsp (5 mL) dried Mexican oregano + ½ tsp (2 mL) onion flakes + ¼ to ½ tsp (1 to 2 mL) garlic flakes + ½ tsp (2 mL) cumin seeds + ¼ to ½ tsp (1 to 2 mL) crushed red pepper flakes

## Merguez

*North African beef sausage spiced and colored red with fiery harissa. Often grilled or served as an accompaniment to couscous.*

### If You Don't Have It

Substitute 1 lb (500 g) merguez sausage with:

- 1 lb (500 g) chorizo
- 1 lb (500 g) andouille
- 1 lb (500 g) spicy kielbasa
- 1 lb (500 g) hot Italian sausage
- 1 lb (500 g) hot links

*See also* HARISSA.

## Meringue Powder

*Convenient, shelf-stable product made of dried egg whites, cornstarch, sugar, and cream of tartar. Can be used as an egg white substitute for meringues or other baked goods or to make confectionery icings.*

### If You Don't Have It

Substitute 1 tbsp (15 mL) meringue powder with:

- 1 tbsp (15 mL) powdered egg white
- 3 tbsp (45 mL) frozen and thawed egg white
- 1 large egg white (to replace reconstituted meringue powder when making meringue)

## Merken

*Also known as mapuche. Chilean spice mix that flavors everything from meat to eggs to soup.*

### If You Don't Have It

Substitute 1 tbsp (15 mL) merken with:
- 1 tbsp (15 mL) Homemade Merken: Combine 3 tbsp (45 mL) smoked ground red aji chile pepper, 2 tsp (10 mL) salt, 1 tsp (5 mL) ground coriander (preferably smoked), and ½ tsp (2 mL) ground cumin (optional). Makes about ¼ cup (60 mL).
- 2 tsp (10 mL) chipotle chile powder + ¾ tsp (3 mL) ground coriander + ¼ tsp (1 mL) salt

## Mescal

*See* TEQUILA.

## Mesclun

*Also known as gourmet salad mix and salad mix. The French word for an assortment of young salad greens.*

| 1 lb (500 g) = |
| 6 cups (1.5 L) |

### If You Don't Have It

Substitute 1 lb (500 g) mesclun with:
- 1 lb (500 g) Homemade Mesclun: Combine 4 oz (125 g) oak leaf lettuce, 2 oz (60 g) arugula, 2 oz (60 g) tatsoi, 2 oz (60 g) frisée, 2 oz (60 g) mizuna, 2 oz (60 g) radicchio, and 2 oz (60 g) mâche or dandelion greens. Makes about 1 pound (500 g).

## Metaxa

*A proprietary Greek spirit blended from aged brandy and sweet wine, and flavored with herbs and spices. The finest type, Metaxa Grande Fine, resembles Spanish Sherry.*

### If You Don't Have It

Substitute 3 tbsp (45 mL) Metaxa with:
- 3 tbsp (45 mL) cognac
- 3 tbsp (45 mL) Armagnac
- 3 tbsp (45 mL) sherry

## Methi

*See* FENUGREEK LEAF.

## Metric Conversion

*See* METRIC CONVERSIONS (PAGE 685).

## Mettwurst

*Also known as Schmierwurst. A spreadable smoked German sausage seasoned with coriander and white pepper.*

### If You Don't Have It

Substitute 1 lb (500 g) Mettwurst with:
- 1 lb (500 g) Teewurst (spicier)
- 1 lb (500 g) liverwurst
- 1 lb (500 g) Braunschweiger (smoked liverwurst)
- 1 lb (500 g) pâté

## Mexi-Bell Chile

*See* CHOOSING FRESH CHILES (PAGE 640).

| | |
|---|---|
| **Mexican Breadfruit** | *See* MONSTERA. |
| **Mexican Chocolate** | *See* CHOCOLATE, MEXICAN. |
| **Mexican Corn Truffle** | *See* HUITLACOCHE. |
| **Mexican Custard Apple** | *See* SAPOTE, WHITE. |
| **Mexican Green Tomato** | *See* TOMATILLO. |
| **Mexican Lime** | *See* LIME. |
| **Mexican Potato** | *See* JICAMA. |

## Meyer Lemon

*Not a true lemon, but believed to be a cross between a lemon and a mandarin orange. Meyer lemons have sweeter and more orange flesh and juice than the common Eureka and Lisbon lemons.*

1 medium Meyer lemon =
¼ to ⅓ cup
(60 to 75 mL) juice =
1 to 3 tbsp
(15 to 45 mL) zest

### If You Don't Have It
Substitute 1 Meyer lemon with:
- 1 large Eureka or Lisbon lemon (smaller; more acidic; add ¼ to ½ tsp/1 to 2 mL sugar if you like)
- ½ tsp (2 mL) orange (larger; sweeter)
- ¾ Eureka or Lisbon lemon + ¼ orange (to replace Meyer lemon juice)
- 1 lime (slightly smaller)
- 1 calamondin (hybrid of kumquat and mandarin orange)
- ¼ grapefruit (larger; sweeter)
- ¼ pummelo (larger; sweeter)

*See also* LEMON.

## Mezcal

*See* TEQUILA.

## Mezzaluna

*Also known as lunetta. Italian "half moon" shaped knife with handles at either end for rocking back and forth over food to chop it.*

### If You Don't Have It
Substitute a mezzaluna with:
- sharp chef's knife used with a rocking motion

## Microplane®

*See* GRATER.

## Microwave Oven

*About the size of a small refrigerator, the first microwave ovens for home use went on sale in 1947. Price: about $3,000.*

### If You Don't Have It

Substitute a microwave oven with:
- steamer (for steaming fish, vegetables, and other foods)
- saucepan and a gas or electric burner (for heating and reheating soups, sauces, and most other foods; add 30 to 50% more cooking time)
- double boiler (for melting chocolate)
- gas or electric oven (for melting chocolate and for cooking and reheating casseroles and other foods that may be cooked in a microwave oven; add 30 to 50% more cooking time)

## Midori

*Glowing green Japanese liqueur that tastes like very sweet honeydew melon.*

### If You Don't Have It

Substitute 3 tbsp (45 mL) midori with:
- 3 tbsp (45 mL) honeydew melon schnapps (less sweet)

### To Vary the Flavor

Substitute 3 tbsp (45 mL) midori with:
- 3 tbsp (45 mL) watermelon liqueur
- 3 tbsp (45 mL) orange liqueur
- 3 tbsp (45 mL) strawberry liqueur
- 3 tbsp (45 mL) raspberry liqueur

## Mielie-Meal

*See* CORNMEAL.

## Milk, Dry

*See* DRY MILK.

## Milk, Fat-Free

*Also known as skim milk and nonfat milk. Fat-free cow's milk can legally contain no more than 0.5% fat. One cup (250 mL) of fat-free milk contains 86 calories and 301 milligrams of calcium.*

### If You Don't Have It

Substitute 1 cup (250 mL) fat-free milk (less than 0.5% fat) with:
- 1/3 cup (75 mL) nonfat dry milk + 3/4 cup (175 mL) water
- 1/4 cup (60 mL) nonfat skim milk + 1 cup (250 mL) minus 3 tbsp (45 mL) water
- 1/2 cup (125 mL) evaporated skim milk + 1/2 cup (125 mL) water (adds slight caramelized flavor)

## Milk, Sour

*See* SOUR MILK.

## Milk, Whole

*Whole cow's milk contains about 3½% fat. Prior to the uniform practice of commercial homogenization that disperses and suspends the fat through the liquid milk, it was possible for the naked eye to see the milkfat rise to the top of a jar and form luscious, thick cream.*

1 quart = 4 cups (1 L)

## If You Don't Have It

Substitute 1 cup (250 mL) whole milk (3.5% fat) with:

- 1 cup (250 mL) minus 3 tbsp (45 mL) fat-free milk + 3 tbsp (45 mL) melted butter or margarine
- 10 tbsp (150 mL) fat-free milk + 6 tbsp (90 mL) half-and-half
- ¾ cup (175 mL) 2% milk + ¼ cup (60 mL) half-and-half
- 1 cup (250 mL) minus 1 tbsp (15 mL) half-and-half + 3 tbsp (45 mL) water (omit 1 tbsp/15 mL butter, shortening, or oil from recipe)
- ½ cup (125 mL) evaporated whole milk + ½ cup (125 mL) water (adds slight caramelized flavor)
- 1 cup (250 mL) minus 3 tbsp (45 mL) water + ¼ cup (60 mL) dry milk
- 1 cup (250 mL) minus 3 tbsp (45 mL) water + ¼ cup (60 mL) nonfat dry milk + 1 tbsp (15 mL) melted butter or margarine

## To Vary the Flavor

Substitute 1 cup (250 mL) whole milk (3.5% fat) with:

- 1 cup (250 mL) raw milk (more complex flavor; unpasteurized; adds beneficial enzymes)
- 1 cup (250 mL) buttermilk (more tangy; for baking, reduce baking powder in recipe by 2 tsp/10 mL and add ½ tsp/2 mL baking soda)
- 1 cup (250 mL) sour cream (more tangy; for baking, creates moister, more tender baked goods; reduce baking powder in recipe by 1 tsp/5 mL, reduce fat by 2 to 3 tbsp/30 to 45 mL, and add ½ tsp/2 mL baking soda)
- 1 cup (250 mL) fruit juice or potato water (for baking)

## For Better Health

Substitute 1 cup (250 mL) whole milk (3.5% fat) with:

- 1 cup (250 mL) acidophilus milk (cow's milk with added beneficial enzymes)
- 1 cup (250 mL) reduced-fat, low-fat, or fat-free milk (2%, 1%, or less than 0.5% fat; thinner consistency; yields less rich results)
- 1 cup (250 mL) lactose-free milk (for the lactose intolerant)
- 1 cup (250 mL) goat's milk (for the lactose intolerant; more tangy taste)
- 1 cup (250 mL) soy milk, rice milk, or almond milk (for the lactose intolerant or vegetarians; may be sweetened)
- 1 cup (250 mL) oat milk (for the lactose intolerant or vegetarians; may be sweetened)

*See also* BUTTERMILK; CREAM; EVAPORATED MILK; MILK, FAT-FREE; SOUR MILK; SWEETENED CONDENSED MILK.

## Millet

*A protein-rich grain that is a staple to nearly one-third of the people on Earth. The whole grains are boiled into hot cereals, simmered in pilafs and ground into flour.*

1 cup (250 mL) =
3½ cups (875 mL) cooked

### If You Don't Have It

Substitute 1 cup (250 mL) millet with:
- 1 cup (250 mL) quinoa
- 1 cup (250 mL) couscous (cooks more quickly)
- 1 cup (250 mL) bulgur
- 1 cup (250 mL) rice
- 1 cup (250 mL) kasha (roasted buckwheat groats; takes more time to cook)

*See also* CHOOSING AMONG WHOLE-GRAIN AND ALTERNATIVE FLOURS (PAGE 648).

## Millet Flour

*See* CHOOSING AMONG WHOLE-GRAIN AND ALTERNATIVE FLOURS (PAGE 648).

## Mimolette

*From the Lille region of France, a semihard golden unpasteurized cow's milk cheese with intense nutty flavor.*

1 lb (500 g) = 4 cups
(1 L) shredded

### If You Don't Have It

Substitute 1 oz (30 g) Mimolette cheese with:
- 1 oz (30 g) Edam
- 1 oz (30 g) Gouda
- 1 oz (30 g) mild Cheddar (to replace aged Mimolette)

## Mini Babybel Cheese

*See* BABYBEL CHEESE.

## Mint

*Also known as herba buena or yerba buena (in Spanish). Peppermint and spearmint may be the most commercially popular varieties, but more than 500 varieties of mint are believed to exist, including apple mint, chocolate mint, ginger mint, horsemint, lamb mint, lemon mint, orange mint, and pineapple mint.*

2 oz (60 g) = 1½ cups
(375 mL) chopped

### If You Don't Have It

Substitute 1 tbsp (15 mL) chopped fresh mint with:
- 1 tsp (5 mL) dried mint
- 1 tsp (5 mL) mint from herbal mint tea bag (will often be peppermint)
- ¼ to ½ tsp (1 to 2 mL) mint extract
- 1 drop oil of peppermint
- 1 to 3 tbsp (15 to 45 mL) crème de menthe (reduce liquid in recipe by 1 to 3 tbsp/15 to 45 mL if necessary; reduce sugar by 1 tsp/5 mL)
- 3 to 4 tbsp (45 to 60 mL) peppermint schnapps (reduce liquid in recipe by 3 to 4 tbsp/45 to 60 mL if necessary)
- 1 tbsp (15 mL) chopped fresh parsley (preferably, add a pinch of dried mint)
- 1 tbsp (15 mL) chopped fresh basil (works well in savory and sweet dishes)

## Mint (cont'd)

### Mint Varieties

Choose 1 tbsp (15 mL) chopped fresh mint from these varieties:

- 1 tbsp (15 mL) chopped fresh spearmint (gentle mint aroma)
- 1 tbsp (15 mL) chopped fresh peppermint (more assertive, peppery mint aroma)
- 1 tbsp (15 mL) chopped fresh pineapple or apple mint (gentle mint and green apple aromas)
- 1 tbsp (15 mL) chopped fresh lemon mint (gentle mint and citrus aromas)

*See also* OIL OF PEPPERMINT; VIETNAMESE MINT.

## Mint Chutney

*Just one of a kaleidoscope of Indian fresh piquant relishes, refreshing mint chutney goes well with biriani, dosas, and samosas.*

### If You Don't Have It

Substitute ½ cup (125 mL) mint chutney with:

- ½ cup (125 mL) Homemade Mint-Cilantro Chutney: Combine ¼ cup (60 mL) fresh mint leaves, ¼ cup (60 mL) fresh cilantro leaves, 3 tbsp (45 mL) coarsely chopped onion, 3 tbsp (45 mL) water, 1 tbsp (15 mL) lime juice, 1 tsp (5 mL) granulated sugar, ⅛ tsp (0.5 mL) salt, and a pinch of cayenne pepper in a small food processor or blender. Makes about ½ cup (125 mL).

## Mint Extract

*A blend of oil of peppermint, oil of spearmint, alcohol, and water, used to flavor candies, frostings, cakes, and cookies.*

### If You Don't Have It

Substitute ½ tsp (2 mL) mint extract with:

- ⅛ tsp (0.5 mL) oil of peppermint

## Mint Oil

*See* OIL OF PEPPERMINT.

## Mint Sauce

*The classic British accompaniment to roast lamb. The properties in mint that aid digestion help to counteract the fatty meat.*

### If You Don't Have It

Substitute 1 cup (250 mL) mint sauce with:

- ½ cup (125 mL) Homemade Mint Sauce: Mix together 1¼ cups (300 mL) apple cider vinegar (or white wine vinegar), ¼ cup (60 mL) water, and 3 tbsp (45 mL) light brown sugar in a saucepan. Bring just to a simmer over medium heat. Remove from heat and stir in ¼ cup (60 mL) minced fresh mint. Let cool to room temperature. Cover and refrigerate for up to 2 days. Makes about 1½ cups (375 mL).

## Mirabelle

*See* PLUM; PLUM BRANDY.

## Mirasol Chile

*See* CHOOSING FRESH CHILES (PAGE 640).

## Mirin

*Also known as Japanese sweet rice wine. Used in Japanese cooking to flavor sauces, glazes, and other dishes. Sold in many supermarkets.*

### If You Don't Have It
Substitute ½ cup (125 mL) mirin with:
- 1½ to 2 tbsp (22 to 30 mL) sugar dissolved in ½ cup (125 mL) dry sherry, vermouth, white wine, or sake
- ½ cup (125 mL) amontillado sherry

## Mirliton

*See* CHAYOTE.

## Miso

*Fermented soybean paste with the addition of barley, rice, or rye. Created in China, miso is now mostly associated with Japanese cuisine, in which it is used to make broths, soups, salad dressings, sauces, pickles, and more.*

> 5 oz (150 g) =
> ½ cup (125 mL)

### If You Don't Have It
Substitute 1 tbsp (15 mL) miso with:
- 1 tbsp (15 mL) Chinese sweet bean paste
- 1 tsp (5 mL) soy sauce
- 2 tsp (10 mL) anchovy paste + ⅛ to ¼ tsp (0.5 to 1 mL) sugar (adds fish flavor)
- ¼ to ½ tsp (1 to 2 mL) salt (less complex flavor)
- 1 tbsp (15 mL) Hoisin sauce (much sweeter; more complex flavors)
- 1 tbsp (15 mL) umeboshi paste (more sour and pungent)

### Miso Varieties
Choose 1 tbsp (15 mL) miso from these varieties:
- 1 tbsp (15 mL) white or shiro miso (pale yellow color; very mild, salty-sweet flavor)
- 1 tbsp (15 mL) yellow or shinshu miso (golden yellow color; mellow salty flavor)
- 1 tbsp (15 mL) barley or mugi miso (reddish brown color; pronounced salty-sweet flavor)
- 2 to 3 tsp (10 to 15 mL) red or sendai miso (reddish yellow color; pronounced salty and pungent flavor)
- 2 to 3 tsp (10 to 15 mL) dark or hatcho miso (reddish brown color; thicker; very strong salty and pungent flavor)

## Mitmita

*Ethiopia's hottest and reddest spice blend consists of ground African bird's eye chile, cardamom, cloves, and salt, sometimes with the addition of cinnamon, cumin, coriander, and/or ginger. It seasons kitfo, a minced raw beef dish, and rests on tables to season vegetables and injera (flatbread).*

### If You Don't Have It
Substitute 1 tbsp (15 mL) mitmita with:
- 1 tbsp (15 mL) Homemade Mitmita: Combine 2 tbsp (30 mL) ground dried African bird's eye, piri-piri, or malagueta chile (or cayenne) with 2½ tsp (12 mL) salt, 1 tsp (5 mL) ground cardamom, and ⅛ tsp (0.5 mL) ground cloves. If you like, add ¼ tsp (1 mL) ground coriander, ¼ tsp (1 mL) ground cumin, and ⅛ tsp (0.5 mL) ground cinnamon or allspice. Makes about 3 tablespoons (45 mL).
- 1 tbsp (15 mL) berbere (less heat)
- 1 tbsp (15 mL) harissa

## Mitsuba

*Also known as honeywort, trefoil, Japanese chervil, and Japanese wild parsley. Mitsuba means "three leaves," and refers to this herb's three-part leaf shape, a remarkable doppleganger for Italian flat-leaf parsley. The flavor combines aromas of angelica, celery, and parsley; and the herb is used in three primary ways: for clear soups (called ito-mitsuba); blanched and chilled as an appetizer (nemitsuba, which has the most intense aroma); and for garnishing (kiri-mitsuba, the mildest flavor).*

### If You Don't Have It
Substitute 1 tbsp (15 mL) fresh mitsuba leaves with:
- 1 tsp (5 mL) celery leaves + 1 tsp (5 mL) angelica leaves + 1 tsp (5 mL) parsley leaves

### To Vary the Flavor
Substitute 1 tbsp (15 mL) fresh mitsuba leaves with:
- 1 tbsp (15 mL) watercress
- 1 tbsp (15 mL) chopped sorrel

## Mixed Spice

*Also known as British mixed spice and pudding spice. An English baking standard used to season a variety of desserts and baked goods.*

### If You Don't Have It
Substitute 1 tsp (5 mL) mixed spice with:
- 1 tsp (5 mL) Homemade Mixed Spice: Combine 4 tsp (20 mL) ground cinnamon, 2 tsp (10 mL) ground coriander, (optional), 1 tsp (5 mL) ground allspice, ½ tsp (2 mL) ground nutmeg, ½ tsp (2 mL) ground ginger, and ¼ tsp (1 mL) ground cloves. Makes about 2½ tablespoons (37 mL).
- 1 tsp (5 mL) pumpkin pie spice
- 1 tsp (5 mL) apple pie spice

## Mixer, Electric

*Tools that beat, mix, or whip foods. Stationary mixers are powerful and come with attachments, such as dough hooks, meat grinders, or ice crushers that expand their utility. Portable mixers are smaller, lighter, and easier to store.*

### If You Don't Have It
Substitute an electric mixer with:
- rotary beater
- whisk

## Mixiote

*See* MAGUEY LEAF.

## Miyoga

*Pinkish white bullet-shaped flower buds of wild ginger with a crunchy texture and mildly bitter ginger taste and floral aroma. Often used as winter vegetable in Japanese soups and salads.*

### If You Don't Have It

Substitute 1 cup (250 mL) miyoga with:
- 1 cup (250 mL) wild ginger buds (a related flower)
- 1 cup (250 mL) minced green or young ginger (no crunchy texture; less complex aroma)

*See also* GINGER, WILD BUD.

## Mizithra

*See* MYZITHRA.

## Mizuna

*Also known as kyona. Of Chinese origin, this mustardy-cabbagey incised-leaf green is beloved in Japan. Use younger leaves in salads and mature leaves for cooking.*

### If You Don't Have It

Substitute 1 cup (250 mL) mizuna with:
- 1 cup (250 mL) tender mustard greens
- 1 cup (250 mL) tatsoi
- 1 cup (250 mL) tender arugula
- 1 cup (250 mL) mibuna (longer, smooth, slender leaves; more mild flavor)
- 1 cup (250 mL) komatsuna or tendergreen (longer, broader leaves; milder flavor similar to young spinach)

## Mochi

*See* VARIETIES OF RICE (PAGE 664).

## Mochiko

*See* RICE FLOUR, SWEET.

## Modified Cornstarch

*See* CLEAR JEL.

## Molasses

*Most supermarkets sell unsulfured molasses, which has a lighter, cleaner taste than sulfured molasses, which is processed with sulfur dioxide as a preservative.*

> 8 oz (250 g) =
> 1 cup (250 mL)

### If You Don't Have It

Substitute 1 cup (250 mL) molasses with:
- 1 cup (250 mL) honey, dark corn syrup, or maple syrup
- ¾ cup (175 mL) light or dark brown sugar dissolved in ¼ cup (60 mL) hot water or liquid in recipe
- ¾ cup (175 mL) granulated sugar dissolved in ¼ cup (60 mL) hot water or liquid in recipe + 1¼ tsp (6 mL) cream of tartar (for baking; cream of tartar adds acidity present in molasses)
- 1 cup (250 mL) golden syrup (much lighter in flavor)
- 2 cups (500 mL) brown rice syrup (reduce liquid in recipe by 1 cup/250 mL if necessary)
- 1¾ cups (425 mL) barley malt syrup (reduce liquid in recipe by ¾ cup/175 mL if necessary)

## Molasses (cont'd)

### Molasses Varieties

Choose 1 cup (250 mL) molasses from these varieties:

- 1 cup (250 mL) dark molasses (often used in American baked goods; dark brown, thick, mildly sweet)
- 1 cup (250 mL) light or Barbardos molasses (often used like pancake syrup; lighter brown color and milder, sweeter flavor than dark molasses)
- 1 cup (250 mL) blackstrap molasses (used less often in cooking; slightly higher in nutrients; very dark brown to black; thicker; more bitter flavor)

## Molcajete y Tejolote

*See* MORTAR AND PESTLE

## Mold

*See* PAN SIZE EQUIVALENTS (PAGE 678).

## Monkey Peach

*See* KIWIFRUIT.

## Monkfish

*Also known as anglerfish, bellyfish, frogfish, goosefish, lotte, and sea devil. A firm-fleshed, low-fat fish with a sweet, mild flavor that is, optimistically, compared to lobster.*

### If You Don't Have It

Substitute 1 lb (500 g) monkfish with:

- 1 lb (500 g) blackfish
- 1 lb (500 g) lobster
- 1 lb (500 g) carp
- 1 lb (500 g) grouper
- 1 lb (500 g) red snapper
- 1 lb (500 g) tilefish
- 1 lb (500 g) wolffish

## Monkfish Liver

*Also known as ankimo, foie de lotte and monkfish foie gras. Remarkably similar to the pale pink-orange color, rich texture and earthy flavor of foie gras, this Japanese delicacy is traditionally steamed and served with ponzu sauce. It's equally delicious poached and pan-seared.*

### If You Don't Have It

Substitute 1 lb (500 g) monkfish liver with:

- 1 lb (500 g) foie gras
- 1 lb (500 g) Pâté de foie gras
- 1 lb (500 g) cod liver

## Monosodium Glutamate

*Also known as MSG. Commercially available as Accent, Mei Yen Seasoning, aji-no-moto, Ve-Tsin, and other products. Identified by Japanese scientists in the 1920s, MSG is a white powder derived from glutamic acid found in seaweed, certain vegetables, and other plants. It is flavorless in itself but acts to intensify the flavor of other foods.*

### If You Don't Have It
Substitute 1 tsp (5 mL) monosodium glutamate with:
- 1 to 2 tsp (5 to 10 mL) powdered dulse (a sea vegetable)

## Monstera

*Also known as ceriman, Mexican breadfruit, and Swiss cheese plant. It takes a year for monstera to ripen, during which time it increasingly resembles a large ear of corn covered with green hexagonal scales that eventually bulge and separate. When fully ripe, its toxic oxalic acid content reduces to safe levels and the kernels may be scraped away, revealing inner fruit with lush tropical aromas calling to mind bananas and pineapple.*

### If You Don't Have It
Substitute 1 lb (500 g) monstera with:
- 1 lb (500 g) jackfruit
- 8 oz (250 g) pineapple + 8 oz (250 g) bananas

## Montasio

*Cow's milk cheese from northeastern Italy's Friuli-Venezia Giulia region is used to make* frico, *the regional specialty fried cheese.*

1 lb (500 g) = 4 cups (1 L) shredded

### If You Don't Have It
Substitute 1 oz (30 g) Montasio cheese with:
- 1 oz (30 g) Carnia
- 1 oz (30 g) medium-ripe Asiago (less complex flavor)

## Montbriac

*Also known as Rochebaron. Imagine crumbly Roquefort and oozy Brie in a single cheese. Made in the Auvergne region of France, Montbriac is a soft pasteurized cow's milk cheese speckled with blue Penicillium roqueforti mold. Inside its blue-gray ash, Montbriac hints at mushroom, celery, and garlic and becomes deliciously runny when ripe.*

### If You Don't Have It
Substitute 1 oz (30 g) Montbriac with:
- 1 oz (30 g) blue Brie such as Cambozola
- 1 oz (30 g) Bleu de Bresse
- 1 oz (30 g) Blue Castello

## Monterey Jack

*See* JACK CHEESE.

## Montrachet

*Ash-coated logs of tangy chèvre from French Burgundy. At its best when young and fresh.*

8 oz (250 g) =
1 cup (250 mL)

### If You Don't Have It
Substitute 1 oz (30 g) Montrachet with:
- 1 oz (30 g) Crottin de Chavignol (soft to firm texture and mild to nutty flavor, depending on age)
- 1 oz (30 g) Selles-sur-Cher (semifirm texture; sweet, nutty flavor; covered with black ash)
- 1 oz (30 g) Bûcheron (softer texture; usually covered with black ash or a white rind)
- 1 oz (30 g) Banon (softer texture; wrapped in chestnut leaves)
- 1 oz (30 g) aged chèvre (firmer texture; stronger flavor)

### To Vary the Flavor
Substitute 1 oz (30 g) Montrachet with:
- 1 oz (30 g) mascarpone (smoother; less complex flavor)
- 1 oz (30 g) cream cheese (smoother; less complex flavor)

*See also* CHÈVRE.

## Moonshine

*See* WHISKEY.

## Moose

*A large North American member of the deer family — the counterpart of the European elk — that can*

### If You Don't Have It
Substitute 1 lb (500 g) moose with:
- 1 lb (500 g) elk
- 1 lb (500 g) caribou
- 1 lb (500 g) red, fallow, or white-tailed deer

*weigh up to 1,300 pounds (650 kg). Moose is valued for its meat, and, according to one Inuit chronicler, the nose is the tastiest morsel.*

- 1 lb (500 g) reindeer
- 1 lb (500 g) antelope
- 1 lb (500 g) gazelle

*See also* VENISON.

## Mora Chile

*See* CHOOSING DRIED CHILES (PAGE 642).

## Morbier

*A French semisoft, raw unpasteurized cow's milk cheese. The pale yellow paste is divided into two layers by a thin flavorless layer of ash. One layer is the cheese from the morning milking and the other from the evening milking.*

### If You Don't Have It

Substitute 1 oz (30 g) Morbier with:

- 1 oz (30 g) Fontina
- 1 oz (30 g) Vacherin Fribourgeois
- 1 oz (30 g) Raclette

## Morcilla

*This blood sausage is a required ingredient in Fabada Asturiana, the famous bean stew of northwest Spain.*

### If You Don't Have It

Substitute 1 lb (500 g) Morcilla with:

- 1 lb (500 g) Blutwurst (German blood sausage)
- 1 lb (500 g) boudin rouge (Cajun blood sausage)
- 1 lb (500 g) Zungenwurst (German blood sausage; includes tongue)

## Morel

*See* SHUFFLING MUSHROOMS (PAGE 654).

## Morello Cherry

*See* CHERRY.

## Moringa

*See* DRUMSTICK.

## Morita Chile

*See* CHOOSING DRIED CHILES (PAGE 642).

## Mörk Sirap

*See* SWEDISH SYRUP.

## Mornay Sauce

*See* BÉCHAMEL.

## Moro

*See* ORANGE, BLOOD.

## Mortadella

*This signature sausage from Bologna is composed*

### If You Don't Have It

Substitute 1 lb (500 g) mortadella with:

- 1 lb (500 g) bologna (less complex flavor)

## Mortadella (cont'd)

*of finely ground pork, studded with bits of fat, peppercorns, and pistachios. Some mortadella sausages can weigh as much as 180 pounds (90 kg).*

- 1 lb (500 g) galantina (chunkier; more complex flavor)
- 1 lb (500 g) olive loaf (adds olive flavor)
- 1 lb (500 g) semidry or summer sausage such as Thuringer, Landjäger, or Lebanon bologna

### For Better Health
Substitute 1 lb (500 g) mortadella with:
- 1 lb (500 g) Gelbwurst (lower in fat and calories)

## Mortar and Pestle

*A combination tool used to grind and mix various foods. The mortar is shaped like a bowl, the pestle fashioned like a thick stick with a rounded end that conforms to the bowl. Can be made of porcelain, wood, stone, marble, or other hard materials. In Mexico, the term for mortar and pestle is molcajete y tejolote.*

### If You Don't Have It
Substitute a mortar and pestle with:
- coffee or spice grinder (for finely grinding small amounts of dry ingredients such as spices)
- rolling pin or heavy skillet (for coarsely crushing)
- food processor (for crushing larger amounts or wet ingredients such as in pesto)

## Mostarda

*Italian condiment of sugar-saturated fruit flavored with mustard essence.*

### If You Don't Have It
Substitute 1 cup (250 mL) mostarda with:
- 1 cup (250 mL) candied fruit + 3 drops mustard essence (or 1½ tsp/7 mL pure mustard oil or ½ tsp/2 mL mustard powder)
- 1 cup (250 mL) glacé fruit + 3 drops mustard essence (or 1½ tsp/7 mL pure mustard oil or ½ tsp/2 mL mustard powder)

## Mouli Grater

*See* GRATER.

## Mountain Cranberry

*See* LINGONBERRY.

## Mountain Pepper

*See* TASMANIAN PEPPER.

## Mozzarella

*Low-moisture mozzarella cheese is typically used in Italian-American cooking.*

### If You Don't Have It
Substitute 1 oz (30 g) mozzarella with:
- 1 oz (30 g) Scamorza
- 1 oz (30 g) Caciocavallo

*High-moisture mozzarella is often served fresh or used in traditional Italian cooking. Bocconcini are "little mouthfuls" of high-moisture mozzarella (the size of ping-pong balls) floating in whey.*

1 lb (500 g) low-moisture mozzarella = 4 cups (1 L) shredded

- 1 oz (30 g) provolone
- 1 oz (30 g) string cheese
- 1 oz (30 g) queso blanco
- 1 oz (30 g) Bel Paese
- 1 oz (30 g) Muenster
- 1 oz (30 g) Gouda
- 1 oz (30 g) Fontina

## Mozzarella Varieties

Choose 1 oz (30 g) mozzarella from these varieties:
- 1 oz (30 g) burrata (creamy, oozy center made from mozzarella and fresh cream)
- 1 oz (30 g) mozzarella di buffalo (sweeter, moister, more complex taste than cow's milk mozzarella)
- 1 oz (30 g) smoked mozzarella (adds smoke flavor)

*See also* BURRATA.

## Muenster

*Also known as Munster. True French Muenster is a soft, yellow pungent cow's milk cheese with an orange rind. It is one of only a few cheeses to ripen from the inside out. American and other versions are white and mild.*

1 lb (500 g) = 4 cups (1 L) shredded

### If You Don't Have It

Substitute 1 oz (30 g) Muenster cheese with:
- 1 oz (30 g) Beaumont
- 1 oz (30 g) Reblochon
- 1 oz (30 g) Monterey Jack
- 1 oz (30 g) mozzarella
- 1 oz (30 g) Gouda
- 1 oz (30 g) Havarti
- 1 oz (30 g) Bel Paese
- 1 oz (30 g) Fontina

## Muesli

*Swiss nutritionist Dr. Bircher-Benner created this healthful "mixture" in the late 1800s. Typical ingredients include raw or toasted grains, such as oats, wheat, millet, and barley, mixed with various dried fruits, nuts, bran, wheat germ, and honey or sugar.*

### If You Don't Have It

Substitute 1 cup (250 mL) muesli with:
- 1 cup (250 mL) granola (very similar)

## Muffin Pan

*See* PAN SIZE EQUIVALENTS (PAGE 678).

## Mulato Chile

*See* CHOOSING DRIED CHILES (PAGE 642).

## Mulberry

The black mulberry is the species most often grown for its fruit. Although to the casual eye it looks like a blackberry, it is actually a sorosis like the pineapple. The fruit forms a cluster of small berries, each with surface lobes that are formed from one of a cluster of flowers.

> 1 pint fresh =
> 2 cups (500 mL)

### If You Don't Have It
Substitute 1 cup (250 mL) mulberries with:
- 1 cup (250 mL) blackberries (smaller; firmer)
- 1 cup (250 mL) loganberries (smaller; red color)
- 1 cup (250 mL) boysenberries (smaller; slightly sweeter)
- 1 cup (250 mL) olallieberries (sweeter)
- 1 cup (250 mL) raspberries (smaller; red color; sweeter)

## Mulberry, Dried

High in the cancer-fighting antioxidant, resveratrol, dried white mulberries are the size of large raisins and have a crunchy texture similar to dried figs.

### If You Don't Have It
Substitute 1 cup (250 mL) dried mulberries with:
- 1 cup (250 mL) golden raisins
- 1 cup (250 mL) dried figs

## Mullet

Also known as silver mullet and striped (black) mullet. Members of the gray mullet family are fairly fat, with firm flesh, and pleasantly nutty taste.

### If You Don't Have It
Substitute 1 lb (500 g) mullet with:
- 1 lb (500 g) sea bass
- 1 lb (500 g) ocean perch
- 1 lb (500 g) grouper
- 1 lb (500 g) orange roughy

*See also* RED MULLET.

## Mulling Spice Mix

A combination of various flavorings, such as herbs, spices, dried fruit, and sugar, which impart a warm and complex flavor when heated with beer, cider, wine, or other beverages.

### If You Don't Have It
Substitute 1 tsp (5 mL) ground mulling spice mix with:
- 1 tsp (5 mL) Homemade Mulling Spice Mix: Combine 1 to 2 three-inch (7.5 cm) cinnamon sticks (or $\frac{1}{2}$ to 1 tsp/2 to 5 mL ground cinnamon) + 2 to 4 whole cloves (or a big pinch of ground cloves) + 2 to 4 whole allspice berries (or a big pinch of ground allspice) + 1 sliced orange. If using ground spices, tie them in cheesecloth or a coffee filter with kitchen string or a clean twist-tie. Makes enough to mull 3 cups (750 mL) cider or red wine.

## Mulukhiyya

*See* JUTE LEAF.

## Mung Bean

*See* THE WIDE WORLD OF DRIED BEANS (PAGE 637).

## Mung Bean Noodles

*See* A SNAPSHOT OF ASIAN NOODLES (PAGE 656).

## Mung Bean Sprouts

*Germinated mung beans are widely used in the Chinese kitchen for salads and stir-fried dishes. Crisp fresh bean sprouts may be refrigerated in a plastic bag for up to a week.*

> 1 lb (500 g) = 1 quart =
> 4 cups (1 L)

### If You Don't Have It
Substitute 1 cup (250 mL) mung bean sprouts with:
- 1 cup (250 mL) sunflower sprouts
- 1 cup (250 mL) pea shoots
- 1 cup (250 mL) julienned snow peas
- 1 cup (250 mL) soybean sprouts

## Munster

*See* MUENSTER.

## Muscadine Grape

*See* GRAPE, TABLE; MUSCADINE JELLY.

## Muscadine Jelly

*A preserve made from a grape native to the southeastern United States. The musky-tasting purple grapes are also used to make scuppernong wine.*

### If You Don't Have It
Substitute 1 cup (250 mL) scuppernong or muscadine jelly with:
- 1 cup (250 mL) red currant jelly
- 1 cup (250 mL) grape jelly

## Muscovado Sugar

*See* SUGAR, RAW.

## Mushrooms, Dried

*Drying is an excellent method of keeping many mushrooms. Most dried mushrooms have a much more intense flavor than their fresh counterparts.*

> 2 to 3 oz (60 to 90 g)
> dried and reconstituted
> = 1 lb (500 g) fresh

### If You Don't Have It
Substitute 1½ oz (45 g) dried mushrooms with:
- 8 oz (250 g) sliced fresh mushrooms
- 4 oz (125 g) drained canned sliced mushrooms

*See also* SHUFFLING MUSHROOMS (PAGE 654).

## Mushrooms, Fresh

*Cooks often say to clean mushrooms by dry wiping because they soak up water during rinsing. Scientist Harold McGee refuted that theory and recommends rinsing.*

1 lb (500 g) fresh =
5 cups (1.25 L) sliced =
6 cups (1.5 L) chopped =
2 cups (500 mL) cooked

### If You Don't Have It

Substitute 8 oz (250 g) sliced fresh mushrooms with:

- 4 oz (125 g) drained canned sliced mushrooms
- 1½ oz (45 g) dried mushrooms + ¾ cup (175 mL) boiling water

*See also* TRUFFLE; SHUFFLING MUSHROOMS (PAGE 654).

## Mushrooms, Powdered

*Often used to enhance the flavor of sauces, soups, stews, and flour coatings, this powder is made from ground dried mushrooms.*

### If You Don't Have It

Substitute 1 tbsp (15 mL) powdered mushrooms with:

- 3 tbsp (45 mL) whole dried mushrooms (pulverized in spice grinder if powder is needed)
- 4 oz (125 g) fresh mushrooms
- 2 oz (60 g) canned mushrooms

## Musk Lime

*See* CALAMONDIN.

## Muskmelon

*See* CANTALOUPE; CASABA; CHARENTAIS MELON; CRENSHAW MELON; GALIA MELON; HONEYDEW MELON; OGEN MELON; PERSIAN MELON; SANTA CLAUS MELON.

## Muskrat

*Also known as marsh rabbit. Semiaquatic muskrats must be trapped in the wild near the salty marshes where they dwell. They have lean, tender, very flavorful meat with a fine grain and deep-pink color similar to hare. Muskrat is so popular in Ohio that firehouses and churches hold muskrat suppers as fund-raisers.*

### If You Don't Have It

Substitute 1 lb (500 g) muskrat with:

- 1 lb (500 g) hare
- 1 lb (500 g) rabbit
- 1 lb (500 g) chicken

*See also* RABBIT.

## Mussels

*Smaller mussels are more tender than large ones. Choose live mussels with shells that are intact and closed, or if open, that snap shut when tapped.*

1 lb (500 g) medium =
9 to 12 mussels =
¾ to 1 cup
(175 to 250 mL) meat

### If You Don't Have It

Substitute 1 lb (500 g) mussels with:
- 1 lb (500 g) oysters
- 1 lb (500 g) soft-shelled or littleneck clams
- 1 lb (500 g) cockles
- 1 lb (500 g) scallops

### Mussel Varieties

Choose 1 lb (500 g) mussels from these varieties:
- 1 lb (500 g) blue mussels (shell is 2 to 3 inches/5 to 7.5 cm long and dark blue or black)
- 1 lb (500 g) New Zealand green mussels (shell is 3 to 4 inches/ 7.5 to 10 cm and green)
- 1 lb (500 g) Prince Edward Island mussels (farm-raised; beardless shell is 2 inches/5 cm long and dark blue or black)

## Mustard Essence

*Also known as volatile oil of mustard. Distilled from black or brown mustard seeds, this essential oil contains up to 92% allyl isothiocyanate, the pungent compound found in horseradish and wasabi (in lower concentrations). It is the key to the nose-filling aroma of mostarda, a classic northern Italian condiment made from candied fruit.*

### If You Don't Have It

Substitute 3 drops mustard essence with:
- 1 to 2 tsp (5 to 10 mL) pure mustard oil (less pungent)
- ½ tsp (2 mL) mustard powder
- 1 to 2 tsp (5 to 10 mL) grated horseradish or wasabi (removed from the preparation before serving)

*See also* MUSTARD OIL.

## Mustard Greens

*The plant species* Brassica juncea *has as many as 17 subspecies that produce leafy greens that vary greatly in appearance and pungency. From the American soul food classic southern mustard — which is also known as curled mustard and southern curled mustard — to Asian wrapped heart mustard — which is also known as dai gai choy,*

### If You Don't Have It

Substitute 1 lb (500 g) mustard greens with:
- 1 lb (500 g) broccoli raab
- 1 lb (500 g) arugula
- 1 lb (500 g) turnip greens
- 1 lb (500 g) radish greens
- 1 lb (500 g) collards
- 1 lb (500 g) escarole
- 1 lb (500 g) kale
- 1 lb (500 g) Chinese kale
- 1 lb (500 g) mature spinach
- 1 lb (500 g) green chard

## Mustard Greens (cont'd)

swatow mustard/cabbage, and heading mustard — these greens feature prominently in the cooking of Asia, India, and Africa.

---

1 lb (500 g) fresh =
6 to 7 cups
(1.5 to 1.75 L) leaves

1 lb (500 g) fresh =
1⅓ to 2 cups
(325 to 500 mL) cooked

10 oz (300 g) frozen =
1¼ cups (300 mL)
cooked

---

## Mustard Oil

In India, mustard oil has been used for cooking and massages for centuries. The pungent oil contains 25 to 45% erucic acid, a compound once thought to be toxic to humans but now considered a potential benefit to cardiovascular health. The oil's pungency is tamed when heated, and Indian cooks usually heat the oil until smoking then lower the heat to cooking temperature. Due to its erucic acid content, mustard oil sold in Europe and North America is often labeled "for external use only."

## Mustard Green Varieties

Choose 1 lb (500 g) mustard greens from these varieties:

- 1 lb (500 g) curled or American mustard (long, slender, pale green stems; large, bright green rippled leaves with frilly edges; sharp, hot flavor)
- 1 lb (500 g) wrapped heart mustard or dai gai choy (wide, curved, pale green stems, branching toward wide, bright green leaves; extremely sharp, hot flavor)
- 1 lb (500 g) leaf (bamboo) mustard or juk gai choy (smaller than dai gai choi; straight narrow or slightly wide pale green stems; flat, bright green leaves; mild to slightly strong sharp flavor)
- 1 lb (500 g) red-in-snow mustard (long, slender, pale green stems; large tear-drop shaped leaves with jagged edges; slightly sweet and mildly peppery flavor)
- 1 lb (500 g) Japanese (purple, red or giant-leaf) mustard (miniature purple/red mustard greens often sold for salad mixes; mature greens have long, slender, pale green stems; broad, rippled leaves are green on one side and purple on the other; extremely sharp flavor when mature)
- 1 lb (500 g) garlic (jack-by-the-hedge) mustard (small teardrop shape green leaves with pungent mustard and garlic aromas)

### If You Don't Have It

Substitute 1 tbsp (15 mL) mustard oil with:

- 1 tbsp (15 mL) canola oil + ½ tsp (2 mL) mustard powder
- 4 to 5 drops mustard essence (more pungent)

See also MUSTARD ESSENCE.

## Mustard, Powdered

*Also known as dry mustard. The vivid yellow-and-red Colman's Mustard tin is one of the most recognizable product packages in the world.*

1 oz (30 g) =
5 tbsp (75 mL)

### If You Don't Have It

Substitute 1 tsp (5 mL) powdered mustard with:

- 1 tbsp (15 mL) prepared mustard minus 1 tsp (5 mL) liquid from recipe
- 1¼ to 1½ tsp (6 to 7 mL) mustard seeds (pulverized in spice grinder if powder is needed)

## Mustard, Prepared

*An internationally varied condiment prepared from ground mustard seeds, liquid (water, vinegar, wine, beer, or grape must), and other seasonings. More than 700 million pounds (325 million kg) of mustard are consumed annually around the world. Canada takes the title for mustard cultivation champion, growing about 90% of the world's supply.*

1 oz (30 g) =
3 tbsp (45 mL)

### If You Don't Have It

Substitute 1 tbsp (15 mL) prepared mustard with:

- 1 tsp (5 mL) powdered mustard + 1 to 2 tsp (5 to 10 mL) vinegar or water
- 1 tsp (5 mL) mustard seeds
- 1 tsp (5 mL) caraway seeds
- 1 tsp (5 mL) prepared horseradish
- 1 tsp (5 mL) mayonnaise

### Prepared Mustard Varieties

Choose 1 tbsp (15 mL) prepared mustard from these varieties:

- 1 tbsp (15 mL) Dijon mustard (smooth or grainy texture; mild to sharp flavor)
- 1 tbsp (15 mL) Chinese mustard (smooth texture; sharp flavor)
- 1 tbsp (15 mL) Creole mustard (grainy texture; very sharp flavor)
- 1 tbsp (15 mL) hot mustard (smooth or grainy texture; very sharp flavor)
- 1 tbsp (15 mL) German mustard (smooth or grainy texture; mild to sharp flavor)

## Mustard Seed

*White (yellow) and brown (Asian) are the two major commercial types. White seeds are mild; the brown more assertive. Whole seeds are used for pickling and seasoning. Ground seeds are the basis for prepared mustards.*

### If You Don't Have It

Substitute 1 tsp (5 mL) mustard seeds with:

- ¾ to 1 tsp (4 to 5 mL) powdered mustard
- 1 tbsp (15 mL) prepared mustard minus 1 tsp (5 mL) liquid from recipe

### Mustard Seed Varieties

Choose 1 tsp (5 mL) mustard seeds from these varieties:

- 1 tsp (5 mL) yellow (white) mustard seeds (sharp flavor; often used to make prepared yellow mustard)
- 1 tsp (5 mL) brown mustard seeds (very sharp flavor; often used in Indian cooking)
- 1 tsp (5 mL) black mustard seeds (very sharp flavor; often used in Indian cooking)

## Mutton

*See* LAMB.

## Myrtle Pepper

*See* ALLSPICE.

## Mysost

*Also known as primost. Scandinavian cheese created by caramelizing cow's milk whey.*

### If You Don't Have It

Substitute 1 oz (30 g) mysost with:

- 1 oz (30 g) gjetost

*See also* GJETOST.

## Myzithra

*Also known as Mizithra. A Greek sheep's milk cheese made from the whey of feta and kefalotyri, available both fresh and aged. The fresh resembles cottage cheese. The aged is pungent, somewhat like Italian ricotta salata, and makes an excellent grating cheese.*

1 lb (500 g) fresh =
4 cups (1 L) crumbled

1 lb (500 g) aged =
4 cups (1 L) grated

### If You Don't Have It

Substitute 1 oz (30 g) Myzithra cheese with:

- 1 oz (30 g) feta (to replace fresh Myzithra)
- 1 oz (30 g) manouri (to replace fresh Myzithra)
- 1 oz (30 g) cotija (fresh or aged; to replace fresh or aged Myzithra)
- 1 oz (30 g) aged ricotta salata (to replace aged Myzithra for grating)
- 1 oz (30 g) Pecorino Romano (to replace aged Myzithra for grating)
- 1 oz (30 g) Parmesan (to replace aged Myzithra for grating)

# Naan to Nutritional Yeast

## Naan

*Also known as nan. Indian white-flour flatbread. The traditional preparation uses dough that is lightly leavened by airborne yeast starter. A pleasant smoky note is added when baked in a tandoor oven.*

**If You Don't Have It**

Substitute 1 naan with:

- 1 roti (a generic term for Indian flatbread; similar to chapati; usually made with whole wheat flour)
- 1 chapati (wheat-flour flatbread with little or no fat; less puffy)
- 1 paratha (griddle-cooked whole wheat flatbread with fat in the dough; richer; more flaky)
- 1 poori (deep-fried flatbread made with whole wheat flour; crisper)
- 1 whole wheat pita bread (similar to naan)
- 1 whole wheat flour tortilla

## Nameko

*See* SHUFFLING MUSHROOMS (PAGE 654).

## Nam Pla

*See* FISH SAUCE.

## Nam Prik

*See* CHILE PASTE.

## Nan

*See* NAAN.

## Nangka

*See* JACKFRUIT.

## Napa Cabbage

*Also known as celery cabbage, Chinese cabbage, da bai cai, hakusai, and wong bok. Growing in tightly clustered heads of ivory stalks rimmed with pale green ruffled leaves, this indigenous Chinese cabbage is sweeter and less assertive than European cabbages. It's enjoyed as much for its texture as its flavor and appears raw or cooked in many dishes.*

---

1 lb (500 g) =
3½ to 4½ cups
(875 mL to 1.125 L)
sliced = 1½ to 2 cups
(375 to 500 mL) cooked

1 small head =
1½ lbs (750 kg)

---

### If You Don't Have It

Substitute 1 lb (500 g) napa cabbage with:

- 1 lb (500 g) bok choy (larger, darker green leaves; firmer, juicier stems)
- 1 lb (500 g) savoy cabbage (stronger flavor)
- 1 lb (500 g) green chard (less cabbagey flavor)
- 1 lb (500 g) green or red cabbage (sturdier leaves; stronger flavor)
- 1 lb (500 g) collard greens (thinner, firmer, deeper green stems; larger, darker green leaves)

### Napa Cabbage Variety

Substitute 1 lb (500 g) napa cabbage with this variety:

- 1 lb (500 g) Michihili (similar, but more elongated with firmer, crunchier stems)

*See also* BOK CHOY.

## Naseberry

*See* SAPODILLA.

## Nasturtium

*A flower with ruffled blooms in vivid shades of yellow, red, and orange, nasturtiums taste as good as they look. The flowers, along with the leaves and stems, have a pleasant peppery appeal as part of salads, sandwiches, and spreads. Often, nasturtiums are used simply to accessorize a dish.*

### If You Don't Have It

Substitute 1 cup (250 mL) nasturtium with

- 1 cup (250 mL) marigolds (to replace nasturtium flowers)
- 1 cup (250 mL) pansies (to replace nasturtium flowers)
- 1 cup (250 mL) watercress or other cress (to replace nasturtium leaves)

*See also* CRESS; PICKING EDIBLE FLOWERS (PAGE 650).

## Natal Plum

*See* CARISSA.

## Natto

*Nutty, savory, and pungent fermented soybeans with a gooey texture. A common accompaniment to breakfast rice in Japan.*

### If You Don't Have It

Substitute ½ cup (125 mL) natto with

- ½ cup (125 mL) fermented black beans
- ½ cup (125 mL) fermented bean paste

## Natural Cocoa

*See* COCOA POWDER, UNSWEETENED.

## Navel Orange

*See* ORANGE, SWEET.

## Navy Bean

*See* THE WIDE WORLD OF DRIED BEANS (PAGE 637).

## Nectarine

*A variety of peach without the fuzz.*

> 1 lb (500 g) =
> 3 to 4 medium = 2 cups
> (500 mL) chopped =
> 2½ cups (625 mL) sliced =
> 1½ cups (375 mL)
> puréed

### If You Don't Have It
Substitute 1 lb (500 g) nectarines with:
- 1 lb (500 g) peaches
- 1 lb (500 g) plums
- 1 lb (500 g) apricots
- 1 lb (500 g) cherries

## Nectarine, Dried

*Like dried apricots, these are often treated with sulfur dioxide but also available untreated.*

> 1 lb (500 g) =
> 2½ to 3 cups
> (625 to 750 mL) =
> 5½ cups (1.375 L)
> cooked

### If You Don't Have It
Substitute 1 oz (30 g) dried nectarines with:
- 1 oz (30 g) dried peaches
- 1 oz (30 g) dried apricots

## Neopolitan Liqueur

*See* GALLIANO.

## Nettles

*Also known as stinging nettles. Only the young shoots and leaf tops of this defensive plant are eaten. They must be cooked to get rid of formic acid, which can irritate the skin, found in the fibers on the leaves.*

> 1 lb (500 g) fresh =
> 1⅓ to 2 cups
> (325 to 500 mL) cooked

### If You Don't Have It
Substitute 1 lb (500 g) nettles with:
- 1 lb (500 g) curly endive or frisée
- 1 lb (500 g) escarole
- 1 lb (500 g) kale
- 1 lb (500 g) spinach

## Neufchâtel

*A French soft white unripened cow's milk cheese that is mild when young and more pungent with age.*

> 8 oz (250 g) =
> 1 cup (250 mL)

### If You Don't Have It
Substitute 1 lb (500 g) Neufchâtel with:
- 1 lb (500 g) cream cheese (higher in fat)
- 1 lb (500 g) mascarpone (higher in fat)
- 1 lb (500 g) Boursin cheese (adds herb flavors)

*See also* CREAM CHEESE.

## Neutral Spirits

*Also known as ethanol, ethyl alcohol, everclear, and grain alcohol. Neutral spirits are 190 proof, clear, and tasteless. Aging in wood creates grain spirits with flavor nuances.*

### If You Don't Have It
Substitute 3 tbsp (45 mL) neutral spirits with:
- ¼ cup (60 mL) 100-proof vodka (reduce liquid in recipe by 3 tbsp/45 mL)
- 3 tbsp (45 mL) grain spirits (wood-aged; mellower flavor)

*See also* VODKA.

## New Mexican Red Chile

*See* CHILE POWDER; CHOOSING DRIED CHILES (PAGE 642); CHOOSING FRESH CHILES (PAGE 640).

## New Zealand Spinach

*Also known as Botany Bay greens and tetragonia. A relative of the ice plant, this Pacific Rim native is not related to spinach apart from its vivid green leaves. A cooking vegetable, the flavor is mild and the texture creamy.*

> 1 lb (500 g) fresh =
> 10 cups (2.5 L) =
> 6 to 8 cups
> (1.5 to 2 L) cooked

### If You Don't Have It
Substitute 1 lb (500 g) New Zealand Spinach with:
- 1 lb (500 g) amaranth leaves
- 1 lb (500 g) callaloo
- 1 lb (500 g) chard leaves
- 1 lb (500 g) Chinese kale
- 1 lb (500 g) spinach

## Ngali Nut

*See* PILI NUT.

## Ngo Gai

*See* SAWLEAF HERB.

## Ngo Om

*See* RICE PADDY HERB.

## Niçoise Olive

*See* CHOOSING AMONG OLIVES (PAGE 659).

## Nigella

*Also known as kalonji and ketza. Sometimes mistakenly called black onion seeds, these tiny black seeds have nothing to do with onion seeds. Nutty and peppery, the seeds are frequently used in the Middle East and India.*

### If You Don't Have It

Substitute 1 tsp (5 mL) nigella seeds with:

- 1 tsp (5 mL) cumin seeds, especially black cumin seeds
- 1 tsp (5 mL) ajwain
- 1 tsp (5 mL) caraway seeds

## Nisa

*See* QUEIJO DE NISA.

## Nixtamal

*Also known as maiz nixtamalado. These lime-treated, partially cooked, dried starchy corn kernels are sold refrigerated or frozen in Mexican groceries. An essential for the Mexican pork stew posole and other special dishes.*

1 lb (500 g) whole = 1¼ cups (300 mL)

### If You Don't Have It

Substitute 1 cup (250 mL) nixtamal with:

- 1 cup (250 mL) hominy (fully cooked; softer)

## Nocino

*See* WALNUT LIQUEUR.

## Nökkelost

*Also known as kuminost. Danish semifirm cheese enhanced with caraway seeds, cloves, and cumin.*

1 lb (500 g) = 4 cups (1 L) shredded

### If You Don't Have It

Substitute 1 oz (30 g) Nökkelost with:

- 1 oz (30 g) Leyden (firmer)
- 1 oz (30 g) Gouda (no cumin or caraway flavors)
- 1 oz (30 g) Edam (less rich; no cumin or caraway flavors)

## Nondairy Whipped Topping

*See* WHIPPED TOPPING.

## Nonfat Milk

*See* MILK, FAT-FREE.

## Nonpareils

*From the French term meaning "without equal," these colored sugar dots are the size of a pinhead and used to decorate cakes, candies, and cookies.*

### If You Don't Have It
Substitute 1 tbsp (15 mL) nonpareils with:
- 1 tbsp (15 mL) dragées
- 1 tbsp (15 mL) jimmies
- 1 tbsp (15 mL) colored sugar sprinkles (decorating sugar)
- 1 tbsp (15 mL) mini M&Ms

## Nonreactive Cookware

*See* EARTHENWARE; ENAMELWARE; STAINLESS-STEEL COOKWARE.

## Nonstick Cookware

*Chemist Roy J. Plunkett is the patron saint of dishwashers everywhere. Researching chlorofluorocarbon refrigerants in a DuPont laboratory in 1938, Plunkett accidentally discovered the polymer that came to be Teflon®. An awards luncheon for Plunkett in 1960 also served to introduce Teflon® bakeware to the public. Each guest left the luncheon with a Teflon®-coated muffin pan.*

### If You Don't Have It
Substitute nonstick cookware with:
- well-seasoned cast-iron cookware + little or no fat, oil, or oil spray (after years of use most cast-iron pans are virtually nonstick)
- anodized aluminum cookware + a small amount of fat, oil, or oil spray (anodized aluminum is relatively low-stick)
- enameled cast-iron cookware + a small amount of fat, oil, or oil spray
- copper, stainless-steel, or clad metal stainless cookware + a fair amount of fat, oil, or oil spray (first heat the fat for the best prevention against sticking)

## Noodles

*See* EGG NOODLE; PASTA, DRIED RIBBONS; PASTA, DRIED STRANDS; A SNAPSHOT OF ASIAN NOODLES (PAGE 656).

## Nopale

*Also known as cactus leaf. After removing the thorns with a vegetable peeler, the fleshy pads of the prickly pear cactus taste like green beans touched with lemon.*

| 1 lb (500 g) fresh = 3 cups (750 mL) cut into strips |
| --- |

### If You Don't Have It
Substitute 1 lb (500 g) fresh nopales with:
- 1 lb (500 g) okra
- 1 lb (500 g) green beans
- 1 lb (500 g) asparagus

### Nopale Varieties
Choose 1 lb (500 g) nopales from these varieties:
- 1 lb (500 g) nopalitos or chopped nopales (often sold canned)
- 1 lb (500 g) acitróns (candied nopales)

## Ñora Chile Peppers

*See* CHOOSING DRIED CHILES (PAGE 642).

## Nori

*Also known as sushi nori and yaki-nori (when toasted). Japanese seaweed that is dried and pressed into beautiful sheets that range in color from dark green to purple black.*

### If You Don't Have It

Substitute 1 oz (30 g) nori with:

- 1 oz (30 g) sea lettuce
- 1 oz (30 g) rice paper
- 1 oz (30 g) dumpling wrappers
- plastic wrap or a silicone mat (for making maki rolls without nori or any wrapper)

*See also* LAVER.

## Nuoc Cham

*In the Vietnamese kitchen, this dipping condiment adds vibrancy to many dishes. To prepare it, nuoc nam (fish sauce) is seasoned with red chilies, garlic, lime juice, ginger, and sugar.*

### If You Don't Have It

Substitute 1 cup (250 mL) nuoc cham with:

- 1 cup (250 mL) Homemade Nuoc Cham: Dissolve ¼ to ⅓ cup (60 to 75 mL) granulated sugar in 3 tbsp (45 mL) hot water. Stir in ⅓ cup (75 mL) fresh lime juice, ⅓ cup (75 mL) nuoc nam or other fish sauce, 1 to 2 minced garlic cloves, and 1 seeded and minced Thai, cayenne, or serrano chile. Let stand for 15 to 20 minutes to blend flavors. Makes about 1 cup (250 mL).

## Nuoc Nam

*See* FISH SAUCE.

## Nut

*In botanical terms, a nut is a dry single-seeded fruit that doesn't split open along a seam when mature. Acorns, chestnuts, and hazelnuts are true nuts. In culinary terms, a nut is any of various seeds and fruits with an edible kernel surrounded by a hard covering. The almond is part of a fruit called a drupe, the Brazil nut is a seed enclosed with other seeds in a capsule, and the peanut is a legume. Other non-nut nuts are cashews, pistachios, and walnuts.*

1 lb (500 g) in shell =
1⅔ cups (400 mL) shelled

1 lb (500 g) shelled =
3 to 4 cups (750 mL to 1 L)
whole = 2¾ to 3¾ cups
(675 to 925 mL) chopped

4 oz (125 g) = ¾ to 1 cup
(175 to 250 mL) chopped

### If You Don't Have It

Substitute 1 cup (250 mL) nuts with:

- 2 to 4 tbsp (30 to 60 mL) nut oil, such as almond, hazelnut, macadamia, pecan, pistachio, or walnut (for baking and cooking; will add nut flavor but not texture of whole nuts; reduce fat in recipe by 2 to 4 tbsp/30 to 60 mL)
- 1 cup (250 mL) chocolate chips (for baking)

### To Vary the Flavor

Substitute 1 cup (250 mL) nuts with:

- 1 cup (250 mL) toasted nuts (more aromatic; toast nuts in dry pan until fragrant)

### For Better Health

Substitute 1 cup (250 mL) nuts with:

- ½ cup (125 mL) toasted nuts, finely chopped (toasting intensifies flavor of nuts so you can use less; finely chopping them better distributes the flavor)
- 1 cup (250 mL) toasted rolled oats (for baking, especially to top baked goods)
- 1 cup (250 mL) Grape-Nuts cereal (for baking; crunchier and less rich)

*See also* ALMOND PASTE; ALMOND, SWEET; BRAZIL NUT; BUTTERNUT; CASHEW; CHESTNUT; HAZELNUT; MACADAMIA NUT; PEANUT; PECAN; PINE NUT; PISTACHIO; WALNUT.

## Nutella

*See* GIANDUJA.

## Nut Flour

*See* ALMOND FLOUR; CHOOSING AMONG WHOLE-GRAIN AND ALTERNATIVE FLOURS (PAGE 648).

## Nut Meal

*Also known as ground nuts and frangipane (almond meal). Nut meal has more oil and is coarser than commercial nut flours, which are finely ground from nuts that have already been pressed for their oil.*

> 4 oz (125 g) nuts =
> 1 cup (250 mL)
> ground nut meal

### If You Don't Have It
Substitute 1 cup (250 mL) nut meal with:
- 1 cup (250 mL) Homemade Nut Meal: Grind about 2 cups (500 mL) chilled whole nuts, such as almonds, hazelnuts, pecans, or walnuts, in a nut mill or food processor. If using a food processor, add 1 to 3 tbsp (15 to 45 mL) granulated sugar and use short pulses just until the nuts resemble cornmeal (the sugar and pulsing help to prevent the nut meal from turning to nut butter; reduce sugar in recipe if necessary). Makes about ½ cup (125 mL).
- 1 cup (250 mL) nut flour (drier, finer texture)

*See also* CHOOSING AMONG WHOLE-GRAIN AND ALTERNATIVE FLOURS (PAGE 648).

## Nutmeg

*Oval brown nutmeg seeds keep their flavor for months, or even years, when stored in a cool, dry, dark cupboard. For finest aroma and flavor, grate the seed on a specially designed nutmeg grater or on a fine rasp-style grater.*

### If You Don't Have It
Substitute 1 tsp (5 mL) ground or grated nutmeg with:
- 1 tsp (5 mL) ground mace
- 1 tsp (5 mL) ground allspice
- 1 to 1½ tsp (5 to 7 mL) ground cinnamon
- 1 tsp (5 mL) apple pie spice (adds cinnamon and allspice flavors)
- 1 tsp (5 mL) pumpkin pie spice (adds cinnamon, allspice, and ginger flavors)

## Nutmeg Grater

*See* GRATER.

## Nutritional Yeast

*See* YEAST, NUTRITIONAL.

# Oak Leaf Lettuce
## to Oyster Sauce

## Oak Leaf Lettuce

*See* LEAF LETTUCE.

## Oat Bran

*The outer casing of the oat groat is very high in heart-healthy soluble fiber.*

### If You Don't Have It
Substitute 1 cup (250 mL) oat bran with:
- 1 cup (250 mL) wheat bran
- 1 cup (250 mL) rice bran
- 1 cup (250 mL) wheat germ

## Oat Flour

*There is no gluten in oat flour, so for baked goods that need gluten's protein structure to rise and trap air bubbles, a flour with gluten must be added to the mix. Generally, oat flour can replace up to one-third of wheat flour in a recipe.*

> 1 lb (500 g) =
> 3 cups (750 mL)

### If You Don't Have It
Substitute 1 cup (250 mL) oat flour with:
- 1¼ cups (300 mL) old-fashioned oatmeal, ground in blender or food processor to the consistency of flour

*See also* CHOOSING AMONG WHOLE-GRAIN AND ALTERNATIVE FLOURS (PAGE 648).

## Oat Groats

*Whole oat grains that are cleaned, toasted, hulled, and cleaned a second time. They are prepared as a cereal or a cooked grain for pilafs, salads, or stuffings.*

1 cup (250 mL) =
2 to 2½ cups
(500 to 625 mL) cooked

### If You Don't Have It
Substitute 1 cup (250 mL) oat groats with:
- 1 cup (250 mL) rye berries
- 1 cup (250 mL) wheat berries (takes longer to cook)
- 1 cup (250 mL) hulled or whole-grain barley (takes longer to cook)
- 1 cup (250 mL) triticale berries or groats (takes longer to cook)
- 1 cup (250 mL) spelt berries or groats (takes longer to cook)
- 1 cup (250 mL) Kamut© berries or groats (takes longer to cook)
- 1 cup (250 mL) kasha (cooks faster)
- 1 cup (250 mL) brown rice (cooks faster)

## Oat Milk

*Fortified substitute for those who can't or don't want to drink cow's milk. Produced by straining cooked and flavored oats.*

### If You Don't Have It
Substitute 1 cup (250 mL) oat milk with
- 1 cup (250 mL) Homemade Oat Milk: Put 5 cups (1.25 L) water in a large saucepan and bring to a boil over high heat. Add a pinch of salt and 1 cup (250 mL) old-fashioned rolled oats. Reduce heat to medium-low and simmer gently until oats are very soft and liquid is reduced to level of oats, 30 to 40 minutes. If you like, add ½ to ¾ tsp (2 to 3 mL) vanilla extract. Sweeten to taste with ¼ to ½ cup (60 to 125 mL) brown rice syrup, maple syrup, honey, or sugar. Purée with an immersion blender or in a food processor or blender. Strain through cheesecloth or a fine-mesh sieve set over a large bowl or pitcher. Refrigerate up to 5 days and shake before using. Makes about 3 cups (750 mL).
- 1 cup (250 mL) soy, rice, or almond milk
- 1 cup (250 mL) cow's or goat's milk

## Oats, Old-Fashioned

*Also known as rolled oats. According to British food authority Alan Davidson, "… it is commonly held that the disproportionately large measure of success and fame achieved by Scottish people on the world stage is partly or even primarily the result of a diet including oatmeal, especially porridge."*

### If You Don't Have It
Substitute 1 cup (250 mL) old-fashioned rolled oats with:
- 1 cup (250 mL) barley flakes (rolled barley)
- 1 cup (250 mL) steel-cut, Irish or Scotch oats (cut oat groats; smaller pieces; takes more time to cook; chewier and more flavorful)
- 1 cup (250 mL) oat groats (larger pieces; takes much longer to cook; much chewier)

### To Vary the Flavor
Substitute 1 cup (250 mL) old-fashioned rolled oats with:
- 1 cup (250 mL) nuts (for baking, especially to top baked goods)

| |
|---|
| 1 cup (250 mL) =<br>3½ oz (105 g) =<br>1¾ cups (425 mL) cooked<br>1 lb (500 g) =<br>5 cups (1.25 L) uncooked |

## To Save Time
Substitute 1 cup (250 mL) old-fashioned rolled oats with:
- 1 cup (250 mL) quick-cooking rolled oats (cooks faster; smaller pieces; less chewy)

## Oaxaca Cheese

*See* ASADERO.

## Obsttortenform

*See* PAN SIZE EQUIVALENTS (PAGE 678).

## Oca

*A tuber from the Andes with a knobby shape resembling fingerling potatoes. The thin skin may be pink, red, or yellow, and the flesh is moist, crisp, waxy, sweet, and sour.*

| |
|---|
| 1 lb (500 g) = 3½ to<br>4 cups (875 mL to 1 L)<br>chopped or sliced |

### If You Don't Have It
Substitute 1 lb (500 g) oca with:
- 1 lb (500 g) sunchokes
- 1 lb (500 g) arrowhead
- 1 lb (500 g) arracacha
- 1 lb (500 g) boniato
- 1 lb (500 g) artichoke hearts (softer texture; similar flavor)
- 1 lb (500 g) potatoes (drier texture; less complex flavor)

## Ocean Perch

*Also known as, Norway haddock and redfish. In the 1930s, a shortage of freshwater yellow perch inspired marketers to substitute a similar, cheaper creature, the redfish, and dub it ocean perch. A member of the rockfish family, ocean perch is not a true perch. Redfish fillets have a firm flake, white flesh, and a taste just slightly more assertive than cod.*

### If You Don't Have It
Substitute 1 lb (500 g) ocean perch with:
- 1 lb (500 g) porgy
- 1 lb (500 g) red snapper
- 1 lb (500 g) weakfish
- 1 lb (500 g) whiting
- 1 lb (500 g) mullet

### Ocean Perch Varieties
Choose 1 lb (500 g) Pacific ocean perch from these varieties:
- 1 lb (500 g) Pacific rockfish
- 1 lb (500 g) bocaccio
- 1 lb (500 g) yelloweye rockfish
- 1 lb (500 g) yellowtail rockfish
- 1 lb (500 g) widow rockfish

*See also* PERCH.

## Octopus

*The Japanese catch about half of the world's octopus. It is often blanched briefly, then is thinly sliced and served with a dip. Octopus is also frequently prepared* nimono *style, in a long-simmered stew to tenderize it.*

### If You Don't Have It

Substitute 1 lb (500 g) octopus with:

- 1 lb (500 g) squid
- 1 lb (500 g) cuttlefish (more tender)

## Ogbono Nut

*Also known as dika, etima, irvingia, odika nuts. Nuts from the mango-like fruit of a tropical rain forest tree (*Irvingia gabonensis*). Like egusi seeds, ogbono nuts are used to thicken and flavor an African soup of the same name. They have a similar mucilaginous texture when ground and cooked.*

### If You Don't Have It

Substitute ½ cup (125 mL) ogbono nuts with:

- ½ cup (125 mL) egusi seeds (similar texture)
- 1½ cups (375 mL) cut okra (similar texture)
- 1 tbsp (15 mL) ground baobab leaves (similar texture)
- ½ cup (125 mL) pumpkin seeds
- ½ cup (125 mL) sunflower seeds
- ½ cup (125 mL) pine nuts

## Ogen Melon

*An Israeli melon that is similar to honeydew.*

2 lbs (1 kg) =
3 cups (750 mL) diced

### If You Don't Have It

Substitute 1 cup (250 mL) chopped Ogen melon with:

- 1 cup (250 mL) chopped honeydew melon
- 1 cup (250 mL) chopped Galia melon
- 1 cup (250 mL) chopped Santa Claus melon
- 1 cup (250 mL) chopped cantaloupe
- 1 cup (250 mL) chopped Persian melon

## Oil

*Oils are liquid at room temperature, while fats (such as butter and vegetable shortening) are solid at room temperature. Recipes that refer to unspecified "oil" generally mean vegetable oil, which includes a wide variety of oils made from nuts, seeds, or other plant sources. The most common vegetable oils are*

### If You Don't Have It

Substitute ¼ cup (60 mL) vegetable oil with:

- ¼ cup (60 mL) melted butter, margarine, bacon drippings, shortening, or lard (for sautéing and frying)
- 2 tbsp (30 mL) vegetable oil + 2 tbsp (30 mL) butter (for sautéing and frying; combines flavor of butter with higher smoke point of oil)
- cooking oil spray (or 1 tbsp/15 mL oil) and a nonstick pan (for sautéing; reduces total calories and fat; heat the pan thoroughly before cooking to help prevent sticking)

*canola oil and soybean oil, which are interchangeable. Olive oil can also replace canola oil and soybean oil for salad dressings, sautéing, and even baking if using a light-flavored olive oil.*

## To Vary the Flavor
Substitute ½ cup (125 mL) vegetable oil with:
- ½ cup (125 mL) "light" butter (adds butter flavor with fewer calories and less fat than butter due mostly to the addition of water; works best as a spread, in frostings and toppings, or melted for drizzling; in pie and pastry doughs, chill light butter and shred before quickly mixing with dry ingredients; in pancake and quick bread batters, omit 2 tbsp/30 mL milk or other liquid from recipe per ½ cup/125 mL light butter used)
- ¼ cup (60 mL) oil + ¼ cup (60 mL) butter (for baking; especially quick breads; increase baking time slightly; baked goods will be slightly more tender)
- ½ cup (125 mL) vegetable oil + 2 tsp (10 mL) toasted sesame oil (best for dressings and uncooked or gently cooked sauces)
- ⅓ cup (75 mL) vegetable oil + 2½ tsp (12 mL) highly flavored nut or seed oil such as walnut, pecan, almond, hazelnut, macadamia, pistachio, or pumpkin oil (best for dressings and uncooked or gently cooked sauces)

## For Better Health
Substitute ½ cup (125 mL) vegetable oil with:
- ¼ cup (60 mL) buttermilk + ¼ cup (60 mL) well-drained, unsweetened applesauce or baby food prunes (for baking; puréed prunes work best with darker batters and doughs, such as chocolate or spice batters)
- ½ cup (125 mL) fat-free, fruit-based butter and oil replacement such as Smucker's "Baking Healthy" (for baking only)
- ¼ cup (60 mL) fat-free, fruit-based butter and oil replacement such as Sunsweet "Lighter Bake"(for baking only)
- ½ cup (125 mL) flaxseed oil (for dressings and uncooked sauces; flaxseed oil is rich in the same heart-healthy omega-3 fatty acids found in fish; avoid heating flaxseed oil, which destroys its omega-3's)

*See also* BUTTER; CHILE OIL; OLIVE OIL; SESAME OIL; SUBSTITUTING OILS (PAGE 658).

## Oil of Bitter Almonds

*The essential flavoring oil extracted from bitter almonds, which need to be heated to destroy the poisonous prussic acid that they contain.*

### If You Don't Have It
Substitute 1 drop oil of bitter almonds with:
- ¼ to ½ tsp (1 to 2 mL) almond extract

## Oil of Lemon

*See* LEMON OIL.

## Oil of Orange

*See* ORANGE OIL.

## Oil of Peppermint

*Although it's used for countless flavorings and fragrances, perhaps the most beloved use is to give candy canes that aroma of Christmas.*

### If You Don't Have It
Substitute 1 drop oil of peppermint with:
- 1 drop oil of spearmint (slightly milder)
- 1/8 to 1/4 tsp (0.5 to 1 mL) mint extract
- 1 tbsp (15 mL) chopped fresh mint
- 1 tsp (5 mL) dried mint

## Oka

*A semisoft cheese made by Trappist monks in Quebec, Canada. It has wonderful melting properties and a nutty taste.*

1 lb (500 g) = 4 cups
(1 L) shredded

### If You Don't Have It
Substitute 1 oz (30 g) oka cheese with:
- 1 oz (30 g) Port Salut
- 1 oz (30 g) Raclette
- 1 oz (30 g) Morbier

## Okara

*The white, flaky by-product of tofu production is high in fiber and protein. Look for it in Asian markets where fresh tofu is stocked.*

### If You Don't Have It
Substitute 1 lb (500 g) okara with:
- 1 lb (500 g) firm tofu (moister; slice into slabs and put a heavy skillet on top to press out excess liquid)

## Okra

*African slaves introduced this green pod vegetable to the American South, where it gained great interest, particularly as a thickener for the wonderful Louisiana gumbo.*

1 lb (500 g) fresh =
2¼ cups (550 mL)
chopped and cooked

10 oz (300 g) frozen =
1¼ cups (300 mL)
chopped

15½ oz (440 mL) can =
1¾ cups (425 mL)
chopped

### If You Don't Have It
Substitute 2 cups (500 mL) okra (for thickening) with:
- 1 tbsp (15 mL) filé powder
- 1 cup (250 mL) nopales, sliced
- 2 tsp (10 mL) cornstarch mixed with 1 tbsp (15 mL) cold water

### To Vary the Flavor
Substitute 2 cups (500 mL) okra with:
- 2 cups (500 mL) green beans
- 2 cups (500 mL) asparagus
- 2 cups (500 mL) broccoli

## Olallieberry

*This cross between a youngberry and a loganberry resembles blackberry. Delightful snatched from the bramble to the mouth.*

1 pint fresh =
2 cups (500 mL)

### If You Don't Have It
Substitute 1 cup (250 mL) olallieberries with:
- 1 cup (250 mL) Marionberries (slightly more tart)
- 1 cup (250 mL) loganberries (red color)
- 1 cup (250 mL) youngberries (dark red color)
- 1 cup (250 mL) boysenberries (slightly more tart)
- 1 cup (250 mL) raspberries (sweeter)
- 1 cup (250 mL) blackberries (slightly more tart)

*See also* BLACKBERRY; MARIONBERRY.

## Old Bay Seasoning

*In 1939, German-American immigrant Gustav Brunn settled in Baltimore and developed a blend of more than a dozen herbs and spices that would become Old Bay Seasoning. Synonymous with the Chesapeake Bay and crabs, Old Bay is also used to flavor many other dishes.*

### If You Don't Have It
Substitute 1 tbsp (15 mL) Old Bay Seasoning with:
- 1 tbsp (15 mL) Homemade Old Bay Seasoning: In a spice grinder or with a mortar and pestle, combine 1 tbsp (15 mL) celery salt or 1 tsp (5 mL) celery seeds, 2 tsp (10 mL) salt, 3 whole bay leaves, ¾ tsp (3 mL) brown mustard seeds or ½ tsp (2 mL) mustard powder, ½ tsp (2 mL) black peppercorns or ½ tsp (2 mL) ground black pepper, 10 allspice berries or ¼ tsp (1 mL) ground allspice, 10 whole cloves or ¼ tsp (1 mL) ground cloves, ½ tsp (2 mL) sweet paprika, ⅛ tsp (0.5 mL) cayenne pepper, ⅛ tsp (0.5 mL) ground ginger, ⅛ tsp (0.5 mL) ground mace, ⅛ tsp (0.5 mL) cardamom seeds (removed from pods or ⅛ tsp/0.5 mL ground cardamom), and a pinch of ground cinnamon. Grind to a coarse powder and store in an airtight container. Makes about 2 tablespoons (30 mL).
- 1 tbsp (15 mL) crab boil
- 1 tbsp (15 mL) pickling spice

*See also* CRAB BOIL SEASONING.

## Oleomargarine
*See* MARGARINE.

## Oliebollen
*See* DOUGHNUT.

## Olive Loaf

*This cold cut is bologna studded with green olives.*

### If You Don't Have It
Substitute 1 lb (500 g) olive loaf with:
- 1 lb (500 g) mortadella (includes cubes of pork fat and garlic flavor)
- 1 lb (500 g) bologna
- 1 lb (500 g) galantina (more chunky)

### For Better Health
Substitute 1 lb (500 g) olive loaf with:
- 1 lb (500 g) Gelbwurst (less fat and fewer calories)

# Olive Oil

*The primary table oil of the Mediterranean basin is now recognized internationally for its health-giving properties and its distinctive flavor. Numerous varieties of olives, which are adapted to the growing conditions of different regions, are grown for oil. After the ripe olives are gathered, stems and leaves are removed and the olives are washed in preparation for the first cold-pressing, which yields oil of the highest quality and finest flavor. Keeping the temperature of the oil below 86°F (30°C) is critical to maintain the distinct characteristics of the oil. If the temperature climbs higher, the oil cannot be considered cold-pressed. Up to 90% of the oil is obtained from the olives during the first cold pressing. The remaining 10% is extracted in refineries that use heat and/or chemical processes to remove the oil remaining in the paste. Although it may appear that darker green oil is more intensely flavored, the color is not a reliable indicator of flavor. Greener oils may simply be pressed from greener olives earlier in the season. Different varieties of olives produce oil in varying shades of green and gold. Plus, most oils (unless they are a boutique bottling from a single olive grove)*

## If You Don't Have It

Substitute ½ cup (125 mL) olive oil (for cooking) with these other cooking oils:

- ½ cup (125 mL) corn oil (similar smoke point of 410°F/210°C; mild flavor; yellow color; fat content is 13% saturated, 62% polyunsaturated, and 25% monounsaturated)
- ½ cup (125 mL) untoasted sesame seed oil (415°F/213°C smoke point; mild nutty flavor; light yellow color; fat content is 18% saturated, 41% polyunsaturated, and 41% monounsaturated)
- ½ cup (125 mL) canola or rapeseed oil (435°F/224°C smoke point; flavorless; light yellow color; fat content is 6% saturated, 32% polyunsaturated, and 62% monounsaturated)
- ½ cup (125 mL) grapeseed oil (445°F/229°C smoke point; mild flavor; fat content is 13% saturated, 70% polyunsaturated, and 17% monounsaturated)
- ½ cup (125 mL) peanut oil (450°F/230°C smoke point; neutral yet rich flavor; golden color; fat content is 17% saturated, 35% polyunsaturated, and 48% monounsaturated)
- ½ cup (125 mL) safflower oil (450°F/230°C smoke point; flavorless; light texture; fat content is 9% saturated, 76% polyunsaturated, and 15% monounsaturated)
- ½ cup (125 mL) soybean oil (450°F/230°C smoke point; light color; fat content is 14% saturated, 61% polyunsaturated, and 25% monounsaturated)

## Olive Oil Varieties

Choose ½ cup (125 mL) olive oil from these varieties:

- ½ cup (125 mL) extra virgin olive oil (made from first cold-pressing; acid content of 1% or less; golden to deep green color; very full, rich flavor; best for uncooked or gently heated dishes)
- ½ cup (125 mL) virgin olive oil (made from first cold-pressing; acid content of 1 to 3%; slightly less rich flavor than extra virgin oil; good for sautéing)
- ½ cup (125 mL) fine or fino olive oil (a blend of virgin and extra virgin oils; acid content of 1 to 3%; slightly less rich flavor than extra virgin oil; good for sautéing)
- ½ cup (125 mL) olive oil or pure olive oil (extracted with chemical solvents and refined; may be a blend of refined and virgin oils; acid content higher than 3%; generally, a lower quality oil; good for frying)
- ½ cup (125 mL) pumace olive oil (extracted with chemical solvents and refined; acid content higher than 3%; the lowest quality oil available; good for frying due to a relatively high smoke point of 460 to 470°F/238 to 243°C)
- ½ cup (125 mL) light or extra light olive oil (highly refined and filtered oil that's lighter in color and flavor than other olive oils; same fat and calorie content as other olive oils; good

*are blends of several olive varieties, perhaps from various growing areas. The various olive oil grades, from extra virgin to extra light, are defined here.*

for baking when you don't want a noticeable olive flavor; good for frying due to a relatively high smoke point of 460 to 470°F/238 to 243°C)

*See also* BUTTER; OIL; SUBSTITUTING OILS (PAGE 658).

## Olives

*The Roman Cato's manual On Farming (circa 175 BC) devotes more space to olive growing and oil making than to any other single topic.*

15 large or 36 small ripe pitted olives =
1 cup (250 mL) chopped

4½ oz (140 g) can =
⅔ cup (150 mL) chopped

### If You Don't Have It
Substitute ½ cup (125 mL) olives with:
- 2 to 3 tbsp (30 to 45 mL) capers (for salty, pickled flavor)
- ½ cup (125 mL) caper berries (as a cocktail garnish)
- ½ cup (125 mL) cocktail onions (as a cocktail garnish)

*See also* CHOOSING AMONG OLIVES (PAGE 659).

## Olympia Oyster

*See* OYSTER.

## Omelet Pan

*The French take their omelet making so seriously that they designed a special skillet with a flat bottom, shallow sloping sides, and a long handle to facilitate the preparation.*

### If You Don't Have It
Substitute an omelet pan with:
- crêpe pan (for small omelets)
- 6-inch (15 cm) to 10-inch (25 cm) sauté pan or skillet (for small and large omelets)

## Onaga

*See* SNAPPER.

## Onion Flakes

*For all those cooks who tear up at the very thought of peeling an onion, dehydrated chopped onions exist.*

¼ cup (60 mL) = 1 cup (250 mL) raw, chopped

1 tbsp (15 mL) onion flakes = 1 tsp (5 mL) onion powder =
1 small onion
(½ cup/125 mL chopped)

### If You Don't Have It
Substitute 1 tbsp (15 mL) onion flakes with:
- 2 to 3 tbsp (30 to 45 mL) jarred minced onion
- ¾ to 1 tsp (3 to 5 mL) onion powder
- ¾ to 1 tsp (3 to 5 mL) onion salt (reduce salt by ½ to 1 tsp/ 2 to 5 mL)
- ¾ tsp (3 mL) liquid onion seasoning
- ½ cup (125 mL) chopped fresh or frozen onion
- ⅔ cup (150 mL) chopped leeks, green onions, or scallions (white and light green parts only)

## Onion, Green

*Also known as bunching. Immature onions with long, slender green tops and small, rounded white bulbs. Scallions look very similar but have straight rather than rounded "bulbs" and a slightly milder flavor.*

1 bunch = 5 oz (150 g) =
10 green onions =
1 cup (250 mL) chopped
(white part only) =
3½ cups (875 mL)
chopped (white and
green parts)

### If You Don't Have It

Substitute 1 bunch green onions (white and green parts) with:
- 1 bunch scallions (slightly milder flavor)
- 1 bunch ramps (wild leeks; milder flavor)
- 3 to 4 cups (750 mL to 1 L) chopped leeks (milder flavor)
- 3 cups (750 mL) chopped shallots (more complex flavor)
- 3 to 4 cups (750 mL to 1 L) chopped chives (milder flavor; best raw or lightly cooked)

### To Vary the Flavor

Substitute 1 bunch green onions with:
- 1 bunch green garlic (adds mild garlic flavor)
- 3 cups (750 mL) chopped garlic chives (adds garlic flavor)
- 3 cups (750 mL) chopped Chinese garlic stems (adds pungent garlic flavor and crunch)

*See also* CHIVES; SCALLION.

## Onion, Instant Minced

*Dehydrated chopped onions that are slightly larger than onion flakes.*

1 tbsp (15 mL) instant
minced onion = 1¾ tsp
(8 mL) onion flakes =
½ to ¾ tsp (3 mL)
onion powder =
½ tsp (2 mL) small onion
(¼ cup/60 mL chopped)

### If You Don't Have It

Substitute 1 tbsp (15 mL) instant minced onion with:
- 1¾ tsp (8 mL) onion flakes
- ½ to ¾ tsp (2 to 3 mL) onion powder
- ½ to ¾ tsp (2 to 3 mL) onion salt (reduce salt by ½ tsp/2 mL)
- ½ tsp (2 mL) liquid onion seasoning
- ¼ cup (60 mL) chopped fresh or frozen onion
- ⅓ cup (75 mL) chopped leeks, green onions, or scallions (white and light green parts only)

## Onion, Little

*These diminutive onions are as appealing for their shape as for their mild allium flavor. When pickled, little pearl onions embellish the Gibson cocktail. Other varieties of little onions are discussed right.*

4 oz (125 g) =
15 to 30 little onions

### If You Don't Have It

Substitute 1 lb (500 g) any little onions with:
- 1 lb (500 g) green onion bulbs, trimmed
- 1 lb (500 g) shallots (more complex flavor)
- 1 lb (500 g) small storage onions (best for cooking, rather than pickling or creaming)

### Little Onion Varieties

Choose 1 lb (500 g) any little onions from these varieties:
- 1 lb (500 g) pearl onions (tiny, white, oval or round bulbs; mildly sweet; best for pickling or creaming whole)
- 1 lb (500 g) boiling onions (small, oval or round bulbs that are white, yellow, or red; best for cooking whole)
- 1 lb (500 g) cipollini or Italian pearl onions (small, round bulbs with a flattened shape and yellow or red color; sweeter than boiling onions; best for cooking whole)

## Onion Powder

*Dehydrated onions ground into convenient powder form.*

1 tsp (5 mL) onion powder = 1 tbsp (15 mL) onion flakes = 1 small onion (½ cup/125 mL chopped)

### If You Don't Have It

Substitute 1 tsp (5 mL) onion powder with:
- 1 tbsp (15 mL) onion flakes
- 2 to 3 tbsp (30 to 45 mL) jarred minced onion
- ¾ to 1 tsp (3 to 5 mL) onion salt (reduce salt by ½ to 1 tsp/ 2 to 5 mL)
- ¾ tsp (3 mL) liquid onion seasoning
- ½ cup (125 mL) chopped fresh or frozen onion
- ⅔ cup (150 mL) chopped leeks, green onions, or scallions (white and light green parts only)

### To Vary the Flavor

Substitute 1 tsp (5 mL) onion powder with:
- ¼ to ½ tsp (1 to 2 mL) asafetida powder (more pungent; more complex garlic and onion flavor)
- ½ to 1 tsp (2 to 5 mL) garlic powder (adds garlic flavor)

## Onion Salt

*A condiment of onion powder mixed with salt.*

### If You Don't Have It

Substitute 1 tsp (5 mL) onion salt with:
- ½ tsp (2 mL) onion powder + ½ tsp (2 mL) salt
- 1 tbsp (15 mL) onion flakes (add salt to taste)
- 2 to 3 tbsp (30 to 45 mL) jarred minced onion (add salt to taste)
- ¾ tsp (3 mL) liquid onion seasoning (add salt to taste)
- ½ cup (125 mL) chopped fresh or frozen onion (add salt to taste)
- ⅔ cup (150 mL) chopped leeks, green onions, or scallions (white and light green parts only; add salt to taste)

### To Vary the Flavor

Substitute 1 tsp (5 mL) onion salt with:
- 1 tsp (5 mL) Beau Monde® Seasoning (adds celery seeds)
- 1 tsp (5 mL) seasoned salt (adds paprika and other flavors)
- ½ tsp (2 mL) table salt (no onion flavor)

## Onion Soup Mix

*When Lipton's introduced dry Onion Soup Mix in 1952, the course of party dips was forever altered.*

1⅜ oz (40 g) pkg = ¼ cup (60 mL)

### If You Don't Have It

Substitute ¼ cup (60 mL) onion soup mix with:
- ¼ cup (60 mL) Homemade Onion Soup Mix: Combine 3 tbsp (45 mL) instant minced onion, 2 tbsp (30 mL) beef bouillon (crushed or granules), ½ tsp (2 mL) onion powder, ¼ tsp (1 mL) parsley flakes (optional), ⅛ tsp (0.5 mL) ground celery seeds, a pinch of ground black pepper, a pinch of sweet paprika, and salt to taste. Makes about ¼ cup (60 mL). To make soup, dissolve mix in 4 cups (1 L) boiling water. To make dips, combine with 2 cups (500 mL) sour cream or plain yogurt.

## Onion, Storage

*True to their name, storage onions are long keeping because they are high in sulfur and low in water. These pungent onions are available year-round; best cooked to temper the sharp flavor. Onions should be firm and heavy for their size. Avoid onions that have sprouted, have an odor, or have green or moldy blemishes. Store onions in a cool dark spot in a container that allows air to circulate.*

> 1 lb (500 g) =
> 4 to 5 medium =
> 4 cups (1 L) chopped =
> 1½ cups (375 mL)
> caramelized
> 1 medium = ¾ to 1 cup
> (175 to 250 mL) chopped

### If You Don't Have It

Substitute 1 medium storage onion (1 cup/250 mL chopped) with:

- 1 cup (250 mL) chopped sweet onion (sweeter; moister; works well cooked or uncooked; reduce sugar if necessary to balance sweetness)
- 1 cup (250 mL) frozen chopped onion
- 1 cup (250 mL) chopped shallots (mellower, more complex flavor)
- 1¼ cups (300 mL) chopped leeks, green onions, or scallions (white and light green parts only)
- ⅓ cup (75 mL) jarred minced onion
- 2 tbsp (30 mL) dried onion flakes
- 1½ to 2 tsp (7 to 10 mL) onion powder
- 1½ to 2 tsp (7 to 10 mL) onion salt (reduce salt by ½ to 1 tsp/2 to 5 mL)
- 1½ tsp (7 mL) liquid onion seasoning

### Storage Onion Varieties

Choose 1 medium storage onion (1 cup/250 mL chopped) from these varieties:

- 1 cup (250 mL) chopped yellow globe onions (widely used among home cooks; relatively pungent, complex flavor; best for cooking)
- 1 cup (250 mL) chopped white globe onions (white color; less pungent, less complex flavor than yellow onions; good for cooking; can be used raw if pieces are rinsed)
- 1 cup (250 mL) chopped Spanish onions (larger and slightly sweeter but otherwise very similar to yellow or white globe onions; good for cooking; can be used raw if pieces are rinsed)
- 1 cup (250 mL) chopped red or Italian red onions (purplish red and white color; slightly sweeter and less pungent than yellow globe onions; good for cooking; can be used raw if pieces are rinsed)
- 1 cup (250 mL) chopped Bermuda onions (white or yellow color; slightly sweeter and less pungent than yellow globe onions; good for cooking; can be used raw if pieces are rinsed)

*See also* ONION, SWEET.

## Onion, Sweet

*Sweet onions are seasonal, usually available from April to August, depending upon the growing region. They are crisp and juicy, served raw or lightly cooked. Vidalia from*

### If You Don't Have It

Substitute 1 cup (250 mL) chopped sweet onion with:

- 1 cup (250 mL) chopped storage onion (less sweet; less moist; best for cooking; if using raw, rinse to soften pungency; add sugar if necessary to balance sweetness)
- 1 cup (250 mL) frozen chopped onion
- 1 cup (250 mL) chopped shallots (more complex flavor)

*Georgia, Walla Walla from Washington, Maui from Hawaii, and other sweet onions have flavor characteristics particular to their growing area.*

1 medium = 1½ to 2 cups (375 to 500 mL) chopped

- 1¼ cups (300 mL) chopped leeks, green onions, or scallions (white and light green parts only)
- ⅓ cup (75 mL) instant minced onion
- 2 tbsp (30 mL) onion flakes
- 1½ to 2 tsp (7 to 10 mL) onion powder
- 1½ to 2 tsp (7 to 10 mL) onion salt (reduce salt by ½ to 1 tsp/2 to 5 mL)
- 1½ tsp (7 mL) liquid onion seasoning

## Sweet Onion Varieties

Choose 1 cup (250 mL) chopped sweet onion from these varieties:

- 1 cup (250 mL) chopped Vidalia onions (pale yellow color; crunchy, juicy texture; sweet, mild, and pleasantly pungent flavor; best raw or lightly cooked)
- 1 cup (250 mL) chopped Maui onions (pale yellow color; crunchy, juicy texture; sweet, mild, and pleasantly pungent flavor; best raw or lightly cooked)
- 1 cup (250 mL) chopped Walla Walla onions (pale yellow color; crunchy, juicy texture; sweet, mild, and pleasantly pungent flavor; best raw or lightly cooked)
- 1 cup (250 mL) chopped Texas Supersweet or other Texas sweet onions (white, pale yellow, or red color; crunchy, juicy; sweet, mild, and slightly more pungent than Vidalia onions; best raw or lightly cooked)
- 1 cup (250 mL) chopped Sweet Imperial or other California sweet onions (pale yellow or red; crunchy, juicy; sweet, mild, and slightly more pungent than Vidalia onions; best raw or lightly cooked)
- 1 cup (250 mL) chopped Grand Canyon, NuMex, Mayan, or OSO Sweet onions (pale yellow or red; crunchy, juicy; sweet, mild, and slightly less complex flavor than Vidalia onions; best raw or lightly cooked)

*See also* ONION, STORAGE.

### Ono

*See* MACKEREL; WAHOO.

### Onza Chile

*See* CHOOSING DRIED CHILES (PAGE 642).

### Opal Basil

*See* BASIL.

### Opo Squash

*See* CUCUZZA.

## Orange, Blood

*Mediterranean citrus with garnet-flecked orange flesh or completely garnet flesh. The juice can be light or dark burgundy. Full-bodied orange flavor with a hint of plum or raspberry.*

> 1 lb (500 g) = 3 medium
> = 1 to 1¼ cups
> (250 to 300 mL) juice

### If You Don't Have It

Substitute 1 blood orange with:

- 1 navel orange (orange flesh)
- 1 to 2 Mandarin oranges (such as tangerines; sweeter)

### Blood Orange Varieties

Choose 1 blood orange from these varieties:

- 1 Moro orange (deep burgundy flesh and juice; sweet-tart flavor with hint of raspberries)
- 1 Sanguinelli orange (garnet-flecked flesh and juice; sweet-tart flavor with a hint of plum)

## Orange Extract

*Like all flavoring extracts, store this flavoring in a cool, dark place, and keep the lid on tightly. Properly stored, it will maintain its flavor for a long time, only gradually losing potency.*

### If You Don't Have It

Substitute ½ tsp (2 mL) orange extract with:

- 1 to 2 drops orange oil + ¼ tsp (1 mL) vodka (optional)
- 2 to 3 tsp (10 to 15 mL) orange liqueur (reduce liquid in recipe by 2½ tsp/12 mL if necessary)
- 1 tsp (5 mL) orange zest
- ½ to ¾ tsp (2 to 3 mL) orange flower water

### To Vary the Flavor

Substitute ½ tsp (2 mL) orange extract with:

- ½ tsp (2 mL) lemon extract
- ¾ tsp (3 mL) vanilla extract
- ¾ tsp (3 mL) rum extract

## Orange Flower Water

*The orange flower water of Provence is renowned. The "water" is a distillate produced like cognac or whisky. It takes about 4 pounds (2 kg) of flower petals to make 1 quart (1 L).*

### If You Don't Have It

Substitute ½ tsp (2 mL) orange flower water with:

- ¼ to ½ tsp (1 to 2 mL) orange extract
- 1 to 2 drops orange oil + ¼ tsp (1 mL) vodka (optional)
- 2 to 3 tsp (10 to 15 mL) orange liqueur (reduce liquid in recipe by 2½ tsp/12 mL if necessary)
- 1 tsp (5 mL) orange zest

### To Vary the Flavor

Substitute ½ tsp (2 mL) orange flower water with:

- ½ tsp (2 mL) rose water
- ¼ to ½ tsp (1 to 2 mL) lemon extract
- ¾ tsp (3 mL) vanilla extract
- ¾ tsp (3 mL) rum extract

## Orange Juice

*The Florida Department of Citrus developed the process for making frozen concentrated orange juice in 1945. The patent on the technology was given to the U.S. government to advance the nation's frozen food industry.*

1 medium sweet orange
= 6 to 8 tbsp
(90 to 120 mL) juice

### If You Don't Have It
Substitute 1 cup (250 mL) fresh orange juice with:
- ¼ cup (60 mL) frozen orange juice concentrate + ¾ cup (175 mL) water
- 2 cups (500 mL) brewed orange herbal tea (may add other flavors; reduce liquid in recipe by 1 cup/250 mL if necessary)
- 1 cup (250 mL) blood orange juice (sweeter)
- 1 cup (250 mL) sour orange juice (much more bitter; excellent for marinades)

### To Vary the Flavor
Substitute 1 cup (250 mL) fresh orange juice with:
- 1 cup (250 mL) pineapple juice (sweeter)
- 1 cup (250 mL) grapefruit juice (more tart)
- 1 cup (250 mL) fruit nectar such as mango or peach (thicker; sweeter)

## Orange Liqueur

*What do the Alfonso special, elephant's kick, margarita, morning glory, and Santa Cruz rum daisy have in common? None of these cocktails would exist without a splash of orange liqueur.*

### If You Don't Have It
Substitute 2 tbsp (30 mL) orange liqueur with:
- 2 tsp (10 mL) orange extract (reduce liquid in recipe by 4 tsp/20 mL if necessary)
- 2 to 4 drops orange oil + ½ tsp (2 mL) vodka (optional; reduce liquid in recipe by 2 tbsp/30 mL if necessary)
- 2 tsp (10 mL) orange zest
- 1 to 1½ tsp (5 to 7 mL) orange flower water
- 1 tbsp (15 mL) orange juice concentrate (add 1 tbsp/15 mL liquid to recipe if necessary)
- 3 tbsp (45 mL) orange juice (reduce liquid in recipe by 1 tbsp/15 mL if necessary)
- 2 tbsp (30 mL) Midori (honeydew melon liqueur)

### Orange Liqueur Varieties
Choose 2 tbsp (30 mL) orange liqueur from these varieties:
- 2 tbsp (30 mL) Cointreau (colorless; relatively dry but slightly sweeter than Grand Marnier; complex, balanced flavor; made from curaçao sour orange and sweet orange peels)
- 2 tbsp (30 mL) Citrónge (similar to Cointreau; colorless; relatively dry but slightly sweeter than Grand Marnier; complex flavor; made from Haitian sour orange and Jamaican sweet orange peels)
- 2 tbsp (30 mL) curaçao (sweeter than Cointreau; less complex flavor; amber, clear, orange, or blue color; made from curaçao sour orange and sweet orange peels)
- 2 tbsp (30 mL) Triple Sec (colorless; sweeter than curaçao; less complex flavor; made from curaçao sour orange and sweet orange peels)
- 2 tbsp (30 mL) Grand Marnier (amber color; relatively dry;

## Orange Liqueur (cont'd)

complex, balanced flavor; made from Haitian sour orange and sweet orange peels)

- 2 tbsp (30 mL) Bauchant (similar to Grand Marnier; amber color; relatively dry; complex flavor; made from curaçao sour orange and sweet orange peels)
- 2 tbsp (30 mL) Gran Torres (amber color; medium-dry; mild orange flavor; made from sweet orange peels)
- 2 tbsp (30 mL) mandarin liqueur (sweeter than most orange liqueurs)
- 2 tbsp (30 mL) kumquat liqueur (more sweet-tart flavor than most orange liqueurs)
- 2 tbsp (30 mL) Sabra (chocolate-flavored orange liqueur)

## Orange Oil

*Also known as oil of orange. An essential oil extracted from the zest of oranges; used in flavorings. Two other essential oils from oranges are used mainly in perfumery. Oil of petitgrain is taken from the leaves and twigs. Oil of neroli is derived from the blossoms.*

### If You Don't Have It

Substitute 1 drop orange oil with:

- $\frac{1}{4}$ to $\frac{1}{2}$ tsp (1 to 2 mL) orange extract (less concentrated; evaporates at high temperatures; reduce liquid in recipe by $\frac{1}{2}$ tsp/2 mL if necessary)
- 1 to $1\frac{1}{2}$ tsp (5 to 7 mL) orange zest

### To Vary the Flavor

Substitute 1 drop orange oil with:

- 1 drop lemon oil
- $\frac{3}{4}$ tsp (3 mL) vanilla extract (evaporates at high temperatures; reduce liquid in recipe by $\frac{3}{4}$ tsp/3 mL if necessary)

## Orange Peel

*See* CITRUS PEEL, CANDIED; ORANGE ZEST.

## Orange Roughy

*This mild, white-fleshed fish was christened by Australians and New Zealanders because its skin is orange and rough. The same fish swims in waters off South Africa, where it is known by the less fortunate moniker* slimehead.

### If You Don't Have It

Substitute 1 lb (500 g) orange roughy with:

- 1 lb (500 g) ocean perch
- 1 lb (500 g) blackfish
- 1 lb (500 g) flounder
- 1 lb (500 g) sole
- 1 lb (500 g) haddock
- 1 lb (500 g) red snapper
- 1 lb (500 g) tilapia

## Orange, Sour

*Also known as bitter orange. The juice of sour oranges was a popular flavoring in medieval Europe. In fact, the sour orange arrived in Europe some 500 years prior to*

### If You Don't Have It

Substitute 1 medium sour orange with:

- 1 calamondin (hybrid of mandarin orange and kumquat; sweeter)
- 2 to 3 kumquats (smaller; acidic flesh; sweet peel)
- $\frac{1}{2}$ to 1 sweet orange (larger; much sweeter)
- 1 mandarin orange (much sweeter)
- 1 lime (for candying the peel)

*the sweet (both types of citrus originated in China.) Today, sour oranges have limited commercial use. The Seville is raised mostly in Spain for the production of British orange marmalade. The peel of another sour orange, the diminutive Bergamot, is an ingredient in Earl Grey tea and is also candied. An essential oil, called essence of bergamot, is extracted from the peel for use in perfumes and confections.*

1 medium sour orange = 2 to 3 tbsp (30 to 45 mL) juice = 1/3 to 1/2 cup (75 to 125 mL) chopped = 1 to 2 tbsp (15 to 30 mL) grated zest

- 1 to 2 tbsp (15 to 30 mL) sweet orange juice + 4 to 6 tsp (20 to 30 mL) lime or lemon juice (to replace 3 tbsp/45 mL sour orange juice)

## Sour Orange Varieties

Choose 1 sour orange from these varieties:
- 1 Spanish Bittersweet or Daidai orange (oblong; used for juice, peel, and essential oil)
- 1 Bergamot orange (often candied or used to make Earl Grey tea)
- 1 Seville orange (often used for juice, marmalade, and to make orange liqueurs)
- 1 to 2 Chinotto oranges (often candied)

*See also* ORANGE, SWEET.

# Orange, Sweet

*Numerous varieties of sweet oranges are cultivated for their juice and for eating out-of-hand. Many agree that the seedless navel orange may be the best eating orange. Kept in a high humidity atmosphere at about 35°F (2°C), oranges will maintain their appetizing qualities for nearly 2 months.*

1 medium = 1/3 to 1/2 cup (75 to 125 mL) juice = 3/4 cup (175 mL) chopped = 2 to 3 tbsp (30 to 45 mL) grated zest

## If You Don't Have It

Substitute 1 sweet orange with:
- 1 large blood orange (sweeter; garnet or garnet-flecked flesh)
- 2 mandarin oranges (smaller; sweet-tart)
- 1 to 2 sour oranges (smaller; much more bitter)
- 2 calamondin (hybrid of kumquat and mandarin orange; smaller; more tart)
- 1 Meyer lemon (more tart and lemony)
- 4 to 6 kumquats (more tart; best for eating out of hand)
- 1/4 to 1/2 tsp (1 to 2 mL) pummelo (larger; more tart)
- 1/2 tsp (2 mL) grapefruit (larger; more tart)
- 1 to 2 limes (smaller; more tart)
- 1 large lemon (smaller; more tart)

## Sweet Orange Varieties

Choose 1 fresh sweet orange from these varieties:
- 1 navel-type orange such as Dream Navel, Cara Cara, or California Navel (often seedless; peels and segments easily; best for eating out-of-hand)
- 1 Valencia-type orange such as Valencia, Rhode Red, Kona, or Hamlin (often seeded; extremely juicy; sweet-tart flavor; best for juicing)

*See also* ORANGE, BLOOD; ORANGE FLOWER WATER; ORANGE JUICE; ORANGE LIQUEUR; ORANGE OIL; ORANGE, SOUR; ORANGE ZEST.

## Orange Zest

*No doubt the term "zest" was chosen for the thin outer skin of oranges and other citrus because of the excitement its aromatic essential oils bring to so many foods.*

> 1 medium sweet orange =
> 2 to 3 tbsp
> (30 to 45 mL) grated zest

### If You Don't Have It

Substitute 1 tbsp (15 mL) grated orange zest with:

- 1 tbsp (15 mL) dried orange peel
- 1½ tsp (7 mL) orange extract

### To Vary the Flavor

Substitute 1 tsp (5 mL) grated orange zest with:

- 1 tsp (5 mL) mandarin orange zest
- 1 tsp (5 mL) calamondin zest
- 1 tsp (5 mL) kumquat zest
- 1 tsp (5 mL) lemon or lime zest
- 1 tsp (5 mL) finely chopped candied orange peel (reduce sugar in recipe by ¼ tsp/1 mL if necessary)

## Oregano

*The "pizza herb" is not one specific plant but rather various species of marjoram that carry the characteristic oregano flavor — a combination of sweet/pungent mint and thyme. Many culinary experts say that oregano's full flavoring potential is realized when the leaves are dried rather than fresh.*

> ½ oz (15 g) fresh =
> ½ cup (125 mL) chopped

### If You Don't Have It

Substitute 1 tbsp (15 mL) fresh oregano leaves with:

- 1 tsp (5 mL) dried oregano leaves

### To Vary the Flavor

Substitute 1 tbsp (15 mL) fresh oregano leaves with:

- 1 tbsp (15 mL) fresh marjoram
- 1 tbsp (15 mL) fresh thyme
- 1 tbsp (15 mL) fresh sweet basil
- 1 tbsp (15 mL) fresh summer savory
- 1 to 2 tsp (5 to 10 mL) fresh sage
- 1 tbsp (15 mL) fresh parsley
- 1 tsp (5 mL) dried Italian seasoning (adds thyme and basil flavors)
- 1 tsp (5 mL) dried Greek seasoning (adds onion, garlic, black pepper, mint and cinnamon flavors)
- 1 tsp (5 mL) Herbes de Provence (adds flavors such as thyme, savory, lavender, fennel, and bay leaf)

## Orgeat Syrup

*This sweet almond beverage flavoring — enhanced with rose water or orange-flower water — appears in the mai tai, scorpion, and other cocktails.*

### If You Don't Have It

Substitute 2 tbsp (30 mL) orgeat syrup with:

- 2 tbsp (30 mL) Homemade Simple Syrup (see recipe, page 552) + ⅛ to ¼ tsp (0.5 to 1 mL) almond extract + 1 to 2 drops rose water or orange flower water
- 2 tbsp (30 mL) almond liqueur such as Amaretto + 1 to 2 drops rose water or orange flower water (less sweet; add 1 to 3 tsp/5 to 15 mL sugar to recipe if necessary to balance sweetness)
- 2 tbsp (30 mL) crème d'amande or crème de noyaux + 1 to 2 drops rose water or orange flower water (thicker texture, pink color)

### To Vary the Flavor

Substitute 2 tbsp (30 mL) orgeat syrup with:

- 2 tbsp (30 mL) falernum (adds lime and ginger flavors)

## Ormer

*See* ABALONE.

## Orzo

*See* PASTA, DRIED SOUP.

## Osetra

*See* CHANGING ROE (PAGE 666).

## Ossau-Iraty Brebis Pyrenees

*A traditional, unpasteurized, semisoft cheese from the French Western Pyrenees, which takes its name from two regions, Ossau and Iraty. Made exclusively from the milk of Manech ewes, the cheese is usually shaped in a wheel with a natural rind.*

1 lb (500 g) = 4 cups (1 L) shredded

### If You Don't Have It
Substitute 1 oz (30 g) Ossau-Iraty Brebis Pyrenees cheese with:
- 1 oz (30 g) Etorki
- 1 oz (30 g) Prince de Claverolle
- 1 oz (30 g) Comté

## Ostrich

*It doesn't taste like chicken! This big African bird, now raised as game on specialty ranches, tastes like beef.*

### If You Don't Have It
Substitute 1 lb (500 g) ostrich with:
- 1 lb (500 g) rhea
- 1 lb (500 g) emu
- 1 lb (500 g) beef (fattier)
- 1 lb (500 g) turkey

## Otaheite Gooseberry

*Also known as cheremai, grosella, Malay gooseberry. Although botanically unrelated, this fruit looks and taste similar to a gooseberry. The yellow pigments in the flesh turn red when cooked with sugar for making jams and jellies.*

### If You Don't Have It
Substitute 1 cup (250 mL) Otaheite gooseberries with:
- 1 cup (250 mL) gooseberries
- 1 cup (250 mL) fresh red or white currants
- 1 cup (250 mL) cape gooseberries (sweeter)

## Ouzo

*See* ANISE LIQUEUR.

## Oven

*According to culinary etymologist Mark Morton, the word* oven *sprang from an Indo-European word that meant "fire-pot" and morphed into the Old English word* ofn *near the 10<sup>th</sup> century. By the 1300s, the term was spelled* oven *as it is today.*

### To Vary the Flavor

Substitute a conventional gas or electric oven with:
- brick oven (excellent for baking; absorbs moisture and creates a crisp crust)
- tandoor oven (made of brick and clay; excellent for breads and meats; absorbs moisture and creates a crisp crust)

### To Save Time

- convection oven (an oven with forced hot air to speed cooking; not recommended for delicate mixtures such as soufflés and meringues)
- microwave oven (speeds heating; best for reheating casseroles or other foods that would be reheated in an oven; not recommended for reheating bread and baked goods)

## Ovenproof Pan

*Skillets with handles fashioned from the same heatproof material as the pan — cast iron, stainless clad aluminum or steel, and others — are convenient for searing foods on the stovetop and finishing the cooking in the oven.*

### If You Don't Have It

Substitute an ovenproof pan with:
- plastic- or rubber-handled pan (wrap the handle in several layers of heavy-duty foil to protect it from heat)

## Oyster

*"Unique in a group of foods that includes truffles, lobster, artichokes, mangoes, passion fruit, and a score of other 'love' foods, oysters are food for the initiated few," write Joan Reardon and Ruth Ebling in* Oysters: A Culinary Celebration. *"Often compared to a seductive woman, there is a mystery, a subtlety, a quality that defies explanation about them. No other food evokes such strong feelings of utter bliss or revulsion; no other food has been written about more eloquently or more trivially."*

### If You Don't Have It

Substitute 1 lb (500 g) oysters with:
- 1 lb (500 g) smoked oysters
- 1 lb (500 g) mussels (more delicate)
- 1 lb (500 g) cockles
- 1 lb (500 g) soft-shell clams (for frying)
- 1 lb (500 g) littleneck or cherrystone clams (for serving on the half-shell)
- 1 lb (500 g) scallops
- 1 lb (500 g) abalone (tougher)

### Oyster Varieties

Choose 1 lb (500 g) oysters from these varieties:
- 1 lb (500 g) Eastern, Atlantic or bluepoint oysters (native to North American Atlantic Coast from Canada to the Gulf of Mexico; elongated, layered, gray to brown shell; 2 to 4 inches/5 to 10 cm long; often eaten on the half-shell)
- 1 lb (500 g) Pacific Japanese oysters (usually farmed and harvested at 6 inches/15 cm long; gray to brown shell)
- 1 lb (500 g) Olympia (native to the U.S. Pacific Coast; 1 to 1½-inch/2.5 to 4 cm shell)

1 cup (250 mL) shucked =
13 to 19 medium

3.7 oz (105 g)
can smoked =
14 to 16 oysters

- 1 lb (500 g) European or belon oyster (native to France; farmed in the United States; 1½ to 3-inch/4 to 7.5 cm, rounded, and slightly flattened shell; often eaten on the half-shell)

*See also* OYSTER LIQUOR.

## Oyster Knife

*A sturdy knife with a stubby handle is essential for opening oysters safely. To use, insert the tip into the hinge of the scrubbed oyster shell to pry open. After opening, use the blade to cut under the oyster to release it from the shell.*

### If You Don't Have It

Substitute an oyster knife with:

- another thick, dull knife such as a small spreading knife or spackling knife
- microwaving the oysters until they open (about 20 seconds) or steaming them until they open (about 4 minutes)

## Oyster Liquor

*The juice that spills from freshly shucked oysters often used to flavor chowders, stuffings, and sauces.*

### If You Don't Have It

Substitute 1 cup (250 mL) oyster liquor with:

- 1 cup (250 mL) fresh or bottle clam juice
- 1 cup (250 mL) fish stock
- 1 cup (250 mL) dashi
- ½ cup (125 mL) chicken broth + ½ cup (125 mL) water

## Oyster Mushroom

*See* SHUFFLING MUSHROOMS (PAGE 654).

## Oyster Sauce

*A classic Chinese sauce that is a powerful concentration of oysters, soy sauce, salt, and other seasonings. Thai oyster sauces tend to have richer oyster flavor than Chinese oyster sauces.*

### If You Don't Have It

Substitute 1 tbsp (15 mL) oyster sauce with:

- 1 tbsp (15 mL) vegetarian oyster sauce (made with mushrooms and vegetable protein instead of oysters)
- 2 tsp (10 mL) soy sauce or teriyaki sauce + 1 tsp (5 mL) canning liquid from canned oysters + pinch of sugar (if using soy sauce)
- 2 dozen finely chopped shucked oysters and their liquid simmered for 20 minutes, strained, and the remaining liquid boiled down to 1 tbsp (15 mL)

# Pacific Oyster to Puya

| | |
|---|---|
| **Pacific Oyster** | *See* OYSTER. |
| **Pacific Pompano** | *See* BUTTERFISH. |
| **Paczi** | *See* DOUGHNUT. |

**Paglia-Style Cheese**

*"Heretical as it may sound," writes Steven Jenkins in his Cheese Primer, "there is evidence that the Italians make better Brie than the French." He's referring to Piedmont's Paglia-style cheeses, soft-ripened cow's milk cheese originally aged in piles of loose straw, known as paglia in Italian. Paglietta, Paglierina, and Pagliola are popular names for these paper-wrapped discs.*

**If You Don't Have It**
Substitute 1 oz (30 g) paglia-style cheese with:
- 1 oz (30 g) Brie
- 1 oz (30 g) Camembert

**Pale Ale**     *See* BEER.

## Palillo

*See* TURMERIC.

## Palm Sugar

*See* JAGGERY.

## Pan

*See* SPECIFIC TYPES; PAN SIZE EQUIVALENTS (PAGE 678).

## Pancake Syrup

*See* MAPLE SYRUP.

## Pancake Turner

*See* TURNER.

## Pancetta

*Cured Italian pork belly, the same cut as American bacon, although generally not smoked like American bacon, except in some Alpine provinces. In Spain, a related unsmoked bacon is known as tocino. A similar French bacon called ventrèche is often used to make lardons.*

1 lb (500 g) = 16 slices

### If You Don't Have It

Substitute 1 slice (about 1 oz/30 g) pancetta with:
- 1 slice (about 1 oz/30 g) guanciale (cured hog jowl)
- 1 thick slice (about 1 oz/30 g) American slab bacon (adds smoke flavor; drop in boiling water for 2 minutes to reduce smoke flavor)
- 1 oz (30 g) Canadian bacon (adds smoke flavor)
- 1 oz (30 g) salt pork (saltier; fattier; best as flavoring in soups, stews, and sauces)
- 1 oz (30 g) prosciutto
- 1 oz (30 g) smoked ham (adds smoke flavor)
- 1 oz (30 g) smoked sausage (adds smoke flavor)

## Panch Phoran

*A Bengali spice mix that typically includes the seeds of cumin, fennel, fenugreek, mustard, and nigella.*

### If You Don't Have It

Substitute 1 tbsp (15 mL) panch phoran with:
- 1 tbsp (15 mL) Homemade Panch Phoran: Combine 1½ tsp (7 mL) brown mustard seeds, 1¼ tsp (6 mL) nigella seeds, 1 tsp (5 mL) cumin seeds, ¾ tsp (3 mL) fenugreek seeds, ½ tsp (2 mL) fennel seeds. Makes about 1½ tablespoons (22 mL).
- 1 tbsp (15 mL) garam masala

## Pandanus

*See* SCREWPINE LEAF.

## Paneer

*See* PANIR.

## Panela Cheese

*Fresh, crumbly white cheese of Mexican origin.*

8 oz (250 g) =
1 cup (250 mL)

### If You Don't Have It

Substitute 1 oz (30 g) panela with:
- 1 oz (30 g) dry-cured cottage cheese

*See also* PILONCILLO.

## Panettone

*A fixture of Italian Christmas celebrations, this cupola-shaped, brioche-like cake is typically studded with raisins and candied fruits.*

### If You Don't Have It

Substitute 1 lb (500 g) panettone with:

- 1 lb (500 g) ciambellone (unyeasted Italian coffee cake)
- 1 lb (500 g) kulich (Russian sweet yeast bread; usually has icing; tall, cylindrical shape)
- 1 lb (500 g) Kugelhopf (central European sweet yeast bread; tall, ring shape)
- 1 lb (500 g) brioche (French yeast bread; richer; less sweet or not sweet )
- 1 lb (500 g) fruitcake

## Panettone Pan

*See* PAN SIZE EQUIVALENTS (PAGE 678).

## Panir

*Also known as paneer. Indian fresh pressed cheese produced from cow's or water buffalo's milk. It is pressed to remove excess moisture. Often served diced and sautéed, it also appears in many vegetarian dishes.*

> 8 oz (250 g) =
> 1 cup (250 mL)

### If You Don't Have It

Substitute 1 oz (30 g) panir with:

- 1 oz (30 g) farmer cheese
- 1 oz (30 g) pot cheese
- 1 oz (30 g) firm tofu, cubed
- 1 oz (30 g) feta cheese, cubed and rinsed to remove excess salt
- 1 oz (30 g) dry-curd cottage cheese

*See also* CHENNA.

## Panko

*Also known as panko bread crumbs and Japanese bread crumbs. Coarser than fine dry bread crumbs, panko make light and crispy gratin toppings and coatings for deep-fried foods.*

> 8 oz (250 g) =
> 2⅓ cups (575 mL)

### If You Don't Have It

Substitute 1 cup (250 mL) panko with:

- 3 to 4 slices or large chunks bread, shredded (preferably with a food processor shredding disc) and baked on a baking sheet at 300°F/150°C until dry, about 5 minutes
- 1 cup (250 mL) bread crumbs
- ¾ cup (175 mL) cracker crumbs
- 1 cup (250 mL) crushed melba toasts
- 1 cup (250 mL) matzo meal
- 1 cup (250 mL) crushed tortilla chips
- 1 cup (250 mL) crushed dry-bagged stuffing mix
- 1 cup (250 mL) crushed pretzels
- 1 cup (250 mL) crushed cornflakes
- 1 cup (250 mL) crushed potato chips

## Pans

*See* SPECIFIC TYPES; PAN SIZE EQUIVALENTS (PAGE 678).

## Pansy

*See* PICKING EDIBLE FLOWERS (PAGE 650).

## Papadam

*See* PAPPADAM.

## Papalo

*Also known as papaloquelite. Mexican herb with broad, oval-shaped leaves tastes like a more potent and slightly bitter cilantro. Said to be an acquired taste, papalo is almost always used raw.*

### If You Don't Have It
Substitute 1 tbsp (15 mL) chopped fresh papalo with:
- 3 to 4 tsp (15 to 20 mL) chopped fresh cilantro
- 4 tsp (20 mL) chopped fresh pipicha
- 1 tbsp (15 mL) chopped fresh culantro or culentro (more bitter flavor)
- 1 tbsp (15 mL) chopped fresh parsley

*See also* PIPICHA.

## Papaw

*Also known as pawpaw. A custard apple fruit of a small North American tree that is related to tropical cherimoya. The smooth, sweet yellow pulp tastes like creamy banana and pear. When referred to as "pawpaw," it is confused with the totally unrelated papaya.*

### If You Don't Have It
Substitute 1 lb (500 g) papaws with:
- 1 lb (500 g) blue java or ice cream bananas (sweet ice cream–like flavor)
- 1 lb (500 g) Orinoco bananas (strawberry flavor)
- 1 lb (500 g) burro bananas (slight lemon flavor)
- 1 lb (500 g) dwarf or finger bananas
- 1 lb (500 g) red bananas (best for baking)
- 1 lb (500 g) manzano bananas (drier flesh; strawberry-apple flavor)
- 1 lb (500 g) yellow Cavendish bananas

*See also* CHERIMOYA.

## Papaya

*Also known as lechosa. A wonderful fruit that grows in tropics spanning the globe. In appearance, papaya resembles a large pear-shaped melon. When ripe, the skin is blotchy yellow orange over green and the flesh yields to the touch. The sweet orange flesh is smooth, compact, and delicately scented.*

1 medium = 10 to 12 oz (300 to 375 g) = 1½ to 2 cups (375 to 500 mL) chopped or sliced

### If You Don't Have It
Substitute 1 lb (500 g) papaya with:
- 1 lb (500 g) ababai
- 1 lb (500 g) babaco
- 1 lb (500 g) pepino
- 1 lb (500 g) mango
- 1 lb (500 g) peaches
- 1 lb (500 g) nectarines

*See also* ABABAI; PAPAW; PAPAYA, GREEN.

## Papaya, Dried

*Flame-orange pieces of freeze-dried papaya sometimes coated with sugar.*

### If You Don't Have It
Substitute 1 cup (250 mL) dried papaya with:
- 1 cup (250 mL) dried mango
- 1 cup (250 mL) dried peaches
- 1 cup (250 mL) dried nectarines
- 1 cup (250 mL) dried apricots
- 1 cup (250 mL) dried cantaloupe

## Papaya, Green

*Also known as unripe papaya. Larger unripe fruits are cooked as a vegetable or made into pickles. In Thai kitchens, long strands of peeled green papaya are used to make refreshing salads.*

2 lbs (1 kg) = 4½ to 6 cups (1.125 to 1.5 L)

### If You Don't Have It
Substitute 1 lb (500 g) green papaya with:
- 1 lb (500 g) chayote

*See also* PAPAYA.

## Papaya Leaf

*The leaves of this tropical fruit tree contain about 2% papain, a protein-digesting enzyme widely used in commercial meat tenderizers. South American cooks sometimes wrap meats in papaya leaves for a similar tenderizing effect.*

### If You Don't Have It
Substitute 4 oz (125 g) papaya leaves with:
- 1 cup (250 mL) acid-based marinade (for tenderizing)
- 4 oz (125 g) banana leaves (for wrapping; no tenderizing effect)

## Pappadam

*Also known as papad, papadam, and poppadum. Wafer-thin Indian flatbreads made from lentil flour may be plain or seasoned with peppers, garlic, and other flavorings.*

### If You Don't Have It
Substitute 1 lb (500 g) pappadam with:
- 1 lb (500 g) crisp lavash
- 1 lb (500 g) water crackers

### To Vary the Flavor
Substitute 1 lb (500 g) pappadam with:
- 1 lb (500 g) shrimp chips

## Paprika

*Also known as Hungarian pepper and Spanish pepper. Dried and ground sweet pimentos achieve their glory in Hungarian cuisine, particularly to flavor and color paprikás, which the rest of the world calls goulash. Depending upon the peppers used, paprika can vary from sweetly mild to very hot.*

### If You Don't Have It

Substitute 1 tbsp (15 mL) paprika with:
- 1 tbsp (15 mL) ancho chile powder (darker reddish brown color; earthier, fruitier aromas)
- pinch of cayenne pepper (much hotter)
- pinch of ground chipotle powder (adds smokiness and heat)
- 1 tbsp (15 mL) chili powder (slightly more pungent; adds flavors of cumin, oregano, and other spices)

### Paprika Varieties

Choose 1 tbsp (15 mL) paprika from these varieties:
- 1 tbsp (15 mL) pimentón or Spanish paprika (oak-smoked paprika that may be mild or hot)
- 1 tbsp (15 mL) sweet Hungarian paprika (milder, more complex flavor than Spanish paprika)
- 1 tbsp (15 mL) hot Hungarian paprika (somewhat pungent, more complex flavor than Spanish paprika)

## Paradise Nut

*Also known as monkey pot nut and sapucaya nut. This wild specimen grows in Brazil and Guyana and is said to have a superb, distinctive flavor. Like its relative the Brazil nut, the paradise nut grows inside a big, woody container.*

1 lb (500 g) =
3⅓ cups (825 mL)

### If You Don't Have It

Substitute 1 cup (250 mL) paradise nuts with:
- 1 cup (250 mL) Brazil nuts
- 1 cup (250 mL) macadamia nuts

*See also* BRAZIL NUT.

## Paraffin Wax

*Also known as baker's wax and canning wax. A small amount of melted wax can be mixed into chocolates to forestall melting.*

### If You Don't Have It

Substitute 1 tbsp (15 mL) paraffin wax with:
- 2 to 3 tsp (10 to 15 mL) vegetable shortening (for chocolate confections; less firm)

## Parameswaran's Pepper

*See* PEPPERCORN.

## Paratha

*Also known as parata, Indian flaky bread — often stuffed with spicy vegetable or meat mixtures — that is fried or cooked on a griddle.*

### If You Don't Have It

Substitute 1 paratha with:

- 1 naan (puffy flatbread made from refined wheat flour and cooked on the walls of a tandoor or clay-lined oven; less rich; sometimes flavored with garlic, herbs, or other aromatics)
- 1 poori (deep-fried flatbread made with whole wheat flour; crisper)
- 1 chapati (flatbread made with whole wheat flour and little or no fat)
- 1 roti (a generic term for Indian flatbread; similar to chapati; usually made with whole wheat flour)
- 1 whole wheat pita bread (similar to naan)
- 1 whole wheat flour tortilla

## Parchment Paper

*Also known as baking paper or cooking parchment. If you don't have a nonstick baking pan, make it nonstick by lining the pan with parchment paper. The paper saves cleanup time, too, because you just throw it away when finished.*

### If You Don't Have It

Substitute parchment paper with:

- aluminum foil (for lining baking pans; for cooking "en papillote" or steaming food in a parchment paper package, use pieces of aluminum foil or foil cooking bags)
- silicone baking mat (for lining baking pans)
- nonstick baking sheet
- plastic resealable bag (to replace a parchment paper cone for piping icings or fillings)

## Parfait d'Amour

*A liqueur fashionable in the 19th century — redolent of spices, vanilla, orange, and flowers — that's making something of a comeback.*

### If You Don't Have It

Substitute 1 oz (30 g) Parfait d'Amour with:

- 1 oz (30 g) crème de rose (lighter color; adds vanilla aroma)
- 1 oz (30 g) crème de violette (purple color; violet flower aroma)
- 1 oz (30 g) curaçao + 1 drop rose water + 1 small drop vanilla extract + 1 small drop almond extract (use colored curaçao)

## Parisienne Sauce

*See* VELOUTÉ.

## Parma Ham

*See* PROSCIUTTO.

## Parmesan

*True Parmesan is an Italian cow's milk grana (grating cheese) made only in the legally designated*

### If You Don't Have It

Substitute 1 oz (30 g) Parmesan with:

- 1 oz (30 g) Grana Padano
- 1 oz (30 g) Pecorino Romano (sharper)

*Parmigiano-Reggiano zone encompassing Parma, Reggio nell'Emilia, Bologna, Modena, and Mantua.*

- 1 oz (30 g) aged Asiago (milder)
- 1 oz (30 g) aged Manchego (milder)
- 1 oz (30 g) dry Jack cheese (more nutty flavor)

---

| 4 oz (125 g) = 1 cup (250 mL) grated |
|---|

### For Better Health
Substitute 1 oz (30 g) Parmesan cheese with:

- 1 oz (30 g) Sapsago (more herbal flavor; lower in fat)

---

## Parrot Fish

*Also known as uhu. Parrot Fish are named for their beak-like teeth, which are designed to chomp on coral. They filter out the nutritious algae and excrete the sand.*

### If You Don't Have It
Substitute 1 lb (500 g) parrot fish with:

- 1 lb (500 g) blue-striped snapper or taape

---

## Parsley

*The leaves of this agreeable herb come two ways: flat (Italian) and curly.*

| 1 oz (30 g) = 1 cup (250 mL) chopped |
|---|

### If You Don't Have It
Substitute 1 tbsp (15 mL) chopped fresh parsley with:

- 1 tbsp (15 mL) chopped fresh chervil
- 1 tsp (5 mL) dried parsley or chervil (much less flavorful)
- 1 tbsp (15 mL) chopped fresh cilantro (adds grassy, citrusy aromas)
- 1 tbsp (15 mL) chopped fresh tarragon (adds anise aroma)
- 1 tbsp (15 mL) chopped fresh basil (adds clove aromas)
- 1 tbsp (15 mL) chopped fresh mint (adds menthol aromas)

---

## Parsley Root

*A root-vegetable subspecies of parsley is favored in parts of Europe as an ingredient in soups, stews, or vegetable side dishes.*

| 1 lb (500 g) = 3 cups (750 mL) chopped = 2 cups (500 mL) cooked |
|---|

### If You Don't Have It
Substitute 1 cup (250 mL) chopped parsley root with:

- ½ cup (125 mL) chopped celeriac + ½ cup (125 mL) chopped carrots (milder)
- 1 cup (250 mL) chopped celeriac (milder)
- 1 cup (250 mL) chopped carrots + pinch of celery seeds
- 1 cup (250 mL) chopped turnips + pinch of celery seeds
- 1 cup (250 mL) chopped parsnips + pinch of celery seeds

---

## Parsnip

*Underutilized roots related to carrot, celeriac and parsley root.*

| 1 lb (500 g) = 3 cups (750 mL) chopped = 2 cups (500 mL) cooked |
|---|

### If You Don't Have It
Substitute 1 cup (250 mL) chopped parsnips with:

- 1 cup (250 mL) chopped carrots
- 1 cup (250 mL) chopped arracacha
- 1 cup (250 mL) chopped turnips
- 1 cup (250 mL) chopped salsify
- 1 cup (250 mL) chopped celeriac

## Parsnip (cont'd)

- 1 cup (250 mL) chopped parsley root
- 1 cup (250 mL) chopped taro
- 1 cup (250 mL) chopped burdock

## Partridge

*An important game bird in Europe and central Asia. The bird has a small chicken-like shape and is plump and tasty.*

### If You Don't Have It

Substitute 1 lb (500 g) partridge with:

- 1 lb (500 g) grouse
- 1 lb (500 g) quail
- 1 lb (500 g) pheasant
- 1 lb (500 g) squab
- 1 lb (500 g) Cornish game hen

### Partridge Varieties

Choose 1 lb (500 g) partridge from these varieties:

- 1 lb (500 g) grey or English partridge
- 1 lb (500 g) red-legged or French partridge

## Pasilla

*See* CHOOSING DRIED CHILES (PAGE 642).

## Passion Fruit

*Also known as maracuja. The exquisite aroma and taste of this exotic fruit is unique. The name is a reference to the fruit's blossom resembling various details of the Passion of Christ.*

| 12 to 14 passion fruits = about 1 cup (250 mL) juice, pulp, or purée |

### If You Don't Have It

Substitute 1 cup (250 mL) passion fruit pulp or juice with:

- 1 cup (250 mL) canned passion fruit nectar (to replace fresh passion fruit juice)
- ½ cup (125 mL) pineapple juice + ½ cup (125 mL) Key lime juice (to replace fresh passion fruit juice)
- 1 cup (250 mL) guava pulp (to replace passion fruit pulp)

### Passion Fruit Varieties

Choose 1 cup (250 mL) passion fruit pulp from:

- 1 cup (250 mL) maracuja or purple passion fruit pulp (the true passion fruit; reddish purple-brown skin, often wrinkled, or pale yellow skin; intensely aromatic greenish orange, sweet-tart pulp)
- 1 cup (250 mL) granadilla pulp (slightly larger than maracuja; orange skin with specks of white; milder, pale gray, sweet-tart pulp)

## Passion Fruit Liqueur

*Tasting of honey, jasmine, and lemon, the intense essence of passion fruit flavors this liqueur.*

### If You Don't Have It

Substitute 2 tbsp (30 mL) passion fruit liqueur with:

- 2 tbsp (30 mL) passion fruit syrup (nonalcoholic)
- 1 tbsp (15 mL) passion fruit nectar + 1 tbsp (15 mL) brandy (less sweet)

### To Vary the Flavor

Substitute 2 tbsp (30 mL) passion fruit liqueur with:

- 2 tbsp (30 mL) fruit brandy such as apricot brandy (less sweet)

## Passover Crackers

*See* MANDLEN; MATZO.

## Pasta, Dried Ribbons

*Thin pasta ribbons, such as linguine, marry well with thin, smooth sauces. Wide ribbons, such as pappardelle, go best with thick, smooth sauces or sauces with small chunks. To substitute regular dried lasagna with no-boil or oven-ready lasagna, add 25% more sauce or liquid, which will be absorbed by the no-boil lasagna.*

> 1 lb (500 g) = 8 cups (2 L) cooked

### If You Don't Have It

Substitute 1 lb (500 g) dried pasta ribbons with these varieties:
- 1 lb (500 g) dried fettuccine, lasagna, linguine, pappardelle, or tagliatelle
- 8 oz (250 g) dried wide egg noodles
- 1 lb (500 g) dried wide Asian wheat noodles

### For Better Health

Substitute 1 lb (500 g) dried pasta ribbons with:
- 1 lb (500 g) dried whole wheat pasta ribbons (higher fiber)
- 1 lb (500 g) dried Jerusalem artichoke pasta ribbons (higher fiber)
- 1 lb (500 g) dried quinoa pasta ribbons (gluten-free)
- 1 lb (500 g) dried spelt pasta ribbons (low-gluten)
- 1 lb (500 g) dried Kamut® pasta ribbons (low-gluten)
- 1 lb (500 g) dried rice pasta ribbons (gluten-free)
- 1 lb (500 g) dried wide Asian rice noodles (gluten-free)

## Pasta, Dried Shapes

*When cooking various shaped pastas together, choose similar sizes so they cook at the same rate. Large shapes and tubes, such as rigatoni, go best with sauces that have large chunks. Small shapes and tubes, such as macaroni, go best with smooth sauces or sauces that have small chunks.*

> 1 lb (500 g) dried = 8 cups (2 L) cooked

### If You Don't Have It

Substitute 1 lb (500 g) dried pasta shapes with these varieties:
- 1 lb (500 g) dried elbow macaroni, medium shells, rotini, twists, spirals, wagon wheels, bow ties, mostaccioli, penne, radiatore, rigatoni, or ziti

### For Better Health

Substitute 1 lb (500 g) dried pasta shapes with:
- 1 lb (500 g) dried whole wheat pasta shapes (higher fiber)
- 1 lb (500 g) dried Jerusalem artichoke pasta shapes (higher fiber)
- 1 lb (500 g) dried quinoa pasta shapes (gluten-free)
- 1 lb (500 g) dried spelt pasta shapes (low-gluten)
- 1 lb (500 g) dried Kamut® pasta shapes (low-gluten)
- 1 lb (500 g) dried rice pasta shapes (gluten-free)

*See also* EGG NOODLE; A SNAPSHOT OF ASIAN NOODLES (PAGE 656).

## Pasta, Dried Soup

*"A vegetable soup can tell you where you are in Italy almost as precisely as a map,"* writes Italian cooking authority Marcella Hazan. For instance, she says, the soups of the south are "founded on tomato, garlic, and olive oil, often filled out with pasta."

1 lb (500 g) =
8 cups (2 L) cooked

## Pasta, Dried Strands

*Thin strands, such as angel hair, go best with thin sauces. Thick strands, such as perciatelli, go well with thick sauces or sauces with small chunks.*

1 lb (500 g) dried =
7 to 8 cups
(1.75 to 2 L) cooked

## Pasta Filata Cheese

### If You Don't Have It
Substitute 1 lb (500 g) dried soup pasta with these varieties:
- 1 lb (500 g) acini de pepe, ditalini, elbow macaroni, orzo, pastina, rizo, or rosamarina

### If You Don't Have It
Substitute 1 lb (500 g) dried pasta strands with these varieties:
- 1 lb (500 g) dried angel hair, capellini, bucatini, perciatelli, spaghetti, or vermicelli
- 1 lb (500 g) dried Asian wheat noodles
- 8 oz (250 g) dried egg noodles

### For Better Health
Substitute 1 lb (500 g) dried pasta strands with:
- 1 lb (500 g) dried whole wheat pasta strands (higher fiber)
- 1 lb (500 g) dried Jerusalem artichoke pasta strands (higher fiber)
- 1 lb (500 g) dried buckwheat pasta or soba noodles (higher fiber)
- 1 lb (500 g) dried quinoa pasta strands (gluten-free)
- 1 lb (500 g) dried spelt pasta strands (low-gluten)
- 1 lb (500 g) dried Kamut® pasta strands (low-gluten)
- 1 lb (500 g) dried rice pasta strands (gluten-free)
- 1 lb (500 g) dried Asian rice noodles (gluten-free)
- 1 medium-large (6 lb/3 kg) spaghetti squash, cooked (7 to 8 cups/1.75 to 2 L cooked strands; adds squash flavor but makes a novel and more nutritious alternative to pasta and can be served just like spaghetti; pierce a whole spaghetti squash once or twice then bake at 375°F/190°C until tender, about 40 minutes; cool slightly and cut lengthwise, pouring spaghetti-like strands into a bowl or onto plates)

*See also* EGG NOODLE; A SNAPSHOT OF ASIAN NOODLES (PAGE 656).

*See* CACIOCAVALLO; MOZZARELLA; PROVOLONE; SCAMORZA.

## Pasta, Filled

Ingredients for pasta fillings are seemingly limitless. The morsels are classified according to the various ways of folding and sealing the pasta.

| 1 lb (500 g) = 5⅓ cups (1.325 L) cooked |
| --- |

### If You Don't Have It

Substitute 1 lb (500 g) frozen filled pasta with these varieties:
- 1 lb (500 g) frozen filled agnolotti, capelletti, ravioli, tortellini, or tortelloni

## Pasta, Fresh

Also known as pasta fresca. Created from soft wheat flour and eggs, fresh pasta is more akin to egg noodles than to macaroni-style factory pasta made with semolina flour.

| 1½ lbs (750 g) = 8 cups (2 L) cooked |
| --- |

### If You Don't Have It

Substitute 1 lb (500 g) fresh pasta with:
- 1 lb (500 g) egg roll wrappers (especially for filled pasta)
- 1 lb (500 g) won ton skins (especially for filled pasta; smaller than egg roll wrappers)
- 1 lb (500 g) dumpling wrappers (especially for filled pasta; thinner than egg roll wrappers; round instead of square corners)
- 1 lb (500 g) empanada wrappers (especially for filled pasta; round)

## Pasta Machine

This chrome tool for rolling and cutting pasta dough clamps to the counter.

### If You Don't Have It

Substitute a roller-type pasta machine with:
- heavy rolling pin, sharp knife, and plenty of time

## Pastis

See ANISE LIQUEUR.

## Pastrami

Highly seasoned beef brisket or round that is dry-cured, smoked, and cooked.

### If You Don't Have It

Substitute 1 lb (500 g) pastrami with:
- 1 lb (500 g) corned beef (less tender)

## Pastry

See PIE CRUST, PASTRY.

## Pastry Bag

A simple but ingenious cone-shaped bag, usually made of plastic or canvas. Frosting and mashed potatoes are just two of the foods that pass through pastry bags.

### If You Don't Have It

Substitute a pastry bag (for piping frostings and fillings) with:
- plastic resealable bag (fill bag and cut off one corner)
- parchment paper (roll into a cone and fill)

## Pastry Blender

*A series of U-shaped sturdy metal wires attached to a handle. Used to cut butter or other fat into a flour mixture for making pie crusts, biscuits, and other baked goods.*

### If You Don't Have It

Substitute a pastry blender with:
- food processor (for cutting fat into dry ingredients and making pastry dough)
- knife and hands (chop fat into small pieces and mix quickly into dry ingredients with fingers; if your hands are warm, run them under cold water to help prevent them from melting the fat)
- fork tines (for cutting fat into dry ingredients)
- table knives (use two knives to cut fat into dry ingredients)

## Pastry Brush

*Useful tool for applying glazes and marinades, these brushes are made in many sizes and materials.*

### If You Don't Have It

Substitute a pastry brush with:
- clean, unused paint brush of similar size

## Pastry Cloth

*A large canvas cloth makes rolling and transferring pie dough an easy task. Rubbing flour into the fibers makes the cloth an excellent nonstick surface. After each use, the cloth should be brushed well to remove all fat residue before storing.*

### If You Don't Have It

Substitute a pastry brush with:
- large silicone baking mat

## Pastry Cutter

*See* BENCH KNIFE.

## Pastry Flour

*See* FLOUR, PASTRY.

## Pastry Shell

*See* PATTY SHELL.

## Pastry Wheel

*Fluted-edge pastry wheels that cut decorative designs in doughs are called jagging wheels or pastry jaggers.*

### If You Don't Have It

Substitute a pastry wheel with:
- pizza wheel
- sharp knife

## Patagonian Toothfish

*Also known as Chilean sea bass and merluza negra. Coldwater fish ranging widely from the Southern Atlantic and Pacific to the Indian and Antarctic Oceans. Many environmental watch groups have placed Patagonian Toothfish on its red list of fish likely to be sourced from unsustainable fisheries.*

### If You Don't Have It
Substitute 1 lb (500 g) Patagonian Toothfish with:
- 1 lb (500 g) black cod
- 1 lb (500 g) sablefish

## Pâté

*In classic French cuisine, a seasoned finely ground meat mixture (terrine) baked in pastry. In modern parlance, the term has come to refer to the forcemeat mixture with or without a crust. Pâté de foie gras is puréed fatty goose liver that may also contain up to 20 percent pork liver, eggs, truffles, or other ingredients.*

### If You Don't Have It
Substitute 1 lb (500 g) pâté with:
- 1 lb (500 g) liverwurst
- 1 lb (500 g) Braunschweiger (smoked liverwurst)

### To Vary the Flavor
Substitute 1 lb (500 g) pâté de foie gras with:
- 1 lb (500 g) goose liver, duck liver, pork liver, or chicken liver pâté made with plenty of butter and some liquid lecithin to emulsify

### For Better Health
- 1 lb (500 g) fava bean pâté made with plenty of butter and some liquid lecithin to emulsify

## Pâte Brisée

*See* PIE CRUST, PASTRY.

## Patis

*See* FISH SAUCE; SHRIMP SAUCE.

## Pattypan Squash

*Also known as scallopini (when young). Pale green or bright yellow summer squash with a fetching scalloped border, often delivers more in looks than taste.*

1 lb (500 g) = 3 cups (750 mL) chopped

### If You Don't Have It
Substitute 1 lb (500 g) pattypan squash with:
- 1 lb (500 g) yellow squash
- 1 lb (500 g) zucchini
- 1 lb (500 g) cucuzza
- 1 lb (500 g) fuzzy gourd

## Patty Shell

A cup-shaped puff pastry shell that can be filled with various creamed dishes. Fresh ones are sold in some bakeries. Frozen unbaked shells are stocked in supermarkets.

### If You Don't Have It

Substitute 1 lb (500 g) patty shells with:
- 1 lb (500 g) barquettes (boat-shaped pastry shells)
- 1 lb (500 g) phyllo shells or knafa (less rich; more crisp; shape knafa into shells in ramekins or muffin cups)

*See also* PUFF PASTRY.

## Pátzcuaro Chile

*See* CHOOSING DRIED CHILES (PAGE 642).

## Pawpaw

*See* PAPAW.

## Pea

*See* PEAS, EDIBLE POD; PEA SHOOTS; PEAS, SHELLING; PEAS, SPLIT.

## Pea Bean

*See* THE WIDE WORLD OF DRIED BEANS (PAGE 637).

## Peach

China gave the world one of its most prized pleasures in this fruit. Of the two basic categories, freestone peaches are eaten as fresh fruit, while clingstones (with flesh that sticks to the stone) are most often commercially canned. Donut peaches (aka flat or saucer peaches) tend to have softer flesh and less acid.

> 1 lb (500 g) fresh =
> 4 medium =
> 2½ cups (625 mL)
> chopped or sliced =
> 1½ cups (375 mL) purée

### If You Don't Have It

Substitute 1 lb (500 g) peaches with:
- 1 lb (500 g) nectarines
- 1 lb (500 g) apricots
- 1 lb (500 g) plums
- 1 lb (500 g) apriums (cross between an apricot and plum)
- 1 lb (500 g) pluots (cross between a plum and an apricot)
- 1 lb (500 g) cherries
- 1 lb (500 g) mango
- 1 lb (500 g) papaya

## Peach, Dried

Sulfur dioxide is often added to commercially dried fruit to improve shelf life and color.

> 1 lb (500 g) =
> 3 cups (750 mL)

### If You Don't Have It

Substitute 1 lb (500 g) dried peaches with:
- 1 lb (500 g) dried apricots
- 1 lb (500 g) dried nectarines
- 1 lb (500 g) dried cherries

## Peanut

*Also known as goobers and ground nuts. Spaniards and Portuguese slave traders transported these legumes from South America to Europe and Africa. African slaves introduced them to the American South.*

> 1 lb (500 g) =
> 3½ to 4 cups
> (875 mL to 1 L)
> chopped = 4 cups (1 L)
> ground meal

### If You Don't Have It

Substitute 1 cup (250 mL) peanuts with:
- 1 cup (250 mL) cashews
- 1 cup (250 mL) almonds
- 1 cup (250 mL) pistachios
- 1 cup (250 mL) pine nuts
- 1 cup (250 mL) walnuts
- 1 cup (250 mL) pecans

*See also* NUT.

## Peanut Butter

*In the late 1800s, a physician in St. Louis ground peanuts into a spread for his patients with bad teeth. At the 1904 Louisiana Purchase Exposition in St. Louis, it was promoted as a health food, but the oil separated from the grainy solids. In 1933, a California packer homogenized the peanuts into a stable butter marketed as Skippy Churned Peanut Butter.*

### If You Don't Have It

Substitute 1 cup (250 mL) peanut butter with:
- 1 cup (250 mL) Homemade Peanut Butter: Put 2 cups (500 mL) roasted peanuts (skins removed) and ¼ tsp (1 mL) salt in a blender or food processor fitted with metal blade. Process, gradually adding 4 to 6 tbsp (60 to 90 mL) vegetable oil and/or peanut oil, until the mixture forms a paste. Add sugar to taste. Makes 1½ cups (375 mL).
- 1 cup (250 mL) almond butter
- 1 cup (250 mL) cashew butter
- 1 cup (250 mL) gianduja (chocolate-hazelnut spread)
- 1 cup (250 mL) tahini (pronounced sesame flavor)

### For Better Health

Substitute 1 cup (250 mL) peanut butter with:
- 1 cup (250 mL) sunflower butter (for those with tree nut allergies)
- 1 cup (250 mL) soynut butter (for those with tree nut allergies; less fat; milder flavor)

## Peanut Butter Chips

*Also known as peanut butter morsels. Sweetened peanut butter candies shaped like chocolate morsels used for baking and snacks.*

> 6 oz (175 g) =
> 1 cup (250 mL)

### If You Don't Have It

Substitute 1 cup (250 mL) peanut butter chips with:
- 1 cup (250 mL) butterscotch chips
- 1 cup (250 mL) cinnamon chips
- 1 cup (250 mL) chocolate chips
- 1 cup (250 mL) chopped nuts

## Peanut Liqueur

*A low-proof cream liqueur infused with the flavor of peanuts. Castries is the most popular brand, named for the capital city of St. Lucia, where it is produced.*

### If You Don't Have It

Substitute 3 tbsp (45 mL) peanut liqueur with:

- 3 tbsp (45 mL) crème do noix (walnut cream liqueur)
- 2 tbsp (30 mL) walnut, almond, or hazelnut liqueur + 1 tbsp (15 mL) light or heavy cream

## Peanut Oil

*See* SUBSTITUTING OILS (PAGE 658).

## Pear

*An atypical fruit that ripens well off the tree, pear varieties number in the thousands.*

> 1 lb (500 g) fresh =
> 3 medium =
> 2 cups (500 mL) sliced

### If You Don't Have It

Substitute 1 lb (500 g) pears with:

- 1 lb (500 g) apples
- 1 lb (500 g) Asian pears (more crisp)
- 1 lb (500 g) quinces

*See also* PICKING PEARS (PAGE 661).

## Pear Brandy

*Clear pear-flavored eau de vie from France and Switzerland. The finest brands encapsulate a whole Williams pear (the European name for Bartlett) inside each bottle. The painstaking process involves placing an individual bottle over a budding fruit and allowing the fruit to ripen in the bottle before it is filled with brandy.*

### If You Don't Have It

Substitute 2 tbsp (30 mL) pear brandy with:

- 2 tbsp (30 mL) apple brandy such as Calvados or applejack
- 1 tbsp (15 mL) cognac or brandy + 1 tbsp (15 mL) pear nectar
- 2 tbsp (30 mL) other fruit brandy such as cherry brandy

## Pear, Dried

*High concentrations of sugar in dried pears ward off bacteria and help the fruit remain supple.*

> 1 lb (500 g) dried =
> 2¾ cups (675 mL) =
> 5½ cups (1.375 L) cooked

### If You Don't Have It

Substitute 1 oz (30 g) dried pears with:

- 1 oz (30 g) dried Asian pears
- 1 oz (30 g) dried apples

## Peas, Edible Pod

*Also known as mangetout (England and France), snow pea, and sugar snap pea. Truly a no-waste vegetable, snow peas and sugar snap peas require little, if any, cooking to enjoy.*

1 lb (500 g) =
3 cups (750 mL)

### If You Don't Have It

Substitute 1 lb (500 g) edible pod peas with:

- 1 lb (500 g) mung bean sprouts
- 1 lb (500 g) fresh edamame or fava beans
- 1 lb (500 g) asparagus
- 1 lb (500 g) broccoli

### Edible Pod Pea Varieties

Choose 1 oz (30 g) edible pod peas from these varieties:

- 1 lb (500 g) sugar snap peas (sweet, crisp, rounded pods with medium-size peas)
- 1 lb (500 g) snow peas (medium-sweet, crisp-tender, flattened pods with small peas)

## Pea Shoots

*Also known as dau miu, pea leaves, pea tendrils, pea vines, and tohbyo. Charming jade green leaves of fresh snap peas or snow peas are festooned with whimsical curlicues. Delicious added to salads. In classic Chinese cooking, the leaves are added to soup, steamed, or stir-fried.*

1 lb (500 g) fresh =
10 cups (2.5 L)

### If You Don't Have It

Substitute 1 cup (250 mL) pea shoots with:

- 1 cup (250 mL) mung bean sprouts
- 1 cup (250 mL) baby spinach leaves (less sweet)
- 1 cup (250 mL) garden or upland cress (more peppery)

## Peas, Shelling

*The most glamorous incarnation of the common fresh garden pea is the French* petits pois *harvested when young and sweet. The sugar in shelled peas starts to turn to starch the moment they are picked. If you can't grow your own or buy from a farmer, the best choice may be frozen baby peas.*

1 lb (500 g) fresh in pod =
5 oz (150 g) shelled =
1 cup (250 mL) shelled

### If You Don't Have It

Substitute 1 lb (500 g) fresh shelling peas (weighed in shell) with:

- 1 lb (500 g) fresh black-eyed peas or other cowpeas (southernpeas; pale green and cream or pink color with black "eye" at center)
- 1 lb (500 g) fresh lima beans (green color)
- 1 lb (500 g) fresh edamame (green color)
- 1 lb (500 g) fresh cranberry beans (cream and red-speckled color)
- 1 lb (500 g) fresh Dragon Tongue beans (deep reddish brown and cream color)
- 1 lb (500 g) fresh Tongue of Fire beans (green and red color)
- 1 lb (500 g) fresh Romano beans (green color)
- 1 lb (500 g) fresh Kentucky Wonder or runner beans (green color)

*See also* BEAN, FRESH SHELLING; BLACK-EYED PEA, FRESH.

## Peas, Split

*Also known as field peas.
A variety of green or
yellow peas cultivated to
be dried. After drying, they
split along a natural seam.
In India, peas are stewed
into a variety of dals. In
the west, green split pea
soup with ham is a classic.*

> 1 lb (500 g) =
> 2⅓ cups (575 mL) dried
> = 5 cups (1.25 L) cooked

### If You Don't Have It

Substitute 1 lb (500 g) green or yellow split peas with:

- 1 lb (500 g) lentils
- 1 lb (500 g) dried black-eyed peas

*See also* SWITCHING LENTILS (PAGE 653).

## Pecan

*This luminary of the hickory
family is synonymous
with the American South.
The name comes from the
Algonquin word* paccan
*which refers to hickories.*

> 1 lb (500 g) in shell =
> 2 cups (500 mL) shelled
>
> 1 lb (500 g) shelled =
> 4 cups (1 L) halves =
> 3¾ cups (925 mL)
> chopped

### If You Don't Have It

Substitute 1 cup (250 mL) shelled pecans with:

- 2 to 4 tbsp (30 to 60 mL) pecan oil (for baking and cooking; will add nut flavor but not texture of whole nuts; reduce fat in recipe by 2 to 4 tbsp/30 to 60 mL)
- 1 cup (250 mL) walnuts
- 1 cup (250 mL) hazelnuts
- 1 cup (250 mL) hickory nuts
- 1 cup (250 mL) pistachios
- 1 cup (250 mL) macadamia nuts
- 1 cup (250 mL) Brazil nuts

### For Better Health

Substitute 1 cup (250 mL) pecans with:

- 1 cup (250 mL) rolled oats, toasted (for baking)

*See also* NUT.

## Pecan Meal

*See* NUT MEAL.

## Pecorino

*A sharp, sheep's milk
cheese,* pecorino romano
*is produced in the regions
of Lazio and Sardinia, as
well as Grosseto province
in Tuscany. Locatelli is
among the most popular
brands of pecorino romano
in the United States.
Pecorino toscano is made
only from milk drawn*

### If You Don't Have It

Substitute 1 oz (30 g) pecorino cheese (for grating) with:

- 1 oz (30 g) aged Nisa or Serpa
- 1 oz (30 g) Parmesan (slightly milder and less salty)
- 1 oz (30 g) Grana Padano
- 1 oz (30 g) aged Asiago
- 1 oz (30 g) aged Manchego
- 1 oz (30 g) dry Jack cheese (more nutty flavor)

*between September and June. Pecorino siciliano is studded with whole black peppercorns. Pecorino sardo, (fiore sardo), is made on the island of Sardinia.*

---

1 lb (500 g) young =
4 cups (1 L) shredded

4 oz (125 g) aged =
1 cup (250 mL) grated

---

## For Better Health
Substitute 1 oz (30 g) pecorino cheese (for grating) with:
- 1 oz (30 g) sapsago (more herbal flavor; lower in fat)

*See also* ROMANO.

## Pectin

*Glue-like plant fiber that traps water and creates a smooth viscous gel in gummy candies, fruit jams, and jellies. If you are sensitive to sulfites, use powdered pectin. Unlike liquid pectin, it doesn't contain sulfites. Use about 4 tsp (20 mL) powdered pectin or 2 tbsp (30 mL) liquid pectin to jell 2 cups (500 mL) of liquid.*

## If You Don't Have It
Substitute 2 tbsp (30 mL) liquid pectin with:
- 4 tsp (20 mL) powdered pectin
- 1 tbsp (15 mL) unflavored gelatin powder or granules

## To Vary the Flavor
Substitute 2 tbsp (30 mL) liquid pectin with:
- 2½ cups (625 mL) finely chopped and cooked high-pectin fruit such as quince, gooseberries, sour plums, or tart apples

## Peel
*See* PIZZA PEEL.

## Peeler
*See* VEGETABLE PEELER.

## Pemmican

*Loaves or small cakes composed of a paste of pulverized ground meat or fish, hot fat, and dried berries or other fruits. Of Native American origin.*

## If You Don't Have It
Substitute 1 oz (30 g) pemmican with:
- 1 oz (30 g) beef jerky (less complex flavor)
- 1 oz (30 g) biltong (spicier; more complex flavor)

## For Better Health
Substitute 1 oz (30 g) pemmican with:
- 1 oz (30 g) turkey jerky (leaner)
- 1 oz (30 g) vegetarian jerky (leaner)

*See also* BILTONG; JERKY.

## Penca
*See* MAGUEY LEAF.

## Penne
*See* PASTA, DRIED SHAPES.

## Pepicha

*See* PIPICHA.

## Pepino

*Also known as melon pear and treemelon. A glossy gold and violet skinned fruit related to eggplant with a mild taste and melon-like texture.*

1 lb (500 g) =
3 cups (750 mL)

### If You Don't Have It

Substitute 1 lb (500 g) pepinos with:

- 1 lb (500 g) babacos
- 1 lb (500 g) tamarillos
- 1 lb (500 g) papaya
- 1 lb (500 g) pears
- 1 lb (500 g) Charentais melon or cantaloupe
- 1 lb (500 g) prickly pears

## Pepita

*See* PUMPKIN SEED.

## Peppadew™ Piquanté Pepper

*Peppadews, the vivid red sweet-hot South African peppers, are available jarred or in the delicatessen section of some supermarkets.*

8 oz (250 g) drained =
1 cup (250 mL)

### If You Don't Have It

Substitute 1 cup (250 mL) Peppadew™ Piquanté peppers with:

- 1 cup (250 mL) peperoncini
- 1 cup (250 mL) pickled cherry peppers
- 1 cup (250 mL) pimentos
- 1 cup (250 mL) red Anaheim chiles
- 1 cup (250 mL) red New Mexico chiles
- 1 cup (250 mL) sun-dried tomatoes

## Pepper

*See* BELL PEPPER; PEPPERCORN; CHOOSING DRIED CHILES (PAGE 642); CHOOSING FRESH CHILES (PAGE 640).

## Peppercorn

*The berry of the climbing vine pepper plant (piper nigrum) native to India and Indonesia is the most popular spice in the world. Green peppercorns are immature berries usually packed in brine. White peppercorns are mature, skinned, dried berries. Black peppercorns are the most popular type. They are slightly underripe berries that turn dark after they dry.*

### If You Don't Have It

Substitute 1 tsp (5 mL) peppercorns with:

- 1½ tsp (7 mL) ground pepper
- 1 tsp (5 mL) cubeb (adds mint and allspice aromas)
- 1 tsp (5 mL) Tasmanian peppercorns (softer, more fruity aroma)
- 1 tsp (5 mL) Java long pepper (adds citrus aromas; more searing heat)
- 1 tsp (5 mL) grains of paradise (adds cardamom aromas)
- 1 tsp (5 mL) crushed Selim Kili pepper (adds eucalyptus and nutmeg aromas; slightly bitter)

*Tellicherry and Lampong are considered the finest types of black pepper.*

---

1 tsp (5 mL) peppercorns
= 1½ tsp (7 mL)
ground pepper

---

## Peppercorn Varieties

Choose 1 tsp (5 mL) peppercorns from these varieties:
- 1 tsp (5 mL) black peppercorns (strong, almost hot flavor)
- 1 tsp (5 mL) white peppercorns (smaller and hotter but less aromatic than black peppercorns)
- 1 tsp (5 mL) green peppercorns (milder than black peppercorns; usually pickled)
- 1 tsp (5 mL) true pink peppercorns (milder than black peppercorns with berry-like aromas; usually pickled)
- 1 tsp (5 mL) Parameswaran's black peppercorns (a mixture of high-quality Panniyor and Karimunda varieties of *piper nigrum* with clean pepper aroma and heat)
- 1 tsp (5 mL) Parameswaran's white peppercorns (soaked to remove outer black husk; less complex aroma; more pointed heat)

## To Vary the Flavor

Substitute 1 tsp (5 mL) peppercorns with:
- 1 tsp (5 mL) pink peppercorns (milder; not a true peppercorn)
- 1 tsp (5 mL) Szechuan pepper (milder; adds citrus aromas; not a true peppercorn)
- ¼ to ½ tsp (1 to 2 mL) cayenne pepper (spicier)
- ½ to 1 tsp (2 to 5 mL) black or yellow mustard seeds (sharper)

*See also* CUBEB; GRAINS OF PARADISE; LONG PEPPER; PINK PEPPERCORN; SELIM KILI PEPPER; SZECHUAN PEPPER; TASMANIAN PEPPER

## Pepper Leaf

*See* BETEL LEAF.

## Pepper Mill

*Former* New York Times *restaurant critic Bryan Miller once wrote, "The disparity between a restaurant's price and food quality rises in direct proportion to the size of the pepper mill.*

### If You Don't Have It

Substitute a pepper mill with:
- mortar and pestle
- spice grinder or clean coffee grinder

## Peppermint

*See* MINT.

## Peppermint Extract

*See* MINT EXTRACT.

## Peppermint Oil

*See* OIL OF PEPPERMINT.

## Peppermint Schnapps

*Created in the 1930s, this is the first popular single-flavored liqueur bearing the schnapps name. It generally has a higher proof than other fruit schnapps liqueurs.*

### If You Don't Have It

Substitute 2 tbsp (30 mL) peppermint schnapps with:
- 1 to 2 tbsp (15 to 30 mL) crème de menthe (thicker; sweeter)
- ¼ to ½ tsp (1 to 2 mL) peppermint extract
- 1 drop oil of peppermint

## Pepperoncini

*Italian-style pickled sweet-hot chiles similar in taste and appearance to small Anaheim chiles.*

8 oz (250 g) drained =
1 cup (250 mL)

### If You Don't Have It

Substitute 1 cup (250 mL) pepperoncini with:
- 1 cup (250 mL) pickled cherry peppers
- 1 cup (250 mL) pickled Anaheim chiles
- 1 cup (250 mL) cup Peppadew™ Piquanté peppers
- 1 cup (250 mL) pickled pimientos
- 1 cup (250 mL) other pickled peppers

*See also* CHOOSING FRESH CHILES (PAGE 640).

## Pepperoni

*Firm, dry, ready-to-eat Italian sausage prepared from beef and pork. Generally sliced very thin, it's most popular on pizza but also makes a good appetizer or addition to pasta.*

### If You Don't Have It

Substitute 1 oz (30 g) pepperoni with:
- 1 oz (30 g) Calabrese sausage
- 1 oz (30 g) soppressata
- 1 oz (30 g) other dry Italian salami

*See also* SALAMI.

## Pequín Chile

*See* CHOOSING DRIED CHILES (PAGE 642).

## Percebe

*See* BARNACLE.

## Perch

*True perch is a moderate-size freshwater fish with two dorsal fins that originated in Eurasia and was introduced in other waters as a prize for anglers. The term perch has been widely misapplied to a number of similar-seeming marine life. The Eastern European fish called pike-perch (zander) is also unrelated.*

### If You Don't Have It

Substitute 1 lb (500 g) with:
- 1 lb (500 g) pike
- 1 lb (500 g) porgy
- 1 lb (500 g) rockfish
- 1 lb (500 g) red snapper
- 1 lb (500 g) grouper

*See also* OCEAN PERCH; PIKE.

## Perilla

*Also known as Japanese basil, shiso, and sesame leaf. This annual herb has been cultivated in Japan since the 8$^{th}$ century. The jagged-edged green shiso leaf, minty and refreshing, is used in salads, sushi, sashimi, tempura, and other dishes. A reddish-purple variety, called akajiso, is used to color pickled plums (umeboshi).*

### If You Don't Have It

Substitute 1 fresh perilla leaf with:
- 2 to 3 fresh peppermint leaves (to replace green perilla leaves as garnish)
- 2 to 3 fresh lemon basil or cinnamon basil leaves (to replace green perilla leaves as garnish)
- 2 to 3 fresh purple ruffle basil leaves (to replace red perilla leaves; adds clove-like flavors)

### Perilla Varieties

Choose 1 fresh perilla leaf from these varieties:
- 1 fresh green shiso leaf or aojiso (Japanese bright green leaf with jagged edges; highly aromatic perfume reminiscent of mint)
- 1 fresh red shiso leaf or akajiso (Japanese ruffled maroon leaf with jagged edges; less aromatic than green shiso leaf; often used for color and flavor in pickled foods such as umeboshi plums and ginger)
- 1 fresh tía tô leaf (Vietnamese perilla with jagged edges and green color on top but purple on bottom; peppery, cinnamony aroma)
- 1 fresh deulkkae or kkaennip leaf (Korean perilla similar to Vietnamese perilla with a minty, fresh apple aroma; often sold canned with chile powder between the leaves)

## Periwinkle

*Also known as bigaro, sea snail, or winkle. A univalve mollusk that resembles a big snail with a similar spiral-shaped shell. The most common edible specimen grows in the north Atlantic attached to rocks, wharves, and pilings.*

### If You Don't Have It

Substitute 1 lb (500 g) periwinkles with:
- 1 lb (500 g) whelks
- 1 lb (500 g) limpets
- 1 lb (500 g) snails
- 1 lb (500 g) scallops
- 1 lb (500 g) cockles
- 1 lb (500 g) clams
- 1 lb (500 g) oysters

## Pernod

*See* ANISE LIQUEUR.

## Persian Lime

*See* LIME.

## Persian Melon

*Large sweet muskmelon with salmon-color flesh. Late summer is the peak season.*

> 1 medium = 5 lbs (2.5 kg)
> = 7½ cups (1.875 L) diced

### If You Don't Have It
Substitute 1 cup (250 mL) chopped Persian melon with:
- 1 cup (250 mL) chopped Crenshaw melon
- 1 cup (250 mL) chopped cantaloupe
- 1 cup (250 mL) chopped Santa Claus melon
- 1 cup (250 mL) chopped honeydew melon
- 1 cup (250 mL) chopped casaba melon

## Persimmon

*Also known as kaki. A flame orange astringent fruit of both Chinese and North American origin, persimmons must be extremely ripe to be palatable. An outstanding source of vitamin A, the fruit is also high in fiber and a good source of potassium.*

> 1 lb (500 g) =
> 3 to 4 medium
>
> 1 medium =
> 9 oz (275 g) =
> ¾ cup (175 mL) pulp

### If You Don't Have It
Substitute 1 lb (500 g) persimmons with:
- 1 lb (500 g) cashew apples
- 1 lb (500 g) plums
- 1 lb (500 g) pumpkin purée (to replace puréed persimmons)
- 1 lb (500 g) applesauce (to replace puréed persimmons)

### Persimmon Varieties
Choose 1 lb (500 g) persimmons from these varieties:
- 1 lb (500 g) Hachiya persimmons (teardrop-shaped; flame orange skin and very soft flesh when ripe; reminiscent of plums with a tangy edge when ripe; tannic and bitter-tasting when unripe)
- 1 lb (500 g) Fuyu persimmons (smaller and rounder than Hachiya persimmons; slightly milder flavor than Hachiyas; flesh is firm when ripe)

## Persimmon, Dried

*Native Americans dried ripe wild persimmons and formed the paste into bricks to eat during the winter months.*

### If You Don't Have It
Substitute 1 cup (250 mL) dried persimmons with:
- 1 cup (250 mL) dried plums (prunes)
- 1 cup (250 mL) dried apricots
- 1 cup (250 mL) dried peaches

## Pesto

*The word translates from Italian as "pounded." Undoubtedly the most famous type is the basil pesto from Genoa, which traditionally is ground into a paste with a pestle in a mortar.*

### If You Don't Have It
Substitute 1 cup (250 mL) pesto with:
- 1 cup (250 mL) Homemade Pesto: Put 2 chopped garlic cloves, 10 cups (2.5 L) loosely packed fresh basil, 2 cups (500 mL) grated Parmigiano-Reggiano cheese, ¾ cup (175 mL) pine nuts, ¾ tsp (3 mL) salt, and ⅛ tsp (0.5 mL) ground black pepper in a food processor or blender. Blend until finely chopped, about 30 seconds. Scrape down sides of bowl then turn on machine and gradually add ¾ cup (175 mL) extra virgin olive oil, blending to a loose paste, about 20 seconds. For thinner pesto, add more oil. Taste and add more salt and pepper if necessary.

Spoon into airtight containers and refrigerate for up to 1 week or freeze for up to 1 year. Replace the basil with cilantro, parsley, or other leafy herbs if you like. Makes about 2¼ cups (550 mL).

## To Vary the Flavor
Substitute 1 cup (250 mL) pesto with:
- 1 cup (250 mL) tapenade (saltier; strong olive flavor)

## Peter Heering

*See* CHERRY LIQUEUR.

## Petit Suisse

*Also known as the popular brand name Gervais. A rich, French cheese with tangy sweet flavor and the consistency of very soft cream cheese.*

8 oz (250 g) =
1 cup (250 mL)

## If You Don't Have It
Substitute 1 oz (30 g) Petit Suisse with:
- 1 oz (30 g) Robiola Piemonte
- 1 oz (30 g) Caprini
- 1 oz (30 g) fromage blanc
- 1 oz (30 g) cream cheese

## Pezsgö

*See* WINE, SPARKLING.

## Pheasant

*The flesh of female pheasants is plumper, juicier, and more tender than that of the males. Very young hens are delicious roasted.*

1 average = 3 lbs (1.5 kg)

## If You Don't Have It
Substitute 1 lb (500 g) pheasant with:
- 1 lb (500 g) guinea fowl
- 1 lb (500 g) grouse
- 1 lb (500 g) quail
- 1 lb (500 g) partridge
- 1 lb (500 g) squab
- 1 lb (500 g) Cornish hen (fattier)

## Phyllo

*Also known as filo. Fresh phyllo dough may be found in Greek or Middle Eastern food stores. Most supermarkets carry packaged frozen phyllo dough.*

## If You Don't Have It
Substitute 1 lb (500 g) phyllo dough with:
- 1 lb (500 g) strudel dough
- 1 lb (500 g) puff pastry (less crisp)

## To Save Time
Substitute 1 lb (500 g) phyllo dough with:
- 1 lb (500 g) kadaif or knafa preshredded phyllo dough (best for top and bottom crusts; does not roll into turnovers like phyllo sheets; toss the thawed dough with butter instead of brushing with butter)

## Physalis

*See* CAPE GOOSEBERRY.

## Piadina

*Thin Italian flatbread similar to Mexican wheat flour tortillas. It can be slathered with Nutella or stuffed with cheese, cured meat, and vegetables to make a sandwich.*

### If You Don't Have It

Substitute 1 piadina with:
- 1 wheat flour tortilla (firmer; can be more brittle)
- 1 piece soft lavash (chewier)
- 1 chapati (chewier)
- 1 naan (puffier)
- 1 round of pita bread (puffier)

---

## Pickerel

*See* PIKE.

---

## Pickled Ginger

*See* GINGER, PICKLED.

---

## Pickled Pork

*Many Creole cooks consider pickled pork (pickle meat) the essential ingredient in a proper pot of red beans.*

### If You Don't Have It

Substitute 8 oz (250 g) pickled pork with:
- 8 oz (250 g) Homemade Pickled Pork: Combine 2 cups (500 mL) distilled white vinegar, ½ cup (125 mL) mustard seeds, 6 peeled garlic cloves, 2 tbsp (30 mL) hot pepper sauce, 2 tbsp (30 mL) kosher salt, 1 tbsp (15 mL) granulated sugar, 1 tbsp (15 mL) celery seed, 2 bay leaves, and 10 peppercorns in a stainless-steel or other nonreactive saucepan. Bring to a boil over high heat and boil for 3 minutes. Remove and add 3 cups (750 mL) ice to cool. Put 2 lbs (1 kg) cubed boneless pork shoulder blade (Boston butt) in an airtight container or containers and add the cooled liquid to cover the pork. Cover tightly and refrigerate for at least 3 days. Use within 2 weeks. Makes about 2 lbs (1 kg).
- 8 oz (250 g) ham hocks
- 8 oz (250 g) smoked ham
- 8 oz (250 g) tasso
- 8 oz (250 g) smoked or pickled pig's feet
- 8 oz (250 g) smoked or pickled pork neck bones

---

## Pickles

*See* SPECIFIC TYPES.

---

## Pickling Spice

*This spice blend was a much more common cupboard staple in the days when fruits and vegetables were canned in home kitchens. Contemporary usage calls for pickling spice in a variety of dishes from chutney to sauerbraten.*

### If You Don't Have It

Substitute 1 tbsp (15 mL) pickling spice with:
- 1 tbsp (15 mL) Homemade Pickling Spice: Combine 1 broken 3-inch (7.5 cm) cinnamon stick, 4 to 5 crushed bay leaves, 1 to 2 broken small dried chile peppers (or 1 to 2 tsp/5 to 10 mL crushed red pepper flakes), 2 tbsp (30 mL) mustard seeds, 1 tbsp (15 mL) whole allspice, 1 tbsp (15 mL) coriander seeds, 1 tbsp (15 mL) black or white peppercorns, 1 tbsp (15 mL) ground ginger, 1 tbsp (15 mL) dill seeds, 2 tsp (10 mL) cardamom seeds (scraped from pods; optional),

and 1 tsp (5 mL) whole cloves. Store in an airtight container. Makes about ½ cup (125 mL).
- 1 tbsp (15 mL) crab boil
- 1 tbsp (15 mL) Old Bay seasoning

## Picon

*Spanish raw cow's milk cheese (sometimes with added sheep and goat's milk) that is naturally blued from mold spores circulating in the aging caves.*

4 oz (125 g) =
1 cup (250 mL) crumbled

### If You Don't Have It
Substitute 1 oz (30 g) Picon with:
- 1 oz (30 g) Cabrales
- 1 oz (30 g) Gamonedo
- 1 oz (30 g) Roquefort

## Picoroco

*See* BARNACLE.

## Pie Cherry

*See* CHERRY.

## Pie Crust, Crumb

*For those with pastry phobia, a crumb crust is easy to execute. Simply combine cookie crumbs with butter or other fat, perhaps some spices, and press into the pie pan before baking.*

### If You Don't Have It
Substitute 1 crumb crust with:
- 1 Homemade Graham Cracker Crumb Crust: Mix together 1½ cups (375 mL) crushed graham crackers (about 21 squares), 3 tbsp (45 mL) packed brown sugar, 3 tbsp (45 mL) melted butter, and ½ to 1 tsp (2 to 5 mL) cinnamon (optional). Press into greased 9-inch (23 cm) pie pan and bake at 350°F (180°C) until light brown, about 8 minutes. Let cool and fill.

### To Vary the Flavor
Substitute 1½ cups (375 mL) crumbs for crust with:
- 1½ cups (375 mL) crushed gingersnaps (about 22)
- 1½ cups (375 mL) crushed vanilla wafer cookies (about 33)
- 1½ cups (375 mL) crushed chocolate wafer cookies (about 32)
- 1½ cups (375 mL) crushed Oreo cookies (about 21, including cookie filling); omit sugar from crust
- 1½ cups (375 mL) crushed wheat, bran or corn flakes (about 4½ cups/1.125 L)
- 1½ cups (375 mL) crushed saltine crackers (about 42); omit sugar from crust and adjust salt in filling (for savory fillings)

## Pie Crust, Crumb (cont'd)

### For Better Health
Substitute 1 crumb crust with:
- ½ tsp (2 mL) of cookie crumbs in recipe plus equal amount of crushed saltine or other table crackers (omit salt from recipe)

*See also* PIE CRUST, PASTRY.

## Pie Crust, Pastry

*Also known as pâte brisée (France). "I was taught to make tender, flaky pastry as if it were one word, tenderflaky," writes cooking authority Shirley Corriher. "Nothing could be further from the truth — tenderness is one characteristic, flakiness a totally different characteristic."*

### If You Don't Have It
Substitute one 9-inch (23 cm) pie crust with:
- 1 sheet from half a 15-oz (425 g) package refrigerated pie crust sheets (not in a tin)

### To Vary the Flavor
Substitute one 9-inch (23 cm) pie crust with:
- 1 sheet puff pastry, rolled into a 9-inch (23 cm) circle (richer)

### For Better Health
Replace one 9-inch (23 cm) pie crust with:
- 3 sheets (6 half-sheets) phyllo dough layered with cooking spray, oil, or melted butter

*See also* PIE CRUST, CRUMB.

## Pie Pan

*See* PAN SIZE EQUIVALENTS (PAGE 678).

## Pie Plant

*See* RHUBARB.

## Pie Weights

*Heavy metal pellets used to weigh down a pie crust while blind baking (baking the crust without a filling).*

### If You Don't Have It
Substitute pie weights with:
- dried beans

## Pigeon

*See* SQUAB.

## Pigeon Pea

*See* THE WIDE WORLD OF DRIED BEANS (PAGE 637).

## Pig's Feet

*See* PICKLED PORK.

## Pike

*A freshwater family of game fish with long bodies and formidable teeth that includes small pickerels and large muskellunge (muskie). The walleyed pike is not a pike but rather a perch.*

### If You Don't Have It
Substitute 1 lb (500 g) pike with:
- 1 lb (500 g) walleye

*See also* PERCH.

## Pilchard

*A small, oily European Atlantic fish that's a shelf staple either canned in oil or tomato sauce.*

### If You Don't Have It

Substitute 1 lb (500 g) pilchards with:

- 1 lb (500 g) sardines
- 1 lb (500 g) shad
- 1 lb (500 g) herring
- 1 lb (500 g) mackerel
- 1 lb (500 g) bluefish

*See also* SARDINES.

## Pili Nut

*Native to the Phillipines, pili nuts are prone to rancidity because they contain more than 70% fat. The flavor is somewhere between sweet almonds, pumpkin seeds, Brazil nuts, and macadamia nuts. A related nut, the kenari nut (aka Java almond, kekuna, galip or ngali nut) can be found in Malaysia and Indonesia.*

### If You Don't Have It

Substitute 1 cup (250 mL) pili nuts with:

- 1 cup (250 mL) sweet almonds (less oily)
- ¼ cup (60 mL) sweet almonds + ¼ cup (60 mL) pumpkin seeds + ¼ cup (60 mL) Brazil nuts + ¼ cup (60 mL) macadamia nuts

## Piloncillo

*Also known as panela, panocha and rapadura. Mexican or South American unrefined cane sugar shaped into a hard truncated cone (piloncillo) or a block (panela or rapadura). Sometimes available in lighter (blanco or claro) or darker (oscuro or prieto), the flavor and color is like molassesy brown sugar.*

1-inch (2.5 cm) tall cone =
1 oz (30 g) =
2 tbsp (30 mL)

### If You Don't Have It

Substitute 1 cup (250 mL) (about 7 oz/210 g) piloncillo with:

- 1 cup (250 mL) dark brown sugar + 1 to 2 tbsp (15 to 30 mL) molasses
- 1 cup (250 mL) jaggery
- 1 cup (250 mL) black sugar (stronger molasses flavor)

*See also* JAGGERY; SUGAR, BLACK; SUGAR, DARK BROWN; SUGAR, GRANULATED; SUGAR, LIGHT BROWN.

## Pimento

*See* ALLSPICE.

## Pimentón

*See* PAPRIKA.

## Pimiento

*Also known as pimento. A red, heart-shaped pepper that is dried to be ground into paprika. Also famous as the stuffing for green olives.*

> 1 lb (500 g) = 2 large = 2½ cups (625 mL) chopped = 3 cups (750 mL) sliced

### If You Don't Have It
Substitute 2 tbsp (30 mL) chopped pimiento with:
- 2 to 3 tbsp (30 to 45 mL) chopped fresh red bell pepper
- 1 tbsp (15 mL) dried red bell pepper + 2 tbsp (30 mL) hot water

*See also* CHOOSING FRESH CHILES (PAGE 640).

## Pimm's

*Summer in England for a certain segment of society is impossible without a refreshing Pimm's Cup, a cocktail made with Pimm's #1, soda, and a twist. The gin-based quinine and herbal liqueur was created in the 1800s by London oyster bar owner James Pimm.*

### If You Don't Have It
Substitute 2 tbsp (30 mL) Pimm's Cup #1 with:
- 2 tbsp (30 mL) gin + ½ tsp (2 mL) granulated sugar dissolved in ½ tsp (2 mL) water + dash of Angostura bitters

## Pineapple

*The introduction of plastic-wrapped peeled and cored pineapples in supermarkets was a joyful innovation for fanciers of fresh pineapple.*

> 1 medium pineapple = 5 cups (1.25 L) cubes
>
> 1 cup (250 mL) chopped = 10 oz (300 g)

### If You Don't Have It
Substitute 1 cup (250 mL) chopped fresh pineapple with:
- 1 cup (250 mL) chopped canned pineapple
- 1 cup (250 mL) papaya
- 1 cup (250 mL) guava
- 1 cup (250 mL) mango
- 1 cup (250 mL) feijoa

### Pineapple Variety
Choose 1 cup (250 mL) chopped fresh pineapple from this variety:
- 1 cup (250 mL) chopped golden pineapple (sweeter; juicier)

## Pineapple, Candied

*Also known as crystallized pineapple and glacé pineapple. Choose candied pineapple that has good color and some pliability.*

### If You Don't Have It
Substitute 1 oz (30 g) candied pineapple with:
- 1 oz (30 g) candied papaya

## Pineapple Guava

*See* FEIJOA.

## Pineapple Juice

*Available either natural or sweetened in cans, bottles, or as frozen concentrate, this tropical juice graces many cocktails and punches.*

### If You Don't Have It
Substitute 1 cup (250 mL) pineapple juice with:
- 1 cup (250 mL) orange juice
- 1 cup (250 mL) grapefruit juice
- 1 cup (250 mL) fruit nectar such as mango or peach (thicker; sweeter)

## Pine Nut

*Also known as pignoli and piñon. Oily, distinctively flavored seeds extracted from the inside of pinecones. European pine nuts are slimmer and longer than more triangular (and less expensive) Asian pine nuts. Some species of pine nuts may cause other foods to taste metallic and bitter for several days.*

> 8 oz (250 g) =
> 1½ cups (375 mL)

### If You Don't Have It
Substitute 1 cup (250 mL) shelled pine nuts with:
- 1 cup (250 mL) walnuts
- 1 cup (250 mL) almonds
- 1 cup (250 mL) pecans
- 1 cup (250 mL) cashews
- 1 cup (250 mL) pistachios
- 1 cup (250 mL) peanuts

*See also* NUT.

## Pinga

*See* CACHAÇA.

## Pink Banana Squash

*See* BANANA SQUASH.

## Pink Bean

*See* THE WIDE WORLD OF DRIED BEANS (PAGE 637).

## Pink Peppercorn

*Pink or red berries of schinus trees that are sold as pink peppercorns. Not true pink peppercorns, which come from the same Piper nigrum vines that produce black, white, and green peppercorns.*

### If You Don't Have It
Substitute 1 tsp (5 mL) pink peppercorns with:
- 1 tsp (5 mL) freeze-dried green peppercorns
- 1 tsp (5 mL) white peppercorns (smaller, stronger)
- 1 tsp (5 mL) black peppercorns (stronger)
- 1 tsp (5 mL) Szechuan pepper (adds citrus aromas)
- ½ tsp (2 mL) ground pepper

*See also* PEPPERCORN.

## Pinto Bean

*See* THE WIDE WORLD OF DRIED BEANS (PAGE 637).

## Pipicha

*An herb from Oaxaca, Mexico with long, slender leaves that resemble tarragon but taste of pine, citrus, cilantro, and mint.*

### If You Don't Have It
Substitute 1 tbsp (15 mL) chopped fresh pipicha with:
- 1 tbsp (15 mL) chopped fresh cilantro
- 1 tbsp (15 mL) chopped fresh culantro or culentro (more bitter flavor)
- 2 tsp (10 mL) chopped fresh papalo

## Pippali

*See* LONG PEPPER.

## Piquin Chile

*See* CHOOSING AMONG DRIED CHILES (PAGE 642).

## Piri-Piri

*See* CHOOSING AMONG DRIED CHILES (PAGE 642).

## Pisco

*A typical Chilean or Peruvian grape brandy that is not wood aged. The Pisco Sour is the signature cocktail of Peru.*

### If You Don't Have It
Substitute 2 tbsp (30 mL) pisco with:
- 2 tbsp (30 mL) grappa
- 2 tbsp (30 mL) cognac
- 2 tbsp (30 mL) Armagnac

## Pismo Clam

*See* SWAPPING CLAMS (PAGE 645).

## Pistachio

*A rich and subtle-tasting nut with a beige shell and lovely pale green fruit. Convenient for nibblers because the shell of mature pistachios is partially split open. Some commercial suppliers color pistachios red with vegetable dyes, a practice which has its detractors and its advocates.*

1 lb (500 g) in shell = 2 cups (500 mL) shelled

1 lb (500 g) shelled = 3½ to 4 cups (875 mL to 1 L)

50 shelled nuts = 2 oz (60 g) = ½ cup (125 mL)

### If You Don't Have It
Substitute 1 cup (250 mL) unsalted pistachio nuts with:
- 1 cup (250 mL) salted pistachios, rinsed under cool water
- 2 to 4 tbsp (30 to 60 mL) pistachio oil (for baking and cooking; will add nut flavor but not texture of whole nuts; reduce fat in recipe by 2 to 4 tbsp/30 to 60 mL)

### To Vary the Flavor
Substitute 1 cup (250 mL) unsalted pistachio nuts with:
- 1 cup (250 mL) pine nuts
- 1 cup (250 mL) almonds
- 1 cup (250 mL) hazelnuts
- 1 cup (250 mL) cashews

*See also* NUT.

## Pita Bread

*Also known as pocket bread. Circular Middle Eastern flatbread that splits horizontally to create two pouches that can be filled with meats, vegetables, or other stuffings.*

### If You Don't Have It
Substitute 1 lb (500 g) pita bread with:
- 1 lb (500 g) lavash (thinner)
- 1 lb (500 g) Barbari bread
- 1 lb (500 g) sangak bread (whole wheat sourdough)
- 1 lb (500 g) naan (thicker)
- 1 lb (500 g) flour tortilla (thinner)
- 1 lb (500 g) small baked pizza crust

*See also* PIZZA CRUST.

## Pitaya

*Also known as apple cactus, dragon fruit, and strawberry pear. A Latin American cactus fruit ranging in color from pink to yellow. The grainy flesh is studded with seeds.*

### If You Don't Have It
Substitute 1 cup (250 mL) pitaya with:
- 1 cup (250 mL) kiwifruit

## Pitomba

*Aromatic Brazilian fruit with golden pulp and a tart, resinous flavor. Pitomba is similar to apricots but slightly more bitter and frequently made into jams, jellies, preserves, and drinks in Brazil. Pitomba shrubs (Eugenia luschnathiana) are often used for coastal topiary landscaping as the flowers emit a pleasant perfume and the shrubs can thrive in salty soil.*

1 lb (500 g) fresh =
8 to 14 = 2½ cups
(625 mL) sliced or halved

### If You Don't Have It
Substitute 1 lb (500 g) pitomba with:
- 1 lb (500 g) apricots
- 1 lb (500 g) apriums (a hybrid of apricot and plum; very apricot-like)
- 1 lb (500 g) small peaches
- 1 lb (500 g) small nectarines

## Pizza Crust

*"It is generally assumed by all relevant historians, including the typically chauvinistic Neapolitan ones, that no date can*

### If You Don't Have It
Substitute 1 (18-inch/45 cm) pizza crust with:
- 1 (18-inch/45 cm) focaccia
- 1 (18-inch/45 cm) refrigerated or frozen pizza shell
- 1 tube (10 oz/300 g) refrigerated pizza dough, rolled into an 18-inch (45 cm) round

## Pizza Crust (cont'd)

*be put on the beginnings of the bread part of the pizza. Flatbreads like it go back forever. The word 'pizza' is obviously related to the word 'pita,'" writes Arthur Schwartz in Naples at Table.*

- 1 piece fresh, refrigerated, or frozen bread dough rolled into an 18-inch (45 cm) round
- 1 (18-inch/45 cm) prebaked pizza crust (such as Boboli)
- 2 wide loaves baked French or Italian bread, halved lengthwise
- 3 to 4 (6-inch/15 cm) rounds pita bread

*See also* PITA BREAD.

## Pizza Pan

*Round, square or rectangular metal pan with or without a rim for baking pizza. Deep-dish pizza pans tend to be round and at least 1-inch (2.5 cm) deep.*

### If You Don't Have It
Substitute a pizza pan with:
- 2 cake pans (for individual pizzas)
- springform pan (for deep-dish pizza)
- similar size and shape baking pan

## Pizza Peel

*Wide, flat wooden or metal paddle used to shuffle pizzas, calzones, breads, and other doughs into a hot oven. The tapered front edge also allows retrieval of the cooked pizza or bread from the hot oven.*

### If You Don't Have It
Substitute a pizza peel with:
- large wooden cutting board well-dusted with cornmeal (for shuffling into the oven)
- large rimless baking sheet well-dusted with cornmeal (for shuffling into and retrieving from the oven)

## Pizza Wheel

*Also known as a pizza cutter. Designed to cut pizzas into wedges, this rolling round cutter can also mince herbs and cut rolled fresh pasta into various shapes.*

### If You Don't Have It
Substitute a pizza wheel with:
- long sharp knife and one or two straight-down cuts

## Plaice

*Also known as Canadian plaice and sand dab (North America). A saltwater flatfish of the flounder family. It has a fine-textured flesh and mild flavor.*

### If You Don't Have It
Substitute 1 lb (500 g) plaice with:
- 1 lb (500 g) sole
- 1 lb (500 g) flounder
- 1 lb (500 g) brill
- 1 lb (500 g) turbot
- 1 lb (500 g) haddock

## Plain Flour

*See* FLOUR, ALL-PURPOSE.

## Plantain

*Also known as cooking banana, plátano, and plátano macho. Best used when still green, plantain has a squash-like flavor and is often used as a potato substitute in Latin America and some African countries.*

> 2 medium =
> 1¼ lbs (625 g) = 2 cups
> (500 mL) cooked slices

### If You Don't Have It
Substitute 1 lb (500 g) plantains with:
- 1 lb (500 g) potatoes (to replace unripe green or yellow plantains)
- 1 lb (500 g) yams (to replace unripe green or yellow plantains)
- 1 lb (500 g) sweet potatoes (to replace unripe green or yellow plantains)
- 1 lb (500 g) breadfruit (to replace green or yellow plantains)
- 1 lb (500 g) jackfruit (to replace green or yellow plantains)
- 1 lb (500 g) underripe bananas (to replace ripe black plantains)

## Plastic Wrap

*Various clinging clear sheets used to wrap and cover foods; can be made from polyethylene, polyvinylidene chloride and polyvinyl chloride.*

### If You Don't Have It
Substitute plastic wrap with:
- plastic bags (for storing food; or cut bags to use as plastic wrap)
- wax paper (for wrapping food and covering food to be microwaved)
- aluminum foil (for wrapping food)

## Plett Pan

*Round griddle, usually cast iron, with several round shallow indentations, usually 3-inch (7.5 cm) diameter each, for making small Swedish pancakes.*

### If You Don't Have It
Substitute a plett pan with:
- a flat griddle or skillet, dropping about 2 tbsp (30 mL) batter for each 3-inch (7.5 cm) pancake

## Pleurotus

*See* SHUFFLING MUSHROOMS (PAGE 654).

## Plugra

*See* BUTTER.

## Plum

*Also known as fresh prune. A drupe related to apricot, peach, and particularly cherry, modern commercial plums are either of Japanese or European origin.*

### If You Don't Have It
Substitute 1 lb (500 g) plums with:
- 1 lb (500 g) plumcots (a hybrid of equal parts plum and apricot)
- 1 lb (500 g) pluots (hybrid of plum and apricot that's closer to a plum)

## Plum (cont'd)

*Japanese plums, such as Santa Rosa, are originally from China and are the clingstone type. Most have crimson to dark red skin with juicy, yellow or reddish flesh. European freestone plums are smaller, denser, and less juicy, with blue or purple skin and golden flesh. These are the plums that are dried into prunes. Varieties include Italian and Empress. The small, tart Damson plums are typically made into preserves.*

> 1 lb (500 g) fresh =
> 2½ cups (625 mL) sliced;
> 2 cups (500 mL) cooked

- 1 lb (500 g) apriums (hybrid of apricot and plum that's closer to an apricot)
- 1 lb (500 g) apricots
- 1 lb (500 g) nectarines
- 1 lb (500 g) peaches
- 1 lb (500 g) cherries
- 1 lb (500 g) loquats
- 1 lb (500 g) mangoes

### Plum Varieties

Choose 1 lb (500 g) plums from these varieties:
- 1 lb (500 g) Friar plums (popular Japanese variety; large, round; purple black skin; pale, juicy, sweet flesh)
- 1 lb (500 g) Santa Rosa plums (popular Japanese variety; medium-size, round; red skin speckled with tiny yellow spots; sweet-tart flesh)
- 1 lb (500 g) Red Beauty plums (Japanese variety; small, round; bright red skin; yellow, mildly sweet flesh)
- 1 lb (500 g) greengage plums (Japanese variety; small, round; green to yellow skin; sweet-tart flesh)
- 1 lb (500 g) Kelsey plums (Japanese variety; small, oval; green to yellow skin; sweet flesh)
- 1 lb (500 g) Damson plums (small, oval European variety; deep purple skin; sweet-tart flesh)
- 1 lb (500 g) Mirabelle plums (small, oval European variety; yellow to red skin; sweet-tart flesh)
- 1 lb (500 g) Italian prune plums (small, oval European variety; green to purple skin; sweet flesh)

*See also* PRUNE; SLOE.

## Plum Brandy

*A European eau de vie that's much appreciated in France, Germany, and Eastern European countries.*

### If You Don't Have It

Substitute 2 tbsp (30 mL) plum brandy with:
- 2 tbsp (30 mL) other fruit brandy such as apricot brandy
- 2 tbsp (30 mL) grappa
- 2 tbsp (30 mL) sloe gin

### Plum Brandy Varieties

Choose 2 tbsp (30 mL) plum brandy from these varieties:
- 2 tbsp (30 mL) slivovitz (colorless; bittersweet; may be made from different plum varieties)
- 2 tbsp (30 mL) quetsch (colorless; bittersweet; made with Alsatian quetch plums)
- 2 tbsp (30 mL) mirabelle (colorless; sweet; made with golden Mirabelle plums)

*See also* CRÈME DE PRUNELLE.

## Plumcot

*See* PLUM.

## Plum, Dried

*See* PRUNE.

## Plum Sauce

*Also known as Chinese duck sauce. A thick, sweet-tart Chinese sauce made from plums, apricots, vinegar, and sugar. In traditional Cantonese cooking, used as a dipping sauce for rich duck or goose.*

### If You Don't Have It

Substitute 1 cup (250 mL) plum sauce with:

- 1 cup (250 mL) Homemade Plum Sauce: Combine 1 cup (250 mL) apricot or plum jam, 2 to 3 tbsp (30 to 45 mL) rice vinegar or cider vinegar, 2 to 3 tsp (10 to 15 mL) grated fresh ginger, 1 tsp (5 mL) sugar, 1 finely minced small garlic clove, $\frac{1}{4}$ tsp (1 mL) crushed red pepper flakes, and $\frac{1}{4}$ tsp (1 mL) salt in a small saucepan. Bring to a boil over high heat. Reduce heat to medium-low and simmer gently for 5 minutes. Taste and add more vinegar, salt, or sugar if necessary. Cool and refrigerate in an airtight container for up to 2 weeks. Makes about 1 cup (250 mL).
- 1 cup (250 mL) mango chutney (chunkier; spicier)

## Pluot

*See* PLUM.

## Poblano

*See* CHOOSING DRIED CHILES (PAGE 642); CHOOSING FRESH CHILES (PAGE 640).

## Pocket Bread

*See* PITA BREAD.

## Pod Pea

*See* PEAS, EDIBLE POD.

## Poha

*See* CAPE GOOSEBERRY.

## Poire Williams

*See* PEAR BRANDY.

## Polenta

*The Italian version of cornmeal mush was once a staple in parts of northern Italy.*

1 lb (500 g) = 3 cups (750 mL) uncooked

1 cup (250 mL) = 5½ oz (165 g) = 4 cups (1 L) cooked

### To Save Time

Substitute 1 lb (500 g) homemade chilled polenta with:

- 1 lb (500 g) prepared polenta (available in the produce aisle of many grocery stores)

*See also* POLENTA MEAL.

## Polenta Meal

*Ground dried white or yellow corn used to make polenta.*

### If You Don't Have It
Substitute 1 cup (250 mL) polenta meal with:
- 1 cup (250 mL) cornmeal (preferably stone-ground)
- 1 cup (250 mL) corn grits (preferably stone-ground)

*See also* POLENTA.

## Pollock

*Also known as pollack. A member of the cod family found in the North Atlantic. The flesh is white and firm with a mild flavor.*

### If You Don't Have It
Substitute 1 lb (500 g) pollock with:
- 1 lb (500 g) cod
- 1 lb (500 g) plaice
- 1 lb (500 g) flounder
- 1 lb (500 g) sole
- 1 lb (500 g) brill
- 1 lb (500 g) turbot
- 1 lb (500 g) haddock
- 1 lb (500 g) blackfish

## Polynesian Chestnut

*See* MAPE.

## Pomegranate Juice

*Also known as Chinese apple. To easily juice a pomegranate, roll the whole fruit back and forth on a hard surface with your palms until all the juice sacs have popped. Insert a straw into the pomegranate and tilt to extract the juice into a cup.*

> 4 to 6 large =
> 1 quart (1 L) juice
>
> 1 large = ¾ to 1 cup
> (175 to 250 mL) juice

### If You Don't Have It
Substitute 1 cup (250 mL) fresh pomegranate juice with:
- 1 cup (250 mL) bottled pomegranate juice (less flavorful; may be from concentrate)
- 3 tbsp (45 mL) pomegranate concentrate, pomegranate syrup, or pomegranate molasses (much more concentrated flavor; add 13 tbsp (195 mL) liquid to recipe if necessary to dilute and add volume)

### To Vary the Flavor
Substitute 1 cup (250 mL) fresh pomegranate juice with:
- ⅓ cup (75 mL) grenadine (may add alcohol and other flavors; add ⅔ cup/150 mL liquid to recipe if necessary)
- 1 cup (250 mL) cranberry juice (more tart; lighter red color)
- ⅓ cup (75 mL) red currant syrup (thicker; sweeter; add ⅔ cup/150 mL liquid to recipe if necessary)
- ⅓ cup (75 mL) raspberry syrup (thicker; sweeter; add ⅔ cup/150 mL liquid to recipe if necessary)

## Pomegranate Molasses

The secret sweet-tart ingredient in Middle Eastern dishes like muhammara, a pesto-like dip made with ground walnuts, puréed roasted red peppers, olive oil, and cumin.

### If You Don't Have It

Substitute 1 tbsp (15 mL) pomegranate molasses with:

- 1 tbsp (15 mL) Homemade Pomegranate Molasses: Bring 4 cups (1 L) 100% pomegranate juice, ½ cup (125 mL) sugar, and 1 tbsp (15 mL) lemon juice to a boil in a medium saucepan. Reduce the heat to medium-low and simmer until syrupy and reduced to 1 cup (250 mL) in volume, about 1 to 1¼ hours. Makes 1 cup (250 mL).
- 1½ tsp (7 mL) honey + 1½ tsp (7 mL) lemon juice
- 1 tbsp (15 mL) grenadine (sweeter)

## Pomegranate Seed, Dried

Also known as anardana. In Indian and Middle Eastern cooking, used as a souring agent or condiment.

### If You Don't Have It

Substitute 1 tbsp (15 mL) dried pomegranate seeds with:

- 1 tbsp (15 mL) lemon or lime juice (as a souring agent)

## Pomelo

See PUMMELO.

## Pomfret

See BUTTERFISH.

## Pompano

Also known as yellowtail (from the Pacific) and jack (worldwide). Considered to be one of the finest-eating saltwater fish, this small blue green and silver fish has firm flesh and rich flavor.

### If You Don't Have It

Substitute 1 lb (500 g) pompano with:

- 1 lb (500 g) butterfish
- 1 lb (500 g) mahi-mahi
- 1 lb (500 g) tuna

See also AMBERJACK; BUTTERFISH.

## Pom Pom Mushroom

See SHUFFLING MUSHROOMS (PAGE 654).

## Pont-l'Évêque

Also known as Moyaux cheese. Savory and piquant French cow's milk cheese with a hint of tangy sweetness. The ridged brown crust (from the straw mats on which it is cured) is edible and the cheese itself is yellow and supple.

### If You Don't Have It

Substitute 1 oz (30 g) Pont-l'Évêque with:

- 1 oz (30 g) Reblochon
- 1 oz (30 g) Camembert (milder)
- 1 oz (30 g) Livarot (stronger)
- 1 oz (30 g) Maroilles (stronger)

## Ponzu

*A Japanese dipping sauce often served with sashimi and chirinabe, a one-pot dish of fish, tofu and vegetables.*

### If You Don't Have It

Substitute 1 cup (250 mL) ponzu with:

- 1 cup (250 mL) Homemade Ponzu Sauce: Combine ½ cup (125 mL) tamari or soy sauce, ¼ cup (60 mL) lemon juice, 2 tbsp (30 mL) lime juice, 3 tbsp (45 mL) rice vinegar, 3 tbsp (45 mL) dried bonito flakes (optional), 1 tbsp (15 mL) mirin, and a 1 to 2-inch (2.5 to 5 cm) square of kombu (optional). Let stand for 24 hours at room temperature (or overnight if not using bonito flakes and kombu). Strain before using (don't bother straining if not using bonito flakes and kombu). Makes about 1 cup (250 mL).

### To Vary the Flavor

Substitute 1 cup (250 mL) ponzu with:

- 1 cup (250 mL) tare, yakitori or teriyaki sauce

## Popcorn

*Popping corn retains some moisture in the center when dried yet has such a tough hull that when heated, steam pressure builds inside to about 380ºF (193ºC), which explodes the hull and turns the kernel inside out. The steam puffs up the exterior to a deliciously flaky texture.*

### If You Don't Have It

Substitute 1 cup (250 mL) popped popcorn with:

- 1 cup (250 mL) puffed rice, puffed kamut or other puffed grains

## Popover Pan

*A baking pan similar to a muffin pan but with deep, tapered cups to accommodate the egg batter that bakes up high into light airy popovers, an American twist on British Yorkshire pudding.*

### If You Don't Have It

Substitute a popover pan with:

- A deep-cup muffin pan with 2- to 3-inch (5 to 7.5 cm) diameter cups
- Individual 2- to 3-inch (5 to 7.5 cm) diameter deep ramekins or custard cups

*See also* PAN SIZE EQUIVALENTS (PAGE 678).

## Poppadum

*See* PAPPADAM.

## Poppy Seed

*While narcotic prior to ripening, poppy seeds yield wonderful benign cooking seeds when ripened. The*

### If You Don't Have It

Substitute 1 cup (250 mL) poppy seeds with:

- 1 cup (250 mL) canned prepared poppy seeds (to replace 1 cup/250 mL ground poppy seeds for fillings) *dark bluish black poppy seeds are favored for pastries and breads in Eastern Europe. In India, a smaller, off-white poppy seed thickens curries and sauces. When roasted, the seeds contribute a nutty note to spice mixtures.*

> 5 oz (150 g) =
> 1 cup (250 mL)

## To Vary the Flavor

Substitute 1 cup (250 mL) poppy seeds with:

- 1 cup (250 mL) sesame seeds (to replace whole seeds as a topping)

## Porgy

*Also known as scup, sea bream, and sheepshead. This low-fat and delectably flavored fish inhabits oceans around the world.*

## If You Don't Have It

Substitute 1 lb (500 g) porgy with:

- 1 lb (500 g) croaker
- 1 lb (500 g) spot
- 1 lb (500 g) pompano
- 1 lb (500 g) rockfish
- 1 lb (500 g) ocean perch
- 1 lb (500 g) bluefish

## Pork

*Select raw pork that is moist and firm to the touch. Loin cuts should be a pale pink with pure white fat. Shoulder and leg cuts will be darker with a slightly coarser texture. Avoid cuts that are dry, gray, red, or otherwise discolored. Because of consumer demand, pork is now bred to be lean, which means it can easily dry out if overcooked. Use an instant-read thermometer to gauge the exact moment when pork is safe to eat but still succulent. The internal temperature should read 160°F (71°C). Remove a roast from the heat when it reads 155°F (68°C) because the temperature will rise to 160°F (71°C) as it rests.*

## If You Don't Have It

Substitute 1 lb (500 g) pork with:

- 1 lb (500 g) boar (darker; leaner; stronger-tasting)
- 1 lb (500 g) lamb
- 1 lb (500 g) veal
- 1 lb (500 g) beef
- 1 lb (500 g) turkey
- 1 lb (500 g) chicken

*See also* BOAR.

## Pork Brawn

*See* HEADCHEESE.

## Pork Lard

*See* LARD.

## Pork Souse

*See* HEADCHEESE.

## Port

*Also known as porto. A sweet fortified wine named for the Portuguese shipping city of Oporto. Vintage ports can be long-lived, often developing character for 50 or more years.*

### If You Don't Have It
Substitute 2 tbsp (30 mL) port with:
- 2 tbsp (30 mL) banyuls
- 2 tbsp (30 mL) Madeira
- 2 tbsp (30 mL) dry vermouth
- 2 tbsp (30 mL) Lillet Rouge
- 2 tbsp (30 mL) dry red wine + ¼ tsp (1 mL) brown sugar
- 2 tbsp (30 mL) beef stock (for sauces)

### Port Varieties
Choose 2 tbsp (30 mL) port from these general varieties:
- 2 tbsp (30 mL) vintage port (made from a single vintage; aged the longest)
- 2 tbsp (30 mL) tawny port (light amber color; made from a blend of vintages; ages less than vintage port)
- 2 tbsp (30 mL) ruby port (bright red color; made from a blend of lesser-quality vintages; aged only 2 years or less)

*See also* BANYULS.

## Porter

*See* BEER.

## Portobello Mushroom

*See* SHUFFLING MUSHROOMS (PAGE 654).

## Port Salut

*A mild semisoft cow's milk cheese that originated in a monastery in Brittany. The cylinders have an orange rind that covers a pale yellow interior.*

> 1 lb (500 g) = 4 cups (1 L) grated or shredded

### If You Don't Have It
Substitute 1 oz (30 g) Port Salut with:
- 1 oz (30 g) Saint Paulin
- 1 oz (30 g) Esrom
- 1 oz (30 g) Tilsit
- 1 oz (30 g) Havarti
- 1 oz (30 g) Oka
- 1 oz (30 g) Muenster

## Portuguese Sweet Bread

*Also known as pao duce. A domed crown typically tops this sweet, airy loaf.*

### If You Don't Have It
Substitute 1 lb (500 g) Portuguese sweet bread with:
- 1 lb (500 g) challah
- 1 lb (500 g) brioche

## Posole

*See* HOMINY.

## Potash

*Also known as bicarbonate of potash and potassium bicarbonate. A compound of "pot" and "ash," the term potash comes from the method of making potassium carbonate by soaking wood ashes then evaporating the solution in large iron pots, leaving behind a white residue. Old recipes for eastern European baked goods sometimes call for potash as the leavening. The modern equivalent is baking soda (sodium bicarbonate).*

> 1 tbsp (15 mL) = 4 oz (125 g) = 7 g

### If You Don't Have It
Substitute 1 tsp (5 mL) potash (potassium bicarbonate) with:
- 1 tsp (5 mL) baking soda (sodium bicarbonate)

## Potato

*Russet Burbank is the most widely known high-starch baking potato. Other types include low-starch boilers, such as round red, and medium-starch all-purpose potatoes, such as Yukon Gold.*

> 1 lb (500 g) = 2 small russet = 4 medium Yukon Gold = 10 creamers = 4 cups (1 L) chopped = 1¾ cups (425 mL) cooked and mashed

### If You Don't Have It
Substitute 1 lb (500 g) potatoes with:
- 1 lb (500 g) cassava
- 1 lb (500 g) yautía or malanga
- 1 lb (500 g) taro
- 1 lb (500 g) sweet potatoes
- 1 lb (500 g) parsnips
- 1 lb (500 g) sunchokes
- 1 lb (500 g) jicama
- 1 lb (500 g) unripe green or yellow plantains

*See also* CHOOSING AMONG POTATOES (PAGE 662).

## Potato Chips

*One day in 1853, at Moon's Lake House in Saratoga Springs, New York, a customer kept returning french fries to chef George Crum because they were too thick. Reputedly, Crum sliced the potatoes increasingly thinner and gave birth to potato chips.*

### If You Don't Have It

Substitute 1 lb (500 g) potato chips with:

- 1 lb (500 g) sweet potato or other vegetable chips
- 1 lb (500 g) bagel chips
- 1 lb (500 g) tortilla chips

### For Better Health

Substitute 1 lb (500 g) potato chips with:

- 1 lb (500 g) pretzels

## Potato Flour

*See* CHOOSING AMONG WHOLE-GRAIN AND ALTERNATIVE FLOURS (PAGE 648).

## Potato Ricer

*See* RICER.

## Pot Cheese

*A slightly drier version of cottage cheese.*

### If You Don't Have It

Substitute 1 oz (30 g) pot cheese with:

- 1 oz (30 g) cottage cheese, drained in cheesecloth (may add more liquid)
- 1 oz (30 g) ricotta cheese, drained in cheesecloth (may add more liquid)
- 1 oz (30 g) farmer cheese (firmer)
- 1 oz (30 g) hoop cheese (firmer)
- 1 oz (30 g) panir
- 1 oz (30 g) cream cheese (especially for dips; may add more liquid)
- 1 oz (30 g) sour cream (especially for dips; may add more liquid)

## Potsticker Wrappers

*See* WON TON SKINS.

## Poultry

*See* CHICKEN; DUCK; GOOSE; GUINEA FOWL; PHEASANT; TURKEY.

## Poultry Seasoning

*The herb sage is often the constant in this flavoring blend designed for fowl.*

### If You Don't Have It

Substitute 1 tsp (5 mL) poultry seasoning with:

- 1 tsp (5 mL) Homemade Poultry Seasoning: Combine $3/4$ tsp (3 mL) dried thyme, $1/2$ tsp (2 mL) crushed or rubbed sage, $1/2$ tsp (2 mL) dried marjoram, $1/4$ tsp (1 mL) ground black pepper, and a pinch of nutmeg (optional). Makes about 2 teaspoons (10 mL).

## Poultry Shears

*Heavy-duty kitchen shears make quick work of cutting up chicken, duck, and other poultry. Good-quality poultry shears have slip-proof handles and slightly curved blades. One of the blades is typically serrated for gripping and cutting through bones.*

### If You Don't Have It

Substitute poultry shears with:
- cleaver
- heavy chef's knife

## Pound Cake

*Said to date from the early 1700s, the traditional recipe for pound cake was easy to recall: 1 pound of butter, 1 pound of sugar, 1 pound of flour, and 1 pound of eggs.*

### If You Don't Have It

Substitute 1 lb (500 g) pound cake with:
- 1 lb (500 g) butter cake (lighter texture; lower in fat)
- 1 lb (500 g) génoise (lighter texture; less moist)
- 1 lb (500 g) sponge cake (lighter texture; lower in fat)
- 1 lb (500 g) ladyfingers (lighter texture; lower in fat)
- 1 lb (500 g) angel food cake (lighter, more airy texture; lower in fat)

## Powdered Egg White

*Pasteurized dried egg whites, available in many supermarkets, are an economical, convenient, shelf-stable alternative to fresh egg whites.*

### If You Don't Have It

Substitute 1 tbsp (15 mL) powdered egg white with:
- 1 tbsp (15 mL) meringue powder
- 2 tbsp (30 mL) frozen and thawed egg white (to replace reconstituted powdered egg white)
- 1 large egg white (to replace reconstituted powdered egg white)

## Powdered Milk

*See* DRY MILK.

## Powdered Mustard

*See* MUSTARD, POWDERED.

## Powdered Sugar

*See* SUGAR, CONFECTIONER'S.

## Pozole

*See* HOMINY.

## Praline

*A brittle candy made with almonds or hazelnuts and caramelized sugar that can be used as a pastry*

### If You Don't Have It

Substitute 1 cup (250 mL) praline with:
- 1 cup (250 mL) Homemade Praline: Combine 1½ cups (375 mL) granulated sugar and 1 cup (250 mL) almonds or hazelnuts (with skins) in a heavy saucepan over low heat.

## Praline (cont'd)

*ingredient or a dessert garnish. To make praline powder, grind cooled praline in a food processor until it resembles the texture of cornmeal.*

Stir now and then until the sugar melts. Cook until sugar is deep amber (about 315°F/157°C). Pour mixture onto a greased baking sheet, spreading quickly with a wooden spoon. Let cool completely then crack into small pieces. Makes about 2 cups (500 mL).

*See also* PRALINE PASTE.

## Praline Paste

*A creamy confection made from almond or hazelnut butter and sugar.*

### If You Don't Have It
Substitute 1 cup (250 mL) praline paste with:
- 1 cup (250 mL) Homemade Praline Paste: Grind 2 cups (500 mL) Homemade Praline (see recipe, page 439) in a food processor or blender until the texture of cornmeal. Add 2 large egg whites and 1 tsp (5 mL) almond or hazelnut liqueur; blend until smooth. Makes about 1½ cups (375 mL).
- 1 cup (250 mL) chopped roasted nuts mixed with 1 cup (250 mL) granulated sugar

### To Vary the Flavor
Substitute 1 cup (250 mL) praline paste with:
- 1 cup (250 mL) hazelnut or other nut paste
- 1 cup (250 mL) gianduja (adds chocolate flavor)
- 1 cup (250 mL) sweetened chestnut purée

## Prawn

*In North America, the term prawn refers to freshwater crustaceans, such as Hawaii blue prawns, that resemble shrimp.*

1 lb (500 g) in shell =
11 to 15

### If You Don't Have It
Substitute 1 lb (500 g) freshwater prawns with:
- 1 lb (500 g) crayfish
- 1 lb (500 g) jumbo shrimp
- 1 lb (500 g) Dublin bay prawns
- 1 lb (500 g) spiny or rock lobster (larger)
- 1 lb (500 g) Maine lobster (larger)

*See also* DUBLIN BAY PRAWN; SHRIMP.

## Pre-Gel Starch

*Pre-gelatinized (pre-cooked) starch, which quickly thickens mixtures whether hot or cold. People with gluten intolerances sometimes use pre-gel starch to provide elasticity in bread doughs. Use about 1 tsp (5 mL) pre-gel starch per cup (250 mL) of gluten-free flour.*

### If You Don't Have It
Substitute 1 tsp (5 mL) pre-gel starch with:
- 1 tsp (5 mL) xanthan gum
- ¾ tsp (3 mL) guar gum
- 1 tsp (5 mL) ground flaxseed
- 2 tbsp (30 mL) cornstarch

## Prepared Mustard

*See* MUSTARD, PREPARED.

## Preserved Lemon

*Also known as salt-cured lemon. Essential in Moroccan cooking, these lemons are cured for several months in salty brine.*

### If You Don't Have It
Substitute 1 preserved lemon with:
- 1 Homemade Preserved Lemon: Cut 4 small lemons (preferably thin-skinned) lengthwise into quarter sections starting from the flower end and cutting down to within about ¼ inch (0.5 cm) of the stem end, keeping quarters attached to each other at the stem end. Open up the almost-quartered lemons like flowers and put them in a large glass bowl or wide-mouthed jar. Sprinkle with 1¾ cups (425 mL) Kosher salt and ¼ cup (60 mL) granulated sugar and toss to coat, especially the cut sides. Cover and refrigerate for at least 1 month or for up to 6 months, stirring the lemons or inverting jar to redistribute the juices. Makes 4.

### To Save Time
Substitute 1 preserved lemon with:
- 1 chopped lemon and 2 tsp (10 mL) salt simmered in 2 cups (500 mL) water for 10 minutes
- 1 sliced lemon, 1 tsp (5 mL) salt, and pinch of sugar heated in 2 tsp (10 mL) olive oil over medium-low heat until lemon is very tender, 20 to 30 minutes

### To Vary the Flavor
Substitute 1 preserved lemon with:
- ½ cup (125 mL) dry-cured olives

## Preserves

*Similar to jam, preserves are made from much larger or whole pieces of fruit.*

### If You Don't Have It
Substitute 1 cup (250 mL) preserves with:
- 1 cup (250 mL) jam (smoother consistency)
- 1 cup (250 mL) jelly (thinner consistency)

## Pressure Cooker

*Because steam builds up inside this pressurized cooking pot, the foods contained inside cook at a very high temperature, which means they cook in a fraction of the time of traditional methods.*

### If You Don't Have It
Substitute a pressure cooker with:
- large pot with a tight-fitting lid (generally, you can sauté or bring foods to a boil then reduce heat and simmer as you would in a pressure cooker; triple or quadruple the cooking time; increase liquid by 20 to 40% to compensate for moisture loss)

## Pretzel

*In the American town of Lititz, Pennsylvania, the first commercial pretzel factory was established in 1861.*

### If You Don't Have It
Substitute 1 lb (500 g) pretzels with:
- 1 lb (500 g) potato chips (to replace hard pretzels)
- 1 lb (500 g) sweet potato or other vegetable chips (to replace hard pretzels)
- 1 lb (500 g) bagel chips (to replace hard pretzels)
- 1 lb (500 g) tortilla chips (to replace hard pretzels)
- 1 lb (500 g) nuts (to replace hard pretzels)
- 1 lb (500 g) crackers (to replace hard pretzels)
- 1 lb (500 g) Grape-Nuts cereal (to replace crushed hard pretzels)
- 1 lb (500 g) bagels (to replace soft pretzels)
- 1 lb (500 g) bialys (to replace soft pretzels)

## Prickly Ash

*See* KINOME LEAF; SZECHUAN PEPPER.

## Prickly Pear

*Also known as Barbary fig, and cactus pear. Pear-shaped cactus fruit with flesh that varies in color from pale green to magenta.*

1 large = ½ cup (125 mL) chopped or puréed

### If You Don't Have It
Substitute 1 lb (500 g) prickly pears with:
- 1 lb (500 g) pepinos
- 1 lb (500 g) tamarillos
- 1 lb (500 g) Charentais melon or cantaloupe
- 1 lb (500 g) honeydew or Ogen melon
- 1 lb (500 g) golden or red watermelon
- 1 lb (500 g) pears

## Prickly Pear Cactus

*See* NOPALE.

## Primost

*See* MYSOST.

## Processed Cheese

*Also known as American cheese. Velveeta is the king of processed cheese, introduced by Kraft in 1928.*

1 oz (30 g) = 1 slice

### If You Don't Have It
Substitute 1 oz (30 g) processed cheese with:
- 1 oz (30 g) American cheese
- 1 oz (30 g) processed cheese spread such as Cheez Whiz (moister)
- 1 oz (30 g) Bel Paese

*See also* AMERICAN CHEESE.

## Prosciutto

*Ham that is salt- and air-cured, produced from pork leg in various styles in different parts of Italy. Its distinction in terms of fragrance and sweetness is attributed to unique climatic conditions. The finest examples are generally acknowledged to be* prosciutto di Parma *and* prosciutto di San Daniele.

> 1 lb (500 g) =
> 32 thin slices

### If You Don't Have It
Substitute 1 lb (500 g) prosciutto with:
- 1 lb (500 g) speck (adds smoky juniper aromas)
- 1 lb (500 g) culatello (less fatty; soaked in wine during aging)
- 1 lb (500 g) Serrano or Iberico ham
- 1 lb (500 g) Ardennes ham (adds smoke flavor)
- 1 lb (500 g) Bayonne ham (adds mild smoke flavor)
- 1 lb (500 g) Westphalian ham (adds juniper and mild smoke flavors)
- 1 lb (500 g) York ham (adds mild smoke flavor)
- 1 lb (500 g) Smithfield ham (add smoke flavor)
- 1 lb (500 g) Yunnan ham (adds smoke flavor)
- 1 lb (500 g) bresaola (less fatty; stronger flavor)

## Prosecco

*See* WINE, SPARKLING.

## Provolone

*Sharp southern Italian cow's milk cheese. The largest* provoloni *can be as long as 6 feet (1.8 m).*

> 1 lb (500 g) = 4 cups
> (1 L) shredded

### If You Don't Have It
Substitute 1 oz (30 g) provolone with:
- 1 oz (30 g) caciocavallo
- 1 oz (30 g) scamorza
- 1 oz (30 g) mozzarella
- 1 oz (30 g) fontina
- 1 oz (30 g) young Asiago

## Prune

*Also known as dried plums. Southwest France is the best place to be a prune. There, dried plums get to steep in Armagnac, the wonderful brandy of the region.*

> 1 lb (500 g) = 2½ cups
> (625 mL) = 4 to 4½ cups
> (1 to 1.125 L) cooked

### If You Don't Have It
Substitute 1 lb (500 g) prunes with:
- 1 lb (500 g) dried figs
- 1 lb (500 g) Chinese dates
- 1 lb (500 g) medjool dates
- 1 lb (500 g) raisins
- 1 lb (500 g) dried persimmons
- 1 lb (500 g) dried blueberries, cherries, or cranberries
- 1 lb (500 g) dried apricots

*See also* PLUM; PRUNE, SOUR.

## Prune Juice

Made by puréeing stewed prunes, prune juice contains the natural laxative dihydrophenylisatin.

### If You Don't Have It
Substitute 1 cup (250 mL) prune juice with:
- 1 cup (250 mL) Homemade Prune Juice: Put 3¾ (925 mL) cups water and ¾ (175 mL) cup pitted prunes (dried plums) in a medium saucepan. Bring to a boil over high heat then reduce the heat to low, cover and simmer for 3 hours. Purée in a blender or food processor. Makes about 4 cups (1 L).
- 1 cup (250 mL) water + ½ to 2 tsp (2 to 10 mL) psyllium seed husks (as a laxative)

## Prunelle

See CRÈME DE PRUNELLE; PLUM BRANDY.

## Prune Purée

Also known as lekvar and prune butter. Sometimes used instead of butter to make lower-fat chocolate or heavily spiced baked goods. Use ⅓ cup (75 mL) prune purée in place of ½ cup (125 mL) butter.

### If You Don't Have It
Substitute 1 cup (250 mL) prune purée with:
- 1 cup (250 mL) Homemade Prune Purée: Purée 1 cup (250 mL) pitted prunes and ½ cup (125 mL) water in a blender or food processor until smooth. Makes about 1⅓ cups (325 mL).
- 1 cup (250 mL) baby food prunes

### To Vary the Flavor
Substitute 1 cup (250 mL) prune purée with:
- 1 cup (250 mL) apple butter
- 1 cup (250 mL) well-drained applesauce
- 1 cup (250 mL) fat-free, fruit-based butter and oil replacement such as Sunsweet "Lighter Bake"

## Prune, Sour

Dried sour plums used in Middle Eastern cooking.

### If You Don't Have It
Substitute 1 sour prune with:
- 1 umeboshi
- 1 ordinary prune soaked overnight in tamarind water or vinegar

## Psyllium Seed Husks

Also known as isabgol. The high-fiber husks of seeds from a plant native to India and Pakistan. Pysllium powder is the primary ingredient in laxative products like Metamucil. It is always taken with plenty of water, which it absorbs instantly.

### If You Don't Have It
Substitute 1 to 2 tsp (5 to 10 mL) psyllium seed husks + 1 cup (250 mL) water with:
- 1 to 2 tsp (5 to 10 mL) Metamucil + 1 cup (250 mL) water (as a laxative)
- 1 cup (250 mL) prune juice (as a laxative)
- 1 cup (250 mL) oat bran (for dietary fiber)

## Pudding Spice

*See* MIXED SPICE.

## Puff Pastry

*Also known as pâte feuilletée. A triumph of the French kitchen, this flaky pastry is made by placing thin rolled sheets of chilled butter between sheets of flour-water dough then repeatedly folding and rolling the packet. During baking, the water in the butter creates steam that causes the thin dough layers to puff up into hundreds of flaky layers.*

### If You Don't Have It
Substitute 1 lb (500 g) puff pastry with:
- 1 lb (500 g) phyllo dough (less puffy)
- 1 lb (500 g) pie dough (denser and less puffy; less rich; best for replacing puff pastry crust in pies)

*See also* PATTY SHELL.

## Pulasan

*Closely related to rambutans, these popular southeast Asian fruits have short spines on their dark red skins and, inside, a small amount of sweet, delicate pulp surrounding an easily removed seed.*

> 1 lb (500 g) fresh =
> 2 cups (500 mL)

### If You Don't Have It
Substitute 1 cup (250 mL) peeled and seeded fresh pulasans with:
- 1 cup (250 mL) peeled and seeded rambutans (slightly less sweet)
- 1 cup (250 mL) peeled and seeded longans
- 1 cup (250 mL) peeled and seeded fresh or canned litchis

*See also* LITCHI; RAMBUTAN.

## Pulla Chile

*See* CHOOSING AMONG DRIED CHILES (PAGE 642).

## Pullman Pan

*Also known as a pan de mie. A long, rectangular baking pan with a slide-on lid used to bake a soft-crusted loaf with perfectly square sides. Like the Pullman railroad car, the Pullman pan was named for 19<sup>th</sup> century American inventor George Mortimer Pullman.*

### If You Don't Have It
Substitute a Pullman pan with:
- another loaf pan, preferably 2-quart (2 L) volume, covered with a flat baking sheet weighted down with a heavy, heatproof weight, such as a brick

## Pulque

*Of Aztec origin, this thick white Mexican beverage is fermented from various agave plants.*

### If You Don't Have It

Substitute 2 tbsp (30 mL) pulque with:
- 2 tbsp (30 mL) tequila (clear or amber color; higher alcohol)
- 2 tbsp (30 mL) mezcal (clear or amber color; higher alcohol)

## Pummelo

*Also known as Chinese grapefruit and shaddock (England). This Malaysian ancestor of grapefruit can weigh as much as 25 pounds (12.5 kg).*

### If You Don't Have It

Substitute 1 cup (250 mL) pummelo segments with:
- 1 cup (250 mL) grapefruit segments (more acidic)
- 1 cup (250 mL) Ugli™ fruit segments
- 1 cup (250 mL) sweet orange segments
- 1 cup (250 mL) tangelo segments

## Pumpernickel Bread

*A dark, slightly sour bread with a high proportion of rye flour to wheat flour.*

### If You Don't Have It

Substitute 1 lb (500 g) pumpernickel bread with:
- 1 lb (500 g) rye bread (especially marbled or sourdough rye)
- 1 lb (500 g) Russian black bread
- 1 lb (500 g) limpa bread (more aromatic)

*See also* BLACK BREAD.

## Pumpernickel Flour

*See* CHOOSING AMONG WHOLE-GRAIN AND ALTERNATIVE FLOURS (PAGE 648).

## Pumpkin

*Is pumpkin a fruit or a vegetable? It's actually a large versatile winter squash that may be a stuffing for savory* tortelli di zucca *or the spiced sweetened custard for Thanksgiving pie.*

1 lb (500 g) fresh =
1 cup (250 mL)
cooked and mashed

1 15 oz (425 g) can =
1¾ cups (425 mL)
mashed

1 29 oz (875 g) can =
3½ cups (875 mL)
mashed

### If You Don't Have It

Substitute 1 cup (250 mL) chopped fresh pumpkin with:
- 1 cup (250 mL) canned pumpkin purée (to replace mashed pumpkin)
- 1 cup (250 mL) chopped butternut squash
- 1 cup (250 mL) chopped buttercup squash
- 1 cup (250 mL) chopped sweet dumpling squash
- 1 cup (250 mL) chopped Hubbard squash
- 1 cup (250 mL) chopped calabaza
- 1 cup (250 mL) chopped sweet potato

## Pumpkin Leaf

*Like other dark leafy greens, pumpkin leaves are high in iron and vitamin A. They often show up in African stews. Use young tender leaves for the most pleasant texture when cooked.*

1 lb (500 g) fresh =
10 cups (2.5 L) = 1½ cups
(375 mL) cooked

### If You Don't Have It
Substitute 1 lb (500 g) pumpkin leaves with:
- 1 lb (500 g) amaranth or Chinese spinach (especially to replace tender young pumpkin leaves)
- 1 lb (500 g) spinach beet (a variety of beet grown for the leaves; larger, broader, slightly tougher leaves)
- 1 lb (500 g) New Zealand spinach (more narrow leaves)
- 1 lb (500 g) red or green chard (slightly tougher leaves; thicker stems; slightly sweeter)
- 1 lb (500 g) turnip greens (smaller, teardrop-shaped, paler green leaves; more peppery flavor)
- 1 lb (500 g) beet greens (these often have reddish tinged stems)
- 1 lb (500 g) spinach (slightly more bitter)

## Pumpkin Pie Spice

*American pumpkin pie, or pudding, as it was known in Colonial times, was not seasoned with its now-trademark warm spice mix until the 1800s, when clipper ships made spices a more common, affordable commodity.*

### If You Don't Have It
Substitute 1 tsp (5 mL) pumpkin pie spice with:
- 1 tsp (5 mL) Homemade Pumpkin Pie Spice: Combine ½ tsp (2 mL) ground cinnamon, ¼ tsp (1 mL) ground nutmeg, ¼ tsp (1 mL) ground ginger, and ⅛ tsp (0.5 mL) ground cloves. Makes about 1 teaspoon (5 mL).
- 1 tsp (5 mL) apple pie spice

## Pumpkin Seed

*Also known as pepitas when shelled. The seed shells, which house the seeds, are also edible when roasted.*

### If You Don't Have It
Substitute 1 cup (250 mL) pumpkin seeds with:
- 1 cup (250 mL) Homemade Roasted Pumpkin Seeds: Remove seeds from the pumpkin cavity, separating the seeds from the pulp and fiber. Rinse well in a colander under cold water then spread the seeds on a kitchen towel to dry. Spread the dry seeds on a baking sheet in a single layer. Toss with oil to coat and roast at 250°F (120°C) until golden, stirring now and then, for about 1 hour. Sprinkle with salt or other seasonings if desired. Store in an airtight container at room temperature for up to 3 months or in the refrigerator for up to 1 year.
- 2 to 4 tbsp (30 to 60 mL) pumpkin seed oil (for baking and cooking; will add toasted pumpkin seed flavor but not texture of whole seeds; reduce fat in recipe by 2 to 4 tbsp/30 to 60 mL)
- 1 cup (250 mL) other winter squash seeds
- 1 cup (250 mL) dried guajes
- 1 cup (250 mL) sunflower seeds

*See also* WINTER SQUASH SEED.

## Pumpkin Seed Oil

*See* SUBSTITUTING OILS (PAGE 658).

## Punt e Mes

*Carpano brand sweetened fortified wine served as an aperitivo. It contains quinine, which stimulates production of digestive enzymes and hence appetite.*

### If You Don't Have It

Substitute 2 tbsp (30 mL) Punt e Mes with:

- 2 tbsp (30 mL) Lillet Rouge
- 2 tbsp (30 mL) Dubonnet Rouge
- 2 tbsp (30 mL) Byrrh
- 2 tbsp (30 mL) Raphael
- 2 tbsp (30 mL) Fernet Branca
- 2 tbsp (30 mL) Campari
- 2 tbsp (30 mL) dry vermouth + dash of Angostura bitters

## Pupulu

*See* BETEL LEAF.

## Pure Gluten

*See* SEITAN.

## Pure Grain Alcohol

*See* NEUTRAL SPIRITS.

## Purple Laver

*See* LAVER.

## Purslane

*Also known as pursley, pussley, and verdolagas. A green of ancient origin and international usage, now rediscovered by gourmet diners. Wild purslane offers more interesting flavor than cultivated. The juicy pad-like leaves are tart like sorrel. Older leaves respond well to cooking.*

4 oz (125 g) = 2 cups (500 mL) chopped

### If You Don't Have It

Substitute 1 lb (500 g) purslane with:

- 1 lb (500 g) sorrel
- 1 lb (500 g) spinach
- 1 lb (500 g) garden cress or watercress
- 1 to 2 tbsp (15 to 30 mL) file powder (for thickening soups and stews)
- 1½ to 2 cups (375 to 500 mL) okra (for thickening soups and stews)

## Puya

*See* CHOOSING AMONG DRIED CHILES (PAGE 642).

# Qaimaaq to Qurut

## Qaimaaq

*See* KAYMAK.

## Quahog

*See* SWAPPING CLAMS (PAGE 645).

## Quail

Commercially raised in Europe, these tiniest of game birds are related to partridges. American quail are birds from a different family. Types of quail include blue quail, bobwhites, brown quails, bush quails, California quails, and mountain quails.

### If You Don't Have It
Substitute 1 lb (500 g) quail with:
- 1 lb (500 g) partridge
- 1 lb (500 g) squab
- 1 lb (500 g) young pheasant
- 1 lb (500 g) grouse
- 1 lb (500 g) guinea fowl
- 1 lb (500 g) Cornish hen (fattier)

## Quail Egg

Considered a gourmet delicacy, the tiny speckled shells vary in color, including white, blue, and brown.

### If You Don't Have It
Substitute 5 quail eggs with:
- 1 extra-large chicken egg, especially from a pasture-raised hen
- 1 small duck egg (richer; more flavorful)

## Quail Grass

*A popular leafy green vegetable (Celosia argentea) in South America, Southeast Asia and Nigeria, where it is known as soko yokoto, meaning, "make husbands fat and happy."*

### If You Don't Have It
Substitute 1 lb (500 g) quail grass with:
- 1 lb (500 g) spinach
- 1 lb (500 g) amaranth or Chinese spinach
- 1 lb (500 g) New Zealand spinach (flatter, more narrow leaves than spinach)

## Quandong

*Also known as desert or sweet quandong. The fruit of an Australian outback bush often eaten dried.*

### If You Don't Have It
Substitute 1 lb (500 g) dried quandongs with:
- 1 lb (500 g) dried apricots
- 1 lb (500 g) dried peaches
- 1 lb (500 g) dried nectarines

## Quark

*A fresh-curd skim milk cheese that's a phenomenon in Germany, accounting for about half the total cheese consumed in that country.*

> 8 oz (250 g) =
> 1 cup (250 mL)

### If You Don't Have It
Substitute 1 oz (30 g) quark with:
- 1 oz (30 g) sour cream, fromage blanc, or yogurt cheese
- ½ oz (15 g) ricotta cheese + ½ oz (15 g) sour cream, blended
- ½ oz (15 g) cream cheese or mascarpone + ½ oz (15 g) cream, blended
- ½ oz (15 g) drained cottage cheese + ½ oz (15 g) yogurt, blended

## Quatre Épices

*In classic French cuisine, "four spices" is used in charcuterie, terrines, and pâtés. Despite its name, the blend often contains more than four spices.*

### If You Don't Have It
Substitute 1 tsp (5 mL) quatre épices with:
- 1 tsp (5 mL) Homemade Savory Quatre Épices: Combine 1¾ tsp (8 mL) ground white pepper, ¾ tsp (3 mL) ground allspice, ½ tsp (2 mL) ground nutmeg, and ¼ tsp (1 mL) ground cloves. Makes about 1 tablespoon (15 mL).
- 1 tsp (5 mL) Homemade Sweet Quatre Épices: Combine 1 tsp (5 mL) ground cinnamon, 1 tsp (5 mL) ground nutmeg, 1 tsp (5 mL) ground allspice, and ¼ tsp (1 mL) ground cloves. Makes about 1 tablespoon (15 mL).
- 1 tsp (5 mL) Spice Parisienne or épices fines (more complex flavor; may include white pepper and herbs; if so, use to replace savory quatre épices)
- ½ tsp (2 mL) ground white or black pepper + ½ tsp (2 mL) pumpkin pie spice or apple pie spice (to replace savory quatre épices)
- 1 tsp (5 mL) apple pie spice or pumpkin pie spice (to replace sweet quatre épices)

*See also* SPICE PARISIENNE.

## Queensland Blue Squash

*Gray-green to jade-green winter squash from Australia. Its fine-textured, sweet orange flesh makes it perfect for pies.*

### If You Don't Have It

Substitute 1 lb (500 g) Queensland blue squash with:

- 1 lb (500 g) Jarrahdale squash
- 1 lb (500 g) golden delicious
- 1 lb (500 g) buttercup squash
- 1 lb (500 g) sugar pumpkin
- 1 lb (500 g) butternut squash

## Queijo de Nisa

*Semifirm raw sheep's milk cheese from Portugal. The sheep feed on cardoon thistle and their milk is then coagulated with thistle instead of animal rennet. Nisa has a robust taste with a grassy, sharp finish similar to other sheep's milk cheeses. It is often aged until hard and used as a grating cheese.*

### If You Don't Have It

Substitute 1 oz (30 g) queijo de nisa with:

- 1 oz (30 g) aged Serpa
- 1 oz (30 g) Pecorino toscano
- 1 oz (30 g) Manchego
- 1 oz (30 g) Parmesan

*See* SERPA.

## Queso Añejo

*Mexican for "aged cheese." Also known as "Cotija" after North America's most widely distributed queso añejo, which is made in Cotija, Michoacan, Mexico.*

4 oz (125 g) =
1 cup (250 mL) grated

### If You Can't Find It

Substitute 1 oz (30 g) queso añejo or Cotija with:

- 1 oz (30 g) Pecorino Romano
- 1 oz (30 g) Parmesan
- 1 oz (30 g) aged Asiago
- 1 oz (30 g) dry Jack

## Queso Asadero

*See* ASADERO.

## Queso Blanco

*See* QUESO FRESCO.

## Queso Chihuahua®

*See* ASADERO.

## Queso Fresco

*Also known as queso blanco, queso ranchero, and queso de metate (when the cheese curds have been smoothed on the metate,*

### If You Don't Have It

Substitute 1 oz (30 g) queso fresco with:

- 1 oz (30 g) pressed, salted farmer cheese
- 1 oz (30 g) young goat cheese
- 1 oz (30 g) feta cheese (rinsed to remove some salt)

## Queso Fresco (cont'd)

*a traditional grinding stone). This Mexican, white, fresh cheese resembles farmer cheese in texture.*

> 4 oz (125 g) =
> 1 cup (250 mL) crumbled

- 1 oz (30 g) Monterey Jack cheese
- 1 oz (30 g) dry cottage cheese + ⅛ tsp (0.5 mL) salt

## Queso Gamonedo

*See* GAMONEDO.

## Queso Ibores

*See* SIERRA IBORES.

## Queso Manchego

*See* MANCHEGO.

## Quetsch

*See* PLUM BRANDY.

## Quiche Pan

*See* PAN SIZE EQUIVALENTS (PAGE 678).

## Quince

*A wonderfully aromatic fruit that can be roughly shaped like a pear or an apple. The flavor also evokes pear and apple, as well as pineapple and guava. Quince requires cooking, and its abundant natural pectin makes it well-suited to jellies and preserves.*

> 1 lb (500 g) = 3 to
> 4 medium = 1½ cups
> (375 mL) chopped

### If You Don't Have It

Substitute 1 lb (500 g) quinces with:
- 1 lb (500 g) tart apples such as Granny Smith or pippin (sweeter)
- 1 lb (500 g) Asian pears (sweeter)
- 1 lb (500 g) Bosc pears (sweeter; softer flesh)

*See also* DULCE DE MEMBRILLO.

## Quinine Water

*See* TONIC WATER.

## Quinoa

*Pride of the Andes, this ultra-nutritious grain has a pleasantly nutty taste and sprightly texture that belie its healthfulness. Before using quinoa, rinse it in a strainer to remove the naturally bitter saponin that coats the surface of the seeds.*

1½ cups (375 mL) =
9 oz (275 g) =
4 cups (1 L) cooked

## Quinoa Flour

## Qurut

*Fermented milk or yogurt that is salted, dried, and saved for times when fresh dairy products are unavailable. Qurut is made from the Middle East to Central Asia in both fresh and dry forms.*

### If You Don't Have It
Substitute 1 cup (250 mL) quinoa with:
- 1 cup (250 mL) millet
- 1 cup (250 mL) couscous, especially whole wheat (cooks more quickly)
- 1 cup (250 mL) bulgur
- 1 cup (250 mL) cracked wheat (takes longer to cook)
- 1 cup (250 mL) rice
- 1 cup (250 mL) kasha (roasted buckwheat groats; takes more time to cook)

*See also* CHOOSING AMONG WHOLE-GRAIN AND ALTERNATIVE FLOURS (PAGE 648).

### If You Don't Have It
Substitute ½ cup (125 mL) qurut with:
- ½ cup (125 mL) kashk
- ½ cup (125 mL) yogurt cheese + pinch of salt
- ½ cup (125 mL) crème fraîche + pinch of salt
- ½ cup (125 mL) sour cream + pinch of salt

*See also* KASHK.

# Rabbit to Rye Whiskey

## Rabbit

These domesticated rodents have fine, all-white-fleshed meat. Fresh and frozen rabbits, whole or cut up, are available in some specialty food markets. Rabbit can replace chicken in many recipes.

### If You Don't Have It
Substitute 1 lb (500 g) rabbit with:
- 1 lb (500 g) hare
- 1 lb (500 g) turkey
- 1 lb (500 g) chicken
- 1 lb (500 g) duck

See also HARE; MUSKRAT.

## Raclette

A mellow, Gruyère-like Swiss cow's milk cheese. The traditional way of serving raclette is to set a hunk of the cheese in front of an open fire and scrape the resulting melted cheese onto dark bread.

1 lb (500 g) = 4 cups (1 L) shredded

### If You Don't Have It
Substitute 1 oz (30 g) Raclette with:
- 1 oz (30 g) Gruyère
- 1 oz (30 g) Emmental
- 1 oz (30 g) Jarlsberg
- 1 oz (30 g) Appenzeller
- 1 oz (30 g) Reblochon
- 1 oz (30 g) oka
- 1 oz (30 g) fontina

## Radicchio

*The Italian word for all chicory, which range in color from cream to garnet. In North America, the word usually refers to the Chioggia variety, which has a round compact head and variegated white and garnet leaves. The bittersweet leaves are enjoyed in salads, braises, and many other ways.*

1 medium head =
8 to 10 leaves

### If You Don't Have It

Substitute 1 lb (500 g) radicchio with:
- 1 lb (500 g) Belgian endive, especially red-tipped
- 1 lb (500 g) chicory
- 1 lb (500 g) curly endive
- 1 lb (500 g) escarole
- 1 lb (500 g) arugula
- 1 lb (500 g) watercress
- 1 lb (500 g) red oak-leaf lettuce (less bitter)

### Radicchio Varieties

Choose 1 lb (500 g) radicchio from these varieties:
- 1 lb (500 g) Chioggia (most popular North American variety; compact, round head; wide white stems and maroon leaves; bitter, slightly sweet flavor; crunchy and chewy texture)
- 1 lb (500 g) Verona (similar to Chioggia but head is looser and slightly more oval in shape; thicker, narrower stems; brighter maroon-color leaves; similar flavor and texture)
- 1 lb (500 g) Early Treviso (elongated, loose head with white stems and maroon leaves; similar in shape to loose-headed mature bok choy; flavor and texture similar to Chioggia)
- 1 lb (500 g) Late Treviso (elongated, semiloose head with slender white stems and maroon leaves that twirl together at the top; flavor and texture slightly more bitter than Chioggia)
- 1 lb (500 g) Castelfranco (round, loose head with delicate out-turned leaves similar to a rose; cream-color stems with pale yellow and maroon-speckled leaves; milder flavor and more tender texture than Chioggia)

*See also* CHICORY; ENDIGIA.

## Radish

*Christmas Eve in Oaxaca, Mexico is called the Night of the Radishes because of the custom of carving big radishes into the shapes of animals.*

8 oz (250 g) =
10 to 14 radishes =
1½ cups (375 mL) sliced

### If You Don't Have It

Substitute 1 lb (500 g) radishes with:
- 1 lb (500 g) jicama (sweeter; add a pinch of pepper or horseradish for more bite)
- 1 lb (500 g) turnips or parsnips (for soups and stews; add a pinch of pepper or horseradish for more bite)

### Radish Varieties

Choose 1 lb (500 g) radishes from these varieties:
- 1 lb (500 g) table radishes (the American favorite; red, pink, or white peel; slightly peppery, crisp, and juicy flesh)
- 1 lb (500 g) Asian radishes (such as white daikon, green-skinned moo, or red-fleshed beauty heart; generally peppery-sweet, crisp, and juicy flesh)
- 1 lb (500 g) black radishes (black peel; firmer, drier, more assertive flesh that's similar to horseradish)

## Radish Greens

*On average, Americans eat 400 million pounds of radishes every year, mostly in salads. Ironically, the greens are usually tossed into the trash, but they add a wonderful arugula-like bite to salads and can be cooked like other leafy greens.*

### If You Don't Have It

Substitute 1 lb (500 g) radish greens with:
- 1 lb (500 g) mustard greens
- 1 lb (500 g) turnip greens
- 1 lb (500 g) beet greens
- 1 lb (500 g) watercress
- 1 lb (500 g) arugula

## Radish Sprouts

*Also known as kaiware sprouts. Crisp, peppery sprouts made from seeds of Japanese daikon. The seeds can also be pressed for radish oil, which ancient Egyptians used before olive oil was widely produced.*

### If You Don't Have It

Substitute ¼ cup (60 mL) radish sprouts with:
- ¼ cup (60 mL) broccoli sprouts (more peppery)
- ¼ cup (60 mL) fenugreek sprouts (slightly bitter)
- ¼ cup (60 mL) alfalfa sprouts (sweeter)
- ¼ cup (60 mL) buckwheat sprouts (less peppery)
- ¼ cup (60 mL) sunflower sprouts (more nutty)
- ¼ cup (60 mL) mung bean sprouts (thicker and more crisp)

## Rainbow Runner

*Also known as Hawaiian salmon, kamanu, and runner. A member of the large Jack family found in tropical Atlantic and Pacific waters. Mostly a game fish, it is rarely seen in markets.*

### If You Don't Have It

Substitute 1 lb (500 g) rainbow runner with:
- 1 lb (500 g) parrot fish
- 1 lb (500 g) amberjack
- 1 lb (500 g) pompano
- 1 lb (500 g) yellowtail
- 1 lb (500 g) mahi-mahi

## Rainbow Trout

*See* TROUT.

## Raisin

*In 1876, Scottish immigrant William Thompson developed a variety of sweet seedless grapes with thin skin. The variety dried well. Today 95% of California raisins — which comprise 50% of the world's supply — are processed from Thompson seedless grapes.*

15 oz (425 g) =
2½ cups (625 mL)

### If You Don't Have It

Substitute 1 cup (250 mL) raisins with:
- 1 cup (250 mL) finely chopped dried apricots
- 1 cup (250 mL) finely chopped soft prunes
- 1 cup (250 mL) finely chopped soft dates
- 1 cup (250 mL) dried berries such as blueberries or cranberries
- 1 cup (250 mL) dried cherries

### Raisin Varieties

Choose 1 cup (250 mL) raisins from these varieties:
- 1 cup (250 mL) dark raisins (usually sun-dried Thompson seedless grapes)
- 1 cup (250 mL) golden raisins or sultanas (usually dried

Thompson seedless grapes treated with sulfur dioxide to retain color; moister and plumper than dark raisins)
- 1 cup (250 mL) currants (dried Zante grapes; firmer and sweeter than dark raisins)
- 1 cup (250 mL) Muscat raisins (dried Muscat grapes; sweeter and more musky aroma than dark raisins)

*See also* CURRANT, DRIED.

## Raki

*See* ANISE LIQUEUR.

## Rambutan

*This tropical fruit looks like a small, spiny sea creature. Inside, the sweet translucent flesh tastes like its relative, the litchi, although a little more acidic. The fruit is available canned in syrup.*

1 lb (500 g) fresh = 2 cups (500 mL)

### If You Don't Have It
Substitute 1 cup (250 mL) peeled and seeded fresh rambutans with:
- 1 cup (250 mL) peeled and seeded longans (sweeter)
- 1 cup (250 mL) peeled and seeded fresh or canned litchis
- 1 cup (250 mL) peeled and seeded pulasans

*See also* LITCHI; PULASAN.

## Ramekin

*Stoneware baking dish that looks like a shrunken straight-sided soufflé dish.*

### If You Don't Have It
Substitute 3-oz (90 mL) ramekins with:
- 3-oz (90 mL) custard cups

## Ramen

*See* A SNAPSHOT OF ASIAN NOODLES (PAGE 656).

## Ramp

*Also known as wild leek. This wild onion grows throughout the Appalachian Chain, but it is in West Virginia that the pungent vegetable comes into its glory at springtime celebrations. The towns of Elkins, Richwood, and Helvetia are well-known for their ramp festivals.*

1 lb (500 g) = 2 cups (500 mL) trimmed and chopped = 1 cup (250 mL) cooked

### If You Don't Have It
Substitute 1 lb (500 g) ramps with:
- 1 lb (500 g) leeks (white and light green parts only; milder, less complex flavor)
- 1 lb (500 g) green onions (white and light green parts only; less complex flavor)
- 1 lb (500 g) shallots (sweeter)
- 1 lb (500 g) sweet or storage onions (less complex flavor)
- 1 lb (500 g) garlic chives (adds garlic flavor)
- 1 lb (500 g) Chinese garlic stems (sharper garlic flavor; adds crunch)

## Rangpur

*Also known as mandarin lime. This orange-skinned citrus is similar to mandarin orange but more acidic.*

1 rangpur = 2 to 3 tbsp (30 to 45 mL) juice = ⅓ to ½ cup (75 to 125 mL) chopped = 1 to 2 tbsp (15 to 30 mL) grated zest

### If You Don't Have It

Substitute 1 rangpur with
- 1 calamondin
- 1 lemon
- 1 lime
- ½ lime + ¼ mandarin orange, blood orange, or navel orange

## Rapeseed Oil

*See* SUBSTITUTING OILS (PAGE 658).

## Rapini

*See* BROCCOLI RAAB.

## Ras el Hanout

*An essential spice mixture in Algeria, Morocco, and Tunisia. For the most intense aromas, use whole spices and toast them before grinding to a powder.*

### If You Don't Have It

Substitute 1 tsp (5 mL) ras el hanout with:
- 1 tsp (5 mL) Homemade Ras el Hanout: Combine 2 tbsp (30 mL) ground ginger, 1 tbsp (15 mL) ground cumin, 2 tsp (10 mL) ground coriander, 2 tsp (10 mL) ground cinnamon, 2 tsp (10 mL) ground nutmeg, 2 tsp (10 mL) ground allspice, 2 tsp (10 mL) ground cardamom, 1½ tsp (7 mL) ground black pepper, 1½ tsp (7 mL) turmeric, 15 saffron threads (crushed), ¼ tsp (1 mL) ground cloves, and ¼ tsp (1 mL) cayenne pepper. Makes about ½ cup (125 mL).
- 1 tsp (5 mL) garam masala

## Rasp

*See* GRATER.

## Raspberry

*Because they are so fragile, the finest raspberries are picked ripe from the bush. Choose packaged raspberries that are dry with no moisture stains at the bottom of the container. Highly perishable, raspberries should be consumed within 2 to 3 days of purchase.*

### If You Don't Have It

Substitute 1 cup (250 mL) raspberries with:
- 1 cup (250 mL) strawberries
- 1 cup (250 mL) loganberries (hybrid of blackberries and raspberries)
- 1 cup (250 mL) boysenberries (hybrid of blackberries, raspberries, and loganberries)
- 1 cup (250 mL) olallieberries (hybrid of youngberries and loganberries)
- 1 cup (250 mL) tayberries (hybrid of blackberries and raspberries)
- 1 cup (250 mL) blackberries

½ pint fresh =
1⅓ cups (325 mL)

1 lb (500 g)
loose-pack frozen =
3⅜ cups (844 mL)

10 oz (300 g)
frozen in syrup =
1¾ cups (425 mL)

## Raspberry Varieties

Choose 1 cup (250 mL) raspberries from these varieties:

- 1 cup (250 mL) red raspberries
- 1 cup (250 mL) yellow or golden raspberries
- 1 cup (250 mL) thimbleberries such as black raspberries

## Raspberry Brandy

*See* FRAMBOISE.

## Raspberry Liqueur

*Sweetened raspberry-flavored spirit, not to be confused with framboise (raspberry) eau de vie. French Chambord ranks among the most popular black raspberry liqueurs.*

## If You Don't Have It

Substitute 2 tbsp (30 mL) raspberry liqueur with:

- 2 tbsp (30 mL) crème de framboise (sweeter; heavier body)
- 2 tbsp (30 mL) framboise (less sweet; higher alcohol)
- 2 tbsp (30 mL) raspberry schnapps (less sweet; higher alcohol)
- 2 tbsp (30 mL) raspberry syrup (sweeter; no alcohol)
- 1 tsp (5 mL) raspberry extract (add 5 tsp/25 mL liquid to recipe if necessary)

## To Vary the Flavor

Substitute 2 tbsp (30 mL) raspberry liqueur with:

- 2 tbsp (30 mL) black raspberry liqueur (slightly more astringent flavor)
- 2 tbsp (30 mL) blackberry liqueur (more astringent flavor)
- 2 tbsp (30 mL) cherry liqueur
- 2 tbsp (30 mL) orange liqueur
- 2 tbsp (30 mL) cassis liqueur
- 2 tbsp (30 mL) crème de fraise (strawberry flavor; sweeter; heavier body)

*See also* FRAMBOISE.

## Rattlesnake Bean

*See* THE WIDE WORLD OF DRIED BEANS (PAGE 637).

## Ravioli

*See* PASTA, FILLED.

## Raw Milk

*See* MILK, WHOLE.

## Raw Sugar

*See* SUGAR, RAW.

## Razor Clam

*See* SWAPPING CLAMS (PAGE 645).

## Reamer

*A hand-held tool with a large, ridged, conical point designed for extracting juice from halved citrus.*

### If You Don't Have It

Substitute a reamer with:

- handheld, table-top, or electric juicer
- fork

## Reblochon Cheese

*Purchase this uncooked French cow's milk cheese from a reliable vendor to ensure perfect ripeness. When overripe, the cheese becomes unpleasantly bitter.*

### If You Don't Have It

Substitute 1 oz (30 g) Reblochon with:

- 1 oz (30 g) Pont-l'Évêque
- 1 oz (30 g) Beaumont
- 1 oz (30 g) Brie
- 1 oz (30 g) Camembert
- 1 oz (30 g) Muenster
- 1 oz (30 g) Esrom
- 1 oz (30 g) Port Salut

## Recao

*See* SAWLEAF HERB.

## Red Banana

*See* BANANA.

## Red Bean

*See* THE WIDE WORLD OF DRIED BEANS (PAGE 637).

## Red Bean Paste

*Also known as sweet red bean paste. Used as a filling in many Chinese sweets, this mixture of azuki beans, sugar, lard, and vanilla is sold canned in smooth and chunky versions.*

### If You Don't Have It

Substitute 1 cup (250 mL) sweet red bean paste with:

- 1 cup (250 mL) Homemade Sweet Red Bean Paste: Soak 8 oz (250 g; 1 generous cup/250 mL) rinsed and picked over azuki or other small red beans in water to cover overnight. Drain and cover with fresh water in a medium pot. Bring to a boil then reduce heat and simmer gently until beans are very tender, 1½ to 2 hours. Remove from heat, drain and let cool. For a chunky paste, return beans to pot and mash until chunky. For a smooth paste, force softened beans through a fine mesh strainer, discarding pulp in the strainer. Return the beans to the pot and stir in 1 cup (250 mL)

## Red Bell Pepper

*See* BELL PEPPER.

## Red Bush

*See* TEA.

## Red Cabbage

*This crucifer takes it gorgeous garnet hue from anthocyanins, which are water-soluble and turn a dingy gray blue when cooked. But anthocyanins retain their color in the presence of acidity. The moral: add some lemon juice or vinegar to help retain the color of cooked red cabbage.*

1 lb (500 g) =
3½ to 4½ cups
(875 mL to 1.125 L)
shredded = 2 cups
(500 mL) cooked

### If You Don't Have It
Substitute 1 lb (500 g) red cabbage with:
- 1 lb (500 g) green cabbage
- 1 lb (500 g) Brussels sprouts
- 1 lb (500 g) savoy cabbage (milder)
- 1 lb (500 g) napa cabbage (milder; more delicate)

## Red Chile Powder
*See* CHILE POWDER.

## Red Chile Sauce
*See* CHILE PASTE; CHILE SAUCE.

## Red Currant
*See* CURRANT, FRESH.

## Red Currant Jelly
*See* CURRANT JELLY.

## Red Date
*See* CHINESE DATE, FRESH.

## Red Delicious Apple
*See* PICKING APPLES (PAGE 636).

## Red Endive
*See* ENDIGIA.

## Redfish
*See* CROAKER.

## Red Leaf Lettuce
*See* LEAF LETTUCE.

## Red Lily Ginger
*See* GINGER, WILD BUD.

## Red Mullet

This reddish pink sea creature is a Mediterranean member of the goatfish family, not a true mullet. It is enjoyed in Europe for its lean, firm flesh.

### If You Don't Have It
Substitute 1 lb (500 g) red mullet with:
- 1 lb (500 g) red snapper
- 1 lb (500 g) black sea bass
- 1 lb (500 g) smelt
- 1 lb (500 g) trout

See also MULLET.

## Red Mustard

See MUSTARD GREENS.

## Red Pepper Flakes

See CAYENNE PEPPER.

## Red Shiso

See PERILLA.

## Red Snapper

The winner of the popularity contest in this 200+ species typically comes to market in the 2 to 8-pound (1 to 4 kg) range. Smaller red snapper are often sold whole, while larger fish are cut into steaks and fillets.

### If You Don't Have It
Substitute 1 lb (500 g) red snapper with:
- 1 lb (500 g) silk snapper
- 1 lb (500 g) vermilion (generally of lesser quality than red snapper)
- 1 lb (500 g) yellowtail or other snapper (generally of lesser quality than red snapper)
- 1 lb (500 g) blackfish
- 1 lb (500 g) black sea bass
- 1 lb (500 g) striped bass
- 1 lb (500 g) grouper
- 1 lb (500 g) haddock
- 1 lb (500 g) halibut
- 1 lb (500 g) tilefish
- 1 lb (500 g) turbot

See also SNAPPER.

## Red Sorrel

See HIBISCUS.

## Refried Beans

Also known as frijoles refritos. Mexican cooking authority Diana Kennedy explains why these cooked beans fried only once are called refried. "The Mexicans have a habit of qualifying a word to

### If You Don't Have It
Substitute 1 cup (250 mL) refried beans with:
- 1 cup (250 mL) Homemade Refried Beans: Heat 2 tbsp (30 mL) lard, bacon drippings, or vegetable oil in a large skillet over medium heat. Add ¾ cup (175 mL) chopped onion and sauté until almost browned, 5 to 8 minutes. Add 2 minced garlic cloves and cook for 2 minutes. Add 4 cups (1 L) cooked or canned black beans and mash to a chunky purée with a potato masher or wooden spoon. Stir in 1 cup (250 mL)

*emphasize the meaning by adding the prefix re-. They will get the oil very hot (requemar), or something will be very good (retebien). Thus refrito means well fried, which they certainly are, since they are fried until they are almost dry."*

cooking or canning liquid and 2 tsp (10 mL) chopped fresh epazote or oregano and cook over medium-low heat until slightly soupy, about 10 minutes, or until almost dry, about 15 minutes. Add salt to taste. Makes about 4 cups (1 L).

## For Better Health

Substitute 1 cup (250 mL) refried beans with:

- 1 cup (250 mL) cooked or canned black beans, mashed with ¼ cup (60 mL) canning or cooking liquid
- 1 cup (250 mL) cooked or canned pinto beans, mashed with ¼ cup (60 mL) canning or cooking liquid

## Refrigerator

*Also known as the fridge. The electric appliance that exiled the icebox was first manufactured successfully for the home kitchen in 1916 by the Kelvinator Company.*

## If You Don't Have It

Substitute a refrigerator with:

- cooler filled with ice
- putting well-covered food outdoors when the outdoor temperature is between 32 and 40°F (0 and 4°C).

## Reindeer

*A large deer particularly valued as game meat in Scandinavia and Russia. The flavor is superior to its relative the caribou.*

## If You Don't Have It

Substitute 1 lb (500 g) reindeer with:

- 1 lb (500 g) caribou
- 1 lb (500 g) red, fallow, or white-tailed deer
- 1 lb (500 g) elk
- 1 lb (500 g) antelope
- 1 lb (500 g) gazelle

*See also* VENISON.

## Rémoulade

*See* MAYONNAISE.

## Rennet

*Soft cheeses like cream cheese, cottage cheese, and panir are made with an acid like lactic acid or citric acid, which gently coagulates milk into solid curds and liquid whey (which is drained off). Hard cheeses are coagulated with rennet, which is a complex of enzymes extracted from the stomach lining of*

## If You Don't Have It

Substitute 1 tsp (5 mL) liquid natural calves' rennet with:

- ½ tsp (2 mL) double-strength natural calves' rennet
- 1 tablet powdered natural calves' rennet
- 1 tsp (5 mL) liquid genetically modified rennet (adding natural pepsin will produce results closer to that of natural calves' rennet)
- 1 tsp (5 mL) liquid vegetable rennet or non-GMO microbial rennet (may produce cheese with a slightly bitter taste, especially the longer the cheese ages)

## Rennet (cont'd)

*calves. Rennet's active enzyme, chymosin, can also be reproduced in molds (so-called vegetable rennet) and, with the help of genetic modification, it can be produced in some bacteria (genetically modified rennet). In 2008, about 85% of commercial U.S. cheeses were made with genetically modified rennet. Most artisanal cheesemakers prefer the qualities of more expensive yet traditional natural calves' rennet.*

## Rhea

*A threatened species of large, flightless, omniverous South American bird. The rhea has a powerful immune system that enables injured birds to heal rapidly.*

### If You Don't Have It

Substitute 1 lb (500 g) rhea with:
- 1 lb (500 g) ostrich
- 1 lb (500 g) emu
- 1 lb (500 g) beef (fattier)
- 1 lb (500 g) buffalo
- 1 lb (500 g) turkey
- 1 lb (500 g) chicken

## Rhubarb

*Although rhubarb is botanically a vegetable, it's treated as a tart fruit and typically prepared with plenty of sugar.*

> 1 lb (500 g) fresh =
> 2 cups (500 mL)
> chopped and cooked

### If You Don't Have It

Substitute 1 lb (500 g) rhubarb with:
- 1 lb (500 g) cranberries
- 1 lb (500 g) gooseberries (for tartness; green color)
- 1 lb (500 g) quinces
- 1 lb (500 g) sorrel (for tartness; green color; much more tender)

## Ricard

*See* ANISE LIQUEUR.

## Rice

*Rice grains, the seeds of a type of grass, sustain about half of the world's population. Brown*

### If You Don't Have It

Substitute 1 cup (250 mL) uncooked white rice with:
- 1 cup (250 mL) uncooked converted rice (more fluffy and separate grains when cooked; slightly increase cooking time)
- 2 cups (500 mL) uncooked orzo pasta (cooks faster)

*rice, with only the hull removed, is closest to the naturally harvested state. The intact bran layers contribute nutty flavor, slightly chewy texture, and a wealth of nutrients and fiber. It requires more liquid and takes longer to cook than white rice, although a quick-cooking brown rice is now marketed. Rice that is milled, or polished, becomes white rice. Depending upon the variety, the grains themselves can be long, medium, or short. Parboiled or converted rice is rough rice soaked in warm water under pressure, steamed, and dried before milling. This procedure gelatinizes the starch and ensures that the grains separate after cooking. It also retains more nutrients than conventionally milled white rice, but it takes a few minutes longer to cook. Instant rice, also known as quick-cooking rice, is milled, completely cooked, enriched, and dehydrated. Preparation takes only a few minutes.*

---

1 cup (250 mL)
long-grain white rice =
3 cups (750 mL) cooked

1 cup (250 mL)
medium-grain white rice =
3 cups (750 mL) cooked

1 cup (250 mL)
short-grain white rice =
3 cups (750 mL) cooked

1 cup (250 mL) brown
or whole-grain rice =
4 cups (1 L) cooked

---

- 1¼ cups (300 mL) uncooked couscous (cooks much faster)
- ¾ cup (175 mL) uncooked pearl barley (chewier; more complex flavor; increase liquid and cooking time)

## To Save Time
Substitute 1 cup (250 mL) uncooked white rice with:
- 1 cup (250 mL) uncooked instant or quick white rice (cooks faster; less flavorful than white rice)
- 1 cup (250 mL) uncooked instant or quick brown rice (cooks faster; less flavorful than brown rice)

## For Better Health
Substitute 1 cup (250 mL) uncooked white rice with:
- 1 cup (250 mL) uncooked brown rice (higher in fiber; chewier; more complex, nutty flavor; increase liquid and slightly increase cooking time)
- 1 cup (250 mL) uncooked wild rice (higher in fiber; chewier; more complex, nutty flavor; increase liquid and cooking time)
- 1¼ cups (300 mL) uncooked whole wheat couscous (high in fiber)
- 1 cup (250 mL) uncooked quinoa (higher in fiber, protein, and other nutrients)
- ¾ cup (175 mL) uncooked millet (higher in fiber and other nutrients)
- ¾ cup (175 mL) uncooked pearl barley (higher in fiber; increase liquid and cooking time; especially to replace short-grain or medium-grain rice)
- ¾ cup (175 mL) uncooked hulled or whole-grain barley (higher in fiber; chewier; more complex flavor; increase liquid and cooking time)
- 1 cup (250 mL) uncooked bulgur (higher in fiber; chewier; more nutty flavor; increase liquid and cooking time)
- 1⅓ cups (325 mL) uncooked wheat berries (higher in fiber; chewier; more nutty flavor; increase liquid and cooking time)
- 1½ cups (375 mL) uncooked kasha (higher in fiber; chewier; more earthy flavor; increase liquid and cooking time)
- 1¼ cups (300 mL) uncooked rye berries (higher in fiber; chewier; more nutty flavor; increase liquid and cooking time)
- 1 cup (250 mL) uncooked Kamut® berries or groats (higher in fiber; chewier; more nutty flavor; increase liquid and cooking time)
- 1⅓ cups (325 mL) uncooked triticale berries or groats (higher in fiber; chewier; more nutty flavor; increase liquid and cooking time)
- 1⅓ cups (325 mL) uncooked spelt berries or groats (higher in fiber; chewier; more nutty flavor; increase liquid and cooking time)

*See also* WILD RICE; VARIETIES OF RICE (PAGE 664).

## Rice Bran

*Bran is the outer cuticle layers and germ directly beneath the hull that remain intact in brown rice but are stripped off when white rice is polished. Rice bran has a sweet, nutty flavor and is rich in vitamins, minerals, and fiber.*

12 oz (375 g) =
3 cups (750 mL)

### If You Don't Have It
Substitute 1 cup (250 mL) rice bran with:
- 1 cup (250 mL) oat bran
- 1 cup (250 mL) wheat bran
- 1 cup (250 mL) wheat germ

## Rice Cake

*Packaged snack discs prepared from puffed rice and a variety of flavorings. A favorite among dieters.*

### If You Don't Have It
Substitute 1 rice cake with:
- ½ cup (125 mL) popcorn

## Rice Cooker

*Electrical pot specially designed to cook rice and keep it warm until serving time. In general, all ingredients are combined using 10 to 20% less liquid than you would using the top-of-the-range method (use ¼ to ½ cup/50 to 125 mL less per cup/250 mL of rice).*

### If You Don't Have It
Substitute a rice cooker with:
- saucepan with a tight-fitting lid (use 10 to 20% more liquid or ¼ to ½ cup/60 to 125 mL more per cup/250 mL of rice)
- pressure cooker (reduce liquid by 20% and reduce cooking time by 60 to 70%)

## Rice Cracker

*Crisp Asian snack crackers prepared from rice flour, often seasoned with soy sauce, seaweed, chilies, or many other flavorings.*

### If You Don't Have It
Substitute 1 lb (500 g) rice crackers with:
- 1 lb (500 g) crisp lavash
- 1 lb (500 g) water crackers
- 1 lb (500 g) bagel chips
- 1 lb (500 g) tortilla chips
- 1 lb (500 g) potato chips
- 1 lb (500 g) sweet potato or other vegetable chips
- 1 lb (500 g) pretzels

## Rice Flour

*See* RICE FLOUR, SWEET; CHOOSING AMONG WHOLE-GRAIN AND ALTERNATIVE FLOURS (PAGE 648).

## Rice Flour, Sweet

*Also known as glutinous rice flour, mochi flour, mochiko, and sweet rice powder. Made from highly starchy varieties of glutinous rice, this flour is used in many Asian countries as the base for dumplings and other sweets. Also an excellent thickener that, like tapioca, doesn't separate after freezing and thawing.*

### If You Don't Have It

Substitute 1 tbsp (15 mL) sweet rice flour (for thickening) with:

- 1½ to 2 tbsp (22 to 30 mL) quick-cooking tapioca (does not separate when frozen)
- 2 tsp (10 mL) arrowroot powder (separates when frozen)
- 2 to 3 tbsp (30 to 45 mL) kudzu powder (separates when frozen)
- 1 tbsp (15 mL) cornstarch (separates when frozen)
- 2 tbsp (30 mL) instant or all-purpose flour (cook a few minutes after thickening to cook out raw flour taste; separates when frozen)
- 2 tsp (10 mL) potato starch or instant mashed potato flakes (separates when frozen)

## Rice Milk

*Liquid extracted from cooked rice and used as a dairy substitute.*

### If You Don't Have It

Substitute 1 cup (250 mL) rice milk with:

- 1 cup (250 mL) almond milk
- 1 cup (250 mL) oat milk
- 1 cup (250 mL) sweetened soy milk
- 1 cup (250 mL) cow's milk
- 1 cup (250 mL) acidophilus milk (adds beneficial enzymes)
- 1 cup (250 mL) lactose-free milk (for the lactose intolerant)
- 1 cup (250 mL) goat's milk (for the lactose intolerant; more tangy taste than cow's milk)

## Rice Noodles

*See* A SNAPSHOT OF ASIAN NOODLES (PAGE 656).

## Rice Paddy Herb

*Also known as ngo om. This green herb with long oval leaves and a sawtooth edge (Limnophila aromatica) thrives in wet rice paddies. It is widely used in South Vietnamese soups for its sharp lemony aroma and whiffs of cumin.*

### If You Don't Have It

Substitute 1 cup (250 mL) rice milk with:

- 1 cup (250 mL) almond milk
- 1 cup (250 mL) oat milk
- 1 cup (250 mL) sweetened soy milk
- 1 cup (250 mL) cow's milk
- 1 cup (250 mL) acidophilus milk (adds beneficial enzymes)
- 1 cup (250 mL) lactose-free milk (for the lactose intolerant)
- 1 cup (250 mL) goat's milk (for the lactose intolerant; more tangy taste than cow's milk)

## Rice Paper

*Also known as spring roll wrappers. Southeast Asian circular or triangular shaped sheets made from rice flour and water. They*

### If You Don't Have It

Substitute 1 lb (500 g) rice paper with:

- 1 lb (500 g) phyllo dough
- 1 lb (500 g) dumpling wrappers (thicker; round)
- 1 lb (500 g) thinly rolled fresh pasta (cut to desired shape)
- 1 lb (500 g) egg roll wrappers (thicker)

## Rice Paper (cont'd)

*are generally available dried and require soaking before using so they soften enough to allow them to be rolled up. The papers are used to wrap ingredients.*

- 1 lb (500 g) won ton skins (thicker)
- 1 lb (500 g) empanada wrappers (thicker; round)

## Ricer

*Also known as a potato ricer. Looking like a garlic press on steroids, this lever-operated plunger forces cooked potatoes, carrots, turnips, or other soft foods through a perforated template to purée them.*

### If You Don't Have It

Substitute a ricer with:
- food mill
- hand-held potato masher
- medium-mesh sieve and back of wooden spoon
- electric mixer
- blender or food processor (not recommended for mashing potatoes and other starchy rootsand tubers; results are too gummy)

## Rice Sticks

*See* A SNAPSHOT OF ASIAN NOODLES (PAGE 656).

## Rice Vinegar

*See* CHOOSING VINEGAR (PAGE 674).

## Rice Wine

*See* MIRIN; SAKE.

## Ricotta

*The name means "re-cooked." This fresh Italian cheese is pleasantly granular and lightly sweet. In Italy, most ricottas are made by cooking the whey drained from producing mozzarella, provolone, or other cheeses. In the U.S., skim or whole milk is often added to the whey.*

8 oz (250 g) =
1 cup (250 mL)

### If You Don't Have It

Substitute 1 oz (30 g) ricotta cheese with:
- 1 oz (30 g) Myzithra
- 1 oz (30 g) cottage cheese, puréed until smooth
- 1 oz (30 g) farmer cheese (firmer)
- 1 oz (30 g) pot cheese (firmer)
- 1 oz (30 g) hoop cheese (firmer)
- 1 oz (30 g) fromage blanc
- 1 oz (30 g) mashed firm tofu (for texture; much less flavorful)

## Ricotta Salata

*Also known as canestrata. Ricotta that is allowed to drain more than the fresh version to become drier in texture. It is also salted.*

### If You Don't Have It

Substitute 1 oz (30 g) ricotta salata with:
- 1 oz (30 g) feta (stronger flavor; rinse to reduce saltiness)
- 1 oz (30 g) Manouri (creamier)
- 1 oz (30 g) Haloumi (may add mint flavor)
- 1 oz (30 g) aged Myzithra (to replace aged ricotta salata)

4 oz (125 g) = 1 cup
(250 mL) crumbled

- 1 oz (30 g) Cotija (may be soft or firm)
- 1 oz (30 g) Pecorino Romano (to replace aged ricotta salata; sharper flavor)
- 1 oz (30 g) Parmesan (to replace aged ricotta salata)

## Ring Bologna

*Also known as fleischwurst. This cooked beef and pork sausage is flexible enough to be shaped into a ring and narrow enough that slices fit on a single cracker. It is available in coarse and fine textures, and the Pennsylvania Dutch often reheat it and serve it with bread or potato salad.*

### If You Don't Have It
Substitute 1 lb (500 g) ring bologna with:
- 1 lb (500 g) bologna (softer, wider, and finer texture)
- 1 lb (500 g) mortadella (softer and wider with cubes of pork fat and garlic flavor)
- 1 lb (500 g) knackwurst (softer)
- 1 lb (500 g) Kielbasa (softer)

### For Better Health
Substitute 1 lb (500 g) ring bologna with:
- 1 lb (500 g) chicken or turkey ring bologna (lower in fat and calories)

*See also* BOLOGNA; LEBANON BOLOGNA

## Ring Dove

*See* SQUAB.

## Ring Mold

*See* PAN SIZE EQUIVALENTS (PAGE 678).

## Risotto Rice

*See* VARIETIES OF RICE (PAGE 664).

## Ritz Cracker

*See* CRACKER.

## Roasted Red Pepper

*See* BELL PEPPER, ROASTED RED.

## Roasting Rack

*A flat or adjustable V-shaped metal rack on which to hold meat or fowl above the bottom of the roasting pan. Because hot air can circulate, the entire roast browns and crisps evenly.*

### If You Don't Have It
Substitute a roasting rack with:
- upper oven rack with pan set on lower oven rack
- cooling rack set in roasting pan or rimmed baking sheet

## Robiola Lombardia

*A creamy cow's milk cheese that originated in the Lombardy town of Robbio.*

### If You Don't Have It

Substitute 1 oz (30 g) Robiola Lombardia with:

- 1 oz (30 g) Taleggio
- 1 oz (30 g) Reblochon
- 1 oz (30 g) Pont-l'Évêque

*See also* ROBIOLA PIEMONTE.

## Robiola Piemonte

*Also known as Robiola di Roccaverano. A well-known variation of Robiola Lombardia, named after a village in Piedmont, is made from goat's milk, sheep's milk, cow's milk or sometimes a mixture of the trio.*

### If You Don't Have It

Substitute 1 oz (30 g) Robiola Piemonte:

- 1 oz (30 g) caprini or creamy young chèvre
- ½ oz (15 g) ricotta + ½ oz (15 g) mascarpone, blended
- 1 oz (30 g) Petit Suisse

*See also* ROBIOLA LOMBARDIA.

## Rocambole

*See* GARLIC.

## Rochebaron

*See* MONTBRIAC.

## Rock and Rye

*This is a citrus liqueur that's based on rye whiskey. A piece of rock candy floats in every bottle.*

### If You Don't Have It

Substitute 2 tbsp (30 mL) rock and rye with:

- 2 tbsp (30 mL) Southern Comfort

## Rock Candy

*See* SUGAR, ROCK.

## Rock Cornish Hen

*See* CHICKEN.

## Rocket

*See* ARUGULA.

## Rockfish

*See* OCEAN PERCH; STRIPED BASS.

## Rock Lobster

*See* SPINY LOBSTER.

## Rock Salt

*See* TRADING SALTS (PAGE 668).

## Rock Sugar

*See* SUGAR, ROCK.

## Rocoto Chile

*See* CHOOSING FRESH CHILES (PAGE 640).

## Roe

*See* CHANGING ROE (PAGE 666).

## Rolled Barley

*See* BARLEY FLAKES.

## Rolled Oats

*See* OATS, OLD-FASHIONED.

## Rolling Pin

*A solid, heavy cylindrical tool used primarily to roll dough but also to crush crackers, flatten cutlets, and perform other tasks. Pins are fashioned from wood, marble, ceramic, glass, and plastic.*

### If You Don't Have It
Substitute a rolling pin with:
- wine bottle
- clean, heavy-duty cardboard tube (such as one from a poster or poster mailing tube) wrapped in plastic wrap

## Romaine Lettuce

*Also known as Cos lettuce. Leaf of choice for the classic Caesar salad.*

1 lb (500 g) =
6 cups (1.5 L) pieces

### If You Don't Have It
Substitute 1 lb (500 g) Romaine lettuce with:
- 1 lb (500 g) crisphead lettuce such as Iceberg, Great Lakes, or Imperial (rounder, crisper leaves; less flavorful; more watery)
- 1 lb (500 g) butterhead lettuce such as Bibb or Boston (smaller, more tender leaves; less watery)
- 8 oz (250 g) leaf lettuce such as oak or lollo (smaller, more tender leaves; less watery)
- 8 oz (250 g) mâche (tender leaves; bittersweet, slightly nutty flavor)

## Romanesco

*Also known as broccoli romanesco. Similar to broccoflower but with beautiful conical florets in the repeating shape of a fractal. The plant thrives in Italy between Rome and Naples but doesn't do as well in California.*

1 lb (500 g) fresh =
2½ to 3 cups (625 to 750 mL) florets = 1½ to 2 cups (375 to 500 mL) chopped

### If You Don't Have It
Substitute 1 lb (500 g) broccoli Romanesco with:
- 1 lb (500 g) Broccoflower (very similar, but with round florets)
- 1 lb (500 g) cauliflower (white color; stronger cabbage flavor)
- 1 lb (500 g) broccoli (darker green color; softer texture; stronger flavor)
- 8 oz (250 g) cauliflower + 8 oz (250 g) broccoli (stronger flavor)

## Romano

*Also known as Pecorino Romano. A style of pungent, hard Italian grating cheese produced from sheep's milk.*

### If You Don't Have It
Substitute 1 oz (30 g) Romano cheese with:
- 1 oz (30 g) Parmesan (slightly milder)
- 1 oz (30 g) Grana Padano
- 1 oz (30 g) aged Asiago (slightly sweeter)
- 1 oz (30 g) aged Manchego (milder)
- 1 oz (30 g) dry Jack cheese (more nutty)

### Romano Varieties
Choose 1 oz (30 g) Romano cheese from these varieties:
- 1 oz (30 g) Pecorino Romano (made with sheep's milk; sharp, salty, delicate fruity aromas)
- 1 oz (30 g) Caprino Romano (made with goat's milk; sharper than Pecorino Romano)
- 1 oz (30 g) Vacchino Romano (made with cow's milk; much milder than Pecorino Romano)

### For Better Health
Substitute 1 oz (30 g) Romano cheese with:
- 1 oz (30 g) Sapsago (lower in fat and calories; more herbal flavor)

*See also* PECORINO.

## Romeritos

*Although they look like rosemary (romeritos means "little rosemary" in Spanish), these acidic little greens (Suaeda torreyana) taste closer to purslane. They form the basis of a dish of shrimp fritters with mole sauce traditionally served at Christmas and Lent in Mexico.*

### If You Don't Have It
Substitute 1 lb (500 g) romeritos with:
- 1 lb (500 g) purslane
- 1 lb (500 g) sorrel
- 1 lb (500 g) spinach

## Romesco

*Spain's answer to Italy's pesto, romesco features almonds, hazelnuts, roasted garlic, roasted peppers (and sometimes roasted tomatoes), olive oil, vinegar, and fresh bread puréed to a coarse red-orange sauce. Traditionally, romesco*

### If You Don't Have It
Substitute ½ cup (125 mL) romesco with:
- ½ cup (125 mL) Homemade Romesco: Halve lengthwise, core and seed 3 plum tomatoes and 2 red bell peppers and place on a baking sheet cut sides down. Slice a head of garlic in half through its equator and put the bottom half on the baking sheet cut side up (discard top half or save for another use). Drizzle the vegetables with 2 tbsp (30 mL) olive oil and roast at 400°F (200°C) until garlic is browned and tomato and pepper skins are partially charred, 1 hour. Cover with foil and let stand 15 minutes. Squeeze the garlic from its

*is made with dried ñora peppers, a mild Spanish chile often smoked or sundried and to make Spanish pimentón (smoked paprika). A similar sauce known as Savitxada is made with garlic-rubbed toast instead of fresh bread and traditionally served at spring onion festivals (calçotades) in Valls, Spain.*

skin into a food processor or blender. Peel the tomatoes and peppers and add to the processor. Meanwhile, tear open 1 oz (30 g) Nora peppers (4 to 5) or 1 large ancho chile and discard seeds. Toast the chile in 1 tbsp (15 mL) olive oil for 15 seconds per side then soak in hot water for 30 minutes. Toast ¼ cup (60 mL) blanched or sliced almonds (preferably Marcona) and ¼ cup (60 mL) blanched hazelnuts in the same pan then transfer to the processor with the oil. Transfer the chile to the processor (reserve soaking water) along with ¼ cup (60 mL) olive oil, 2 tbsp (30 mL) sherry vinegar or red wine vinegar, 1 large slice (1 oz/30 g) torn country bread (crust removed), 1 tsp (5 mL) pimentón or smoked paprika, and 1 tsp (5 mL) salt. Process to a coarse purée, adding chile soaking water as necessary to make thick, spoonable sauce. Makes about 2½ cups (625 mL).

## To Vary the Flavor
Substitute ½ cup (125 mL) romesco with:
- ½ cup (125 mL) pesto (seasoned basil and pine nut purée)
- ½ cup (125 mL) tapenade (seasoned olive purée)

## Rondelé

*A Wisconsin brand of European-style soft cheeses.*

8 oz (250 g) =
1 cup (250 mL)

### If You Don't Have It
Substitute 1 oz (30 g) Rondelé with:
- 1 oz (30 g) boursin
- 1 oz (30 g) Alouette
- 1 oz (30 g) herbed cream cheese + 1½ tsp (7 mL) softened butter

## Rooibos

*See* TEA.

## Root Beer

*Originally, this foamy beverage was prepared with sassafras. Today it is a blend of anise, cinnamon, cloves, ginger, juniper, licorice, lemon oil, orange oil, sarsaparilla, vanilla, and wintergreen.*

### If You Don't Have It
Substitute 1 cup (250 mL) root beer with:
- 1 cup (250 mL) birch beer
- 1 cup (250 mL) cola (less aromatic)
- 1 cup (250 mL) ginger beer (sharper flavor)

## Root Vegetables

*See* SPECIFIC TYPES.

## Roquefort

*Genuine French Roquefort takes its blue cheese character from sheep's milk, naturally occurring Peniciullium roqueforti bacteria, and the constant conditions of the aging caves.*

> 4 oz (125 g) =
> 1 cup (250 mL) crumbled

### If You Don't Have It

Substitute 1 oz (30 g) Roquefort with:
- 1 oz (30 g) Gorgonzola
- 1 oz (30 g) Maytag Blue
- 1 oz (30 g) Stilton
- 1 oz (30 g) Cashel Blue
- 1 oz (30 g) Fourme d'Ambert
- 1 oz (30 g) Bleu d'Auvergne
- 1 oz (30 g) Bleu des Causses
- 1 oz (30 g) Danish Blue

## Rose

*See* PICKING EDIBLE FLOWERS (PAGE 650).

## Rose Apple

*Also known as Malabar plum. The crisp, juicy flesh of this pear-shaped fruit (Syzygium jambos) tastes similar to Asian pears with a hint of bitterness and a rose-like aroma.*

### If You Don't Have It

Substitute 1 lb (500 g) rose apples with:
- 1 lb (500 g) Asian pears + $\frac{1}{4}$ tsp (1 mL) rose water
- 1 lb (500 g) tart, crisp apples + $\frac{1}{4}$ tsp (1 mL) rose water

## Rose Essence

*A far more concentrated form of rose water, which Indian cooks use to flavor beverages and desserts.*

### If You Don't Have It

Substitute 1 tsp (5 mL) rose essence with:
- 1 tbsp (15 mL) rose water
- 2 tbsp (30 mL) rose syrup (sweeter; reduce liquid in recipe by a scant 2 tbsp/30 mL if necessary)

### To Vary the Flavor

Substitute 1 tsp (5 mL) rose essence with:
- 1 tbsp (15 mL) other flower-based water such as orange flower water
- 1 to $1\frac{1}{2}$ tsp (5 to 7 mL) almond or vanilla extract

*See also* ROSE SYRUP; ROSE WATER.

## Rose Hip, Dried

*Also known as rose haw. Even when dried, the nutrient-rich fruit of the rose plant contains about 2000 mg of vitamin C in just $3\frac{1}{2}$ ounces (105 g).*

### If You Don't Have It

Substitute 1 cup (250 mL) dried rose hips with:
- 1 cup (250 mL) dried hibiscus flowers
- 1 cup (250 mL) Red Zinger herbal tea bags (adds rose hips, peppermint, and other herbs)

## Rose Hip, Fresh

*The red-orange fruits of the rose plant make delicious sweet-tart jams, pies, and syrups with a rosé color and aromatic apple-like flavor. According to Liz Druitt, author of* The Organic Rose Garden, *the species with the best tasting hips are* Rosa canina, Rosa rugosa rubra, Hansa, Old Blush, *and* Dortmund.

### If You Don't Have It
Substitute 1 cup (250 mL) fresh rose hips with:
- 1 cup (250 mL) fresh acerola
- 1 cup (250 mL) red currants
- 1 cup (250 mL) pitted cherries

## Roselle

*See* HIBISCUS.

## Rosemary

*When you purchase fresh rosemary for a recipe and don't use all of it, you can easily dry or freeze the remainder for future use. Wash the branches and dry thoroughly on a towel. Place in a small paper bag to dry in a cool pantry or place in a resealable bag and store in the freezer.*

### If You Don't Have It
Substitute 1 tbsp (15 mL) chopped fresh rosemary with:
- 1 to 2 tsp (5 to 10 mL) crushed dried rosemary

### To Vary the Flavor
Substitute 1 tbsp (15 mL) chopped fresh rosemary with:
- 2 tsp (10 mL) chopped fresh sage or thyme
- 1 tbsp (15 mL) chopped fresh summer savory
- 1 tbsp (15 mL) chopped fresh basil or oregano

## Rose Syrup

*Also known as rose-scented syrup. Essence of rose combined with a sugar syrup. This floral sweetener is used in the Middle East, India, and Southeast Asia in desserts and beverages.*

### If You Don't Have It
Substitute 1 tbsp (15 mL) rose syrup with:
- 1½ tsp (7 mL) rose water (less sweet)
- ½ tsp (2 mL) rose essence (less sweet)

### To Vary the Flavor
Substitute 1 tbsp (15 mL) rose syrup with:
- 1 tbsp (15 mL) other flavored syrup, such as almond, hazelnut, orange, or vanilla

*See also* ROSE ESSENCE; ROSE WATER.

## Rose Water

*In the Middle East, India, and China, this intense distillation of rose petals is used as a food flavoring.*

### If You Don't Have It
Substitute 1 tsp (5 mL) rose water with:
- ¼ to ½ tsp (1 to 2 mL) rose essence
- 2 tsp (10 mL) rose syrup (sweeter)

## Rose Water (cont'd)

### To Vary the Flavor

Substitute 1 tsp (5 mL) rose water with:

- 1 to 2 tbsp (15 to 30 mL) Parfait d'Amour (adds rose, orange, and vanilla aromas, sweetness, and alcohol)
- 1 to 2 tbsp (15 to 30 mL) crème de rose (adds rose and vanilla aromas, sweetness, and alcohol)
- 1 to 2 tbsp (15 to 30 mL) crème de violette (adds violet flower aroma, sweetness, alcohol,and purple color)
- 1 tsp (5 mL) flower-based water such as orange flower water
- ¼ to ½ tsp (1 to 2 mL) vanilla or almond extract

*See also* ROSE ESSENCE; ROSE SYRUP.

## Rotary Beater

*In* The Eggbeater Chronicles, *by collectibles author Don Thornton, you'll find a history and pictorial guide to more than 700 different eggbeater designs, including water-powered, glass plunger, and rotary cranked models.*

### If You Don't Have It

Substitute a rotary beater with:

- whisk
- fork
- pastry blender
- electric mixer

## Roti

*Indian whole wheat flatbread cooked on a griddle. When the roti is held over an open flame for a few seconds to complete cooking, it puffs like a balloon.*

### If You Don't Have It

Substitute 1 roti with:

- 1 chapati (flatbread made with whole wheat flour and little or no fat)
- 1 paratha (griddle-cooked whole wheat flatbread with fat in the dough; richer; more flaky)
- 1 poori (deep-fried flatbread made with whole wheat flour; crisper)
- 1 naan (more puffy flatbread made from refined wheat flour and cooked on the walls of a tandoor or clay-lined oven; sometimes flavored with garlic, herbs, or other aromatics)
- 1 whole wheat pita bread (similar to naan)
- 1 whole wheat flour tortilla

*See also* CHAPATI.

## Rotisserie

*A cooking implement that automates the ancient method of slowly revolving meat or poultry over heat to roast and baste simultaneously.*

### If You Don't Have It

Substitute a rotisserie with:

- stationary roasting rack and very frequent turning (food may be less moist and less evenly browned; save yourself the trouble and get a rotisserie)

## Roucou

*See* ANNATTO SEED.

## Roux

*A cooked mixture of flour and fat used for thickening sauces, soups, and stews. White roux and blond roux — cooked until slightly golden — are made with butter and used for delicately colored dishes. Brown roux can be made with butter or the drippings from pork or beef roasts. Cooked to a walnut color, brown roux is used for more robust soups and sauces. In Creole and Cajun roux, lard is often used and the mixture may be cooked for an hour or until very dark and deeply flavored.*

### If You Don't Have It

Substitute ½ cup (125 mL) roux with:

- ½ cup (125 mL) beurre manié (¼ cup/60 mL softened butter + ¼ cup/60 mL flour, kneaded together; less flavorful)
- ¼ cup (60 mL) instant flour (less flavorful)
- ¼ cup (60 mL) all-purpose flour + ½ cup (125 mL) cold water, whisked together (less flavorful)
- 2 tbsp (30 mL) cornstarch, potato starch, or rice starch + ¼ cup (60 mL) cold water, whisked together (less flavorful)
- 3 tbsp (45 mL) arrowroot + ¼ cup (60 mL) cold water, whisked together (less flavorful)
- 4 tsp (20 mL) instant mashed potato flakes (less flavorful)
- 5 tbsp (75 mL) tapioca starch + ½ cup (125 mL) cold water, whisked together (less flavorful)
- ¼ cup (60 mL) cornmeal (adds mild corn flavor)

### Roux Varieties

Choose ½ cup (125 mL) roux from these varieties:

- ½ cup (125 mL) white roux (cooked until beige and not browned; best for light or cream-based sauces and soups)
- ½ cup (125 mL) blond roux (cooked until golden or lightly browned; slightly more flavorful than white roux; best for light or cream-based sauces and soups)
- ½ cup (125 mL) brown roux (cooked until deeply browned and richly toasted or nutty in flavor and aroma; best for dark sauces, soups, and stews)

## Royal Ann Cherry

*See* CHERRY.

## Royal Cumin

*See* CUMIN.

## Royal Icing

*Stiff, meringue-based icing used to decorate cookies and cakes and glue together gingerbread houses.*

### If You Don't Have It

Substitute 1 cup (250 mL) Royal Icing with:

- 1 cup (250 mL) Homemade Royal Icing: Put 4 cups (1 L) confectioner's (icing) sugar, 3 tbsp (45 mL) meringue powder, and ⅓ cup (75 mL) warm water in the bowl of a mixer. Add 1 tsp (5 mL) vanilla, other flavoring, and/or food coloring if you like. Beat until stiff peaks form when beaters are lifted, 7 to 10 minutes. You can also replace the meringue powder and water with 3 oz (90 g) pasteurized egg whites or 3 raw egg whites from a trusted source, gently beating the whites first then adding the sugar and flavorings/colorings, and beating until stiff. Makes about 3 cups (750 mL).

## Royal Icing (cont'd)

- 1 cup (250 mL) Homemade Egg-Free Royal Icing: Dissolve ¼ oz (7 g) unflavored gelatin in a 1¼ cups (300 mL) hot water and let stand until cool but not set. Place ¼ cup (60 mL) of mixture in the bowl of a mixer and beat for 2 minutes. Add 4 cups (1 L) confectioner's (icing) sugar, 1 tsp (5 mL) vanilla, other flavoring, and/or food coloring and beat until stiff peaks form when beaters are lifted, 7 to 10 minutes. Makes about 3 cups (750 mL).

## Rubber Spatula

*See* SPATULA.

## Ruby Port

*See* PORT.

## Rum

*Fermented sugarcane juice that is distilled and aged. May be flavored with spices or tropical fruits.*

### If You Don't Have It

Substitute 2 tbsp (30 mL) rum with:

- ¾ to 1 tsp (3 to 5 mL) rum extract or brandy extract + 2 tbsp (30 mL) apple cider or water
- 2 tbsp (30 mL) brandy
- 2 tbsp (30 mL) bourbon

### Rum Varieties

Choose 2 tbsp (30 mL) rum from these varieties:

- 2 tbsp (30 mL) light, white, or silver rum (colorless; light body; light, dry flavor)
- 2 tbsp (30 mL) flavored rum, such as coconut rum (colorless; light body; lightly sweet flavor infused with tropical aromas such as coconut)
- 2 tbsp (30 mL) gold or amber rum (amber color; medium body; aged longer than light rum; more flavorful and less harsh-tasting than white rum)
- 2 tbsp (30 mL) añejo rum (similar to gold or amber rum but aged longer)
- 2 tbsp (30 mL) spiced rum (colorless or amber color; light to medium body; flavored with spices such as vanilla)
- 2 tbsp (30 mL) dark rum (dark amber color; medium to full body; aged longer than gold or amber rum; more complex, molasses-like flavor than gold or amber rum; Jamaican rum is a dark rum)
- 2 tbsp (30 mL) Demerara rum (dark amber color; medium to full body; more complex flavor than white or amber rum; may be higher in alcohol than other dark rums)

*See also* RUM EXTRACT.

## Rumberry

*See* GUAVABERRY LIQUEUR.

## Rum Extract

*Good for adding rum flavor — with only a trace amount of the alcohol found in rum — to cakes, pies, breads, and savory fruit dishes.*

### If You Don't Have It

Substitute 1 tsp (5 mL) rum extract with:

- 2 to 3 tbsp (30 to 45 mL) rum (omit 2 to 3 tbsp/30 to 45 mL liquid from recipe if necessary)

### To Vary the Flavor

Substitute 1 tsp (5 mL) rum extract with:

- 1 tsp (5 mL) brandy extract
- 1 tsp (5 mL) vanilla extract

## Runner Bean

*See* PEAS, SHELLING.

## Rusk

*See* ZWIEBACK.

## Russian Black Bread

*See* BLACK BREAD.

## Russian Easter Bread

*See* KULICH.

## Rutabaga

*Also known as Canadian, Russian, Swedish, and yellow turnip. The Rodney Dangerfield of the vegetable world, this golden globe root vegetable deserves far more respect in the kitchen than it gets. Newly harvested sweet rutabagas are delightful tossed into salads and stir-fries. The vegetable may also be steamed, mashed, sautéed, or roasted until caramelized.*

> 1 medium = 1½ to 2 lbs
> (750 g to 1 kg) =
> 4 to 5 cups
> (1 to 1.25 L) cubed

### If You Don't Have It

Substitute 1 cup (250 mL) chopped rutabaga with:

- 1 cup (250 mL) chopped turnips (sweeter)
- 1 cup (250 mL) chopped broccoli stems (sweeter, milder)
- 1 cup (250 mL) chopped kohlrabi bulb (sweeter, milder)
- 1 cup (250 mL) chopped Asian radishes such as daikon (more peppery)
- 1 cup (250 mL) chopped black radishes (much sharper and hotter flavor)

## Rye Bread

*Dark, hearty breads made from rye flour (often with some wheat flour) are preferred in northeastern Europe, Scandinavia, and in parts of North America settled by immigrants from these areas. The characteristic acidic flavor comes from the sourdough leavening.*

### If You Don't Have It

Substitute 1 lb (500 g) rye bread with:

- 1 lb (500 g) pumpernickel bread
- 1 lb (500 g) limpa bread (more aromatic)
- 1 lb (500 g) Russian black bread

## Rye Flour

*See* CHOOSING AMONG WHOLE-GRAIN AND ALTERNATIVE FLOURS (PAGE 648).

## Rye Whiskey

*See* WHISKEY.

# Saan Choi to Szechuan Pepper

## Saan Choi

*See also* BASELLA.

## Saanen

A Swiss cheese of amazing longevity, sometimes edible for 200 years. Traditionally, a child's birth is commemorated with an individual saanen cheese. Tiny pieces are consumed on special occasions during the person's lifetime. In some cases, the cheese outlives the person.

4 oz (125 g) =
1 cup (250 mL) grated

### If You Don't Have It
Substitute 1 oz (30 g) Saanen with:
- 1 oz (30 g) Sbrinz
- 1 oz (30 g) Spalen or Sparen
- 1 oz (30 g) aged Asiago
- 1 oz (30 g) Parmesan (slightly sharper)
- 1 oz (30 g) Grana Padano (slightly sharper)
- 1 oz (30 g) dry Jack cheese (more nutty flavor)

### For Better Health
Substitute 1 oz (30 g) Saanen with:
- 1 oz (30 g) Sapsago (more herbal flavor; lower in fat)

## Sablefish

Also known mistakenly as Alaska cod, black cod, and butterfish. Neither butterfish nor cod, this oily Pacific Northwest fish is excellent for smoking. Often sold as smoked black cod.

### If You Don't Have It
Substitute 1 lb (500 g) sablefish with:
- 1 lb (500 g) black cod
- 1 lb (500 g) butterfish
- 1 lb (500 g) mackerel
- 1 lb (500 g) whitefish
- 1 lb (500 g) salmon
- 1 lb (500 g) blackfish
- 1 lb (500 g) grouper
- 1 lb (500 g) smoked black cod (cured fish; adds smoke flavor)

*See also* BLACK COD; BUTTERFISH.

## Sabra Liqueur

*From Israel, a chocolate-orange sweetened spirit.*

### If You Don't Have It

Substitute 2 tbsp (30 mL) Sabra liqueur with:
- 2 tbsp (30 mL) orange liqueur (omits chocolate flavor)
- 2 tbsp (30 mL) crème de cacao (sweeter)
- 2 tbsp (30 mL) Cheri Suisse (combines chocolate and cherry flavors)
- 2 tbsp (30 mL) Vandermint (combines chocolate and mint flavors)
- 2 tbsp (30 mL) Tiramisù liqueur (combines chocolate, coffee, and almond flavors)

*See also* ORANGE LIQUEUR.

## Saenkanter

*See* GOUDA.

## Safflower

*Also known as bastard saffron, false saffron, and kasubha. Related to sunflowers and thistles, the stunning orange flowers of this plant have long been substituted for the much more expensive saffron.*

### If You Don't Have It

Substitute 1 tsp (5 mL) crushed dried safflower florets with:
- ½ tsp (2 mL) turmeric + ½ tsp (2 mL) mild paprika (for yellow orange color; adds more pungent flavor)
- 1 to 1½ tsp (5 to 7 mL) annatto seeds (for yellow orange color; steep the seeds in hot water or oil liquid until richly colored then drain and use the colored liquid, discarding the seeds)
- 2 drops yellow food coloring + 1 drop red food coloring mixed into water or other liquid in the recipe (for yellow orange color)
- 10 to 15 crushed saffron threads (for yellow orange color; adds earthy, floral aromas; much more expensive)

*See also* SAFFRON.

## Safflower Oil

*See* SUBSTITUTING OILS (PAGE 658).

## Saffron

*This most expensive of seasonings is found in the orange red stigmas of the crocus flower. It takes 70,000 flowers — the stigmas of which must be harvested by hand — to yield a pound of saffron. Saffron has a spicy aroma, pleasantly bitter flavor, and a gorgeous red gold hue.*

10 to 15 threads = pinch = ⅛ to ¼ tsp (0.5 to 1 mL) powder

### If You Don't Have It

Substitute 10 to 15 crushed saffron threads with:
- 1 tsp (5 mL) crushed dried safflower florets (for yellow orange color; much milder, less complex aroma; much less expensive)
- ½ tsp (2 mL) turmeric + ½ tsp (2mL) mild paprika (for yellow orange color; adds more pungent flavor)
- 1 to 1½ tsp (5 to 7 mL) annatto seeds (for yellow orange color; steep the seeds in hot water or oil liquid until richly colored then drain and use the colored liquid, discarding the seeds)
- 2 drops yellow food coloring + 1 drop red food coloring mixed into water or other liquid in the recipe (for yellow orange color)

*See also* SAFFLOWER; TURMERIC.

## Saga Blue

*A luxurious Danish double- or triple-crème cheese with subtle blue veining, mellow flavor, and an edible white rind.*

### If You Don't Have It
Substitute 1 oz (30 g) Saga blue with:
- 1 oz (30 g) Bleu de Bresse
- 1 oz (30 g) Cambozola
- 1 oz (30 g) Blue Castello
- 1 oz (30 g) Danish Blue
- 1 oz (30 g) Gorgonzola (more pungent, complex flavor)

## Sage

*An evergreen perennial of the mint family, this robustly flavored herb worked its way into European kitchens in the 16$^{th}$ century.*

> 1 oz (30 g) rubbed sage =
> 1 cup (250 mL)
>
> 1 oz (30 g) ground sage =
> ¼ cup (60 mL)

### If You Don't Have It
Substitute 1 tbsp (15 mL) chopped fresh sage with:
- 1 tsp (5 mL) dried sage
- 1 tbsp (15 mL) chopped fresh pineapple sage (adds pineapple aromas)

### To Vary the Flavor
Substitute 1 tbsp (15 mL) chopped fresh sage with:
- 3 to 4 tsp (15 to 20 mL) chopped fresh summer savory
- 1 tbsp (15 mL) chopped fresh rosemary
- 3 to 4 tsp (15 to 20 mL) chopped fresh thyme, basil, or oregano
- 1 to 2 tsp (5 to 10 mL) poultry seasoning (sage and other herbs such as thyme and marjoram)

## Sage Derby

*See* DERBY.

## Sago

*A light starch used for thickening, obtained from sago and other palms. It is processed into flour, meal, and pearls similar to tapioca. Most widely used in India, Southeast Asia, Central and South America, the Caribbean, and among native Australians.*

### If You Don't Have It
Substitute 1 tbsp (15 mL) sago flour or pearls (for thickening) with:
- 1 tbsp (15 mL) tapioca flour or pearls
- 2 tsp (10 mL) arrowroot powder
- 1 heaping tbsp (15 mL) all-purpose flour
- 1½ tsp (7 mL) cornstarch, potato starch, or rice starch

## Sahlab

*Also known as salep. The starchy bulbs of certain orchids (Orchis mascula) dried and powdered to thicken and flavor Middle Eastern milk beverages of the same name. In Turkey, sahlab is a precious aphrodisiac also used to thicken dondurma (Turkish ice cream). "Behold the Satyrion root, is it not formed like the male privy parts?" wrote the 16th century Swiss toxicologist Paracelsus, "Accordingly, magic discovered it and revealed that it can restore a man's virility and passion."*

### If You Don't Have It

Substitute 1 tsp (5 mL) powdered sahlab (flour) with:
- 1 tsp (5 mL) cornstarch
- 1 to 1½ tsp (5 to 7 mL) arrowroot

## Saint Agur

*Creamy, spicy cow's milk blue from Auvergne in south-central France. Delicious spread on raisin bread, with pears, or savored with a glass of Sauternes.*

### If You Don't Have It

Substitute 1 oz (30 g) Saint Agur with:
- 1 oz (30 g) Bleu d'Auvergne
- 1 oz (30 g) Bleu de Gex
- 1 oz (30 g) Fourme d'Ambert
- 1 oz (30 g) Cambozola
- 1 oz (30 g) Stilton

## Saint Albray

*This mild and spicy soft cheese made at the base of the French Pyrenees is instantly recognizable by the scalloped shape of its whitish red rind.*

### If You Don't Have It

Substitute 1 oz (30 g) Saint Albray with:
- 1 oz (30 g) Camembert
- 1 oz (30 g) Brie
- 1 oz (30 g) Explorateur

## Saint André

*Velvety French triple-crème cheese is delightful paired with ripe pineapple, mangoes, or other tropical fruits.*

### If You Don't Have It

Substitute 1 oz (30 g) Saint André with:
- 1 oz (30 g) Brillat-Savarin
- 1 oz (30 g) Explorateur
- 1 oz (30 g) Boursault
- 1 oz (30 g) Gratte-Paille

## Sainte-Maure de Touraine

*Log-shaped goat's cheese from central France that has straw in the center to aerate the cheese.*

### If You Don't Have It

Substitute 1 oz (30 g) Sainte-Maure de Touraine with:
- 1 oz (30 g) Crottin de Chavignol (soft to firm texture and mild to nutty flavor, depending on age)
- 1 oz (30 g) Selles-sur-Cher (semifirm texture; sweet, nutty flavor; covered with black ash)

## Saint John's Bread

*See* CAROB.

## Saint-Marcellin

*A creamy, unpasteurized, natural-rind cheese made from cow's or goat's milk. Usually round in shape with a wrinkly, whitish rind. The young cheese varies in texture from runny to firm. The flavor is yeasty, nutty, and fruity.*

### If You Don't Have It

Substitute 1 oz (30 g) Saint-Marcellin with:
- 1 oz (30 g) Banon

## Saint-Nectaire

*A semisoft French cheese from Auvergne in south-central France. Patches of white, yellow, and red mold grow on the rind during cellar ripening.*

### If You Don't Have It

Substitute 1 oz (30 g) Saint-Nectaire with:
- 1 oz (30 g) Tomme de Savoie
- 1 oz (30 g) Beaumont
- 1 oz (30 g) Reblochon

## Saint Paulin

*Originally made by Trappist Monks, this is France's first pasteurized milk cheese. St. Paulin is a pleasant dessert or table cheese. It is creamy in texture but firm enough to slice. Beware of imitation cheeses that are encased in an inedible plastic rind.*

1 lb (500 g) = 4 cups (1 L) shredded

### If You Don't Have It

Substitute 1 oz (30 g) Saint Paulin with:
- 1 oz (30 g) Port Salut
- 1 oz (30 g) Esrom
- 1 oz (30 g) Tilsit
- 1 oz (30 g) Havarti
- 1 oz (30 g) Oka
- 1 oz (30 g) Muenster

## Sake

*Japanese brewed alcoholic rice drink that plays a major role in the country's cuisine. It's ranked with soy sauce, miso, and dashi in terms of essential ingredients.*

### If You Don't Have It

Substitute ½ cup (125 mL) sake with:
- ½ cup (125 mL) Shaoxing wine
- ½ cup (125 mL) dry vermouth
- ½ cup (125 mL) dry sherry
- ½ cup (125 mL) flat beer (preferably lager)

## Sake Lees

*Also known as kasu. The by-product of making sake, this fermented rice mash has a yeasty aroma and umami-rich flavor, and is often used in Japanese soups and marinades. The lees' texture is pliable like clay and it is formed into dough-like sheets or balls.*

### If You Don't Have It

Substitute 1 cup (250 mL) sake lees with:
- 1 cup (250 mL) sake (for flavor only; texture is liquid instead of solid)

## Salad Burnet

*An herb with a cucumber aroma used in salads, to season vegetables, and brewed into tea.*

2 oz (60 g)= 1½ cups (375 mL) chopped

### If You Don't Have It

Substitute 1 tbsp (15 mL) fresh salad burnet with:
- 1 tbsp (15 mL) fresh borage or country borage

## Salad Spinner

*A utensil that makes quick, easy work of drying greens, herbs, and other delicate ingredients.*

### If You Don't Have It

Substitute a salad spinner with:
- clean pillowcase (especially for large amounts of greens; shake or spin washed greens in pillowcase until dry)
- colander or large mesh strainer (wash greens in colander or strainer then cover with kitchen towel and shake over sink until dry)
- kitchen towels (wash greens, put on towel and pat dry with more towels)

## Salak

*Also known as snake fruit. Fig-shaped fruit (Salacca zalacca) of a small palm tree native to Indonesia and Malaysia. Peeling*

### If You Don't Have It

Substitute 1 lb (500 g) peeled and seeded salak with:
- 8 oz (250 g) peeled and cored apple + 8 oz (250 g) peeled and cored pineapple

*away its scaly brown, snake-like skin reveals three lobes resembling garlic in texture and color but tart apple and pineapple in flavor.*

## Salak Varieties
Choose 1 lb (500 g) salak from these varieties:
- 1 lb (500 g) Pondoh (pungent aroma)
- 1 lb (500 g) Bali (less aromatic; slightly tart)
- 1 lb (500 g) Gula Pasir (sweeter; smaller)

## Salamander

*A tool used for caramelizing or browning the surface of certain dishes. It is a wooden-handled iron rod attached to a heavy iron disc that is heated until red hot. It's named for a mythical lizard said to survive in fire.*

### If You Don't Have It
Substitute a salamander with:
- broiler
- blowtorch (especially for crème brûlée)

## Salami

*The Italian term for a variety of seasoned ground meat products, usually pork based, that are packed in casing. The three basic types are fresh, dry-aged, and cooked (cotto). Salt is probably the only ingredient common to all salami. Pepper, spices, and other seasonings are added depending upon individual formulas. The fineness of the grind, the amount of added fat, and whether or not the meat is marinated also affect the resulting product. Fresh salami, such as pork sausage (salsiccia), contains raw meat and must be cooked before eating. Dry-aged salami, such as* finocchiona, *are "cured" by hanging in dry, crisp air. Cotto or cooked salami, such as* mortadella, *are cooked but still must be refrigerated and eaten shortly after purchase.*

### If You Don't Have It
Substitute 1 lb (500 g) salami with:
- 1 lb (500 g) pepperoni
- 1 lb (500 g) Spanish chorizo
- 1 lb (500 g) cured Portuguese chouriço or linguiça
- 1 lb (500 g) prosciutto
- 1 lb (500 g) summer sausage

### Salami Varieties
Choose 1 lb (500 g) salami from these popular varieties:
- 1 lb (500 g) Milanese or Milano salami (made with pork and beef; gently seasoned with garlic and pepper)
- 1 lb (500 g) Genovese or Genoa salami (made with pork and veal; well-seasoned with pepper and garlic)
- 1 lb (500 g) Alessandri and alpino (made with pork; dry; coarse texture)
- 1 lb (500 g) finocchiona salami (made with pork; coarse texture; seasoned with fennel seeds)
- 1 lb (500 g) sopressata (made with pork; slightly flattened shape; dry and well-seasoned with pepper)
- 1 lb (500 g) Neapolitan or Napoli salami (made with pork and beef; long and thin; spicy with red and black pepper)
- 1 lb (500 g) Sardinian or Sardo salami (made with pork; spicy with red pepper)
- 1 lb (500 g) Calabrian or Calabrese sausage or salami (made with pork; short and squat; dry and spicy with red pepper)
- 1 lb (500 g) kosher salami (made only with beef; cooked; moist)

*See also* MORTADELLA; PEPPERONI.

## Salep

*See* SAHLAB.

## Salicornia

*Also known as glasswort, samphire, sea bean, and sea pickle. A crunchy, juicy, salty-tasting green sea plant, salicornia shouldn't be confused with rock samphire, a different sea plant that grows along the coasts of France and the U.K.*

### If You Don't Have It
Substitute 1 lb (500 g) salicornia with:
- 1 lb (500 g) haricots verts or young green beans, dipped in boiling water for 10 to 20 seconds and salted (softer)
- 1 lb (500 g) thin asparagus, dipped in boiling water for 10 to 20 seconds and salted (softer)
- 1 lb (500 g) caper berries (for a briny garnish; softer)
- 1 lb (500 g) gherkins or very crisp pickles (for a briny garnish; softer)

## Salmon

*This delicious and healthful fish swims only in waters of the Northern Hemisphere. Once a prized game catch, it was typically caught in spring as it began its journey from the ocean upriver to the spot where it was born to lay its own eggs. Due to declining fish populations, in large part because of river pollution, salmon are now widely raised in fish farms. Most Atlantic salmon sold in North American markets is farmed. Pacific salmon comes mostly from Alaska, and may be farmed or wild-caught. Pacific includes several varieties such as Chinook, coho, sockeye, pink, and chum salmon, often categorized by season as spring, summer or fall salmon, according to when adults return to fresh water.*

### If You Don't Have It
Substitute 1 lb (500 g) salmon with:
- 1 lb (500 g) trout
- 1 lb (500 g) char
- 1 lb (500 g) striped bass
- 1 lb (500 g) swordfish
- 1 lb (500 g) marlin
- 1 lb (500 g) tuna

### Salmon Varieties
Choose 1 lb (500 g) salmon from these varieties:
- 1 lb (500 g) Chinook or king salmon (flesh is pale to deep red, high-fat, soft, and succulent with pronounced flavor)
- 1 lb (500 g) coho or silver salmon (flesh is pink to reddish orange, high-fat, and firm with rich flavor)
- 1 lb (500 g) sockeye, blueback, or red salmon (flesh is dark red, high-fat, and firm with strong flavor; often canned)
- 1 lb (500 g) pink or humpback salmon (flesh is pink, medium-fat, and firm with delicate flavor)
- 1 lb (500 g) chum or dog salmon (flesh is pale to bright orange, relatively low-fat, and firm with mild flavor)

### To Vary the Flavor
Substitute 1 lb (500 g) salmon with:
- 1 lb (500 g) smoked salmon (cured fish; adds smoke flavor)

*See also* SALMON, CANNED; SMOKED SALMON; CHANGING ROE (PAGE 666).

## Salmon, Canned

*In 1985, the Alaska Seafood Marketing Institute promoted canned salmon by popularizing a salmon burger consisting of the canned fish mixed with mayonnaise, bread crumbs, and Parmesan cheese served on a hamburger bun.*

6 oz (170 g) can =
⅔ to ¾ cup
(150 to 175 mL) drained

### To Vary the Flavor
Substitute 1 (6-oz/170 g) can salmon with:
- 1 (6-oz/170 g) can tuna
- 1 (6-oz/170 g) can mackerel

## Salsa

*Accordingly to culinary etymologist Mark Morton, the term* salsa *is a Medieval Latin word that originally meant "salty seasoning" and became the French word* sauce. *It is still Spanish for "sauce," and in Mexico, salsa always includes chiles.*

### If You Don't Have It
Substitute 1 cup (250 mL) fresh salsa with:
- 1 cup (250 mL) spicy tomato chutney
- 1 cup (250 mL) spicy tomato relish
- 1 cup (250 mL) prepared taco sauce (smoother)
- 1 cup (250 mL) spicy tomato ketchup (smoother; sweeter)
- 1 cup (250 mL) refrigerated salsa (sold in tubs in the refrigerated produce section of many grocery stores)
- 1 cup (250 mL) jarred salsa + 1 tbsp (15 mL) chopped fresh cilantro + 1 tsp (5 mL) fresh lime juice

### Salsa Varieties
Choose 1 cup (250 mL) salsa from these basic varieties:
- 1 cup (250 mL) Homemade Pico de Gallo (Fresh Tomato Salsa): Mix together 1 lb (500 g; about 2) seeded and finely chopped tomatoes, 2 to 3 seeded and finely chopped jalapeño peppers, 1 minced garlic clove, ¼ cup (60 mL) finely chopped and rinsed onion, ¼ cup (60 mL) chopped fresh cilantro, the juice of 2 small limes, and ½ tsp (2 mL) salt. Makes about 2 cups (500 mL).
- 1 cup (250 mL) Homemade Mexican Salsa Verde: In a large hot skillet, pan-roast 1 lb (500 g) husked tomatillos, 1 whole unpeeled garlic clove, 3 cored and seeded jalapeño peppers (halved lengthwise), and 1 small white onion (halved) until the vegetables are lightly charred all over, 3 to 5 minutes per side. Transfer to a food processor or blender and add ¼ cup (60 mL) chopped fresh cilantro, 1 tsp (5 mL) salt, ½ tsp (2 mL) sugar, and ⅓ cup (75 mL) water. Process to a coarse purée, adding more water as necessary to create a loose, spoonable sauce. Makes about 2 cups (500 mL).
- 1 cup (250 mL) Salsa Ranchera: In a large hot skillet, pan-roast 2 lbs (1 kg; about 4 large) cored and seeded

## Salsa (cont'd)

tomatoes (halved lengthwise) and 5 cored and seeded serrano or 3 cored and seeded jalapeño peppers (halved lengthwise) until the vegetables are lightly charred all over, 3 to 5 minutes per side. Transfer to a food processor or blender and add 2 peeled and coarsely chopped garlic cloves. Process until slightly chunky. Sauté 2 tbsp (30 mL) minced fresh onion in 2 tbsp (30 mL) canola oil in a large skillet until soft, 2 to 3 minutes. Add the purée and boil over medium-high heat until the mixture reduces in volume by about half, scraping the pan bottom now and then. Season with ½ tsp (2 mL) salt. Makes about 1½ cups (375 mL).

## Salsiccia

See SALAMI; SAUSAGE.

## Salsify

*Also known as oyster plant and white salsify. Looking like gnarled, hairy white carrots, this root tastes like delicate cooked artichoke heart. A related root, black salsify (also known as black oyster plant and scorzonera) is a dark brown-skinned, straighter root that tastes of coconut mixed with artichoke.*

> 1 lb (500 g) fresh =
> 4 to 5 roots = 3 cups
> (750 mL) chopped =
> 2 cups (500 mL) cooked

### If You Don't Have It
Substitute 1 lb (500 g) salsify with:
- 1 lb (500 g) artichoke hearts
- 1 lb (500 g) sunchokes
- 1 lb (500 g) Chinese artichokes
- 1 lb (500 g) cardoons
- 1 lb (500 g) burdock
- 1 lb (500 g) parsnips
- 1 lb (500 g) arracacha

### Salsify Varieties
Choose 1 lb (500 g) salsify from these varieties:
- 1 lb (500 g) salsify or white salsify (pale skin; multiple roots and hairy-looking rootlets; mild flavor reminiscent of artichoke hearts and sunchokes)
- 1 lb (500 g) scorzonera or black salsify (brown skin on a single root; slightly thicker and longer than white salsify; mild flavor reminiscent of artichoke hearts, coconut, and sunchokes)

## Salt

*The most common salt is table salt, a fine-grain refined salt with additives that prevent it from clumping. The trace element iodine is often added to table salt, a practice that began as a preventive measure against hypothyroidism. Many cooks use table salt for baking and salt shakers but prefer Kosher and sea salts for cooking.*

### If You Don't Have It
Substitute 1 tsp (5 mL) table salt with:
- 1 to 1½ tsp (5 to 7 mL) seasoned salt (adds other flavors such as paprika, onion, celery, and/or garlic)
- 1½ to 2 tsp (7 to 10 mL) Beau Monde® Seasoning (adds onion and celery flavors)
- 2 tsp (10 mL) soy sauce (adds dark color)
- 3 to 4 tsp (15 to 20 mL) anchovy paste (adds fish flavor)
- 1 tsp (5 mL) powdered dulse or other seaweed (adds briny flavor; for soups and stews)
- 2 tbsp (30 mL) yellow or shinshu miso (for sauces, soups and stews)

1 tsp (5 mL) table salt =
1 tsp (5 mL) fine-grained
sea salt = 1⅛ to 1½ tsp
(5.5 to 7 mL) Kosher salt
= ¼ oz (7 g)

1 lb (500 g) = 2 cups
(500 mL) Kosher salt

- 4 to 6 tsp (20 to 30 mL) dark or hatcho miso (for sauces, soups and stews)

## For Better Health
Substitute 1 tsp (5 mL) salt with:
- 1 to 2 tsp (5 to 10 mL) ground dried seaweed such as dulse
- 2 tsp (10 mL) Italian seasoning (usually salt-free)
- 2 tsp (10 mL) herbal salt substitute such as Mrs. Dash® (salt-free)
- 1 tsp (5 mL) salt substitute such as No Salt® or Lite Salt® (may contain some sodium and taste slightly bitter)
- 1 to 2 tbsp (15 to 30 mL) chopped fresh herbs (for flavor; bay leaf also enhances the savory flavor of low-sodium sauces and soups)
- 1 tsp (5 mL) lemon zest or juice (for flavor; especially good with vegetables)

*See also* HERBAL SALT SUBSTITUTE; SEASONED SALT; TRADING SALTS (PAGE 668).

## Salt Block

*Unrefined blocks of salt can be heated like stones and used as cookware or chilled and used as tableware.*

### If You Don't Have It
Substitute a salt block with:
- a wood plank (for grilling)
- a hot flat stone (for cooking)
- a cold flat stone (for tableware)

## Salt Cod

*Also known as bacalao (Spanish), baccalà (Italian), and morue (French). Salting and partially drying cod started as a prerefrigeration method of preserving the fish. Not to be confused with stockfish, which is dried but not salted cod.*

### If You Don't Have It
Substitute 1 lb (500 g) salt cod with:
- 1 lb (500 g) other salted and dried fish such as mackerel

*See also* COD.

## Salt-Cured Lemon

*See* PRESERVED LEMON.

## Saltine

*See* CRACKER.

## Salt Mill

*A device for grinding coarse salt. Look for types that have a grinder made from a substance other than carbon steel, which will corrode on contact with salt.*

### If You Don't Have It
Substitute a salt mill with:
- pepper mill
- mortar and pestle
- heavy pan or rolling pin for crushing

## Salt Plank

*See* SALT BLOCK.

## Salt Pork

*Also known as pickled pork. A layer of pork belly fat with some lean streaks that is preserved by salting. Prior to refrigeration, the use of salt pork was much more common than it is now.*

> 4 oz (125 g) =
> 1 cup (250 mL) cracklings

### If You Don't Have It
Substitute 4 oz (125 g) salt pork with:
- 4 oz (125 g) bacon (leaner; adds smoke flavor)
- 4 oz (125 g) ham (leaner)
- 4 oz (125 g) pancetta (leaner)
- 4 oz (125 g) fatback (not salted; add salt as necessary)
- 4 oz (125 g) hog jowls or cheeks (adds smoke flavor)
- 4 oz (125 g) guanciale (leaner)
- 1 ham hock (may add smoke flavor)

## Salt Substitute

*See* SALT.

## Sambal Bajak

*See* CHILE PASTE.

## Sambal Oelek

*See* CHILE PASTE.

## Sambhar Masala

*A unique Indian spice blend featuring toasted and ground split peas and lentils. Used to make sambhar, the popular South Indian stew.*

### If You Don't Have It
Substitute 1 tbsp (15 mL) sambhar masala with:
- 1 tbsp (15 mL) Homemade Sambhar Masala: Toast 1 tbsp (15 mL) yellow split peas (chana dal), 1 tbsp (15 mL) split black lentils (urad dal), 1 tbsp (15 mL) coriander seeds, 1 tsp (5 mL) cumin seeds, 1 tsp (5 mL) fenugreek seeds, 1 tsp (5 mL) brown mustard seeds, 3 fresh curry leaves (optional), and 4 dried cayenne chiles (stems removed) in a dry skillet over medium heat until fragrant, 5 minutes. Grind in a spice grinder to a coarse powder then mix with 1 tsp (5 mL) ground turmeric, ½ tsp (2 mL) salt, and ½ tsp (2 mL) asafetida powder (optional). Makes about ¼ cup (60 mL).
- 2 tsp (10 mL) garam masala + 1 tsp (5 mL) yellow split peas (chana dal) toasted and ground

*See also* CHAAT MASALA; GARAM MASALA; PANCH PHORAN.

## Sambuca

*See* ANISE LIQUEUR.

## Samp

*See* HOMINY.

## Samphire

*See* SALICORNIA.

## Samsoe

*Foremost Danish cow's milk cheese is Swiss-style with a yellow paste and small random holes. Mild and nutty, it's a good cooking and eating cheese.*

> 1 lb (500 g) = 4 cups (1 L) shredded

### If You Don't Have It

Substitute 1 oz (30 g) Samsoe with:
- 1 oz (30 g) Tybo (slightly milder)
- 1 oz (30 g) Danbo (may add caraway flavor)
- 1 oz (30 g) Emmental (drier; more complex flavor)
- 1 oz (30 g) Gouda

*See also* TYBO.

## Sand Dab

*See* PLAICE.

## Sangak Bread

*Long, whole wheat sourdough Iranian flatbread with a pebbled surface. Sangak is traditionally baked on a bed of small, hot river stones.*

### If You Don't Have It

Substitute 1 lb (500 g) sangak bread with:
- 1 lb (500 g) Barbari bread
- 1 lb (500 g) lavash (thinner)
- 1 lb (500 g) pita bread
- 1 lb (500 g) naan (thicker)
- 1 lb (500 g) flour tortilla (thinner)

## Sanguinelli

*See* ORANGE, BLOOD.

## Sansho

*See* KINOME LEAF; SZECHUAN PEPPER

## Santa Claus Melon

*Also known as Christmas melon. At peak season in December, the outside of this fruit resembles a watermelon but inside it's more like a honeydew melon.*

> 2 lbs (1 kg) = 3 cups (750 mL) diced

### If You Don't Have It

Substitute 1 cup (250 mL) chopped Santa Claus melon with:
- 1 cup (250 mL) chopped honeydew melon
- 1 cup (250 mL) chopped Galia melon
- 1 cup (250 mL) chopped Ogen melon
- 1 cup (250 mL) chopped casaba melon
- 1 cup (250 mL) chopped Crenshaw melon (orange flesh)
- 1 cup (250 mL) chopped Persian melon (orange flesh)
- 1 cup (250 mL) cantaloupe (orange flesh)

## Santaka

*See* CHOOSING FRESH CHILES (PAGE 640).

## Sante Fe Grande

*See* CHOOSING FRESH CHILES (PAGE 640).

## Sapodilla

*Also known as naseberry. The fruit of a Central American tree that also produces chicle, from which chewing gum is made. The juicy, translucent flesh tastes, surprisingly, a bit like maple syrup.*

1 lb (500 g) fresh =
2½ cups (625 mL) sliced

### If You Don't Have It

Substitute 1 lb (500 g) sapodillas with:
- 1 lb (500 g) pears
- 1 lb (500 g) mamey sapote
- 1 lb (500 g) white sapote
- 1 lb (500 g) cherimoya
- 1 lb (500 g) mango
- 1 lb (500 g) apricot

## Sapote, White

*Also known as Mexican custard apple, zapote and zapote blanco. A Latin American fruit with cream-color flesh that's the consistency of custard. Depending upon the variety, white sapote tastes of peach, lemon, mango, caramel, or vanilla. Often mistakenly called sapote and sapota.*

2 white sapotes = 1 cup
(250 mL) mashed pulp

### If You Don't Have It

Substitute 1 lb (500 g) white sapote with:
- 1 lb (500 g) peaches
- 1 lb (500 g) mango
- 1 lb (500 g) sapodillas
- 1 lb (500 g) cherimoya

### Sapote Varieties

Choose 1 lb (500 g) white sapote from these varieties:
- 1 lb (500 g) black sapote (color and texture of chocolate pudding, for which it makes a novel substitute)
- 1 lb (500 g) mamey sapote (salmon-color flesh with a flavor reminiscent of apricots)

*See also* MAMEY SAPOTE.

## Sapsago

*Also known as Schabzierger. A cone-shaped, low-fat cheese produced in Switzerland. The pale green color and herbal flavor come from a clover called melilot.*

4 oz (125 g) =
1 cup (250 mL) grated

### If You Don't Have It

Substitute 1 oz (30 g) Sapsago with:
- 1 oz (30 g) Parmesan (higher in fat; less herbal flavor)
- 1 oz (30 g) Romano (higher in fat; less herbal flavor)
- 1 oz (30 g) dry Jack cheese (higher in fat; more nutty flavor)
- 1 oz (30 g) aged Asiago (higher in fat; less herbal flavor)

## Sapucaya Nut

*See* PARADISE NUT.

## Sardines

*Not a true variety of fish but rather a generic term applied to various small silvery saltwater fish such as herring, pilchard, and sprats. Said to be a name given to small pilchards — one of the first fish to be packed in oil — caught off the coast of Sardinia.*

### If You Don't Have It
Substitute 1 lb (500 g) sardines with:
- 1 lb (500 g) anchovies
- 1 lb (500 g) small herring
- 1 lb (500 g) small pilchards
- 1 lb (500 g) sprats
- 1 lb (500 g) shad
- 1 lb (500 g) smelts
- 1 lb (500 g) small mackerel

### To Vary the Flavor
Substitute 1 lb (500 g) sardines with:
- 1 lb (500 g) smoked sardines (cured fish; adds smoke flavor)

## Saskatoon Berry

*See* JUNEBERRY.

## Satsuma Orange

*See* MANDARIN ORANGE.

## Saucer Peach

*See* PEACH.

## Sauces

*See* SPECIFIC TYPES.

## Sausage

*Broadly defined, sausage is a seasoned ground meat mixture stuffed into tubular casings or molded into special shapes.*

### For Better Health
Substitute 1 lb (500 g) pork sausage with:
- 1 lb (500 g) turkey sausage (less fat and fewer calories)
- 1 lb (500 g) vegetarian sausage (less fat and fewer calories)

*See also* SPECIFIC TYPES.

## Sausage Casings

*Tubular sheaths into which ground meat mixtures are stuffed to make sausage. "Don't tie your dog to a leash of sausages."*
*–French proverb*

### If You Don't Have It
Substitute natural sausage casings with:
- cheesecloth and string (to shape sausages for poaching; remove cloth and string for grilling or frying the sausage)

### Sausage Casing Varieties
Choose sausage casings from these varieties:
- natural casing (outer layer of cattle, hog, or sheep intestines; provides traditional snap in cooked sausages; need to be soaked, rinsed, and kept refrigerated; suitable for smoking; beef casings average 2 to 4 inches/5 to 10 cm diameter; hog casings average 1 to 2 inches/2.5 cm to 5 cm diameter; sheep casings average ¾ to 1¼ inches/2 to 3 cm diameter)

## Sausage Casings (cont'd)

- collagen casing (made from hides of cattle or hogs; needs no preparation; uniform sizes; usually adheres to meat; fairly thin; use extra-thick casings to support weight of meat if hung in a smoker; edible if thin)
- fibrous sausage casing (artificial casing made from wood pulp, cellulose, protein and/or plastic; inedible; often used for salami; smoke and moisture permeable)
- plastic sausage casing (artificial casing made from plastic; adheres to meat; not smoke and moisture permeable)

## Sauté Pan

*A wide pan with curved sides designed to brown cutlets, chops, and other foods.*

### If You Don't Have It
Substitute a sauté pan with:
- frying pan or skillet
- wide saucepan
- wok

## Savitxada

*See* ROMESCO.

## Savoiardi

*See* LADYFINGERS.

## Savory

*Known in parts of Europe as the bean herb because its pleasant spicy nature benefits beans, peas, and lentils. Summer savory is milder and the spiky leaves are more tender than those of winter savory.*

> 1 oz (30 g) fresh =
> ⅔ cup (150 mL)

### If You Don't Have It
Substitute 1 tbsp (15 mL) chopped fresh savory with:
- 1 tsp (5 mL) dried savory

### To Vary the Flavor
Substitute 1 tbsp (15 mL) chopped fresh savory with:
- 2 to 3 tsp (10 to 15 mL) chopped fresh thyme
- 1 to 1½ tsp (5 to 7 mL) chopped fresh thyme + 1 to 1½ tsp (5 to 7 mL) chopped fresh mint
- 1 to 2 tsp (5 to 10 mL) chopped fresh sage
- 2 to 3 tsp (10 to 15 mL) chopped fresh rosemary
- 1 tsp (5 mL) Herbes de Provence (adds other flavors such as thyme, marjoram, lavender, rosemary, fennel, and bay leaf)

## Savoy Cabbage

*Mellower in flavor than common green cabbage, the leaves of savoy cabbage are also more tender and crinkled.*

> 1 lb (500 g) =
> 3½ to 4½ cups
> (875 mL to 1.125 L)
> thinly sliced =
> 2 cups (500 mL) cooked

### If You Don't Have It
Substitute 1 lb (500 g) savoy cabbage with:
- 1 lb (500 g) green cabbage (more crisp; stronger flavor)
- 1 lb (500 g) napa cabbage (wider, white, crunchy stems; more delicate, pale green, mild-tasting leaves)
- 1 lb (500 g) bok choy (wider, white, crunchy stems; larger, darker green leaves)
- 1 lb (500 g) Brussels sprouts

*See also* CABBAGE.

## Sawleaf Herb

*Also known as culantro, ngo gai, and recao. A green herb (*Eryngium foetidum*) with long serrated leaves and aromas of cilantro, basil, and mint. Sawleaf herb flavors the Puerto Rican base recipes for recaito and sofrito and provides the alluring aromas in Vietnamese pho soups.*

### If You Don't Have It

Substitute 1 tbsp (15 mL) chopped fresh sawleaf herb with:

- 1 tbsp (15 mL) chopped fresh rice paddy herb
- 1 tbsp (15 mL) chopped fresh Vietnamese mint
- 1 tbsp (15 mL) chopped fresh cilantro
- 1 tbsp (15 mL) chopped fresh lemon basil
- 1 tsp (5 mL) fresh mint + 1 tsp (5 mL) fresh basil + 1 tsp (5 mL) fresh cilantro

## Sbrinz

*A cow's milk grating cheese from Switzerland that is aged for 2 to 3 years. The golden cheese has a brownish rind. Aged for under 2 years, the cheese is called spalen.*

> 4 oz (125 g) =
> 1 cup (250 mL) grated

### If You Don't Have It

Substitute 1 oz (30 g) Sbrinz with:

- 1 oz (30 g) Saanen
- 1 oz (30 g) Spalen or Sparen (younger)
- 1 oz (30 g) aged Asiago
- 1 oz (30 g) Parmesan (slightly sharper)
- 1 oz (30 g) Grana Padano (slightly sharper)
- 1 oz (30 g) dry Jack cheese (more nutty flavor)

## Scallion

*Members of the onion family with a white, straight-sided bottom and dark green leaves, both of which are edible. They are slightly milder in flavor than immature green or spring onions.*

> 1 bunch = 5 oz (150 g) =
> 10 scallions =
> 1 cup (250 mL) chopped
> (white part only) =
> 3½ cups (875 mL)
> chopped (white and
> green parts)
>
> 1 medium = 2 to 3 tbsp
> (30 to 45 mL) chopped

### If You Don't Have It

Substitute 1 bunch scallions (white and green parts) with:

- 1 bunch green onions (slightly stronger flavor)
- 1 bunch ramps (wild leeks; milder flavor)
- 3 to 4 cups (750 mL to 1 L) chopped leeks (milder flavor)
- 3 to 4 cups (750 mL to 1 L) chopped chives (milder flavor; best raw or lightly cooked)

### To Vary the Flavor

Substitute 1 bunch scallions with:

- 1 bunch green garlic (adds mild garlic flavor)
- 3 cups (750 mL) chopped garlic chives (adds mild garlic flavor)
- 3 cups (750 mL) chopped Chinese garlic stems (adds pungent garlic flavor and crunch)

*See also* ONION, GREEN.

## Scallopini

*See* PATTYPAN SQUASH.

## Scallop

*The fan-shaped shell, joined by the muscle that is called a scallop, is a beloved artistic motif. Scallops fall into two basic groups by size. Bay scallops are about ½ inch (1 cm) in diameter and sea scallops are about 1½ inches (4 cm) in diameter. Fresh scallops should be ivory to pale pink in color. If they are bright white, shiny, and clumping together, they have most likely been soaked in brine, which dilutes the flavor and increases the weight (and price). For the best quality and value, look for unsoaked, or "dry," scallops, which remain separate and retain their ivory or pale pink color.*

> 1 lb (500 g) =
> 100 bay scallops
> or 30 sea scallops

### If You Don't Have It

Substitute 1 lb (500 g) scallops with:
- 1 lb (500 g) shark (less creamy)
- 1 lb (500 g) skate (less creamy)
- 1 lb (500 g) mussels (more delicate)
- 1 lb (500 g) clams (smoother)
- 1 lb (500 g) cockles (smoother)
- 1 lb (500 g) oysters (smoother)
- 1 lb (500 g) whelks (tougher)
- 1 lb (500 g) abalone (tougher)
- 1 lb (500 g) shrimp (firmer)
- 1 lb (500 g) lobster (firmer)
- 1 lb (500 g) monkfish (firmer)
- 1 lb (500 g) cod (flakier)

### Scallop Varieties

Choose 1 lb (500 g) scallops from these varieties:
- 1 lb (500 g) bay scallops (about ½ inch/1 cm in diameter; delicate, moist texture; very sweet flavor; usually available only in winter in eastern North America)
- 1 lb (500 g) calico scallops (about ½ inch/1 cm in diameter; less delicate texture than bay scallops; sweet flavor; best when very briefly and gently cooked)
- 1 lb (500 g) sea scallops (about 1½ inch/4 cm in diameter; firmer than bay scallops; mildly sweet flavor)

## Scamorza

*Also known as scamorze and scamorzo. Fashioned in small ovals or gourd shapes, this mild Italian cheese is like a firm, salty mozzarella. It is sometimes available smoked.*

> 1 lb (500 g) = 4 cups
> (1 L) shredded

### If You Don't Have It

Substitute 1 oz (30 g) scamorza with:
- 1 oz (30 g) mozzarella (moister)
- 1 oz (30 g) Caciocavallo
- 1 oz (30 g) provolone
- 1 oz (30 g) string cheese
- 1 oz (30 g) queso blanco
- 1 oz (30 g) young kashkaval
- 1 oz (30 g) Bel Paese
- 1 oz (30 g) Muenster
- 1 oz (30 g) Gouda
- 1 oz (30 g) Fontina

## Schinkenwurst

*Also known as Bierschinken and ham bologna. A German cold cut with chunks of ham suspended in a bologna sausage.*

### If You Don't Have It
Substitute 1 lb (500 g) Schinkenwurst with:
- 1 lb (500 g) Bierwurst (firmer)
- 1 lb (500 g) cervelat (firmer)
- 1 lb (500 g) Jagdwurst (firmer)
- 1 lb (500 g) Bierschinken (includes pistachios)
- 1 lb (500 g) mortadella (may include pistachios)

## Schmaltz

*Rendered chicken fat used in Ashkenazi Jewish cooking as a spread and frying fat. It is sometimes flavored with apple, onion, and other seasonings.*

### If You Don't Have It
Substitute 1 cup (250 mL) schmaltz with:
- 1 cup (250 mL) Homemade Schmaltz: Put skin and fat from 4 medium chickens (4 to 5 packed cups/1 to 1.25 L) in a deep nonstick skillet or sauté pan and cook over low heat until fat melts. Increase heat to medium-low and add 1 sliced medium onion (and ½ cup/125 mL grated apple and/or 1 sliced garlic clove, if you like). Cook until the onions are golden brown. Let cool slightly then strain the fat into a glass jar or other airtight container, discarding solids (or use solids for another purpose). Refrigerate for up to 6 months. Makes about 2 cups (500 mL).
- 1 cup (250 mL) rendered, strained duck fat (preferably rendered with onions in pan)
- 1 cup (250 mL) rendered, strained goose fat (preferably rendered with onions in pan)
- 1 cup (250 mL) margarine or vegetable shortening (preferably heated with onions then strained; much less flavorful)

### For Better Health
- 1 cup (250 mL) vegetable oil (preferably heated with onions then strained; much less flavorful)

## Schnapps
*See* SPECIFIC TYPES.

## Scone

*A Scottish/British quick bread traditionally cooked on a griddle but now most often baked. Similar in texture to American biscuits.*

### If You Don't Have It
Substitute 1 scone with:
- 1 wedge shortcake
- 1 American biscuit (preferably made with sugar in dough)
- 1 crumpet (less sweet; less crumbly; more airy)
- 1 English muffin (less sweet; less crumbly; more airy)
- 1 croissant (preferably sweetened; richer; flakier)

## Scorzonera
*See* SALSIFY.

## Scotch
*See* WHISKEY.

## Scotch Bonnet

*See* CHOOSING FRESH CHILES (PAGE 640).

## Scotch Salmon

*See* SMOKED SALMON.

## Scrapple

*Enjoyed mostly in northeastern America, this savory Pennsylvania Dutch pudding loaf is made from pork scraps, cornmeal mush, and seasonings. After it firms, scrapple is sliced and fried.*

### If You Don't Have It

Substitute 1 lb (500 g) scrapple with:
- 1 lb (500 g) goetta (a similar loaf made with sausage and oatmeal)
- 1 lb (500 g) loose breakfast sausage
- 1 lb (500 g) hash
- 1 lb (500 g) bacon

## Screwpine Leaf

*Also known as bai toey (Thailand), kewra (India), la dua (Vietnam), daun pandan (Malaysia and Indonesia), pandanus and rampe leaf (Sri Lanka). The palm-like leaves of the screwpine tree average about 2 feet (61 cm) in length. Their sweet, grassy flavor lends a subtle fragrance and green color to many southeast Asian dishes. Look for screwpine leaves fresh, frozen, or dried in Asian markets. Green pandan paste and essence are also available. Kewra, a floral-scented essence used in sweet and savory dishes, is made from the flowers of a related variety of pandanus.*

### If You Don't Have It

Substitute 1 fresh screwpine leaf with:
- ½ to 1 tsp (2 to 5 mL) screwpine or pandan powder
- ½ tsp (2 mL) pandan paste
- 1 drop pandan essence or kewra essence + 1 small drop green food coloring
- 1 drop green food coloring (for color only)

## Scrod

*See* COD.

## Scungilli

*See* WHELK.

## Scup

*See* PORGY.

## Scuppernong Grape

*See* GRAPE, TABLE; MUSCADINE JELLY.

## Sea Bass

*See* BLACK SEA BASS.

## Sea Bean

*See* SALICORNIA.

## Sea Bream

*See* PORGY.

## Sea Devil

*See* MONKFISH.

## Sea Legs

*See* SURIMI.

## Sea Lettuce

*An ocean vegetable that spans the globe. The crinkled leaves turn from pale to dark green as the plant matures.*

### If You Don't Have It

Substitute 1 oz (30 g) sea lettuce with:
- 1 oz (30 g) kelp
- 1 oz (30 g) nori
- 1 oz (30 g) wakame
- 1 oz (30 g) dulse

## Sea Pickle

*See* SALICORNIA.

## Sea Salt

*See* SALT; TRADING SALTS (PAGE 668).

## Sea Snail

*See* PERIWINKLE.

## Seasoned Salt

*Regular table salt blended and packaged with various seasonings for convenience. Popular types include celery salt, garlic salt, onion salt, and proprietary blends such as Lawry's Seasoned Salt.*

### If You Don't Have It

Substitute 1 tsp (5 mL) seasoned salt with:
- 1 tsp (5 mL) Homemade Seasoned Salt: Combine 1 tbsp (15 mL) salt, 1/8 tsp (0.5 mL) paprika, 1/8 tsp (0.5 mL) granulated sugar, a pinch of onion powder, and a pinch of garlic powder. Makes 1 generous tablespoon (15 mL).
- 1 tsp (5 mL) Beau Monde® Seasoning
- 1/2 tsp to 3/4 tsp (2 to 3 mL) table salt
- 1/2 tsp (2 mL) Mei Yen seasoning

### For Better Health

Substitute 1 tsp (5 mL) seasoned salt with:
- 1 tsp (5 mL) herbal salt substitute (no sodium)

*See also* HERBAL SALT SUBSTITUTE; SALT.

## Sea Trout

*See* CROAKER.

| | |
|---|---|
| **Sea Vegetables** | *See* AGAR; ARAME; CARRAGEEN; DULSE; HIJIKI; KOMBU; LAVER; NORI; SALICORNIA; SEA LETTUCE; WAKAME. |
| **Seaweed** | *See* ARAME; CARRAGEEN; DULSE; HIJIKI; KOMBU; LAVER; NORI; WAKAME. |
| **Seckel Pear** | *See* PICKING PEARS (PAGE 661). |

**Seitan**

*Also known as wheat meat. A vegetarian meat replacement produced from wheat gluten(aka instant gluten flour and vital gluten flour), the same high-protein wheat product added to all-purpose flour to create high-protein bread flour. Seitan's bland flavor and chewy texture lend it to a variety of seasonings.*

### If You Don't Have It
Substitute 1 lb (500 g) seitan with:
- 1 lb (500 g) tempeh (stronger flavor)
- 1 lb (500 g) extra-firm tofu, pressed of excess water (softer texture)
- 1 lb (500 g) extra-firm tofu, frozen then pressed of excess water (more spongy texture)
- 1 lb (500 g) portobello mushroom caps (adds mushroom flavor)
- 1 lb (500 g) prepared vegetarian meat substitute (available refrigerated and frozen in many grocery stores)

| | |
|---|---|
| **Sekt** | *See* WINE, SPARKLING. |
| **Self-Rising Cornmeal** | *See* CORNMEAL, SELF-RISING. |
| **Self-Rising Flour** | *See* FLOUR, SELF-RISING. |

**Selim Kili Pepper**

*Also known as African pepper, Ethiopian pepper, grains of selim, Guinea pepper and kimba pepper. Slender, elongated dried pods of an African bush with aromas of eucalyptus and nutmeg in the seedpods and slightly bitter heat in the seeds.*

### If You Don't Have It
Substitute 1 tsp (5 mL) crushed selim kili pepper with:
- 1 tsp (5 mL) cubeb (adds mint and allspice aromas)
- 1 tsp (5 mL) Tasmanian peppercorns (softer, more fruity aroma)
- 1 tsp (5 mL) grains of paradise (adds cardamom aromas)
- 1 tsp (5 mL) long pepper (add citrus aromas)
- 1 tsp (5 mL) black peppercorns (less complex)

| | |
|---|---|
| **Selles-sur-Cher** | *See* CHÈVRE. |
| **Seltzer** | *See* SODA WATER. |

## Semolina

*See* FLOUR, SEMOLINA.

## Sendai Miso

*See* MISO.

## Senjed

*See* CHINESE DATE, DRIED.

## Sereh

*See* LEMONGRASS.

## Serpa

*Name-protected Southern Portuguese cheese traditionally made from the raw milk of Merino sheep but now more often made from that of Lacaune sheep (the French breed used to make Roquefort) because Lacaune produce more milk. Like queijo de Nisa, Serpa is coagulated not with animal rennet but with cardoon thistle, which gives it a slightly bitter edge. The cheese is often eaten when springy-soft, creamy, and young (after a month or so of aging) but is also aged longer to develop its pungency.*

> 4 oz (125 g) =
> 1 cup (250 mL) grated

### If You Don't Have It
Substitute 1 oz (30 g) serpa with:
- 1 oz (30 g) serra da estrella
- 1 oz (30 g) young queijo de nisa

## Serrano Chile

*See* CHOOSING DRIED CHILES (PAGE 642); CHOOSING FRESH CHILES (PAGE 640).

## Serrano Ham

*Spanish "mountain ham" that is dry-salted and aged for a year or more.*

### If You Don't Have It
Substitute 1 oz (30 g) Serrano ham with:
- 1 oz (30 g) Iberico ham
- 1 oz (30 g) prosciutto (di Parma or di San Daniele)
- 1 oz (30 g) Ardennes ham (adds smoke flavor)
- 1 oz (30 g) Bayonne ham (adds smoke flavor)
- 1 oz (30 g) Westphalian ham (adds smoke and juniper flavors)
- 1 oz (30 g) York ham (adds smoke flavor)
- 1 oz (30 g) Smithfield or other Virginia ham (adds smoke flavor)

## Sesame Butter

*A thick paste made from ground toasted unhulled sesame seeds. It's similar to tahini but thicker and darker. Store opened sesame butter in the refrigerator.*

### If You Don't Have It

Substitute 1 cup (250 mL) sesame butter with:

- 1 cup (250 mL) tahini or sesame paste (thinner and slightly sweeter)
- 1 cup (250 mL) minus 2 tbsp (30 mL) almond, cashew or peanut butter + 2 tbsp (30 mL) toasted sesame oil
- 1 cup (250 mL) almond, cashew or peanut butter

*See also* TAHINI.

## Sesame Chili Oil

*See* CHILE OIL; SESAME OIL, TOASTED.

## Sesame Leaf

*See* PERILLA.

## Sesame Oil, Toasted

*Also known as dark sesame oil. Of Chinese origin, the oil extracted from roasted sesame seeds is often used as a pungent flavoring for marinades and sauces.*

### If You Don't Have It

Substitute 1 tsp (5 mL) toasted sesame oil with:

- 2 tsp (10 mL) sesame seeds, toasted, crushed and mixed with 1 tsp (5 mL) peanut oil (adds texture of crushed seeds to dish)
- 2 tsp (10 mL) tahini (thicker than oil and lacks toasted flavor)
- 1 tsp (5 mL) hot chili sesame oil (adds spicy flavor)

*See also* SESAME OIL, UNTOASTED; SUBSTITUTING OILS (PAGE 658).

## Sesame Oil, Untoasted

*Cooking oil pressed from sesame seeds is high in polyunsaturated fatty acids and has good keeping qualities. It is very highly esteemed in Japan.*

### If You Don't Have It

Substitute 1 tbsp (15 mL) untoasted sesame oil with:

- ½ tsp (2 mL) toasted sesame oil + 2½ tsp (12 mL) vegetable oil

*See also* SESAME OIL, TOASTED; SUBSTITUTING OILS (PAGE 658).

## Sesame Paste

*See* TAHINI.

## Sesame Salt

*See* GOMASHIO.

## Sesame Seed

*Also known as benne seeds. Minuscule seeds of a very tall annual herb of African and Indian origin. Distinctively nutty and sweet, the seeds are widely*

### If You Don't Have It

Substitute 1 tbsp (15 mL) sesame seeds with:

- 1 tbsp (15 mL) white or black poppy seeds
- 1 tbsp (15 mL) pumpkin seeds (much larger)
- 1 tbsp (15 mL) finely chopped peanuts
- 1 tbsp (15 mL) finely chopped almonds
- 1 tbsp (15 mL) finely chopped cashews

*employed as a flavoring ingredient in Eastern Mediterranean, Middle Eastern, Indian, Chinese, and Japanese cooking. Depending upon the variety, sesame seeds can be white, yellow, brown, or black.*

| 1 oz (30 g) = |
| 3 tbsp (45 mL) |

### Sesame Seed Varieties

Choose 1 tbsp (15 mL) sesame seeds from these varieties:

- 1 tbsp (15 mL) muki goma or hulled white sesame seeds (white color; mild sesame flavor)
- 1 tbsp (15 mL) shiro goma or unhulled white sesame seeds (beige color; mild sesame flavor; slightly more bitter)
- 1 tbsp (15 mL) kuro goma or black sesame seeds (stronger sesame flavor)

## Seven-Spice Seasoning

*See* SHICHIMI TOGARASHI.

## Seville Orange

*See* ORANGE, SOUR.

## Sevruga Caviar

*See* CHANGING ROE (PAGE 666).

## Shad

*This large member of the herring family tastes good but challenges cooks (and diners) with its many tiny bones. The American Micmac tribe has a legend that shad was formerly a porcupine that asked the Great Spirit Manitou to change it into another creature. The spirit turned the porcupine inside out and tossed it into a river, where it became a shad. The roe from shad is a springtime delicacy.*

### If You Don't Have It

Substitute 1 lb (500 g) shad with:

- 1 lb (500 g) herring (smaller)
- 1 lb (500 g) sardines (smaller)
- 1 lb (500 g) pilchards
- 1 lb (500 g) smelt
- 1 lb (500 g) mackerel
- 1 lb (500 g) bluefish
- 1 lb (500 g) blackfish

*See also* HERRING: CHANGING ROE (PAGE 666).

## Shaddock

*See* PUMMELO.

## Shahi Jeera

*See* CUMIN.

## Shalal

*Stark white, salty, Syrian cow's milk cheese woven into strands.*

### If You Don't Have It

Substitute 1 oz (30 g) shalal with:

- 1 oz (30 g) Armenian string cheese
- 1 oz (30 g) American string cheese

## Shallot

*An allium that's much loved in French and Asian cooking. Smaller and more delicately flavored than an ordinary round onion, a shallot divides into a cluster of small bulbs with skins that are grayish brown, golden, pale pink, or red.*

---

1 lb (500 g) = 4 cups (1 L) chopped

1 medium shallot = ½ to 1 oz (15 to 30 g) = 1 tbsp (15 mL) minced

---

### If You Don't Have It
Substitute 1 chopped shallot with:
- 1 tsp (5 mL) freeze-dried shallots (much less flavorful)

### To Vary the Flavor
Substitute 1 chopped shallot with:
- ¼ cup (60 mL) chopped ramps or wild leeks (light part only)
- ¼ cup (60 mL) chopped leeks or storage onions + ½ tsp (2 mL) minced garlic (red onions work well)
- ¼ cup (60 mL) chopped green onions or scallions (white and light green parts part only)
- ¼ cup (60 mL) chopped sweet or storage onions (more pungent; red onions work well)

---

## Shanghai Bok Choy

*See* BOK CHOY.

---

## Shanklish

*Also known as sorke. Syrian cow's or sheep's milk cheese typically formed into balls, rolled in za'atar spice blend, Aleppo chile powder, or thyme and served with mezze appetizers. As it ages, soft and mild-tasting shanklish becomes increasingly crumbly and pungent.*

### If You Don't Have It
Substitute 1 oz (30 g) shanklish with:
- 1 oz (30 g) aged goat cheese
- 1 oz (30 g) sheep's milk feta cheese

---

## Shao Mai Skins

*See* WON TON SKINS.

---

## Shaoxing Wine

*Chinese yellow grain rice wine. Its unique flavor is essential in many Chinese dishes.*

### If You Don't Have It
Substitute ½ cup (125 mL) Shaoxing wine with:
- ½ cup (125 mL) sake
- ½ cup (125 mL) dry vermouth
- ½ cup (125 mL) dry sherry
- ½ cup (125 mL) flat beer (preferably lager)

## Shark

*Edible species include angel shark, dogfish, hammer-head shark, and porbeagle. Despite their terrifying reputation, the odds are stacked against the shark. For each person a shark attacks, one million sharks are captured by fishermen.*

**If You Don't Have It**

Substitute 1 lb (500 g) shark with:
- 1 lb (500 g) mahi-mahi
- 1 lb (500 g) pompano
- 1 lb (500 g) swordfish
- 1 lb (500 g) marlin
- 1 lb (500 g) tuna

## Sharlyn Melon

*The netted outer layer covers a greenish orange rind. The sweet white flesh tastes like a blend of cantaloupe and honeydew melon.*

> 2 lbs (1 kg) =
> 3 cups (750 mL) diced

**If You Don't Have It**

Substitute 1 cup (250 mL) chopped Sharlyn melon with:
- 1 cup (250 mL) chopped Spanish melon (pale green flesh)
- 1 cup (250 mL) chopped Ogen melon (greener flesh)
- 1 cup (250 mL) chopped Galia melon (greener flesh)
- 1 cup (250 mL) chopped Crenshaw melon (orange flesh)
- 1 cup (250 mL) chopped Persian melon (orange flesh)
- 1 cup (250 mL) chopped Charentais melon (orange flesh)
- 1 cup (250 mL) chopped cantaloupe (orange flesh)
- 1 cup (250 mL) chopped honeydew melon (pale green flesh)

## Sharpening Steel

*Also known as a butcher's steel. A steel doesn't really sharpen a knife blade; it only keeps the blade honed after it has been sharpened on a stone.*

**If You Don't Have It**

Substitute a sharpening steel with:
- whetstone (to sharpen the blade)
- electric knife-sharpener or honer

## Sheep Butter

*Often used in Greek and Middle Eastern cooking. It has a more assertive aroma compared to cow's milk butter, and its lower melting point makes it easier to spread on phyllo dough for dishes such as baklava.*

**If You Don't Have It**

Substitute ½ cup (125 mL) sheep butter with:
- ½ cup (125 mL) goat butter (slightly less assertive)
- ½ cup (125 mL) cow butter (milder aroma; waxier texture; yellow color; lower in calories, protein, unsaturated fats, calcium, potassium, and vitamin A; higher melting point)

*See also* BUTTER; GOAT BUTTER.

## Sheepshead

*See* PORGY.

## Shelal

*See* SHALAL.

## Shelling Bean

*See* BLACK-EYED PEA, FRESH; CRANBERRY BEAN, FRESH; EDAMAME; FAVA BEAN; LIMA BEAN; PEAS, SHELLING.

## Shelling Pea

*See* PEAS, SHELLING.

## Sherbet

*See* SORBET.

## Sherry

*This fortified wine, developed in the southern Spanish city of Jerez, is now internationally imitated with varying levels of success. The Spanish solera system produces wines of consistent quality year after year by using recently made sherry to top off older wines. Sherries come in a range of colors, flavors, and sweetness. Fino is pale and very dry, best enjoyed young and served chilled. Manzanilla is like a fino but with a hint of saltiness from the seaside town in which it is produced. Amontillado, a medium sherry also known as milk sherry, is aged longer and is typically sweeter, darker, and more mellow than a fino. Oloroso, also known as cream or golden sherry, is darker, sweeter, and the most robust. Best enjoyed at room temperature.*

### If You Don't Have It

Substitute 2 tbsp (30 mL) sherry with:
- 2 tbsp (30 mL) dry vermouth (especially for sauces and soups)
- 2 tbsp (30 mL) sake (especially for sauces and soups)
- 2 tbsp (30 mL) dry white wine + pinch of sugar (especially for sauces and soups)
- 2 tbsp (30 mL) Madeira (darker color)
- 2 tbsp (30 mL) Port (redder color)
- 2 tbsp (30 mL) unsweetened orange juice or apple juice + $\frac{1}{8}$ tsp (0.5 mL) vanilla extract (to replace sweet sherry)

### Sherry Varieties

Choose 2 tbsp (30 mL) sherry from these varieties:
- 2 tbsp (30 mL) fino sherry (very dry, light-bodied, and pale silvery gold in color; delicate flavor; often served chilled)
- 2 tbsp (30 mL) Manzanilla sherry (a type of fino sherry; very dry, light-bodied, and pale silvery gold in color; delicate flavor with a whiff of sea air; often served chilled)
- 2 tbsp (30 mL) Amontillado or milk sherry (an aged fino sherry; medium-dry, medium-bodied, and light gold in color; stronger, more nutty flavor than fino sherries)
- 2 tbsp (30 mL) oloroso sherry (sweet, medium- to full-bodied, and golden in color; stronger, more complex flavor than fino or Amontillado sherries)
- 2 tbsp (30 mL) cream sherry (a type of oloroso sherry; sweet, medium- to full-bodied, and golden in color; fuller flavor than fino or Amontillado sherries)
- 2 tbsp (30 mL) Amoroso sherry (a type of oloroso sherry; sweet, medium- to full-bodied, and golden in color; fuller flavor than fino or Amontillado sherries)

## Shichimi Togarashi

*Also known as seven-spice powder. "Shichimi togarashi is a popular condiment used to enhance the flavor of noodle, hot-pot, and stir-fried dishes," writes Hiroko Shimbo, author*

### If You Don't Have It

Substitute 1 tsp (5 mL) shichimi togarashi with:
- 1 tsp (5 mL) Homemade Shichimi Togarashi: Toast 1 tbsp (15 mL) crushed red pepper flakes, 2 tsp (10 mL) whole Szechuan peppercorns (or use untoasted powdered sansho leaves), and 1 tsp (5 mL) white sesame seeds in a dry skillet over medium heat until fragrant, 2 to 4 minutes. Let cool

*of The Japanese Kitchen. "At noodle restaurants in Japan, a small glass or wooden jar of seven-spice powder appears on every table."*

and mix with 1 tsp (5 mL) dried orange peel (preferably mandarin orange), 1 tsp (5 mL) crushed nori or dark green seaweed, $\frac{1}{4}$ tsp (1 mL) white poppy seeds, and $\frac{1}{4}$ tsp (1 mL) hemp seeds (optional). Coarsely grind in a spice grinder, clean coffee grinder, or with a mortar and pestle. Makes about 3 tablespoons (45 mL).

- $\frac{3}{4}$ tsp (3 mL) cayenne pepper + $\frac{1}{4}$ tsp (1 mL) sesame seeds (much less flavorful)

## Shiitake

*See* SHUFFLING MUSHROOMS (PAGE 654).

## Shimeji

*See* SHUFFLING MUSHROOMS (PAGE 654).

## Shinshu Miso

*See* MISO.

## Shiso

*See* PERILLA.

## Shokupan

*In Japanese, the word literally means "eating bread." This white, rectangular loaf — enriched with eggs, butter, and cream — is an adaptation of Western factory bread.*

### If You Don't Have It

Substitute 1 lb (500 g) shokupan with:
- 1 lb (500 g) brioche
- 1 lb (500 g) challah (less rich)
- 1 lb (500 g) croissants (less eggy, more airy texture)
- 1 lb (500 g) Kugelhopf (filled with dried and candied fruit and nuts)

## Shortbread

*This crumbly, buttery cookie is traditionally linked with the yule season in Scotland. It is baked in a round decorative earthenware mold, which is notched around the edges to represent beams of sunlight.*

### If You Don't Have It

Substitute 1 lb (500 g) shortbread cookies with:
- 1 lb (500 g) butter cookies (more crisp)

## Shortcake

*A rich, sweet, and tender biscuit — either baked as a single large round or individual rounds.*

### If You Don't Have It

Substitute 1 wedge shortcake with:
- 1 scone
- 1 American biscuit (preferably made with sugar in dough)
- 1 slice pound cake (richer; moister; sweeter)
- 1 crumpet (less sweet; less crumbly; more airy)

## Shortening

*See* VEGETABLE SHORTENING.

## Shottsuru

*See* FISH SAUCE.

## Shoyu

*See* SOY SAUCE.

## Shredder

*See* GRATER.

## Shrimp

*While marketing names vary shrimp are classified by size indicating the number of shrimp per pound.*

1 lb (500 g) in shell =
8 oz (250 g) shelled =
2 cups (500 mL) cooked

1 lb (500 g) colossal =
10 or fewer shrimp

1 lb (500 g) jumbo =
11 to 15 shrimp

1 lb (500 g) extra-large =
16 to 20 shrimp

1 lb (500 g) large =
21 to 30 shrimp

1 lb (500 g) medium =
31 to 35 shrimp

1 lb (500 g) small =
36 to 45 shrimp

1 lb (500 g) miniature =
about 100 shrimp

### If You Don't Have It

Substitute 1 lb (500 g) shrimp with:

- 1 lb (500 g) prawns (especially to replace jumbo shrimp)
- 1 lb (500 g) Dublin Bay prawns (especially to replace jumbo shrimp)
- 1 lb (500 g) crayfish (especially to replace rock shrimp)
- 1 lb (500 g) crab (less firm)
- 1 lb (500 g) lobster (more expensive; firmer)
- 1 lb (500 g) scallops (moister)

### Shrimp Varieties

Choose 1 lb (500 g) shrimp from these popular varieties:

- 1 lb (500 g) brown, gray, California or bay shrimp (tiny shrimp that turn brown or gray when briefly cooked)
- 1 lb (500 g) northern or pink shrimp (pink body; small to medium size; found in the Atlantic and Pacific)
- 1 lb (500 g) Gulf pink shrimp (red or light brown shell; relatively large)
- 1 lb (500 g) Pacific white shrimp (medium-size with a somewhat clear shell and blue green hues on the legs and tail; among the popular farmed varieties)
- 1 lb (500 g) Gulf brown and white shrimp (brown are medium-size with a brown shell; white are medium-size with a somewhat clear shell and blue green hues on the legs and tail)
- 1 lb (500 g) California or Monterey spot prawns (actually a type of shrimp; white spots on body; medium to relatively large)
- 1 lb (500 g) black tiger shrimp (grayish black strips on a thick shell; relatively large; popular farmed variety)

*See also* PRAWN; SHRIMP, DRIED.

## Shrimp Boil

*See* CRAB BOIL.

## Shrimp Chips

*Chinese snack that's popular in Indonesia, these crisp nibblers are made from tapioca flour and shrimp paste. When dropped into hot oil, shrimp chips puff up instantaneously.*

### If You Don't Have It

Substitute 1 lb (500 g) shrimp chips with:
- 1 lb (500 g) crackling or fried pork rinds (crunchier; adds pork flavor)
- 1 lb (500 g) pappadam (thinner; more brittle; lacks shrimp flavor)
- 1 lb (500 g) crisp lavash (thinner; lacks shrimp flavor)
- 1 lb (500 g) water crackers (thinner; more brittle; lacks shrimp flavor)

## Shrimp, Dried

*Small dried shrimp are often used in Asian and Latin American kitchens for their concentrated pungent seafood flavor. They are available whole, chopped, or ground into powder.*

### If You Don't Have It

Substitute 1 oz (30 g) whole dried shrimp with:
- 1 oz (30 g) whole dried crayfish (less fishy aroma)

## Shrimp Paste

*Also known as bagoong, blacang, kapi, and terasi. Pungent seasoning paste made from fermented shrimp.*

### If You Don't Have It

Substitute 1 tsp (5 mL) shrimp paste with:
- 1 mashed anchovy fillet (less pungent)
- 1 tsp (5 mL) anchovy paste (less pungent)

*See also* SHRIMP SAUCE.

## Shrimp Sauce

*Also known as patis (Philippines) and hom ha (Hong Kong). This moist version of shrimp paste is used as a condiment and seasoning in Southeast Asian cookery.*

### If You Don't Have It

Substitute 1 tbsp (15 mL) shrimp sauce with:
- 1 tbsp (15 mL) fish sauce (less pungent)
- 2 mashed anchovy fillets or 2 tsp (10 mL) anchovy paste + 1 tsp (5 mL) soy sauce (less pungent; thicker)

*See also* SHRIMP PASTE.

## Shropshire Blue

*A relatively new blue cheese created in the 1970s by Mrs. Hutchinson Smith in Shropshire, England. Shropshire Blue is similar to Stilton in shape and texture but with a sharper flavor and bright orange color created with annatto.*

### If You Don't Have It

Substitute 1 oz (30 g) Shropshire Blue with:
- 1 oz (30 g) Blue Cheshire (mellower)
- 1 oz (30 g) Stilton (slightly mellower; lacks orange color)
- 1 oz (30 g) Blue Wensleydale (lacks orange color)
- 1 oz (30 g) Roquefort (lacks orange color)
- 1 oz (30 g) Maytag Blue (lacks orange color)
- 1 oz (30 g) Gorgonzola (creamier; lacks orange color)

## Sichuan Pepper

*See* SZECHUAN PEPPER.

## Sierra Ibores

*Also known as queso Ibores. Traditional Spanish unpasteurized goat's milk cheese that is now produced commercially in small modern dairies. The rind is rubbed with paprika and olive oil, while the cheese itself is firm, almost crumbly, yet buttery on the tongue.*

### If You Don't Have It

Substitute 1 oz (30 g) Sierra Ibores with:
- 1 oz (30 g) aged Manchego (made with sheep's milk)
- 1 oz (30 g) Romano (especially Caprino Romano made with goat's milk)
- 1 oz (30 g) Parmesan (made with cow's milk)
- 1 oz (30 g) aged Asiago (made with cow's milk)

## Sieve

*See* STRAINER.

## Sifter

*Washing a flour sifter is likely to gum up the works. To clean, simply tap the sifter to remove all solid particles then wipe with a clean dry paper towel.*

### If You Don't Have It

Substitute a sifter with:
- fine-mesh strainer or sieve
- fine-holed shaker (for quickly sifting small amounts of a single ingredient such as confectioner's sugar, flour, or cocoa powder for dusting)

## Silken Tofu

*See* TOFU.

## Silkie

*See* CHICKEN, BLACK.

## Silverwasser

*Also known as Silberwasser. "Silver water" is a European herbal liqueur made glamorous by adding particles of silver.*

### If You Don't Have It

Substitute 2 tbsp (30 mL) Silverwasser with:
- 2 tbsp (30 mL) Goldwasser (includes gold instead of silver flakes)
- 2 tbsp (30 mL) Kümmel
- 2 tbsp (30 mL) aquavit
- 2 tbsp (30 mL) Liqueur d'Or
- 2 tbsp (30 mL) Strega

## Simple Syrup

*See* SUGAR SYRUP.

## Single-Malt Scotch

*See* WHISKEY.

## Single-Malt Whiskey

*See* WHISKEY.

## Skate

*Also known as skate wing and ray. The fins (wings) are the edible part of this fish and have a flavor and texture reminiscent of scallops. To remove the characteristic ammonia odor, skate is soaked in acidulated water before cooking.*

### If You Don't Have It

Substitute 1 lb (500 g) skate with:
- 1 lb (500 g) sea scallops
- 1 lb (500 g) crab

## Skewer

*From Italian* spiedini *to Indonesian* satay, *long thin pointed rod is utilized by cooks around the world as an efficient tool to hold small pieces of food together during cooking.*

### If You Don't Have It

Substitute metal skewers with:
- double metal skewers (these have two long prongs to prevent food from spinning around)
- bamboo skewers (soak in liquid for 20 minutes to prevent burning; food cooks slightly more slowly because wood doesn't conduct heat as well as metal)
- stiff rosemary sprigs (remove leaves from sprigs or let the leaves be; adds wonderful rosemary aroma)
- stiff stainless-steel wire (in a pinch)

### To Save Time

Substitute metal skewers with:
- no skewers (if chunks of food are large enough to be grilled without falling through the grill rack, just toss them on the grill)

## Skillet

*See* FRYING PAN.

## Skim Milk

*See* MILK, FAT-FREE.

## Skipjack

*See* TUNA, FRESH.

## Skyr

*Yogurt-like dairy product made from skim milk in Iceland. It is close to Greek strained yogurt in texture but tastes slightly more sour.*

### If You Don't Have It

Substitute 1 cup (250 mL) skyr with:
- 1 cup (250 mL) Greek strained yogurt or yogurt cheese
- 1 cup (250 mL) kefir cheese
- 1 cup (250 mL) quark (richer texture)
- 1 cup (250 mL) cream cheese
- 1 cup (250 mL) mascarpone
- 1 cup (250 mL) fromage blanc
- 1 cup (250 mL) sour cream

## Slippery Vegetable

*See* BASELLA.

## Slivki

*See* SMETANA.

## Slivovitz

*See* PLUM BRANDY.

## Sloe

*A wild, European purple plum with bitingly tart yellow flesh. Sweetened, they make wonderful jam and jellies.*

### If You Don't Have It
Substitute 1 lb (500 g) sloes with:

- 1 lb (500 g) Damson, Mirabelle, greengage or other tart plums

*See also* PRUNE; SLOE GIN.

## Sloe Gin

*A sweet, gin-based liqueur flavored with sloe plums. It is aged in wood-barrels and has a red color.*

### If You Don't Have It
Substitute 2 tbsp (30 mL) sloe gin with:

- 2 tbsp (30 mL) Homemade Sloe Gin: Freeze 1 lb (500 g) washed fresh sloes until the skins burst, about 2 to 3 days (or pick fresh sloes after the first frost has burst the skins; alternatively, prick the skins to expose the fruit to the gin). Separate the frozen sloes from one another and put them in a large glass jar or bottle to thaw along with $1\frac{1}{2}$ tsp (7 mL) chopped fresh almonds and 2 whole cloves, if you like. Pour in 2 cups (500 mL) gin and 1 cup (250 mL) brown or granulated sugar. Seal and store in a cupboard or other dark place, shaking the jar several times a week until the sugar dissolves, about 4 to 6 weeks. Then shake about once a week for another 2 to 3 months. Strain the liquid into a glass jar or bottle (discard the sloes or save them to make a tipsy crisp or crumble). Let the sloe gin age in the bottle for at least 3 more months before drinking. Makes about 2 cups (500 mL).
- 2 tbsp (30 mL) prunelle (pale green to dark amber plum brandy; sweeter and thicker; made from sloes)
- 2 tbsp (30 mL) slivovitz (colorless plum brandy; bittersweet; may be made from different plum varieties)
- 2 tbsp (30 mL) quetsch plum brandy (colorless plum brandy; bittersweet; made with Alsatian quetch plums)
- 2 tbsp (30 mL) Mirabelle (colorless plum brandy; sweet; made with golden Mirabelle plums)
- 2 tbsp (30 mL) grappa
- 2 tbsp (30 mL) other fruit brandy such as apricot

*See also* GIN; SLOE.

## Slotted Spoon

*A large spoon perforated with slots or holes enabling foods to be lifted out of a pot and drained simultaneously.*

### If You Don't Have It

Substitute a slotted spoon with:
- Chinese spider strainer
- small mesh strainer
- tongs or pasta spoon (for plucking or scooping foods out of hot liquid)
- colander nested in larger heatproof bowl or pot (for draining foods and saving liquid)

## Slow Cooker

*An electric pot, such as Crock-Pot®, designed to cook foods very slowly over the course of several hours.*

### If You Don't Have It

- covered casserole or heavy heatproof dish and an oven or burner set to low (for stews and braises; requires more attention from the cook)

## Smelt

*Also known as sparling. This small silvery fish spawns a cult following each spring when warm days and rainy evenings trigger their annual runs from lakes to tributary streams. Easily caught at night in nets, the fish are tasty when battered, fried, and eaten whole.*

### If You Don't Have It

Substitute 1 lb (500 g) smelt with:
- 1 lb (500 g) shad
- 1 lb (500 g) pilchards
- 1 lb (500 g) anchovies (smaller; stronger flavor)
- 1 lb (500 g) sardines (smaller; stronger flavor)
- 1 lb (500 g) herring (smaller)
- 1 lb (500 g) mackerel

### Smelt Varieties

Choose 1 lb (500 g) smelt from these varieties:
- 1 lb (500 g) rainbow smelt (primarily Atlantic variety)
- 1 lb (500 g) whitebait (Pacific variety)
- 1 lb (500 g) eulachon or candlefish (Pacific variety)

## Smetana

*Also known as tejfel and slivki. An Eastern European version of crème fraîche but thicker, more sour tasting, and with a higher fat content (averaging 40% fat compared to 28% fat in crème fraîche). Unlike sour cream, it won't curdle when boiled. Consistency and fat content vary from runny (10% fat) to thick (70% fat).*

### If You Don't Have It

Substitute 1 cup (250 mL) Smetana with:
- ¾ cup (175 mL) crème fraîche + ¼ cup (60 mL) heavy cream
- ¾ cup (175 mL) sour cream + ¼ cup (60 mL) heavy cream
- ½ cup (125 mL) kaymak + ½ cup (125 mL) yogurt (preferably Greek or strained yogurt)
- ½ cup (125 mL) clotted cream + ½ cup (125 mL) yogurt (preferably Greek or strained yogurt)

*See also* CREAM, CLOTTED; CRÈME FRAÎCHE; KAYMAK; SOUR CREAM.

## Smithfield Ham

*See* VIRGINIA HAM.

## Smoke

*See* WOOD SMOKE.

## Smoked Fish

*See* FINNAN HADDIE; SMOKED SALMON; SPECIFIC FISH VARIETIES.

## Smoked Salmon

*Many different styles exist but basically fall into one of two categories: cold-smoked or hot-smoked. Cold-smoking, which usually produces a more delicate result, is done in temperatures ranging from 70 to 90°F (21 to 32°C) for as briefly as a day or as long as several weeks. Danish-smoked, Irish-smoked, and Scotch-smoked are all cold-smoked, regional Atlantic salmon. The generic moniker "smoked salmon" typically refers to cold-smoked Pacific varieties. European kippered salmon is a split whole salmon that is brined and cold-smoked. Indian-cured salmon, a type of jerky, is brined before cold-smoking for up to 2 weeks. Lox is brined (sometimes with sugar added) before cold-smoking. Often lox is referred to on the Eastern seaboard as Nova or Nova Scotia salmon. Hot-smoking is done in temperatures ranging from 120 to 180°F (48 to 82°C) for a period from 6 to 12 hours. American style kippered salmon is brined and hot-smoked. "Squaw candy" is strips of salt-sugar brined salmon that are hot-smoked.*

### If You Don't Have It

Substitute 1 lb (500 g) smoked salmon with:

- 1 lb (500 g) gravlax (unsmoked salmon; adds dill flavor)
- 1 lb (500 g) cured or smoked arctic char
- 1 lb (500 g) smoked trout
- 1 lb (500 g) smoked black cod or sablefish
- 1 lb (500 g) smoked sturgeon
- 1 lb (500 g) smoked bluefish
- 1 lb (500 g) smoked mackerel
- 1 lb (500 g) smoked haddock or finnan haddie

### Smoked Salmon Varieties

Choose 1 lb (500 g) smoked salmon from these varieties:

- 1 lb (500 g) lox (salt-cured, sometimes with sugar, and cold-smoked)
- 1 lb (500 g) nova or Nova Scotia salmon (cold-smoked Atlantic salmon, often from the eastern coast of North America)
- 1 lb (500 g) Scotch salmon (cold-smoked Atlantic salmon from Scotland; often less salty than lox)
- 1 lb (500 g) Irish salmon (cold-smoked Atlantic salmon from Ireland; often less salty than lox)
- 1 lb (500 g) Danish or Dutch salmon (cold-smoked Atlantic salmon from Denmark; often less salty than lox)
- 1 lb (500 g) "squaw candy" (sweet strips of brine-cured, hot-smoked salmon)
- 1 lb (500 g) kippered salmon (brined, hot-smoked salmon steak, fillet, or chunks)

*See also* GRAVLAX.

## Smoker Box

*A feature of modern gas grills that holds wood chips or chunks to provide smoke in the cooking chamber. Stovetop smokers are sometimes referred to as smoker boxes and are similarly constructed with a covered pan to set over a burner and a rack to hold the food inside the pan with smoldering wood chips beneath or beside the food.*

### If You Don't Have It
Substitute a smoker box with:
- smoking packet (wrap a single layer of soaked wood chips in foil, poke large holes in the top, and place directly over a gas burner set to low)
- smoking tray (put a single layer of soaked wood chips in a disposable aluminum or crimped foil tray and place directly over a gas burner set to low)
- a small amount of liquid smoke in the marinade, baste, or sauce for the grilled food

*See also* WOOD SMOKE.

## Snails

*"Yes, I really do think, in fact I am almost sure, that the snails this year will be finer, sweeter, plumper, truly more delicious than ever before," says Papazi in M.F.K. Fisher's Serve It Forth.*

| 1 lb (500 g) = 5 dozen = 2½ cups (625 mL) |
| 1 dozen = 3 oz (90 g) = ½ cup (125 mL) out of the shell |

### If You Don't Have It
Substitute 1 lb (500 g) land snails with:
- 1 lb (500 g) periwinkles (sea snails)
- 1 lb (500 g) limpets

*See also* PERIWINKLE.

## Snake Mackerel
*See* ESCOLAR.

## Snake Gourd
*See* CUCUZZA.

## Snake Melon
*See* CUCUMBER.

## Snapper

*There are more than 200 varieties of this medium-size tasty tropical fish with quick-to-snap jaws sporting canine-like teeth. Red snapper is a household name but others are blubberlip*

### If You Don't Have It
Substitute 1 lb (500 g) snapper with:
- 1 lb (500 g) blackfish
- 1 lb (500 g) black sea bass
- 1 lb (500 g) striped bass
- 1 lb (500 g) grouper
- 1 lb (500 g) haddock
- 1 lb (500 g) halibut

## Snapper (cont'd)

*snapper, Malabar blood snapper, mutton snapper, schoolmaster, silk snapper, and spotted rose snapper.*

### Snapper Varieties

Choose 1 lb (500 g) snapper from these varieties:

- 1 lb (500 g) red snapper (medium; pinkish red over entire body; black edge on tail; firm texture; mild flavor; similar to silk snapper and vermilion snapper)
- 1 lb (500 g) vermilion snapper (small; red upper body flecked with yellow and a series of narrow, dotted blue stripes; firm texture; mild flavor; similar to red snapper)
- 1 lb (500 g) silk snapper (small; pinkish upper body with yellow hues; pinkish yellow fins; black edge on tail; firm texture; mild flavor; similar to red snapper)
- 1 lb (500 g) yellowtail snapper (small to medium; wide, yellow stripe from eye to tail; large yellow forked tail; firm texture; mild flavor)
- 1 lb (500 g) mutton snapper (medium; olive green upper body with light blue stripes, especially below eye; lower fins tinged with red; firm texture; mild flavor)
- 1 lb (500 g) school master snapper (small to medium; grayish brown with yellow tinge and reddish tinge near eye; golden yellow fins; dotted or solid blue line beneath eye; firm texture; mild flavor)
- 1 lb (500 g) gray snapper (small to medium; grayish brown upper body with faint reddish vertical rows; darker brown or black near eye; firm texture; mild flavor)

*See also* RED SNAPPER.

## Snow Crab

*See* CHOOSING AMONG CRABS (PAGE 647).

## Snow Peas

*See* PEAS, EDIBLE POD.

## Snow Pea Shoots

*See* PEA SHOOTS.

## Soba

*See* A SNAPSHOT OF ASIAN NOODLES (PAGE 656).

## Sockeye Salmon

*See* SALMON.

## Soda Cracker

*See* CRACKER.

## Soda Water

*Also known as carbonated water, club soda, and seltzer. Bottled bubbly water with a touch of sodium bicarbonate.*

### If You Don't Have It

Substitute 1 cup (250 mL) soda water with:

- 1 cup (250 mL) sparkling mineral water (may be less fizzy)

## Soft-Shell Clam

*See* SWAPPING CLAMS (PAGE 645).

## Soft-Wheat Flour

*See* FLOUR, CAKE.

## Sole

*"At the top-tier fish restaurants, you will be served grilled sole correctly. I was served such a sole in a Paris brasserie...,"* writes Gina Mallet in Last Chance to Eat. *"The fish arrived hot from the grill — a fine fish that filled the plate, for my inspection. Next, the waiter whisked away the plate and boned the fish. He cut all around it, then pulled the spine out in a single movement without disturbing the fish at all. The sole came back to me looking just the same but boneless, with a thick pat of* maître d'butter *melting on top...."*

### If You Don't Have It
Substitute 1 lb (500 g) sole with:
- 1 lb (500 g) turbot
- 1 lb (500 g) brill
- 1 lb (500 g) flounder
- 1 lb (500 g) plaice or dab
- 1 lb (500 g) cod
- 1 lb (500 g) haddock
- 1 lb (500 g) pollock
- 1 lb (500 g) whiting

### Sole Varieties
Choose 1 lb (500 g) sole from these varieties:
- 1 lb (500 g) Channel or Dover sole (fine, firm texture; mild, superb flavor)
- 1 lb (500 g) sand or French sole (smaller than Dover sole; fine, firm texture; mild flavor)
- 1 lb (500 g) thickback sole (smaller than Dover sole, with a thicker back; fine, firm texture; mild flavor)

*See also* FLOUNDER.

## Somen

*See* A SNAPSHOT OF ASIAN NOODLES (PAGE 656).

## Soncoya

*See* ILAMA.

## Sonho

*See* DOUGHNUT.

## Sonoma Jack

*See* JACK CHEESE.

## Sope

*In Mexican cooking, a small griddle-fried disc of fresh corn tortilla dough, filled with various mixtures.*

### If You Don't Have It
Substitute 1 sope with:
- 1 chalupa
- 1 arepa
- 1 gordita
- 1 corn tortilla (thinner and stiffer)

## Sopressata

*See* SALAMI.

## Sorbet

*French for sherbet, sorbet is a water-based frozen dessert often flavored with fruit. Some sorbets and sherbets include milk or cream.*

### If You Don't Have It

Substitute 1 cup (250 mL) sorbet with:

- 1 cup (250 mL) granita (grainy Italian water-based frozen dessert)
- 1 cup (250 mL) gelato (ice cream made without eggs)
- 1 cup (250 mL) frozen yogurt
- 1 cup (250 mL) ice cream

*See also* GRANITA.

## Sorghum Flour

*Ground from the seeds of a cereal grass, this coarse flour lacks gluten and is mostly eaten cooked as porridge, especially by those intolerant of gluten.*

### If You Don't Have It

Substitute 1 cup (250 mL) sorghum flour with:

- ½ cup (125 mL) yellow cornmeal + ½ cup (125 mL) white cornmeal

## Sorghum Molasses

*Also known as sorghum or sorghum syrup. Certain cultivars of the cereal grass sorghum are grown for the sweet sap in their thick stems, which is processed into syrup. It is dark brown with a taste close to sugarcane molasses. In America during the 1800s, sorghum molasses provided a cheap alternative to maple syrup.*

### If You Don't Have It

Substitute 1 cup (250 mL) sorghum molasses with:

- 1 cup (250 mL) golden syrup (thicker)
- 1 cup (250 mL) light or dark corn syrup (less sweet; dark will add darker amber color and caramel flavor)
- 1 cup (250 mL) molasses (darker; less sweet)
- 1 cup (250 mL) honey (sweeter)
- 1 cup (250 mL) pure maple syrup (thinner; adds maple flavor)

## Sorke

*See* SHANKLISH.

## Sorrel

*Garden sorrel is also known as belleville sorrel, sour dock, and sour grass. Dock sorrel is also called herb patience and spinach dock. A sour green leaf, both*

### If You Don't Have It

Substitute 1 lb (500 g) sorrel with:

- 1 lb (500 g) arugula (more bitter and nutty, less sour flavor)
- 1 lb (500 g) mature spinach + 1 tbsp (15 mL) lemon zest

*wild and cultivated, that becomes more sour with maturity. It can be used raw in salads or cooked into its characteristic sauce-like consistency.*

> 1 oz (30 g) fresh =
> 1⅓ cups (325 mL)

## Sorrel Varieties

Choose 1 lb (500 g) sorrel from these varieties:

- 1 lb (500 g) cultivated or garden sorrel (the most common variety; grass green, elongated, oval, and silken leaves 5 to 9 inches/12.5 to 23 cm long with two points near the stem; tart, citrus-like flavor)
- 1 lb (500 g) sour grass or sheep sorrel (small, grass green, stretched-out oval, silken leaves 2 to 3 inches/5 to 7.5 cm long with two points near the stem; milder than garden sorrel; especially good for salads)
- 1 lb (500 g) sour, yellow or curly dock (deep green, ruffled plume-shaped leaves 4 to 10 inches/10 to 25 cm long, often tinged with red on the stems; more bitter and tough than garden sorrel; becomes more tender and pleasantly sour when cooked)
- 1 lb (500 g) bitter or broadleaf dock (deep green, broad, heart-shaped leaves 3 to 4 inches/7.5 to 10 cm long and tinged with red on the stems; similar to curly dock but more pedestrian, less complex flavor)

## Soubise Sauce

*See* BÉCHAMEL.

## Soufflé Dish

*The classic round French ceramic baking dish with straight striated sides is designed to promote even heat distribution and ensure a high rise to a soufflé.*

### If You Don't Have It

Substitute a soufflé dish with:

- ovenproof baking dish + a foil or parchment "collar" wrapped around the lip of the dish to help facilitate rising (soufflé may not rise as high)

## Soup Nut

*See* MANDLEN.

## Sour Cherry

*See* CHERRY.

## Sour Cream

*Also known as crema Salvadoreña (in Central America). Commercially cultured dairy product that contains from 18 to 20% butterfat. Its creamy tanginess enhances everything from dips to desserts.*

> 8 oz (250 g) =
> 1 cup (250 mL)

### If You Don't Have It

Substitute 1 cup (250 mL) sour cream with:

- 1 cup (250 mL) soy sour cream (adds light beany flavor)
- 1 cup (250 mL) plain yogurt (more tart; baked goods will be slightly less moist)
- 1 cup (250 mL) drained yogurt (for cheesecake or other dishes in which you want the yogurt to set)
- 1 cup (250 mL) crème fraîche
- ⅓ cup (75 mL) melted unsalted butter + ¾ cup (175 mL) buttermilk, soured milk, or plain yogurt (for baking)
- ⅓ cup (75 mL) melted unsalted butter + ¾ cup (175 mL) milk + 1 tsp (5 mL) lemon juice (for baking)

## Sour Cream (cont'd)

- 1 cup (250 mL) evaporated milk (especially Milnot brand) or whole milk + 1 tbsp (15 mL) vinegar or lemon juice (let stand 5 minutes before using)
- 1 cup (250 mL) cottage cheese (or ½ cup/125 mL cottage cheese + ½ cup/125 mL plain yogurt) blended with 2 tbsp (30 mL) whole milk or buttermilk and 1 to 2 tbsp (15 to 30 mL) lemon juice
- 6 oz (175 g) cream cheese (¾ cup/175 mL) + 3 tbsp (45 mL) whole milk

### For Better Health

Substitute 1 cup (250 mL) sour cream with:
- 1 cup (250 mL) reduced-fat or fat-free sour cream
- 1 cup (250 mL) quark (richer texture than reduced-fat sour cream)
- 1 cup (250 mL) reduced-fat or fat-free plain yogurt
- 1 cup (250 mL) fat-free evaporated milk + 1 tbsp (15 mL) lemon juice

*See also* CREAM, CLOTTED; CRÈME FRAÎCHE; KAYMAK; SMETANA.

## Sourdough Bread

*Characteristically tangy bread, traditionally associated with San Francisco, takes its special flavor from the starter, or leavening mixture, which is populated with wild strains of yeast.*

### If You Don't Have It

Substitute 1 lb (500 g) sourdough bread with:
- 1 lb (500 g) relatively tight-crumbed French bread (slightly less tart flavor)
- 1 lb (500 g) relatively tight-crumbed Italian bread (slightly less tart flavor)

## Sour Grass

*See* SORREL.

## Sour Milk

*Milk that has been commercially soured with the addition of certain bacteria to produce a tangier, thickened product.*

### If You Don't Have It

Substitute 1 cup (250 mL) sour milk with:
- 1 tbsp (15 mL) lemon juice or distilled vinegar + enough milk to equal 1 cup (250 mL) (let stand 5 to 10 minutes before using)
- 1 cup (250 mL) buttermilk
- 1 cup (250 mL) plain yogurt

## Sour Orange

*See* ORANGE, SOUR.

## Sour Prune

*See* PRUNE, SOUR.

## Soursop

*Also known as corossol, guanabana, and prickly custard apple. This spiky-skinned tropical American fruit yields acidic, watery flesh. Lives up to its full potential in drinks such as the Puerto Rican carato and Brazilian champola, in which sweetened soursop juice is mixed with milk or water, and colored pink or green.*

### If You Don't Have It

Substitute 1 lb (500 g) soursop with:

- 1 lb (500 g) cherimoya (smaller)
- 1 lb (500 g) atemoya (smaller; hybrid of sweetsop and cherimoya)
- 1 lb (500 g) sweetsop (smaller)

*See also* ATEMOYA; CHERIMOYA; SWEETSOP.

## Souse

*See* HEADCHEESE.

## Southern Comfort

*Potent (100 proof) American liqueur based on bourbon and peaches.*

### If You Don't Have It

Substitute 2 tbsp (30 mL) Southern Comfort with:

- 2 tbsp (30 mL) rock and rye
- 1 tbsp (15 mL) peach schnapps + 1 tbsp (15 mL) bourbon

### For Better Health

Substitute 2 tbsp (30 mL) Southern Comfort with:

- 2 tbsp (30 mL) peach nectar + dash of cider vinegar (no alcohol)

## Soybean Curd

*See* TOFU.

## Soybean, Dried

*See* THE WIDE WORLD OF DRIED BEANS (PAGE 637).

## Soybean, Fermented

*See* FERMENTED BEAN PASTE; FERMENTED BLACK BEAN; NATTO.

## Soybean, Green

*See* EDAMAME.

## Soybean, Roasted

*See* SOY NUT.

## Soybean Sprouts

*In Chinese cooking, these sprouts are typically cooked in soups and braised dishes. Sprouted soybeans have a yellow tip and more assertive flavor than mung bean sprouts.*

### If You Don't Have It

Substitute 1 cup (250 mL) soybean sprouts with:

- 1 cup (250 mL) mung bean sprouts
- 1 cup (250 mL) julienned snow peas

*See also* MUNG BEAN SPROUTS.

## Soy Cheese

*Imitation cheese made from soy milk may seem like a great alternative for vegans or those with dairy allergies, but many soy cheeses contain the milk protein* casein *to improve flavor and melting qualities. Check labels if you are concerned.*

### If You Don't Have It
Substitute 1 oz (30 g) soy cheese with:
- 1 oz (30 g) cow's milk cheese (usually richer; melts better)

## Soy Flour

*See* CHOOSING AMONG WHOLE-GRAIN AND ALTERNATIVE FLOURS (PAGE 648).

## Soy Ice Cream

*Creamy frozen dessert made from soy milk and either partially hydrogenated soybean oil or palm oil.*

### If You Don't Have It
Substitute 1 cup (250 mL) soy ice cream with:
- 1 cup (250 mL) cow's milk ice cream (usually richer and creamier)
- 1 cup (250 mL) frozen yogurt

## Soy Margarine

*See* MARGARINE.

## Soy Mayonnaise

*Also known as tofu mayonnaise. For those keen on avoiding eggs or saturated fat, tofu replaces the egg in this product.*

### If You Don't Have It
Substitute 1 cup (250 mL) soy mayonnaise with:
- 1 cup (250 mL) mayonnaise (contains eggs)
- 1 cup (250 mL) soy sour cream
- 1 cup (250 mL) soy yogurt

## Soy Milk

*The whitish, opaque liquid obtained from pressed ground soybeans is widely marketed as a healthful alternative to dairy milk. It has more protein than cow's milk with less fat and sodium. Calcium is commonly added to make the nutrient content comparable to cow's milk.*

### If You Don't Have It
Substitute 1 cup (250 mL) soy milk with:
- 1 cup (250 mL) Homemade Soy Milk: Bring 4 cups (1 L) water to a boil. Whisk together 2 cups (500 mL) plain soy flour and 2 cups (500 mL) cold water then whisk the mixture into the boiling water and return to a boil. Reduce the heat to medium-low and gently simmer for 30 minutes, stirring now and then. Strain into a bowl through a sieve or colander lined with cheesecloth, nylon mesh (such as clean nylon stockings), or coffee filters (straining will take longer if using coffee filters). Whisk in $\frac{1}{4}$ to $\frac{1}{2}$ cup (60 to 125 mL) confectioner's (icing) sugar, $\frac{1}{4}$ to $\frac{1}{2}$ tsp (1 to 2 mL) vanilla extract, and a pinch of salt, if you like. Makes about $5\frac{1}{2}$ cups (1.375 L).
- 1 cup (250 mL) minus 2 tbsp (30 mL) water + $\frac{1}{4}$ cup (60 mL) powdered soy milk

## To Vary the Flavor

Substitute 1 cup (250 mL) soy milk with:

- 1 cup (250 mL) cow's milk (less sweet; may have more grassy or barnyardy aroma)

## For Better Health

Substitute 1 cup (250 mL) soy milk with:

- 1 cup (250 mL) lactose-free cow's milk (for the lactose-intolerant)
- 1 cup (250 mL) acidophilus cow's milk (adds beneficial enzymes)
- 1 cup (250 mL) goat's milk (for the lactose intolerant; more tangy taste)
- 1 cup (250 mL) rice milk (for the lactose intolerant or vegetarians; may be sweetened)
- 1 cup (250 mL) almond milk (for the lactose intolerant or vegetarians; may be sweetened)
- 1 cup (250 mL) oat milk (for the lactose intolerant or vegetarians; may be sweetened)

## Soy Nut Butter

*Similar to other nut butters but made with roasted soybeans, which are lower in total fat and milder in flavor.*

### If You Don't Have It

Substitute 1 cup (250 mL) soy nut butter with:

- 1 cup (250 mL) peanut butter
- 1 cup (250 mL) almond butter
- 1 cup (250 mL) cashew butter
- 1 cup (250 mL) gianduja (chocolate-hazelnut spread)
- 1 cup (250 mL) tahini (sesame paste)

## Soy Nut

*Dry roasted soybeans that, like roasted peanuts, make crunchy nibblers.*

### If You Don't Have It

Substitute 1 cup (250 mL) soy nuts with:

- 1 cup (250 mL) Homemade Soy Nuts: Soak 1 cup (250 mL) dried soybeans in water to cover for 8 to 16 hours. Rinse, drain, and pat dry with paper towels. Spread in a single layer on a baking sheet and roast at 350°F (180°C) until golden brown, 45 minutes to 1 hour, shaking the pan occasionally. Remove and season with salt, curry powder or other seasoning blend. Reduce oven to 200°F (100°C) and bake until crispy, $1\frac{1}{2}$ to 2 hours. Makes about 1 cup (250 mL).
- 1 cup (250 mL) almonds, peanuts, or other nuts (less crunchy)

## Soy Sauce

*Also known as shoyu (Japanese). A complex, salty brown condiment that's inextricably bound with the cuisines of China, Japan, and other Asian countries. At its most basic, soy sauce is the liquid produced from a long and complex process of fermenting soy beans. Numerous styles exist, just a few of which are described right. One important distinction to note is that Japanese soy sauces (except for tamari) include roasted wheat in the mash, which makes them sweeter than Chinese soy sauces. The Chinese sauces are made primarily from soybeans, sometimes with small amounts of other grains added.*

## If You Don't Have It
Substitute 1 tbsp (15 mL) soy sauce with:
- 1 tbsp (15 mL) Maggi Seasoning (darker; more complex flavor)
- scant ¾ tsp (3 mL) Kosher salt + ½ tsp (2 mL) granulated sugar dissolved in 1 tbsp (15 mL) hot water (lighter color; less complex flavor)
- 1 tbsp (15 mL) teriyaki sauce (sweeter; thicker)
- 1 tbsp (15 mL) kecap (sweeter, more complex)

## Soy Sauce Varieties
Choose 1 tbsp (15 mL) soy sauce from these varieties:
- 1 tbsp (15 mL) light Chinese soy sauce (thin, light-brown, salty sauce; made mostly with soybeans; used often in cooking)
- 1 tbsp (15 mL) dark Chinese soy sauce (dark brown, somewhat salty sauce; thicker and aged longer than light Chinese soy sauce; includes molasses, which enhances sweetness; made mostly with soybeans; used often as a table sauce)
- 1 tbsp (15 mL) Japanese shiro (thin, very light brown, fairly sweet sauce; made mostly with wheat and a relatively low amount of soybeans)
- 1 tbsp (15 mL) Japanese usukuchi (light brown, salty and sweet sauce; sweetness is enhanced through the addition of amasake, a fermented rice drink)
- 1 tbsp (15 mL) Japanese koikuchi (medium brown, gently salty sauce; made with equal parts soybeans and wheat; the most widely used soy sauce in Japan)
- 1 tbsp (15 mL) Japanese saishikomi (dark brown, rich, strong-flavored, gently salty sauce; made with soybeans and wheat)
- 1 tbsp (15 mL) Japanese tamari (dark brown, rich, strong-flavored, gently salty, lightly sweet sauce; made with soybeans and very little or no wheat; similar to dark Chinese soy sauce)
- 1 tbsp (15 mL) Thai sweet black soy sauce (dark brown to black, rich, strong-flavored, gently salty, fairly sweet sauce; made with soybeans; similar to Indonesian kecap)

## For Better Health
Substitute 1 tbsp (15 mL) soy sauce with:
- 1 tbsp (15 mL) low-sodium soy sauce

## Soy Sour Cream

*Soy milk treated with a souring agent to simulate dairy sour cream. It can replace regular sour cream in any recipe.*

### If You Don't Have It

Substitute 1 cup (250 mL) soy sour cream with:
- 1 cup (250 mL) sour cream (contains cow's milk)
- 1 cup (250 mL) quark (contains cow's milk)
- 1 cup (250 mL) crème fraîche (contains cow's milk)
- 1 cup (250 mL) soy mayonnaise (less tart)
- 1 cup (250 mL) soy yogurt (for dips and soups; more tart)
- 1 cup (250 mL) drained soy yogurt (for cheesecake or other dishes in which you want the yogurt to set)
- 6 oz (175 g) soy cream cheese (¾ cup/175 mL) + 3 tbsp (45 mL) soy milk

## Soy Yogurt

*Also known as soygurt. Lactose-free replacement for yogurt is produced by treating soy milk with "good" bacteria. Look for it plain or fruit-flavored in natural food stores.*

### If You Don't Have It

Substitute 1 cup (250 mL) soy yogurt with:
- 1 cup (250 mL) yogurt (contains cow's milk)
- 1 cup (250 mL) low-lactose yogurt (contains cow's milk; for the lactose intolerant)
- 1 cup (250 mL) goat's milk yogurt (contains goat's milk; for the lactose intolerant)
- 1 cup (250 mL) soy sour cream (thicker; less tart)
- 1 cup (250 mL) cow's milk sour cream (contains cow's milk; thicker; less tart)
- 1 cup (250 mL) silken tofu, blended until smooth (thicker; less tart)
- 1 cup (250 mL) buttermilk (contains cow's milk; thinner; best for baking, dressings, and gently cooked or uncooked sauces)
- 1 cup (250 mL) quark (richer texture)

## Spaetzle

*Also known as spätzle. German for "little sparrow," this tiny egg dumpling is sometimes made with dough firm enough to be rolled like noodles. But, a more entertaining way to make spaetzle is to push the dough through the holes of a colander into a pot of boiling water.*

### If You Don't Have It

Substitute 1 lb (500 g) spaetzle with:
- 1 lb (500 g) egg barley (tarhonya)
- 1 lb (500 g) egg noodles
- 1 lb (500 g) won ton skins

## Spaghetti

*See* PASTA, DRIED STRANDS.

## Spaghetti Squash

*Also known as vegetable spaghetti. The uncanny resemblance to strands of spaghetti is the calling card of this mild-tasting squash. After the whole squash is cooked, typically by roasting, it is halved and the seeds are removed. The golden flesh is then raked with a fork to separate the filaments. The vegetable can be served as a side dish or sauced and enjoyed like pasta.*

1 medium =
5 lbs (2.5 kg) = 6 cups
(1.5 L) cooked strands

### If You Don't Have It
Substitute 1 cup (250 mL) cooked spaghetti squash with:
- 1 cup (250 mL) cooked spaghetti or other strand pasta
- 1 cup (250 mL) cooked butternut squash (solid squash instead of strands; creamier)
- 1 cup (250 mL) cooked buttercup squash (solid squash instead of strands; creamier)
- 1 cup (250 mL) cooked banana squash (solid squash instead of strands; creamier; more fruity aromas)
- 1 cup (250 mL) cooked delicata squash (solid squash instead of strands)

## Spalen

*See* SBRINZ.

## Spam

*Since its creation by the Hormel Company in the 1920s, this canned seasoned pork product has fathered a family of products including Spam® Hickory Smoked Flavored and Spam® Hot & Spicy. As the product promotion says, Spam® is Crazy Tasty!™*

### If You Don't Have It
Substitute 12 oz (375 g) spam with:
- 12 oz (375 g) canned ham
- 12 oz (375 g) wet-cured ham

### For Better Health
Substitute 12 oz (375 g) spam with:
- 12 oz (375 g) "lite" Spam (fewer calories; less fat; less sodium)

## Spanish Brandy

*See* BRANDY DE JEREZ.

## Spanish Mackerel

*See* MACKEREL.

## Spanish Melon

*Sweet and succulent with flavor like Crenshaw and color like honeydew. This muskmelon has*

### If You Don't Have It
Substitute 1 cup (250 mL) chopped Spanish melon with:
- 1 cup (250 mL) chopped Crenshaw melon (orange flesh)
- 1 cup (250 mL) chopped Sharlyn melon (pale green flesh)

*a large egg shape with
a ribbed green rind.*

```
   2 lbs (1 kg) =
3 cups (750 mL) diced
```

- 1 cup (250 mL) chopped casaba melon (cream-color flesh)
- 1 cup (250 mL) chopped Ogen melon (green flesh)
- 1 cup (250 mL) chopped Galia melon (green flesh)
- 1 cup (250 mL) chopped Persian melon (orange flesh)
- 1 cup (250 mL) chopped cantaloupe (orange flesh)
- 1 cup (250 mL) chopped honeydew melon (pale green flesh)

## Spanish Olive

*See* CHOOSING AMONG OLIVES (PAGE 659).

## Spanish Onion

*See* ONION, STORAGE.

## Spanish Pepper

*See* PAPRIKA.

## Sparkling Mineral Water

*Bottled water taken from a
source such as a spring or
lake. The water contains
natural carbonation and
dissolved minerals.*

### If You Don't Have It
Substitute 1 cup (250 mL) sparkling mineral water with:
- 1 cup (250 mL) soda water, seltzer, club soda, or carbonated water (may be more fizzy)
- 1 cup (250 mL) still mineral water (no fizz)

## Sparkling Wine

*See* WINE, SPARKLING.

## Sparling

*See* SMELT.

## Spatula

*Stirring, scraping, and
spreading: spatulas
perform these tasks and
more. These tools come in
many sizes and materials
including wood, stainless
steel, rubber, plastic,
acrylic, and silicone.*

### If You Don't Have It
Substitute a spatula with:
- pancake turner (for turning and gentle scraping or stirring)
- clean flexible spackling knife or dough scraper (for spreading or stirring)

## Spätzle

*See* SPAETZLE.

## Spearfish

*See* MARLIN.

## Spearmint

*See* MINT.

## Speck

*Smoked prosciutto from the Alto Adige region of Italy. Aromas of juniper permeate the pork legs throughout a months-long air-curing and cold-smoking process.*

> 1 lb (500 g) =
> 32 thin slices

### If You Don't Have It
Substitute 1 lb (500 g) speck with:
- 1 lb (500 g) prosciutto (no smokiness or juniper aromas)
- 1 lb (500 g) culatello (less fatty; soaked in wine during aging)
- 1 lb (500 g) Westphalian ham (similar juniper and mild smoke aromas)
- 1 lb (500 g) Serrano or Iberico ham
- 1 lb (500 g) Ardennes ham
- 1 lb (500 g) Bayonne ham
- 1 lb (500 g) York ham
- 1 lb (500 g) Smithfield ham
- 1 lb (500 g) Yunnan ham
- 1 lb (500 g) smoked bacon
- 1 lb (500 g) pancetta (unsmoked)

*See also* FATBACK; LARD.

## Spelt

*See* FARRO.

## Spelt Flour

*See* CHOOSING AMONG WHOLE-GRAIN AND ALTERNATIVE FLOURS (PAGE 648).

## Spiced Ham

*See* DEVILED HAM; SPAM.

## Spiced Rum

*See* RUM.

## Spice Parisienne

*Also known as épices fines and sel épice. American term for a bottled spice blend based on the French classic sel épice (spiced salt).*

### If You Don't Have It
Substitute 1 tsp (5 mL) Spice Parisienne with:
- 1 tsp (5 mL) Homemade Spice Parisienne: Combine 1 to 2 crushed bay leaves, 1 tsp (5 mL) ground white pepper, 1 tsp (5 mL) ground black pepper, ½ tsp (2 mL) ground nutmeg, ½ tsp (2 mL) ground mace, ½ tsp (2 mL) ground allspice, ½ tsp (2 mL) crushed dried rosemary, ½ tsp (2 mL) dried thyme, ¼ tsp (1 mL) ground cloves, and ⅛ tsp (0.5 mL) ground cinnamon. Add salt to taste. Makes about 2 tablespoons (30 mL).

### To Vary the Flavor
Substitute 1 tsp (5 mL) Spice Parisienne with:
- 1 tsp (5 mL) savory quatre épices (for savory dishes)
- 1 tsp (5 mL) sweet quatre épices (for sweet and savory dishes)
- ½ tsp (2 mL) ground white or black pepper + ½ tsp (2 mL) pumpkin pie spice or apple pie spice

## Spices

*See* SPECIFIC TYPES.

## Spider Strainer

*See* STRAINER.

## Spike©

*Nutrition guru Gaylord Hauser developed this all-purpose seasoning blend of 39 herbs, vegetables, spices, and salt.*

### If You Don't Have It

Substitute 1 tsp (5 mL) Spike© seasoning with:

- 1 tsp (5 mL) seasoned salt
- 1 tsp (5 mL) Beau Monde® Seasoning
- ½ tsp (2 mL) table salt

### For Better Health

Substitute 1 tsp (5 mL) Spike© seasoning with:

- 1 tsp (5 mL) herbal salt substitute such as Mrs. Dash©
- 1 tbsp (15 mL) chopped fresh herbs

## Spinach

*"On the subject of spinach: divide into little piles. Rearrange again into new piles. After five or six maneuvers, sit back and say you are full," advises Delia Ephron in* How to Eat Like a Child.

1 lb (500 g) fresh =
10 cups (2.5 L) =
1½ cups (375 mL) cooked

10 oz (300 g) frozen =
1½ cups (375 mL) =
1 cup (250 mL) cooked
and drained

### If You Don't Have It

Substitute 1 lb (500 g) spinach with:

- 1 lb (500 g) amaranth or Chinese spinach (especially to replace tender baby spinach)
- 1 lb (500 g) New Zealand spinach (flatter, more narrow leaves than spinach)
- 1 lb (500 g) spinach beet (a variety of beet grown for the leaves; larger, broader, slightly tougher leaves)
- 1 lb (500 g) beet greens (these often have reddish-tinged stems)
- 1 lb (500 g) red or green chard (slightly tougher leaves; thicker stems; slightly sweeter)
- 1 lb (500 g) turnip greens (smaller, teardrop-shaped, paler green leaves; more peppery flavor)
- 1 lb (500 g) kale (larger, tougher, ruffled leaves)
- 1 lb (500 g) sorrel, especially the smaller sheep sorrel (more delicate, pale green leaves; more tart flavor)
- 1 lb (500 g) arugula (smaller, more delicate, pale-green leaves; more bitter and nutty flavor)
- 1 lb (500 g) watercress (smaller, more delicate pale-green leaves; more peppery flavor)

### Spinach Varieties

Choose 1 lb (500 g) spinach from these popular varieties:

- 1 lb (500 g) flat-leaf or garden spinach (small, flat, delicate, pale green leaves, sometimes with two points near the tender stem; mild bittersweet flavor; preferred for salads)
- 1 lb (500 g) curly leaf spinach (large, crinkly, dark green leaves; rather tough stems; mild bitter flavor; often sold in cellophane bags or frozen)

## Spiny Lobster

*Also known as rock lobster and langouste. Crustaceans of the family Palinuridae are lobsters with no claws that flourish in waters warmer than North Atlantic lobster.*

### If You Don't Have It

Substitute 1 lb (500 g) spiny lobster with:

- 1 lb (500 g) Maine lobster
- 1 lb (500 g) Dublin Bay prawns
- 1 lb (500 g) crayfish
- 1 lb (500 g) jumbo shrimp
- 1 lb (500 g) crab
- 1 lb (500 g) scallops

## Spiral-Sliced Ham

*See* HAM, WET-CURED.

## Spit Roaster

*See* ROTISSERIE.

## Splenda©

*See* SUCRALOSE.

## Split Peas

*See* PEAS, SPLIT; SWITCHING LENTILS (PAGE 653).

## Sponge Cake

*Also known as sunshine cake. Sponge cake is the fraternal twin of angel food cake. The only major difference is that it is made with egg yolks and egg whites, instead of egg whites only.*

### If You Don't Have It

Substitute 1 lb (500 g) sponge cake with:

- 1 lb (500 g) angel food cake (lighter, more airy texture; lower in fat)
- 1 lb (500 g) génoise (moister; slightly less sweet; tighter crumb)
- 1 lb (500 g) soft or soaked crisp ladyfingers (especially for tiramisù)
- 1 lb (500 g) butter cake (moister and richer)
- 1 lb (500 g) pound cake (moister, denser texture)

## Spot

*See* CROAKER.

## Sprat

*A small, oily fish at home in the North Atlantic. Small sprats that are packed in oil are known as brisling or brisling sardines. Sprats also come smoked.*

### If You Don't Have It

Substitute 1 lb (500 g) sprats with:

- 1 lb (500 g) sardines
- 1 lb (500 g) smelt
- 1 lb (500 g) anchovies (smaller)
- 1 lb (500 g) pilchards (larger)
- 1 lb (500 g) shad (larger)
- 1 lb (500 g) mackerel
- 1 lb (500 g) smoked sprats (cured fish; adds smoke flavor)

## Springform Pan

*See* PAN SIZE EQUIVALENTS (PAGE 678).

## Spring Ginger

*See* GINGER, FRESH.

## Spring Mix

*See* MESCLUN.

## Spring Roll Wrapper

*See* RICE PAPER.

## Sprouts

*See* ALFALFA SPROUTS; BROCCOLI SPROUTS; BUCKWHEAT SPROUTS; FENUGREEK SPROUTS; MUNG BEAN SPROUTS; PEA SHOOTS; RADISH SPROUTS; SOYBEAN SPROUTS.

## Squab

*These farm-raised pigeons are members of the dove family. They are generally marketed at about 4 weeks, weighing about 1 pound (500 g). The meat is dark and tender.*

### If You Don't Have It
Substitute 1 lb (500 g) squab with:
- 1 lb (500 g) pigeon
- 1 lb (500 g) quail
- 1 lb (500 g) grouse
- 1 lb (500 g) pheasant
- 1 lb (500 g) partridge
- 1 lb (500 g) Cornish hen (fattier)

## Squash Blossom

*See* PICKING EDIBLE FLOWERS (PAGE 650).

## Squash Seed

*See* WINTER SQUASH SEED.

## Squash, Summer

*See* PATTYPAN SQUASH; YELLOW SQUASH; ZUCCHINI.

## Squash, Winter

*See* ACORN SQUASH; BANANA SQUASH; BUTTERCUP SQUASH; BUTTERNUT SQUASH; DELICATA SQUASH; HUBBARD SQUASH; KABOCHA SQUASH; PUMPKIN; SPAGHETTI SQUASH; SWEET DUMPLING SQUASH.

## Squid

*Also known as calamari and ika (Japanese). A cephalopod that is well-loved in Japan and Europe but underutilized elsewhere. Its mild flesh responds best to either quick cooking or long simmering. Anything in between renders the squid tough.*

1 lb (500 g) = 3 squid (6 inches/15 cm each) = 8 to 10 oz (250 to 300 g) cleaned

### If You Don't Have It
Substitute 1 lb (500 g) squid with:
- 1 lb (500 g) cuttlefish (larger; more tender)
- 1 lb (500 g) baby octopus (firmer; tenderize by simmering in salted water or by pounding)

## Squirrel

*The common gray squirrel was once so popular in North America that the 1962 edition of* The Joy of Cooking *featured several recipes and step-by-step instructions for skinning and cleaning squirrel.*

### If You Don't Have It

Substitute 1 lb (500 g) squirrel with:
- 1 lb (500 g) rabbit (more tender meat)
- 1 lb (500 g) hare (pinker meat)
- 1 lb (500 g) chicken (lighter, more tender meat)

## Stainless-Steel Cookware

*Stainless steel — an alloy of iron, carbon, and chromium — is often wrapped around a core of aluminum or copper to create nonreactive clad metal cookware with improved heat conductivity.*

### If You Don't Have It

Substitute stainless-steel cookware with:
- glass cookware (nonreactive; poor heat conduction; good heat retention)
- enamelware (nonreactive; good heat conduction and retention if enameled cast iron; poor heat conduction if enameled steel)
- earthenware (nonreactive; poor heat conduction; good heat retention)

## Staka

*See* GOAT BUTTER.

## Star Anise

*Possibly the prettiest spice in the world, this brown pod is shaped like a lacy eight-pointed star with a seed in each segment. In China, it is widely used in cooking and in teas.*

> 1 whole star =
> ½ tsp (2 mL) ground

### If You Don't Have It

Substitute 1 whole star anise with:
- ½ tsp (2 mL) ground star anise
- ¾ tsp (3 mL) crushed anise seeds + pinch of ground allspice (less complex flavor)
- ½ tsp (2 mL) Chinese five-spice powder (includes mostly star anise plus fennel seed, cinnamon, Szechuan peppercorns, and cloves)
- 1 tbsp (15 mL) anise or licorice liqueur (weaker anise flavor; adds alcohol and liquid)
- ¼ to ½ tsp (1 to 2 mL) anise extract

*See also* CHINESE FIVE-SPICE POWDER.

## Star Apple

*Also known as caimito. Cut this baseball-size fruit in half and behold its white star-shaped core.*

> 1 lb (500 g) = 2 to 3 star apples = 2 cups (500 mL) sliced

### If You Don't Have It

Substitute 1 lb (500 g) star apples with:
- 1 lb (500 g) star fruit (more yellow color)
- 1 lb (500 g) kiwifruit (green color)

## Star Fruit

*See* CARAMBOLA.

## Steak Sauce

*In 1824, chef Henderson William Brand created a groundbreaking steak sauce for King George IV. Rumor has it that the king was so pleased with the new sauce, he proclaimed it "A number 1" or A1 for short.*

### If You Don't Have It
Substitute 1 tbsp (15 mL) steak sauce with:

- 1 tbsp (15 mL) Homemade Steak Sauce: In a small saucepan, combine 3 tbsp (45 mL) balsamic vinegar, 3 tbsp (45 mL) apple cider vinegar, 3 tbsp (45 mL) water, 2 tbsp (30 mL) tomato paste, 2 tbsp (30 mL) soy sauce, 2 tbsp (30 mL) orange juice, a 4-inch (10 cm) strip of orange zest, 1 tbsp (15 mL) finely chopped onion, 1 tbsp (15 mL) Dijon mustard, 1 tbsp (15 mL) molasses, 1 tbsp (15 mL) chopped raisins, 1½ tsp (7 mL) honey, 1 tsp (5 mL) tamarind paste concentrate, 1 small smashed garlic clove left in one piece, 1 bay leaf, a pinch of dried thyme, pinch of ground coriander, pinch of ground cloves, pinch of ground cinnamon, pinch of ground ginger, and pinch of cayenne pepper. Stir until smooth then bring to a simmer over medium heat. Reduce the heat to low and simmer gently, stirring often, until thick, 10 to 15 minutes. Discard the orange zest and bay leaf. Let cool slightly then purée until smooth in a food processor or blender. Taste and add salt as necessary. Let cool and refrigerate for up to 3 months. Makes about ¾ cup (175 mL).
- 1 tbsp (15 mL) HP sauce
- 1 tbsp (15 mL) Worcestershire sauce (thinner, less sweet, tangier from tamarind)
- 2 tsp (10 mL) ketchup + 1 tsp (5 mL) Worcestershire sauce

*See also* WORCESTERSHIRE SAUCE.

## Steamer

*Any cooking vessel or basket that cooks food by suspending the food on a rack over simmering water. Includes bamboo steamers, perforated metal "insert" types that fit inside larger saucepans, and collapsible metal types.*

### If You Don't Have It
Substitute a steamer with:

- Makeshift steamer: crumple balls of foil to line the bottom of a wide pot or deep sauté pan that has a tight-fitting lid. Place a small metal colander, strainer, or wire rack (such as a cooling rack or one from a toaster oven) over the foil balls to use as a steaming basket. Add about 1 inch (2.5 cm) of water to the bottom of the pot, cover, and simmer, adding food to the makeshift basket.
- Use a heatproof (ovenproof) plate set over a metal trivet or clean, empty tuna can with both ends removed (to make a ring on which to prop the plate). Set the trivet or can-ring in the pot, add water, and place the food on the plate. Cover and simmer to steam.

## Steamer (cont'd)

### To Save Time
Substitute a steamer with:

- Microwave oven: excels at steaming foods. Place vegetables, chicken, or fish in a microwave-safe container. Put the thick ends of the food toward the middle and add a small amount of liquid such as water or stock (or none at all if the food is very liquidy). Cover tightly with plastic wrap and cook on High power until the food is just cooked through.

## Steamer Clam

*See* SWAPPING CLAMS (PAGE 645).

## Steel

*See* SHARPENING STEEL.

## Stem Lettuce

*See* CELTUCE.

## Sterlet Caviar

*See* CHANGING ROE (PAGE 666).

## Sterno©

*Also known as canned heat. Sterno gel is a canned portable cooking fuel made from denatured alcohol, water, and gel. It is used in a variety of situations from tabletop to campsite.*

### If You Don't Have It
Substitute Sterno© with:

- tea candles
- warming tray
- gas burner set on lowest possible setting

## Stevia

*A plant of South American origin, extracts of which are up to 300 times sweeter than ordinary table sugar. Since 1977, stevia has grown to capture more than 40% of the sweetener market in Japan. In the U.S., the Food and Drug Administration categorizes it as an unsafe food additive and approves its sale only as a "dietary supplement." One European study of stevia's effect on rats found a decrease in male fertility.*

### If You Don't Have It
Substitute ¼ tsp (1 mL) liquid stevia with:

- 1 cup (250 mL) granulated sugar
- 1¾ cups (425 mL) unsifted confectioner's (icing) sugar
- 1 cup (250 mL) packed light or dark brown sugar
- 1 cup (250 mL) superfine (castor) sugar
- 1 cup (250 mL) turbinado sugar
- 1 cup (250 mL) date sugar
- ⅔ cup (150 mL) granulated fructose or fruit sugar (fructose tends to make baked goods moister, darker, and chewier)
- 1 cup (250 mL) minus 2 tbsp (30 mL) honey (for baking, reduce liquid in recipe by 3 tbsp/45 mL; add ¼ tsp/1 mL baking soda to neutralize acidity of honey)
- ¾ cup (175 mL) maple syrup (for baking, reduce liquid in recipe by 3 to 4 tbsp/45 to 60 mL; add scant ¼ tsp/1 mL baking soda to neutralize acidity of maple syrup)
- ½ cup (125 mL) sugar + 6 tbsp (90 mL) honey, maple syrup, or corn syrup (in baking, reduce liquid in recipe by

2 tbsp/25 mL, or add 2 tbsp/25 mL flour if there is no other liquid in recipe; reduce oven temperature by 25°F/14°C)
- ½ cup (125 mL) granulated sugar + ½ cup (125 mL) molasses + ½ tsp (2 mL) baking soda (reduce liquid in recipe by 2 tbsp/25 mL, or add 2 tbsp/25 mL flour if there is no other liquid in recipe)
- ¾ cup (175 mL) granulated sugar + ¼ cup (60 mL) maple sugar

## For Better Health
Substitute ¼ tsp (1 mL) liquid stevia with:
- 1 cup (250 mL) Sucanat (powdered organic sugarcane juice, which retains all its vitamins and minerals)
- ½ cup (125 mL) granulated sugar + ½ cup (125 mL) sugar-free sugar substitute such as sucralose, Splenda© or DiabetiSweet© (for best balance of reduced calories, flavor, and browning in baking)
- 1 cup (250 mL) sugar-free sugar substitute such as sucralose, Splenda© or DiabetiSweet© (calorie-free; may leave slight aftertaste and browning will not occur in baking because there is no sugar to caramelize)

## Sticky Rice

*See* VARIETIES OF RICE (PAGE 664).

## Stilton

*A superstar of the cheese world, Stilton is a golden, rich, crumbly British blue-veined cheese. Purists say it should be savored alone with only a glass of port or dry red wine for accompaniment.*

4 oz (125 g) = 1 cup (250 mL) crumbled

### If You Don't Have It
Substitute 1 oz (30 g) Stilton with:
- 1 oz (30 g) Shropshire Blue (more pungent; bright orange color)
- 1 oz (30 g) Roquefort (slightly softer; more pungent)
- 1 oz (30 g) Gorgonzola (creamier; more pungent)
- 1 oz (30 g) Cashel Blue
- 1 oz (30 g) Maytag Blue

### To Vary the Flavor
Substitute 1 oz (30 g) Stilton with:
- 1 oz (30 g) Huntsman cheese (a layer of Stilton sandwiched between two layers of Double Gloucester)

## Stinging Nettles

*See* NETTLES.

## Stinking Gum

*See* ASAFETIDA.

## Stock, Beef

*Few home cooks these days go to the time, effort, and expense to make stocks from scratch; but fortunately,*

### If You Don't Have It
Substitute 1 cup (250 mL) beef stock with:
- 1 cup (250 mL) boiling water + 1 tsp (5 mL) beef base or instant beef bouillon granules, 1 beef bouillon cube, or

## Stock, Beef (cont'd)

*many commercial renderings are available. Most of these products tend to be salty, so adjust additional salt in the recipe accordingly. Liquid broths are available in supermarkets packed in steel cans or aseptic packages. Concentrated forms of stock, which have the advantage of requiring less storage space, include bouillon cubes and granules as well as jarred or frozen concentrated meat pastes, also known as stock base. The paste is reconstituted with water to create stock.*

- 1 envelope beef bouillon (may be higher in sodium and less flavorful)
- 1 cup (250 mL) aseptically packaged or canned beef broth (may be higher in sodium and less flavorful)
- 1 cup (250 mL) cold or room temperature aseptically packaged or canned beef broth + $\frac{1}{8}$ to $\frac{1}{4}$ tsp (1 mL) unflavored powdered or granulated gelatin, mixed in saucepan then reheated until gelatin dissolves (improves texture)

### To Vary the Flavor

Substitute 1 cup (250 mL) beef stock with:

- 1 cup (250 mL) red wine or beer (to replace up to half of beef stock in sauces and stews)
- 1 cup (250 mL) vegetable stock, broth, or reconstituted base or bouillon (may be less robust in flavor; use roasted vegetable stock to intensify flavor)

### For Better Health

- 1 cup (250 mL) low-sodium beef broth

## Stock, Chicken

*The natural choice of flavoring liquid for poultry soups, braised dishes, stews, gravies, and sauces. Low-salt versions allow you to salt to taste or reduce the broth to a glaze without it becoming overly salty.*

### If You Don't Have It

Substitute 1 cup (250 mL) chicken stock with:

- 1 cup (250 mL) boiling water + 1 tsp (5 mL) chicken base or instant chicken bouillon granules, 1 chicken bouillon cube, or 1 envelope chicken bouillon (may be higher in sodium and less flavorful)
- 1 cup (250 mL) aseptically packaged or canned chicken broth (may be higher in sodium and less flavorful)
- 1 cup (250 mL) cold or room temperature aseptically packaged or canned chicken broth + $\frac{1}{8}$ to $\frac{1}{4}$ tsp (0.5 to 1 mL) unflavored powdered or granulated gelatin, mixed in saucepan then reheated until gelatin dissolves (improves texture of broth)
- 1 cup (250 mL) aseptically packaged or canned chicken broth + 2 tbsp (30 mL) chopped leftover chicken bones, brought to a boil in a saucepan then gently simmered for 30 minutes and strained before using (improves texture and flavor of broth)

### To Vary the Flavor

Substitute 1 cup (250 mL) chicken stock with:

- 1 cup (250 mL) dry white wine, vermouth or sherry (to replace up to half of chicken stock in sauces and stews)
- 1 cup (250 mL) vegetable stock, broth, or reconstituted base or bouillon (may be less robust in flavor; use roasted vegetable stock to intensify flavor)

### For Better Health

- 1 cup (250 mL) low-sodium chicken broth

## Stock, Fish

*Also known as fish fumet. From the home cook's perspective, the easiest, fastest stock to make from scratch. Only the frames of white-fleshed fish should be used. Oilier fish such as bluefish or mackerel would overpower the flavor.*

### If You Don't Have It

Substitute 1 cup (250 mL) fish stock with:

- 1 cup (250 mL) Homemade Fish Stock: Combine ¾ cup (175 mL) bottled clam juice, ½ cup (125 mL) water, ½ cup (125 mL) dry white wine, ½ cup (125 mL) sliced onion, and 2 to 3 sprigs parsley in a saucepan. Simmer over medium heat until reduced to 1 cup (250 mL), about 30 minutes, then strain. Makes about 1 cup (250 mL).
- 1 cup (250 mL) boiling water + ½ tsp (2 mL) lobster, clam, or chicken base or instant fish or chicken bouillon granules, ½ tsp (2 mL) fish or chicken bouillon cube, or ½ tsp (2 mL) envelope fish or chicken bouillon

### To Vary the Flavor

Substitute 1 cup (250 mL) fish stock with:

- ½ cup (125 mL) aseptically packaged or canned chicken broth + ½ cup (125 mL) water (less flavorful)
- 1 cup (250 mL) dry white wine, vermouth, or sherry (to replace up to half of fish stock in sauces and stews)
- 1 cup (250 mL) reconstituted instant dashi or dashi-no-moto (more fishy, less fresh flavor)
- 1 cup (250 mL) chicken stock or broth + 2 tbsp (30 mL) dulse (seaweed) flakes or a 1-inch (2.5 cm) square of kombu, brought to a boil, removed from heat and cooled for 5 minutes, then strained (not as flavorful)
- 1 cup (250 mL) vegetable stock, broth, or reconstituted base or bouillon (less aromatic and flavorful)

## Stock, Veal

*Brown veal stock is the most flavorful and versatile stock of the French repertoire. A properly made veal stock will acquire a deep golden brown color from oven-roasting the bones before they are simmered with water and aromatic vegetables and herbs. It will also jell when refrigerated. It is the basis for numerous gravies, sauces, soups, and stews. Bones with a good proportion of meat and cartilage, such as veal breast, are essential.*

### If You Don't Have It

Substitute 1 cup (250 mL) veal stock with:

- 1 cup (250 mL) cold or room temperature aseptically packaged or canned chicken or beef broth + ⅛ to ¼ tsp (0.5 to 1 mL) unflavored powdered or granulated gelatin, mixed in saucepan then reheated until gelatin dissolves (improves texture of broth)
- 1 cup (250 mL) aseptically packaged or canned chicken broth + 2 tbsp (30 mL) chopped leftover chicken bones, brought to a boil in a saucepan then gently simmered for 30 minutes and strained before using (improves texture and flavor of broth)
- 1 cup (250 mL) boiling water + 1 tsp (5 mL) chicken or beef base or instant chicken or beef bouillon granules, 1 chicken or beef bouillon cube, or 1 envelope chicken or beef bouillon (less rich; less flavorful)
- 1 cup (250 mL) aseptically packaged or canned chicken or beef broth (may be higher in sodium and less flavorful)
- 1 cup (250 mL) dry white wine, vermouth or sherry (to replace up to half of veal stock in sauces and stews)

## Stock, Veal (cont'd)

- 1 cup (250 mL) vegetable stock, broth, or reconstituted base or bouillon (may be less robust in flavor; use roasted vegetable stock to intensify flavor)

## Stock, Vegetable

*For vegetarians or those just trying to cut down on meat consumption, a tasty vegetable stock will add immeasurable flavor to many dishes. When making your own stock, try adding vegetables or herbs to match the flavor of the dishes you'll be making. For instance, add ginger to the stock to complement Asian dishes. Or add a few sprigs of fresh cilantro to the stock to marry with Mexican dishes. Experiment with vegetables and seasonings, but avoid very strong-tasting vegetables such as broccoli.*

### If You Don't Have It

Substitute 1 cup (250 mL) vegetable stock with:

- 1 cup (250 mL) Homemade Vegetable Stock: Combine 2 cups (500 mL) chopped onions, 2 cups (500 mL) chopped carrots, 1 cup (250 mL) chopped celery, 4 halved garlic cloves, 4 sprigs parsley, 1 to 2 bay leaves, and a few sprigs of thyme in a large saucepan. Cover with cold water by 1 inch (2.5 cm). Simmer over medium heat until vegetables are tender, about 1 hour. Pour through a fine-mesh strainer into a heatproof container, pressing on solids. Discard solids. Season to taste with salt and pepper. Let cool. Refrigerate in airtight containers for 1 week or freeze for up to 6 months. Makes about 4 cups (1 L).
- 1 cup (250 mL) boiling water + 1 tsp (5 mL) vegetable or chicken base or instant vegetable or chicken bouillon granules, 1 vegetable or chicken bouillon cube, or 1 envelope vegetable or chicken bouillon
- 1 cup (250 mL) aseptically packaged or canned vegetable broth (may be higher in sodium and less flavorful)
- 1 cup (250 mL) roasted vegetable stock (roast vegetables at 475°F/240°C until well-browned before making stock; intensifies flavors)
- 1 cup (250 mL) cold or room temperature aseptically packaged or canned vegetable or chicken broth + $\frac{1}{8}$ to $\frac{1}{4}$ tsp (0.5 to 1 mL) unflavored powdered or granulated gelatin, mixed in saucepan then reheated until gelatin dissolves (improves texture of broth)

### To Vary the Flavor

Substitute 1 cup (250 mL) vegetable stock with:

- 1 cup (250 mL) aseptically packaged or canned chicken broth (may be higher in sodium and less flavorful; adds chicken flavor)
- 1 cup (250 mL) dry white wine, vermouth or sherry (to replace up to half of vegetable stock in sauces and stews)

### For Better Health

- 1 cup (250 mL) low-sodium vegetable broth

## Stone Crab

*See* CHOOSING AMONG CRABS (PAGE 647).

## Stoneware

A sturdy type of cookware made from glazed pottery that's fired at temperatures of up to 2200°F (1204°C). After passing the test of fire, these chip-resistant pans are ideal for slow cooking and baking in either conventional or microwave ovens.

### If You Don't Have It
Substitute stoneware with:
- earthenware
- porcelain
- heatproof glass

## Stout

See BEER.

## Stracchino

Also known as stracchino di crescenza. Various types of cheeses in Northern Italy are made from cows' milks combined from morning and evening milkings and called stracchino. Gorgonzola and taleggio are both stracchino cheeses. Crescenza or stracchino di crescenza is another type.

### If You Don't Have It
Substitute 1 oz (30 g) young stracchino di crescenza with:
- 1 oz (30 g) mascarpone (creamier)
- 1 oz (30 g) cream cheese (creamier)

### For Better Health
Substitute 1 oz (30 g) young stracchino with:
- 1 oz (30 g) Neufchâtel (creamier)

See also TALEGGIO.

## Strained Yogurt

See YOGURT CHEESE.

## Strainer

Also known as Chinese spider strainer or a sieve. They can be shaped as cones, drums, or bowls, but strainers all have a mesh bottom designed to strain liquids from solids or sift dry ingredients.

### If You Don't Have It
Substitute a strainer with:
- colander
- tongs, pasta spoon, or slotted spoon (for plucking or scooping foods out of hot liquid)
- Chinese spider strainer (for skimming or scooping foods out of hot liquid)
- sifter (for sifting ingredients)
- fine-holed shaker (for quickly sifting small amounts of a single ingredient such as confectioner's sugar or cocoa powder)

See also COLANDER.

## Strawberry

*Wild strawberries are indigenous to both the Old and New Worlds. In 19ᵗʰ century England, Michael Keens produced a strawberry of remarkable size and taste. Almost all varieties in cultivation today are descended from it.*

1 pint = 24 medium = 36 small = 2½ cups (625 mL) whole = 1¾ cups (425 mL) sliced = 1¼ cups (300 mL) puréed

20 oz (600 g) pkg frozen whole strawberries = 4 cups (1 L) = 2¼ cups (550 mL) puréed

10 oz (300 g) pkg in syrup = 1¼ cups (300 mL)

### If You Don't Have It

Substitute 1 pint strawberries with:

- 1 pint raspberries (red color; slightly more tart)
- 1 pint loganberries (red color; slightly more tart)
- 1 pint tayberries (red color; slightly more tart)
- 1 pint blueberries (purple color; slightly more tart)
- 2 cups (500 mL) guava pulp (pinkish orange color)
- 2 cups (500 mL) peeled kiwifruit (green color; slightly more tart)

*See also* FRAISES DES BOIS.

## Strawberry, Dried

*Dr. William Butler, a 17ᵗʰ century British writer, was among the first to recommend eating oysters only in months that have an "R" in them. He also wrote in praise of the strawberry, "Doubtless God could have made a better berry, but doubtless God never did."*

### If You Don't Have It

Substitute 1 cup (250 mL) dried strawberries with:

- 1 cup (250 mL) dried raspberries (slightly less sweet)
- 1 cup (250 mL) dried cherries (more tart)
- 1 cup (250 mL) dried cranberries (more tart)
- 1 cup (250 mL) dried blueberries (dark blue color)
- 1 cup (250 mL) raisins

## Strawberry Liqueur

*See* CRÈME DE FRAISE.

## Strawberry Pear

*See* PITAYA.

## Strawberry Preserves

*One of many attempts to extend our enjoyment of strawberries beyond their botanical seasons.*

### If You Don't Have It

Substitute ½ cup (125 mL) strawberry preserves with:

- ½ cup (125 mL) raspberry or blueberry preserves
- ½ cup (125 mL) guava paste
- ½ cup (125 mL) other tropical fruit preserves

## Strawberry Tomato

*See* CAPE GOOSEBERRY.

## Straw Mushroom

*See* SHUFFLING MUSHROOMS (PAGE 654)

## Strega

Made from more than 70 herbs, this anise-tasting liqueur is named "witch" but that doesn't seem to deter the many Italians who enjoy it. Strega may be clear or a glistening yellow green color.

### If You Don't Have It

Substitute 2 tbsp (30 mL) Strega with:
- 2 tbsp (30 mL) Chartreuse (green or yellow color)
- 2 tbsp (30 mL) Izarra (green or yellow color)
- 2 tbsp (30 mL) Liqueur d'Or (includes gold flakes)
- 2 tbsp (30 mL) Bénédictine (deep amber color)
- 2 tbsp (30 mL) sambuca (colorless; licorice flavor)

## String Bean

*See* GREEN BEAN.

## String Cheese

Semihard, mild white cheese that's typically formed into strips. It's popular for snacking because it's easy to eat out-of-hand.

### If You Don't Have It

Substitute 1 oz (30 g) string cheese with:
- 1 oz (30 g) firm mozzarella, cut into strips
- 1 oz (30 g) Scamorza, cut into strips
- 1 oz (30 g) Caciocavallo, cut into strips

## Striped Bass

Also known as rock, rockfish, and striper. A highly sought after true bass of the eastern U.S. coast. The white flesh is firm, well-flavored, and only moderately high in fat. Wild striped bass has olive green, silvery skin marked by up to 8 longitudinal black stripes. Less flavorful farmed striped bass is a hybrid of wild striped bass and white bass. It's easy to distinguish the farmed striped because of its shorter stubbier body and a stripe pattern that appears broken up.

### If You Don't Have It

Substitute 1 lb (500 g) striped bass with:
- 1 lb (500 g) blackfish
- 1 lb (500 g) rockfish
- 1 lb (500 g) black sea bass
- 1 lb (500 g) grouper
- 1 lb (500 g) red snapper
- 1 lb (500 g) swordfish

## Striped Mullet

*See* MULLET.

## Striper

*See* STRIPED BASS.

## Strudel Dough

A central European gossamer pastry dough similar to phyllo. Typically, many layers are piled on one another to create a crescendo of crispness after baking.

### If You Don't Have It
Substitute 1 lb (500 g) strudel dough with:
- 1 lb (500 g) phyllo dough
- 1 lb (500 g) puff pastry (less crisp)

## Stuffing Cubes

*See* CROUTONS.

## Sturgeon

Fine-tasting fish that has been compared in flavor and texture to veal. Sturgeon, particularly from the Black Sea and the Caspian Sea, is most sought after for its caviar.

### If You Don't Have It
Substitute 1 lb (500 g) sturgeon with:
- 1 lb (500 g) swordfish
- 1 lb (500 g) tuna
- 1 lb (500 g) mahi-mahi
- 1 lb (500 g) halibut
- 1 lb (500 g) smoked sturgeon

*See also* CHANGING ROE (PAGE 666).

## Su

*See* CHOOSING VINEGAR (PAGE 674).

## Sucanat

Also known as granulated sugarcane juice, dehydrated sugarcane juice, and unrefined natural sugar. "Su-ca-nat" is short for sugarcane natural. Unlike commercial "brown sugar" which is molasses-flavored granulated sugar, Sucanat is comprised of brown porous granules that result from crushing the sugarcane, extracting the juice, and rapidly evaporating the syrup. It retains most of the nutrients that are naturally occurring in the sugarcane.

### If You Don't Have It
Substitute 1 cup (250 mL) Sucanat with:
- 1 cup (250 mL) granulated sugar (more highly refined; fewer nutrients and minerals)
- 1¾ cups (425 mL) unsifted confectioner's (icing) sugar
- 1 cup (250 mL) packed light or dark brown sugar (more highly refined; fewer nutrients and minerals)
- 1 cup (250 mL) superfine (castor) sugar
- 1 cup (250 mL) turbinado sugar
- 1 cup (250 mL) date sugar
- ⅔ cup (150 mL) granulated fructose or fruit sugar (fructose tends to make baked goods moister, darker, and chewier)
- 1 cup (250 mL) minus 2 tbsp (30 mL) honey (for baking, reduce liquid in recipe by 3 tbsp/45 mL; add ¼ tsp/1 mL baking soda to neutralize acidity of honey)
- ¾ cup (175 mL) maple syrup (for baking, reduce liquid in recipe by 3 to 4 tbsp/45 to 60 mL; add scant ¼ tsp/1 mL baking soda to neutralize acidity of maple syrup)

1 lb (500 g) = 2¼ cups (550 mL) packed

- ½ cup (125 mL) granulated sugar + 6 tbsp (90 mL) honey, maple syrup, or corn syrup (in baking, reduce liquid in recipe by 2 tbsp/30 mL, or add 2 tbsp/30 mL flour if there is no other liquid in recipe; reduce oven temperature by 25°F/14°C)
- ½ cup (125 mL) granulated sugar + ½ cup (125 mL) molasses + ½ tsp (2 mL) baking soda (reduce liquid in recipe by 2 tbsp/30 mL, or add 2 tbsp/30 mL flour if there is no other liquid in recipe)
- ¾ cup (175 mL) granulated sugar + ¼ cup (60 mL) maple sugar

## For Better Health

Substitute 1 cup (250 mL) Sucanat with:

- ½ cup (125 mL) Sucanat + ½ cup (125 mL) sugar-free sugar substitute such as sucralose, Splenda© or DiabetiSweet© (for balance of reduced calories, flavor, and browning in baking)
- 1 cup (250 mL) sugar-free sugar substitute such as sucralose, Splenda© or DiabetiSweet© (calorie-free; may leave slight aftertaste and browning will not occur in baking because there is no sugar to caramelize)
- ⅛ to ¼ tsp (0.5 to 1 mL) liquid stevia (calorie-free; probiotic, which promotes growth of healthy bacteria in digestive system; may leave slight licorice-like aftertaste and browning will not occur in baking because there is no sugar to caramelize)

## Sucralose

*A calorie-free sweetener made from sugar by a chemical process that replaces three hydrogen-oxygen groups on the sugar molecule with three chlorine atoms. Because the body does not recognize sucralose as a carbohydrate, it passes through the body without being broken down for energy. It is stable and can be used in cooking and baking. The most widely available brand, Splenda®, is interchangeable with sucralose in all the following substitutions.*

## If You Don't Have It

Substitute 1 cup (250 mL) sucralose with:

- 1 cup (250 mL) granulated sugar (adds calories; aids in browning)
- 1¾ cups (425 mL) unsifted confectioner's (icing) sugar (adds calories; aids in browning)
- 1 cup (250 mL) packed light or dark brown sugar (adds calories; aids in browning; makes baked goods moister and chewier)
- 1 cup (250 mL) superfine (castor) sugar (adds calories; aids in browning)
- 1 cup (250 mL) turbinado sugar (adds calories; aids in browning)
- 1 cup (250 mL) date sugar (adds calories; aids in browning)
- ⅔ cup (150 mL) granulated fructose or fruit sugar (adds calories; fructose tends to make baked goods moister, darker, and chewier)

## Sucralose (cont'd)

- 1 cup (250 mL) minus 2 tbsp (30 mL) honey (adds calories; for baking, reduce liquid in recipe by 3 tbsp/45 mL; add ¼ tsp/1 mL baking soda to neutralize acidity of honey; makes baked goods moister and chewier; reduce oven temperature by 25°F/14°C)
- ¾ cup (175 mL) maple syrup (adds calories; for baking, reduce liquid in recipe by 3 to 4 tbsp/45 to 60 mL; add scant ¼ tsp/1 mL baking soda to neutralize acidity of maple syrup)
- ½ cup (125 mL) granulated sugar + 6 tbsp (90 mL) honey, maple syrup, or corn syrup (adds calories; for baking, reduce liquid in recipe by 2 tbsp/25 mL, or add 2 tbsp/25 mL flour if there is no other liquid in recipe; reduce oven temperature by 25°F/14°C)
- ½ cup (125 mL) granulated sugar + ½ cup (125 mL) molasses + ½ tsp (2 mL) baking soda (adds calories; for baking, reduce liquid in recipe by 2 tbsp/25 mL or add 2 tbsp/25 mL flour if there is no other liquid in recipe)
- ¾ cup (175 mL) granulated sugar + ¼ cup (60 mL) maple sugar (adds calories)

### For Better Health
Substitute 1 cup (250 mL) sucralose with:
- 1 cup (250 mL) Sucanat (adds calories; powdered organic sugarcane juice, which retains all its vitamins and minerals)
- ½ cup (125 mL) granulated sugar + ½ cup (125 mL) sugar-free sugar substitute such as Splenda® or DiabetiSweet® (adds calories; for best balance of reduced calories, flavor, and browning in baking)
- 1 cup (250 mL) sugar-free sugar substitute such as DiabetiSweet© (calorie-free; may leave slight aftertaste and browning will not occur in baking because there is no sugar to caramelize)
- ¼ tsp (1 mL) liquid stevia (calorie-free; probiotic, which promotes growth of healthy bacteria in digestive system; may leave slight licorice-like aftertaste and browning will not occur in baking because there is no sugar to caramelize)

## Suet

*The solid, white fat found around the kidneys and loins of beef and other animals. Suet is a traditional component of many British recipes for pastries, puddings, and mincemeats.*

1 lb (500 g) ground = 3¾ cups (925 mL)

### If You Don't Have It
Substitute ½ cup (125 mL) suet with:
- ½ cup (125 mL) vegetarian suet such as Atora (made from vegetable fat; same calories and fat content as beef suet; suitable for vegetarians)
- ½ cup (125 mL) vegetable shortening (moister)
- ½ cup (125 mL) rendered and solidified beef, chicken, or pork fat (moister)
- ½ cup (125 mL) butter (moister)

## Suey Gow Wrappers

*See* WON TON SKINS.

## Sufganiyah

*See* DOUGHNUT.

## Sugar Apple

*See* SWEETSOP.

## Sugar, Black

*Japanese unrefined brown sugar pressed into firm yet moist rectangular blocks. Intense molasses flavor.*

1 lb (500 g) =
3 to 3¼ cups
(750 to 800 mL)

### If You Don't Have It
Substitute 1 cup (250 mL) black sugar with:
- 1 cup (250 mL) piloncillo (Mexican unrefined brown sugar)
- 1 cup (250 mL) jaggery (Indian unrefined brown sugar)
- 1 cup (250 mL) dark brown sugar + 1 tbsp (15 mL) molasses
- 1 cup (250 mL) light brown sugar + 2 tbsp (30 mL) molasses
- ¾ cup (175 mL) granulated sugar + ⅓ cup (75 mL) molasses
- 1 cup (250 mL) palm sugar

## Sugar, Chinese

*See* SUGAR, ROCK.

## Sugar, Confectioner's

*Also known as powdered sugar and icing sugar. Granulated sugar that's pulverized to a powder and mixed with about 3% cornstarch to prevent clumping. It dissolves almost instantly in icings and frostings. It's also sprinkled on pastries for decorative effect. The number of Xs on the package indicates the degree of fineness. XXXX is finer than XXX.*

1 lb (500 g) = 3½ to
4 cups (875 mL to 1 L)
unsifted = 4½ to 5 cups
(1.125 to 1.25 L) sifted

### If You Don't Have It
Substitute 1 cup (250 mL) confectioner's sugar with:
- ½ cup (125 mL) plus 1½ tbsp (22 mL) granulated sugar plus ¾ tsp (3 mL) cornstarch (optional) finely ground in a blender or small food processor

*See also* SUGAR, GRANULATED.

## Sugar, Dark Brown

*Use dark brown sugar
instead of light brown sugar
for a deeper molasses flavor
in cooking, baking, spice
rubs, and marinades. To
measure accurately, always
pack the sugar firmly into
a measuring cup.*

1 lb (500 g) = 2¼ cups
(550 mL) packed

### If You Don't Have It
Substitute 1 packed cup (250 mL) dark brown sugar with:
- 1 packed cup (250 mL) light brown sugar + 1 tbsp (15 mL) molasses
- 1 cup (250 mL) granulated sugar + 2 to 3 tbsp (30 to 45 mL) molasses
- 1 cup (250 mL) turbinado sugar
- 1 cup (250 mL) Muscovado sugar (more moist; reduce liquid in recipe by 1 to 2 tsp/5 to 10 mL)
- 1 cup (250 mL) chopped jaggery (more firm)
- 1 cup (250 mL) chopped piloncillo (more firm)
- 1 cup (250 mL) chopped black sugar (more firm; strong molasses flavor)

### For Better Health
Substitute 1 packed cup (250 mL) dark brown sugar with:
- 1 cup (250 mL) sugar-free sugar substitute such as sucralose, Splenda© or DiabetiSweet© + ¼ cup (60 mL) molasses (fewer calories; may leave slight aftertaste and browning will not occur in baking because there is less sugar to caramelize)

*See also* JAGGERY; PILONCILLO; SUGAR, BLACK; SUGAR, GRANULATED.

## Sugar, Decorating

*Also known as coarse
sugar, crystal sugar, and
sugar crystals. Sparkling
clear pellets that are four
times as large as those
in granulated sugar are
employed for decorating
pastries. They are sold in
cake-decorating supply
shops, specialty pastry
catalogs, online, and
some supermarkets.*

### If You Don't Have It
Substitute 1 cup (250 mL) decorating sugar with:
- 1 cup (250 mL) Homemade Colored Decorating Sugar: Put 1 cup (250 mL) decorating or granulated sugar in a glass jar with a tight-fitting lid. Add 8 to 10 drops food coloring, seal, and shake immediately and vigorously until sugar is evenly colored. Makes 1 cup (250 mL).
- 1 cup (250 mL) turbinado sugar (slightly smaller, blond-color crystals)
- 1 cup (250 mL) Demerara sugar (slightly smaller, light brown color crystals)

### To Vary the Flavor
Substitute 1 cup (250 mL) decorating sugar with:
- 1 cup (250 mL) Homemade Cinnamon Sugar (adds cinnamon flavor; smaller crystals; see recipe, page 549)
- 1 cup (250 mL) Homemade Vanilla Sugar (adds vanilla flavor; smaller crystals; see recipe, page 549)
- 1 cup (250 mL) nonpareils (solid white color)
- 1 cup (250 mL) jimmies (various colors and flavors)

*See also* SUGAR, ROCK.

## Sugar, Granulated

*Also known as white sugar. These medium-size white crystals are processed from sugarcane and also, to a lesser degree in the marketplace, from sugar beets. Some product labels specify "pure cane sugar" while others do not. Although scientists detect no chemical difference between the two, many bakers and jam makers contend that cane sugar produces more consistent results. Many vegetarians prefer beet sugar because some cane sugar is whitened using animal bones. Aside from its obvious role as a sweetener, sugar helps maintain moistness in baked goods, stabilizes egg whites for meringue, prevents some food from spoilage, and gives many cooked foods a golden color. Sugar cubes are granulated sugar that is "glued" together with syrup and molded in tiny blocks.*

---

1 lb (500 g) = 2 to
2¼ cups (500 to 550 mL)

1 tsp (5 mL) = two
½-inch (1 cm) sugar cubes

---

## If You Don't Have It

Substitute 1 cup (250 mL) granulated sugar with:

- 1¾ cups (425 mL) unsifted confectioner's (icing) sugar (may make baked goods less crisp)
- 1 cup (250 mL) packed light or dark brown sugar (slightly higher calories, minerals, and other nutrients; makes baked goods moister and chewier)
- 1 cup (250 mL) superfine or castor sugar (smaller crystals)
- 1 cup (250 mL) turbinado sugar (larger crystals)
- ⅔ cup (150 mL) granulated fructose or fruit sugar (fructose tends to make baked goods moister, darker, and chewier)

## To Vary the Flavor

Substitute 1 cup (250 mL) granulated sugar with:

- 1 cup (250 mL) date sugar
- 1 cup (250 mL) minus 2 tbsp (30 mL) honey, agave nectar, or brown rice syrup (for baking, reduce liquid in recipe by 3 tbsp/45 mL; add ¼ tsp/1 mL baking soda to neutralize acidity; makes baked goods moister and chewier; reduce oven temperature by 25°F/14°C)
- ¾ cup (175 mL) maple syrup (for baking, reduce liquid in recipe by 3 to 4 tbsp/45 to 60 mL; add scant ¼ tsp/1 mL baking soda to neutralize acidity of maple syrup)
- ¾ cup (175 mL) barley malt syrup (for baking, reduce liquid in recipe by 3 to 4 tbsp/45 to 60 mL)
- ½ cup (125 mL) granulated sugar + 6 tbsp (90 mL) honey, maple syrup, or corn syrup (in baking, reduce liquid in recipe by 2 tbsp/30 mL, or add 2 tbsp/30 mL flour if there is no other liquid in recipe; reduce oven temperature by 25°F/14°C)
- ½ cup (125 mL) granulated sugar + ½ cup (125 mL) molasses + ½ tsp (2 mL) baking soda (for baking, reduce liquid in recipe by 2 tbsp/30 mL, or add 2 tbsp/30 mL flour if there is no other liquid in recipe; adds molasses flavor)
- ¾ cup (175 mL) granulated sugar + ¼ cup (60 mL) maple sugar
- 1 cup (250 mL) Homemade Vanilla Sugar: Combine 2 whole vanilla beans and 2 cups (500 mL) granulated sugar in an airtight container and store at room temperature indefinitely. Shake the container occasionally. The vanilla beans will flavor the sugar within 1 to 2 weeks. Remove vanilla sugar as necessary and replace with an equal amount of granulated sugar. Replace vanilla beans when they give up their flavor. Makes 2 cups (500 mL). To substitute 1 cup (250 mL) vanilla sugar, use 1 cup (250 mL) sugar + ½ tsp (2 mL) vanilla extract.
- 1 cup (250 mL) Homemade Cinnamon Sugar: Combine 1 cup (250 mL) granulated sugar and 2 to 3 tbsp (30 to 45 mL) cinnamon in an airtight container and store at room

## Sugar, Granulated (cont'd)

temperature indefinitely. Or combine 6 cinnamon sticks and 4 cups (1 L) sugar in an airtight container and store at room temperature indefinitely. Shake the container occasionally. The cinnamon sticks will flavor the sugar within 1 to 2 weeks. Remove cinnamon sugar as necessary and replace with an equal amount of granulated sugar. Replace cinnamon sticks when they give up their flavor. Makes 4 cups (1 L).

### For Better Health

Substitute 1 cup (250 mL) granulated sugar with:

- ¾ cup (175 mL) granulated sugar (fewer calories; sugar can often be reduced by one-quarter of the amount called for; makes baked goods slightly less sweet and more pale and dry)
- 1 cup (250 mL) Sucanat (powdered organic sugarcane juice, which retains all its vitamins and minerals)
- ½ cup (125 mL) granulated sugar + ½ cup (125 mL) sugar-free sugar substitute such as Splenda® or DiabetiSweet® (for best balance  of reduced calories, flavor and browning in baking)
- 1 cup (250 mL) sugar-free sugar substitute such as sucralose, Splenda© or DiabetiSweet© (calorie-free; may leave slight aftertaste and browning will not occur in baking because there is no sugar to caramelize)
- ⅛ to ¼ tsp (0.5 to 1 mL) liquid stevia (calorie-free; probiotic, which promotes growth of healthy bacteria in digestive system; may leave slight licorice-like aftertaste and browning will not occur in baking because there is no sugar to caramelize)

*See also* DATE SUGAR; MAPLE SUGAR; SUGAR, DARK BROWN; SUGAR, LIGHT BROWN

## Sugar, Light Brown

*Made by mixing granulated sugar with molasses. Generally, the lighter the brown color, the less molasses is added. To keep the sugar soft after opening a package, place a strip of orange zest, about 3 inches by 1 inch (7.5 by 2.5 cm) in the bag. Seal tightly and store inside a resealable plastic bag.*

1 lb (500 g) =
2¼ cups (550 mL) packed

### If You Don't Have It

Substitute 1 packed cup (250 mL) light brown sugar with:

- 1 cup (250 mL) sugar + 1 to 2 tbsp (15 to 30 mL) molasses
- ½ cup (125 mL) dark brown sugar + ½ cup (125 mL) granulated sugar
- 1 cup (250 mL) turbinado sugar (less moist; larger crystals)

### For Better Health

Substitute 1 cup (250 mL) light brown sugar with:

- ¾ cup (175 mL) light brown sugar (sugar can often be reduced by one-quarter of the amount called for; makes baked goods slightly less sweet and more pale and dry)
- ½ cup (125 mL) light brown sugar + ½ cup (125 mL) sugar-free brown sugar substitute such as Brown Sugar Twin© (for best balance of reduced calories, flavor and browning in baking)
- 1 cup (250 mL) sugar-free brown sugar substitute such as Brown Sugar Twin© (may leave slight aftertaste and browning will not occur in baking because there is no sugar to caramelize)

*See also* JAGGERY; PILONCILLO; SUGAR, BLACK; SUGAR, DARK BROWN; SUGAR, GRANULATED.

## Sugar, Palm

*Also known as coconut sugar, gur, and jaggery. Coarse dark sugar derived from the sap of various palm trees or from sugarcane juice. Some manufacturers classify palm sugar as gur and sugarcane as jaggery. This sweetener adds complex wine-like flavor and aroma to many dishes.*

### If You Don't Have It
Substitute 1 cup (250 mL) palm sugar with:
- 1 cup (250 mL) jaggery
- 1 cup (250 mL) piloncillo
- 1 cup (250 mL) dark brown sugar + 2 tsp (10 mL) molasses
- 1 cup (250 mL) muscovado sugar

*See also* JAGGERY; PILONCILLO; SUGAR, BLACK.

## Sugar, Raw

*Resembling brown sugar in looks only, raw sugar is the residue remaining after cane sugar is processed to remove molasses and refine the sugar crystals. In its natural state, raw sugar may contain fibers, molds, and other contaminants, therefore commercially marketed raw sugar is purified.*

> 1 lb (500 g) =
> 3 to 3¼ cups
> (750 to 800 mL)

### If You Don't Have It
Substitute 1 cup (250 mL) raw sugar with:
- 1 cup (250 mL) palm sugar
- 1 cup (250 mL) light or dark brown sugar
- 1 cup (250 mL) granulated sugar (drier; less molasses-like flavor)

### Raw Sugar Varieties
Choose 1 cup (250 mL) raw sugar from these varieties:
- 1 cup (250 mL) turbinado sugar (steam-cleaned raw sugar; coarse, blond-color crystals; mild molasses flavor)
- 1 cup (250 mL) Demerara sugar (from Guyana; dry, coarse crystals; slightly stronger molasses flavor)
- 1 cup (250 mL) Muscovado or Barbados sugar (very moist, fine crystals; stronger molasses flavor)

### For Better Health
Substitute 1 cup (250 mL) raw sugar with:
- 1 cup (250 mL) Sucanat (powdered organic sugarcane juice, which retains all its vitamins and minerals)

*See also* SUGAR, BLACK; SUGAR, DARK BROWN; SUGAR, GRANULATED; SUGAR, LIGHT BROWN.

## Sugar, Rock

*Also known as Chinese sugar and rock candy. The largest-size crystals of decorating sugar, available as brown sugar, white sugar, or colored sugar.*

### If You Don't Have It
Substitute 1 rock sugar crystal with:
- 2 to 3 tsp (10 to 15 mL) decorating sugar (smaller crystals)
- 2 to 3 tsp (10 to 15 mL) granulated sugar (much smaller crytals; sweeter; less caramelized flavor)

*See also* SUGAR, DECORATING; SUGAR, GRANULATED.

## Sugar Snap Pea

*See* PEAS, EDIBLE POD.

## Sugar, Superfine

*Also known as bar sugar, caster sugar, and castor sugar (British). Ground finer than granulated sugar, superfine sugar dissolves more easily.*

1 lb (500 g) =
2⅓ cups (575 mL)

### If You Don't Have It
Substitute 1 cup (250 mL) superfine sugar with:
- 1 cup (250 mL) + 1 tsp (5 mL) granulated sugar finely ground in a blender or small food processor

*See also* SUGAR, GRANULATED.

## Sugar Syrup

*Also known as simple syrup. A solution of sugar and water cooked just until the sugar crystals dissolve. These syrups can be of thin, medium, or heavy consistency depending upon the ratio of sugar to water. They have many applications in confectionery and beverages.*

### If You Don't Have It
Substitute 1 cup (250 mL) sugar syrup with:
- 1 cup (250 mL) Homemade Simple Syrup: Combine 1 cup (250 mL) water and 1 cup (250 mL) granulated sugar in a small saucepan. Bring to a boil over high heat. Then reduce heat to medium or medium-low and gently simmer until sugar is dissolved and mixture is syrupy, 3 to 5 minutes. Let cool and refrigerate in an airtight container for up to 1 month. Makes about 1 cup (250 mL).
- 1 cup (250 mL) Homemade Heavy Syrup: Combine 1 cup (250 mL) water and 1⅓ cups (325 mL) granulated sugar in a small saucepan. Bring to a boil over high heat. Then reduce heat to medium or medium-low and gently simmer until sugar is dissolved and mixture is syrupy, 3 to 5 minutes. Let cool and refrigerate in an airtight container for up to 1 month. Makes about 1 cup (250 mL).
- 1 cup (250 mL) Homemade Medium Syrup: Combine 1 cup (250 mL) water and ½ cup (125 mL) granulated sugar in a small saucepan. Bring to a boil over high heat. Then reduce heat to medium or medium-low and gently simmer until sugar is dissolved and mixture is syrupy, 3 to 5 minutes. Let cool and refrigerate in an airtight container for up to 1 month. Makes about 1 cup (250 mL).
- 1 cup (250 mL) Homemade Thin Syrup: Combine 1 cup (250 mL) water and ¼ cup (60 mL) granulated sugar in a small saucepan. Bring to a boil over high heat. Then reduce heat to medium or medium-low and gently simmer until sugar is dissolved and mixture is syrupy, 3 to 5 minutes. Let cool and refrigerate in an airtight container for up to 1 month. Makes about 1 cup (250 mL).

## Sugar, Turbinado

*See* SUGAR, RAW.

## Sujuk

*Also known as soujouk and yershig. Spicy Lebanese beef sausage.*

### If You Don't Have It

Substitute 1 lb (500 g) sujuk with:
- 1 lb (500 g) pepperoni
- 1 lb (500 g) sopressata (made with pork; slightly flattened shape; dry and well-seasoned with black pepper)
- 1 lb (500 g) Neapolitan or Napoli salami (made with pork and beef; long and thin; spicy with red and black pepper)
- 1 lb (500 g) Sardinian or Sardo salami (made with pork; spicy with red pepper)
- 1 lb (500 g) Calabrian or Calabrese sausage or salami (made with pork; short and squat; dry and spicy with red pepper)
- 1 lb (500 g) other spicy salami

## Sultana

*See* RAISIN.

## Sulze

*See* HEADCHEESE.

## Sumac

*The tart berries (drupes) of the Sicilian or elm-leafed sumac are used whole or powdered in Middle Eastern cookery, particularly in parts of Syria, northern Iraq, and other remote areas where fresh lemons are rare.*

1 tsp (5 mL) whole berries = 1½ tsp (7 mL) ground sumac

### If You Don't Have It

Substitute 1 tsp (5 mL) ground sumac with:
- ¾ tsp (3 mL) whole sumac berries
- 1 tsp (5 mL) finely grated lemon zest
- 1 to 2 tsp (5 to 10 mL) lemon juice
- 1 to 2 tsp (5 to 10 mL) cider vinegar
- 1 tsp (5 mL) za'atar (combines sumac, thyme, sesame seeds, and salt)
- 1 tsp (5 mL) salt-free lemon pepper seasoning
- 1 tsp (5 mL) herbal salt substitute (most have high proportion of lemon)

## Summer Sausage

*The generic term for any semidry sausage that does not require refrigeration. Contrary to its name, summer sausage is traditionally prepared in the autumn during hunting seasons in North America and Europe.*

### If You Don't Have It

Substitute 1 lb (500 g) summer sausage with:
- 1 lb (500 g) salami or other dry sausage
- 1 lb (500 g) pepperoni
- 1 lb (500 g) Bierwurst
- 1 lb (500 g) Blockwurst
- 1 lb (500 g) bologna

### Summer Sausage Varieties

Choose 1 lb (500 g) summer sausage from these varieties:
- 1 lb (500 g) Thuringer (smoked; made with beef and ham or pork fat; mildly tangy flavor)
- 1 lb (500 g) Lebanon bologna (heavily smoked and dark; made with coarsely chopped beef; tart, tangy flavor)

## Summer Sausage (cont'd)

- 1 lb (500 g) Landjäger (heavily smoked and dark; made with beef; links are slightly flattened in shape; tart flavor)

*See also* CERVELAT; LANDJÄGER; LEBANON BOLOGNA; THURINGER.

## Summer Savory

*See* SAVORY.

## Summer Squash

*See* PATTYPAN SQUASH; YELLOW SQUASH; ZUCCHINI.

## Sunchoke

*Also known as Jerusalem artichoke and topinambour. A mild and crisp, native North American tuber that can be eaten raw in salads or cooked as a side dish.*

> 1 lb (500 g) =
> 12 medium = 2½ cups
> (625 mL) peeled
> and sliced

### If You Don't Have It
Substitute 1 lb (500 g) sunchokes with:
- 1 lb (500 g) oca
- 1 lb (500 g) arrowhead
- 1 lb (500 g) arracacha
- 1 lb (500 g) salsify
- 1 lb (500 g) artichoke hearts (softer texture)
- 1 lb (500 g) water chestnuts (sweeter)
- 1 lb (500 g) jicama (sweeter)
- 1 lb (500 g) potatoes (drier texture; less complex flavor)

## Sun-Dried Tomato

*Best quality sun-dried tomatoes should be deep red in color, fleshy and flexible with a rich piquant tomato flavor.*

> 1 lb (500 g) = 2¾ cups
> (675 mL) sun-dried
> tomato halves
>
> 1 tbsp (15 mL) sun-dried
> tomato paste = 3 to 5
> sun-dried tomatoes

### If You Don't Have It
Substitute 3 to 5 sun-dried tomatoes with:
- 1 tbsp (15 mL) sun-dried tomato paste
- 1 tbsp (15 mL) tomato paste (less intense tomato flavor)
- 1 to 2 fresh plum tomatoes (less intense tomato flavor; more watery)

## Sunflower Butter

*A popular alternative to peanut butter among those with peanut and tree-nut allergies due to sunflower butter's similar fat content and rich mouthfeel.*

### If You Don't Have It
Substitute 1 cup (250 mL) peanut butter with:
- 1 cup (250 mL) soy nut butter (for those with tree nut allergies; less fat; milder flavor)
- 1 cup (250 mL) almond butter
- 1 cup (250 mL) cashew butter
- 1 cup (250 mL) peanut butter
- 1 cup (250 mL) tahini (sesame seed paste)

### To Vary the Flavor
Substitute 1 cup (250 mL) sunflower butter with:
- 1 cup (250 mL) gianduja or Nutella (chocolate-hazelnut spread)

## Sunflower Oil

See SUBSTITUTING OILS (PAGE 658).

## Sunflower Seed

*Iron-rich seeds of the sunflower plant are eaten as a snack, a condiment, or an addition to breads and other baked goods. They are sold plain and salted.*

7 oz (210 g) unshelled = 2½ cups (625 mL) unshelled = ¾ cup (175 mL) kernels

### If You Don't Have It
Substitute 1 cup (250 mL) sunflower seeds with:
- 1 cup (250 mL) pumpkin seeds (larger; green)
- 1 cup (250 mL) sesame seeds (smaller)
- 1 cup (250 mL) pine nuts (larger)
- 1 cup (250 mL) almonds, peanuts, or other snacking nuts

## Sunflower Sprouts

*Hulled sunflower kernels that are soaked for a day or so to sprout.*

### If You Don't Have It
Substitute 1 cup (250 mL) sunflower sprouts with:
- 1 cup (250 mL) mung bean sprouts
- 1 cup (250 mL) soybean sprouts
- 1 cup (250 mL) julienned snow peas

## Superfine Sugar

See SUGAR, SUPERFINE.

## Surimi

*Japanese-style fake shellfish is made by an ancient method dating back to 1100 BC. Mild white-fleshed fish is processed into a flavorless paste then seasoned with natural or artificial shellfish flavoring.*

### If You Don't Have It
Substitute 1 lb (500 g) surimi with:
- 1 lb (500 g) real crabmeat (much better flavor)
- 1 lb (500 g) lobster (firmer)
- 1 lb (500 g) shrimp (firmer)
- 1 lb (500 g) scallops
- 1 lb (500 g) monkfish
- 1 lb (500 g) cod

### Surimi Varieties
Choose 1 lb (500 g) surimi from these varieties:
- 1 lb (500 g) chikuwa (tube-shaped surimi snack)
- 1 lb (500 g) crab sticks or sea legs (usually made from Alaskan pollock, crab flavoring, and red food coloring; key element in California sushi roll)
- 1 lb (500 g) hanpen (white triangles often served in soup)
- 1 lb (500 g) kamaboko (half-logs often colored pink on top, sliced crosswise into half-moons and served cold with dipping sauces or served in soup)

## Sürke

See SHANKLISH.

## Sushi Mat

Also known as a sushi roller or sudare. Looks like a place mat made of tiny bamboo slats. It is used to roll and shape the hot cooked seasoned rice for sushi.

### If You Don't Have It
Substitute a sushi mat with:
- flexible plastic place mat
- flexible silicone baking sheet

## Sushi Nori

See NORI.

## Suze

A French bittersweet herbal liqueur. Its most pronounced essence is gentian, also one of the flavors in angostura bitters.

### If You Don't Have It
Substitute 2 tbsp (30 mL) Suze with:
- 2 tbsp (30 mL) Punt e Mes
- 2 tbsp (30 mL) Amer Picon
- 2 tbsp (30 mL) Byrrh
- 2 tbsp (30 mL) Campari

## Swai

See CATFISH.

## Swedish Limpa Bread

See LIMPA BREAD.

## Swedish Syrup

Made from beet sugar, golden Swedish light syrup (ljus sirap) is typically poured over pancakes, while chocolate-brown Swedish dark syrup (mörk sirap) shows up in breads, cookies, and other baked goods.

> 16 fluid oz (454 mL) =
> 2 cups (500 mL)

### If You Don't Have It
Substitute 1 cup (250 mL) Swedish light syrup (ljus sirap) with:
- 1 cup (250 mL) golden syrup
- 1 cup (250 mL) light corn syrup

### If You Don't Have It
Substitute 1 cup (250 mL) Swedish dark syrup (mörk sirap) with:
- 1 cup (250 mL) light molasses

## Sweet Acidophilus Milk

See MILK, WHOLE.

## Sweet-and-Sour Sauce

*Many cuisines feature sweet and sour sauces, but the sugary, vinegary, red-tinged sauce in Americanized Chinese food has come to define the genre.*

### If You Don't Have It
Substitute 1 cup (250 mL) sweet and sour sauce with:
- 1 cup (250 mL) Homemade Sweet-and-Sour Sauce: In a saucepan, combine ¾ cup (175 mL) granulated sugar, ⅓ cup (75 mL) rice vinegar, ⅔ cup (150 mL) water, ¼ cup (60 mL) soy sauce, 1 tbsp (15 mL) ketchup, and 2 tbsp (30 mL) cornstarch. Stir over medium heat until the mixture boils and thickens. Makes about 2 cups (500 mL).
- 1 cup (250 mL) agrodolce (Italian sweet and sour sauce)
- 1 cup (250 mL) gastrique (French sweet and sour sauce)

## Sweet Cherry

*See* CHERRY.

## Sweet Cicely

*See* CHERVIL; CICELY.

## Sweet Dumpling Squash

*Pretty, little winter squash with green stripes on a cream rind when harvested but turning pale orange in storage. The cooked flesh is mealier than other squash, with a fresh taste hinting of corn. Unlike most winter squashes, the skin is thin enough to eat.*

> 1 lb (500 g) =
> 1 cup (250 mL)
> cooked and mashed

### If You Don't Have It
Substitute 1 cup (250 mL) chopped sweet dumpling squash with:
- 1 cup (250 mL) chopped delicata squash
- 1 cup (250 mL) chopped butternut squash (tougher peel)
- 1 cup (250 mL) chopped buttercup squash (tougher peel)
- 1 cup (250 mL) chopped pumpkin (tougher peel)
- 1 cup (250 mL) chopped sweet potato

## Sweetened Condensed Milk

*Milk reduced by evaporation then sweetened. A 14-oz (398 mL) can is made from 1 quart (1 L) whole milk and 7 ounces (210 g) of granulated sugar. An essential ingredient for genuine Key lime pie.*

> 14-oz (398 mL) can =
> 1¼ cups (300 mL)

### If You Don't Have It
Substitute 1 14-oz (398 mL) can sweetened condensed milk (8% to 10% fat) with:
- 1 cup (250 mL) evaporated milk + 1¼ cups (300 mL) granulated sugar, heated until sugar dissolves

### For Better Health
Substitute 1 14-oz (398 mL) can sweetened condensed milk with:
- 1 14-oz (398 mL) can fat-free sweetened condensed milk

*See also* EVAPORATED MILK.

## Sweet Fish

*See* AYU.

## Sweet Gherkin

*Pickles that are named for a variety of tiny cucumbers.*

### If You Don't Have It
Substitute 1 cup (250 mL) sweet gherkins with:
- 1 cup (250 mL) cornichons (more tart)
- 1 cup (250 mL) bread and butter pickles
- 1 cup (250 mL) small whole or sliced dill pickles (more tart)

## Sweet Gooseberry

*See* GOOSEBERRY.

## Sweet Marjoram

*See* MARJORAM.

## Sweet Orange

*See* ORANGE, BLOOD.

## Sweet Pepper

*Pod vegetables that are called sweet to distinguish them from their hot cousins, the chile peppers. Sweet peppers include red pimientos, Cubanelles, yellow banana peppers, and the most common bell peppers. Freshly picked peppers keep fine at room temperature for several days. For longer storage, refrigerate in a perforated plastic bag.*

1 lb (500 g) bell peppers =
2 large = 2½ cups
(625 mL) chopped =
3 cups (750 mL) sliced

1 lb (500 g) Cubanelles,
banana peppers or
pimientos = 2½ cups
(625 mL) chopped

### If You Don't Have It
Substitute 1 cup (250 mL) chopped fresh sweet peppers with:
- 1 cup (250 mL) chopped fresh Anaheim peppers (spicier)
- 1 cup (250 mL) chopped fresh poblano peppers (spicier)
- ½ cup (125 mL) dried bell peppers

### Sweet Pepper Varieties
Choose 1 cup (250 mL) chopped fresh sweet peppers from these popular varieties:
- 1 cup (250 mL) chopped fresh bell peppers (bell-shaped; sweet and juicy with thick walls; green, red, yellow, orange, purple, or brown colors; the most popular sweet pepper variety)
- 1 cup (250 mL) chopped fresh, canned, or bottled pimiento (heart-shaped; sweet, juicy, and more complex flavor than bell peppers; red color; often used fresh to stuff olives or dried to make paprika)
- 1 cup (250 mL) chopped fresh banana peppers (long and banana-shaped; sweet and slightly less juicy than bell peppers; pale yellow color)
- 1 cup (250 mL) chopped fresh Cubanelle peppers (long and banana-shaped but more tapered than banana peppers; sweet and slightly less juicy but more complex flavor than bell peppers; yellow to red color)
- 1 cup (250 mL) chopped fresh bull's horn peppers (thin, curved shape; sweet and less juicy than bell peppers; green color)

*See also* BELL PEPPER; CHILE PEPPER; PIMIENTO.

## Sweet Potato

*"Sweet potatoes, potatoes, and yams are not related,"* writes produce authority Elizabeth Schneider. *Orange-fleshed sweet potatoes, such as the Beauregard, Jewel, and Garnet, are preferred only in North America and Europe. In Asia, where sweet potatoes are a major food crop, varieties are typically ivory in color with a medium sweet flavor and creamy texture. Yams, the name U.S. markets commonly misapply to sweet potatoes, are large white-fleshed bland tropical tubers.*

1 lb (500 g) fresh = 3 medium = 3½ to 4 cups (875 mL to 1 L) chopped or sliced

15½ oz (440 mL) can = 1½ to 1¾ cups (375 to 425 mL)

## Sweet Red Bean Paste

## Sweet Rice Flour

### If You Don't Have It
Substitute 1 cup (250 mL) chopped sweet potatoes with:
- 1 cup (250 mL) chopped sweet pumpkin
- 1 cup (250 mL) chopped butternut squash (more firm)
- 1 cup (250 mL) chopped buttercup squash (more firm)
- 1 cup (250 mL) chopped dumpling squash (lighter orange flesh)
- 1 cup (250 mL) chopped white or cushcush yams (white flesh; more starchy; less sweet)
- 1 cup (250 mL) chopped russet potatoes (white flesh; more starchy; less sweet)

### Sweet Potato Varieties
Choose 1 cup (250 mL) chopped sweet potatoes from these varieties:
- 1 cup (250 mL) chopped orange-flesh sweet potatoes (the most common variety; brown or reddish skin; orange flesh; soft and sweet flesh when cooked)
- 1 cup (250 mL) chopped white-flesh sweet potatoes (tan skin; cream-color flesh; soft and sweet flesh when cooked)
- 1 cup (250 mL) chopped boniato (red or brown skin; sometimes more lumpy in shape than orange-flesh sweet potatoes; white flesh; less sweet and more dry, starchy flesh than orange-flesh sweet potatoes)
- 1 cup (250 mL) chopped Asian, Japanese, or Korean sweet potatoes (reddish skin; cream-color flesh; slightly less sweet and slightly drier than orange-flesh sweet potatoes)

*See also* BONIATO; YAM.

*See* RED BEAN PASTE.

*See* RICE FLOUR, SWEET.

## Sweetsop

*Also known as sugar apple. This fruit of a tropical American tree is popular in Latin America, the West Indies, and India. The scaly, green skin protects the luscious custard-like fruit within. The seeds are poisonous and should not be eaten.*

1 sweetsop = 12 oz to 1 lb (375 to 500 g)

### If You Don't Have It
Substitute 1 lb (500 g) sweetsop with:
- 1 lb (500 g) cherimoya (larger)
- 1 lb (500 g) atemoya (hybrid of sweetsop and cherimoya)
- 1 lb (500 g) soursop (larger)

*See also* ATEMOYA; CHERIMOYA; SOURSOP.

## Sweet Spice

*See* MIXED SPICE.

## Swiss Chard

*See* CHARD.

## Swiss Cheese

*Also known as American-style Swiss cheese. Countless generic cheeses — pale yellow, nutty flavored, riddled with holes — attempt to recreate Switzerland's esteemed Emmental and Gruyère.*

### If You Don't Have It
Substitute 1 oz (30 g) Swiss cheese with:
- 1 oz (30 g) Emmental
- 1 oz (30 g) Gruyère
- 1 oz (30 g) Jarlsberg
- 1 oz (30 g) slice provolone (to replace slices of Swiss for sandwiches)

## Swiss Cheese Plant

*See* MONSTERA.

## Swordfish

*The "steak" of seafood, the firm, succulent, mild flesh of this large sea fish has become very popular with diners.*

### If You Don't Have It
Substitute 1 lb (500 g) swordfish with:
- 1 lb (500 g) marlin
- 1 lb (500 g) tuna
- 1 lb (500 g) shark
- 1 lb (500 g) mahi-mahi
- 1 lb (500 g) grouper
- 1 lb (500 g) halibut

## Syrup

*See* SPECIFIC TYPES.

## Szechuan Pepper

*Also known as flower pepper, Japanese pepper, sansho pepper, and Sichuan or Szechwan pepper. Dried berries of the prickly ash tree with a peppery taste, citrus aroma, and lingering fizzy sensation on the tongue. When ground, the dried berries are known as sansho in Japanese cooking. A common addition to Chinese five-spice powder and the Japanese spice blend called shichimi togarashi.*

## If You Don't Have It
Substitute 1 tbsp (15 mL) Szechuan peppercorns with:
- $2\frac{1}{2}$ tsp (12 mL) sansho (ground Japanese prickly ash berries)
- 2 tsp (10 mL) black peppercorns + 1 tsp (5 mL) finely grated lemon zest
- 1 tbsp (15 mL) salt-free lemon-pepper seasoning

## To Vary the Flavor
Substitute 1 tbsp (15 mL) Szechuan peppercorns with:
- 1 to $1\frac{1}{2}$ tbsp (15 to 22 mL) shichimi togarashi (spicier; combines Szechuan peppercorns, dried red chiles, sesame and/or poppy seeds, dried orange peel, and nori)

*See also* KINOME LEAF; PEPPERCORN.

# Tabasco to Tybo

## Tabasco®

See HOT PEPPER SAUCE; CHOOSING FRESH CHILES (PAGE 640).

## Tabil

*A blazing Tunisian spice paste that's similar to harissa but even hotter. Among its components are cilantro, coriander seeds, caraway seeds, garlic, sweet peppers, and chile peppers.*

### If You Don't Have It
Substitute 1 tbsp (15 mL) tabil with:
- 1 tbsp (15 mL) Homemade Tabil: Toast 1 tsp (5 mL) caraway seeds and 1 tsp (5 mL) coriander seeds in a dry skillet over medium heat until fragrant, about 2 minutes. Grind to a powder in a spice grinder, blender, or with a mortar and pestle (preferred method). If using a spice grinder, transfer to a blender or small food processor and add 1 large chopped garlic clove, 1 to 1½ tsp (5 to 7 mL) cayenne pepper, and 1 tbsp (15 mL) vegetable oil. Grind to a paste and add salt to taste. Makes about ¼ cup (60 mL).

### To Vary the Flavor
Substitute 1 tbsp (15 mL) tabil with:
- 1 tbsp (15 mL) harissa (a similar spice paste from Tunisia; adds paprika and cumin flavors)
- 1 tbsp (15 mL) chile paste
- 1 tbsp (15 mL) berbere
- 1 to 3 tsp (5 to 15 mL) hot sauce (less aromatic)

*See also* HARISSA.

## Taco Sauce

*A bottled condiment that is the Mexican-American adaptation of a traditional Mexican sauce made from roasted tomatoes, hot chiles, onion, garlic, and sometimes spices such as cumin.*

### If You Don't Have It
Substitute 1 cup (250 mL) taco sauce with:
- 1 cup (250 mL) enchilada sauce (often spicier)
- 1 cup (250 mL) tomato salsa (chunkier)
- 1 cup (250 mL) chili sauce

## Taco Seasoning Mix

*Americanized Mexican spice blend typically used to season ground beef for tacos.*

1¼ oz (35 g) pkg =
¼ cup (60 mL)

### If You Don't Have It
Substitute 1 tbsp (15 mL) taco seasoning mix with:
- 1 tbsp (15 mL) Homemade Taco Seasoning Mix: Combine 2 tsp (10 mL) pure chile powder, ¼ tsp (1 mL) dried oregano, ¼ tsp (1 mL) ground cumin, ⅛ tsp (0.5 mL) garlic powder, ⅛ tsp (0.5 mL) onion powder, and a pinch of cayenne pepper. Add salt to taste. Makes about 1 tablespoon (15 mL).
- 1 tbsp (15 mL) chili powder

## Taco Shell

*See* TORTILLA, CORN.

## Tahini

*Thick paste of ground sesame seeds that's essential in many Middle Eastern specialties, including baba ghanoush and hummus.*

### If You Don't Have It
Substitute 1 cup (250 mL) tahini with:
- 1 cup (250 mL) sesame seeds ground in a blender with enough untoasted sesame oil, peanut oil, or vegetable oil to create a smooth paste
- ¾ cup (175 mL) peanut butter, almond butter, or cashew butter + ¼ cup (60 mL) untoasted sesame oil (more peanutty flavor)
- 1 cup (250 mL) peanut butter, almond butter, or cashew butter

*See also* SESAME BUTTER; SESAME SEED.

## Tahitian Chestnut

*See* MAPE.

## Tahiti Lime

*See* LIME.

## Tailed Pepper

*See* CUBEB.

## Taiwan Bok Choy

*See* BOK CHOY.

## Taleggio

*A soft, buttery Stracchino-style Italian cheese made from cow's milk in the Taleggio Valley near Bergamo in the Lombardy region.*

### If You Don't Have It

Substitute 1 oz (30 g) Taleggio with:

- 1 oz (30 g) Robiola Lombardia
- 1 oz (30 g) Fontina
- 1 oz (30 g) Beaumont
- 1 oz (30 g) Reblochon

*See also* STRACCHINO.

## Tamari

*See* SOY SAUCE.

## Tamarillo

*Also known as tree tomato. A gorgeous tree fruit indigenous to South America, this pointed egg-shaped fruit has glossy red or golden skin and deep apricot flesh marked by whorls of purple seeds.*

1 lb (500 g) = 5 medium
= 2 cups (500 mL)
chopped

### If You Don't Have It

Substitute 1 lb (500 g) tamarillos with:

- 1 lb (500 g) pepinos
- 1 lb (500 g) babacos (less flavorful)
- 1 lb (500 g) papaya (less tart)
- 1 lb (500 g) plum tomatoes (less tart)

## Tamarind Concentrate

*Also known as asam jawa and tamarind paste. The tart dried pulp of the pods from an Asian shade tree. Tamarind concentrate is the most widely used form. From it, tamarind "juice" or water is made by soaking 1 cup (250 mL) of tamarind concentrate in 4 cups (1 L) hot water then straining and pressing on the solids to extract the juice.*

### If You Don't Have

Substitute 1 tbsp (15 mL) tamarind concentrate or paste with:

- 1½ tbsp (22 mL) mango powder or amchur (for acidity)
- 1 to 1½ tbsp (15 to 22 mL) lime or lemon juice (for acidity)
- 1 tbsp (15 mL) Worcestershire sauce (less acidic; adds other flavors, including vinegar, molasses, anchovies, onion, and garlic)

## Tandoori Paste

*Also known as tandoori coloring. A seasoning and coloring mixture of herbs, aromatics and spices that give tandoori chicken its distinctive reddish hue and spicy flavor. The paste is often mixed with yogurt to make a marinade for chicken prior to roasting in a tandoor.*

### If You Don't Have It
Substitute 1 cup (250 mL) tandoori paste with:
- 1 cup (250 mL) Homemade Tandoori Paste: Combine 8 to 10 finely minced garlic cloves, $\frac{1}{4}$ cup (60 mL) finely minced fresh ginger, 1 tbsp (15 mL) garam masala (see page 230), 1 tbsp (15 mL) paprika, 2 tsp (10 mL) ground coriander, 1 tsp (5 mL) ground cumin, $\frac{1}{2}$ to 1 tsp (2 to 5 mL) cayenne pepper, and 2 to 3 tbsp (30 to 45 mL) vegetable oil or enough to make a thick paste. If you like, stir in $\frac{1}{2}$ tsp (2 mL) yellow food coloring and $\frac{1}{4}$ tsp (1 mL) red food coloring for color.

## Tandoor Oven

*A style of clay oven found in countries from the Middle East to India. It is a large clay jar with an opening at the bottom for adding and removing fuel. Flatbreads are slapped onto the heated vertical walls of the tandoor, where they quickly bake by a combination of radiant heat and convection. As the heat subsides somewhat, casseroles and other dishes are placed in the oven to bake.*

### If You Don't Have It
Substitute a tandoor oven with:
- brick oven
- charcoal or gas grill (to help get a crisp crust, use a ceramic-type grill such as the Big Green Egg; or use any other grill and a pizza stone or unglazed quarry tiles to absorb moisture)

## Tangelo

*A cross between the pummelo and the tangerine, this citrus has juicy, tart-sweet flesh with few seeds. The skin is loose and size varies from that of a tangerine to a small grapefruit. The Minneola is the most common variety in the U.S.*

1 lb (500 g) = 4 medium = 2 cups (500 mL) sections

### If You Don't Have It
Substitute 1 tangelo with:
- 1 mandarin orange (typically orange flesh; sweet flavor with honey aromas)
- 1 Moro or blood orange (red flesh; sweet-tart, complex flavor)
- 1 navel orange (orange flesh; sweeter)
- 1 Rangpur or mandarin lime (sweet-tart; complex mandarin and lime aromas)
- 1 calamondin (orange flesh; acidic)
- $\frac{1}{2}$ to 1 grapefruit (typically pink or white flesh; sweetly tart flavor)

## Tangelo (cont'd)

## Tangelo Varieties

Choose 1 tangelo from these varieties:

- 1 Minneola (orange flesh; sweet-tart flavor with honey aromas)
- 1 Nocatee (white to yellow flesh; sweetly tart like grapefruit)
- 1 Sampson (yellow orange flesh; tart flavor; best for juicing or as an ornamental)

## Tangerine

*See* MANDARIN ORANGE.

## Tango Lettuce

*See* LEAF LETTUCE.

## Tapenade

*Intense paste of ripe olives, capers, anchovies, olive oil, lemon juice and seasonings is one of the glories of Provençal cooking. It enlivens raw vegetables, cooked fish or seafood, various meats, and other preparations.*

### If You Don't Have It

Substitute 1 cup (250 mL) tapenade with:

- 1 cup (250 mL) Homemade Tapenade: Put 1 cup (250 mL) pitted black olives (oil-cured, Niçoise, or Kalamata), 1 cup (250 mL) loosely packed fresh parsley leaves, 3 tbsp (45 mL) extra virgin olive oil, 2 tbsp (30 mL) drained capers, 5 anchovy fillets or 2½ tsp (12 mL) anchovy paste, 1 chopped garlic clove, 2 tsp (10 mL) chopped fresh thyme leaves, 2 tsp (10 mL) lemon juice, and ¼ tsp (1 mL) ground black pepper in a small food processor, blender or large mortar. Pulse or grind until finely minced but not completely puréed. Refrigerate for up to 1 month. Makes about 1½ cups (375 mL).

### To Vary the Flavor

Substitute 1 cup (250 mL) tapenade with:

- 1 cup (250 mL) basil pesto
- 1 cup (250 mL) sun-dried tomato paste
- 1 cup (250 mL) roasted red pepper pesto

## Tapioca

*From the roots of the cassava plant comes pearl tapioca, which looks like beads or pearls and is often used to make tapioca pudding. Granulated quick-cooking or instant tapioca is very convenient for thickening fruit pies to a clear gel. Ground tapioca flour or starch thickens pies, puddings, stews, and sauces without leaving behind any of the swollen beads of pearl tapioca.*

### If You Don't Have It

Substitute 1 tbsp (15 mL) quick-cooking tapioca (for thickening) with:

- 1½ to 2 tsp (7 to 10 mL) sweet rice flour (does not separate when frozen)
- 2 to 3 tsp (10 to 15 mL) tapioca flour or cassava flour (does not separate when frozen)
- 2 tbsp (30 mL) small pearl tapioca, soaked (or, to approximate tapioca flour, ground in a clean spice grinder or with a mortar and pestle; does not separate when frozen)
- 2 to 3 tsp (10 to 15 mL) gari (fermented, roasted, and ground cassava; best for thickening stews)
- 2 to 3 tsp (10 to 15 mL) sago flour or pearls
- 2 tsp (10 mL) arrowroot powder (separates when frozen)
- 1 heaping tbsp (15 mL) all-purpose flour (cook a few minutes after thickening to cook out raw flour taste; separates when frozen)

1 lb (500 g) pearl tapioca
= 2¾ cups (675 mL) =
7½ cups (1.875 L) cooked

1 lb (500 g) quick-
cooking tapioca =
3 cups (750 mL) =
7½ cups (1.875 L) cooked

- 1½ to 2 tsp (7 to 10 mL) cornstarch, potato starch, or rice starch (separates when frozen)

## Taratezak

*Peppery-tasting herb in the mustard family.*

1 oz (30 g) =
1 cup (250 mL)

### If You Don't Have It
Substitute 1 cup (250 mL) taratezak with:
- 1 cup (250 mL) watercress
- 1 cup (250 mL) arugula
- 1 cup (250 mL) radish greens
- 1 cup (250 mL) baby spinach leaves + a pinch of pepper
- 1 cup (250 mL) tender dandelion greens

## Tare

*See* PONZU; TERIYAKI SAUCE.

## Tarhonya

*See* EGG BARLEY.

## Taro

*Also known as dasheen and malanga. Small, dark, rough-skinned cormels of taro have a moist bland flesh. The larger barrel-shaped dark shaggy roots have dense flesh that tastes of coconut, potato, and chestnut. In Africa, taro (cocoyam or kontomire) leaves are also used to make a stew called kontomire. Mature spinach or Swiss chard can stand in for the sturdy leaves, which are also known as elephant ears.*

1 lb (500 g) = 3½ to
4 cups (875 mL to 1 L)
chopped or sliced =
2 cups (500 mL)

### If You Don't Have It
Substitute 1 lb (500 g) taro with:
- 1 lb (500 g) yautía or malanga
- 1 lb (500 g) cassava
- 1 lb (500 g) boniato
- 1 lb (500 g) potatoes
- 1 lb (500 g) parsnips

*See also* CALLALOO; YAUTÍA.

## Tarragon

*The distinctive anise flavor of this herb is most associated with the French kitchen in dishes where it flavors vinegar and seasons dishes such as* poulet à l'estragon *and* sauce béarnaise.

> 1 oz (30 g) fresh leaves = ⅔ cup (150 mL)
>
> 1 oz (30 g) dried leaves = 1 cup (250 mL)

### If You Don't Have It

Substitute 1 tbsp (15 mL) chopped fresh tarragon with:

- 1 tbsp (15 mL) chopped fresh cicely
- 1 tbsp (15 mL) chopped fresh chervil (milder anise flavor)
- 1 tbsp (15 mL) chopped fresh fennel leaves (milder anise flavor)
- 1 tbsp (15 mL) chopped fresh fines herbes (usually includes tarragon, chervil, chives, and parsley)
- 1 tbsp (15 mL) chopped fresh parsley
- 1 tsp (5 mL) dried tarragon (much less flavorful)
- 1 tbsp (15 mL) chopped fresh dill (particularly with chicken, fish, eggs, and cheese)

## Tartar Sauce

*See* MAYONNAISE.

## Tart Pan

*See* PAN SIZE EQUIVALENTS (PAGE 678).

## Tasajo

*Also known as carne seca (dried meat). The primary difference between jerky and Latin American and Spanish tasajo is that North American jerky may consist of highly processed chopped, formed meat. Tasajo consists of marinated strips of whole-muscle meat that are usually smoke-dried.*

### If You Don't Have It

Substitute 4 oz (125 g) tasajo with:

- 4 oz (125 g) tasso
- 4 oz (125 g) jerky
- 4 oz (125 g) pemmican
- 4 oz (125 g) biltong

*See also* JERKY; TASSO.

## Tasmanian Pepper

*Also known as mountain pepper. The plump, purple-black dried berries of this native Australian bush are soft enough to split by hand, releasing complex hibiscus and cardamom aromas. The pleasant, lingering pungency on the tongue is attributed to a flavor compound known as polygodial.*

### If You Don't Have It

Substitute 1 tsp (5 mL) Tasmanian pepper with:

- 1 tsp (5 mL) cubeb (adds mint and allspice aromas)
- 1 tsp (5 mL) Java long pepper (adds citrus aromas; more searing heat)
- 1 tsp (5 mL) grains of paradise (adds cardamom aromas)
- 1 tsp (5 mL) crushed selim kili pepper (adds eucalyptus and nutmeg aromas; slightly bitter)
- 1 tsp (5 mL) black peppercorns (less complex)

## Tasso

*Spiced and smoked piece of pork or beef used in Cajun cooking as a seasoning ingredient.*

### If You Don't Have It
Substitute 4 oz (125 g) tasso with:
- 4 oz (125 g) smoked ham, Canadian bacon, slab bacon, or hog jowl + 1 tbsp (15 mL) Cajun seasoning
- 4 oz (125 g) Cajun andouille
- 4 oz (125 g) spicy smoked sausage

## Tatsoi

*Also known as flat cabbage and rosette bok choy. Sometimes growing flat, sometimes in a bouquet, this variety of bok choy has celery-color stems and dark green puckered leaves. More strongly flavored than other bok choy. Young tiny leaves are good in salads. Larger leaves are wonderful in soups and stir-fries.*

1 lb (500 g) =
6 cups (1.5 L) chopped

### If You Don't Have It
Substitute 1 lb (500 g) tatsoi with:
- 1 lb (500 g) Shanghai or baby bok choy (for cooking; not fresh salads)
- 1 lb (500 g) mizuna
- 1 lb (500 g) baby spinach leaves
- 1 lb (500 g) arugula (more bitter and peppery, less cabbagey flavor)
- 1 lb (500 g) escarole
- 1 lb (500 g) broccoli raab (for cooking)
- 1 lb (500 g) mustard greens (for cooking)

*See also* BOK CHOY.

## Tautog

*See* BLACKFISH.

## Tayberry

*Named after the Tay River in Scotland, where this blackberry-raspberry hybrid was developed in the late 1970s, the tayberry tastes similar to a loganberry with a bit more zest.*

1 pint fresh =
2 cups (500 mL)

### If You Don't Have It
Substitute 1 cup (250 mL) tayberries with:
- 1 cup (250 mL) loganberries (hybrid of blackberries and raspberries; dark red color)
- 1 cup (250 mL) boysenberries (hybrid of blackberries, raspberries, and loganberries; reddish purple color)
- 1 cup (250 mL) olallieberries (hybrid of youngberries and loganberries; dark purple color; larger; sweeter)
- 1 cup (250 mL) blackberries (larger; darker purple color)
- 1 cup (250 mL) youngberry (larger; red color)
- 1 cup (250 mL) raspberries (sweeter; red color)

## Tea

*Across the globe, tea is consumed more than any other beverage except water. Various types of black tea have a single thing in common: they are all forms of the plant* Camellia sinensis, *the leaves of which are typically brewed for their astringent, slightly bitter flavor. Herbal teas, on the other hand, are prepared with various leaves, flowers, or fruits but never any from* Camellia sinensis. *Red tea usually refers to rooibos, a South African plant (red bush) whose ruddy needle-like leaves are brewed into a delicious amber herbal tea.*

---

1 lb (500 g) = 6½ cups (1.625 L) loose tea = 200 brewed cups (6 oz/175 g each)

1 teabag = 2 grams = 1½ to 2 tsp (7 to 10 mL) loose tea

---

### If You Don't Have It
Substitute 1 cup (250 mL) strong brewed tea with:
- 1 cup (250 mL) brewed coffee

### To Vary the Flavor
Substitute 1 cup (250 mL) strong brewed tea with:
- 1 cup (250 mL) brewed chai (spicier, sweeter, includes milk)

### For Better Health
Substitute 1 cup (250 mL) strong brewed tea with:
- 1 cup (250 mL) brewed decaffeinated tea
- 1 cup (250 mL) brewed rooibos or other herbal tea
- 1 cup (250 mL) brewed roasted chicory (caffeine-free)

*See also* SWITCHING TEA (PAGE 670).

## Tea Melon

*Also known as sweet cucumber. An Asian mini-melon resembling a tiny cucumber with yellow skin, crisp flesh, and a mildly sweet taste. It's most often found preserved in spiced honey or soy sauce in Asian markets, where it goes by the name of Chinese pickle, which is served as a condiment or incorporated into many Asian dishes.*

### If You Don't Have It
Substitute 1 lb (500 g) tea melon with:
- 1 lb (500 g) lemon cucumber (round, yellow skin, slightly sweet taste)
- 1 lb (500 g) small pickling or Kirby cucumbers (larger, bumpy, greener skin, less sweet)
- 1 lb (500 g) sweet gherkins (to replace Chinese pickle)

## Teewurst

*A smoky, spreadable sausage similar to liverwurst. Germans enjoy it spread on bread or crackers at teatime.*

### If You Don't Have It
Substitute 1 lb (500 g) Teewurst with:
- 1 lb (500 g) Braunschweiger
- 1 lb (500 g) liverwurst
- 1 lb (500 g) Mettwurst
- 1 lb (500 g) pâté

## Teff

*Also known as tef. The seeds of a North African species of lovegrass. Similar to millet but much tinier. Teff is high in protein, containing all eight essential amino acids. It is extensively cultivated in Ethiopia, India, and Australia.*

> 2 cups (500 mL) =
> 4 cups (1 L) cooked

### If You Don't Have It
Substitute 1 cup (250 mL) teff with:
- 1 cup (250 mL) quinoa
- 1 cup (250 mL) millet
- 1 cup (250 mL) couscous, especially whole wheat (cooks more quickly)
- 1 cup (250 mL) bulgur
- 1 cup (250 mL) cracked wheat (takes longer to cook)
- 1 cup (250 mL) brown rice (takes longer to cook)
- 1 cup (250 mL) kasha (roasted buckwheat groats; takes longer to cook)

## Teff Flour

*See* CHOOSING AMONG WHOLE-GRAIN AND ALTERNATIVE FLOURS (PAGE 648).

## Tejfel

*See* SMETANA.

## Teleme

*A soft and tangy cow's milk cheese associated with Northern California. As it ages, the flavor becomes more assertive and the texture more runny.*

### If You Don't Have It
Substitute 1 oz (30 g) Teleme with:
- 1 oz (30 g) Touloumi (made with goat's milk)
- 1 oz (30 g) Monterey Jack

*See also* TOULOUMI.

## Tempeh

*Also known as tempe. Made from fermented cooked soybeans, this meat replacement has a mild mushroom-like aroma, earthy flavor, and toothsome texture. Because it holds its shape well and absorbs seasonings, it is used as the base for numerous vegetarian prepared foods.*

### If You Don't Have It
Substitute 1 lb (500 g) tempeh with:
- 1 lb (500 g) firm tofu, drained and pressed (softer and moister; more bland)
- 1 lb (500 g) seitan (chewier; more bland)
- 1 lb (500 g) vegetarian meat substitutes (available in the frozen section of most grocery stores)
- 1 cup (250 mL) textured vegetable protein, reconstituted in 1½ to 2 cups (375 to 500 mL) vegetable stock (to replace crumbled tempeh; less chewy; less flavorful)

## Temperature

*See* TEMPERATURE EQUIVALENTS (PAGE 681).

## Temple Orange

*See* MANDARIN ORANGE.

## Tempura Oil

*A combination of safflower oil and untoasted sesame oil traditionally used in Japan for deep-frying pieces of batter-dipped vegetables and fish.*

### If You Don't Have It
Substitute 1 cup (250 mL) tempura oil with:
- ½ cup (125 mL) safflower or soybean oil + ½ cup (125 mL) untoasted sesame oil
- 1 cup (250 mL) safflower oil

## Tenderizer

*See* MEAT TENDERIZER, POWDERED.

## Tennessee Whiskey

*See* WHISKEY.

## Tentsuyu

*Japanese dipping sauce that cools and flavors foods hot from the fryer such as tempura. Typically, a mixture of mirin, dashi, soy sauce, and sugar.*

### If You Don't Have It
Substitute 1 cup (250 mL) tentsuyu with:
- 1 cup (250 mL) Homemade Tentsuyu: Combine 1 cup (250 mL) heated dashi or reconstituted dashi-no-moto, ¼ cup (60 mL) tamari or soy sauce, 2 tbsp (30 mL) mirin (or 1 to 2 tsp/5 to 10 mL granulated sugar plus 2 tbsp/25 mL sake), 2 tbsp (30 mL) sake or dry vermouth or sherry, and 1 to 2 tsp (5 to 10 mL) freshly grated ginger. Makes about 1½ cups (375 mL).
- 1 cup (250 mL) teriyaki sauce
- 1 cup (250 mL) soy sauce

## Tepín Chile

*See* CHOOSING DRIED CHILES (PAGE 642); CHOOSING FRESH CHILES (PAGE 640).

## Tequila

*A distinctive Mexican liquor produced by fermenting and distilling the sweet sap of the blue agave cactus. Not to be confused with mezcal, a very similar liquor, which may be made from any mixture of agave species, anywhere in Mexico. By law, tequila can only be made in the states*

### If You Don't Have It
Substitute 2 tbsp (30 mL) tequila with:
- 2 tbsp (30 mL) pulque (thicker; milky-white; lower in alcohol)
- 2 tbsp (30 mL) vodka (less flavorful)
- 2 tbsp (30 mL) light rum
- 2 tbsp (30 mL) grappa

### Tequila Varieties
Choose 2 tbsp (30 mL) tequila from these varieties:
- 2 tbsp (30 mL) tequila blanco, white, or silver tequila (colorless; unaged or aged 1 to 2 months; fiery and peppery with gasoline aromas in lesser-quality versions; often used for mixed drinks)

of Guanajuato, Jalisco, Michoacan, Mayarit, and Tamaulipas and must contain 51% blue agave (the remainder is mostly sugarcane). Tequilas labeled 100% blue agave are often of better quality. Four categories exist. Blanco, also known as white, plata, or silver, captures the herbaceous character of the newly distilled liquor. Joven abocado, also known as gold, is a colored and flavored blanco. Resposado may also be colored and flavored but must be aged in wood for between 2 and 12 months, a process that contributes hints of vanilla and spice. Añejo is aged for 1 to 3 years to create a tequila complex and elegant enough for sipping.

- 2 tbsp (30 mL) tequila joven abocado or gold tequila (gold color; silver tequila with added coloring and flavoring; often used for mixed drinks)
- 2 tbsp (30 mL) tequila reposado or rested tequila (pale straw to gold color; aged 2 to 12 months; spirited yet softer, mellowed flavor, often with aromas of vanilla; may contain added coloring and flavoring; good for sipping or uncomplicated mixed drinks such as margaritas)
- 2 tbsp (30 mL) añejo or aged tequila (gold to deep amber color; aged at least 1 year but preferably longer; smooth, complex flavor often with hints of vanilla and mild oak; best for sipping)
- 2 tbsp (30 mL) mezcal (clear or pale straw and potent; harsh, smoky flavor that's often sweetened or softened with fruits, herbs, or nuts; made from any mixture of agave, anywhere in Mexico; often marketed with a worm in the bottle; often used for mixed drinks or shots)

## Terasi

*See* SHRIMP PASTE.

## Teriyaki Sauce

*Also known as tare and yakitori sauce. A Japanese mixture of sweetened soy sauce and rice wine that serves as an all-purpose marinade, basting sauce, and dipping sauce, especially for yakitori (literally, grilled chicken). Basic tare (Japanese for sauce) also flavors soups and other dishes.*

### If You Don't Have It
Substitute ½ cup (125 mL) teriyaki sauce with:
- ½ cup (125 mL) Homemade Basic Tare or Teriyaki Sauce: In a medium saucepan, combine ⅔ cup (150 mL) soy sauce (preferably tamari), ⅔ cup (150 mL) mirin, ⅓ cup (75 mL) sake, 2½ tbsp (37 mL) granulated sugar or 2 tbsp (30 mL) honey. For teriyaki sauce, add 1 tbsp (15 mL) minced fresh ginger and 2 tsp (10 mL) minced fresh garlic. Simmer over medium heat until slightly thickened, 5 minutes. Makes about 1½ cups (375 mL).
- ⅓ cup (75 mL) soy sauce + 3 tbsp (45 mL) rice vinegar + 2 to 3 tsp (10 to 15 mL) sugar or honey (less complex flavor)

### To Vary the Flavor
Substitute ½ cup (125 mL) teriyaki sauce with:
- ½ cup (125 mL) ponzu sauce (adds citrus, dried fish, and seaweed flavors)
- ½ cup (125 mL) kecap (thicker, sweeter, less complex flavor)
- ½ cup (125 mL) Maggi Seasoning (darker, more assertive, more complex flavor)

## Testerbranntwein

*See* GRAPPA.

## Tête de Moine

*Semifirm Swiss raw cow's milk cheese that literally means "monk's head" and is older that the Confederation of Switzerland itself. Rich, summer milk creates a sumptuous pale caramel cheese that becomes so pungent that it is traditionally shaved into paper-thin rosettes made with a special cheese scraper known as a girolle.*

### If You Don't Have It
Substitute 1 oz (30 g) Tête de Moine with:
- 1 oz (30 g) French Girollin
- 1 oz (30 g) Comte
- 1 oz (30 g) aged Appenzeller

*See also* GIROLLE.

## Tetragonia

*See* NEW ZEALAND SPINACH.

## Texmati Rice

*See* VARIETIES OF RICE (PAGE 664).

## Textured Vegetable Protein

*Also known as TVP, textured soy protein (TSP), and vegetable protein. A neutrally flavored dried granular ingredient produced from refined soybean meal. It's used as a ground meat extender in many processed foods. Vegetarians often cook it as a meat substitute. It's most commonly available as granules but also comes in chunks and flakes. It's sold in natural food stores.*

### If You Don't Have It
Substitute 1 cup (250 mL) reconstituted textured vegetable protein granules with:
- 1 lb (500 g) vegetarian ground beef or crumbles (often a mix of textured vegetable protein, tofu, and seitan; more flavorful)
- 1 lb (500 g) firm tofu, frozen, thawed, and crumbled with a few quick pulses in a food processor (less chewy; less flavorful)
- 1 lb (500 g) tempeh (stronger flavor)
- 1 lb (500 g) prepared seitan (more chewy)
- 1 lb (500 g) ground beef, pork, turkey, or chicken

## Thai Basil

*See* BASIL.

## Thai Chile

*See* CHOOSING FRESH CHILES (PAGE 640).

## Thai Fish Sauce

*See* FISH SAUCE.

## Thai Ginger

*See* GALANGAL.

## Thai Sweet Black Soy Sauce

*See* SOY SAUCE.

## The Laughing Cow

*See* LA VACHE QUI RIT.

## Thermometer

*Meat thermometers take the guesswork out of knowing when roasts, poultry, and even bread are cooked through but not overdone. The older style thermometer is inserted into the food at the beginning of the cooking time and remains throughout the cooking process. More recent advancements have brought us instant-reading and digital thermometers, which only need to be inserted when checking the temperature.*

### If You Don't Have It

Substitute a meat thermometer with:
- The touch test (for steaks): Press your fingertip into the meat. If it's soft, the meat is most likely medium-rare (about 145°F/63°C); if it springs back a bit, the meat is most likely medium (about 160°F/71°C); if it is stiff, the meat is most likely well-done (about 165°F/74°C). These are inexact doneness tests; if the quality or cleanliness of your meat is questionable, use a thermometer to be sure the meat is properly cooked.

*See also* TEMPERATURE EQUIVALENTS (PAGE 681).

## Thimbleberry

*See* RASPBERRY.

## Thompson Grape

*See* GRAPE, TABLE; RAISIN.

## Thuringer

*A group of semidry summer sausages often made with beef, ham, pork fat, and mild spices such as coriander.*

### If You Don't Have It

Substitute 1 lb (500 g) Thuringer with:
- 1 lb (500 g) Landjäger
- 1 lb (500 g) Lebanon bologna
- 1 lb (500 g) other semidry or summer sausage
- 1 lb (500 g) salami or other dry sausage
- 1 lb (500 g) pepperoni

*See also* CERVELAT; SUMMER SAUSAGE.

## Thyme

*"Sun loving, tiny leafed but tough, thyme tastes and smells warm, earthy and flowery. Use it in every kind of long-simmered and red-wine dish, with rabbit, veal and chicken in all their tomatoey forms, in a bouquet garni and marinades and — instead of rosemary — with lamb."* — The Cook Book by Terence and Caroline Conran.

1 oz (30 g) fresh leaves = ⅔ cup (150 mL)

1 oz (30 g) dried leaves = ½ cup (125 mL)

### If You Don't Have It

Substitute 1 tbsp (15 mL) fresh thyme leaves with:
- ¾ to 1 tsp (3 to 5 mL) dried thyme
- 1 tbsp (15 mL) chopped fresh marjoram
- 1 tbsp (15 mL) chopped fresh oregano
- 1 tbsp (15 mL) chopped fresh basil
- 1 tbsp (15 mL) chopped fresh summer savory
- 1 to 2 tsp (5 to 10 mL) chopped fresh sage
- 2 to 3 tsp (10 to 15 mL) chopped fresh rosemary (more pine-like resinous aromas)
- 1 tsp (5 mL) dried Italian seasoning (usually combines thyme, oregano, and basil)
- 1 tsp (5 mL) dried poultry seasoning (usually combines dried thyme, sage, and marjoram)
- 1 tsp (5 mL) Herbes de Provence (often combines thyme, savory, marjoram, lavender, rosemary, fennel seeds, and bay leaves)
- 2 tsp (10 mL) dried ajwain (a southern Indian spice with aromas similar to thyme)

### Thyme Varieties

Choose 1 tbsp (15 mL) fresh thyme leaves from these varieties:
- 1 tbsp (15 mL) fresh garden thyme leaves (small, gray-green leaves with a warming, citrus-like sharpness; includes narrow-leafed French thyme and broad-leafed English thyme)
- 1 tbsp (15 mL) fresh lemon thyme leaves (hybrid of garden thyme and wild thyme; small green leaves; less pungent and more lemony aroma than garden thyme)

## Tia Maria

*See* COFFEE LIQUEUR.

## Tiger Lily Bud

*See* LILY BUD.

## Tiger Nut

*See* CHUFA.

## Tilapia

*Also known as St. Peter's fish. A mild and versatile white-fleshed fish originating in East Africa. It's now a major aqua-cultured specimen.*

### If You Don't Have It

Substitute 1 lb (500 g) tilapia with:
- 1 lb (500 g) porgy
- 1 lb (500 g) black sea bass
- 1 lb (500 g) red snapper
- 1 lb (500 g) orange roughy
- 1 lb (500 g) ocean perch
- 1 lb (500 g) sole
- 1 lb (500 g) flounder

## Ti Leaf

*The shiny green leaves of a tropical Asian/Polynesian plant are used as a pot herb or food wrapper.*

### If You Don't Have It
Substitute ti leaves (as a food wrapper) with:
- banana leaves (adds mild herby-green aroma)
- corn husks (much smaller; adds mild corn aroma)
- hoja santa leaves (much smaller; adds aromas of root beer and fennel)
- parchment paper (no flavor)
- aluminum foil (no flavor; reduce cooking time slightly)

## Tilefish

*Although he tastes good, it's the North Atlantic tilefish's looks that get him noticed. He is one of the most brilliantly colored fish found outside of the tropics. Various body parts are colored bluish green, pinkish purple, yellow, rose, white, red, and spotted yellow.*

### If You Don't Have It
Substitute 1 lb (500 g) tilefish with:
- 1 lb (500 g) blackfish
- 1 lb (500 g) croaker
- 1 lb (500 g) black sea bass
- 1 lb (500 g) halibut
- 1 lb (500 g) grouper
- 1 lb (500 g) red snapper
- 1 lb (500 g) turbot
- 1 lb (500 g) weakfish
- 1 lb (500 g) cod
- 1 lb (500 g) haddock

## Tilsit

*Also known as tilsiter. In the mid-1800s, Dutch settlers in East Prussia had their Gouda cheese hijacked by local molds, yeast, and bacteria. The resulting semisoft, tangy Tilsit cheese is ivory or butter colored with tiny holes.*

> 1 lb (500 g) = 4 cups
> (1 L) shredded

### If You Don't Have It
Substitute 1 oz (30 g) Tilsit with:
- 1 oz (30 g) Havarti (milder)
- 1 oz (30 g) Esrom (stronger)
- 1 oz (30 g) Fontina (more nutty)
- 1 oz (30 g) Monterey Jack
- 1 oz (30 g) brick cheese

## Timbale

*Named after its drum shape, this baking mold is usually high-sided and tapered at the bottom.*

### If You Don't Have It
Substitute a timbale with:
- custard cup
- deep muffin cup
- tall-sided ramekin

## Tipo 00 Flour

*See* FLOUR, ALL-PURPOSE.

## Tiramisù Liqueur

*See* CHOCOLATE LIQUEUR; COFFEE LIQUEUR.

## Tirmis

*See* LUPINI BEAN.

## Toasted Sesame Oil

*See* SESAME OIL, TOASTED; SUBSTITUTING OILS (PAGE 658).

## Tocino

*See* PANCETTA.

## Tofu

*Also known as bean curd and soybean curd. Think of tofu as "cheese" made from "milk" extracted from cooked soybeans instead of cows. Those who love to hate tofu complain that it is bland, but that is one of tofu's strengths. It absorbs flavors beautifully and adapts to numerous ethnic seasonings. It's processed into a variety of textures — silken, soft, firm and extra-firm. It can be found in supermarkets, water-packed in sealed containers, vacuum-packed without water, aseptically packaged, or freeze-dried. In some Asian markets, it is displayed in tubs of water.*

### If You Don't Have It

Substitute 1 lb (500 g) tofu with:

- 1 lb (500 g) tempeh (stronger flavor)
- 1 lb (500 g) prepared seitan (more chewy)
- 1 cup (250 mL) reconstituted textured vegetable protein granules (to replace crumbled tofu)
- 1 lb (500 g) panir (to replace cubed tofu in savory dishes)
- 1 lb (500 g) vegetarian beef, pork, or chicken products (often a mix of textured vegetable protein, tofu, and seitan; more flavorful; available in the frozen section of most grocery stores)
- 1 lb (500 g) beef, pork, turkey, or chicken

### Tofu Varieties

Choose 1 lb (500 g) tofu from these varieties:

- 1 lb (500 g) extra-firm tofu (sold in tubs of water; very firm texture; holds its shape well; good for marinating, grilling, broiling, baking, sautéing, and stir-frying)
- 1 lb (500 g) firm tofu (sold in tubs of water; firm texture; holds its shape fairly well; good for marinating, grilling, broiling, baking, sautéing, and stir-frying; can be mashed and used like ricotta cheese)
- 1 lb (500 g) soft tofu (sold in tubs of water; soft texture; does not hold its shape well; good for baking, sautéing, and stir-frying; can be mashed and used like ricotta cheese)
- 1 lb (500 g) silken tofu (often sold in small aseptic boxes; available in soft and firm varieties; lower in fat than other varieties; very soft, almost creamy texture; does not hold its shape well; best for soups or puréed and used like sour cream, yogurt, or mayonnaise)
- 1 lb (500 g) marinated or flavored tofu (firm or extra-firm tofu marinated with Chinese five-spice powder or other flavors)
- 1 lb (500 g) baked tofu (firm or extra-firm tofu that is baked and usually flavored)
- 1 lb (500 g) smoked tofu (firmer texture; smoke flavor; excellent for grilling)
- 1 lb (500 g) deep-fried tofu or abura-age (firmer texture; chewy surface; excellent for stir-frying)

- 1 lb (500 g) extra-firm tofu, frozen, thawed, and crumbled with a few quick pulses in a food processor (do this at home to make tofu more firm, chewy, and absorbent)
- 1 lb (500 g) pressed tofu (do this at home to make tofu more firm and chewy; cut the block of tofu into slabs, lay the slabs flat and put a heavy weight on top for 20 minutes to press out excess liquid)

### For Better Health
Substitute 1 lb (500 g) tofu with:
- 1 lb (500 g) reduced-fat tofu

*See also* ABURA-AGE; ATSU-AGE.

---

### Tofu Ice Cream

*See* SOY ICE CREAM.

---

### Tofu Sour Cream

*See* SOY SOUR CREAM.

---

### Togarashi

*See* CHOOSING DRIED CHILES (PAGE 642); CHOOSING FRESH CHILES (PAGE 640).

---

### Tokay Grape

*See* GRAPE, TABLE.

---

### Tomatillo

*Also known as Mexican green or husk tomato. Tomatillo is not a green tomato, but it does resemble a small green tomato, if a small green tomato had a papery husk surrounding it. Widely used in Mexican and Guatemalan cooking, tomatillos must be husked and cooked briefly to bring out their full, tart flavor in "green" dishes and sauces.*

> 1 lb (500 g) = 12 to 16 medium tomatillos = 2½ to 3 cups (625 to 750 mL) chopped

### If You Don't Have It
Substitute 1 lb (500 g) tomatillos with:
- 1 lb (500 g) green or red cherry tomatoes (add lime or lemon juice to help mirror the aroma of tomatillos)
- 1 lb (500 g) cape gooseberries (more tart)

## Tomato

*"The total number of dishes around the world in which tomato is the or a main ingredient must amount to thousands,"* writes Alan Davidson in The Oxford Companion to Food. *"For a foodstuff which has come up to the front from almost nowhere in under two centuries, the tomato has proved to have astonishingly vigorous penetrative qualities, so that it is as close to being ubiquitous in the kitchens of the world as any plant food."*

1 lb (500 g) = 3 to
4 medium tomatoes =
8 plum = 25 cherry =
2 cups (500 mL)
chopped

### If You Don't Have It

Substitute 1 lb (500 g) fresh tomatoes with:

- 1½ cups (375 mL) canned whole tomatoes (for cooking, not salads)
- 6 to 8 sun-dried tomato halves, reconstituted in hot water (more chewy; more intense tomato flavor; less watery; for cooking, not salads)
- 3 tbsp (45 mL) tomato paste (to replace cooked tomatoes; more concentrated tomato flavor; add liquid as necessary)
- 1 lb (500 g) tomatillos (slightly more tart; adds apple and citrus aromas; for cooking or salads)
- 1 lb (500 g) red bell peppers + 1 tsp (5 mL) lemon juice (to replace cooked-down tomatoes for sauce; roast, peel, and seed red bell peppers or use jarred roasted red peppers then purée the pepper flesh and add a splash of lemon juice)

### Tomato Varieties

Choose 1 lb (500 g) fresh tomatoes from these varieties:

- 1 lb (500 g) globe or slicing tomatoes (familiar, medium, round tomatoes such as red Early Boy and Early Girl; heirloom varieties may be red, pink, purple, orange, yellow, or green; yellow tomatoes tend to be sweeter and less acidic than red varieties; tender, juicy flesh that's good both raw and cooked)
- 1 lb (500 g) beefsteak tomatoes (similar to globe tomatoes, but larger; includes many heirloom varieties such as the red Mortgage Lifter)
- 1 lb (500 g) plum or Roma tomatoes (oblong, red or yellow tomatoes with thick, dry, flesh; best for sauces or preparations where you don't want a lot of juice)
- 1 lb (500 g) grape tomatoes (baby plum tomatoes; best for snacking and salads)
- 1 lb (500 g) cherry, pear, or currant tomatoes (round or teardrop shaped, red or yellow tomatoes ranging in diameter from the tiny, ½-inch (1 cm) currants to larger 1-inch (2.5 cm) cherries; sweet, juicy flesh; best for snacking, salads, or light sautéing)
- 1 lb (500 g) green tomatoes (unripe tomatoes; firm, slightly acidic flesh; best for frying, broiling, and salsas, chutneys, and relishes)

*See also* SUN-DRIED TOMATO; TOMATO JUICE; TOMATO PASTE; TOMATO PURÉE; TOMATO SAUCE; TOMATO SOUP.

## Tomato Juice

*The official state beverage of Ohio and solace to Bloody Mary lovers everywhere who can rationalize that*

### If You Don't Have It

Substitute 1 cup (250 mL) tomato juice with:

- ½ cup (125 mL) tomato purée or tomato sauce + ½ cup (125 mL) water
- ¼ cup (60 mL) tomato paste + ¾ cup (175 mL) water

*at least they're imbibing vitamin A, lycopene, and other health-giving compounds with their vodka.*

## To Vary the Flavor
Substitute 1 cup (250 mL) tomato juice with:
- 1 cup (250 mL) V8® juice (more complex flavor)
- 1 cup (250 mL) carrot juice (sweeter; orange color)

## Tomato Paste

*If you typically use only small amounts of tomato paste to thicken a sauce, look for it packed in a squeezable tube. Because the tube is virtually air tight, the paste can be refrigerated for months without spoiling.*

### If You Don't Have It
Substitute 1 tbsp (15 mL) tomato paste with:
- 2 to 3 tbsp (30 to 45 mL) tomato purée or tomato sauce (reduce liquid in recipe by 2 to 3 tbsp/30 to 45 mL; or boil tomato purée or sauce until reduced to 1 tbsp/15 mL)

## Tomato Purée

*Briefly cooked tomatoes puréed through a food mill to remove the skin and seeds.*

> 12 cups (3 L) tomato purée = 10 lbs (5 kg) plum tomatoes

### If You Don't Have It
Substitute 1 cup (250 mL) tomato purée with:
- ⅓ cup (75 mL) tomato paste + ⅔ cup (150 mL) water
- 1 cup (250 mL) tomato sauce (slightly thicker; adds other seasonings)

*See also* FOOD MILL.

## Tomato Sauce

*Sauce based on chunky or puréed tomatoes with the addition of aromatics and other seasonings. Vodka is a "secret" ingredient in many chefs' tomato sauces.*

### If You Don't Have It
Substitute 1 cup (250 mL) tomato sauce with:
- ½ cup (125 mL) tomato paste + ½ cup (125 mL) water
- 1 cup (250 mL) seasoned tomato purée
- 1 cup (250 mL) canned stewed tomatoes, blended in a blender until smooth

## Tomato Soup

*Soulmate of the grilled cheese sandwich, icon to pop artist Andy Warhol, and tummy warmer to generations of kids. Two factions square off in the preparation of condensed tomato soup: the milk people and the water people.*

### If You Don't Have It
Substitute 1 (10¾ oz/305 g) can tomato soup with:
- 1 cup (250 mL) tomato sauce + ¼ cup (60 mL) water or milk

## Tomme Crayeuse

*Semisoft, raw cow's milk cheese from Savoie in the French Alps. It was created by French affineur Max Schmidhauser in the late 1990s as a Tomme de Savoie with chutzpah. The dank, dimpled moldy golden rind should be cut away so you can revel in the rich, mushroomy cheese and its pleasant hints of citrus acidity. Well-aged Tomme Crayeuse oozes at the edge and is slightly chalky at the center (crayeuse means chalky in French).*

### If You Don't Have It
Substitute 1 oz (30 g) Tomme Crayeuse with:
- 1 oz (30 g) Tomme de Savoie (milder, less rich)
- 1 oz (30 g) Saint Nectaire
- 1 oz (30 g) Beaumont

## Tomme de Savoie

*From the French Alps, a semifirm, disc-shaped, pale cow's milk cheese that's mild, a bit salty, and fruity with a hint of grass. The rind is thick and gray brown.*

### If You Don't Have It
Substitute 1 oz (30 g) Tomme de Savoie with:
- 1 oz (30 g) Saint Nectaire
- 1 oz (30 g) Beaumont
- 1 oz (30 g) Reblochon

## Tongue Sausage

*Pork, lamb, veal, or beef tongue pieces that have been cooked, pressed into loaves, jellied, and, sometimes, smoked.*

### If You Don't Have It
Substitute 1 lb (500 g) tongue sausage with:
- 1 lb (500 g) Zungenwurst (tongue blood sausage)

## Tonic Water

*Also known as quinine water. A beverage mixer, this carbonated water gets its bitter note from quinine, an alkaloid derived from the bark of the evergreen cinchona tree. Tonic water is also sweetened and flavored with fruit extracts.*

### If You Don't Have It
Substitute 2 tbsp (30 mL) tonic water with:
- 2 tbsp (30 mL) ginger ale (makes an interesting gin and tonic)
- 2 tbsp (30 mL) lemon-lime soda

### For Better Health
Substitute 2 tbsp (30 mL) tonic water with:
- 2 tbsp (30 mL) low-calorie tonic water

## Tonka Bean

*Resembling raisins, these wrinkled black seeds from a leguminous tree native to Guyana are banned from U.S. import by the Federal Drug Administration. The seeds contain coumarin, a compound used to make many popular blood-thinning medications. While large doses of coumarin can be lethal, many cooks use a few tonka beans like vanilla beans here and there in recipes without any ill effects. Tonka beans exude tropical aromas of vanilla, almond, and freshly mown hay, the latter of which comes from the coumarin.*

### If You Don't Have It
Substitute 1 tonka bean with:
- 1 (3 inch/7.5 cm) length of vanilla bean + ½ tsp (2 mL) mahlab
- 1 tsp (5 mL) vanilla extract + ½ tsp (2 mL) almond extract

## Torch Ginger

*See* GINGER, WILD BUD.

## Tortilla Chips

*Deep-fried or baked tortilla wedges come packaged in a variety of seasoning styles. Usually served with salsa, guacamole, or other dips.*

### If You Don't Have It
Substitute 1 lb (500 g) tortilla chips with:
- 1 lb (500 g) Homemade Tortilla Chips: Cut a stack of 5 corn tortillas into 8 wedges like a pizza to make 40 wedges. Spread in a single layer on a large baking sheet (or two small ones) and coat generously with cooking spray. Sprinkle with ¼ to ½ tsp (1 to 2 mL) salt and ¼ to ½ tsp (1 to 2 mL) pure chile powder or other seasonings if you like. Bake at 375°F (190°C) until crisp, about 10 minutes. Makes 40 chips (about 4 oz/125 g).

### To Vary the Flavor
Substitute 1 lb (500 g) tortilla chips with:
- 1 lb (500 g) corn chips
- 1 lb (500 g) potato chips
- 1 lb (500 g) sweet potato or other vegetable chips
- 1 lb (500 g) bagel chips

### For Better Health
Substitute 1 lb (500 g) tortilla chips with:
- 1 lb (500 g) pretzels

## Tortilla, Corn

*The staff of daily life for Mexicans, these flavorful corn flatbreads are used as wrappers, scoops for eggs and beans, and thickeners for soups and stews. For a change of texture, they are fried and then folded so they harden in a U-shape to make taco "shells."*

### If You Don't Have It

Substitute 8 corn tortillas with:

- 8 Homemade Corn Tortillas: Mix 1 cup (250 mL) minus 2 tbsp (30 mL) masa harina with ½ cup (125 mL) hot water and set aside to reconstitute for 30 minutes. Or use 8 oz (250 g) of fresh masa. Gently work cold water into the dough, teaspoon by teaspoon until it is soft and pliable but not sticky. Shape the dough into 7 to 8 balls and cover with plastic wrap. Working with 1 ball at a time and a tortilla press lined with plastic wrap on the top and bottom, press each ball to a thin circle about 6 inches (15 cm) in diameter and no more than ⅛-inch (3 mm) thick. Peel off the top layer of plastic and flip the tortilla into your hand. Peel off the remaining layer of plastic and quickly flip the tortilla onto a dry griddle or heavy skillet preheated to medium. Cook until lightly browned, about 30 seconds per side. Repeat with remaining dough. Makes 7 to 8 tortillas.

### To Vary the Flavor

Substitute 8 corn tortillas with:

- 8 arepas (Venezuelan corn flatbread; thicker and softer)
- 8 chalupas (thicker; softer)
- 8 gorditas (thicker; softer)
- 8 flour tortillas (slightly thinner; softer)

*See also* MASA; MASA HARINA.

## Tortilla, Flour

*Griddle flatbreads made from all-purpose flour and, traditionally, lard or shortening. Most common in the northern states of Mexico.*

### If You Don't Have It

Substitute 8 flour tortillas with:

- 8 corn tortillas (firmer; can be more brittle)
- 8 pieces of soft lavash (chewier)
- 8 chapati (chewier)
- 8 naan (puffier)
- 8 rounds of pita bread (puffier)

## Tortoise

*See* TURTLE.

## Touloumi

*Semisoft, tart goat cheese made on the island of Crete. Greek immigrants in Northern California started making a similar cheese using cow's milk, and it came to be called Teleme.*

### If You Don't Have It

Substitute 1 oz (30 g) Touloumi with:

- 1 oz (30 g) Teleme (made with cow's milk)
- 1 oz (30 g) Monterey Jack

*See also* TELEME.

## Toulouse

*French pork sausage flavored with garlic, wine, and other seasonings. It contributes character to cassoulet and other braises.*

### If You Don't Have It
Substitute 1 lb (500 g) Toulouse with:
- 1 lb (500 g) French andouillette (made with tripe)
- 1 lb (500 g) kielbasa
- 1 lb (500 g) Spanish chorizo
- 1 lb (500 g) Portuguese chouriço or linguiça
- 1 lb (500 g) other mild sausage such Italian sweet sausage

## Touristenwurst

*Ring-shaped, pliable salami made of finely chopped pork and beef.*

### If You Don't Have It
Substitute 1 lb (500 g) touristenwurst with:
- 1 lb (500 g) ring bologna
- 1 lb (500 g) Lebanon bologna (smoked)
- 1 lb (500 g) landjäger (smoked; flattened)
- 1 lb (500 g) Thuringer (spiced)

## Toute-épice
*See* ALLSPICE.

## Tra
*See* CATFISH.

## Trassi
*See* SHRIMP PASTE.

## Treacle

*Also known as black or dark treacle. The British term for the syrup left over after sugar is refined. Very close to molasses with a slightly bitter note.*

### If You Don't Have It
Substitute 1 cup (250 mL) dark treacle with:
- 1 cup (250 mL) molasses (especially blackstrap molasses)
- 1 cup (250 mL) dark corn syrup (slightly thinner; sweeter)
- 1 cup (250 mL) golden syrup or light treacle (lighter color and flavor; less bitter)

*See also* GOLDEN SYRUP.

## Treacle, Light
*See* GOLDEN SYRUP.

## Tree Ear
*See* SHUFFLING MUSHROOMS (PAGE 654).

## Treemelon
*See* PEPINO.

## Tree Tomato
*See* TAMARILLO.

## Trefoil
*See* MITSUBA.

## Tremmocos
*See* LUPINI BEAN.

## Triple Sec

*See* ORANGE LIQUEUR.

## Triticale Flour

*See* CHOOSING AMONG WHOLE-GRAIN AND ALTERNATIVE FLOURS (PAGE 648).

## Trivet

*Ceramic or metal stand on which to sit hot pans or dishes.*

### If You Don't Have It

Substitute a trivet with:

- cooling rack
- oven mitt
- pizza stone or unglazed quarry tiles

## Trompette de la Mort

*See* SHUFFLING MUSHROOMS (PAGE 654).

## Trout

*One of the most common and well-liked fish in the world. Includes brown trout (also known as sea trout), rainbow trout (also known as steelhead), cutthroat trout, brook trout, and lake trout. Trout respond to a variety of cooking methods including poaching, grilling, broiling, frying, and en papillote.*

### If You Don't Have It

Substitute 1 lb (500 g) trout with:

- 1 lb (500 g) salmon (especially to replace rainbow trout)
- 1 lb (500 g) char (especially to replace rainbow trout)
- 1 lb (500 g) shad
- 1 lb (500 g) sablefish
- 1 lb (500 g) ocean perch

### Trout Varieties

Choose 1 lb (500 g) trout from these popular varieties:

- 1 lb (500 g) smoked trout (usually rainbow trout; cured fish; adds smoke flavor)
- 1 lb (500 g) rainbow trout (freshwater species; light purple band along body; black spots on tail fin; often farmed; prepare like salmon)
- 1 lb (500 g) steelhead or salmon trout (a large, saltwater subspecies of rainbow trout that migrates to freshwater to spawn; prepare like salmon)
- 1 lb (500 g) brown, river, or lake trout (freshwater species; greenish brown skin with black spots or mottling; excellent flavor; best cooked simply)
- 1 lb (500 g) brook or speckled trout (freshwater species; smaller than rainbow trout; excellent flavor; best cooked whole and simply)
- 1 lb (500 g) sea trout (include several subspecies, most of which are milder in flavor than freshwater varieties and have white to pale pink flesh)

## Truffle

*The fruiting body of a fungus that grows under certain trees in a*

### If You Don't Have It

Substitute 1 oz (30 g) truffles with:

- 1 to 2 tbsp (15 to 30 mL) truffle oil

*mycorrhizal relationship that benefits both parties. Truffles, which can only be foraged in the wild, cost a fortune for those enamored of their pungent, earthy, mysterious essence. Black truffles are found in France, Spain, and Italy. The best are said to come from Périgord in France. The Piedmontese town of Alba claims dominance in the white truffle arena.*

- 1 to 2 oz (30 to 60 g) fresh porcini mushrooms (less complex flavor)
- 1 oz (30 g) black garlic (sweeter, caramel flavor with hints of garlic)

## Truffle Varieties
Choose 1 oz (30 g) truffles from these popular varieties:
- 1 oz (30 g) black truffles (complex earthy, floral, mushroom-like aroma; best paired with somewhat strongly flavored foods)
- 1 oz (30 g) white truffles (complex, earthy, garlicky, mushroom-like aroma; best paired with delicately flavored foods)
- 1 oz (30 g) summer truffles (complex, woodsy, mushroom-like, relatively delicate aroma and crisp texture; best paired with delicately flavored food)

## Tuaca

*An Italian brand herbal liqueur with the dominant note coming from vanilla.*

## If You Don't Have It
Substitute 2 tbsp (30 mL) Tuaca with:
- 2 tbsp (30 mL) Licor 43™
- 2 tbsp (30 mL) crème de vanille or other vanilla liqueur
- 2 tbsp (30 mL) vanilla vodka (less sweet)

## Tube Pan

*See* PAN SIZE EQUIVALENTS (PAGE 678).

## Tuna, Canned

*Likely the most abundant canned seafood in the world, cooked tuna comes packed in either water or oil. Canned "white tuna" is albacore tuna while "chunk light" is yellowfin or skipjack tuna, which has a slightly stronger flavor. The highest grade, consisting of large pieces, is called "solid" or "fancy." "Chunk" grade is smaller pieces.*

6 oz (170 g) can =
⅔ to ¾ cup
(150 to 175 mL) drained

## To Vary the Flavor
Substitute 1 (6-oz/170 g) can tuna with:
- 1 (6-oz/170 g) can salmon
- 1 (6-oz/170 g) can mackerel

## For Better Health
Substitute 1 (6-oz/170 g) can tuna in oil with:
- 1 (6-oz/170 g) can tuna in water (fewer calories)

## Tuna, Fresh

*Also known as tunny. Tuna's muscles are red, textured, and hearty — much more meat-like than other fish — because tuna's muscles are so powerful. Tuna is a warm-blooded fish that must swim continuously to draw oxygen-rich water over its gills.*

### If You Don't Have It
Substitute 1 lb (500 g) fresh tuna with:
- 1 lb (500 g) swordfish
- 1 lb (500 g) marlin
- 1 lb (500 g) shark
- 1 lb (500 g) bluefish
- 1 lb (500 g) blackfish
- 1 lb (500 g) mahi-mahi
- 1 lb (500 g) striped bass
- 1 lb (500 g) mackerel
- 1 lb (500 g) salmon

### Tuna Varieties
Choose 1 lb (500 g) fresh tuna from these varieties:
- 1 lb (500 g) skipjack, aku, katsuo, or watermelon (weighs 6 to 40 lbs/3 to 20 kg; parallel dark blue stripes on body; relatively lean, pale pink flesh; sometimes canned; sometimes used for sashimi; often dried to make bonito flakes)
- 1 lb (500 g) albacore (weighs 10 to 60 lbs/5 to 30 kg; dark blue black back and silver-gray sides; long pectoral fins; relatively rich, pale pink or white flesh; often canned; sometimes used for sashimi)
- 1 lb (500 g) blackfin (weighs up to 45 lbs/22 kg; black backs; large eyes; oval shaped bodies with yellow on the sides; dark, rich flesh; sometimes used for sashimi)
- 1 lb (500 g) yellowfin or ahi (weighs up to several hundred pounds; has yellow fins; relatively lean, pink flesh; sometimes canned; sometimes used for sashimi)
- 1 lb (500 g) bigeye or ahi (weighs up to several hundred pounds; dark blue black back; yellow pectoral fins and relatively large eyes; relatively rich, crimson flesh; sometimes used for sashimi)
- 1 lb (500 g) bluefin (weighs up to a ton; includes northern and southern varieties; rich, deep crimson flesh; used for high-quality sashimi; endangered by overfishing)

*See also* BONITO.

## Tuong

*See* FERMENTED BEAN PASTE.

## Turban Squash

*Also known as Turk's cap. An old variety of winter squash cultivated mostly for its dramatic appearance. The flesh is yellow and mild. The rind is very tough, but if the squash is*

### If You Don't Have It
Substitute 1 cup (250 mL) chopped turban squash with:
- 1 cup (250 mL) chopped butternut squash (more easily peeled; creamier)
- 1 cup (250 mL) chopped buttercup squash (smaller; similar turban cap)
- 1 cup (250 mL) chopped pumpkin (creamier)

*baked or steamed whole, the top can be sliced off and the insides scooped out to make soup. The empty squash shell then makes a beautiful tureen.*

- 1 cup (250 mL) chopped delicata squash (moister)
- 1 cup (250 mL) chopped sweet potato (sweeter; moister)

See also BUTTERCUP SQUASH.

> 1 lb (500 g) =
> 1 cup (250 mL)
> cooked and mashed

## Turbinado Sugar

See SUGAR, RAW.

## Turbot

*An esteemed European flatfish, almost on a par with Dover sole. Demand exceeds the catch, which is mostly from the Atlantic North Sea.*

### If You Don't Have It
Substitute 1 lb (500 g) turbot with:
- 1 lb (500 g) halibut
- 1 lb (500 g) Dover sole
- 1 lb (500 g) brill

## Turkey

*Dark meat has slightly more fat, calories, and flavor than white meat. To reduce calories by up to 30% in dark meat parts, use skinless turkey or don't eat the skin (leave the skin on during cooking, particularly the breast, to help keep the meat moist). Use bone-in turkey pieces for slightly more flavor.*

> 1 lb (500 g) boneless
> turkey = 3 cups (750 mL)
> cubed

### If You Don't Have It
Substitute 1 lb (500 g) turkey with:
- 1 lb (500 g) chicken
- 1 lb (500 g) rabbit
- 1 lb (500 g) emu
- 1 lb (500 g) ostrich
- 1 lb (500 g) pheasant

### For Better Health
Substitute 1 lb (500 g) turkey with:
- 1 lb (500 g) kosher turkey (raised more humanely with tighter bacterial controls; brined, which makes the meat slightly more salty)
- 1 lb (500 g) free-range turkey (raised more humanely; often fed a vegetarian diet; meat may be slightly less tender but more flavorful)
- 1 lb (500 g) pasture-raised turkey (raised outdoors on a diet with a high percentage of natural forage; meat may be slightly less tender but more flavorful)
- 1 lb (500 g) organic turkey (fed an organic diet)
- 1 lb (500 g) vegetarian turkey products (made with soy protein)
- 1 lb (500 g) extra-firm tofu (more tender; less flavorful; press to extract excess liquid)

## Turkey Bacon

See BACON.

## Turkey Baster

*See* BASTER.

## Turkey, Ground

*Fresh or frozen ground turkey is a blend of white and dark turkey meat or all dark turkey meat with natural portion of skin that is at least 85% lean. Some supermarkets also grind whole boneless, skinless turkey breast that is up to 99% fat-free.*

### If You Don't Have It
Substitute 1 lb (500 g) ground turkey with:
- 1 lb (500 g) ground chicken
- 1 lb (500 g) ground veal
- 1 lb (500 g) ground beef

### For Better Health
- 1 lb (500 g) ground turkey breast (less fat and fewer calories)

## Turkey Jerky

*See* JERKY.

## Turkish Yogurt

*See* YOGURT CHEESE.

## Turmeric

*Also known as Indian or yellow ginger and Indian saffron. A southeast Asian/ Indian rhizome that can be used fresh or ground after it's dried. It's valued as much for its intense reddish golden color as for its astringent flavor. Turmeric is frequently presented as a cheaper alternative to saffron, although it lacks saffron's complexity. A very similar but stronger rhizome known as* palillo *is used both fresh and dried in Peruvian cooking.*

1 tbsp (15 mL) minced fresh = 1/8 to 1/4 tsp (0.5 to 1 mL) ground

### If You Don't Have It
Substitute 2 tbsp (30 mL) chopped fresh turmeric with:
- 1/4 to 1/2 tsp (1 to 2 mL) ground turmeric

### To Vary the Flavor
Substitute 1/4 to 1/2 tsp (1 to 2 mL) ground turmeric with:
- 1/4 to 1/2 tsp (1 to 2 mL) ground ginger + 1 to 2 tsp (5 to 10 mL) minced fresh ginger
- 5 to 7 crushed saffron threads (more expensive; more complex floral aroma)
- 1/2 to 3/4 tsp (2 to 3 mL) annatto seeds steeped in oil or other liquid for 15 minutes, then discarded (for yellow orange color; less pungent flavor)
- 1/2 tsp (2 mL) crushed dried safflower florets (for yellow orange color)
- 1 drop yellow food coloring + 1 small drop red food coloring mixed into water or other liquid (for yellow orange color)
- 1/2 tsp (2 mL) curry powder (includes other ground spices such as coriander, cumin, fenugreek seeds, black pepper, mustard seeds, allspice, cayenne pepper, ginger, and salt)
- 1/2 tsp (2 mL) powdered lesser galangal or 1 tbsp (15 mL) fresh

*See also* SAFFRON.

## Turner

*Typically a flat piece of metal, nylon, or acrylic attached to a long handle, turners flip and/or lift burgers, pancakes, cutlets, cookies, eggs, and more. Some turners are slotted so that fat can drain from the food as it's lifted.*

### If You Don't Have It
Substitute a turner with:
- wide spatula
- clean flexible spackling knife or dough scraper

## Turnip

*A root vegetable related to broccoli and Brussels sprouts. Although turnips can be cultivated in a rainbow of colors, the most common is the lilac and white variety. A small, white Japanese turnip is also appearing in some supermarkets. Turnips can be eaten raw, steamed, or roasted and have a delightful sweet pungency when not overcooked.*

> 1 lb (500 g) =
> 3 to 4 medium =
> 2½ cups (625 mL)
> chopped and cooked

### If You Don't Have It
Substitute 1 cup (250 mL) chopped turnips with:
- 1 cup (250 mL) chopped rutabaga (less sweet)
- 1 cup (250 mL) chopped kohlrabi bulb (sweeter)
- 1 cup (250 mL) chopped parsnips (sweeter)
- 1 cup (250 mL) chopped salsify (milder)
- 1 cup (250 mL) chopped celeriac (stronger flavor with celery aromas)
- 1 cup (250 mL) chopped parsley root (stronger flavor)
- 1 cup (250 mL) chopped broccoli stems (sweeter, milder)
- 1 cup (250 mL) chopped Asian radishes such as daikon (more peppery)
- 1 cup (250 mL) chopped black radishes (much sharper and hotter flavor)

## Turnip Greens

*The leaves that top turnip bulbs can be cooked like mustard leaves, beet leaves, or any other green.*

> 1 lb (500 g) fresh =
> 1⅓ to 2 cups
> (325 to 500 mL) cooked

### If You Don't Have It
Substitute 1 lb (500 g) turnip greens with:
- 1 lb (500 g) mustard greens
- 1 lb (500 g) dandelion greens
- 1 lb (500 g) kohlrabi greens
- 1 lb (500 g) collards
- 1 lb (500 g) kale
- 1 lb (500 g) beet greens
- 1 lb (500 g) green chard leaves (milder)
- 1 lb (500 g) mature spinach (milder)

## Turnip-Rooted Parsley

*See* PARSLEY ROOT.

## Turtle

*The availability of the meat of several varieties of hard-shelled reptiles has been limited by conservation measures. The sea or green turtle is found in temperate salt water. The white or, the preferred, green flesh is often simmered into turtle soup. A smaller species called the terrapin inhabits fresh or brackish water. Its meat is highly regarded, sometimes pounded into a cutlet. Less desirable as food are tortoises, which live on land.*

### If You Don't Have It

Substitute 1 lb (500 g) turtle meat with:
- 1 lb (500 g) alligator or crocodile tail meat
- 1 lb (500 g) chicken or turkey (less chewy)

## Turtle Bean

*See* THE WIDE WORLD OF DRIED BEANS (PAGE 637).

## TVP

*See* TEXTURED VEGETABLE PROTEIN.

## Tybo

*Mild, Danish cow's milk cheese is the color of cream and dotted with holes. The mild taste is similar to Samsoe. Some versions contain caraway seeds.*

1 lb (500 g) = 4 cups (1 L) shredded

### If You Don't Have It

Substitute 1 oz (30 g) Tybo with:
- 1 oz (30 g) Samsoe (slightly more flavorful)
- 1 oz (30 g) Danbo (may add caraway flavor)
- 1 oz (30 g) Emmental (drier; more complex flavor)
- 1 oz (30 g) Gouda

*See also* SAMSOE.

# Udo to Unsweetened Cocoa Powder

## Udo

*Just like asparagus in the West, the young stalks of this plant, which taste like fennel, are a springtime delicacy in Japan.*

1 lb (500 g) = 3½ cups (875 mL) chopped

### If You Don't Have It

Substitute 1 lb (500 g) udo with:
- 1 lb (500 g) fennel bulb (crunchier)
- 1 lb (500 g) bok choy stems (preferably, add 1 tsp/5 mL crushed fennel seeds or 1 tbsp/15 mL anise liqueur such as Pernod or Ricard to add anise flavor)
- 1 lb (500 g) asparagus (preferably, add 1 tsp/5 mL crushed fennel seeds or 1 tbsp/15 mL anise liqueur such as Pernod or Ricard to add anise flavor)

## Udon

*See* A SNAPSHOT OF ASIAN NOODLES (PAGE 656).

## Ugli™ Fruit

*Also known as uniq fruit. A trademarked name for a thick-skinned Jamaican citrus that's thought to be a cross between the mandarin and a grapefruit or pummelo.*

1 medium ugli = 10 oz (300 g) = 1 cup (250 mL) segments

### If You Don't Have It

Substitute 1 cup (250 mL) Ugli™ fruit segments with:
- 1 cup (250 mL) pummelo segments (less sweet)
- 1 cup (250 mL) grapefruit segments (more acidic)
- 1 cup (250 mL) sweet orange segments (sweeter)
- 1 cup (250 mL) tangelo segments (sweeter)

## Uhu

*See* PARROT FISH.

## Umeboshi

*Japanese pickled plums made from ume or green plums that are salt-cured and sun-dried by a time-consuming, complicated process that starts during the rainy season in June and concludes with sunny August days. It is the leaves of the reddish purple variety of shiso that color the plums crimson. Umeboshi are eaten in onigiri, stuffed rice balls, and many other dishes. Umeboshi are among the most concentrated sources of citric acid, a natural energizer. Samurai of the Edo Period (1600-1868) are said to have always carried a supply of umeboshi so they could be alert and ready for action.*

### If You Don't Have It
Substitute 1 umeboshi plum with:
- 1 tsp (5 mL) umeboshi paste or bainiku

### To Vary the Flavor
Substitute 1 umeboshi plum with:
- 1 sour prune
- 6 to 10 vinegar-brined sloes
- 1 tbsp (15 mL) miso
- 1 tsp (5 mL) soy sauce
- ½ tsp (2 mL) sea salt

*See also* PERILLA; PRUNE, SOUR.

## Uni

*See* CHANGING ROE (PAGE 666).

## Uniq Fruit

*See* UGLI™ FRUIT.

## Unsalted Butter

*See* BUTTER.

## Unsweetened Cocoa Powder

*See* COCOA POWDER, UNSWEETENED.

# V8 Juice to Vodka

## V8® Juice

*A blend of tomato, spinach, celery, carrot, beet, lettuce, watercress, and parsley juices.*

### If You Don't Have It
Substitute 1 cup (250 mL) V8® Juice with:
- 1 cup (250 mL) tomato juice (less complex flavor)
- ½ cup (125 mL) tomato purée or tomato sauce + ½ cup (125 mL) water (less complex flavor)
- ¼ cup (60 mL) tomato paste + ¾ cup (175 mL) water (less complex flavor)

### To Vary the Flavor
Substitute 1 cup (250 mL) V8® Juice with:
- 1 cup (250 mL) carrot juice (orange color; sweeter)

## Vache Qui Rit

*See* La Vache Qui Rit.

## Vacherin Fribourgeois

*A Swiss cow's milk cheese with a soft, smooth consistency. It is cured in very damp conditions in order to promote the growth of surface mold.*

### If You Don't Have It
Substitute 1 oz (30 g) Vacherin Fribourgeois with:
- 1 oz (30 g) Fontina
- 1 oz (30 g) Vacherin d'Abondance
- 1 oz (30 g) Morbier
- 1 oz (30 g) Appenzeller

*See also* Vacherin Mont d'Or.

## Vacherin Mont d'Or

*Also known as Vacherin du Haut-Doubs (a French cheese that is very similar). A traditional Swiss cow's milk cheese that is so soft, it can be eaten with a spoon.*

### If You Don't Have It

Substitute 1 oz (30 g) Vacherin Mont d'Or with:
- 1 oz (30 g) Vacherin du Haut-Doubs
- 1 oz (30 g) Reblochon

*See also* VACHERIN FRIBOURGEOIS.

## Vadouvan

*An Indian seasoning base featuring onions, garlic, and spices such as curry, fenugreek, cardamom, coriander, cumin, black pepper, and chile. Traditionally the raw ingredients are sun-dried for days then rolled into balls. Modern versions typically fry the onions and garlic then oven-dry the seasoned mixture.*

### If You Don't Have It

Substitute 1 tbsp (15 mL) vadouvan with:
- 1 tbsp (15 mL) Homemade Vadouvan Base: Heat 3 tbsp (45 mL) oil and 2 tbsp (30 mL) butter in a skillet over medium heat and add 4 finely chopped medium onions and 2 finely chopped large shallots. Cover and cook until soft and lightly browned, 15 minutes. Add 6 finely chopped garlic cloves, 2 tsp (10 mL) ground cumin, 1 tsp (5 mL) ground cardamom, 1 tsp (5 mL) ground fenugreek seeds, 1 tsp (5 mL) whole brown mustard seeds, $\frac{3}{4}$ tsp (3 mL) ground turmeric, $\frac{1}{2}$ tsp (2 mL) ground coriander, $\frac{1}{4}$ tsp (1 mL) grated nutmeg, $\frac{1}{4}$ tsp (1 mL) ground cloves, $\frac{1}{4}$ tsp (1 mL) salt, and pinch of cayenne pepper. Cook for 5 minutes. Spread into a thin layer on a baking sheet and bake at 250°F (120°C) until browned and only slightly moist, 45 minutes. Freeze for up to 6 months. Makes about $\frac{3}{4}$ cup (175 mL).
- 1 tbsp (15 mL) Homemade Vadouvan Powder: Combine 1 tbsp (15 mL) ground cumin, 2 tsp (10 mL) ground cardamom, 2 tsp (10 mL) ground fenugreek seeds, 2 tsp (10 mL) ground brown mustard seeds, $1\frac{1}{2}$ tsp (7 mL) ground turmeric, 1 tsp (5 mL) ground coriander, 1 tsp (5 mL) onion powder, 1 tsp (5 mL) garlic powder, $\frac{1}{2}$ tsp (2 mL) grated nutmeg, $\frac{1}{2}$ tsp (2 mL) ground cloves, $\frac{1}{2}$ tsp (2 mL) salt, $\frac{1}{8}$ tsp (0.5 mL) cayenne pepper. Makes about $\frac{1}{4}$ cup (60 mL).
- 1 tbsp (15 mL) caramelized onions + $\frac{1}{2}$ tsp (2 mL) sautéed garlic + $\frac{1}{2}$ tsp (2 mL) curry powder
- 2 tsp (15 mL) curry powder + $\frac{1}{2}$ tsp (2 mL) onion powder + $\frac{1}{2}$ tsp (2 mL) garlic powder

## Valencia Orange

*See* ORANGE, SWEET.

## Valois Sauce

*See* BÉARNAISE SAUCE.

## Vandermint

*See* CHOCOLATE LIQUEUR.

## Vanilla Bean

*One of the most wonderfully aromatic and complex flavorings in the world comes from the only orchid vanilla planifolia (out of some 20,000 varieties) that has an edible long, thin pod. Vanilla bean is expensive due to the labor and time required to cultivate and process it. Three types of bean are most common. The rich, thin Bourbon-Madagascar vanilla bean, accounting for 75% of the world's supply, comes from islands of Madagascar and Réunion. The thicker Mexican vanilla bean is smooth and rich but scarcer in supply. The Tahitian vanilla bean is the thickest and darkest. It is intensely aromatic, though not as flavorful as the others. Vanilla bean is available whole or as vanilla powder.*

> 1 8-inch (20 cm) vanilla bean = 1 tbsp (15 mL) vanilla extract
>
> 1 2-inch (5 cm) piece vanilla bean = 1 tsp (5 mL) vanilla extract

### If You Don't Have It
Substitute 1 8-inch (20 cm) vanilla bean with:
- 2 to 3 tsp (10 to 15 mL) vanilla extract (for the most flavor, add to custards or other cooked mixtures toward the end of cooking rather than at the beginning)
- 2 to $2\frac{1}{2}$ tsp (10 to 12 mL) vanilla powder (good for baking, because its flavor does not dissipate as readily as vanilla extract when exposed to heat)
- 8 to 12 drops vanilla essence
- $1\frac{1}{2}$ to 2 tbsp (22 to 30 mL) imitation vanilla extract
- 3 tbsp (45 mL) vanilla liqueur (adds alcohol)
- 2 tonka beans (adds bitter almond aroma)

### Vanilla Bean Varieties
Choose 1 8-inch (20 cm) vanilla bean from these varieties:
- 1 8-inch (20 cm) Bourbon or Madagascar vanilla bean (robust aroma and dark, smooth, sweet flavor that hints of fermented fruit; best for baking and long-cooking because the strong flavors withstand heat better than other varieties)
- 1 8-inch (20 cm) Mexican vanilla bean (strong, delicately complex floral aroma and sweet flavor with hints of chocolate and warm spices; good for both hot and cold dishes; buy from a reputable merchant or check the label, as some lesser-quality Mexican vanilla products may contain coumarin, a potential toxin banned by the U.S. Food and Drug Administration)
- 1 8-inch (20 cm) Tahitian vanilla bean (intense floral aroma with sweet flavor and hints of cherry and anise; best for cold preparations such as pastry cream because the strong aroma dissipates with prolonged heat)
- 1 8-inch (20 cm) Java or Indonesian vanilla bean (relatively mild aroma and flavor; these smaller, less expensive beans are often used to make mass-market vanilla extract)

*See also VANILLA ESSENCE; VANILLA EXTRACT; VANILLA POWDER.*

## Vanilla Essence

*Highly concentrated extract of vanilla. Not to be confused with the British vanilla essence or imitation vanilla essence, both of which are synonymous with vanilla extract and imitation vanilla extract, respectively.*

### If You Don't Have It
Substitute 2 drops concentrated vanilla essence with:
- 1-inch (2.5 cm) piece vanilla bean (split or beans scraped from pod; add early in the recipe to allow the most flavor extraction)
- $\frac{1}{2}$ tsp (2 mL) vanilla extract
- $\frac{1}{2}$ tsp (2 mL) vanilla powder (good for baking because its flavor does not dissipate as readily as vanilla extract when exposed to heat)
- $\frac{3}{4}$ tsp (3 mL) imitation vanilla extract

*See also VANILLA BEAN; VANILLA EXTRACT; VANILLA POWDER.*

## Vanilla Extract

*Also known as vanilla essence (British). Pure vanilla extract is extracted by soaking vanilla beans in alcohol. Imitation vanilla extract has a vaguely similar flavor but is entirely artificial and often manufactured from the paper industry's wood-pulp by-products.*

### If You Don't Have It

Substitute 1 tsp (5 mL) pure vanilla extract with:

- 3-inch (7.5 cm) piece vanilla bean (split or beans scraped from pod; add early in the recipe to allow the most flavor extraction)
- 1 to 1½ tsp (5 to 7 mL) Homemade Vanilla Extract: Combine ¾ cup (175 mL) vodka and 1 to 2 split vanilla beans in a large glass jar. Seal and store in a cool, dark place for at least 4 months or indefinitely. To use sooner, jump-start the mixture with 3 tbsp (45 mL) pure vanilla extract and store for at least 2 months. Remove extract as necessary, replacing the vanilla beans when they give up their flavor and the vodka when it begins to run low.
- ½ tsp (2 mL) double-strength vanilla extract
- ¼ tsp (1 mL) triple-strength vanilla extract
- 3 to 5 drops vanilla essence
- ¾ to 1 tsp (3 to 5 mL) vanilla powder (good for baking because its flavor does not dissipate as readily as vanilla extract when exposed to heat)
- 1½ tsp (7 mL) imitation vanilla extract
- 1 tbsp (15 mL) vanilla liqueur

### To Vary the Flavor

Substitute 1 tsp (5 mL) vanilla extract with:

- ½ tsp (2 mL) almond, orange, or lemon extract
- ¼ tsp (1 mL) peppermint extract
- 1 tbsp (15 mL) rum
- 1 tbsp (15 mL) almond liqueur
- ¼ tsp (1 mL) Fiori di Sicilia (a Sicilian flower essence with vanilla and citrus aromas)

*See also* VANILLA BEAN; VANILLA ESSENCE; VANILLA POWDER.

## Vanilla Liqueur

*The generic term for a French sweetened spirit flavored with vanilla.*

### If You Don't Have It

Substitute 2 tbsp (30 mL) vanilla liqueur with:

- 2 tbsp (30 mL) crème de vanille (may be thicker; sweeter)
- 2 tbsp (30 mL) vanilla vodka (less sweet)
- 2 tbsp (30 mL) Tuaca
- 2 tbsp (30 mL) Licor 43

## Vanilla Powder

*Dried vanilla beans that are finely ground. Because the powder holds its flavor when exposed to heat, it is excellent for flavoring baked goods, custards, and other cooked dishes. It is sold in specialty cake decorating supply shops (also catalogs and online), as well as some gourmet markets.*

### If You Don't Have It

Substitute 1 tsp (5 mL) vanilla powder with:
- 1 to 1½ tsp (5 to 7 mL) vanilla extract
- 1½ to 2 tsp (7 to 10 mL) imitation vanilla extract
- 4 to 6 drops vanilla essence

*See also* VANILLA BEAN; VANILLA ESSENCE; VANILLA EXTRACT.

## Vanilla Sugar

*See* SUGAR, GRANULATED.

## Veal

*The meat of a young calf, generally no older than 3 months. "Milk-fed veal" comes from calves that have not been weaned so the flesh remains soft and creamy-white with perhaps a pale pink tinge. "Formula-fed veal" can come from calves as old as 4 months, fed on milk solids, fats, nutrients, and water. This type is not as delicate as milk-fed.*

### If You Don't Have It

Substitute 1 lb (500 g) veal with:
- 1 lb (500 g) pork
- 1 lb (500 g) chicken
- 1 lb (500 g) turkey

## Vegemite©

*See* YEAST EXTRACT.

## Vegetable Oil

*See* SUBSTITUTING OILS (PAGE 658).

## Vegetable Oil Spray

*A commercial product of vegetable oil, lecithin, and a harmless propellant packed into a spray can. It is used to coat cooking and baking pans with the minimum amount of oil to make the surface nonstick.*

### If You Don't Have It

Substitute a 10- to 15-second spray of vegetable oil spray with:
- 1 tsp (5 mL) vegetable oil (to use the least amount, spread to a fine film using a paper towel or pastry brush)
- 1 tsp (5 mL) butter or margarine
- nonstick silicone bakeware (for baking; available as baking sheets or molds in the shapes of most baked goods such as breads, muffins, and cakes; reusable; flexible; does not need to be greased; highly recommended)

## Vegetable Oil Spray (cont'd)

*To make your own oil spray, fill a plastic pump spray bottle with your favorite cooking oil. Adding 2 tablespoons (30 mL) of liquid lecithin per ½ cup (125 mL) of oil helps create a smoother spray but is not absolutely necessary.*

> 10- to 15-second spray = 1 tsp (5 mL) oil

## Vegetable Oil Spray Varieties
Choose vegetable oil spray from these varieties:
- olive oil spray
- butter-flavored vegetable oil spray
- flour and butter-flavored vegetable oil spray (for baking pans)

*See also* BUTTER.

## Vegetable Peeler

*This handy sharp-bladed tool is indispensable for cooks who peel apples for pies or potatoes for mashing. If possible, purchase a peeler from a cookware shop that will let you test drive the implement to make sure it fits your hand well.*

### If You Don't Have It
Substitute a vegetable peeler with:
- paring knife
- countertop peeling-coring-slicing machine
- slicing side of a box grater (to remove vegetable or fruit peels in small pieces)
- citrus zester (to remove small thin strips of peel from fruit or vegetables)

## Vegetable Protein

*See* TEXTURED VEGETABLE PROTEIN.

## Vegetable Shortening

*Also known as Crisco and solid shortening. Produces light and tender baked goods because, unlike butter, it is free of water. But it lacks buttery flavor. A combination of shortening and butter works best for many baked goods.*

> 1 lb (500 g) = 2⅓ cups (575 mL)

### If You Don't Have It
Substitute 1 cup (250 mL) vegetable shortening with:
- 1 cup (250 mL) lard
- 1 cup plus 2 tbsp (280 mL) unsalted butter (adds butter flavor; makes softer cookies)
- 1 cup plus 2 tbsp (280 mL) margarine (makes softer cookies; decrease salt by ⅛ tsp/0.5 mL)
- 1 cup (250 mL) bacon fat (for sautéing and frying)

### To Vary the Flavor
Substitute 1 cup (250 mL) vegetable shortening with:
- ½ cup (125 mL) vegetable shortening + ½ cup (125 mL) unsalted butter (for both flakiness and flavor in biscuits, pie crust and pastries)
- 1 cup (250 mL) coconut butter (sweeter; adds coconut flavor)

## For Better Health

Substitute 1 cup (250 mL) vegetable shortening with:

- ½ cup (125 mL) butter + ½ cup (125 mL) well-drained, unsweetened applesauce, prune purée or baby food prunes (for baking; applesauce works well with lighter-colored or spice batters; puréed prunes work best with darker batters such as chocolate; creates slightly chewier texture; use pastry or cake flour for lighter texture; increase sugar for more crispness)
- ½ cup (125 mL) butter + 6 tbsp (90 mL) vegetable oil (for baking, especially quick breads and some cookie doughs; reduce baking time slightly; baked goods will be slightly more chewy; use pastry or cake flour for lighter texture; increase sugar for more crispness)
- ½ cup (125 mL) butter + ½ cup (125 mL) apple butter (for baking; reduce baking time slightly; baked goods will be slightly more chewy; use pastry or cake flour for lighter texture; adjust sugar if apple butter is sweetened)
- 1 cup (125 mL) fat-free, fruit-based butter and oil replacement such as Smucker's "Baking Healthy" (for baking)
- ½ cup (125 mL) fat-free, fruit-based butter and oil replacement such as Sunsweet "Lighter Bake" (for baking)
- ¾ cup (175 mL) vegetable shortening + ¼ cup (60 mL) apple pectin (for cookies and cakes; makes texture more tender)
- 1 cup (250 mL) marshmallow crème (for fillings and frostings)
- 1 cup (250 mL) oil (for sautéing and frying). Or use a mixture of butter and oil. Or use a nonstick pan coated with cooking oil spray (or 2 to 4 tsp/10 to 20 mL oil or butter) and heat the pan thoroughly.

*See also* BUTTER.

---

## Vegetable Yeast Extract

*See* YEAST EXTRACT.

---

## Velouté

*One of the four French mother sauces, velouté is similar to béchamel in that it starts with a roux (cooked mixture of flour and butter) but incorporates a white stock such as chicken, veal or fish stock instead of incorporating milk. The word* velouté *translates literally from the French to mean "velvetiness."*

### If You Don't Have It

Substitute 1 cup (250 mL) velouté with:

- 1 cup (250 mL) Homemade Basic Velouté: Melt 2 tbsp (30 mL) butter in a heavy saucepan over low heat. Whisk in 3 tbsp (45 mL) all-purpose flour and cook, stirring, for 2 to 3 minutes without darkening. Heat 2 cups (500 mL) chicken, veal, or fish stock just to a simmer in a small saucepan or microwave oven. Remove the flour mixture from the heat and whisk in the hot stock. Return to medium-high heat, bring to a boil, and boil, stirring, for 1 minute. Season with salt and pepper (preferably white). Makes about 2 cups (500 mL).
- 1 cup (250 mL) béchamel (velouté made with milk or cream instead of stock)

## Velouté (cont'd)

### To Vary the Flavor

Substitute 1 cup (250 mL) velouté with:

- 1 cup (250 mL) Parisienne or Allemande sauce (velouté with egg yolks, cream, and lemon juice)
- 1 cup (250 mL) Aurore sauce (velouté with tomato paste or purée)
- 1 cup (250 mL) Suprême sauce (chicken velouté with reduced mushroom liquid)
- 1 cup (250 mL) Bercy sauce (fish velouté with shallots, wine, and lemon juice)
- 1 cup (250 mL) Normandy sauce (fish velouté with mushroom cooking liquid, oyster liquor, egg yolks, and cream)

See also BÉCHAMEL.

## Velveeta

See PROCESSED CHEESE.

## Velvet Apple

See MABOLO.

## Venison

*The meat of deer is dark red, finely grained, typically lean, and often delicious. The term venison is often used to refer to the meat of related animals such as elk, caribou, moose, and reindeer.*

### If You Don't Have It

Substitute 1 lb (500 g) venison with:

- 1 lb (500 g) antelope
- 1 lb (500 g) gazelle
- 1 lb (500 g) buffalo
- 1 lb (500 g) beef (richer; less gamey tasting)

See also CARIBOU; DEER; ELK; MOOSE; REINDEER.

## Ventrèche

See PANCETTA.

## Verbena

See LEMON VERBENA.

## Vermouth

*Fortified white wine liqueurs that some historians date back as medicinals to 400 BC. The name derives form the German for wormwood (wermut or vermut), which was a primary ingredient until, fortunately, someone discovered that it is poisonous. Today, vermouths are concocted*

### If You Don't Have It

Substitute 2 tbsp (30 mL) vermouth with:

- 2 tbsp (30 mL) dry sherry (to replace dry vermouth, especially for sauces and soups)
- 2 tbsp (30 mL) dry white wine (to replace dry vermouth, especially for sauces and soups)
- 2 tbsp (30 mL) Punt e Mes (to replace dry vermouth; red color; more bitter)
- 2 tbsp (30 mL) Madeira (to replace dry vermouth)
- 2 tbsp (30 mL) sake (to replace dry vermouth)
- 2 tbsp (30 mL) Shaoxing wine (to replace dry vermouth)
- 2 tbsp (30 mL) Lillet blanc (to replace sweet vermouth)
- 2 tbsp (30 mL) medium-dry white wine (to replace sweet vermouth)

*with countless herbs, flowers, seeds, and other botanicals. Two basic types exist. Sweet vermouth, developed in Italy in the 1700s, can be clear or tinted reddish brown with caramel. Dry vermouth, also known as French Vermouth, dates from around 1800. Both are enjoyed as apéritifs and as ingredients in various cocktails.*

## To Vary the Flavor
Substitute 2 tbsp (30 mL) vermouth with:
- 1 tbsp (15 mL) dry or French vermouth + 1 tbsp (15 mL) sweet or Italian vermouth (to make "perfect" cocktails such as a perfect Manhattan)

## For Better Health
Substitute 2 tbsp (30 mL) vermouth with:
- 2 tbsp (30 mL) chicken, fish, or vegetable stock (no alcohol; to replace vermouth in sauces or soups)

## Viande

*See* GLACE DE VIANDE.

## Vienna Sausage

*Tiny wieners that are typically available in cans.*

## If You Don't Have It
Substitute 1 lb (500 g) Vienna sausage with:
- 1 lb (500 g) cocktail wieners
- 1 lb (500 g) frankfurters (cut to size as necessary)
- 1 lb (500 g) Bockwurst (made with veal; cut to size as necessary)
- 1 lb (500 g) kielbasa (larger; cut to size as necessary)
- 1 lb (500 g) chipolata (spicier; cook first)

## Vietnamese Fish Sauce

*See* FISH SAUCE.

## Vietnamese Mint

*Also known as Cambodian mint, daun kesom, hot mint, laksa leaf, Vietnamese coriander, and water pepper. Each stem sprouts many pointy leaves with a strong, minty, peppery essence. The herb seasons Vietnamese soups, rice paper rolls, and other dishes.*

2 oz (60 g) = 1½ cups (375 mL) chopped

## If You Don't Have It
Substitute 1 tbsp (15 mL) chopped fresh Vietnamese mint with:
- 1½ tsp (7 mL) chopped fresh cilantro + 1½ tsp (7 mL) chopped fresh peppermint or lemon basil

## Vinegar

*While vinegar ("sour wine" in French) probably produced itself naturally from wine exposed to air, vinegar can be made from any sugary or starchy liquid that can be induced to ferment. It is used prolifically around the world as a flavoring and pickling agent.*

### If You Don't Have It

Substitute 2 tbsp (30 mL) vinegar with:

- 2 tbsp (30 mL) lemon juice or lime juice (for acidulated water, dressings, marinades, sauces, and deglazing pans)
- 2 tbsp (30 mL) mango powder (as a souring agent in curries, chutneys, and soups)
- 1½ to 2 tsp (7 to 10 mL) tamarind concentrate or paste (as a souring agent in curries, chutneys, and soups)
- 2 tbsp (30 mL) wine, sherry, brandy, or port (for deglazing pans)

*See also* CHOOSING VINEGAR (PAGE 674).

## Viola

*See* PICKING EDIBLE FLOWERS (PAGE 650).

## Violet

*See* PICKING EDIBLE FLOWERS (PAGE 650).

## Virginia Ham

*A class of fine American hams noted for their lean meat. The superb example is Smithfield ham, which is processed from razorback pigs. The ham is dry-rubbed with salt and pepper, smoked over hickory and apple wood, and then aged for at least a year.*

### If You Don't Have It

Substitute 4 oz (125 g) Virginia ham with:

- 4 oz (125 g) Smithfield ham (the most famous and often the best Virginia ham)
- 4 oz (125 g) Kentucky ham (also smoked over hickory and apple woods)
- 4 oz (125 g) York ham (lighter smoke flavor)
- 4 oz (125 g) Yunnan ham (lean, dry-cured Chinese ham)
- 4 oz (125 g) Westphalian ham (adds juniper flavor)
- 4 oz (125 g) Ardennes ham
- 4 oz (125 g) Bayonne ham
- 4 oz (125 g) serrano or Iberico ham (lacks smoke flavor)
- 4 oz (125 g) prosciutto (lacks smoke flavor)

## Vital Wheat Gluten

*See* SEITAN.

## Vodka

*A clear, colorless distilled liquor. The finest come from grains such as barley and wheat. Vegetables, such as potatoes and beets, can also be used to make vodka. Vodka is purified by distillation at high proof levels followed by filtration through activated charcoal. Some vodkas are embellished with fruits, peppers, or other flavorings.*

### If You Don't Have It
Substitute 2 tbsp (30 mL) vodka with:
- 1 tbsp (15 mL) neutral spirits (increase liquid in recipe by 1 tbsp/15 mL)
- 1 tbsp (15 mL) grain spirits (wood-aged; mellow flavor; increase liquid in recipe by 1 tbsp/15 mL)
- 2 tbsp (30 mL) gin (adds other flavors such as juniper)
- 2 tbsp (30 mL) white rum (slightly sweeter; mellower, richer flavor if aged)
- 2 tbsp (30 mL) aquavit (adds caraway flavor)
- 2 tbsp (30 mL) tequila (more peppery, herbaceous flavor; mellower, richer flavor if aged)

### To Vary the Flavor
Substitute 2 tbsp (30 mL) vodka with:
- 2 tbsp (30 mL) flavored vodka such as lemon, pepper, or vanilla (some flavored vodkas may be sweeter than unflavored vodka)

*See also* NEUTRAL SPIRITS.

# Wahoo to Wu Gu Ji

## Wahoo

*Also known as ono (Hawaiian). A Pacific game fish with sweet, fine, moderately high-fat flesh. The beautiful iridescent dark blue stripes on the sides of wahoo fade when the fish dies. The flavor is often compared to albacore.*

### If You Don't Have It
Substitute 1 lb (500 g) wahoo with:
- 1 lb (500 g) king mackerel
- 1 lb (500 g) mahi-mahi (moister; sweeter)
- 1 lb (500 g) swordfish
- 1 lb (500 g) mako shark
- 1 lb (500 g) tuna

*See also* MACKEREL.

## Wakame

*A delicate, brown seaweed that is very important in Japanese cooking for soups and salads. Available fresh in spring, it is semidried or dried for year-round consumption.*

### If You Don't Have It
Substitute 1 oz (30 g) wakame with:
- 1 oz (30 g) dulse (similar brine flavor; maroon-brown color)
- 1 oz (30 g) arame (similar brine flavor; reddish or greenish brown color; long, slender shape)
- 1 oz (30 g) kombu or kelp (stronger brine flavor; dark brown to black color)
- 1 oz (30 g) hijiki (stronger brine flavor; black color; long, slender shape)

## Walla Walla

*See* ONION, SWEET.

## Walleye

*See* PIKE.

# Walnut

*The most common commercially grown walnuts are the English (Persian), which are marketed in the shell, as halves, and as pieces. American black walnuts are a different species, with a thick, blackish brown shell and a much more pronounced taste. Predominantly used for desserts and baked goods, walnuts are also delicious in many savory dishes.*

---

1 lb (500 g) in shell =
2 cups (500 mL) nuts

1 lb (500 g) shelled =
3¾ cups (925 mL) halves
= 3½ cups (875 mL)
chopped

---

## If You Don't Have It

Substitute 1 cup (250 mL) walnuts with:

- 2 to 4 tbsp (30 to 60 mL) walnut oil (for baking and cooking; will add nut flavor but not texture of whole nuts; reduce fat in recipe by 2 to 4 tbsp/30 to 60 mL)
- 2 to 4 tbsp (30 to 60 mL) walnut liqueur (for baking and cooking; adds nut flavor and alcohol but not texture of whole nuts; reduce liquid in recipe by 2 to 4 tbsp/30 to 60 mL)

## To Vary the Flavor

Substitute 1 cup (250 mL) walnuts with:

- 1 cup (250 mL) butternuts
- 1 cup (250 mL) pine nuts
- 1 cup (250 mL) pecans
- 1 cup (250 mL) almonds
- 1 cup (250 mL) hazelnuts

## Walnut Varieties

Choose 1 cup (250 mL) walnuts from these popular varieties:

- 1 cup (250 mL) Persian or English walnuts (the most common type)
- 1 cup (250 mL) American black walnuts (thicker, harder shell; stronger, more complex, and slightly more bitter flavor that withstands heat better than English walnuts)

*See also* BUTTERNUT; NUT; NUT MEAL.

---

# Walnut Liqueur

*Traditionally, Italian nocino, a walnut liqeur made from green walnuts, is consumed on November 2, All Souls' Day, to honor the departed. A similar liqueur is now mass produced by several popular brands including Nocciole, Nocello, and Nocino.*

## If You Don't Have It

Substitute 2 tbsp (30 mL) walnut liqueur with:

- 2 tbsp (30 mL) crème de noix (thicker; sweeter)
- 2 tbsp (30 mL) water + ½ to ¾ tsp (2 to 3 mL) walnut extract (or skip the water and reduce liquid in recipe by a scant 2 tbsp/30 mL)

## To Vary the Flavor

Substitute 2 tbsp (30 mL) walnut liqueur with:

- 2 tbsp (30 mL) almond liqueur, hazelnut liqueur, coffee liqueur, or chocolate liqueur

---

# Walnut Meal

*See* NUT MEAL.

---

# Walnut Oil

*See* SUBSTITUTING OILS (PAGE 658).

---

# Walu

*See* ESCOLAR.

## Wasabi

The root of a Japanese herb, grated into a fine pale green paste, adds hot pungency to sushi, sashimi, and other dishes. The fresh root is rarely available outside of Japan. When buying wasabi paste or powder, look for the words "100% grated hon-wasabi" on the label. Lesser quality imitation "wasabi" paste and powder are made with horseradish, mustard, and colorings such as spinach powder.

### If You Don't Have It

Substitute 1 tbsp (15 mL) freshly grated wasabi with:

- 1 tbsp (15 mL) wasabi paste
- 1 tbsp (15 mL) wasabi powder + 2 to 3 tsp (10 to 15 mL) water (mix, cover, and let rest for 15 minutes)
- 1 tbsp (15 mL) finely grated fresh horseradish (white color; less pungent; mix with a ¼ drop of green food coloring if you like)
- 1 tbsp (15 mL) well-drained prepared horseradish (white color; coarser texture; less pungent; mild vinegar flavor; mix with a ¼ drop of green food coloring if you like)
- 1 tbsp (15 mL) mustard powder + 1 tsp (5 mL) water (mix, cover, and let rest for 15 minutes; yellow color; hotter at the back of the throat and less aromatically pungent)

## Water

See BOILING WATER; SPARKLING MINERAL WATER.

## Water Caltrop

Also known as horned water chestnut and ling jiao. These black nuts look remarkably similar to a bull's head with horns. They are often made into necklaces but the hard shells can also be cracked to extract the grainy nutmeat, which tastes similar to a water chestnut. Water caltrops must be cooked before eating to kill harmful toxins.

### If You Don't Have It

Substitute 1 cup (250 mL) cooked water caltrops with:

- 1 cup (250 mL) cooked water chestnuts (sweeter and crunchier)

## Water Chestnut

Look for fresh water chestnuts in Asian markets. The pale, sweet flesh tastes of apple, sunchoke, and sugarcane.

8 oz (250 g) can = 24 to 28 water chestnuts = 1 cup (250 mL) sliced

### If You Don't Have It

Substitute 1 cup (250 mL) fresh water chestnuts with:

- 1 cup (250 mL) canned water chestnuts (less sweet, less crisp, and less nutty)
- 1 cup (250 mL) chopped jicama (less nutty)
- 1 cup (250 mL) chopped cooked or canned lotus root
- 1 cup (250 mL) chopped sunchokes (less sweet and nutty)
- 1 cup (250 mL) chopped cooked or canned bamboo shoots (for stir-fries; less crisp)

## Water Chestnut Powder

*Also known as water chestnut flour. Dried and ground water chestnuts are used in Asian cooking for thickening or for dredging foods. It is available in Asian markets and some natural food stores.*

### If You Don't Have It
Substitute 1 tbsp (15 mL) water chestnut powder (for thickening) with:
- 1 tbsp (15 mL) cornstarch
- 2 tbsp (30 mL) all-purpose flour (cook a few minutes after thickening to cook out raw flour taste)
- 2 tsp (10 mL) arrowroot (a better choice if thickened food will be frozen or cooked for a long time; also makes sauces more glossy)

## Water Cracker

*See* CRACKER.

## Watercress

*See* CRESS.

## Watermelon

*Cleopatra probably enjoyed cool, sweet, refreshing slices of watermelon on many a sweltering afternoon. The melon was cultivated in Egypt for a good 2,000 years before she ascended the throne.*

> 2 lbs (1 kg) =
> 3 cups (750 mL) diced

### If You Don't Have It
Substitute 1 cup (250 mL) chopped watermelon with:
- 1 cup (250 mL) chopped honeydew melon (less crisp; less watery)
- 1 cup (250 mL) chopped Galia melon (less crisp; less watery)

## Water Spinach

*Also known as swamp cabbage. A thick-stemmed, green-leafed water plant that's common in China and Southeast Asia, prepared in stir-fries or with highly seasoned sauces. It's relatively high in protein and iron.*

### If You Don't Have It
Substitute 1 lb (500 g) water spinach shoots and leaves with:
- 1 lb (500 g) sweet potato shoots and leaves

## Wax Bean

*See* GREEN BEAN.

## Wax Chile

*See* CHOOSING FRESH CHILES (PAGE 640).

## Wax Paper

*Also known as greaseproof paper and waxed paper. Thomas Alva Edison, inventor of the phonograph, light bulb, and motion picture camera, also created wax paper.*

### If You Don't Have It

Substitute wax paper with:
- parchment paper (for lining baking pans)
- aluminum foil (for lining baking pans and wrapping food)
- plastic wrap (for wrapping food)

## Weakfish

*See* CROAKER.

## Wehani Rice

*See* VARIETIES OF RICE (PAGE 664).

## Weisswurst

*Also known as white sausage. Mildly seasoned fresh German veal sausages. Often paired with potato salad.*

### If You Don't Have It

Substitute 1 lb (500 g) Weisswurst with:
- 1 lb (500 g) French boudin blanc (delicate flavor)
- 1 lb (500 g) Cajun boudin blanc (spicier, more complex flavor)
- 1 lb (500 g) white Bratwurst (mild flavor)
- 1 lb (500 g) Bockwurst (mild flavor)

## Wensleydale

*A British whole milk cheese with a flavor akin to a sour version of Cheddar. A renowned blue Wensleydale is more rare and expensive.*

1 lb (500 g) = 4 cups (1 L) shredded

### If You Don't Have It

Substitute 1 oz (30 g) Wensleydale with:
- 1 oz (30 g) Cheshire
- 1 oz (30 g) Cheddar

## West Indian Cherry

*See* ACEROLA.

## Westphalian Ham

*A notable German ham that is dry-salted, soaked in salt brine, and then scrubbed with fresh water to remove excess sodium. The ham is smoked over beech and juniper wood.*

### If You Don't Have It

Substitute 4 oz (125 g) Westphalian ham with:
- 4 oz (125 g) York ham (mild flavor; may be lightly or heavily smoked)
- 4 oz (125 g) Virginia ham such as Smithfield ham (smoked over hickory and apple woods)
- 4 oz (125 g) Kentucky ham (smoked over hickory and apple woods)

- 4 oz (125 g) Bradenham ham (sweeter; black exterior)
- 4 oz (125 g) Black Forest ham (stronger flavor; black exterior)
- 4 oz (125 g) Ardennes ham
- 4 oz (125 g) Bayonne ham

## Wet-Cured Ham

*See* HAM, WET-CURED.

## Wheat Beer

*See* BEER.

## Wheat Berries

*Whole wheat kernels with only the inedible hull removed. Soaking wheat berries for several hours in cold water significantly reduces the cooking time. They make a chewy, nutritious addition to cooked grain salads. Both red and white hard wheat berries (typically ground for bread flour) are chewier, higher in protein, and take longer to cook than red or white soft wheat berries (typically ground for pastry flour).*

> 1 cup (250 mL) whole wheat berries = 2½ cups (625 mL) cooked

### If You Don't Have It
Substitute 1 cup (250 mL) wheat berries with:
- 1 cup (250 mL) cracked wheat (takes less timeto cook)
- 1 cup (250 mL) bulgur (takes less time to cook)
- 1 cup (250 mL) rye berries (takes less time to cook)
- 1 cup (250 mL) kasha (takes less time to cook)
- 1 cup (250 mL) triticale berries or groats
- 1 cup (250 mL) spelt berries or groats
- 1 cup (250 mL) Kamut® berries or groats

*See also* FARRO.

## Wheat Bran

*The rough covering of wheat berries is a wealth of dietary fiber. The bran is packaged and sold in supermarkets and can be used to add fiber to a variety of dishes, from meat loaf to breads.*

### If You Don't Have It
Substitute 1 cup (250 mL) wheat bran with:
- 1 cup (250 mL) oat bran
- 1 cup (250 mL) rice bran
- 1 cup (250 mL) wheat germ

## Wheat Germ

*The most nutritious part of the wheat berry contains vitamins, minerals, and protein. Wheat germ is sold in its natural form as well as toasted. Because of its high natural oil content, it should be stored in the refrigerator or freezer to delay rancidity.*

### If You Don't Have It

Substitute 1 cup (250 mL) wheat germ with:

- 1 cup (250 mL) wheat bran
- 1 cup (250 mL) oat bran
- 1 cup (250 mL) rice bran

### For Better Health

Substitute 1 cup (250 mL) wheat germ with:

- 1 cup (250 mL) ground flaxseed (higher in beneficial omega-3 fatty acids)

## Wheatmeal Biscuit

*See* GRAHAM CRACKER.

## Wheat Meat

*See* SEITAN.

## Whelk

*A large marine snail with a decorative shell and large foot muscle that is typically pounded into steaks to tenderize before cooking.*

### If You Don't Have It

Substitute 1 lb (500 g) whelks with:

- 1 lb (500 g) periwinkles
- 1 lb (500 g) limpets
- 1 lb (500 g) conch
- 1 lb (500 g) snails

## Whipped Cream

*Whipped cream is not what it used to be. Prior to the Second World War, raw heavy cream could be frothed into unctuous drifts almost by stirring alone. Cream is more difficult to whip today because it is pasteurized or ultra-pasteurized, a procedure that destroys an enzyme that encourages the fat globules to clump together. To get the best possible results from supermarket creams, choose fresh whipping cream that is at least 30% fat. If possible, buy heavy cream that is 36% fat or more. Chill the bowl, beaters, and*

### If You Don't Have It

Substitute 1 cup (250 mL) freshly whipped cream with:

- 1 cup (250 mL) canned whipped cream
- 1 cup (250 mL) frozen nondairy whipped topping, thawed
- 1 envelope nondairy whipped topping mix, prepared according to instructions

### For Better Health

Substitute 1 cup (250 mL) freshly whipped cream with:

- 12-oz (375 g) can Milnot evaporated milk (at room temperature or chilled), whipped
- 12-oz (375 g) can evaporated milk, chilled overnight, mixed with 1 tbsp (15 mL) lemon juice, and whipped until stiff (less fat; to flavor, beat in 1 tsp/5 mL vanilla extract and ¼ cup/ 50 mL confectioner's sugar)
- 1 cup (250 mL) canned reduced-fat whipped cream
- 1 cup (250 mL) frozen light nondairy whipped topping, thawed
- 1 cup (250 mL) Homemade Whipped Cream Substitute: Combine 1 cup (250 mL) dry whole milk and ⅔ cup (150 mL) cold water in a glass bowl. Freeze until beginning to ice over. Beat with chilled beaters on high speed until soft peaks

*cream in the freezer for 15 minutes before whipping.*

½ cup (125 mL) heavy or whipping cream = 1 cup (250 mL) whipped

form when beaters are lifted. Add 1 tbsp (15 mL) lemon juice and beat until stiff peaks form when beaters are lifted. To flavor, beat in 1 tsp (5 mL) vanilla extract and ¼ cup (60 mL) confectioner's (icing) sugar. Chill until serving. Makes about 1½ cups (375 mL).

## Whipped Topping

*Also known as nondairy whipped topping. A packaged fluffy whipped cream replacement manufactured from processed vegetable oils and high fructose corn syrup.*

### If You Don't Have It
Substitute 1 cup (250 mL) frozen nondairy whipped topping with:
- 1 envelope nondairy whipped topping mix, prepared according to package instructions

### To Vary the Flavor
Substitute 1 cup (250 mL) frozen nondairy whipped topping with:
- 1 cup (250 mL) whipped cream (richer, fresher flavor)

### For Better Health
Substitute 1 cup (250 mL) frozen nondairy whipped topping with:
- 1 cup (250 mL) light frozen nondairy whipped topping

## Whipping Cream

*See* CREAM, WHIPPING; WHIPPED CREAM.

## Whisk

*Also known as a whip. A utensil that beats ingredients as it whips air into the mixture. The tool is comprised of looped wires attached to a handle.*

### If You Don't Have It
Substitute a whisk with:
- electric mixer with beaters
- rotary beater
- fork (for light whisking)
- pastry blender (for light whisking)

## Whiskey

*Also known as whisky (Canada and British Isles). "The water of life" in Ireland and Scotland traveled to North America with immigrants. Barley, rye, or corn is fermented and distilled to produce this amber liquor. Factors affecting the final quality and taste are the type of grain, the water source,*

### If You Don't Have It
Substitute 2 tbsp (30 mL) whiskey (for cooking and baking) with:
- 2 tbsp (30 mL) cognac, brandy, or rum
- 1 to 1½ tsp (5 to 7 mL) vanilla extract (add 4½ to 5 tsp/22 to 25 mL water or apple cider if necessary to replace lost liquid volume)
- ¾ to 1 tsp (3 to 5 mL) rum extract or brandy extract (add 5 to 5¼ tsp/25 to 26 mL water or apple cider if necessary to replace lost liquid volume)

## Whiskey (cont'd)

*the yeast, the distillation method, and the aging. "Straight whiskey," such as bourbon, Tennessee whiskey, and rye whiskey, must contain 51% of a single grain and cannot be higher than 160 proof. It is aged in oak for 2 years and may be diluted with water to no less than 80 proof. "Blended whiskey" is a mix of at least two 100-proof straight whiskeys blended with neutral spirits, grain spirits, or light whiskeys. "Light whiskey," generally used for blending, is distilled to more than 160 proof then diluted with water. It acquires distinction from aging in charred oak barrels. "Single-malt whiskey" is made exclusively with malted barley by a single distiller. Single malt Scotch whiskeys and Irish Whiskeys are richly flavored and tend to be pricey.*

## Whiskey Varieties

Choose 2 tbsp (30 mL) whiskey from these varieties:

- 2 tbsp (30 mL) bourbon (includes small-batch bourbon blended from select barrels and single-barrel bourbon made from a single barrel; bourbon is straight whiskey made from a mash of 51 to 79% corn; aged in new, charred, white-oak barrels for at least 2 years; bottled at 80 to 125 proof; amber color; lightly sweet, smoky flavor)
- 2 tbsp (30 mL) Tennessee whiskey (straight whiskey similar to bourbon; made from a mash of at least 51% corn or another single grain; filtered through sugar-maple charcoal, which imparts a sweeter flavor than bourbon)
- 2 tbsp (30 mL) corn whiskey, moonshine, or white lightning (similar to bourbon and Tennessee whiskey; made from a mash of more than 80% corn; less smooth flavor)
- 2 tbsp (30 mL) rye whiskey (similar to bourbon; made from a mash of at least 51% rye, often with barley and wheat comprising the rest; the predominance of rye gives it a strong, spicy flavor)
- 2 tbsp (30 mL) Scotch whiskey (includes single-malt Scotch, made only from malted barley; and blended Scotch, made from malted barley and unmalted barley, corn, and wheat; Scotch is smokier than other whiskeys because the malted barley is dried over burning peat or turf)
- 2 tbsp (30 mL) Irish whiskey (includes single-malt and blended Irish whiskeys; typically blended and made from malted or unmalted barley, corn, rye, oats, or other grains; aged in wood for at least 4 years in used casks, which impart unique aromas; exceptionally smooth and light flavor resulting from three distillations)
- 2 tbsp (30 mL) Canadian whiskey (blended whiskey made from rye, corn, barley, and wheat; aged in wood for at least 3 years in used casks, which impart unique aromas; smooth, light flavor)

## White Chocolate

*See* CHOCOLATE, WHITE.

## White Currant

*See* CURRANT, FRESH.

## Whitefish

*A North American lake fish with delicate flavor is marketed either as whole fish or in fillets. Smoked whitefish is also produced as is the roe for caviar.*

### If You Don't Have It

Substitute 1 lb (500 g) whitefish with:

- 1 lb (500 g) pike
- 1 lb (500 g) perch
- 1 lb (500 g) walleye
- 1 lb (500 g) lake trout

### To Vary the Flavor

Substitute 1 lb (500 g) whitefish with:

- 1 lb (500 g) smoked whitefish (cured fish; adds smoke flavor)

*See also* CHANGING ROE (PAGE 666).

| **Whitefish Caviar** | *See* CHANGING ROE (PAGE 666). |

| **White Lightning** | *See* WHISKEY. |

| **White Pepper** | *See* PEPPERCORN. |

| **White Poppy Seed** | *See* POPPY SEED. |

## White Pudding

*British sausage that contains chicken or pork, a grain such as oatmeal, and seasonings. In the butcher's case, white pudding is the counterpoint to black pudding (blood sausage).*

### If You Don't Have It
Substitute 1 lb (500 g) white pudding with:
- 1 lb (500 g) French boudin blanc (delicate flavor)
- 1 lb (500 g) Cajun boudin blanc (spicier, more complex flavor)
- 1 lb (500 g) German Weisswurst (mild flavor)
- 1 lb (500 g) white Bratwurst (mild flavor)

| **White Rum** | *See* RUM . |

| **White Sapote** | *See* SAPOTE, WHITE. |

| **White Sauce** | *See* BÉCHAMEL. |

## White Sea Bass

*Also known as California or Pacific sea bass and white weakfish. A member of the croaker family that runs from Baja, California to Juneau, Alaska and averages about 7 pounds (3.5 kg).*

### If You Don't Have It
Substitute 1 lb (500 g) white sea bass with:
- 1 lb (500 g) Atlantic croaker
- 1 lb (500 g) black drum
- 1 lb (500 g) red drum or redfish
- 1 lb (500 g) spot
- 1 lb (500 g) kingfish
- 1 lb (500 g) weakfish
- 1 lb (500 g) porgy
- 1 lb (500 g) hake

*See also* CROAKER.

| **White Walnut** | *See* BUTTERNUT. |

## Whiting

*A name applied to different fish in North Atlantic/European and Indo-Pacific waters. The European fish is digestible but dull. The species that are caught near India and Australia are an important food source, offering better flavor and a delicate texture.*

### If You Don't Have It

Substitute 1 lb (500 g) whiting with:

- 1 lb (500 g) hake
- 1 lb (500 g) cod
- 1 lb (500 g) pollock
- 1 lb (500 g) flounder or other flatfish
- 1 lb (500 g) ocean perch
- 1 lb (500 g) red snapper
- 1 lb (500 g) tilefish

## Whole Wheat Flour

*See* FLOUR, WHOLE WHEAT.

## Whortleberry

*See* BILBERRY.

## Wild Leek

*See* RAMP.

## Wild Pecan Rice

*See* VARIETIES OF RICE (PAGE 664).

## Wild Rice

*A cereal grass that grows wild in water in parts of North America, Africa, Southeast Asia, and China. It is not closely related to rice and doesn't lend itself to cultivation. In the upper Midwest U.S., and in several Canadian provinces, the grains are traditionally harvested by Native Americans paddling in canoes through the rice beds.*

1 cup (250 mL) =
3½ to 4 cups
(875 mL to 1 L) cooked

### If You Don't Have It

Substitute 1 cup (250 mL) uncooked wild rice with:

- 1 cup (250 mL) uncooked brown rice (less chewy; less complex flavor; decrease liquid and cooking time slightly)
- 1 cup (250 mL) uncooked brown basmati rice (less chewy; more aromatic, nutty flavor; decrease liquid and cooking time slightly)
- 1 cup (250 mL) wild pecan rice (less chewy; more aromatic, popcorn-like flavor; decrease liquid and cooking time slightly)
- 1 cup (250 mL) uncooked bulgur (less chewy; less complex flavor; decrease liquid and cooking time slightly)

## Wine, Dessert

*Sweet and luscious, perfect as a finale to a great meal or a delightful treat in itself. The finest dessert wines are those that nature sweetens by concentrating the grape sugars in late-harvested grapes infected with the* Botrytis cinerea *mold, known as "noble rot." French Sauternes is an eminent example of a late-harvest dessert wine. Fortified wines, such as port and sherry are also often classified as dessert wines. Fortified wines are made by adding grape brandy to wine to increase the amount of alcohol.*

### If You Don't Have It

Substitute 1 cup (250 mL) dessert wine with:
- 1 cup (250 mL) sparkling grape juice (nonalcoholic)
- 1 cup (250 mL) sparkling cider (nonalcoholic)
- 1 cup (250 mL) grape juice (nonalcoholic)

### To Vary the Flavor

Substitute 1 cup (250 mL) dessert wine with:
- 1 cup (250 mL) coffee or espresso (to accompany dessert)

### Dessert Wine Varieties

Choose 1 cup (250 mL) dessert wine from these popular varieties:
- 1 cup (250 mL) sparkling wine such asasti spumante (sweet, musky flavor from Muscat grapes)
- 1 cup (250 mL) demi-sec or doux champagne (sweet champagnes with more than 3% sugar)
- 1 cup (250 mL) late-harvest wine such as Riesling, Gewürztraminer, Sauvignon Blanc, and Sauternes (sweet wines with a relatively high alcohol content; made from late-harvest grapes infected with a beneficial mold that shrivels the grapes and concentrates their sugar content)
- 1 cup (250 mL) ice wine (sweet wines made from grapes frozen on the vine and pressed while still frozen, which produces a richly flavored, high-sugar wine)
- 1 cup (250 mL) sherry, especially oloroso, Amoroso, or cream sherry (sweet, medium- to full-bodied, and golden in color; full flavor)
- 1 cup (250 mL) Madeira, especially Boal or Malmsey (medium-sweet to sweet and golden in color with rich flavor)
- 1 cup (250 mL) port (sweet; light amber to reddish color; mild or full flavor depending on age and vintage)
- 1 cup (250 mL) banyuls (sweet; lighter amber-red color; mild or full flavor depending on age and vintage)

*See also* BANYULS; PORT; SHERRY.

## Wine, Fortified

*See* BANYULS; MADEIRA; MARSALA; PORT; SHERRY; VERMOUTH.

## Wine, Red

*To make red wine, the juice of crushed grapes is left in contact with the skins to extract color. Tannin is another important component of the extraction. It*

### If You Don't Have It

Substitute 1 cup (250 mL) red wine (for cooking) with:
- ¾ cup (175 mL) red grape juice or currant juice + 2 tbsp (30 mL) red wine vinegar or lemon juice + 2 tbsp (30 mL) water (for marinades)
- 1 cup (250 mL) beef stock (for sauces and stews)
- 1 cup (250 mL) soaking liquid from sun-dried tomatoes or dried mushrooms (for sauces and stews)

## Wine, Red (cont'd)

*contributes structure and body as well as aging potential. The amount of color will depend on the grape type and the length of time that maceration on the skins is permitted. Red wines are typically more robust than whites.*

> 750 mL bottle = 25.4 oz
> = 5 (5-oz) servings

## Wine, Sparkling

*Associated universally with celebration, effervescent wines vary in style and quality. The strict and precise méthode champenoise produces Champagne, the finest sparkling wine in the world, only in the Champagne region of France. All other French sparkling wines are known as* vins mousseux *or* crémant. *Sparklers from other countries using the méthode champenoise include Spanish cava and Italian* franciacorta. *Other good sparkling wines, such as Italian* prosecco *are produced in the charmat or bulk method of tank fermentation followed by bottling under pressure. Cheap sparkling wines have carbon dioxide pumped in by the soda pop method. For both American and European sparkling wines, natural is drier than brut. Brut is drier than extra dry.*

- 1 cup (250 mL) beer (for stews)
- 1 cup (250 mL) Madeira (for sauces and stews; pale to tawny color and dry to sweet flavor)
- 1 cup (250 mL) port (for sauces and stews; sweeter)

### For Better Health
Substitute 1 cup (250 mL) red wine with:
- 1 cup (250 mL) nonalcoholic red wine (sweeter)

### If You Don't Have It
Substitute 1 cup (250 mL) sparkling wine with:
- 1 cup (250 mL) champagne
- 1 cup (250 mL) crisp white wine (no bubbles)

### Sparkling Wine Varieties
Choose 1 cup (250 mL) sparkling wine from these varieties:
- 1 cup (250 mL) champagne (French)
- 1 cup (250 mL) prosecco (Italian)
- 1 cup (250 mL) franciacorta (Italian)
- 1 cup (250 mL) cava (Spanish)
- 1 cup (250 mL) espumante (Portuguese)
- 1 cup (250 mL) sekt (German and Austrian)
- 1 cup (250 mL) pezsgö (Hungarian)
- 1 cup (250 mL) Cap Classique (South African)

### For Better Health
Substitute 1 cup (250 mL) sparkling wine with:
- 1 cup (250 mL) sparkling cider (no alcohol)
- 1 cup (250 mL) sparkling grape juice (no alcohol)

*See also* CHAMPAGNE; WINE, DESSERT.

## Wine, White

*In the making of white wine, after the juice is squeezed from the grapes, it has only the briefest contact with the grape skins. (Some white wines are actually made from red-skinned grapes.) Virtually no color and very little tannin is extracted. While tannins add structure and body to red wines, they may overpower the delicate flavors and aromas of white wines. Depending upon the varietal, white wines should be served chilled, at temperatures ranging from 36° to 50°F (2° to 10°C).*

750 mL bottle = 25.4 oz = 5 (5-oz) servings

### If You Don't Have It

Substitute 1 cup (250 mL) white wine (for cooking) with:
- 1 cup (250 mL) sherry or vermouth (especially for sauces and stews)
- 1 cup (250 mL) sake (especially for sauces and stews)
- 1 cup (250 mL) mirin (especially for sauces and stews; sweeter)
- 1 cup (250 mL) Madeira (for sauces and stews; pale to tawny color and dry to sweet flavor)
- 1 cup (250 mL) chicken or vegetable stock (for sauces and stews)
- 1 cup (250 mL) fish stock (for sauces, soups, and stews; adds briny, fish flavor)
- 1 cup (250 mL) veal stock (for sauces, soups, and stews; adds rich texture)
- ¾ cup (175 mL) white grape juice, apple juice, or apple cider + ¼ cup (60 mL) white wine vinegar or lemon juice (for marinades)

### For Better Health

Substitute 1 cup (250 mL) white wine with:
- 1 cup (250 mL) nonalcoholic white wine (sweeter)

*See also* MIRIN; SAKE.

## Winged Bean

*Also known as goa bean. A nourishing tropical vegetable with edible pods that taste like a combination of pod beans and green beans.*

1 lb (500 g) fresh = 3½ cups (875 mL) whole

### If You Don't Have It

Substitute 1 lb (500 g) winged bean pods with:
- 1 lb (500 g) yard-long beans
- 1 lb (500 g) fresh cranberry beans
- 1 lb (500 g) green beans (less starchy and beany-tasting; sweeter)

## Winkle

*See* PERIWINKLE.

## Winter Melon

*Also known as ash gourd, dung gua (Chinese), jundol (Philippine), petha (India), wax gourd, and white gourd. Winter melons are eaten throughout the summer in China. The icy white flesh, akin in taste to cucumber and summer squash, has a cooling effect. In India, it is crystallized into fruit candy. Winter melons can weigh from 5 to 50 pounds (2.5 to 25 kg) and have a dark green skin with a frosty finish.*

2 lbs (1 kg) =
3 cups (750 mL) diced

### If You Don't Have It

Substitute 1 lb (500 g) winter melon with:
- 1 lb (500 g) cucuzza
- 1 lb (500 g) bottle gourd
- 1 lb (500 g) chayote
- 1 lb (500 g) zucchini
- 1 lb (500 g) yellow squash

*See also* FUZZY GOURD.

## Winter Squash

*See* ACORN SQUASH; BANANA SQUASH; BUTTERCUP SQUASH; BUTTERNUT SQUASH; DELICATA SQUASH; HUBBARD SQUASH; KABOCHA SQUASH; PUMPKIN; SPAGHETTI SQUASH; SWEET DUMPLING SQUASH.

## Winter Squash Seed

*Similar to pumpkin seeds, the seeds of most winter squash can be roasted and eaten as a snack. Butternut, acorn, and hubbard squash seeds all taste good.*

### If You Don't Have It

Substitute 1 cup (250 mL) winter squash seed with:
- 1 cup (250 mL) Homemade Roasted Winter Squash Seeds: Remove seeds from the squash cavity, separating the seeds from the pulp and fiber. Rinse well in a colander under cold water then spread the seeds on a kitchen towel to dry. Spread the dry seeds on a baking sheet in a single layer. Toss with oil to coat and roast at 250°F (120°C) until golden, stirring now and then, for about 1 hour. Sprinkle with salt or other seasonings, if desired. Store in an airtight container at room temperature for up to 3 months or in the refrigerator for up to 1 year.
- 1 cup (250 mL) pumpkin seeds
- 1 cup (250 mL) dried guajes
- 1 cup (250 mL) sunflower seeds
- 2 to 4 tbsp (30 to 60 mL) pumpkin seed oil (for baking and cooking; will add toasted pumpkin seed flavor but not texture of whole seeds; reduce fat in recipe by 2 to 4 tbsp/ 30 to 60 mL)

*See also* PUMPKIN SEED.

## Wok

*A round-bottomed pan popular in Asian cooking.*

### If You Don't Have It

Substitute a wok with:
- slope-sided sauté pan (preferably heavy and nonstick or well-seasoned)

## Wondra

*See* FLOUR, INSTANT.

## Wong Bok

*See* NAPA CABBAGE.

## Won Ton Skins

*Also known as potsticker wrappers and won ton wrappers. Square or round sheets of dough, in varying thicknesses, purchased ready-made to make won tons, egg rolls, and other dough-encased dishes. Thinner varieties are best cooked in liquid, such as wontons cooked in soup. Thicker varieties, such as gyoza wrappers, are best fried.*

### If You Don't Have It

Substitute 1 lb (500 g) won ton skins with:
- 1 lb (500 g) egg roll wrappers (relatively thick; often used for egg rolls)
- 1 lb (500 g) empanada wrappers (round)
- 1 lb (500 g) rolled pasta (cut to desired shape)
- 1 lb (500 g) rice paper (thinner; larger; cut to desired shape; makes crispy dumplings)

### Won Ton Skin Varieties

Choose 1 lb (500 g) won ton skins from these varieties:
- 1 lb (500 g) water dumpling wrappers (relatively thin; round; often used for soups or cooked in liquid)
- 1 lb (500 g) shao mai skins (relatively thin; round; often used for steamed dumplings)
- 1 lb (500 g) gyoza wrappers (thicker; round; often used for pot stickers)
- 1 lb (500 g) suey gow wrappers (may be thin or thick; used for dumplings)

## Wood Ear

*See* SHUFFLING MUSHROOMS (PAGE 654).

## Wood Plank

*Grilling directly on wood planks makes it easier to handle thin delicate foods such as fish fillets and adds smoky aromas from the burning wood. Cedar, alder, maple, and cherry are some of the more popular woods for plank grilling.*

### If You Don't Have It

Substitute wood planks (for grilling) with:
- untreated cedar shingles (or any untreated wood that is about ¼ inch/0.5 cm thick)
- preheated salt block or plank

## Wood Smoke

*Wood smoke is the essential flavor in barbecued food. It can come from wood logs, chunks, chips, shavings, or pellets. You can't barbecue without smoke, but you can get smoke flavor without barbecuing.*

### If You Don't Have It

Substitute wood smoke (for smoke flavor) with:

- liquid smoke
- smoked salt
- smoked pepper, paprika, or other smoked spices
- smoked bacon or ham hock (adds pork flavor)
- chipotle peppers or canning liquid from chipotles en adobo (adds spices and considerable heat)

*See also* LIQUID SMOKE.

## Worcestershire Sauce

*This dark and complex liquid condiment is modeled after an Indian sauce that was fancied by the former governor of Bengal Lord Marcus Sandys. It was in the early 1800s that Sandys commissioned two Worcester (UK) chemists, John Lea and William Perrins, to create a large batch to replicate the Indian sauce. Lord Sandys said the result "tasted filthy" and was nothing like the Indian sauce. A few months later, Lea and Perrins rechecked the mixture to discover it had fermented and matured into a piquant, spicy flavoring. They purchased the recipe from Sandys and began to manufacture the now internationally famous Worcestershire Sauce.*

### If You Don't Have It

Substitute 1 tbsp (15 mL) Worcestershire sauce with:

- 1 tsp (5 mL) tamarind concentrate or paste + 1 tsp (5 mL) soy sauce + 1 tsp (5 mL) apple cider vinegar + dash of hot pepper sauce + small pinch of ground cloves
- 1 tbsp (15 mL) HP sauce (thicker; sweeter)
- 2 tsp (10 mL) soy sauce + 4 drops hot pepper sauce + $\frac{1}{4}$ tsp (1 mL) lemon juice + $\frac{1}{4}$ tsp (1 mL) granulated sugar
- 1 tbsp (15 mL) steak sauce (thicker; sweeter; usually lacks the sour tang of tamarind)
- 1 tbsp (15 mL) vegetarian Worcestershire sauce (made without anchovies)

*See also* STEAK SAUCE.

## Wu Gu Ji

*See* CHICKEN, BLACK.

# Xanthan Gum
## to **XO Sauce**

## Xanthan Gum

*Often combined with guar gum, this thickener, emulsifier, and stabilizer is made by allowing Xanthomonas campestris bacteria to feed on corn sugar. The slippery gum that forms helps to keep ice creams smooth and sauces emulsified. It also lends a richer mouthfeel to low-fat products and serves as a gluten substitute in gluten-free baking (use about $^3/_4$ tsp/3 mL per cup/250 mL of gluten-free flour). To thicken 1 cup (250 mL) liquid, use a heaping $^1/_4$ tsp (1 mL) xanthan gum.*

## If You Don't Have It

Substitute 1 tsp (5 mL) xanthan gum with:

- $^3/_4$ tsp (3 mL) guar gum
- 1 tsp (5 mL) ground flaxseed
- 2 tbsp (30 mL) cornstarch
- 1 tsp (5 mL) pre-gel starch

## XO Sauce

*Rich, spicy Chinese seafood sauce created in Hong Kong in the 1980s and featuring dried scallops, dried shrimp, red chiles, garlic, oil, and dry-cured ham. The name XO comes from the finest cognac ("extra old") and signifies quality and luxury.*

## If You Don't Have It

Substitute 1 tbsp (15 mL) XO sauce with:

- 1 tbsp (15 mL) Homemade XO sauce: Soak 2 tbsp (30 mL) small dried shrimp in boiling water to cover for 1 hour. Combine 1 cup (250 mL) water and ¼ cup (60 mL) dried scallops in a small saucepan. Bring to a boil, then remove from heat and set aside until the water is cool to the touch, 20 minutes. Return the pan to low heat and simmer until the scallops are soft, 15 minutes. Remove from heat and let cool in the liquid. When cool, pluck out the scallops and shred like pulled pork into a bowl, discarding the tough adductor muscle of each scallop. Reserve the scallop soaking liquid. Drain the shrimp and finely chop. Heat ½ cup (125 mL) peanut oil or canola oil in a wok or heavy skillet over medium heat. Add ¼ cup (60 mL) minced fresh onion, 3 minced garlic cloves, and ½ to 1 tsp (2 to 5 mL) crushed red pepper flakes and stir-fry for 2 to 3 minutes. Add the chopped shrimp, shredded scallops, 2 tbsp (30 mL) minced jinhua, Yunnan, or Smithfield Virginia ham, and ¼ tsp (1 mL) ground black pepper. Stir-fry for 2 to 3 minutes. Add the scallop soaking liquid and reduce heat to low. Simmer gently until most of the liquid evaporates and the sauce looks oily, 15 minutes. Let cool completely and refrigerate in an airtight container for up to 3 weeks. Makes about ¾ cup (175 mL).
- 1 tbsp (15 mL) bottled XO sauce
- 1 tbsp (15 mL) bottled oyster sauce + 1 tsp (5 mL) minced Iberico or Virginia ham

# Yakitori Sauce to Yuzu

## Yakitori Sauce

*See* TERIYAKI SAUCE.

## Yam

*Also known as igname (French), ñame (Spanish), and mapuey (Spanish). A bland and starchy tropical tuber that nourishes many of the world's people. Most yams have dark brown, shaggy skin, but types can differ in size and shape from large tubes to small rounds. These include the white yam, purple yam, Chinese yam, and cushcush yam. In the U.S., the term "yam" is often misapplied to sweet potatoes, to which yams bear no resemblance.*

1 lb (500 g) =
3½ to 4 cups
(875 mL to 1 L)
chopped or sliced

### If You Don't Have It
Substitute 1 lb (500 g) yams with:
- 1 lb (500 g) boniato
- 1 lb (500 g) cassava
- 1 lb (500 g) mandiba
- 1 lb (500 g) yautía
- 1 lb (500 g) starchy potatoes such as russets
- 1 lb (500 g) taro
- 1 lb (500 g) oca
- 1 lb (500 g) arracacha
- 1 lb (500 g) arrowhead
- 1 lb (500 g) unripe green plantains
- 1 lb (500 g) orange-flesh sweet potatoes (much softer, moister, sweeter, orange-color flesh)

### Yam Varieties
Choose 1 lb (500 g) yams from these varieties:
- 1 lb (500 g) white or water yams (the most common true yam; white, crisp, mildly sweet flesh)
- 1 lb (500 g) African white yams (similar to white yams; white to pale yellow, crisp, mildly sweet flesh; often used to make the African mash called fufu)
- 1 lb (500 g) purple yams (uncommon variety of white yam; pinkish purple, crisp, mildly sweet flesh; color deepens after cooking)

## Yam (cont'd)

- 1 lb (500 g) cushcush or mapuey yams (cream-color, firm, starchy, mildly sweet flesh; more flavorful and delicately textured than other yams)
- 1 lb (500 g) Chinese yams (cream to yellow color, very mild, dry flesh)

*See also* SWEET POTATO.

## Yankee Bean

*See* THE WIDE WORLD OF DRIED BEANS (PAGE 637).

## Yard-Long Bean

*These skinny flexible pods are at their best when stir-fried, sautéed, pan fried, or deep fried.*

1 lb (500 g) fresh = 3½ cups (875 mL) sliced

### If You Don't Have It
Substitute 1 lb (500 g) yard-long beans with:
- 1 lb (500 g) green beans (sweeter, less starchy, and more crisp)
- 1 lb (500 g) winged-bean pods
- 1 lb (500 g) fresh shelled black-eyed peas or cranberry beans

## Yau Choy

*Also known as yau tsoi, you cai, yu choy, and yu choy sum or green choy sum. A type of bok choy that looks like a thinner-stemmed version of Chinese broccoli with pretty yellow flower buds.*

1 lb (500 g) fresh = 3½ cups (875 mL) chopped

### If You Don't Have It
Substitute 1 lb (500 g) yau choy with:
- 1 lb (500 g) choy sum or flowering Chinese cabbage (similar to bok choy but slightly smaller stems and leaves; often blossoms with clusters of small yellow flowers)
- 1 lb (500 g) Taiwan bok choy (thinner stems; more delicate leaves; very mild cabbage flavor)
- 1 lb (500 g) Shanghai bok choy (short, squat, green stems; often sold as "baby" bok choy; mellow cabbage flavor)
- 1 lb (500 g) Canton bok choy (slightly stronger cabbage flavor)
- 1 lb (500 g) mature bok choy (the variety of bok choy that is common in American markets; sweet; juicy; mild cabbage flavor)
- 1 lb (500 g) Chinese broccoli or gai lan (darker green stems and sweeter, less cabbagey flavor)
- 1 lb (500 g) napa cabbage (paler green yellow color; more tender; great for stir-frying)
- 1 lb (500 g) Green chard (less cabbagey flavor)
- 1 lb (500 g) collards (firmer, greener stems; larger leaves)

*See also* BOK CHOY.

## Yautía

*Also known as coco, cocoyam, malanga (Cuban), tanier, tannia, taro, yautía amarilla, yautía blanca, and yautía lila. The Puerto Rican name of a root vegetable that's native to New World tropics. The cormels are typically long and tapered, with dark shaggy skin that sometimes doesn't completely cover the flesh. Yautía (malanga) is a boiled staple in many countries, eaten with spicy sausages, pungent dried fish, or peppery stews.*

> 1 lb (500 g) = 3½ to 4 cups (875 mL to 1 L) chopped or sliced = 2 cups (500 mL) cooked and mashed

### If You Don't Have It

Substitute 1 lb (500 g) yautía or malanga with:

- 1 lb (500 g) taro
- 1 lb (500 g) cassava
- 1 lb (500 g) mandiba
- 1 lb (500 g) boniato
- 1 lb (500 g) oca
- 1 lb (500 g) arracacha
- 1 lb (500 g) arrowhead
- 1 lb (500 g) unripe green plantains
- 1 lb (500 g) potatoes
- 1 lb (500 g) parsnips
- 1 lb (500 g) orange-flesh sweet potatoes (much softer, moister, sweeter, orange-color flesh)

### Yautía Varieties

Choose 1 lb (500 g) yautía or malanga from these varieties:

- 1 lb (500 g) white yautía or malanga blanca (white flesh with potato-like texture; mild to earthy flavor; the most common variety in North America)
- 1 lb (500 g) purple yautía or malanga lila (light purple flesh with dense, potato-like texture; earthy flavor; color fades to grayish when cooked)
- 1 lb (500 g) yellow yautía or malanga amarilla (pale yellow orange flesh with very dense, potato-like texture; sweet, nutty flavor; often mixed with other ingredients to make pasteles, fufu, and other Latin American dishes)

*See also* TARO.

---

## Yeast, Baker's

*Microscopic single-celled organism that causes breads and other baked goods to rise by creating carbon dioxide as it feasts upon flour, and perhaps sugar, in the dough.*

> ¼ oz (8 g) pkg active dry yeast = 2¼ tsp (11 mL) = 0.6 oz (17 g) cake compressed fresh yeast
>
> 1 large (2 oz/60 g) cake compressed fresh yeast = 3 small (0.6 oz/17 g) cakes compressed fresh yeast = 3 tbsp (45 mL) active dry yeast

### If You Don't Have It

Substitute ¼ oz (8 g) pkg or 2¼ tsp (11 mL) active dry yeast or 0.6 oz (17 g) cake compressed fresh yeast with:

- 2 cups (500 mL) yeast starter (adds flavor of starter, such as tartness of sourdough starter)

### To Save Time

Substitute ¼ oz (8 g) pkg active dry yeast with:

- 2¼ tsp (11 mL) instant or quick-rising yeast (needs only one rise; reduce rising time by 40 to 50%; add to dry ingredients; flavor of bread may be slightly diminished)
- 2¼ tsp (11 mL) bread machine yeast (fine texture; needs only one rise; reduce rising time by 40 to 50%; add to dry ingredients; flavor of bread may be slightly diminished)

## Yeast, Brewer's

*Particular strains of yeast used in beer making. Because it is rich in B vitamins, it is also eaten as a nutritional supplement. It is sold in natural food stores and beer-making equipment shops.*

1 tbsp (15 mL) powdered = 2 tbsp (30 mL) flakes

### If You Don't Have It

Substitute 1 tbsp (15 mL) brewer's yeast with:
- 1 to 1½ tbsp (15 to 22 mL) nutritional yeast (pale yellow color; less bitter and more cheesy flavor)
- 2 to 3 tsp (10 to 15 mL) yeast extract (dark brown paste; stronger, saltier flavor)

### To Vary the Flavor

Substitute 1 tbsp (15 mL) brewer's yeast with:
- 1 tbsp (15 mL) debittered brewer's yeast (less bitter flavor)

*See also* YEAST, NUTRITIONAL.

## Yeast Extract

*A combination of liquids extracted from fresh yeast and fresh vegetables. It can be pourably thin or as thick as paste. It's rich in B vitamins and can be used as a seasoning. Also the base for pungent, salty brown spreads such as Marmite© and Vegemite©.*

### If You Don't Have It

Substitute 1 tbsp (15 mL) yeast extract with:
- 1 tbsp (15 mL) brewer's yeast (flakes or powder)
- 1 tbsp (15 mL) nutritional yeast (milder, more cheesy flavor)
- 1 tbsp (15 mL) dark or hatcho miso (saltier)
- 1 tbsp (15 mL) peanut butter (for spreading on bread; sweeter and milder flavor)

### Yeast Extract Varieties

Choose 1 tbsp (15 mL) yeast extract from these commercial varieties:
- 1 tbsp (15 mL) Vegemite© (pungent and slightly salty; popular in Australia)
- 1 tbsp (15 mL) Marmite© (pungent, salty, and slightly sweet; popular in Britain)
- 1 tbsp (15 mL) Promite© (pungent and slightly sweet)

## Yeast, Nutritional

*A dietary supplement from the same strain as brewer's yeast but with a less bitter flavor. It has a nutty-cheesy taste and is packed with protein and B vitamins. Sold as flakes or powder. Vegans use it to for a dairy-free cheesy flavor, especially on popcorn.*

1 tbsp (15 mL) powdered = 2 tbsp (30 mL) flakes

### If You Don't Have It

Substitute 1 tbsp (15 mL) nutritional yeast with:
- 2 to 3 tsp (10 to 15 mL) brewer's yeast (darker color; more bitter and less cheesy flavor)
- 2 to 3 tsp (10 to 15 mL) yeast extract (dark brown paste; stronger, saltier flavor)
- 1 tbsp (15 mL) grated Parmesan or Cheddar cheese (for cheesy flavor)

*See also* YEAST, BREWER'S.

## Yellow Berry

*See* CLOUDBERRY.

## Yellowfin Tuna

*See* TUNA, FRESH.

## Yellow Soybean Paste

*See* FERMENTED BEAN PASTE.

## Yellow Squash

*A sunny-skinned summer marrow that can have either a straight, semi-straight or crooked neck that is narrower than the base.*

1 lb (500 g) = 3 medium = 3 cups (750 mL) sliced

### If You Don't Have It

Substitute 1 lb (500 g) yellow squash with:
- 1 lb (500 g) zucchini (yellow or green color)
- 1 lb (500 g) pattypan squash (yellow or green color)
- 1 lb (500 g) Zephyr summer squash (hybrid of yellow crookneck, Delicata, and acorn squashes; yellow on one end and green on the other)
- 1 lb (500 g) cucuzza (pale green)
- 1 lb (500 g) bottle gourd (pale green)
- 1 lb (500 g) chayote (cream to pale green)

### Yellow Squash Varieties

Choose 1 lb (500 g) yellow squash from these varieties:
- 1 lb (500 g) yellow crookneck squash (warty and curved near stem end; slightly sweeter than straightneck yellow squash)
- 1 lb (500 g) straightneck yellow squash (smooth and tapered near stem end; milder, less sweet flavor than crookneck squash)

## Yellow Storage Onion

*See* ONION, STORAGE.

## Yellowtail

*See* POMPANO.

## Yerba Buena

*See* MINT.

## Yogurt

*Also known as yoghurt. The Turkish name for this healthful fermented milk product has been adopted into English. Refreshing, protein-rich, and easy to digest, yogurt is even reputed to increase longevity. In its*

### If You Don't Have It

Substitute 1 cup (250 mL) yogurt with:
- 1 cup (250 mL) sour cream (thicker; less tart)
- 1 cup (250 mL) soy sour cream (contains soy milk; thicker; less tart)
- 1 cup (250 mL) crème fraîche (thicker; less tart)
- 1 cup (250 mL) silken tofu, blended until smooth (thicker; less tart)
- 1 cup (250 mL) buttermilk (thinner; best for baking, dressings, and gently cooked or uncooked sauces)

## Yogurt (cont'd)

*myriad mass-produced incarnations, with the addition of sugar and other empty calorie add-ons, yogurt often strays from its healthful roots.*

1 cup (250 mL) =
8 oz (250 g)

- 1 cup (250 mL) kefir (traditionally contains camel's milk; these days, usually contains cow's milk; thinner; more sour-tasting)
- 1 cup (250 mL) quark (richer texture)
- 1 cup (250 mL) mayonnaise (contains eggs; richer texture)

### Yogurt Varieties

Choose 1 cup (250 mL) yogurt from these varieties:
- 1 cup (250 mL) flavored yogurt (sweeter)
- 1 cup (250 mL) soy yogurt (contains soy milk)
- 1 cup (250 mL) low-lactose yogurt (for the lactose intolerant)
- 1 cup (250 mL) goat's milk yogurt (for the lactose intolerant)

### For Better Health

Substitute 1 cup (250 mL) yogurt with:
- 1 cup (250 mL) reduced-fat yogurt (less fat and fewer calories)

## Yogurt Cheese

*Also known as chaka, labneh, strained yogurt, and Turkish or Greek yogurt. A delightfully tangy fresh cheese prepared by straining yogurt through cheesecloth to remove much of the liquid. It makes a thicker alternative to plain yogurt and a delicious spread when mixed with fresh herbs, spices, or other seasonings.*

1 cup (250 mL) =
10 oz (300 g)

### If You Don't Have It

Substitute 1 cup (250 mL) yogurt cheese or strained yogurt with:
- 1 cup (250 mL) Homemade Yogurt Cheese or Strained Yogurt: Put 3 cups (750 mL) plain yogurt into a colander or sieve lined with cheesecloth or a thin kitchen towel. For extra-firm yogurt cheese, cover with a top layer of cheesecloth and weigh down with a bag of beans or another weight. Set the colander or sieve over a deep bowl, loosely cover, and refrigerate overnight or until the yogurt is reduced in volume by at least half (the excess liquid will drain into the bowl). Makes about 1½ cups (375 mL).
- 1 oz (30 g) kefir cheese

### To Vary the Flavor

Substitute 1 oz (30 g) yogurt cheese with:
- 1 cup (250 mL) quark (richer texture)
- 1 cup (250 mL) cream cheese
- 1 cup (250 mL) mascarpone
- 1 cup (250 mL) fromage blanc
- 1 cup (250 mL) sour cream
- 1 cup (250 mL) buttermilk cheese
- 1 cup (250 mL) crème fraîche
- 1 cup (250 mL) silken tofu, blended until smooth
- ½ cup (125 mL) ricotta cheese + ½ cup (125 mL) sour cream, blended
- ½ cup (125 mL) cream cheese + ½ cup (125 mL) cream, blended
- ½ cup (125 mL) cottage cheese + ½ cup (125 mL) yogurt, blended

## Yogurt, Frozen

*Similar in texture to soft ice cream, frozen yogurt took off in popularity in the 1980s as a healthier alternative to ice cream.*

### If You Don't Have It
Substitute 1 cup (250 mL) frozen yogurt with:
- 1 cup (250 mL) ice cream or soy ice cream

### For Better Health
Substitute 1 cup (250 mL) frozen yogurt with:
- 1 cup (250 mL) reduced-fat frozen yogurt (less fat and fewer calories)

## York Ham

*Originally from York, England, this mild, lightly colored style of ham is delectable served hot or cold. It is dry-salted and smoked then aged for several months.*

### If You Don't Have It
Substitute 4 oz (125 g) York ham with:
- 4 oz (125 g) Virginia ham, such as Smithfield (more heavily smoked over hickory and apple woods)
- 4 oz (125 g) Kentucky ham (more heavily smoked over hickory and apple woods)
- 4 oz (125 g) Yunnan ham (lean, dry-cured Chinese ham)
- 4 oz (125 g) Westphalian ham (adds juniper flavor)
- 4 oz (125 g) Ardennes ham
- 4 oz (125 g) Bayonne ham
- 4 oz (125 g) serrano or Iberico ham (lacks smoke flavor)
- 4 oz (125 g) prosciutto (lacks smoke flavor)

## Youngberry

*Distinctively flavored, tart, dark red berry. A cross between the Phenomenal berry (a blackberry/ raspberry hybrid) and the Austin Mayes dewberry developed in Morgan City, Louisiana by B.M. Young in 1905.*

1 pint fresh = 2 cups (500 mL)

### If You Don't Have It
Substitute 1 cup (250 mL) youngberries with:
- 1 cup (250 mL) dewberries (close relative of blackberry)
- 1 cup (250 mL) loganberries (hybrid of blackberries and raspberries; dark red color)
- 1 cup (250 mL) boysenberries (hybrid of blackberries, raspberries, and loganberries; reddish purple color)
- 1 cup (250 mL) olallieberries (hybrid of youngberries and loganberries; dark purple color; larger; sweeter)
- 1 cup (250 mL) tayberries (hybrid of blackberries and raspberries; larger; red color)
- 1 cup (250 mL) blackberries (larger; darker purple color)
- 1 cup (250 mL) raspberries (sweeter; red color)

*See also* DEWBERRY.

## Yuca
*See* CASSAVA.

## Yu Choy Sum
*See* YAU CHOY.

## Yunnan Ham

*A lean, dry-cured Chinese ham similar to Virginia ham.*

### If You Don't Have It

Substitute 4 oz (125 g) Yunnan ham with:

- 4 oz (125 g) Jinhua ham
- 4 oz (125 g) Smithfield ham or other Virginia ham
- 4 oz (125 g) Westphalian ham (adds juniper flavor)
- 4 oz (125 g) Ardennes ham
- 4 oz (125 g) Bayonne ham
- 4 oz (125 g) York ham
- 4 oz (125 g) serrano or Iberico ham (lacks smoke flavor)
- 4 oz (125 g) prosciutto (lacks smoke flavor)

## Yuzu

*A tangerine-size citrus much loved in Japan. Bright green in summer, yuzu turns yellow when it ripens in the fall. The tart zest and juice flavor many dishes, particularly ponzu dressing, in which it is combined with rice vinegar, mirin, soy sauce, and fish broth.*

### If You Don't Have It

Substitute 1 tbsp (15 mL) yuzu with:

- 2 tsp (10 mL) lemon juice + 1 tsp (5 mL) lime juice (to replace yuzu juice)
- 1½ tsp (7 mL) lime juice + 1½ tsp (7 mL) orange or grapefruit juice (to replace yuzu juice)
- 1 tbsp (15 mL) grated lemon and/or lime zest (to replace grated yuzu zest)

# Za'atar to Zwieback

## Za'atar

Also known as zahtar. A Middle Eastern spice blend of dried marjoram, toasted sesame seeds, dried thyme, and sumac. It enhances dips, meats, and vegetables. Often, it's blended with olive oil and salt to accompany hot bread.

### If You Don't Have It
Substitute 1 tbsp (15 mL) za'atar with:
- 1 tbsp (15 mL) Homemade Za'atar: Combine 2 tsp (10 mL) dried thyme, ¾ tsp (3 mL) sumac (optional), ½ tsp (2 mL) toasted sesame seeds, and ⅛ tsp (0.5 mL) salt in a mortar and pestle and coarsely grind.

## Zante Grape

See CHAMPAGNE GRAPE; CURRANT, DRIED.

## Zapote Blanco

See SAPOTE, WHITE.

## Zeppoli

See DOUGHNUT.

## Zester

A tiny-toothed cutting instrument that removes citrus zest in filament-like strands.

### If You Don't Have It
Substitute a zester (for zesting citrus fruit) with:
- fine holes of a box grater
- Microplane® or rasp grater
- paring knife

See also GRATER.

## Zucchini

*Also known as courgette (Britain). Tender-skinned summer squash with mild buttery flavor. In U.S. markets, zucchini is almost always the dark green or cylindrical squash but many other flavorful types exist. Vegetable marrow or marrow squash refers to a large zucchini.*

1 lb (500 g) =
3 medium zucchini =
3 cups (750 mL) sliced

### If You Don't Have It
Substitute 1 lb (500 g) zucchini with:
- 1 lb (500 g) yellow squash (yellow color)
- 1 lb (500 g) pattypan squash (green or yellow color)
- 1 lb (500 g) Zephyr summer squash (hybrid of yellow crookneck, Delicata, and acorn squashes; yellow on one end and green on the other)
- 1 lb (500 g) cucuzza or bottle gourd (pale green)
- 1 lb (500 g) chayote (cream to pale green)

### Zucchini Varieties
Choose 1 lb (500 g) zucchini from these varieties:
- 1 lb (500 g) straightneck or classic zucchini (deep green skin; mild flavor)
- 1 lb (500 g) golden or yellow zucchini (straightneck; bright yellow skin; sweeter than classic zucchini)
- 1 lb (500 g) Costata Romanesca, Roman zucchini, or cocozelle (thick straightneck; dark green and speckled white with raised lengthwise ridges; sweet and juicy)
- 1 lb (500 g) Lebanese or Middle Eastern zucchini (bell-shaped; pale green and shiny skin; firm, sweet, and juicy)
- 1 lb (500 g) round zucchini or globe squash (round balls; dark green skin; few or no seeds; firm, sweet, and juicy)
- 1 lb (500 g) oval or Tatume zucchini (egg-shaped; pale green speckled skin; few or no seeds; very firm and sweet; popular in Mexico)

## Zungenwurst

*Also known as blood tongue sausage. A German blood sausage studded with chunks of pickled tongue meat.*

### If You Don't Have It
Substitute 4 oz (125 g) zungenwurst with:
- 4 oz (125 g) Blutwurst (German)
- 4 oz (125 g) boudin rouge (Cajun)
- 4 oz (125 g) morcilla (Spanish)
- 4 oz (125 g) tongue sausage (no blood)

## Zwieback

*Also known as biscotte and rusk. "Twice-baked" German bread that comes in the form of long thin crackers.*

### If You Don't Have It
Substitute 1 lb (500 g) zwieback with:
- 1 lb (500 g) graham crackers
- 1 lb (500 g) bagel chips
- 1 lb (500 g) crostini or bruschetta
- 1 lb (500 g) Melba toasts
- 1 lb (500 g) dense crackers
- 1 lb (500 g) crisp lavash

# Ingredient Guides

USE THE FOLLOWING CHARTS when substituting one variety of a particular food for another variety of the same food. For instance, certain apple varieties such as Red Delicious are best for eating out of hand, while other apple varieties such as Granny Smith make terrific pies. The charts provide basic information about each food variety, including alternate names for the food, its texture and flavor characteristics, and its best uses or substitutes. A few charts do not include substitutes. For instance, substitutes are not included in the apple chart because so many different apple varieties can be substituted for one another that it would be unhelpful to list them all. In these charts, the food's best uses are offered instead of a lengthy list of substitutes.

# Picking Apples

Choosing the right apple is generally a matter of matching its texture and flavor to its intended use. Crisp, juicy, sweet apples tend to work best for eating out of hand. Tart apples with a more firm texture are better suited for cooking and baking. Some varieties, such as Gala, taste good both raw and cooked. Small crabapples, considered a different species, are very tart and high in pectin making them ideal for jellies, jams, and chutneys. Experiment with different varieties using the table below as a guide. See also Apple (page 30).

| Apple | Texture and Flavor | Best Uses |
|---|---|---|
| Arkansas Black | Crisp, firm, juicy | Eating, sauce |
| Baldwin | Crisp, rough-textured, juicy, spicy | Pie, sauce, eating |
| Braeburn | Crisp, firm, sweet-tart | Eating, sauce, pie |
| Bramley | Firm, rough-textured, juicy, tangy-sweet | Baking, sauce |
| Cortland | Crisp, juicy, tangy, aromatic | Salad, eating, pie, sauce |
| Cox's Orange Pippin | Firm, juicy, tangy, aromatic | Eating, pie, sauce |
| Crispin (Mutsu) | Crisp, juicy, spicy, sweet-tart | Eating, sauce |
| Empire | Crisp, delicate-textured, juicy, sweet-tart | Eating, salad |
| Fuji | Crisp, fine-textured, juicy, tangy, sweet, aromatic | Eating |
| Gala | Crisp, mildly tart, aromatic | Eating, baking, sauce |
| Golden Delicious | Juicy, sweetly aromatic | Eating, salad, sauce, baking |
| Granny Smith | Crisp, firm, juicy, tart | Pie, baking, sauce, eating |
| Gravenstein | Crisp, fine-textured, juicy, mildly tart | Pie, baking, sauce, eating |
| Greening (Rhode Island) | Crisp, juicy, tart | Pie, sauce, eating |
| Idared | Soft-textured, juicy, mildly tart | Pie, sauce, baking |
| Jonagold | Crisp, juicy, sweet-tart | Eating, pie, baking |
| Jonathan | Crisp, fine-textured, juicy, mildly tart | Eating, sauce, pie |
| Lady (Christmas) Apple | Crisp, juicy, intensely sweet | Eating, baking |
| Macoun | Firm, juicy, aromatic | Eating, pie, sauce |
| McIntosh | Soft-textured, juicy, tart, spicy, aromatic | Eating, sauce, pie |
| Newton Pippin | Firm, somewhat fine-textured, tart, aromatic | Eating, pie, sauce |
| Northern Spy | Extra-firm, extra-juicy, sweet | Pie, sauce, eating, baking |
| Red Delicious | Crisp, juicy, mildly tart | Eating |
| Rome Beauty | Crisp, firm, juicy, mildly tart | Baking |

| Apple | Texture and Flavor | Best Uses |
|---|---|---|
| **Spartan** | Crisp, fine-textured, sweet-tart | Eating |
| **Winesap** | Firm, juicy, winey-tasting | Eating, sauce |

# The Wide World of Dried Beans

Freshly cooked dried beans taste richer, less salty, and less mushy than canned beans. But the two can be used interchangeably in many recipes. To remove the salty canning liquid, rinse canned beans in a sieve under running water before using. If cooking dried beans, plan on 1 pound (500 g), (about 2 cups/500 mL), expanding to 4 to 6 cups (1 to 1.5 L) total volume when cooked. To substitute one variety of dried bean for another, see the suggestions below. For information on lentil varieties, see Switching Lentils (page 653). For other legumes, see Bean, Dried (page 54); Legume (page 307); and Peas, Split (page 412).

| Dried Bean | Characteristics | Substitutes |
|---|---|---|
| **Adzuki (azuki)** | Small, round-oval, maroon red, fine-textured, mildly sweet | Black adzuki beans (similar but black color), pink beans (slightly larger), red kidney beans (larger |
| **Anasazi** | Medium, oval kidney shape, brick-red spotted with white (deep pink when cooked), mildly sweet | Pink beans, red kidney beans, cranberry beans |
| **Appaloosa** | Medium, oval kidney shape, white or cream spotted with black or brown | Pink beans, red kidney beans, pinto beans, black beans, tepary beans |
| **Black (turtle)** | Medium-small, oval kidney shape, black with coarse-textured, cream-color interior | Appaloosa beans, calypso beans (milder), black soybeans, small red beans, pink beans, pinto beans |
| **Black-eyed pea** | Small, oval kidney shape, cream with black dot, mildly sweet | Yellow-eye, lady, crowder or other cowpeas, pigeon peas |
| **Calypso** | Small, oval kidney shape, white with black splotch, fine-textured | Cannellini beans, white kidney beans, black beans (stronger flavor) |
| **Cannellini** | Medium, elongated oval kidney shape, white, fine-textured | White kidney beans, Great Northern beans (larger), navy beans (smaller), calypso beans, flageolets (fresher taste) |
| **Chickpea (garbanzo)** | Small, round, bumpy, beige, coarse-textured | Tan tepary beans, white kidney beans, Great Northern beans, large lima beans |
| **Cranberry (borlotti)** | Medium, oval kidney shape, cream speckled with chianti red | Tongues of fire beans, Anasazi beans, pink beans, red beans, pinto beans |
| **European Soldier** | Large, oval kidney shape, ivory with reddish brown markings, mildly sweet | White kidney beans, cannellini beans, red kidney beans, Anasazi beans |

*continued on next page…*

| Dried Bean | Characteristics | Substitutes |
| --- | --- | --- |
| Fava (broad) | Large, flat, earlobe-shape, light brown, mildly bitter | Ful (smaller, rounder fava bean variety used to make the Egyptian dish ful medames; takes longer to cook), lima beans |
| Flageolet (immature kidney bean) | Medium, oval kidney shape, white or light green, delicate texture | Cannellini beans, Great Northern beans, calypso beans, white tepary beans |
| Great Northern | Medium, oval kidney shape, white, coarse-textured | White kidney beans, cannellini beans, navy beans (smaller), lima beans, flageolets (more tender) |
| Jackson Wonder | Medium-large, flattened oval kidney shape, reddish brown speckled with dark brown | Red kidney beans, pink beans, pinto beans, red beans, cranberry beans |
| Lima (baby or sieva) | Medium, round kidney shape, white, delicate texture, sweet | Cannellini beans, navy beans, black-eyed peas, ful (small, round fava beans) |
| Lima (butter or Fordhook) | Extra-large, kidney shape, white, sweet | Christmas limas (brick red marking), Great Northern beans, white kidney beans, cannellini beans, fava beans |
| Marrow | Medium-large, oval, putty-color, creamy texture | Great Northern beans, cannellini beans, white kidney beans, navy beans (smaller) |
| Mung | Small, round-oval, green (yellow interior), soft texture, sweet | Small flageolets, pigeon peas |
| Navy (pea bean or Yankee bean) | Small, round-oval, white, dense texture | French navy beans (egg shape with light green marking), baby lima beans, cannellini beans, Great Northern beans, white kidney beans, white tepary beans |
| Pigeon pea | Small, round, beige or yellow spotted with reddish brown | Yellow-eye, black-eye, lady, crowder or other cowpeas |
| Pink (chili bean) | Medium, round kidney shape, pale reddish brown | Small red beans, pinto beans, rattlesnake beans, red kidney beans, cranberry beans |
| Pinto | Medium, kidney shape, light brown speckled with brown or pink, coarse texture | Pink beans, small red beans, rattlesnake beans, red kidney beans, Anasazi beans, cranberry beans |
| Rattlesnake | Medium, round kidney shape, brown speckled with dark brown, smooth texture | Pinto beans, pink beans, small red beans, red kidney beans, Anasazi beans, cranberry beans |
| Red (small Mexican chili bean) | Medium-small, oval kidney shape, reddish brown, dense texture | Red kidney beans, pink beans, pinto beans, red kidney beans, Anasazi beans, cranberry beans |

| Dried Bean | Characteristics | Substitutes |
|---|---|---|
| **Red kidney** | Medium, kidney shape, deep reddish brown, coarse texture | Small red beans, pink beans, pinto beans, Anasazi beans, cranberry beans |
| **Scarlet Runner** | Large, oval kidney shape, mottled black and lavender, fluffy texture | White, black or other runner beans, cranberry beans, pinto beans, red kidney beans |
| **Soybean** | Small, round, pale yellow, very dense texture | Chickpeas, navy beans |
| **Spanish Tolosana** | Medium, kidney shape, mottled tan and reddish purple | Jackson Wonder beans, red kidney beans, pinto beans, pink beans, cranberry beans |
| **Steuben Yellow-eye** | Medium, oval kidney shape, half cream and half light brown, coarse texture | Navy beans, white kidney beans, Great Northern beans, cannellini beans, baby lima beans |
| **Swedish Brown** | Medium-small, oval shape, caramel brown | Pinto beans, cranberry beans, Great Northern beans, navy beans |
| **Tepary** | Medium-small, flattened oval, tan or white or gold or black color | Navy beans, pinto beans, rattlesnake beans, black beans |
| **Tongues of Fire** | Medium, oval, mottled beige and reddish brown | Cranberry beans, rattlesnake beans, pinto beans, pink beans |
| **Trout (Jacob's Cattle)** | Medium-large, kidney shape, white speckled with brownish purple, coarse texture | Pinto beans, pink beans, Spanish Tolosana beans, white kidney beans |
| **White kidney** | Medium, kidney shape, white, coarse texture | Cannellini beans (creamier), Great Northern beans, navy beans (smaller), flageolets (more tender) |

# Choosing Fresh Chiles

The Scoville heat scale, developed in 1912 by pharmacist Wilbur Scoville, measures a pepper's pungency. Bell or sweet peppers have 0 Scoville heat units; jalapeños have 5,000 to 10,000; and pure capsaicin, the heat-producing substance in chile peppers, clocks in at 16 million Scoville units. The chiles below include composite Scoville ratings from several authoritative sources. Keep in mind that a chile pepper's heat and flavor often fluctuate according to the variety of seeds used and the particular conditions under which the pepper was grown.

| Pepper | Characteristics | Scoville Units | Substitutes |
|---|---|---|---|
| African Bird's Eye | 1/2 to 1 inch (1 to 2.5 cm) long, blunt point, red | 100,000 to 200,000 | Thai, Charleston hot cayenne |
| Ají (green or red) | 4 inches (10 cm) long, 3/4 inch (2 cm) wide, pointed, green or red, fruity | 30,000 to 50,000 | Cayenne, tabasco, arbol |
| Anaheim (green California, red Colorado) | 6 to 8 inches (15 to 20 cm) long, 1 to 1 1/2 inches (2.5 to 4 cm) wide, blunt point, green or red | 500 to 1,500 | New Mexico, poblano, Hungarian cherry pepper, pepperoncini |
| Banana (Sweet) | 5 inches (12.5 cm) long, 1 to 1 1/2 inches (2.5 to 4 cm) wide, blunt point, pale yellow to orange red | 0 to 250 | Bell, cubanelle, mexi-bell, pimiento, Anaheim |
| Bell | 4 to 5 inches (10 to 12.5 cm) long, 3 to 4 inches (7.5 to 10 cm) wide, bell or elongated bell shape, various colors | 0 | Banana, cubanelle, mexi-bell, pimiento, Anaheim |
| Bhut Jolokia (Naga) | 2 to 4 inches (5 to 10 cm) long, 1 inch (2.5 cm) wide, dented elongated bullet shape, bright red or orange | 1,000,000 | Habanero |
| Cachucha | 2 to 3 inches (5 to 7.5 cm) long, 1 1/2 to 2 inches (4 to 5 cm) wide, bell shape, various colors | 0 to 250 | Bell, banana, cubanelle, mexi-bell, pimiento, Anaheim |
| Cayenne (Ginnie) | 4 to 6 inches (10 to 15 cm) long, 1/2 inch (1 cm) wide, pointed, green or red | 10,000 to 40,000 | Serrano, tabasco, ají Colorado, Thai |
| Cherry (Hungarian) | 1 inch (2.5 cm) long, 1 1/2 inches (4 cm) wide, cherry shape, green or red | 100 to 500 | Mexi-bell, pepperoncini, pimiento, Anaheim, New Mexico |
| Chilaca | 8 inches (20 cm) long, 1 inch (2.5 cm) wide, twisted blunt point, dark purple green | 1,000 to 1,500 | Poblano, New Mexico, Anaheim |
| Cubanelle (Italian frying) | 6 inches (15 cm) long, 2 inches (5 cm) wide, elongated bell shape, yellow green or orange red | 0 | Bell, banana, pimiento, mexi-bell, Anaheim |
| Fresno (caribe) | 3 inches (7.5 cm) long, 1 1/2 inches (4 cm) wide, blunt point, green to red, floral | 5,000 to 8,000 | Jalapeño, Santa Fe grande, yellow wax, serrano |
| Güero | 3 to 5 inches (7.5 to 12.5 cm) long, 1 to 1 1/2 inches (2.5 to 4 cm) wide, blunt point, pale yellow | 3,000 to 8,000 | Hungarian wax, Santa Fe grande, Fresno, jalapeño |

| Pepper | Characteristics | Scoville Units | Substitutes |
| --- | --- | --- | --- |
| Habanero | 1½ inches (4 cm) long, 1 inch (2.5 cm) wide, lantern shape, yellow, orange, red or green, fruity | 100,000 to 500,000 | Scotch bonnet, Thai, African bird's eye, Charleston hot cayenne |
| Holland (Dutch) | 4 inches (10 cm) long, 1 to 1½ inches (2.5 to 4 cm) wide, pointed, red | 4,000 to 6,000 | Fresno, jalapeño, yellow wax |
| Hontaka (Japones) | 1 to 2 inches (2.5 to 5 cm) long, ¼ inch (0.5 cm) wide, pointed, red | 15,000 to 30,000 | Santaka, Thai, serrano, cayenne |
| Jalapeño | 2 to 4 inches (5 to 10 cm) long, 1 inch (2.5 cm) wide, blunt point, green or red | 5,000 to 10,000 | Fresno, Sante Fe grande, Holland, serrano, cayenne |
| Malagueta pepper | 1 to 2 inches (2.5 to 5 cm) long, ¾ inch (2 cm) wide, pointed, yellow orange or green, fruity | 8,000 to 30,000 | Thai, Hontaka, Santaka, serrano, cayenne, tabasco |
| Mexi-bell | 3 to 5 inches (7.5 to 12.5 cm) long, 3 to 4 inches (7.5 to 10 cm) wide, bell shape, various colors | 100 to 400 | Pimiento, New Mexico, Hungarian cherry, bell, banana |
| Mirasol | 4 inches (10 cm) long, ¾ inch (2 cm) wide, pointed, red, fruity | 2,500 to 5,000 | Hungarian wax, jalapeño, serrano |
| New Mexico (green or red) | 6 to 8 inches (15 to 20 cm) long, 1½ to 2 inches (4 to 5 cm) wide, blunt point, green or red | 500 to 1,500 | Anaheim, poblano, Hungarian cherry, pepperoncini |
| Pepperoncini | 3 inches (7.5 cm) long, ¾ inch (2 cm) wide, pointed, pale green to red | 100 to 500 | Hungarian wax or cherry, Anaheim, mexi-bell, New Mexico, pimiento |
| Pimiento | 3 to 5 inches (7.5 to 12.5 cm) long, 2 to 3 inches (5 to 7.5 cm) wide, pointed bell shape, red | 0 to 500 | Bell, mexi-bell, Hungarian cherry, banana, New Mexico |
| Poblano | 4 to 5 inches (10 to 12.5 cm) long, 2 to 3 inches (5 to 7.5 cm) wide, dimpled pointed bell shape, dark green or red | 1,250 to 2,500 | Chilaca, Hungarian wax, New Mexico, Anaheim |
| Rocoto (manzano or péron) | 2 to 3 inches (5 to 7.5 cm) long, 2 to 2½ inches (5 to 6 cm) wide, bell or lantern shaped, yellow orange or red | 20,000 to 50,000 | Tabasco, serrano, jalapeño, Thai, Hontaka, Santaka |
| Santaka (Japones) | 1 to 2 inches (2.5 to 5 cm) long, ¼ inch (0.5 cm) wide, pointed, red | 15,000 to 30,000 | Hontaka, Thai, serrano, cayenne |
| Sante Fe Grande | 3 to 5 inches (7.5 to 12.5 cm) long, 1 to 1½ inches (2.5 to 4 cm) wide, blunt point, pale yellow | 3,000 to 8,000 | Güero, Fresno, jalapeño, Hungarian wax |
| Scotch Bonnet | 1½ inches (4 cm) long, 1 inch (2.5 cm) wide, lantern shape, yellow green, orange, or red, fruity | 200,000 to 325,000 | Habanero, Thai, African bird's eye, Charleston hot cayenne |
| Serrano | 1 to 3 inches (2.5 to 7.5 cm) long, ½ inch (1 cm) wide, blunt point, green or red | 10,000 to 25,000 | Cayenne, Hontaka, Santaka, Thai |

*continued on next page…*

| Pepper | Characteristics | Scoville Units | Substitutes |
|--------|-----------------|----------------|-------------|
| Tabasco | 1 to 1½ inches (2.5 to 4 cm) long, ¼ to ½ inch (0.5 to 1 cm) wide, blunt point, yellow orange or red | 30,000 to 50,000 | Rocoto, Thai, serrano, cayenne, malagueta, Hontaka, Santaka |
| Tepín (chiltepin) | ½-inch (1 cm) diameter, round or oval, red | 40,000 to 80,000 | Thai, Tabasco, Serrano, rocoto |
| Thai | 1 to 2 inches (2.5 to 5 cm) long, ¼ inch (0.5 cm) wide, pointed, various colors | 15,000 to 30,000 | Hontaka, Santaka, serrano, cayenne |
| Togarashi (ichimi) | ½ to 1½ inches (1 to 4 cm) long, ¼ to ½ inch (0.5 to 1 cm) wide, pointed, red | 10,000 to 40,000 | Hontaka, Santaka, cayenne, Thai, serrano |
| Wax (yellow or Hungarian) | 4 to 6 inches (10 to 15 cm) long, 1 to 1½ inches (2.5 to 4 cm) wide, blunt point, pale yellow green | 5,000 to 15,000 | Santa Fe grande, güero, serrano, jalapeño, mirasol |

# Choosing Dried Chiles

There is widespread confusion about chile nomenclature due the massive variety of chiles grown around the world. The same chile pepper may have five different names, depending on where it was grown. Fresh chiles are often given a different name when dried, adding to the confusion. In the chart below, I have included alternate names whenever possible. All chiles referred to here are dried or they are the dried versions of fresh chiles that have the same name. The heat level of chiles is measured on a scale from 0 to 16,000,000 "Scoville units." For more information on Scoville heat units, see Choosing Fresh Chiles (page 640).

| Pepper | Characteristics | Scoville Units | Substitutes |
|--------|-----------------|----------------|-------------|
| African Bird's Eye | ½ to 1 inch (1 to 2.5 cm) long, blunt point, red | 100,000 to 200,000 | Piri piri, Malagueta, Thai, Charleston hot cayenne, tepín, piquin |
| Ají Amarillo (cuzqueño) | 4 inches (10 cm) long, ¾ inch (2 cm) wide, pointed, orange, fruity | 30,000 to 50,000 | Ají colorado, cayenne, tabasco, arbol |
| Ají Colorado (cuzqueño) | 4 inches (10 cm) long, ¾ inch (2 cm) wide, pointed, red, fruity | 30,000 to 50,000 | Ají amarillo, cayenne, tabasco, arbol |
| Ají Mirasol (cuzqueño) | 3 to 5 inches (7.5 to 12.5 cm) long, 1 inch (2.5 cm) wide, tapered point, reddish orange, fruity | 1,000 to 3,000 | Ancho, New Mexico, ají panca |
| Ají Panca (cuzqueño) | 3 to 5 inches (7.5 to 12.5 cm) long, 1 inch (2.5 cm) wide, tapered point, ruddy brown, fruity | 500 to 1,000 | Ancho, New Mexico, ají mirasol |
| Aleppo (Halaby) | 4 to 6 inches (10 to 15 cm) long, ½ inch (1 cm) wide, pointed, red | 6,000 to 10,000 | Cayenne, serrano, costeño rojo |
| Ancho (dried poblano) | 4 inches (10 cm) long, 3 inches (7.5 cm) wide, heart-shaped, reddish brown or mahogany, earthy and fruity | 1,250 to 2,500 | Mulato, pasilla, chilhuacle rojo, costeño amarillo, New Mexico |

| Pepper | Characteristics | Scoville Units | Substitutes |
|---|---|---|---|
| **Arbol (de Arbol)** | 2 to 3 inches (5 to 7.5 cm) long, $\frac{1}{4}$ inch (0.5 cm) wide, pointed, shiny red, grassy-hot | 15,000 to 30,000 | Pico de pajaro, serrano, cayenne |
| **Cascabel (bola)** | $1\frac{1}{2}$-inch (4 cm) diameter, round, reddish brown | 1,250 to 2,500 | Chihuacle rojo, costeño amarillo, guajillo, catarina, Ñora, Hungarian cherry pepper |
| **Catarina** | $1\frac{1}{2}$ to 2 inches (4 to 5 cm) long, $\frac{3}{4}$ inch (2 cm) wide, blunt point, red | 2,000 to 4,000 | Costeño amarillo, chilhuacle rojo, guajillo, Hungarian cherry pepper, New Mexico |
| **Cayenne (Ginnie)** | 2 to 4 inches (5 to 10 cm) long, $\frac{1}{2}$ inch (1 cm) wide, pointed, shiny red | 10,000 to 40,000 | Arbol, serrano, ají colorado, Thai |
| **Chilcostle** | 3 to 5 inches (7.5 to 12.5 cm) long, $\frac{1}{2}$ inch (1 cm) wide, pointed, deep red | 3,500 to 5,000 | Catarina, chilhuacle amarillo, costeño amarillo, pepperoncini, pulla |
| **Chilhuacle Amarillo** | 2 to 3 inches (5 to 7.5 cm) long, $1\frac{1}{2}$ inches (4 cm) wide, blunt point, orange red | 1,250 to 2,000 | Chilhuacle negro, chilhuacle rojo, cascabel, catarina, guajillo, costeño amarillo |
| **Chilhuacle Negro** | 2 to 3 inches (5 to 7.5 cm) long, 2 to 3 inches (5 to 7.5 cm) wide, heart-shaped, deep purplish brown, earthy, fruity | 1,250 to 2,000 | Mulato, pasilla, pátzcuaro, ancho |
| **Chilhuacle Rojo** | 2 to 3 inches (5 to 7.5 cm) long, $1\frac{1}{2}$ inches (4 cm) wide, blunt point, reddish brown | 1,250 to 2,000 | Chilhuacle amarillo, cascabel, catarina, guajillo, costeño amarillo |
| **Chipotle (smoked jalapeño)** | 2 to 4 inches (5 to 10 cm) long, 1 inch (2.5 cm) wide, blunt point, grayish chocolate brown | 5,000 to 10,000 | Pasilla de Oaxaca, mora or morita, serrano (a drop of liquid smoke adds smoke flavor) |
| **Costeño (rojo or bandeño)** | 2 to 3 inches (5 to 7.5 cm) long, $\frac{1}{2}$ inch (1 cm) wide, pointed, orange red | 5,000 to 10,000 | Costeño amarillo, chilhuacle rojo, serrano, cayenne, arbol, puya, pico de pajaro |
| **Costeño Amarillo** | 2 to 3 inches (5 to 7.5 cm) long, $\frac{3}{4}$ inch (2 cm) wide, pointed, yellow-red | 1,250 to 2,500 | Costeño rojo, chilhuacle amarillo, cascabel, guajillo, puya, catarina, New Mexico |
| **Guajillo** | 4 to 6 inches (10 to 15 cm) long, 1 inch (2.5 cm) wide, blunt point, shiny brownish orange red | 2,000 to 4,500 | New Mexico, puya, ají mirasol, chilhuacle amarillo or rojo, costeño amarillo, cascabel, ancho, mulato |

*continued on next page…*

| Pepper | Characteristics | Scoville Units | Substitutes |
|--------|-----------------|----------------|-------------|
| Habanero | 1½ inches (4 cm) long, 1 inch (2.5 cm) wide, lantern shape, yellow, orange, red or green, fruity | 100,000 to 500,000 | Scotch bonnet, Thai, African bird's eye, Charleston hot cayenne |
| Malagueta | 1 to 2 inches (2.5 to 5 cm) long, tapered, blunt point, red | 60,000 to 100,000 | Piri piri, African bird's eye, Thai, Jamaican hot, Charleston hot cayenne, tepin, piquin |
| Mora or morita | 1 to 2 inches (2.5 to 5 cm) long, ¼ to ¾ inch (0.5 to 2 cm) wide, blunt point, reddish brown | 5,000 to 10,000 | Chipotle, pasilla de Oaxaca, serrano (a drop of liquid smoke adds smoke flavor) |
| Mulato (dried poblano) | 4 inches (10 cm) long, 2 to 3 inches (5 to 7.5 cm) wide, blunt point, chocolate brown | 1,250 to 2,500 | Ancho, pasilla, chilhuacle rojo, costeño amarillo, New Mexico |
| New Mexico (roasted green or Anaheim) | 5 inches (12.5 cm) long, 1 inch (2.5 cm) wide, blunt point, brownish green | 500 to 1,500 | New Mexico red, Hungarian cherry pepper |
| New Mexico (red or Colorado) | 6 inches (15 cm) long, 1½ inches (4 cm) wide, blunt point, red | 1,000 to 2,500 | Guajillo, ají mirasol, catarina, costeño amarillo, ancho |
| Ñora | 1½-inch (4 cm) diameter, round, reddish brown | 250 to 1,000 | Cascabel, chihuacle rojo, costeño amarillo, guajillo, catarina, Hungarian cherry pepper |
| Onza (rojo) | 3 inches (7.5 cm) long, ½ inch (1 cm) wide, pointed, brick red | 2,500 to 5,000 | Chilhuacle rojo, catarina, cascabel, chilcostle, costeño rojo, guajillo, New Mexico |
| Pasilla (negro) | 6 inches (15 cm) long, 1½ inches (4 cm) wide, blunt point, raisin brown | 1,000 to 1,500 | Mulato, ancho, pasilla de Oaxaca, pátzcuaro, cascabel, chilhuacle negro, costeño amarillo, guajillo |
| Pasilla de Oaxaca | 4 inches (10 cm) long, 1 inch (2.5 cm) wide, blunt point, mahogany red | 4,000 to 8,000 | Pátzcuaro, puya, cascabel, chilcostle, serrano |
| Pátzcuaro | 5 inches (12.5 cm) long, 1 inch (2.5 cm) wide, blunt point, purplish red | 3,000 to 8,000 | Pasilla de Oaxaca, puya, cascabel, chilcostle, serrano |
| Pico de Pajaro | 1 inch (2.5 cm) long, ¼ inch (0.5 cm) wide, pointed, dark orange red | 40,000 to 80,000 | Piquin, tepín, arbol, Thai, ají colorado |
| Piquin (pequín) | ½ inch (1 cm) long, ¼ inch (0.5 cm) wide, oval blunt point, orange red | 50,000 to 100,000 | Tepín, pico de pajaro, cayenne, serrano, arbol |
| Piri piri | ½ to 1 inches (1 to 2.5 cm) long, blunt point, red | 100,000 to 200,000 | African bird's eye, malagueta, Thai, Jamaican hot, Charleston hot cayenne, tepín, piquin |

| Pepper | Characteristics | Scoville Units | Substitutes |
|---|---|---|---|
| **Puya (pulla)** | 4 to 5 inches (10 to 12.5 cm) long, ¾ inch (2 cm) wide, pointed, purplish red | 5,000 to 15,000 | Chilcostle, cascabel, costeño rojo, pátzcuaro, guajillo (milder) |
| **Serrano** | 1½ inches (4 cm) long, ½ inch (1 cm) wide, blunt point, orange red | 10,000 to 25,000 | Arbol, cayenne, costeño rojo |
| **Tepín (chiltepín)** | ½-inch (1 cm) diameter, round or oval, red | 40,000 to 80,000 | Pico de pajaro, piquin, piri-piri, ají colorado, cayenne |
| **Togarashi (ichimi)** | ½ to 1½ inches (1 to 4 cm) long, ¼ to ½ inch (0.5 to 1 cm) wide, pointed, red | 10,000 to 40,000 | Cayenne, Thai, arbol, serrano |

## Swapping Clams

Numbering in the hundreds, clam varieties fall into two main categories: hard-shell clams, which may be eaten raw, and soft-shell clams, which are generally eaten cooked. The soft-shell varieties are named for their thin, brittle shells and long necks that are used to siphon ocean water. While each clam variety has its own taste and texture, substitutions can be made within each of the two main categories.

| | Clam | Shell Diameter | Substitutes |
|---|---|---|---|
| **Hard Shell (Quahog)** | **Butter** | 3 to 5 inch (7.5 to 12.5 cm) | Chowder |
| | **Cherrystone** | 2 to 3 inches (5 to 7.5 cm) | Littleneck |
| | **Chowder (large)** | 3 to 6 inches (7.5 to 15 cm) | Butter, manila |
| | **Littleneck (Atlantic and Pacific)** | 1 to 2 inches (2.5 to 5 cm) | Cherrystone |
| | **Manila (Japanese Littleneck)** | 3 to 4 inches (7.5 to 10 cm) | Littleneck, cherrystone |
| | **Pismo** | 5 to 7 inches (7.5 to 18 cm) | Cherrystone, littleneck |
| | **Ocean Quahog (Mahogany)** | 2 to 3 inches (5 to 7.5 cm) | Cherrystone, littleneck |
| | **Surf (bar or hen clam)** | 4 to 8 inches (10 to 20 cm) | Ocean quahog |
| **Soft Shell (Longneck)** | **Geoduck (mirugai)** | 6 to 8 inches (15 to 20 cm) | Surf clam, abalone |
| | **Razor** | 5 to 8 inches (12.5 to 20 cm) long, ¼ to ½ inch (0.5 to 1 cm) wide | Manila, geoduck (for chowder) |
| | **Steamer** | 1 to 2 inches (2.5 to 5 cm) | Razor |

# Picking Coffee

Buying coffee has become as complex as choosing a decent wine. To substitute one coffee variety for another, keep three things in mind: the origin of the beans, their flavor characteristics, and how darkly the beans are roasted. Lighter roasts exhibit the terroir of the beans' region of origin, while darker roasts reduce acidity, cut sweetness, and exhibit the more toasted and browned flavors of roasting itself. Dark roasting also makes the beans appear oilier on the surface. Roasting levels include light (cinnamon, half city, New England), medium (full city, America, regular, breakfast, brown), dark (high, Italian, Viennese, espresso, continental), and double roast (French). In the Aroma column of the chart below, the descriptive terms range progressively from light roast to dark roast. Aside from roasting, the country of origin has the biggest impact on the taste of coffee beans. Coffees from Latin America and the Caribbean are the most popular worldwide (especially for blends) because they have a clean taste, light body, and bright acidity. On the other side of the globe, the intense, dry heat of Africa and the Arabian Peninsula produces idiosyncratic coffees with more pronounced wine-like acidity and dried fruit aromas. In Asia and Hawaii, the beans brew into a more floral cup of coffee. Here's a road map to world's major coffee-producing regions and their popular coffee varietals. Ask your coffee seller for the best grade available (such as "AA" or "Supremo"), and keep in mind that the best "high-grown" coffees are grown in the mountains at least 3,000 feet above sea level. If you're looking for the most expensive coffee beans available, try civet coffee, which is found in the droppings of the catlike civet; the indigestible coffee beans ferment in the animal's stomach acids and create into an unusually smooth brew with a chocolate taste and neglible bitterness.

| | Coffee Origin and Name | Body | Acidity | Aroma |
|---|---|---|---|---|
| **Arfica/ Arabian Peninsula** | **Ethiopia Yirgacheffe** | light | bright | cedar, orange blossoms, chocolate-covered dried berries |
| | **Kenya AA** | medium | bright | tangerine, black currant, malt |
| | **Tanzania Hope AA** | medium | gentle | volkamer lemon, apricot, raisins |
| | **Uganda Bugisu** | medium | gentle | baked apple, sun-dried tomato, brown butter |
| | **Yemen Mocha** | full | bright | cardamom, tobacco, chocolate fudge |
| **Latin America/Caribbean** | **Brazil Bourbon Santos** | full | gentle | currant, pecan, caramel |
| | **Brazil Cerrado** | full | gentle | cedar, sweet tomato, milk chocolate |
| | **Brazil Tres Fazendas** | full | gentle | hazelnut, caramel, Tennessee whiskey |
| | **Colombia Bucaramanga** | full | gentle | pear, cashew, vanilla |
| | **Colombia Medellin** | full | gentle | butter, toast, milk chocolate |
| | **Costa Rica Monte Crisol** | full | gentle | blueberry, almond, butter |
| | **Costa Rica Tarrazu** | medium | gentle | cinnamon, milk chocolate, tobacco |
| | **Guatemala Antigua** | medium | bright | nectarines, allspice, bittersweet chocolate |
| | **Guatemala Huehuetenango** | medium | bright | peaches, cinnamon, cocoa nibs |
| | **Jamaica Blue Mountain** | full | bright | champagne, allspice, semisweet chocolate |
| | **Mexico Chiapas** | medium | bright | citrus, pumpkin seed, Mexican chocolate |
| | **Nicargua Segovia** | medium | gentle | almond nougat, peaches, milk chocolate |

| | Coffee Origin and Name | Body | Acidity | Aroma |
|---|---|---|---|---|
| Latin America/ Caribbean | Panama Boquette | medium | gentle | honey, butter, butterscotch |
| | Peru Cepi Café | light | bright | cinnamon, corn, almonds |
| | Peru Chanchamayo | light | gentle | clove, cherimoya, hazelnuts |
| Asia/Pacific | Dragon Flores Bajawa | heavy | low | nectarine, walnut, vanilla |
| | Hawaii Kona | heavy | gentle | plumeria, cardamom, molasses |
| | Sumatra IKA | heavy | low | laksa, candied orange, brown butter |
| | Sumatra Mandheling | heavy | low | parsley, soil, musk |
| | Timor Cooperativa | heavy | low | cilantro, black cherry, milk chocolate |

# Choosing Among Crabs

Crab devotees often prefer either she-crabs or he-crabs, but both can be delicious. To tell a male from a female, turn a whole crab over and look at the underside of the shell. On she-crabs, you'll see a wide, triangular, off-white "apron" on the underside of the shell. Males (also called jimmies) have a longer, more narrow, T-shaped apron on the underside.

| Crab | Shell Diameter | Substitutes |
|---|---|---|
| Blue (Chesapeake blue) | 4 to 6 inches (10 to 15 cm) | Dungeness |
| Dungeness | 6 to 8 inches (15 to 20 cm) | Blue |
| King | 5 to 7 inches (12.5 to 18 cm) | Snow |
| Peekytoe | 3 to 6 inches (7.5 to 15 cm) | Dungeness, blue |
| Snow | 3 to 5 inches (7.5 to 12.5 cm) | King |
| Stone (morro) | 3 to 6 inches (7.5 to 15 cm) | Blue crab claws |

# Choosing Among Wheat Flours

Different varieties of wheat flour produce different textures in baked goods. When choosing among flours, consider the protein content. Generally, you can substitute up to half of the flour called for with another flour of similar protein content. For yeast breads requiring a sturdy structure, choose high-protein flour (12 to 14% protein). For quick breads and pastry requiring a lighter structure, choose lower-protein flour (7 to 11% protein). Here's a guide based on the percentage of protein in common types of wheat flour.

| Flour Type | % Protein | Best Uses |
| --- | --- | --- |
| Cake | 7 to 9 | Cakes, particularly those high in sugar |
| Pastry | 8 to 9 | Biscuits, cookies, pie crusts, pastries |
| Whole wheat pastry | 9 to 10 | Quick breads |
| All-purpose | 8 to 11 | Quick breads, yeast breads, cakes, cookies, and everyday baking |
| Self-rising | 8 to 11 | Quick breads |
| Bread | 12 to 14 | Pizza crusts, yeast breads, and bread machine recipes |
| Semolina | 12 to 16 | Pasta |
| Durum | 12 to 16 | Pasta |
| Graham | 14 | Combine with other flours in breads |
| Whole wheat | 14 | Combine with other flours in breads |

# Choosing Among Whole-Grain and Alternative Flours

Generally, a whole-grain or alternative flour can be substituted for up to half of the all-purpose flour called for in quick bread and yeast bread recipes. Whole-grain flours add fiber while varying the flavor and texture of baked goods. Use the guide below to replace all-purpose flour with alternative flours. To make homemade flour from whole grains such as barley, millet, oats, quinoa, rice, and teff, grind the grain in a food processor to the texture of flour.

| Flour | Protein Content | Gluten Content | Taste | Best Uses |
| --- | --- | --- | --- | --- |
| Almond | High | Gluten-free | Mild, sweet, nutty | Breads, cookies, pastry |
| Amaranth | High | Gluten-free | Assertive, nutty | Quick breads |
| Barley | Low | Low-gluten | Earthy, mild, sweet flavor, chewy texture | Quick breads, some cookies |
| Buckwheat | Low | Gluten-free | Earthy and mild or strong (if buckwheat groats are roasted) | Quick breads (especially pancakes), dumplings, noodles (soba); creates tender baked goods; pairs well with fruits like apples, cherries, and pumpkin; gray color |

| Flour | Protein Content | Gluten Content | Taste | Best Uses |
|-------|-----------------|----------------|-------|-----------|
| **Chestnut** | Low | Gluten-free | Nutty, smoky (if chestnuts are roasted) | Quick breads, noodles, pizza dough |
| **Chickpea (garbanzo, gram)** | High | Gluten-free | Mild, not beany | Quick breads, yeast breads |
| **Corn** | Low | Gluten-free | Nutty, corn flavor | Quick breads, yeast breads; pairs well with higher-gluten flours |
| **Kamut©** | Low | Medium Low-gluten | Nutty, earthy | Quick breads, yeast breads, substitute 1:1 for all-purpose flour |
| **Millet (bajri)** | High | Gluten-free | Mild, slightly nutty | Quick breads, makes baked goods very crumbly; pairs well with cornmeal, oat flour, or rye flour |
| **Oat** | High | Gluten-free | Sweet, earthy | Quick breads, cookies, yeast breads (in combination with high-gluten flour); creates moister more chewy texture; pairs well with whole wheat flour, rye flour, millet flour |
| **Potato** | Low | Gluten-free | Mild potato flavor | Yeast breads (in combination with high-gluten flour) |
| **Pumpernickel (dark rye)** | Low | Low-gluten | Earthy and strong | Yeast breads (this flour is coarsely ground, dark rye flour used to make pumpernickel bread) |
| **Quinoa** | High | Gluten-free | Mild, nutty | Quick breads, yeast breads (in combination with high-gluten flour); pairs well with cornmeal, oat flour, barley flour, and buckwheat flour |
| **Rice** | Low | Gluten-free | Mild, earthy (white rice flour) or nutty (brown rice flour) | Quick breads, dumplings, noodles; makes baked goods more crumbly; pairs well with oat flour |
| **Rye** | Low | Low-gluten | Earthy and mild to strong (depending upon fineness of grind) | Quick breads, yeast breads (in combination with high-gluten flour); knead gently and increase yeast to improve rise in yeast breads |
| **Soy** | Very high | Gluten-free | Mild, slightly beany | Quick breads, yeast breads (in combination with high-gluten flour); adds moisture to baked goods; high in fat |
| **Spelt** | High | Low-gluten | Mild, nutty | Quick breads, yeast breads |
| **Teff** | High | Gluten-free | Mild to rich molasses flavor (depending on whether light or dark) | Quick breads, especially spice breads; yeast breads (in combination with high-gluten flour) |
| **Triticale** | High | Low-gluten | Mild, earthy | Quick breads, yeast breads (in combination with high-gluten flour); hybrid of rye and wheat; knead yeast breads gently |

# Picking Edible Flowers

Most edible flowers make beautiful garnishes. They can also bring color and flavor to salads, soups, sauces, desserts, and beverages. Only use edible flowers that have not been sprayed with harmful chemicals. Look for them in gourmet shops and farmer's markets (or your own organic garden) rather than in florist shops.

| Flower | Color | Flavor | Best Uses |
|---|---|---|---|
| Begonia | Shades of white, yellow or red | Sweet and lemony | Fruit salads, desserts |
| Borage | Blue or pink | Cool, refreshing, and cucumber-like | Salads, cold soups, beverages, crystallized |
| Calendula | Yellow orange | Earthy and saffron-like | Crumbled like saffron |
| Carnation (Dianthus) | Shades of white, pink, or red | Peppery like cloves or nutmeg | Desserts, wine, crystallized |
| Chive Blossom | Pink or lavender | Mild onion flavor | Salads, soups, fish or egg dishes |
| Clary | Shades of white, pink, and lavender | Mild sage aroma | Salads |
| Daisy | Yellow and white | Mild clover or mint flavor | Salads |
| Dandelion | Yellow | Honey flavor (when young) or bitter (when old) | Salads, infusions, wine |
| Daylily | Various colors | Sweet and crunchy | Salads, stuffed as an appetizer, desserts |
| Johnny Jump-Up (Viola) | White, yellow, or purple | Wintergreen flavor | Salads, cold soups, desserts, beverages |
| Lavender | Light purple | Sweet and citrusy | Desserts, baking, beverages, soups, salads, sauces |
| Lilac | Light purple | Lemony | Salads |
| Marigold | Yellow or orange | Spicy and citrusy, sometimes bitter | Salads, soups |
| Nasturtium | Various colors | Peppery like watercress | Salads, sandwiches, egg dishes |
| Pansy | White, yellow, or purple | Mildly grassy | Salads, soups, fruit salads, desserts |
| Rose | Various colors | Sweet and fruity | Salads, fruit salads, desserts, syrups, sweet sauces, jams |
| Squash Blossom | Yellow or orange with green | Mildly sweet squash flavor | Salads, egg dishes, stuffed as an appetizer |
| Violet | Purple and white | Sweet wintergreen flavor | Salads, desserts, beverages, crystallized |

# Spooning Up Honey

Bees make honey from the nectar of hundreds of different flowers. The individual nectar characteristics determine the color and flavor of the resulting honey—from crystal-clear, mild and citrusy to dark brown, assertive, and malty. As with wine, changes in climate and growing conditions alter the nectar and the color and flavor of honey from year to year. Note that some honeys taste like their source, but others do not. Buckwheat honey tastes remarkably similar to buckwheat, but blueberry honey may taste nothing like blueberries. The tendency to crystallize also varies from honey to honey and is determined by the proportion of fructose to glucose in the honey. The lower the fructose, the more likely the honey will crystallize. While most commercial honeys are blended from several types of flower nectar, better-quality honeys are unblended. Wildflower honey is an unblended honey from unidentified flowers. Monofloral honeys are unblended and come from the primary flower from which the bees have gathered nectar. Here's a guide to monofloral honey varietals to help match the color, flavor, and aroma when substituting one honey for another.

| Honey Varietal | Color | Flavor, Aroma, and Attributes |
| --- | --- | --- |
| Acacia | Clear to pale amber | Floral, mildly tangy, doesn't crystallize |
| Alfalfa | Clear | Very mild, occasionally with a hint of spice, often a blend of honeys |
| Apple Blossom | Light to medium amber | Apple-like aroma |
| Aster | Clear to light amber | Varies by region, crystallizes quickly |
| Avocado | Dark amber | Bold, rich flavor |
| Basswood | Dark amber | Assertive with a hint of pepper |
| Blackberry | Light amber | Delicate with a faint berry aroma |
| Blueberry | Medium amber | Occasionally has traces of berry aroma |
| Buckwheat | Dark brown | Strong malty buckwheat flavor |
| Canola | Clear to light amber | Delicate, only mildly acidic, crystallizes easily |
| Chestnut | Chestnut brown | Bold, spicy, nutty, slightly bitter |
| Clover | Clear to amber | Delicate, slightly tart, crystallizes easily |
| Cranberry | Medium amber | Mild, fruity aroma, slightly tart |
| Eucalyptus | Dark | Mild fruit and menthol aroma |
| Fireweed | Light to medium amber | Mild fruit flavor, rich body |
| Gallberry | Dark amber | Slightly tart |
| Goldenrod | Light amber | Strong taste with hints of beeswax |
| Heather | Dark amber | Dark caramel taste, slightly bitter |
| Huckleberry | Dark amber | Full-bodied |
| Kamahi | Light amber | Rich, full-bodied |
| Lavender | Medium amber | Lavender aroma |
| Leatherwood | Dark amber | Robust and spicy |

*continued on next page…*

| Honey Varietal | Color | Flavor, Aroma, and Attributes |
|---|---|---|
| Lehua | Golden | Rich and buttery with floral aroma, crystallizes readily to make honey cream |
| Linden | Pale amber | Spicy |
| Nodding Thistle | Light amber | Delicate, floral |
| Orange Blossom | Light to dark amber | Citrus aroma |
| Pine Honey | Dark amber | Rich molasses aroma |
| Poplar | Medium amber | Robust |
| Pumpkin | Medium amber | Delicate with mild winter squash aroma |
| Raspberry | Light golden and opaque | Slight berry aroma, crystallizes readily to make honey cream |
| Rata | Clear | Mild, yet buttery with some minerality |
| Rewarewa | Burnt umber | Full-bodied with malt aroma |
| Rosemary | Pale amber | Rich pine aroma |
| Safflower | Medium to dark amber, sometimes with a light green glow | Full-bodied |
| Sage | Medium amber | Mild herb aroma |
| Sage, Black Button | Medium amber | Mild herb aroma, slow to crystallize |
| Sage, Purple | Clear | Gentle flavor, slow to crystallize |
| Sage, White | Sunny yellow | Slightly tart, floral aroma |
| Saw Palmetto | Medium amber | Herb and citrus aromas with hints of aged wood |
| Silkweed | Dark amber | Assertive, spicy |
| Sourwood | Medium amber | Spicy, aromas of ginger |
| Sunflower | Light to medium amber | Sharp floral aroma, crystallizes readily |
| Tawari | Light amber | Butterscotch aroma |
| Thyme | Light amber | Herb and charred grass aromas |
| Tupelo | Golden, often with a green glow | Full-flavored, medium body; slow to crystallize |
| Viper's Bugloss (Borage) | Light amber | Delicate with floral aromas |
| Wildflower | Medium amber | Varies from mild to robust and acidic, depending on flowers |

# Switching Lentils

In botanical terms, lentils include several varieties of the *Lens culinaris* family, all of which are small, flat, disc-shaped legumes. However, in culinary parlance, Indian cooks also use the term "lentils" or "dal" to refer to similar skinned and split peas or beans that cook relatively quickly and do not need to be soaked, such as split mung beans (moong dal). Unsplit whole beans are often referred to by Indian cooks as "gram." The chart below includes substitutes for popular lentils and other split peas or beans that are cooked like lentils. To find substitutes for other legumes, see specific entries listed alphabetically in the A to Z section.

| | Legume | Interior Color | Substitutes |
|---|---|---|---|
| Lentils | **Beluga lentil** | Black | French green lentils |
| | **Brown lentil (green lentil)** | Brown or green | French green lentils (firmer), yellow lentils |
| | **French green lentil (Puy lentils)** | Brown or green | Beluga lentils, brown lentils (softer) |
| | **Red lentil** | Orange pink | Masoor dal (cooks faster), yellow lentils |
| | **Yellow lentil** | Yellow | Yellow moong dal, yellow split peas, toor dal (firmer), channa dal (firmer) |
| Dal | **Channa dal (split chickpea relative)** | Pale yellow | Toor dal, yellow split peas, yellow lentils (softer), yellow moong dal (cooks faster) |
| | **Masoor dal (split red lentils)** | Orange pink | Red lentils (takes longer to cook), yellow lentils |
| | **Matar dal (split green or yellow peas)** | Green or pale yellow | Yellow moong dal, yellow lentils, channa dal |
| | **Moong dal (split mung beans)** | Cream (green skins) | Yellow moong dal (cooks faster), brown lentils, yellow lentils |
| | **Moong dal, yellow (split and husked mung beans)** | Yellow | Yellow split peas, yellow lentils, toor dal (firmer), moong dal (takes longer to cook) |
| | **Toor dal (split pigeon peas)** | Yellow | Channa dal, yellow split peas, yellow lentils |
| | **Urad dal (split black lentils)** | Cream (black skins) | Whole pigeon peas, split black-eyed peas, beluga lentils (softer) |
| | **Urad dal chilka (split and husked black lentils)** | Cream | Val dal (larger) |
| | **Val dal (split lablab beans)** | Ivory | Urad dal chilka (smaller), split black-eyed peas |

# Shuffling Mushrooms

Mushrooms are the fruiting bodies of edible fungi. Most have a similar flavor chemistry based on glutamate, the savory flavor component that is now understood as umami, the fifth detectable flavor after sweet, sour, salty, and bitter. For this reason, many mushrooms are interchangeable for flavor purposes. But each mushroom has a unique flavor, texture, and color. Use the guide below to make more accurate fresh mushroom substitutions. Keep in mind that many dried and reconstituted mushrooms, such as porcinis and morels, make a fair substitute for fresh. In general, 1 pound (500 g) fresh mushrooms equals 2 to 3 ounces (60 to 90 g) dried. For more information on dried mushrooms, see Mushrooms, Dried (page 359) and Mushrooms, Powdered (page 360).

| Mushroom | Characteristics | Substitutes |
| --- | --- | --- |
| Beech (Brown Clamshell, Hon-Shimeji) | White to light brown clustered caps; firm, crunchy texture; mild, nutty flavor | Enoki (more delicate), oyster, white button |
| Blewit (Blue Foot) | Violet gray cap and stem; meaty texture; earthy, somewhat spicy flavor | Matsutake (spicier), shiitake |
| Cauliflower | Large, pale yellow white, cauliflower-like, ruffled, layered lobes on a rooting stalk; firm, yet supple texture; nutty, sweet flavor | Pom pom (firmer) |
| Chanterelle, Black Trumpet (Trompette de la Mort) | Charcoal to black trumpet-shaped caps on thick white stems; delicate texture; rich, smoky, fruity flavor | Golden chanterelle (more delicate flavor), hedgehog |
| Chanterelle, Golden (Egg Mushroom, Girolle, Pfifferling) | Golden yellow funnel-shaped caps on tapered, hollow, yellow stems; firm, yet supple texture; earthy, nutty flavor and apricot-like aroma | White chanterelle, yellow foot chanterelle (less flavorful), hedgehog, royal trumpet or king oyster |
| Chanterelle, White | Pale white, funnel-shaped caps on pale white stems; firm, yet supple texture; earthy, nutty flavor with fruity aroma | Golden chanterelle, hedgehog, royal trumpet or king oyster |
| Chanterelle, Yellow Foot | Brown, funnel-shaped caps on yellow stems; firm, yet supple texture; earthy flavor with plum-like aroma | Golden chanterelle (more flavorful), hedgehog, royal trumpet or king oyster |
| Chicken-of-the-Woods | Yellow orange overlapping, tiered fruitbody; firm texture (similar to chicken); mild, earthy flavor and citrus-like aroma | Porcini (richer flavor), portobello (richer flavor), shiitake (more woodsy flavor) |
| Cinnamon Cap | Tawny-color clustered caps; firm, yet supple texture; earthy, sweet flavor | Nameko, shiitake, matsutake, golden chanterelle |
| Crimini (Italian brown) | Tan to brown cap; similar to white mushrooms but with denser texture and deeper flavor | White mushrooms, baby portobellos, shiitakes |
| Enoki (snow puff) | Several tiny, white caps joined at the base; delicate, nearly crunchy texture; mild, aromatic flavor | Oyster, white button |

| Mushroom | Characteristics | Substitutes |
|---|---|---|
| Fairy-Ring | Smooth, tawny, conical caps on long beige stem; firm, yet supple texture; mild, earthy flavor | Nameko, cinnamon cap, white button, chanterelle |
| Hedgehog | Creamy white, slightly funnel-shaped caps on white stem; delicate texture; earthy, nutty, flavor | White or golden chanterelle, nameko |
| Honey | Large, amber or light brown, clustering caps on light brown stems; firm, yet supple texture; earthy flavor | Cinnamon cap, nameko, hedgehog, shiitake (richer flavor) |
| Maitake (Hen of the Woods) | Grayish brown, layered cluster of fungus petals fused to a central stalk; firm, yet supple texture; aromatic, woodsy flavor | Oyster, shiitake |
| Matsutake (Pine Mushroom) | Light to dark brown caps; dense, meaty texture; rich, spicy aroma | Blewit (blue color), portobello (more earthy), shiitake |
| Morel | Beige, yellow or black sponge-like, pointed, honeycomb caps on thick, hollow stems; delicate texture; rich, woodsy, nutty flavor | Dried and reconstituted morel, oyster, shiitake, portobello |
| Nameko | Shiny, orange brown clustered caps; firm, yet supple texture; earthy, sweet flavor | Cinnamon cap, shiitake, matsutake, golden chanterelle |
| Oyster (Pleurotus) | Light brown to gray to red flattened caps; velvety, oyster-like texture; mild flavor | White chanterelle, enoki (slightly more crunchy texture) |
| Oyster (Royal trumpet or king oyster) | Light brown trumpet-shaped caps on tender, white stem; delicate texture; mild flavor | Oyster, white chanterelle, matsutake, shiitake |
| Pom Pom (Yamabushitake, bear's head) | White ball-shaped cap with no stem; velvety texture; mild, sweet flavor | King oyster or royal trumpet, white chanterelle, small puffball (firmer) |
| Porcini (Cèpe, King Bolete, Steinpilze) | Smooth, light to dark brown, bun-shaped cap on thick barrel-shaped stem; dense, meaty texture; rich, woodsy, complex flavor | Dried and reconstituted porcini, matsutake, portobello (less complex flavor), hedgehog |
| Portobello (mature crimini) | Dark brown caps up to 6 inches (15 cm) in diameter; meaty texture; rich woodsy flavor | Large crimini (milder), jumbo white mushrooms (even milder), porcini, matsutake |
| Puffball | White ball-shaped cap with no stem; firm texture; mild, earthy flavor | Pom Pom (more delicate), jumbo white |
| Shiitake (Oak, Chinese or black forest) | Golden to dark brown umbrella-shaped caps; spongy, yet meaty texture; rich, woodsy flavor | Golden chanterelle, crimini, oyster, straw |
| Straw | Small, light brown to dark charcoal, conical cap; firm, yet supple texture; mild, earthy, musty flavor | Canned straw mushrooms (less firm), enoki, white button |
| White (Button) | Small (button) to large (jumbo) white to light brown bun-shaped caps; mild, earthy flavor | Crimini (more flavorful), oyster (more delicate) |
| Wood Ear | Earthy flavor; includes tree ear (thick), cloud ear (thin), and silver ear (white) | Dried and reconstituted wood ear, maitake (more flavorful), shiitake (more flavorful) |

# A Snapshot of Asian Noodles

Sheets, ribbons, strands and nests of noodles from China, Japan, Korea, Thailand, Vietnam, Laos, Malaysia, and other Asian countries are made from a variety of starches and vegetables including rice, wheat, buckwheat, soybeans, mung beans, arrowroot, cornstarch, tapioca, seaweed, and sweet potatoes. Noodles often have various names in different languages, many of which are listed below. When substituting one noodle for another, keep in mind that dried rice noodles are usually soaked in cold water then briefly boiled or added to soups during the few minutes of cooking, while dried wheat noodles are boiled like Italian pasta. As with Italian pasta, there are two basic types of Asian wheat noodles: those made with egg, such as lo mein and ramen, and those made with only water, such as chow fun, soba, somen, and udon.

| | Noodle | Characteristics | Substitutes |
|---|---|---|---|
| **Rice Noodles** | **Laksa noodles (Lei fun)** | Thick, white strands | Wide rice noodles, Chinese wheat noodles |
| | **Rice noodles, wide (Jantaboon, sha he fan, sen chan)** | Thick, flat ribbons | Medium rice sticks, somen, linguine or fettuccine |
| | **Rice sticks, medium (Banh pho, ho fun, lai fen, sen lek, kway teow)** | Opaque ribbons | Wide rice noodles, linguine, somen |
| | **Rice sticks, thin (Bun, pancit palabok, sen yai)** | Very thin, opaque or white strands | Cellophane noodles, rice vermicelli, vermicelli |
| | **Rice vermicelli (Sen mee, mi fen, mai fun, pancit bijon, banh hoi, bee hoon)** | Very thin, delicate strands sold in nests | Thin rice sticks, cellophane noodles, wide rice noodles (thicker), vermicelli |
| **Wheat Noodles** | **Chinese egg noodles** | Chewy, round, yellowish strands or flat ribbons | Chinese wheat noodles, egg roll wrappers (sliced into noodles), strand or ribbon pasta such as spaghetti or fettuccine |
| | **Chinese wheat noodles** | Tender round strands | Chinese egg noodles (not as delicate), ramen, strand pasta such as spaghetti |
| | **Chow fun** | Flat, wide wheat noodles | Wide Chinese egg noodles, linguine or fettuccine |
| | **Chow mein** | Thin, round egg noodle strands | Chinese wheat noodles, strand pasta such as thin spaghetti |
| | **Chow mein, fried** | Crunchy, round strands | Ramen, boiled and fried strand pasta such as thin spaghetti |
| | **Hiyamugi** | Narrow, wheat ribbons | Somen, udon |
| | **Hokkien noodles (Mee)** | Thick, round yellow egg noodle strands | Laksa noodles, Shanghai noodles |
| | **Kishimen** | Flat, wide wheat noodle ribbons with slippery texture | Udon, linguine |

| | Noodle | Characteristics | Substitutes |
|---|---|---|---|
| **Wheat Noodles** | **Korean wheat noodles (Gook soo)** | Flat wheat ribbons | Somen, fettuccine |
| | **Lo mein** | Round or flat egg noodle strands or ribbons | Ramen, chow mein, spaghetti, fettuccine |
| | **Ramen** | Thin, egg noodle strands | Lo mein, chow mein, spaghetti |
| | **Shanghai noodles** | Thick, oval wheat noodle strands | Perciatelli, spaghetti, laksa noodles |
| | **Soba** | Strands made with wheat and buckwheat | Whole wheat vermicelli, Korean buckwheat noodles (naeng myun) |
| | **Somen** | Thin, delicate wheat noodle strands | Hiyamugi, vermicelli, rice sticks |
| | **Udon (Kal guksu)** | Thick, flat, slippery ribbons | Kishimen, linguine |
| | **Wonton noodles** | Thin, wide egg noodles | Egg roll wrappers (sliced into noodles) |
| **Other Asian Noodles** | **Arrowroot vermicelli** | Thin, opaque strands made with arrowroot starch | Cellophane noodles, cornstarch noodles |
| | **Bean curd noodles (Gan si, soybean noodles)** | Thin, chewy strands made from tofu | Chinese egg noodles such as chow mein |
| | **Cellophane noodles (Bean threads, bai fun, Chinese vermicelli, fen si, fen szu, glass noodles, sai fun, soo hoon, pancit sotanghon, woon sen, bun tao)** | Thin, translucent, gelatinous strands made from mung bean starch | Harusame, rice vermicelli, thin rice sticks |
| | **Cornstarch noodles (Pancit luglug)** | Thin, gelatinous strands made from cornstarch | Cellophane noodles, arrowroot vermicelli |
| | **Harusame (Japanese vermicelli)** | Thin, translucent strands similar to cellophane noodles but sometimes made from potato, sweet potato, or rice starch | Cellophane noodles, arrowroot vermicelli, cornstarch noodles |
| | **Korean buckwheat noodles (Naeng myun)** | Thin strands made with buckwheat flour and potato starch | Soba, whole wheat vermicelli |
| | **Korean sweet potato vermicelli (Dang myun)** | Chewy strands made from sweet potato starch | Harusame, cellophane noodles, arrowroot vermicelli |
| | **Seaweed noodles** | Long, thin strands made from seaweed | Cellophane noodles, arrowroot vermicelli |
| | **Tapioca sticks (Hu tieu bot loc)** | Thin strands made from tapioca starch | Cellophane noodles, arrowroot noodles |
| | **Yam noodles (Shirataki, ito konnyaku)** | Gelatinous strands made from yams | Cellophane noodles, harusame |

# Substituting Oils

There are two main categories of oils: frying oils and salad oils. Within each category, the oils are generally interchangeable. Frying oils tend be mild in flavor yet they can withstand the high temperatures needed for sautéing and frying. When sautéing or frying with "vegetable oil," corn oil, canola oil, and soybean oil all make good choices. Choose a frying oil with a high smoke point for extended deep-fat frying. To help you choose, the sautéing and frying oils listed below are arranged according to smoke point from lowest to highest. The salad oils, on the other hand, are arranged alphabetically. Salad oils tend to have pronounced flavors that dissipate when exposed to heat. Full-flavored salad oils work best in uncooked or gently heated dishes like dressings, sauces, and desserts. Choose a salad oil with a color and flavor that best complements the dish you are making.

| Sautéing and Frying Oils | Smoke Point | Characteristics |
|---|---|---|
| Coconut Oil | 350°F (180°C) | Mild to rich coconut flavor; light color; fat content is 89% saturated, 3% polyunsaturated, and 8% monounsaturated |
| Corn oil | 410°F (210°C) | Mild flavor; yellow color; fat content is 13% saturated, 62% polyunsaturated, and 25% monounsaturated |
| Olive oil | 410°F (210°C) | Mild to rich olive flavor; pale yellow to deep green color; fat content is 14% saturated, 10% polyunsaturated, and 76% monounsaturated |
| Sesame seed oil (untoasted) | 415°F (213°C) | Mild nutty flavor; light yellow color; fat content is 18% saturated, 41% polyunsaturated, and 41% monounsaturated |
| Canola (rapeseed) oil | 435°F (224°C) | Flavorless; light yellow color; fat content is 6% saturated, 32% polyunsaturated, and 62% monounsaturated |
| Grapeseed oil | 445°F (229°C) | Mild flavor; fat content is 13% saturated, 70% polyunsaturated, and 17% monounsaturated |
| Palm oil | 450°F (230°C) | Mild flavor; red orange color; fat content is 50% saturated, 10% polyunsaturated, and 40% monounsaturated |
| Peanut oil | 450°F (230°C) | Neutral yet rich flavor; golden color; fat content is 17% saturated, 35% polyunsaturated, and 48% monounsaturated |
| Safflower oil | 450°F (230°C) | Flavorless; light texture; fat content is 9% saturated, 76% polyunsaturated, and 15% monounsaturated |
| Soybean oil | 450°F (230°C) | Light color; fat content is 14% saturated, 61% polyunsaturated, and 25% monounsaturated |

| Salad, Sauce, and Flavoring Oils | Characteristics |
|---|---|
| Almond oil | Toasted almond flavor; light yellow color; breaks down with heat; also great in cold desserts |
| Argan oil | Rich, nutty flavor; golden yellow color; breaks down with heat |
| Avocado oil | Rich buttery flavor; light yellow to green color; breaks down with heat |

| Salad, Sauce, and Flavoring Oils | Characteristics |
|---|---|
| **Grapeseed oil** | Mild flavor; pale yellow to green color |
| **Hazelnut oil** | Toasted hazelnut flavor; light golden color; breaks down with heat; also good for baking |
| **Macadamia oil** | Mild to rich macadamia flavor; light color; breaks down with heat |
| **Olive oil** | Mild to rich olive flavor; pale yellow to deep green color; can be used for baking; use extra virgin for uncooked or gently cooked dishes |
| **Pecan oil** | Mild to rich pecan flavor; light golden color; breaks down with heat |
| **Pistachio oil** | Toasted pistachio flavor; deep green color; breaks down with heat |
| **Pumpkin seed oil** | Toasted pumpkin seed flavor; green color; breaks down with heat |
| **Sesame oil (toasted)** | Concentrated toasted sesame flavor; dark amber color; breaks down with heat |
| **Sunflower oil** | Mild flavor; light yellow color; breaks down with heat |
| **Truffle oil** | Mild (white truffle oil) to rich (black truffle oil) and complex, mushroom-like flavor; light amber color; breaks down with heat |
| **Walnut oil** | Rich walnut flavor; amber color; breaks down with heat |

# Choosing Among Olives

Olives are variously marketed by their country of origin (Greece), curing method (oil-cured), and/ or the varietal of the fruit itself (Picual). Color also comes into play, as green olives often taste slightly bitter, while black olives tend to taste richer. For simplicity's sake, the chart below groups olives by the most widely used curing methods: dry-curing and brine-curing. Dry-cured olives are cured in salt, which typically leaves them wrinkled, soft, and salty. They are sometimes packed with oil or herbs. Oil-cured olives are similarly wrinkled and soft, but less salty-tasting. Brine-cured olives are firmer with a sharp, salty flavor due to the salt, vinegar or wine in the brine. Some recipes call for specific olive varieties, while others call for generic categories of olives such as black Greek olives or French oil-cured olives. Use the guide below to choose or substitute olive varieties that have the characteristics you seek.

| | Olive | Characteristics | Substitutes |
|---|---|---|---|
| **Dry-Cured Olives** | **Aleppo** | Black, Middle Eastern, slightly bitter | Moroccan, Nyons |
| | **Gaeta** | Black, small, Italian, often rubbed with oil and flavored with herbs | Niçoise |
| | **Moroccan** | Black, Moroccan, shiny and slightly bitter | Aleppo, Nyons |
| | **Niçoise** | Black, French, small, oily, chewy, sometimes flavored with lemon and garlic | Gaeta |
| | **Nyons** | Black brown, French, shiny, salty, bitter, often packed in oil | Moroccan, Aleppo |

*continued on next page...*

| Olive | Characteristics | Substitutes |
|-------|----------------|-------------|
| **Agrinion** | Green, Greek, large, soft, cracked, tart | Atalanta, Naphlion, Kura |
| **Aleppo** | Green, Middle Eastern, salty, bitter | Kura, Naphlion |
| **Alphonso** | Purple black, Chilean, large, soft, tart, slightly bitter | Kalamata, Gaeta |
| **Amphissa** | Purple black, Greek, large, soft | Kalamata, Gaeta, Alphonso |
| **Arauco** | Green, Spanish, large, flavored with rosemary | Manzanilla |
| **Arbequina** | Green, Spanish, small, mild flavor | Manzanilla (larger) |
| **Atalanta** | Green brown, Greek, soft | Royal, Agrinion |
| **Calabrese** | Green brown, Italian, sharp, often flavored with chile peppers and herbs | Sicilian, Kalamata |
| **Cerignola** | Green (sometimes black), Italian, very large, meaty, mildly sweet | Sicilian (more tart), Calabrese (sharper) |
| **Gaeta** | Brownish purple black, Italian, small, soft, nutty, salty | Ponentine, Kalamata, Alphonso |
| **Kalamata (Calamata)** | Purple black, Greek, almond-shaped, soft, rich, fruity | Royal, Gaeta, Amphissa |
| **Kura** | Green, Middle Eastern, cracked, bitter | Naphlion (more fruity), Agrinion |
| **Ligurian** | Black brown, Italian, small, tart and piquant, sometimes includes stems | Niçoise, Gaeta |
| **Lugano** | Black, Italian, firm and salty | Picual, Ligurian |
| **Manzanilla** | Green, Spanish, crisp, often pitted and stuffed with pimiento or garlic | Arauco, Arbequina, Sevillano, Naphlion |
| **Mission** | Black, Californian, soft, mild, watery flavor | Alphonso (more bitter), Gaeta (more flavorful), Kalamata (more firm and flavorful) |
| **Naphlion** | Dark green, Greek, cracked, crisp, fruity | Agrinion, Kura (more bitter), Aleppo, Manzanilla, Picholine |
| **Niçoise** | Black brown, French, small, chewy and meaty, tart and rich | Ligurian, Kalamata, Gaeta |
| **Picholine** | Green, French, oblong, crisp, tart, sometimes flavored with herbes de Provence | Sevillano, Manzanilla, Naphlion |
| **Picual** | Black, Spanish, firm, nutty | Lugano, Ligurian |
| **Ponentine** | Black, Italian, mild flavor | Gaeta, Cerignola (black), Amphissa, Kalamata |
| **Royal (Victoria)** | Reddish brown, Greek, large, chewy | Kalamata, Atalanta |
| **Sevillano (Queen, Super-Colossal)** | Pale green, Californian, very large, crisp | Manzanilla, Naphlion, Picholine |
| **Sicilian** | Green, large, Sicilian, tart, meaty, often flavored with red pepper or fennel | Calabrese, Manzanilla |

Brine-Cured Olives

# Picking Pears

While pear varieties number in the thousands, the fruit is so fragile that far fewer varieties are commonly available. Use the guide below to find the most popular eating and cooking pears. See also Asian pear (page 38) and Pear (page 410).

|  | Characteristics | Best Uses | Substitutes |
|---|---|---|---|
| **Anjou** | Pale green yellow skin, often russeted; velvety, juicy white flesh; mild and sweet | Eating, cooking | Bartlett, Comice |
| **Bartlett** | Yellow speckled skin blushed pink; juicy, sweet flesh | Eating, cooking | Red Bartlett, Anjou |
| **Bartlett, Red** | Shiny, speckled red skin; buttery-soft, sweet and juicy flesh | Eating, cooking | Bartlett, Anjou |
| **Bosc** | Golden or light brown russeted skin; juicy, firm yet tender white flesh; sweet and mildly tart | Cooking, eating | Seckel (smaller) |
| **Comice** | Yellow green, speckled, russeted skin; soft, velvety, juicy, white flesh; sweet, rich, and aromatic | Eating | Anjou, Red Bartlett, Packham's Triumph |
| **Forelle** | Red speckled skin; firm, grainy, sweet flesh | Cooking | Winter Nellis |
| **Packham's Triumph** | Green yellow speckled skin, sometimes russeted; soft, smooth, succulent flesh; sweet and mildly tart | Eating, cooking | Comice, Anjou, Bartlett |
| **Seckel** | Very small, rounded pear with thick, green and red skin; firm yet tender, juicy flesh; sweet, spicy, and aromatic | Cooking, eating | Bosc (larger) |
| **Winter Nellis** | Small, rounded pear with green or red, russeted skin; firm, grainy, sweet flesh | Cooking | Forelle |

# Choosing Among Potatoes

Potatoes come in three basic types, which determine their best uses. High-starch potatoes, such as russets, are called baking potatoes due to their low-moisture content, which makes them light and fluffy when baked. High-starch potatoes also make excellent mashed potatoes and french fries. Low-starch or waxy potatoes, such as round red-skinned potatoes, are called boiling potatoes because they retain their shape when boiled, which makes them a good choice in salads and stews. New potatoes are also low-starch because they are harvested young before the starch develops. Some low-starch varieties are called creamers due to their moist, firm texture. Medium-starch potatoes, such as Yukon Gold, are called all-purpose potatoes because their starch content falls somewhere in between the two extremes. Fingerlings are named for their small, finger-like shape and may have high-, medium-, or low-starch content. Use the guide below to substitute potatoes within and outside of the three main categories: high-starch, medium-starch, and low-starch. Varieties or alternate names for certain potatoes are listed in parentheses.

| | Potato | Characteristics | Substitutes |
|---|---|---|---|
| **High-Starch Potatoes** | **Russet (Arcadia, Burbank, Butte, Idaho)** | Oval, netted brown skin, white flesh that is mealy and fluffy when cooked | White Rose or other long white (for baking or frying), Yellow Finn, Yukon Gold, or other yellow flesh (for baking, mashing, or frying) |
| **Medium-Starch Potatoes** | **All Blue** | Round, dense, somewhat waxy bluish purple flesh | Purple Peruvian, Peruvian Blue, Russian Blue |
| | **Austrian Crescent** | Fingerling shape, smooth golden skin, somewhat waxy, pale yellow flesh | Banana, Ratte, Ruby Crescent (rosy skin), Bintje |
| | **Banana (Russian Banana)** | Fingerling shape, smooth, golden skin, somewhat waxy, pale yellow flesh | Austrian Crescent, Ratte, Ruby Crescent (rosy skin), Bintje |
| | **Bintje** | Golden skin, somewhat waxy, creamy yellow flesh | Charlotte, Austrian Crescent, Banana, Ratte, Ruby Crescent (rosy skin), Yukon Gold, White Rose or other long white |
| | **California White (Long white)** | Oval, light tan, thin skin, somewhat starchy, somewhat waxy white flesh | White Rose or other long white, Irish Cobbler or other round white |
| | **Caribe** | Purplish blue skin, somewhat starchy, white flesh | Purple Viking, Bintje, Yellow Finn, Yukon Gold, Irish Cobbler or other round white |
| | **Charlotte** | Oval, thin golden skin, somewhat starchy, somewhat waxy, yellow flesh | Yellow Finn, Yukon Gold, White Rose or other long white, Kennebec or other round white |
| | **Desiree** | Oval, thin red skin, somewhat waxy, creamy yellow flesh | Rose Finn Apple, Ruby Crescent, Russian Red, Red Bliss (white flesh), La Soda (white flesh), Bintje (gold skin), Yellow Finn (gold skin), Yukon Gold (gold skin) |
| | **German Butterball** | Rounded, golden skin, somewhat starchy yellow flesh | Yukon Gold, Yellow Finn, Charlotte, Irish cobbler or other round white (white flesh) |
| | **Irish Cobbler (Round white)** | Tan, thin skin, somewhat starchy white flesh | Katahdin or other round white, German Butterball, White Rose or other long white |

| | Potato | Characteristics | Substitutes |
|---|---|---|---|
| **Medium-Starch Potatoes** | Katahdin (Round white) | Light brown skin, somewhat starchy white flesh | Kennebec or other round white, German Butterball, White Rose or other long white |
| | Kennebec (Round white) | Light tan skin, somewhat starchy, somewhat waxy white flesh | Katahdin or other round white, German Butterball, White Rose or other long white |
| | Peruvian Blue | Oval, dark blue skin, somewhat starchy, somewhat waxy, deep purple flesh with sweet, nutty flavor | All Blue, Russian Blue, Purple Peruvian |
| | Purple Peruvian | Fingerling shape, shiny, thick purple skin, somewhat waxy purple flesh | All Blue, Russian Blue, Peruvian Blue |
| | Purple Viking | Striking purple and pink skin, somewhat starchy, white flesh | Caribe, White Rose or other long white, Irish Cobbler or other round white, Bintje, Yellow Finn, Yukon Gold |
| | Ratte | Fingerling shape, golden skin, somewhat waxy, buttery, pale yellow flesh | Austrian Crescent, Banana, Bintje |
| | Red Gold | Oblong, red skin, somewhat waxy, creamy, yellow flesh | Desiree, Ruby Crescent, Bintje (gold skin), Austrian Crescent (gold skin), Banana (gold skin), Ratte (gold skin) |
| | Russian Blue | Blue skin, somewhat waxy, blue flesh with white ring just inside | All Blue, Purple Peruvian, Peruvian Blue |
| | White Rose (Long white) | Oval, light tan, thin skin, somewhat starchy, somewhat waxy white flesh | California White or other long white, Kennebec or other round white, Purple Viking (purple and pink skin) |
| | Yellow Finn | Golden skin, somewhat starchy, buttery-sweet, yellow flesh | Yukon Gold, German Butterball, Caribe (purplish blue skin) |
| | Yukon Gold | Golden skin, somewhat starchy, yellow flesh | Yellow Finn, German Butterball, Caribe (purplish blue skin) |
| **Low-Starch Potatoes** | All Red | Round or oblong, thin red skin, red flesh | Purple Peruvian (purple flesh), Russian Blue (blue flesh) |
| | Anoka | Oblong, pale yellow skin, white flesh | White rose or other long white, Kennebec or other round white, La Soda (rosy skin), Red Bliss (red skin) |
| | La Soda | Small, round, smooth, rosy skin, white flesh | Red Bliss, Desiree (yellow flesh), Rose Finn Apple (yellow flesh), Ruby Crescent (yellow flesh), Russian Red (yellow flesh) |
| | Red Bliss (Round red) | Red, thin skin, white flesh | La Soda, White Rose or other long white (tan skin), Kennebec or other round white (tan skin), Rose Finn Apple (yellow flesh), Ruby Crescent (yellow flesh), Russian Red (yellow flesh) |

*continued on next page…*

| | Potato | Characteristics | Substitutes |
|---|---|---|---|
| **Low-Starch Potatoes** | **Rose Finn Apple** | Fingerling shape, rosy skin, yellow, fruity-sweet flesh | Ruby Crescent, Russian Red, La Soda, Desiree, Austrian Crescent (gold skin), Banana (gold skin), Ratte (gold skin), Bintje (gold skin), Red Bliss (white flesh) |
| | **Ruby Crescent** | Fingerling shape, rosy skin, yellow flesh | Russian Red, La Soda, Desiree, Austrian Crescent (gold skin), Banana (gold skin), Ratte (gold skin), Bintje (gold skin), Red Bliss (white flesh) |
| | **Russian Red** | Fingerling shape, red skin, yellow flesh | Ruby Crescent, La Soda, Desiree, Austrian Crescent (gold skin), Banana (gold skin), Ratte (gold skin), Bintje (gold skin), Red Bliss (white flesh) |

# Varieties of Rice

Rice is generally classified by grain length. Long-grain rice is four to five times as long as it is wide. When cooked, the grains are separate and fluffy. Medium-grain rice is two to three times longer than its width. Cooked medium-grain rice is more moist, tender, and apt to cling together more than long-grain rice. Short-grain rice has a plump, almost round shape. When cooked, short-grain rice tends to be very soft and creamy and/or sticky. Within each length, varieties of rice are generally interchangeable. Other categories of rice include aromatic rice, a set of long-grain varieties that have nutty or floral aromas; risotto rice, a set of short- to medium-grain varieties that get creamy on the surface when cooked; paella rice, a set of medium- to short-grain varieties that get less creamy; sushi rice, a set of Japanese short-grain varieties that get slightly sticky; and glutinous rice, a mildly sweet, very sticky rice. See also Rice (page 464) and Wild Rice (page 616).

| | Rice | Characteristics | Substitutes |
|---|---|---|---|
| **Long-Grain Rices** | **Basmati** | Aromatic, nutty-tasting grains that are dry and fluffy when cooked, available brown or white, often used in Indian cooking | Patna rice (less nutty tasting), Texmati, wehani, wild pecan or other "popcorn" rice, jasmine rice (more floral aroma) |
| | **Converted (Parboiled)** | Husked white rice that is briefly steamed | White rice, brown rice (takes longer to cook) |
| | **Himalayan Red (Bhutanese Red)** | Red, chewy, whole-grain rice, strong nutty flavor | Wehani, long-grain brown rice |
| | **Jasmine (Thai Basmati)** | Aromatic, floral-perfumed grains that are fluffy when cooked, available brown or white, often used in Thai cooking | Basmati (more nutty tasting), Texmati, wehani, wild pecan or other "popcorn" rice, Patna rice (less aromatic) |
| | **Patna** | Aromatic rice often used in Indian cooking | Basmati rice (more nutty tasting), Texmati, wehani, wild pecan or other "popcorn" rice, jasmine rice (more floral aroma) |
| | **Texmati (Della)** | Aromatic, Texan cross between basmati and American long-grain rice, available brown or white | Wild pecan, wehani, other "popcorn" rice, basmati rice (more nutty tasting), Patna rice, jasmine rice (more floral aroma) |

| | Rice | Characteristics | Substitutes |
|---|---|---|---|
| **Long-Grain Rices** | **Wehani** | Aromatic, terra cotta colored, whole-grain (brown) rice with popcorn-like flavor that becomes slightly cracked when cooked | Brown basmati rice, brown rice, wild pecan rice, brown Texmati rice, wild rice |
| | **Wild Pecan** | Aromatic, Louisianian, chewy, nutty-tasting rice with popcorn-like flavor | Wehani, Texmati, or other "popcorn" rice, brown basmati rice, brown rice |
| **Medium-Grain Rices** | **Bahia** | Spanish, slightly sticky, often used for paella | Bomba, granza, Valencia or other Spanish rice; Arborio, Carnaroli or other risotto rice |
| | **Black Japonica** | Aromatic, spicy, mushroom-like flavor | Wehani rice, wild pecan rice, wild rice |
| | **Bomba** | Spanish, slightly sticky, often used for paella | Bahia, granza, Valencia or other Spanish rice; Arborio, Carnaroli or other risotto rice |
| | **Granza** | Spanish, slightly sticky, often used for paella | Bahia, bomba, Valencia or other Spanish rice; Arborio, Carnaroli or other risotto rice |
| | **Valencia** | Spanish, slightly sticky, often used for paella | Bomba, granza, or other Spanish rice; Arborio, Carnaroli or other risotto rice |
| **Short-Grain Rices** | **Arborio** | Fat, ivory grains that release creamy starch when cooked, often used for risotto | Baldo, Carnaroli, nano, Roma or other risotto rice; Bahia, bomba, granza, Valencia or other Spanish rice; pearl barley (chewier, less starchy, makes passable risotto) |
| | **Baldo** | Fat, ivory grains that release creamy starch when cooked, often used for risotto | Arborio, Carnaroli, nano, Roma or other risotto rice; Bahia, bomba, granza, Valencia or other Spanish rice; pearl barley (chewier, less starchy, makes passable risotto) |
| | **Carnaroli** | Fat, ivory grains that release creamy starch when cooked, often used for risotto | Arborio, Carnaroli, nano, Roma or other risotto rice; Bahia, bomba, granza, Valencia or other Spanish rice; pearl barley (chewier, less starchy, makes passable risotto) |
| | **Botan rice** | Ivory-color, mildly sweet, glutinous rice | Thai Purple or other glutinous rice |
| | **Glutinous (Sticky, Sweet, or Mochi Rice)** | Mildly sweet, sticky rice that releases some starch when cooked, available white or russet | Botan rice (white color), Thai Purple rice (purple color) |
| | **Nano (Vialone Nano)** | Fat, ivory grains that release creamy starch when cooked, often used for risotto | Arborio, Baldo, Carnaroli, nano or other risotto rice; Bahia, bomba, granza, valencia or other Spanish rice; pearl barley (chewier, less starchy, makes passable risotto) |
| | **Risotto rice** | See Arborio, Baldo, Carnaroli, Nano, Roma | |

*continued on next page…*

| | Rice | Characteristics | Substitutes |
|---|---|---|---|
| **Short-Grain Rices** | **Roma** | Fat, ivory grains that release creamy starch when cooked, often used for risotto | Arborio, Baldo, Carnaroli, nano or other risotto rice; Bahia, bomba, granza, Valencia or other Spanish rice; pearl barley (chewier, less starchy, makes passable risotto) |
| | **Thai Purple (Thai Black Sticky Rice)** | Purple-color, mildly sweet, sticky rice that releases some starch when cooked | Botan or other glutinous rice |

# Changing Roe

Varieties of fish roe are available in three general categories: hard roe (female eggs), white or soft roe (the milt of male fish), and true caviar (salted eggs of certain varieties of sturgeon). The best caviar is harvested from sturgeon in the Caspian and Black Seas. The term malassol (Russian for "lightly salted") often appears on the finest caviar taken early in the spawning season. The term "pressed caviar" refers to the ripest, most strongly flavored sturgeon eggs, which are taken late in the season and pressed together. Pasteurized roe have been heated to improve shelf life, which creates a slightly firmer texture. Some roe not labeled "caviar" is quite good and can be substituted for true sturgeon caviar, especially when a splash of lemon juice is added. Some connoisseurs prefer these less-expensive substitutes in order to allow overfished sturgeon to recover in the Caspian Sea.

| Roe | Characteristics | Substitutes |
|---|---|---|
| **Bottarga (Sardinian Caviar)** | Amber, salted and sun-dried gray mullet (bottarga di muggine) or tuna (bottarga di tonno) roe, sold in a sausage-like "baffa" or sack to be sliced, shaved, or grated | Tara, cod roe |
| **Bowfin Roe (Choupique, Cajun Caviar)** | Black, small, shiny, firm | Beluga caviar, sevruga caviar, American hackleback roe, paddlefish roe |
| **Capelin Roe (Masago)** | Orange, somewhat translucent, very small, often served with sushi | Smelt roe, flying fish roe, orange lumpfish roe, whitefish roe |
| **Caviar, American Hackleback Sturgeon (Black Pearl Caviar)** | Black, small, buttery, sweet | Beluga caviar, sevruga caviar, black lumpfish roe, paddlefish roe, bowfin roe |
| **Caviar, American Lake Sturgeon** | Light to dark gray, large, soft, mildly sweet | Beluga caviar, American hackleback caviar, paddlefish roe |
| **Caviar, Beluga** | Light to dark gray, large, velvety soft, mildly sweet, from Huso huso sturgeon | American lake sturgeon caviar, American hackleback sturgeon caviar, osetra caviar, sevruga caviar, black lumpfish roe, paddlefish roe, bowfin roe |
| **Caviar, Mandarin** | Grayish green, large, from Chinese white sturgeon | Osetra caviar, beluga caviar , sevruga caviar |

| Roe | Characteristics | Substitutes |
|---|---|---|
| Caviar, Osetra (Oscietra) | Gray to brown, strong flavor, from Acipenser guldenstaedti sturgeon; also includes the rare and superior golden brown grains of "golden," "Imperial," or "sterlet" caviar from the albino sturgeon of this species | Golden paddlefish roe (to replace Imperial osetra), sevruga caviar, beluga caviar, Mandarin caviar, American hackleback caviar, bowfin roe, black lumpfish roe |
| Caviar, Sevruga | Gray to greenish black, small, very strong flavor | Paddlefish roe, American hackleback caviar, osetra caviar, beluga caviar, Mandarin caviar, bowfin caviar, black lumpfish roe |
| Cod Roe | Pale pink, salty, sometimes sold as a paste in tubes, also available smoked | Lobster roe, sea urchin roe, herring roe, tara, bottarga |
| Flying Fish Roe (Tobiko) | Red orange, crunchy | Capelin roe (smaller), smelt roe, golden caviar, salmon roe, trout roe |
| Herring Roe (Kazunoko) | Pink yellow, often pickled, salty, and sold in a shaped mass | Cod roe, shad roe, sea urchin roe |
| Lobster Roe (Coral) | Coral pink when heated | Sea urchin roe, cod roe |
| Lumpfish Roe | Red, orange, or black, small, firm | Beluga caviar, osetra caviar, salmon roe or capelin roe or smelt roe (to replace orange lumpfish roe) |
| Paddlefish Roe | Light to dark steel gray or golden | Sevruga caviar, osetra caviar, beluga caviar , American hackleback roe, bowfin roe |
| Salmon Roe (Red Caviar, Ikura) | Red orange, large, translucent, juicy, also available smoked | Trout roe, orange lumpfish roe, flying fish roe |
| Sea Urchin Roe (Uni) | Red orange to yellow, velvety soft, often served with sushi | Flying fish roe (for sushi), salmon roe, lobster roe |
| Shad Roe | Small roe swaddled in two oblong, translucent membranes | Herring roe |
| Smelt Roe | Orange, somewhat crunchy | Flying fish roe, orange lumpfish roe, capelin roe, trout roe |
| Tara | Salted and dried gray mullet roe; rare; puréed to make Greek taramasalata spread | Cod roe, bottarga |
| Trout Roe | Golden brown orange, firm, sticky, salty | Whitefish roe, salmon roe, flying fish roe, smelt roe, orange lumpfish roe |
| Whitefish Roe (American Golden Caviar) | Pale orange or iridescent gold, crunchy, mild flavor | Trout roe, salmon roe, smelt roe, orange lumpfish roe |

# Trading Salts

There are two basic types of salts: those mined from the earth and those evaporated from the sea. Mined salts are usually refined and include common table salt, kosher salt, pickling salt, rock salt, and the less common, unrefined black salt used in Indian cooking. Sea salts are generally those evaporated from bay or ocean waters bordering various lands around the world such as France and Hawaii. Both salts may be highly refined to remove trace minerals or left unrefined to retain trace minerals. Use fine-grained salts for most baking. Use coarse-grained salt for most cooking, especially because the coarse grains can be pinched up more easily. Reserve the most expensive unrefined coarse sea salts for sprinkling onto foods at the last minute so you will taste their complex flavors before the salt completely dissolves. Use the guide below for other substitutions among types of mined and sea salts.

| | Salt | Characteristics | Substitutes |
|---|---|---|---|
| Mined Salts | Black salt (kala namak, sanchal) | Brown black in lump form, purple pink in powder form, unrefined mineral salt often used in Indian cooking, assertive sulfuric aroma with pleasant smoky taste | Other unrefined sea salt or table salt (may need to use 1½ times as much) |
| | Kosher salt | Coarse refined salt with trace minerals removed | Coarse or flaked sea salt such as Maldon, pickling salt, margarita salt, table salt (finer, use a bit less due to the fine grind) |
| | Margarita salt | Coarse refined salt used to salt rims of Margarita glasses | Kosher salt, coarse sea salt, table salt |
| | Pickling salt (Canning salt) | Fine, non-iodized, refined salt similar to table salt | Kosher salt (use a bit more due to the coarser grind), non-iodized table salt |
| | Popcorn salt | Fine refined table salt used for salting snacks | Table salt |
| | Pretzel salt | Coarse, white refined salt used to salt pretzels | Kosher salt, margarita salt |
| | Rock salt | Coarse refined salt used for making ice cream and nestling oysters | Kosher salt, margarita salt |
| | Table salt | Fine, iodized or non-iodized refined salt used for all-purpose cooking and flavoring | Kosher salt (coarser, use a bit more due to the coarse grind), fine sea salt |
| Sea Salts | Alaea Volcanic | Hawaiian red salt with clean, well-balanced flavor and more than 80 minerals from volcanic clay | Haleakala Ruby |
| | Amabito No Moshio (Seaweed Salt) | Japanese, very fine, pale brown salt infused with umami flavor from Hon'dawara seaweed | Sea salt (preferably Japanese) mixed with ground seaweed |
| | Atlantic Mesquite Smoked Salt | America, medium brown sea salt smoked with mesquite for an assertive flavor | Hickory, oak, alder, cherry or another smoked salt |

| | Salt | Characteristics | Substitutes |
|---|---|---|---|
| Sea Salts | **Bali Kechil Pyramid Salt** | Delicate, hollow pyramids of bright-tasting white salt from an Indonesian island | Maldon salt or Turkish Black Pyramid (charcoal gray color) |
| | **Bamboo Salt (Jukyom)** | Korean salt roasted in bamboo cylinders with yellow mud, smoky, mineral-rich flavor | Other smoked sea salt, black salt |
| | **Barrique Chardonnay** | French fleur de sel smoked over French oak wine casks | Iburi Jio Cherry or another smoked salt |
| | **Celtic Salt** | Light gray, moist, complex mineral flavor | Sel gris |
| | **Fiore di Sale di Cervia** | Italian fleur de sel from the Adriatic coast with mellow flavor | Fleur de sel, Pangasinan Star |
| | **Fleur de Sel (flower of the sea)** | French, white, somewhat moist, complex mineral flavor | Fiore di Sale di Cervia, Pangasinan Star, Celtic salt, Maldon salt |
| | **Haleakala Ruby** | Hawaiian, moist, rich-tasting red salt with 16% trace minerals | Alaea Volcanic |
| | **Halen Mon Gold** | Welsh, oak-smoked salt with delicate, flaky texture | Halen Mon Silver (not smoked), Alder or another smoked flake salt |
| | **Himalayan Pink Salt** | Himalayan 250-million-year-old rose-colored salt containing iron and 84 other minerals | Murray Darling or Alaea Volcanic salt |
| | **Iburi Jio Cherry** | Japanese, fine, somewhat moist salt smoked over cherry wood | Barrique Chardonnay or another smoked salt |
| | **Maldon Salt** | White, thin flakes | Fleur de sel, celtic salt |
| | **Murray Darling Salt** | Australian peach or rose-colored salt with fine, flaky texture | Fine Himalayan pink salt |
| | **Pangasinan Star** | Philippine, medium-fine white salt similar to but lusher than fleur de sel | Fleur de Sel, Fiore di Sale di Cervia |
| | **Sel Gris (French gray salt)** | Gray, moist, complex mineral flavor | Celtic salt, fleur de sel, other sea salt |
| | **Turkish Black Pyramid Salt** | Delicate, hollow pyramidal salt from the Mediterranean combined with activated charcoal | Maldon or Bali Kechil pyramid salt (both white in color) |

# Switching Tea

All tea consists of leaves and/or buds of the plant *Camellia sinensis*. The six major categories of tea varieties correspond to the color of the leaves as they are dried, wilted, bruised, crushed, allowed to oxidize, or otherwise processed before brewing and consumption. White tea is a category of tea harvested in spring from young buds (and sometimes leaves); it is typically air-dried and only slightly wilted and slightly oxidized, a process that showcases the terroir of the growing region in the brewed tea. Green tea consists of young spring tea leaves that are pan-fired (in China) or lightly steamed (in Japan), then rolled or shaped, dried, and minimally oxidized to preserve the highest amount of nutrients in the tea. Light steaming gives Japanese green tea a grassier aroma, more bitter taste, and deeper green color than Chinese green tea. Yellow tea is similar to green tea but is only lightly steamed then rested to smooth out the flavor of the tea. It is air-dried and unoxidized. Oolong tea is a fourth category of tea made from mature tea leaves harvested in summer and fall, which are bruised, partially oxidized, and twisted into strips or rolled into balls. Black tea, the most common category, is wilted, sometimes crushed, and almost always fully oxidized. The category includes many signature teas like Assam and Ceylon as well as blends like Earl Grey, which is infused with bergamot oil, and English Breakfast, a robust blend of Assam, Ceylon, Kenyan, and/or Keemun black teas. All black teas taste astringent from the tannins developed during oxidation.

Black tea was developed in the mid-1600s to help preserve tea for export. Prior to that, most tea was green. Black tea has the most caffeine, while oolong tea has about two-thirds as much caffeine, and green tea about one-third as much. Green, yellow, and white teas, on the other hand, have the highest amounts of *catechins*, antioxidants shown to help protect against heart disease and certain cancers. Puerh tea is the final category of and is based on green tea that is pan-fired to remove excess moisture. The tea is then rolled, twisted, and sundried (known as mao cha). From there, two types of Puerh tea are made: traditional puerh (sheng) is mao cha compressed into flat bricks, cakes, or other shapes and fermented for an extended period to improve flavor. Modern puerh (shou or post-fermented tea) is mao cha that is cooked to speed up the ripening process. Both types are sometimes sold as loose tea but mostly available as compressed shapes. Unlike most teas, which taste best soon after they are produced, puerh tea improves with age, going from sweet and clean-tasting to robust and earthy. Puerh tea is typically infused several times to release its full flavor and aroma. Use the chart below to familiarize yourself with some popular tea varieties, which are generally interchangeable within any single category.

| | Tea Origin | Name Description | Brewed Flavor, Aroma, and Color |
|---|---|---|---|
| White Tea | **China (Fujian Province) Silver Needles or Yin Zhen** | Slender, downy silver/yellow tea harvested in spring from unopened buds; air-dried and barely oxidized | Sweet, evergreen aroma; pale silver liquor |
| | **Nepal White Silver Tips** | Silver and green-brown leaves and buds harvested in spring; air-dried and mildly oxidized | Sweet, rich aroma; light amber liquor |
| | **Sri Lanka Ceylon Silver Tips** | Slender, downy silver/yellow tea harvested in spring; air-dried and lightly oxidized | Honey, pine aroma; light copper liquor |

| | Tea Origin | Name Description | Brewed Flavor, Aroma, and Color |
|---|---|---|---|
| **Yellow Tea** | **China (Anhui Province) Huoshan Huangya** | Slender, green downy tea tinged with purple and/or yellow; air-dried, lightly steamed, and unoxidized | Mildly peppery, fresh grass aroma; rich, green-gold liquor |
| | **China (Hunan Province) Junshan Yinzhen** | Slender, deep green leaves; air-dried, lightly steamed, and unoxidized | Clean, grassy aroma; pale green liquor |
| | **China (Sichuan Province) Mengding Mountain Snow Buds** | Large, plump, moist, deep green buds tinged with yellow; air-dried, lightly steamed, and unoxidized | Bright taste with mild savoriness; green-gold liquor |
| **Green Tea** | **China (Zhejiang Province) Gunpowder** | Moist, deep green-gray leaves harvested in summer and fall and rolled into small or large pellets; pan-fired and minimally oxidized | Well-rounded, honey taste with nutty aroma; pale green-gold liquor |
| | **China (Zhejiang Province) Longjing (Dragon Well)** | Long, flat green leaves sometimes tinged with yellow harvested in spring; available in several varieties and low-to-high grades from 5 to 1 to Superior and Competition; pan-fired and minimally oxidized | Soft body and sharp, clean taste with nutty aroma; pale amber or straw-colored liquor |
| | **China (Jiangsu Province) Dong Ting Bi Luo Chun (Green Snail Spring)** | Moist, deep green leaves tinged with brownish yellow harvested in early spring and rolled into snail-like spirals; pan-fired and minimally oxidized | Rich, grassy taste and nutty, floral aroma; pale golden liquor |
| | **China (Anjui Province) Liu An Gua Pian (Melon Seed)** | Jade green leaves harvested in spring and resembling flat, oval melon seeds; basket-fired and minimally oxidized | Mild, earthy flavor and nutty aroma; straw-colored liquor |
| | **Japan Genmaicha** | Deep green leaves of sencha mixed with toasted, popped rice; oven-fired and minimally oxidized | Bright, sweet grass flavor and roasted rice aroma; pale yellow liquor |
| | **Japan Gyokuro** | Slender, deep green leaves tinged with yellow; oven-fired and minimally oxidized | Robust, slightly savory flavor; pale green liquor |
| | **Japan Hojicha** | Wide, deep brown leaves; charcoal-roasted in porcelain pots and minimally oxidized | Roasted caramel-like aroma; reddish-brown liquor |
| | **Japan Matcha** | Bright green leaves stone-ground to a powder; steamed, air-dried and minimally oxidized | Fresh, grassy aroma; pale green liquor; also used to flavor foods like green tea ice cream |
| | **Japan Sencha** | Slender, dark green leaves harvested in spring; steamed, air-dried and minimally oxidized | Pleasantly bitter, vegetal taste and grassy aroma; green-gold liquor |

*continued on next page…*

| | Tea Origin | Name Description | Brewed Flavor, Aroma, and Color |
|---|---|---|---|
| Oolong Tea | China (Fujian Province) Da Hong Pao (Big Red Robe) | Brownish red leaves twisted into strips; medium-roasted and mostly oxidized | Sweet taste and floral stone-fruit aroma; red-orange liquor |
| | China (Fujian Province) Tie Guanyin | Brown leaves tinged with red and rolled into balls; mostly oxidized | Rich honey taste with hints of minerals; gold-orange liquor |
| | India Darjeeling Oolong | Ruddy brown leaves tinged with green and twisted into strips; pan-fired and partially oxidized | Sweet, spicy taste with muscat aroma; amber liquor tinged with green |
| | Taiwan Bai Hao (Dongfang Meiren) | Brown leaves tinged with deep purple, sometimes with white hairs and white tips, twisted into strips; medium-roasted and mostly oxidized | Clean, sweet flavor with aroma of apricots; reddish-orange liquor |
| | Tawian Li Shan | Large purple-green leaves rolled into balls; medium-roasted and mostly oxidized | Well-rounded honey taste with bright, floral aroma; golden yellow liquor |
| Black Tea | China (Anhui Province) Keemun | Slender, tightly curled black leaves; fully oxidized | Smooth, sweet taste with fruity, floral aroma; bright amber liquor |
| | China (Fujian Province) Lapsang Souchong | Thick brownish green twisted leaves smoke-dried over pine; fully oxidized | Strong smoky taste with pine aroma; rich red liquor |
| | India Assam | Brownish green leaves, sometimes tinged with yellow; fully oxidized | Brisk, malty taste; burgundy liquor; often used as the base for chai |
| | India Darjeeling | Greenish brown twisted leaves, sometimes tinged with yellow; mostly oxidized | Light body and sweet taste with muscat aroma; clear amber liquor |
| | Kenya | Brownish green twisted leaves; fully oxidized | Bright, assertive, earthy taste; rich amber liquor |
| | Nepal | Brownish green twisted leaves; fully oxidized | Bright, clean taste and mountain-fresh aroma; golden amber liquor |
| | Sri Lanka Ceylon | Deep brown twisted leaves; fully oxidized | Clean, crisp taste with citrus aroma; copper-amber liquor |

| | Tea Origin | Name Description | Brewed Flavor, Aroma, and Color |
|---|---|---|---|
| Puerh Tea | China (Yunnan Province) Bulang Mountain Old Banzhang | Pan-fired green/raw puerh (sheng) compressed into large round cakes | Robust, earthy flavor with a hint of sweetness; dark amber-green liquor |
| | China (Yunnan Province) Mengku Growing Area Ancient Mini-Cake | Pan-fired green/raw puerh (sheng) compressed in small round cakes | Mild mineral flavor with floral aroma; dark amber-green liquor |
| | China (Yunnan Province) Nannuo Mountain Golden Buds | Cooked and fermented deep golden brown puerh (shou) compressed into large cakes | Robust, earthy flavor; dark amber liquor |
| | China (Yunnan Province) Nannuo Mountain Wild Arbor | Pan-fired green/raw puerh (sheng) compressed into large round cakes | Slightly astringent yet sweet taste with floral aroma; dark amber-green liquor |
| | China (Yunnan Province) Silver Tuo Cha | Pan-fired green/raw puerh (sheng) with silver tips compressed into small nests | Sweet, mineral flavor; dark amber-green liquor |
| | China (Yunnan Province) Yun Xian | Cooked and fermented deep brown puerh (shou) compressed into large cakes | Robust, earthy flavor; dark amber liquor |

# Choosing Vinegar

Vinegars are made from various foods such as fermented grains (rice vinegar, malt vinegar), fermented grapes (balsamic, champagne, sherry, and wine vinegar), and other fermented fruits (apple cider vinegar, umeboshi plum vinegar). When choosing or substituting vinegars, try to match color and flavor of the vinegar with the color and flavor of the food. Use the chart below as a guide. See also the entry for Vinegar (page 604).

| Vinegar | Characteristics | Substitutes |
|---|---|---|
| **Apple cider** | Amber, tart, mildly fruity-tasting vinegar made from fermented apples, often used with pork, for salads, or to make pickles | Malt vinegar, white wine vinegar, rice vinegar |
| **Balsamic** | Brownish black, mildly acidic, sweet and fruity-tasting vinegar made from concentrated Trebbiano white grape juice, aged in wood barrels for at least 10 years, also available as white balsamic, often used to make vinaigrettes and sauces | Red or white wine vinegar, Chinese black vinegar (more strongly flavored), raspberry or other fruit vinegar (lighter body, less complex taste, more fruity aroma) |
| **Banyuls** | Amber-red, mildly acidic, and sweet with hints of walnuts, vanilla, and ginger, made from Banyuls (fortified sweet French wine), aged for several years | Sherry vinegar, champagne vinegar, aged balsamic vinegar, red wine vinegar |
| **Cane** | Light-color, mildly sweet, made from sugar cane syrup | Champagne vinegar, sherry vinegar, white rice vinegar, coconut vinegar (stronger flavor) |
| **Champagne** | Light-bodied, mildly flavored, often used with seafood, chicken, or salads | White wine vinegar, raspberry or other fruit vinegar, rice vinegar |
| **Chinese black (Chekiang)** | Black rice vinegar often used in Asian cooking | Balsamic vinegar, red rice vinegar, white rice vinegar |
| **Coconut (Suka ng niyog)** | Strong vinegar used sometimes in Southeast Asian and Indian cooking | Cane vinegar, white wine vinegar |
| **Distilled white** | Harsh-tasting white vinegar made from grain alcohol, often used for cleaning and acidulated water | Apple cider vinegar, malt vinegar, lemon juice |
| **Malt** | Amber, mild-tasting vinegar usually made from beer | Cider vinegar, white wine vinegar, lemon juice |
| **Raspberry** | White wine vinegar infused with raspberries | Other fruit vinegar such as blueberry or pineapple, herb vinegar such as tarragon, champagne vinegar, white balsamic vinegar |
| **Red rice (Chinese red vinegar)** | Reddish, salty-tasting rice vinegar often used in Asian cooking | Chinese black vinegar (sweeter), red wine vinegar, white rice vinegar |
| **Red wine** | Reddish, mildly sweet vinegar with pronounced flavor, often used to make vinaigrettes and sauces | White wine vinegar, sherry vinegar, champagne vinegar, balsamic vinegar |

| Vinegar | Characteristics | Substitutes |
|---|---|---|
| **Rice** | Mildly sweet, mildly acidic vinegar made from white rice | Red rice vinegar (red color), champagne vinegar, white wine vinegar |
| **Sherry (Jerez Vinegar)** | Amber, mildly acidic, mildly sweet and fruity-tasting vinegar, aged in barrels for at least 6 years, often used to make vinaigrettes and sauces | Red or white wine vinegar, champagne vinegar, raspberry or other fruit vinegar (lighter body, less complex taste, more fruity aroma), balsamic vinegar (darker, richer) |
| **Tarragon** | White wine vinegar infused with fresh tarragon | Other herb vinegar such as rosemary, fruit vinegar such as raspberry |
| **Umeboshi (Plum Vinegar)** | Salty, somewhat tart and fruity vinegar made from umeboshi plums, often used in Japanese cooking | Red rice vinegar |
| **White wine** | Light-bodied, mildly flavored vinegar, often used with seafood, chicken, or salads | Champagne vinegar, raspberry or other fruit vinegar, rice vinegar, red white vinegar (stronger flavor) |

# Measurement Equivalents

THE FOLLOWING MEASUREMENT EQUIVALENCY TABLES include international equivalents for temperatures, can sizes, pan sizes, Imperial-to-Metric conversions, and common cooking measures such as weight and volume. They also offer charts of the progressive stages of cooked sugar for candy making, the amount of alcohol retained during cooking, and suggested adjustments for cooking and baking at high altitude.

# Pan Size Equivalents

When substituting one pan for another, choose a pan with a similar shape and size. If your substitute pan is deeper than the one you are replacing, lower the oven temperature slightly and increase the cooking time to allow heat to reach the interior. If the substitute pan is shallower, raise the oven temperature slightly and reduce the cooking time. To get accurate width dimensions, measure pans from inside edge to inside edge. For volume, fill the pan with water then measure the water in a measuring cup to the top of the pan. In general, fill pans no more than two-thirds full to allow for expansion when baking.

| Pan Size | Pan Type | Approximate Filled Volume |
| --- | --- | --- |
| 1¾-by ¾-inch (4.5 by 2 cm) | Mini muffin or madeleine cup | 2 tbsp (30 mL) |
| 5-by 1⅜ by ½-inches (12.5 by 3.4 by 1 cm) | Cornstick pan (single stick), barquette shell, or ladyfinger cup | 3½ tbsp (52 mL) |
| 2¾-by 1⅛-inches (7 by 2.8 cm) | Muffin cup | ¼ cup (60 mL) |
| 2¾-by 1⅜-inches (7 by 3.4 cm) | Deep muffin or popover cup | 7 tbsp (105 mL) |
| 3-by 1¼-inches (7.5 by 3 cm) | Jumbo muffin cup | 10 tbsp (150 mL) |
| 3½-by 1¾-inches (8.5 by 4.5 cm) | Round ramekin or custard cup | ¾ cup (175 mL) |
| 5½-by 3-by 2½-inches (14 by 7.5 by 6 cm) | Loaf | 2 cups (500 mL) |
| 1 quart (1 L) | Casserole | 4 cups (1 L) |
| 8-by 1½-inches (20 by 4 cm) | Pie, quiche, round cake, Obsttortenform or Mary Ann | 4 cups (1 L) |
| 11-by 1-inch (27.5 by 2.5 cm) | Tart or quiche | 4 cups (1 L) |
| 9-by 1½-inches (23 by 4 cm) | Pie, quiche, round cake | 5 cups (1.25 L) |
| 7½-by 3-inches (19 by 7.5 cm) | Bundt or Kugelhopf | 6 cups (1.5 L) |
| 8-by 2-inches (20 by 5 cm) | Round cake | 6 cups (1.5 L) |
| 8-by 8-by 1½-inches (20 by 20 by 4 cm) | Square | 6 cups (1.5 L) |
| 10-by 1½-inches (25 by 4 cm) | Pie or quiche | 6 cups (1.5 L) |
| 11-by 7-by 2-inches (27.5 by 18 by 5 cm) | Rectangular | 6 cups (1.5 L) |
| 8½-by 4½-by 2½-inches (21 by 11 by 6 cm) | Loaf | 6 cups (1.5 L) |
| 6-by 4¼-inches (15 by 10.5 cm) | Charlotte, panettone, or round mold | 7½ cups (1.875 L) |
| 2 quart (2 L) | Casserole | 8 cups (2 L) |
| 8-by 8-by 2-inches (20 by 20 by 5 cm) | Square | 8 cups (2 L) |
| 9-by 2-inches (23 by 5 cm) | Deep-dish pie, quiche, or round cake | 8 cups (2 L) |
| 9-by 5-by 3-inches (23 by 12.5 by 7.5 cm) | Loaf | 8 cups (2 L) |

| Pan Size | Pan Type | Approximate Filled Volume |
|---|---|---|
| 9-by 9-by 1½-inches (23 by 23 by 4 cm) | Square | 8 cups (2 L) |
| 9¼-by 2¾-inches (23.5 by 7 cm) | Ring mold | 8 cups (2 L) |
| 9½-by 3¼-inches (24 by 8 cm) | Brioche pan | 8 cups (2 L) |
| 13-by 4-by 4-inches (33 by 10 by 10 cm) | Rectangular Pullman loaf | 8 cups (2 L) |
| 8-by 3-inches (20 by 7.5 cm) | Tube | 9 cups (2.25 L) |
| 9-by 3-inches (23 by 7.5 cm) | Bundt | 9 cups (2.25 L) |
| 9-by 9-by 2-inches (23 by 23 by 5 cm) | Square | 10 cups (2.5 L) |
| 9½-by 2½-inches (24 by 6 cm) | Springform | 10 cups (2.5 L) |
| 15-by 10-by 1-inch (38 by 25 by 2.5 cm) | Jelly Roll | 10 cups (2.5 L) |
| 10-by 2-inches (25 by 5 cm) | Round cake | 11 cups (2.75 L) |
| 10-by 2½-inches (25 by 6 cm) | Springform | 12 cups (3 L) |
| 10-by 3½-inches (25 by 8.5 cm) | Bundt | 12 cups (3 L) |
| 3 quart (3 L) | Casserole | 12 cups (3 L) |
| 13-by 9-by 2-inches (33 by 23 by 5 cm) | Rectangular | 12 cups (3 L) |
| 10-by 4-inches (25 by 10 cm) | Tube | 16 cups (4 L) |
| 14-by 10½-by 2½-inches (35 by 26 by 6 cm) | Roasting | 18 cups (4.5 L) |
| 10-by-5-inches (25 by 12.5 cm) | Round cloche clay oven | 20 cups (5 L) |

# Can and Package Size Equivalents

Some recipes call for specific can and package sizes rather than actual weights and volumes. Use the chart below to substitute standard can and package sizes with an equivalent weight or volume of fresh or frozen food. The sizes are arranged by weight and volume from lowest to highest.

| Standard Can or Package Size | Approximate Weight | Approximate Volume |
|---|---|---|
| $\frac{1}{4}$ | 4 oz (125 g) | $\frac{1}{2}$ cup (125 mL) |
| Evaporated milk | 6 oz (175 g) | $\frac{2}{3}$ cup (150 mL) |
| Frozen juice concentrate | 6 oz (175 g) | $\frac{3}{4}$ cup (175 mL) |
| $\frac{3}{8}$ | 6 oz (175 g) | $\frac{3}{4}$ cup (175 mL) |
| $\frac{1}{2}$ | 8 oz (250 g) | 1 cup (250 mL) |
| 10 oz | 10 oz (300 g) | $1\frac{1}{4}$ cups (300 mL) |
| #1 picnic | $10\frac{1}{2}$ to 12 oz (300 to 375 g) | $1\frac{1}{4}$ cups (300 mL) |
| #1 | 11 oz (325 g) | $1\frac{1}{3}$ cups (325 mL) |
| Condensed milk | 14 oz (425 g) | $1\frac{1}{3}$ cups (325 mL) |
| Condensed milk (Canada) | 10 oz (300 g) | $1\frac{1}{4}$ cups (300 mL) |
| #211 | 12 oz (375 g) | $1\frac{1}{2}$ cups (375 mL) |
| #2 vacuum | 12 oz (375 g) | $1\frac{2}{3}$ cups (400 mL) |
| Evaporated milk | $14\frac{1}{2}$ oz (450 g) | $1\frac{2}{3}$ cups (400 mL) |
| Evaporated milk (Canada) | 12 oz (375 g) | $1\frac{1}{2}$ cups (375 mL) |
| 10 oz (300 g) pack frozen vegetables | 10 oz (300 g) | $1\frac{1}{2}$ to 2 cups (375 to 500 mL) |
| #300 | 14 to 16 oz (425 to 500 g) | $1\frac{3}{4}$ cups (425 mL) |
| #1 juice | 13 oz (400 g) | $1\frac{5}{8}$ cups (450 mL) |
| #1 tall | 16 oz (500 g) | 2 cups (500 mL) |
| #1 square | 16 oz (500 g) | 2 cups (500 mL) |
| #303 | 16 to 17 oz (500 to 525 g) | 2 cups (500 mL) |
| #300 cylinder | 20 oz (625 g) | $2\frac{1}{2}$ cups (625 mL) |
| #2 | 20 oz (625 g) | $2\frac{1}{2}$ cups (625 mL) |
| #303 cylinder | 22 oz (675 g) | $2\frac{2}{3}$ cups (650 mL) |
| #3 squat | 23 oz (700 g) | $2\frac{3}{4}$ cups (675 mL) |
| #3 vacuum | 25 oz (750 g) | 3 cups (750 mL) |
| #2 cylinder | 26 oz (775 g) | $3\frac{1}{3}$ cups (825 mL) |
| #$2\frac{1}{2}$ | 27 to 29 oz (825 to 875 g) | $3\frac{1}{2}$ cups (796 to 875 mL) |
| #$2\frac{1}{2}$ square | 31 oz (925 g) | scant 4 cups (scant 1 L) |
| 16 oz (500 g) bag frozen vegetables | 16 oz (500 g) | 3 to 4 cups (750 mL to 1 L) |

| Standard Can or Package Size | Approximate Weight | Approximate Volume |
|---|---|---|
| #3 | 33½ oz (1 kg) | 4¼ cups (1.05 L) |
| #3 cylinder (46 fl oz) | 51 oz (1.5 kg) | 5¾ cups (1.425 L) |
| #5 | 56 oz (3½ lbs/1.75 kg) | 7 cups (1.75 L) |
| 2 lb (1 kg) coffee | 32 oz (1 kg) | 8 cups (2 L) |
| #10 | 110 to 115 oz (6½ to 7¼ lbs/3.25 to 3.65 kg) | 13 cups (3.25 L) |

# Temperature Equivalents

An oven's actual temperature often varies from the temperature to which the oven has been set. To be absolutely sure your oven temperature is correct, buy an inexpensive oven thermometer at a cookware store and keep it in your oven for reference. For any temperature conversions not listed below, convert Fahrenheit to Celsius by subtracting 32, multiplying by 5, then dividing by 9. To convert Celsius to Fahrenheit, multiply by 9, divide by 5, then add 32.

| Temperature Description | Fahrenheit | Celsius | Gas Mark |
|---|---|---|---|
| Freezer storage | 0° | -18° | N/A |
| Water freezes | 32° | 0° | N/A |
| Refrigerator storage | 40° | 4° | N/A |
| Wine storage | 55° | 13° | N/A |
| Butter is ready for creaming | 67° | 19° | N/A |
| Room temperature | 68° to 72° | 20° to 22° | N/A |
| Yeast dough will rise properly | 85° | 30° | N/A |
| Water is lukewarm | 95° | 35° | N/A |
| Poaching temperature | 160° to 180° | 70° to 82° | N/A |
| Water simmers | 185° to 205° | 85° to 95° | N/A |
| Water boils | 212° | 100° | N/A |
| Very cool oven | 225° | 110° | ¼ |
| Cool oven | 250° | 120° | ½ |
| Very slow oven | 275° | 140° | 1 |
| Slow oven | 300° | 150° | 2 |
| Low oven | 325° | 160° | 3 |
| Moderate oven | 350° | 180° | 4 |
| Moderately hot oven | 375° | 190° | 5 |
| Hot oven | 400° to 425° | 200° to 220° | 6 to 7 |
| Very hot oven | 450° to 475° | 230° to 240° | 8 to 9 |
| Extremely hot oven | 500° | 260° | 9+ |
| Broil | | | Grill |

# Volume Equivalents

Volume conversions from Imperial (U.S.) to metric are not always precise. The equivalents below have been rounded slightly to make measuring easier and avoid odd numerical measurements. For more precise conversions, see the formulas on page 685.

| | IMPERIAL | | | | |
|---|---|---|---|---|---|
| **Descriptive Measures** | **Teaspoons** | **Tablespoons** | **Fluid Ounces** | **Cups** | |
| Dash or pinch | less than ⅛ tsp (dry) | | 0.015 fl oz | | |
| 20 drops | ¼ tsp | | 0.03 fl oz | | |
| 40 drops | ½ tsp | | 0.06 fl oz | | |
| | ¾ tsp | ¼ tbsp | 0.12 fl oz | | |
| | 1 tsp | ⅓ tbsp | 0.15 fl oz | | |
| | 1½ tsp | ½ tbsp | 0.25 fl oz | | |
| | 3 tsp | 1 tbsp | 0.5 fl oz | | |
| | 6 tsp | 2 tbsp | 1 fl oz | ⅛ cup | |
| 1 jigger | 9 tsp | 3 tbsp | 1.5 fl oz | | |
| | 12 tsp | 4 tbsp | 2 fl oz | ¼ cup | |
| | | 5 tbsp + 1 tsp | 3 fl oz | ⅓ cup | |
| | 24 tsp | 8 tbsp | 4 fl oz | ½ cup | |
| | | 10 tbsp + 2 tsp | 5 fl oz | ⅔ cup | |
| | 36 tsp | 12 tbsp | 6 fl oz | ¾ cup | |
| | 42 tsp | 14 tbsp | 7 fl oz | ⅞ cup | |
| | 48 tsp | 16 tbsp | 8 fl oz | 1 cup | |
| | | 32 tbsp | 16 fl oz | 2 cups | |
| | | | 32 fl oz | 4 cups | |
| | | | 64 fl oz | 8 cups | |
| | | | 128 fl oz | 16 cups | |

| IMPERIAL | | | METRIC | |
|---|---|---|---|---|
| Pints | Quarts | Gallons | Milliliters | Liters |
| | | | 0.5 mL | |
| | | | 1 mL | |
| | | | 2 mL | |
| | | | 3 mL | |
| | | | 5 mL | |
| | | | 7 mL | |
| | | | 15 mL | |
| | | | 30 mL | |
| | | | 45 mL | |
| | | | 60 mL | |
| | | | 75 mL | |
| | | | 125 mL | |
| | | | 150 mL | |
| | | | 175 mL | |
| | | | 220 mL | |
| ½ pint | | | 250 mL | 0.25 L |
| 1 pint | ½ quart | | 500 mL | 0.5 L |
| 2 pints | 1 quart | ¼ gallon | 1,000 mL | 1 L |
| 4 pints | 2 quarts | ½ gallon | 2,000 mL | 2 L |
| 8 pints | 4 quarts | 1 gallon | 4,000 mL | 4L |

# Weight Equivalents

Weight conversions from Imperial (U.S.) to metric are not always precise. The equivalents below have been rounded slightly to make measuring easier and avoid odd numerical measurements. For more precise conversions, see the formulas on page 685.

| Ounces | Pounds | Grams | Kilograms |
|---|---|---|---|
| 1 oz | | 30 g | |
| 2 oz | | 60 g | |
| 3 oz | | 90 g | |
| 3.5 oz | | 100 g | |
| 4 oz | ¼ lb | 125 g | |
| 5 oz | ⅓ lb | 150 g | |
| 6 oz | | 175 g | |
| 7 oz | | 210 g | |
| 8 oz | ½ lb | 250 g | |
| 10 oz | | 300 g | |
| 12 oz | ¾ lb | 375 g | |
| 14 oz | | 400 g | |
| 16 oz | 1 lb | 500 g | |
| 24 oz | 1½ lbs | 750 g | |
| | 2 lbs | | 1 kg |
| | 3 lbs | | 1.5 kg |
| | 3½ lbs | | 1.75 kg |
| | 4 lbs | | 2 kg |
| **Quarts** | **Pecks** | **Gallons** | **Bushels** |
| 8 quarts (dry) | 1 peck | | |
| | 4 pecks (dry) | 8 gallons | 1 bushel |

# Metric Conversions

Use the following formulas for precise conversions from Imperial (U.S) to metric measurements. To convert from metric to Imperial, use the same formulas but work backward, dividing by instead of multiplying by the number in the center column. For a list of volume conversions and common weight, see the tables on pages 682 and 684. Note that the measurements on those pages have been slightly rounded, while the formulas below will yield more precise conversions.

| To Convert | Multiply By | To Determine |
|---|---|---|
| Teaspoon | 4.93 | Milliliter |
| Tablespoon | 14.79 | Milliliter |
| Fluid ounce | 29.57 | Milliliter |
| Cup | 236.59 | Milliliter |
| Cup | 0.236 | Liter |
| Pint | 473.18 | Milliliter |
| Pint | 0.473 | Liter |
| Quart | 946.36 | Milliliter |
| Gallon | 3.785 | Liter |
| Ounce | 28.35 | Gram |
| Pound | 0.454 | Kilogram |
| Inch | 2.54 | Centimeter |

# Baking at High Altitude

At high altitudes, foods dry out more quickly due to lower air pressure and thinner, drier air. For yeast breads, no ingredient adjustments are necessary but allow the dough to rise twice before the final rising to develop flavor and texture. Also, keep an eye on yeast dough as it rises to avoid letting it rise beyond the point of doubling. To prevent overrising of yeast dough in the oven, increase the baking temperature by 25°F (14°C) at least during the first 15 minutes. Quick breads require a few more adjustments. Depending on the recipe, you may need to use slightly more liquid, less leavener, less flour, a higher oven temperature, and/or a reduced cooking time

| Altitude Above Sea Level | Sugar (reduce each cup/250 mL by) | Baking Powder or Soda (reduce each tsp/5 mL by) | |
|---|---|---|---|
| 3,000 ft (915 m) | ½ to 1 tbsp (7 to 15 mL) | ⅛ tsp (0.5 mL) | |
| 5,000 ft (1,525 m) | ½ to 2 tbsp (7 to 30 mL) | ⅛ to ¼ tsp (0.5 to 1 mL) | |
| 7,000 ft + (2,135 m +) | 1 to 3 tbsp (15 to 45 mL) | ¼ tsp (1 mL) | |

# Cooking at High Altitude

At altitudes above sea level, atmospheric pressure steadily decreases. The lower air pressure causes liquids in food to heat more slowly because there is less pressure on the surface to retain the heat. For instance, at sea level, water boils at 212°F (100°C). For every 1,000 feet (305 meters) above sea level, the boiling point of water reduces by about 2°F (about 1°C). Thus, at 5,000 feet (1,525 meters), water boils at 203°F (95°C). To compensate for the lower boiling points and thinner,

| Altitude Above Sea Level | Vegetables and Dried Beans (increase cooking time by) | Stewing and Braising (on low heat, increase cooking time by) | |
|---|---|---|---|
| 3,000 ft (915 m) | 20 to 30% | 30 mins | |
| 5,000 ft (1,525 m) | 40 to 50% | 1 hr | |
| 7,000 ft + (2,135 m +) | 60 to 70% | 2 to 3 hrs | |

for cake batters and cookie doughs to achieve the right texture. Use the basic adjustments in the table below then refine your adjustments as necessary. Also, use extra-large eggs, which have additional moisture that compensates for the drier air at high altitudes. Due to the lower air pressure, beat egg whites no further than the soft-peak stage to prevent baked goods from overrising. It also helps to let cake and quick bread batters stand for 15 minutes before baking to allow some of the leavening gases to escape. Fill baking pans only halfway to allow more room for rising.

| Liquid (for each cup/250 mL add) | Temperature and Time (increase temperature and reduce time by) |
| --- | --- |
| 1 to 2 tbsp (15 to 30 mL) | 10 to 15°F (5.5 to 8°C); 2 mins |
| 2 to 4 tbsp (30 to 60 mL) | 25°F (14°C); 5 mins |
| 3 to 4 tbsp (45 to 60 mL) | 25 to 30°F (14 to 17°C); 5 to 10 mins |

drier air, foods cooked above sea level generally require higher temperatures, longer cooking times, and/or more water. Contact your local Cooperative Extension Service or municipal government office to determine the altitude of your kitchen and use the general guide below to make adjustments as necessary.

| Roasting (increase cooking temperature by) | Deep Frying (slightly increase cooking and reduce oil temperature by) |
| --- | --- |
| 10 to 20°F (5.5 to 11°C) | 8 to 10°F (4 to 5.5°C) |
| 20 to 30°F (11 to 17°C) | 10 to 15°F (5.5 to 8°C) |
| 30 to 50°F (17 to 28°C) | 15 to 25°F (8 to 14°C) |

# Alcohol Retention in Cooking

Alcohol evaporates more quickly when heated. The particular rate of evaporation depends of several factors, including the amount of heat applied, the cooking and standing time, and the physical dimensions of the cookware or other vessel containing the alcohol. The biggest determining factor is the total cooking time. For example, the amount of alcohol retained in a pan sauce that simmers for less than 15 minutes can be as high as 40% of the original amount added. On the other hand, long-simmered preparations that cook for more than 2 hours retain only about 5% of the alcohol initially added. Igniting (flambéing) alcohol does very little to reduce alcohol content, retaining about 75% of the original amount added. More alcohol will evaporate simply by allowing the dish to sit at room temperature uncovered overnight than by setting the alcohol ablaze for a few seconds. The chart below, which comes from the U.S. Department of Agriculture's long-running study of nutrient retention factors, shows the amount of alcohol retained during different cooking methods and times.

| Method | Alcohol Retained | Alcohol Evaporated |
|---|---|---|
| Alcohol added to boiling liquid and removed from heat | 85% | 15% |
| Alcohol flamed (flambéed) | 75% | 25% |
| Alcohol stored uncovered overnight, no heat | 70% | 30% |
| Baked 25 minutes, not stirred into mixture | 45% | 55% |
| Baked or simmered 15 minutes, stirred into mixture | 40% | 60% |
| Baked or simmered 30 minutes, stirred into mixture | 35% | 65% |
| Baked or simmered 1 hour, stirred into mixture | 25% | 75% |
| Baked or simmered 1.5 hours, stirred into mixture | 20% | 80% |
| Baked or simmered 2 hours, stirred into mixture | 10% | 90% |
| Baked or simmered 2.5 hours, stirred into mixture | 5% | 95% |

# Stages of Cooked Sugar Concentration

As sugar syrup boils and the water evaporates, it concentrates the amount of sugar in the solution. It also raises the solution's boiling point, which means that you can measure the sugar concentration by taking the solution's temperature. Before the days of candy thermometers, cooks tested the sugar concentration by pouring a drop of the syrup into ice water and observing it as it cooled (many cooks still use this method). If the drop forms a thin, soft thread, it is at the "thread" stage, with a fairly low sugar concentration of 40 to 65%. If it forms hard, brittle shards that crack in the water, it is at the "hard crack" stage with a high sugar concentration of 98 to 99%, appropriate for making butterscotch, brittle, toffee, lollipops, and other hard candies. See the chart below for other stages appropriate for making various candies. After all of the water evaporates, you are left with 100% molten sugar and the sugar itself begins to concentrate, forming light to dark brown caramel suitable for making spun sugar and caramel cages. Throughout the stages of caramelization, sugar develops delicious, complex flavors yet becomes decreasingly sweet. Above 375°F (191°C), cooked sugar eventually turns from brown to black and from sweet to bitter.

| Stage | In ice water, sugar syrup forms: | Temperature | Sugar Concentration | Common Uses |
|---|---|---|---|---|
| Thread | Soft thread | 214 to 220°F (101 to 104°C) | 40 to 65% | Thin, medium, and heavy syrup |
| Soft ball | Soft, flat ball | 234 to 240°F (112 to 116°C) | 80 to 86% | Fudge, fondant, and pralines |
| Firm ball | Firm, pliable thread | 248°F (120°C) | 87% | Rock candy, caramels, and marshmallows |
| Hard ball | Hard, compact ball | 250 to 252°F (121 to 122°C) | 90 to 92% | Nougat and divinity |
| Soft crack | Hard, pliable thread | 270°F (132°C) | 95% | Taffy |
| Hard crack | Hard, brittle thread | 300 to 310°F (149 to 154°C) | 98 to 99% | Butterscotch, brittle, toffee, lollipops, hard candy |
| Very pale caramel | Hard, very brittle thread | 315 to 335°F (157 to 168°C) | 99+% | Pulled sugar |
| Light caramel | Hard, very brittle thread | 340 to 350°F (171 to 177°C) | 100% | Spun sugar |
| Medium caramel | Hard, very brittle thread | 355 to 360°F (179 to 182°C) | 100% | Medium caramel cages |
| Dark caramel | Hard, very brittle thread | 365 to 380°F (185 to 193°C) | 100% | Dark caramel cages |
| Black caramel | Hard, very brittle thread | 410°F (210°C) | 100% | Baker's caramel |

# Acknowledgments

WRITING THIS BOOK HAS BEEN a years-long journey. It took about one year just to develop the list of entries. The substitutions themselves were developed in various ways over several years. Most came from my own experience tinkering in the kitchen. But many came from suggestions given by colleagues, friends, and family. I owe a huge debt of gratitude to all those who generously contributed substitution ideas, including Mark Bowman, Christine Bucher, Bob Dees, Lisa Ekus, Judith Finlayson, Beatrice Flint, Raghavan Iyer, Bonnie Joachim, Jon and Michelle Joachim, Normand LeClair, Karen Levin, Janine MacLachlan, Nick Malgieri, Sharon Sanders, Andrew Schloss, Mark Taylor, and Marc Vetri.

I tested many substitutions with ingredients from local food producers and purveyors. Thanks to George and Melanie DeVault, Rod Wieder, and the other farmers at the Emmaus Farmers Market for carefully growing and producing such wonderful ingredients with which to work. Thanks also to Barbara Hoback at the Allentown Wegman's Cheese Shop for helpful advice and tasty samples of cheeses.

I have combed through and combined a great deal of information in this book, some of which came from well-known and lesser-known books on a variety of cuisines and styles of cooking around the world. Several substitution suggestions appeared in these books, and I would like to thank the authors for offering their wonderful ideas. Please see the Bibliography on page 692 for a list of these authors and their books. I am also grateful for the background information provided by many organizations, including the Almond Board of California, the American Egg Board, the Florida Fish and Wildlife Conservation Commission, the Food and Agricultural Organization of the United Nations, the Horseradish Information Council, the Mushroom Council, the National Hot Dog and Sausage Council, the National Potato Promotion Board, the Oregon Raspberry and Blackberry Commission, the Trade Commission of Spain, the U.S. Apple Association, the USA Rice Federation, and the United States Department of Agriculture.

It's amazing how many people it takes to publish a book of this size — or of any size for that matter. Like building a house, creating a book typically involves dozens of people with very specialized skills. There are project managers who oversee production and keep the book on schedule, writers who transform raw materials into a new edifice and editors who make sure that it is structurally sound, copy editors who check to see that everything is properly and consistently aligned, designers who make the book beautiful, publicity people who market it, and agents who negotiate the deals. Every one of these folks contributes greatly to the book and deserves special mention.

But before I get to that, I must to tell you about a dream I had several months ago. In the dream, I was sitting in my home office writing these acknowledgments and some kind of linguistic blackout prevented me from using any proper names. Instead, I had to use little descriptive snapshots that captured the thanked person in words. I began with my publisher at Robert Rose, Bob Dees. He became "a pleasure to dine with," "a nimble raconteur," and "See also Visionary Thinker." My agent, Lisa Ekus, was, "bursts of brilliant energy," "a wonderful friend and counselor," and "a keen businesswoman." For my editor Carol Sherman, I wrote "patient, steady hand," "thoughtful re-organizer," and "supreme mover of bean sprouts." The phrases "delicious sense of humor," "creative researcher," and "Campari connoisseur," stood in for Sharon Sanders, who helped write the entry introductions. I'm not sure why, but in the dream, all of these descriptive phrases came in sets of three. My wife Christine's triad of unusually long phrases was: "the only person in the world who would put up with weird substitution experiments in our kitchen laboratory," "iron legs and an iron stomach strong enough to watch me sip tamari and Maggi seasoning side by side," and "her veiled look of horror as I mixed yeast extract and barbecue sauce to approximate hoisin sauce." My two sons, August and Maddox, were briefly characterized as "jumping monkeys," "messy eaters," and "willing subjects in the experiment of life."

And so it went with the other unfortunate souls whose names were replaced by phrases, including scores of publishing people such as sales & marketing manager Marian Jarkovich, designers Andrew Smith, Joseph Gisini, Kevin Cockburn, Daniella Zanchetta and Rob Fujimoto, and copy editors Karen Campbell-Sheviak and Jennifer MacKenzie.

I awoke, rubbed the sleep from my eyes, and wrote down bits and pieces of this bizarre dream. Soon, it became clear that not using names wasn't such a hardship. The substitutes worked just fine.

# Bibliography

## Books

Aaron, Chester. *The Great Garlic Book*. Ten Speed Press, 1997.

Amendola, Joseph. *The Bakers' Manual (Fourth Edition)*. John Wiley & Sons, Inc., 1993.

Anderson, Jean. *The Food of Portugal*. William Morrow, 1994.

Andoh, Elizabeth. *Washoku*. Ten Speed Press, 2005.

Andrés, José. *Tapas*. Clarkson Potter, 2005.

Ayto, John. *An A-Z of Food & Drink*. Oxford University Press, 2002.

Barrett, Judith. *Fagioli: The Bean Cuisine of Italy*. Rodale, 2004.

Bartlett, Jonathan. *The Cook's Dictionary and Culinary Reference*. Contemporary Books, 1996.

Bayless, Rick. *Authentic Mexican: Regional Cooking from the Heart of Mexico*. William Morrow, 1987.

_____. *Rick Bayless's Mexican Kitchen*. Scribner, 1996.

Beard, James. *James Beard's American Cookery*. Little, Brown and Company, 1972.

_____. *Beard on Food*. Alfred A. Knopf, 1974.

Beard, James, Milton Glaser, and Burton Wolf. *The Cooks' Catalogue*. Avon Books, 1975.

Beranbaum, Rose Levy. *The Cake Bible*. William Morrow and Company, Inc., 1988.

_____. *The Pie and Pastry Bible*. Scribner, 1998.

_____. *Rose's Heavenly Cakes*. Wiley & Sons, 2009. Bissell, Frances. *The Book of Food*. Henry Holt and Company, 1994.

Bittman, Mark. *How to Cook Everything*. Macmillan, 1998.

_____. *Fish: The Complete Guide to Buying and Cooking*. Macmillan, 1994.

_____. *Leafy Greens*. Macmillan, 1995.

Bloom, Carole. *The International Dictionary of Desserts, Pastries, and Confections*. Hearst Books, 1995.

Brennan, Jennifer. *The Cuisines of Asia*. St. Martin's Press, 1984.

Brillat-Savarin, Jean Anthelme. *The Physiology of Taste*. Counterpoint, 1949.

Brown, Marlene. *The International Produce Cookbook & Guide*. HP Books, 1989.

Casas, Penolope. *The Foods and Wines of Spain*. Alfred A. Knopf, 1982.

Child, Julia. *The Way to Cook*. Alfred A. Knopf, 1989.

_____. *Mastering the Art of French Cooking (Revised Edition)*. Alfred A. Knopf, 2001.

Clingerman, Polly. *The Kitchen Companion*. The American Cooking Guild, 1994.

Conran, Terence and Caroline. *The Cook Book*. Crown Publishers, 1980.

Cost, Bruce. *Asian Ingredients*. William Morrow, 1988.

Culinary Institute of America. *The New Professional Chef (Seventh Edition)*. John Wiley & Sons, 2001.

_____. *Techniques of Healthy Cooking, Professional Edition*. John Wiley & Sons, 2007.

Davidson, Alan. *Seafood: A Connoisseur's Guide and Cookbook*. Simon & Schuster, 1989.

_____. *The Oxford Companion to Food*. Oxford University Press, 1999.

De'Medici, Lorenza. *A Passion for Fruit*. Abbeville Press Publishers, 1999.

DeWitt, Dave. *The Chile Pepper Encyclopedia*. William Morrow, 1999.

Epstein, Becky Sue and Hilary Dole Klein. *Substituting Ingredients (Third Edition)*. Globe Pequot Press, 1996.

Farmer, Fannie Merritt. *The Original Boston Cooking-School Cook Book 1896 (facsimile)*. Crown Publishers, 1973.

Fearnley-Whittingstall, Hugh. *The River Cottage Meat Book*. Hodder and Stoughton, 2004.

Field, Carol. *The Italian Baker*. Harper & Row, 1985.

Friberg, Bo. *The Professional Pastry Chef (Third Edition)*. Van Nostrand Reinhold, 1996.

Gardiner, Anne and Sue Wilson. *The Inquisitive Cook*. Owl Books, 1998.

Goldman, Amy. *The Compleat Squash: A Passionate Grower's Guide to Pumpkins, Squash, and Gourds*. Artisan, 2004.

Green, Karen. *The Great International Noodle Experience*. Atheneum, 1977.

Greene, Bert. *The Grains Cookbook*. Workman, 1988.

Griffith, Fred. *Nuts*. St. Martin's Press, 2003.

Grigson, Jane. *Jane Grigson's Fruit Book*. Atheneum, 1982.

_____. *Jane Grigson's Vegetable Book*. Macmillan, 1979.

Guzman, Elmer. *The Shoreline Chef*. Watermark Publishing, 2003.

Harrison, S.G., G.B. Masefield, and M. Wallis. *The Oxford Book of Food Plants*. Oxford University Press, 1969.

Hawkes, Alex D. *The Flavors of the Caribbean & Latin America*. Viking Press, 1978.

Hazan, Marcella. *Essentials of Classic Italian Cooking*. Alfred A. Knopf, 1998.

Hemphill, Ian. *The Spice and Herb Bible, 2$^{nd}$ Edition*. Robert Rose, 2006.

Herbst, Sharon Tyler. *The New Food Lover's Companion (Third Edition)*. Barron's Educational Series, 2001.

_____. *The New Food Lover's Tiptionary*. William Morrow, 2002.

Hibler, Janie. *The Berry Bible*. HarperCollins, 2004.

Hill, Tony. *Contemporary Encyclopedia of Herbs and Spices*. John Wiley & Sons, 2004.

Hillman, Howard. *Kitchen Science (Revised Edition)*. Houghton Mifflin, 1989.

Hoffman, Matthew and David Joachim (eds). *Prevention's The Healthy Cook*. Rodale, 1997.

Hom, Ken. *Ken Hom's Asian Ingredients*. Ten Speed Press, 1996.

Hosking, Richard. *A Dictionary of Japanese Food*. Tuttle Publishing, 1997.

Iyer, Raghavan. *Betty Crocker's Indian Home Cooking*. Hungry Minds, Inc., 2001.

_____. *660 Curries*. Workman, 2008. Jackson, Michael. *Michael Jackson's Beer Companion (Second Edition)*. Running Press, 1997.

Jenkins, Nancy Harmon. *The Essential Mediterranean*. HarperCollins, 2003.

Jenkins, Steven. *Cheese Primer*. Workman, 1996.

Joachim, David. *Brilliant Food Tips and Cooking Tricks*. Rodale, 2001.

_____. *Fresh Choices*. Rodale, 2004.

Joachim, David and Andrew Schloss. *The Science of Good Food*. Robert Rose, 2008.

Johnson, Paul. *Fish Forever*. Wiley & Sons, 2007.

Kamman, Madeleine. *The New Making of a Cook*. William Morrow, 1997.

Kasper, Lynne Rosetto. *The Splendid Table*. William Morrow, 1993.

Kennedy, Diana. *The Cuisines of Mexico*. Harper & Row, 1972.

Kiple, Kenneth F. and Kriemhild Coneè Ornelas (eds). *The Cambridge World History of Food*. Cambridge, Cambridge University Press, 2000.

Kirby, Jane, R.D. and David Joachim. *Eat Great Lose Weight*. Rodale, 2000.

Kochilas, Diane. *The Glorious Foods of Greece*. Morrow, 2001.

Kowalchik, Claire and William H. Hylton (eds). *Rodale's Illustrated Encyclopedia of Herbs*. Rodale Press, 1987.

Labensky, Steven, Gaye G. Ingram, and Sarah R. Labensky. *Webster's New World Dictionary of Culinary Arts (Second Edition)*. Prentice Hall, 2000

Laessøe, Thomas and Anna Del Conte. *The Mushroom Book*. Dorling Kindersley, 1996.

Lee, Mercédès (ed). *Seafood Lover's Almanac*. National Audubon Society Living Oceans Program, 2000.

Levy, Paul. *The Penguin Book of Food and Drink*. Penguin Books, 1996.

Lichine, Alexis. *Alexis Lichine's New Encyclopedia of Wines & Spirits*. Alfred A. Knopf, 1979.

MacNeil, Karen. *The Wine Bible*. Workman, 2001.

Madison, Deborah. *Vegetarian Cooking for Everyone*. Broadway, 1997.

Malgieri, Nick. *How to Bake*. HarperCollins, 1995.

Mallet, Gina. *Last Chance to Eat: The Fate of Taste in a Fast Food World*. W.W. Norton & Company, 2004.

Mariani, John F. *The Dictionary of Italian Food and Drink*. Broadway Books, 1998.

_____. *The Dictionary of American Food and Drink (Revised Edition)*. Hearst Books, 1994.

May, Tony. *Italian Cuisine*. Italian Wine & Food Institute, 1990.

Mayes, Kathleen and Sandra Gottfried. *Boutique Bean Pot*. Woodbridge, 1992.

McGee, Harold. *The Curious Cook*. North Point Press, 1990.

_____. *On Food and Cooking (Revised Edition)*. Scribner, 2004.

McLagan, Jennifer. *Fat*. Ten Speed Press, 2008. Miller, Mark. *The Great Chile Book*. Ten Speed Press, 1991.

Montagné, Prosper (ed). *Larousse Gastronomique*. Clarkson Potter, 2001.

Morton, Mark. *Cupboard Love: A Dictionary of Culinary Curiosities*. Bain & Cox Publishers, 1996.

Newman, Bettina and David Joachim. *Lose Weight the Smart Low-Carb Way*. Rodale, 2002.

Oliver, Garrett. *The Brewmaster's Table*. Ecco, 2003.

Ortiz, Elizabeth Lambert. *The Encyclopedia of Herbs, Spices, and Flavorings*. Dorling Kindersley, 1992.

Oseland, James. *Cradle of Flavor*. W.W. Norton & Company, 2006.

Page, Karen and Andrew Dornenburg. *The Flavor Bible*. Little, Brown, and Company, 2008.

Patent, Greg. *Baking in America*. Houghton Mifflin, 2002.

Peterson, James. *Vegetables*. William Morrow, 1998.

_____. *Fish & Shellfish*. William Morrow, 1996.

_____. *Sauces: Classic and Contemporary Sauce Making (Second Edition)*. John Wiley & Sons, 1998.

Prudhomme, Paul. *Chef Paul Prudhomme's Louisiana Kitchen*. William Morrow, 1984.

Raichlen, Steven. *Steven Raichlen's Healthy Latin Cooking*. Rodale, 1998.

Reardon, Joan and Ruth Ebling. *Oysters: A Culinary Celebration*. Parnassus Imprints, 1984.

Resnik, Linda and Dee Brock. *Food FAQs*. FAQs Press, 2000.

Revsin, Leslie. *Great Fish, Quick*. Doubleday, 1997.

Roden, Claudia, *Mediterranean Cookery*. Alfred A. Knopf, 1987.

_____. *The New Book of Middle Eastern Food (Revised Edition)*. Alfred A. Knopf, 2000.

Rogers, Ford. *Olives: Cooking with Olives and Their Oils*. Ten Speed, 2002.

Rolland, Jacques L. *The Cook's Essential Kitchen Dictionary*. Robert Rose, 2004.

Rombauer, Irma S., Marion Rombauer Becker, and Ethan Becker. *The Joy of Cooking*. Scribner, 1997.

Rombauer, Irma S. and Marion Rombauer Becker, *The Joy of Cooking*. Bobbs-Merrill, 1975.

Root, Waverley. *Food*. Fireside, 1980.

Ruhlman, Michael. *Ratio*. Scribner, 2009.

Ruhlman, Michael and Brian Polcyn. *Charcuterie*. W.W. Norton & Company, 2005.

Sahni, Julie. *Classic Indian Cooking*. Morrow, 1980.

Sass, Lorna. *Lorna Sass' Complete Vegetarian Kitchen*. Hearst Books, 1992.

Schloss, Andrew. *The Art of the Slow Cooker*. Chronicle Books, 2008.

Schneider, Elizabeth. *Vegetables from Amaranth to Zucchini*. William Morrow, 2001.

_____. *Uncommon Fruits & Vegetables: A Commonsense Guide*. William Morrow, 1986.

Schneider, Sally. *The Improvisational Cook*. William Morrow, 2006.

Schwartz, Arthur. *Naples at Table*. HarperCollins, 1998.

Sheraton, Mimi. *The German Cookbook*. Random House, 1965.

Shimbo, Hiroko. *The Japanese Kitchen*. Harvard Common Press, 2000.

Simmons, Marie. *The Good Egg*. Houghton Mifflin, 2000.

_____. *Things Cooks Love*. Andrews McMeel, 2008.

Simonds, Nina. *Classic Chinese Cuisine*. Houghton Mifflin, 1982.

_____. *Asian Noodles*. Morrow, 1997.

Smith, Andrew F. *Oxford Encyclopedia of Food and Drink in America*. Oxford University Press, 2004.

Stein, Rick. *Rick Stein's Complete Seafood*. Ten Speed Press, 2004.

Susser, Alan. *The Great Citrus Book*. Ten Speed Press, 1997.

Suzuki, Tokiko. *The Essentials of Japanese Cooking*. Japan Publications, 1995.

Taylor, John Martin. *Hoppin' John's Lowcountry Cooking*. Bantam, 1992.

Teubner, Christian. *The Cheese Bible*. Penguin Studio, 1998.

_____. *The Vegetable Bible*. Penguin Studio, 1998.

_____. *The Chicken and Poultry Bible*. Penguin Studio, 1997.

Thompson, David. *Thai Food*. Ten Speed Press, 2002.

Thorne, John, *Simple Cooking*. Viking, 1987.

Trang, Corinne. *Essentials of Asian Cuisine*. Simon & Schuster, 2003.

Tribole, Evelyn. *More Healthy Homestyle Cooking*. Rodale Inc., 2000

Tropp, Barbara. *The Modern Art of Chinese Cooking*. Hearst, 1996.

Tsuji, Shizuo. *Japanese Cooking: A Simple Art*. Kodansha International, 1980.

Underwood, Greer. *The New Gourmet Light (Third Edition)*. Globe Pequot Press, 1999.

Vorhees, Don. *Why Do Donuts Have Holes?* Citadel, 2004.

Waldron, Maggie. *Potatoes: A Country Garden Cookbook*. HarperCollins, 1993.

Weinzweig. Ari. *Zingerman's Guide to Good Eating*. Houghton Mifflin, 2003.

Whiteman, Kate. *The New Guide to Fruit*. Lorenz Books, 1999.

Willan, Anne. *LaVarenne Pratique*. Crown Publishers, 1989.

Williams, Chuck. *Williams-Sonoma Kitchen Companion*. Time Life Books, 2000.

Wolf, Burt. *The New Cooks' Catalogue*. Alfred A. Knopf, 2000.

Wolfert, Paula. *World of Food*. Harper & Row, 1988.

_____. *Mediterranean Grains and Greens*. HarperCollins, 1998.

_____. *The Cooking of the Eastern Mediterranean*. HarperCollins, 1994.

_____. *Mediterranean Cooking (Revised Edition)*. Perennial Currents, 1994.

Wright, Clifford A. *Mediterranean Vegetables*. Harvard Common Press, 2001.

Yepsen, Roger. *Apples*. W.W. Norton & Company, 1994.

Yin-Fei Lo, Eileen. *The Chinese Kitchen*. Morrow, 1999.

_____. *Mastering the Art of Chinese Cooking*. Chronicle Books, 2009.

Young, Grace and Alan Richardson. *The Breath of a Wok*. Simon & Schuster, 2004.

Zanini de Vita, Oretta. *Encyclopedia of Pasta*. University of California Press, 2009.

## Websites

101 Cookbooks. **www.101cookbooks.com**

Agence Partenaire. **www.francefromages.com**

Alberto-Culver Company. Mrs. Dash® Products. **www.mrsdash.com**

Almond Board of California. California Almonds Are In! **www.almondsarein.com**

Amazon. **www.amazon.com**

American Egg Board. **www.aeb.org**

Baking 911. **www.baking911.com**

Barilla Group. **www.barilla.com**

The Chemical Heritage Foundation. **www.chemheritage.org**

Chocolate & Zucchini. **www.chocolateandzucchini.com**

The Cincinnati Enquirer. **www.enquirer.com**

Cocktail DB. **www.cocktaildb.com**

Columbia Encyclopedia, Sixth Edition. **www.encyclopedia.com**

Cooking.com. **www.cooking.com**

Cooking for Engineers. **www.cookingforengineers.com**

The Cook's Thesaurus. **www.foodsubs.com**

Drinks Mixer. **www.drinksmixer.com**

Durkee-Mower Inc. **www.marshmallowfluff.com**

Espana. **www.spain.info**

Fiery Foods. **www.fiery-foods.com**

Florida Fish and Wildlife Conservation Commission. **www.marinefisheries.org**

Food and Agricultural Organization of the United Nations. **www.fao.org**

Food Reference.com. **www.foodreference.com**

The Fruit Pages. **www.thefruitpages.com**

Gammel Dansk. **www.gammeldansk.dk**

GourmetSleuth.com. **www.GourmetSleuth.com**

Greek Products.com. **www.greekproducts.com**

Harper, Douglas. Online Etymology Dictionary. **www.etymonline.com**

Hellenic Electronic Center. **www.greece.org**

Hormel Foods. **www.hormel.com**

Innvista. **www.innvista.com**

Internet Movie Database. **www.imdb.com**

Joy of Baking. **www.joyofbaking.com**

Kraft Foods. **www.kraft.com**

LeRoy Historical Society. **www.jellogallery.org**

McCormick & Co. **www.mccormick.com**

Microsoft Corporation. **www.encarta.msn.com**

Mushroom Council. **www.mushroomcouncil.org**

National Hot Dog and Sausage Council. **www.hot-dog.org**

National Potato Promotion Board. **www.potatohelp.com**

Ochef. **www.ochef.com**

Oregon Raspberry and Blackberry Commission. **www.oregon-berries.com**

Practically Edible. **www.practicallyedible.com**

Rieger, Mark. Mark's Fruit Crops. **www.uga.edu/fruit**

SeaFood Business. **www.seafoodbusiness.com**

Simply Recipes. **www.simplyrecipes.com**

Spice Advice. **www.spiceadvice.com**

Steamy Kitchen. **www.steamykitchen.com**

The New York Times Company. **www.about.com**

Trade Commission of Spain. **www.cheesefromspain.com**

Truestar Health. **www.truestarhealth.com**

U.K. Chile Head. **www.g6csy.net**

Unilever UK. **www.unilever.co.uk**

United States Department of Agriculture, Food Safety and Inspection Service. **www.fsis.usda.gov**

University of Florida. **www.ifas.ufl.edu**

University of Massachusetts Medical School. **www.umassmed.edu**

U.S. Apple Association. **www.usapple.org**

USA Rice Federation. **www.usarice.com**

USDA National Nutrient Database for Standard Reference. **www.nal.usda.gov/fnic/foodcomp/search**

View London. **www.viewlondon.co.uk**

The Webtender. **www.webtender.com**

What's Cooking America. **www.whatscookingamerica.net**

Whyte and Mackay, Ltd. **www.glayva.com**

Wilton Industries, Inc. **www.wilton.com**

Wines on the Internet. **www.wines.com**

# Also Available from Robert Rose

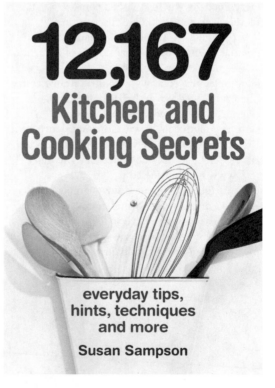
## Visit us at www.robertrose.ca